Modern Financial
Intermediaries and Markets

Modern Financial Intermediaries and Markets

Nasser Arshadi
University of Missouri–St. Louis

Gordon V. Karels
University of Nebraska–Lincoln

Prentice Hall, Upper Saddle River, NJ 07458

Acquisitions Editor: Paul Donnelly
Associate Editor: Gladys Soto
Editorial Assistant: Mary Beth Sanok
Editor-in-Chief: James Boyd
Marketing Manager: Sandra Steiner
Production Editor: Maureen Wilson
Production Coordinator: David Cotugno
Managing Editor: Carol Burgett
Manufacturing Buyer: Kenneth J. Clinton
Manufacturing Supervisor: Arnold Vila
Manufacturing Manager: Vincent Scelta
Senior Designer: Ann France
Design Director: Patricia Wosczyk
Interior Design: Function Thru Form, Inc.
Cover Design: Lorraine Castellano
Illustrator (Interior): Function Thru Form, Inc.
Composition: Rainbow Graphics, Inc.
Cover Art: Jeff Brice Inc.

 Copyright © 1997 by Prentice-Hall, Inc.
A Simon & Schuster Company
Upper Saddle River, New Jersey 07458

Library of Congress Cataloging-in-Publication Data

Arshadi, Nasser.
    Modern financial intermediaries & markets / Nasser Arshadi, Gordon Karels.
        p.   cm.
    Includes index.
    ISBN 0-13-119470-4
    1. Financial institutions—United States.   2. Capital market.
3. Financial instruments.   4. Risk management.   I. Karels, Gordon
V. II. Title.
HG181.A73 1997
332.1'0973—dc20   96-23952
                                                           CIP

Prentice-Hall International (UK) Limited, *London*
Prentice-Hall of Australia Pty. Limited, *Sydney*
Prentice-Hall Canada, Inc., *Toronto*
Prentice-Hall Hispanoamericana, S.A., *Mexico*
Prentice-Hall of India Private Limited, *New Delhi*
Prentice-Hall of Japan, Inc., *Tokyo*
Simon & Schuster Asia Pte. Ltd., *Singapore*
Editora Prentice-Hall do Brasil, Ltda., *Rio de Janeiro*

Printed in the United States of America

10 9 8 7 6 5 4 3 2 1

B R I E F
C O N T E N T S

C O N T E N T S

P R E F A C E

Most of the available textbooks dealing with financial markets and institutions introduce a collection of topics that have no clear theoretical connection with one another. As a result, students simply memorize a set of institutional details that often become obsolete due to changes in regulatory structure, advancements in technology, and the intensification of competition in domestic and international markets. Furthermore, students faced with a list of seemingly unrelated topics have difficulty in prioritizing particular facts and in comprehending and retaining the material for subsequent coursework and employment. In the end, this seemingly straightforward pedagogical methodology only complicates the subject matter. Not surprisingly, students find such texts tedious.

The existing descriptive books have generally shied away from the coverage of modern theoretical and empirical research under the assumption that such topics are too difficult for students to comprehend. Indeed, the very institutional nature of these books does not allow for a thorough integration of theoretical findings and their empirical tests. A decade of teaching such material, however, has proven to us in both undergraduate and graduate courses that students are eager to learn truly relevant theories and related evidence. The challenge for an effective finance instructor is to present complex theories and empirics in a manner that is comprehensible to students. Academics equally dissatisfied with material found in existing texts have settled, as we have, for a compilation of journal articles and special-topic books. We intend to integrate these topics into a single volume through a unified treatment.

As advances in information technology rapidly change the composition of financial instruments and intermediaries, education must also adapt to the new environment by teaching students the nature of the intermediation process, the unique features of intermediaries and instruments, and the trends in the development of new instruments in financial risk management (e.g., derivatives). Understanding the economic foundation of the intermediation process, in addition to the institutional details of today's intermediaries and instruments, will prepare students not only for today's job market but will also help to increase their educational flexibility in adapting to future changes.

Modern Financial Intermediaries and Markets examines firms, intermediaries, financial market instruments, and financial risk management. Advancements in the theory of capital markets and financial intermediation in the last two decades have significantly improved our understanding of these topics and altered traditional perspectives on the roles of capital markets, financial intermediaries, and regulatory structure. We develop the intermediation process as a broad theme which extends beyond the nature and purpose of financial intermediaries to include their influence over the financial instruments and markets in which they operate. For example, we examine the reasons behind commercial bank dominance in the swap market by evaluating the unique features of swap contracts, their primary functions, and the financial positions of customers who demand swaps. This analysis requires us to build a unified framework through which we can explain how a bank is uniquely qualified to produce customer credit information before the bank participates in a swap agreement, bears the risk, and facilitates the customer's sale of stocks and bonds in the capital market.

We wrote this text primarily for financial markets and institutions courses at both the undergraduate and MBA levels, taken either as a general business requirement or as a finance or economics elective. The text will also work well in related courses on money and banking or bank management. Since the book is self-contained, students need no prior knowledge of financial intermediation or capital markets, but may find an introductory economics course useful as a prerequisite.

To assist instructors in teaching, we provide an instructor's manual consisting of solutions to all questions and problems in the book, lecture notes, and overhead transparency masters. We also supply a test bank consisting of multiple choice questions and problems, essays, and word problems. A computerized version of the test bank is also available. We also intend to set up a Web Site to discuss current issues related to subjects discussed in the book. Like most instructors, we have been dissatisfied with the auxiliary material provided by most of the textbooks in the market. Our supplements are carefully prepared to provide detailed teaching and test material, with the intention of reducing instructors' preparation time.

ACKNOWLEDGMENTS

We are indebted to the following reviewers for their many thoughtful suggestions on earlier drafts:

Allen S. Anderson	University of Akron
James C. Baker	Kent State University
Scott W. Barnhart	Clemson University
Keqian Bi	University of San Francisco
E. Tylor Claggett, Jr.	Wake Forest University
Ronnie J. Clayton	University of Central Florida
David Distad	University of California–Berkeley
David Durst	University of Akron
Shane A. Johnson	Bowling Green State University
Inayat U. Mangla	Western Michigan University
Loretta J. Mester	Federal Reserve Bank of Philadelphia
Paul S. Nadler	Rutgers University–Newark
Robert A. Nagy	University of Wisconsin–Green Bay
Suzanne Paranjpe	Wayne State University
Rose M. Prasad	Central Michigan University
Robert I. Webb	University of Virginia

At Prentice Hall we were fortunate to work with many talented people. Paul Donnelly, Senior Finance Editor, has been a valuable friend and a genuine supporter throughout the project. Mary Beth Sanok, Editorial Assistant, coordinated many tasks efficiently. Sheila Lynch, Advertising Copywriter, cheerfully campaigned for this book. Susan McLaughlin, Marketing Manager, proved that marketing a finance book can actually be fun. Maureen Wilson, Production Editor, accommodated us with a tight production schedule. Zanea Rodrigo, Development Editor, provided many useful comments. We are grateful for all their efforts.

I would like to thank my past and present coauthors for their insights. Tom Eyssell, Ed Lawrence, and Don Kummer, through our joint projects, have influenced the material covered in the present text. Gordon Karels, my current coauthor, kept his enthusiasm and sense of humor throughout the project. My other colleagues, David Rose, Robert Sorensen, and D'Anne Hancock, read various chapters and provided valuable comments. My research assistant, Anne Lewis, read most of the chapters and improved the project immensely. I am indebted to my students who during class testing provided valuable written comments: Jay Adams, Tanya Bullock, Isabelle Cordonnier, Jeff Ecker, Ron Gibson, Lars Giesen, Steffen Hoess, Jenny Meyer, Julien Miniconi, and Denise Ritcher.

I thank my parents, sisters, and brother for their personal support and for their help in collecting information about the French financial system. Cherry Claus helped in setting up appointments with officials at Lloyd's of London, LIFFE, and the Bank of England during my visitorship at Imperial College in London. While at the Federal Reserve Board, I benefited from the comments on individual chapters by Tom Durkin, Gregory Elliehausen, and Barbara Lowery, and research assistance by Zach Jonasson.

Many friends provided tremendous support throughout the project for which I am grateful: Nina and Don Murano, Cathy Leonard, Bruce, Dawn, and Holly Grench, and Seymour Katz.

Gordon Karel's Acknowledgments

Chris McClatchey, Chuck Schultz, and Melissa Griswold served as research assistants and provided valuable assistance. I am grateful to my colleagues at UNL—Manferd Peterson, Tom Zorn, George McCabe, George Rejda, Richard Defusco, John Geppert, Kathy Farrell, and Bobbi Schini for their support. I am very grateful to my good friend and former colleague, Arun Prakash, for his suggestions on the text and for all his support and encouragement over the years.

I really want to thank my wife Earla and children, Nikki, Dan, and Kim, for their support and encouragement. It was not easy for them and I very much appreciate their accommodating the time spent on the project. I also want to thank my mother, brothers, sisters, and late father for years of support and friendship.

I want to provide the greatest acknowledgment to my friend and coauthor. His enthusiasm, dedication, and efforts are largely responsible for the success of this project.

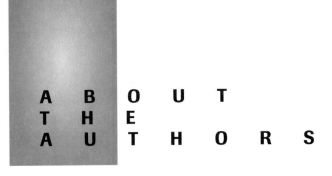

ABOUT THE AUTHORS

Nasser Arshadi is an Associate Professor of Finance at the University of Missouri–St. Louis. His areas of research interest include financial intermediation, capital markets, and corporate finance. His papers have appeared in the *Journal of Money, Credit, and Banking, Journal of Banking and Finance, Journal of Financial Services Research, Journal of Financial Research, Financial Management*, and *Financial Review*. He has published a prior book entitled *The Law and Finance of Corporate Insider Trading: Theory and Evidence*, coauthored with Thomas Eyssell. He has served as a Visiting Scholar at Board of Governors of the Federal Reserve System in Washington, DC, and as a consultant to the American Bankers Association and the Treasury Management Association.

Gordon V. Karels is the Nebraska Bankers Association Professor of Banking at the University of Nebraska–Lincoln. He is currently serving as Associate Dean of the College of Business Administration and has previously served as Graduate Programs Coordinator and MBA Program Director at UNL. He received his doctorate from Purdue University in 1979 and joined the UNL faculty in 1986. Prior to joining the UNL faculty, he served as Chairman of the Economics Department at the University of Nebraska at Omaha and on the faculty at Florida International University. In 1993, he had the distinction of serving as the first Visiting American Business Professor at Technical University Chemnitz (Germany). He has also served as a Visiting Professor at Bayreuth University (Germany).

Dr. Karels has teaching and research interests in the areas of bank management, financial institutions, managerial economics, competitive bidding, and managerial finance. He has published over 25 refereed journal articles, a textbook in financial mathematics, supplemental textbook material in microeconomics, and several cases in bank management. He serves as a consultant on asset-liability management to Information Technology Incorporated and has consulted for the Goodyear Tire and Rubber Company. He has taught numerous management development seminars on financial budgeting and forecasting.

Modern Financial
Intermediaries and Markets

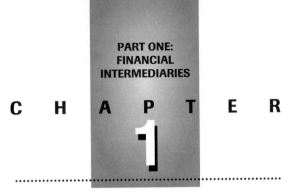

C H A P T E R

1

A Framework for Studying Modern Financial Intermediaries and Markets

OBJECTIVES

This chapter presents a brief introduction to the intermediation process. We begin with a discussion of transaction costs, because their role is central to establishing markets, firms, corporations, financial intermediaries, and financial and derivative instruments. After introducing transaction costs, we describe the intermediation process, and conclude with a synopsis of each chapter.

TRANSACTION COSTS AS THE UNIFYING THEME

Advances in technology and intensified competition in domestic and global markets have led to drastic changes in the intermediation process, requiring a new approach to the study of financial institutions and markets. Since most activities in the intermediation process involve information, the impact of innovative technology on the financial services industry is significant. The ability to collect, process, and analyze large quantities of information quickly and cheaply has expanded market opportunities (e.g., mutual funds, derivatives) and has altered the way traditional markets operate (e.g., home mortgage securitization).

Technology has also contributed to the unbundling of the traditional loan into origination, risk-bearing, funding, and servicing functions, which, in turn, has increased competition in the financial markets for each function. Separating funding from the remaining loan services develops new lines of business for intermediaries in the form of fee-based activities. Securitization, loan sales, and off-balance-sheet activities are examples of fee-based ventures that do not require funding. Fee-based activities are on the rise, while traditional activities such as intermediary loans are on the decline. Whereas corporations once relied on bank loans for a major part of their external financing, they now raise a significant part of their funds through the direct sale of securities in the capital market, facilitated by standby letters of credit obtained from commercial banks.

In market-oriented economies there is an economic rationale for the existence of each and every institution and instrument. The surviving institutions and instruments are those that have the lowest transaction costs. *Transaction costs* are defined as the costs of search and information, contracting and monitoring, and the cost of incentive problems between buyers and sellers of goods and services. We have chosen transaction costs as the unifying theme that links our topics. For example, transaction costs explain why commercial banks are dominant in the swap market. Transaction costs also explain why firms and intermediaries are formed and why businesses are set up as proprietorships, partnerships, or corporations.

THE INTERMEDIATION PROCESS

If individuals and businesses could easily contract with one another for investment, financing, and risk-distribution functions, there would be no need for financial intermediaries. However, certain financial services delivered through intermediaries carry lower transaction costs than would acquiring them in the market. To shed light on the process, we examine five aspects of intermediation:

1. information production
2. risk intermediation
3. monitoring
4. temporal intermediation
5. size intermediation

Information Production

If there were nothing special about a bank, then the bank function could be handled by the local grocery store. If making a commercial loan were a simple transaction, then the checker at the grocery checkout counter could easily perform this task. The difficult part in making a loan is in determining the creditworthiness of the customer. Such a decision is based on an analysis of the expected cash flows of the loan applicant. If the present value of the expected cash flows is greater than the loan value, the loan should be granted. The important difference between a financial intermediary and a nonfinancial firm lies with the role that information plays in the activities of the intermediary.

Information production is the key to the entire intermediation process. Banks, in approving the creditworthiness of a commercial borrower, provide a valuable signal to potential investors as to the overall prospect of the borrower. For this reason, the process of certifying creditworthiness has become a significant source of business income to financial intermediaries. Many companies find it cheaper to obtain funds by entering the more competitive commercial paper market with certification from a bank in the form of a standby letter of credit. This allows some firms to borrow at a lower rate in the market than the rate on a bank loan while paying to the bank for the information production and signaling through a standby letter of credit.

The information-processing function is a complex one. Consider a consumer loan application for a new automobile. The loan application procedure requires the individual to provide information about income, place of employment, length of residence, credit history, and a number of other important considerations. Obviously, the bank cannot take the information provided by the applicant at face value, it must be checked and verified. This process is costly but necessary. In addition to the risk of unreliable information, there is a risk of adverse changes after the fact: The individual can change future cash flows by changing jobs or careers once the loan has been made. The bank is always at a disadvantage concerning the correctness of information about the borrower.

This informational asymmetry between the lender and the borrower requires the financial intermediary to gain expertise in the collection and processing of information. Intermediaries that fail to invest in that expertise will ultimately fail, either because of loan losses or due to conservative lending practices that reduce the volume of lending significantly. This expertise in information production pertains to more than just lending activities. Insurance companies invest heavily in understanding the probabilities of natural outcomes. Investment banks specialize in knowing the institutional demand for new securities. Savings and loans specialize in understanding the retail mortgage market.

Risk Intermediation

Financial intermediaries provide risk intermediation services in two distinct ways: First, they enable their investors to reduce risk by diversification, and second, they help their customers to redistribute their risk exposures by using financial derivatives. An investor who is interested in purchasing equity shares may only afford a few shares in a particular company stock. But this will expose the investor to the unique risk of that company if shares are held in isolation. An equity mutual fund provides the investor with the chance to obtain diversification by buying into shares in a variety of companies. A bank provides a similar service to its customers by pooling their deposits and investing them in a fully diversified portfolio of loans and investments.

The general inclination of individuals and businesses to avoid risk provides the impetus for the development of new instruments. *Risk aversion* is defined as the preference for a certain payoff, as opposed to an uncertain payoff of an expected value. To make a risk-averse person even consider two future payoffs—one certain and the other uncertain—the individual must be compensated for choosing uncertainty by receiving a higher payoff in that case.

Consider an individual who is offered the following choices for a retirement plan. Under Plan A, the individual will receive $500,000 in cash upon retirement from the company at age 65. Under Plan B the individual will receive 100,000 shares of stock in the company, currently selling for $5 per share, upon retirement at age 65. The plan must be chosen now and has no value prior to retirement.

If the individual could wait until the day of retirement to make his choice, the decision would be easy. Plan B would be chosen if the price of the stock was worth more than $5 per share; otherwise Plan A would be chosen. The decision becomes much more difficult when it must be made at a point well before retirement. The decision criterion is still the same—choose the plan with the highest terminal value—but it is much more difficult to calculate the terminal value of Plan B. The final decision depends upon what the individual believes the price of the stock will be at retirement.

Suppose that there is a 50% chance that the stock will be worth $6 and an equal chance that the stock will be worth $4 at retirement. The expected value of Plan B at retirement would be ($4 × 100,000 × 0.5) + ($6 × 100,000 × 0.5) = $500,000. While both plans have the same expected outcome, Plan B exposes the individual to greater variability in future income. Risk-averse individuals will choose the plan with the lower variability in income (i.e., the lower-risk plan) if the expected payment is the same.

Instead of those possible outcomes, however, suppose the stock price will be $10 per share with a probability of 0.5 and worthless with a probability of 0.5 at retirement. This case also has an expected value of $500,000 at retirement, so it is of equal expected value to the plans described above. But this case has more risk, as the individual will now end up with $1,000,000 or nothing at all. A better alternative for someone forced to choose between the two retirement plans would be to find some kind of product that would allow the individual to capture the gains from increases in stock prices but to be protected from declines in stock prices. Such a product would be the equivalent of an insurance policy on the risky retirement plan. A company that could measure and understand the risk on such a product could then write a policy to provide this service and price it in such a way as to make it attractive to the buyer and profitable for the seller.

Pricing products that will help individuals and businesses shed unwanted risks is another line of business for financial intermediaries. Insurance companies are the classic example of businesses that exist primarily to allow individuals to get rid of unwanted risks. For example, life insurance provides protection for survivors from an interruption in their income-consumption stream; health insurance provides protection from catastrophic medical expenses; and hazard insurance provides property protection against losses due to fire, storm, or other natural disasters.

Besides these natural types of risk that individuals attempt to shed, there are also financial risks that businesses and individuals want to avoid. The pension choice example is a type of situation for which markets and products have been developed to offset or reduce such risks. Other examples are mutual funds exposed to a potential downturn in the stock market, banks with large bond portfolios at risk of an upturn in interest rates, and an importer of German machinery concerned with a possible decline in the value of the dollar against the German mark.

The products that have been developed to deal with these types of financial risks are referred to as *derivatives*. In their basic form, derivatives include forwards, futures, swaps, and options, whose prices depend on—are derived from—the prices of some other assets such as stocks, bonds, and currencies. Derivatives are the fastest growing instruments in the financial market. The main reason for this growth is the substantial increase in financial risk caused by recent increases in the volatility of interest rates, foreign exchange rates, and commodity prices. Prior to the late 1970s, there was little reason for banks, savings and loans, and other financial firms to worry about the impact of interest rate changes on the value of their portfolios, primarily because central bank policy was oriented toward keeping interest rates stable. A shift in emphasis by the Federal Reserve from monitoring interest rates to controlling monetary growth has led to wide swings in interest rates and has forced financial firms to devise strategies and products to keep their balance sheets immune from these fluctuations. A similar development occurred in the foreign exchange market in the early 1970s when the fixed exchange rates known as the Bretton Woods Agreements were abandoned in favor of a floating rate. Commodities prices became volatile in the mid-1970s in the aftermath of significant price increases in oil.

Monitoring

An important aspect of the intermediation process that follows risk intermediation is monitoring. When a client applies for a loan, the bank collects and processes information about the cash flow of the applicant and uncertainty surrounding it. If the client meets the bank's credit standards, the loan is made. While the loan is outstanding, the bank monitors the client's cash flow, supervises compliance with loan covenants, and oversees the collateral. While these steps are necessary for successful credit management, they do not guarantee that the loan will be repaid fully and on time. If the borrower experiences financial distress, effective credit management requires working out a resolution that will minimize the cost of the problem loan. This may involve extending the term of the loan, providing additional credit to make the loan current, or making provisions for liquidating the loan or foreclosing on the collateral. Typically, liquidation and foreclosure are considered the options of last resort.

Monitoring is also an essential part of managing revolving loans. A decision to renew a loan is often more significant than issuing a loan for the first time. This decision is based on the credit history of the borrower during the initial phase of the loan. A sound credit policy depends on a thorough monitoring process that enables the bank to make a sensible loan-renewal decision.

Other financial intermediaries also depend on their monitoring skills to perform their functions. Insurance companies carefully follow the behavior of the insured to make sound policy-renewal decisions. Investment banking firms depend on a steady flow of information to improve their underwriting choices with repeat clients.

Temporal Intermediation

Individual borrowers and lenders often have varying maturity preferences. A depositor may want to invest funds for a short term. A borrower may need funds for a long term. A bank provides maturity intermediation by borrowing short and lending long. The interest-rate risk embodied in the long-term loan is greater than the interest-rate risk contained in the short-term deposit. Consequently, the interest rate charged on the loan comprises a premium greater than the premium included in the interest rate paid on the deposit.

Since interest-rate risk cannot be diversified, maturity intermediation exposes the bank to the interest-rate risk. The bank may either bear the risk or transfer it to another party by using interest-rate derivatives such as futures or options. The bank incurs transaction costs in hedging the interest-rate risk using derivatives. If the bank has to bear the hedging cost, what is the advantage of maturity intermediation over a direct exchange of funds between borrower and lender? The advantage lies with economies from two sources. First, an intermediary is generally better equipped with the expertise necessary to manage the interest-rate risk than individual borrowers and lenders. Second, since an intermediary hedges its interest-rate risks in large denominations, economies in large-scale hedging make it superior to hedging many small positions (lower average transaction cost per dollar).

Size Intermediation

A typical depository intermediary raises funds primarily from small deposits and makes loans in large denominations. For example, a mortgage loan is financed by small savings deposits. A money market mutual fund also raises funds from selling its shares in small denominations and then investing them in larger denominations in Treasury securities, among others. Similar examples can be found in insurance and pension fund businesses. Size intermediation can also involve raising funds in large denominations in order to make smaller loans. For example, finance companies raise funds by issuing commercial paper in large denominations and subsequently making smaller loans to individuals and businesses.

A SYNOPSIS OF THE CHAPTERS

In Chapter 2, we ask a basic question: Why do firms exist? The question stimulates a discussion of the factors that lead to the establishment of a firm. The underlying logic in creating a firm is to reduce transaction costs. Since every line of business has an optimal ownership structure, we identify factors that determine ownership structures, including proprietorships, partnerships, and corporations. The discussion proceeds with incentive problems within corporations and solutions to those problems. Information asymmetry is one of the major incentive problems within corporations. We conclude the chapter by introducing financial intermediaries and their role in mitigating the information asymmetry problem.

In Chapter 3 we ask: Why do financial intermediaries exist? We examine the economic reasons for their existence including a discussion of "the lemon problem," the advantages of repeat transactions through intermediaries that reduce transaction costs, and confidentiality embodied in the intermediary loans. The chapter analyzes features unique to intermediary loans and contingent claims and their role in the resolution of the information asymmetry problem. Finally, we discuss organizational efficiencies in stock vs. mutual ownership structures.

Chapter 4, the first of four chapters on depository financial intermediaries, focuses on their basic functions. Commercial banks, savings and loan associations, savings banks, and credit unions are distinguished from other intermediaries by issuing deposit accounts. We begin with an analytical framework defining the general functions of financial intermediaries as brokerage and asset transformation. The brokerage function involves intermediating between parties without taking a risk position. The asset transformation function requires depository intermediaries to undertake liquidity, credit, and interest-rate risks. The "goldsmith analogy" provides an understanding of the origins of banks, the creation of the medium of payment, and the formation of the central bank. This is followed by a historical review of commercial banks, savings and loan associations, savings banks, and credit unions. The last section of this chapter looks at depository institution risks rooted in their liquidity, credit, and interest-rate activities.

Chapter 5 builds on the previous chapter by discussing a set of fast-growing products, including off-balance-sheet activities, loan sales, and securitization. The unbundling of the traditional bank loan provides four distinct functions: origination, risk-bearing, funding, and servicing. This chapter describes how banks may provide the origination function through writing a loan and subsequently selling it without recourse. A combination of the origination and risk-bearing functions is provided through off-balance-sheet products such as standby letters of credit and over-the-counter derivatives. Securitization provides all of the functions of a traditional loan except for funding.

Chapter 6 examines the regulation of depository intermediaries. The discussion begins by asking the fundamental question of why depository intermediaries are regulated. Four federal agencies—the Federal Reserve (Fed), the Office of Comptroller of the Currency (OCC), the Federal Deposit Insurance Corporation (FDIC), and the Securities Exchange Commission (SEC)—create an intricate regulatory system with overlapping responsibilities. The four objectives of regulation are described: safety and soundness, customer and depositor protection, fairness, and information disclosure. The conflicts in achieving these objectives are examined. The current regulations affecting depository intermediaries are classified by objective into four groups and presented in an appendix to Chapter 6.

Chapter 7 continues the discussion of the regulation of depository intermediaries by examining the deposit insurance system. It provides a brief history of deposit insurance in the United States and reviews the circumstances that led to the establishment of the FDIC in 1933. The savings and loan crisis of the 1980s and the moral hazards in the system are investigated. The newly adopted risk-based premium and risk-based capital requirements are studied, and future trends in depository intermediary safety are also discussed.

Chapters 8 and 9 describe the business of nondepository intermediaries. As the term suggests, these intermediaries do not raise their funds through traditional deposits. Notwithstanding this difference, nondepository intermediaries offer many of the same services that depository intermediaries provide. Despite regulatory restrictions, there seems to be a move toward a convergence of depository and nondepository functions. After a discussion of the trends in the financial activities of nondepository intermediaries, Chapter 8 presents a detailed discussion of the insurance business. In addition to the life and property-casualty insurance that is the standard fare, health insurance, annuities, and Lloyd's of London get a comprehensive look. Chapter 9 continues the discussion of nondepository intermediaries by presenting an in-depth account of pension funds, mutual funds, investment banks, and finance companies. Recent data in each of these industries are presented and industry trends are analyzed.

While we have incorporated global issues throughout the text, Chapter 10 examines in detail the globalization of the intermediation process and the regulatory environment governing such transactions.

Chapter 11 is the first of the four chapters on financial markets that constitute Part II. Here we examine market efficiency and describe procedures by which to value financial claims under certainty and uncertainty. While most students may have had a course in corporate finance before using this book, we have assumed no knowledge of corporate finance in discussing valuation issues.

Chapter 12 examines the level and structure of interest rates and the role of the Federal Reserve in monitoring them. Understanding interest rates is important because financial claims are valued based on only two variables: expected cash flows and the appropriate interest rate used to discount them. This chapter discusses the impact of economic factors and government policies with regard to debt financing and taxation on interest rates.

Chapter 13 examines financial markets, including money and capital markets. Short-term securities with less than one year to maturity are known as money market instruments; securities with longer than one year to maturity are referred to as capital market instruments. We look at the general characteristics of financial markets and provide data on deficit and surplus spending units in the economy. The discussion continues by examining in detail domestic, international, and global instruments of money and capital markets. Global equity markets are compared to draw inferences about their efficiency. Risks and returns in emerging equity markets are evaluated to determine the merit of global investment. The chapter concludes with a discussion of the benefits of global portfolio diversification.

While Chapter 13 examines money and capital markets with an emphasis on financial instruments, Chapter 14 continues our study of capital markets with an emphasis on major market transactions, including corporate takeovers, defensive tactics, and insider trading. Corporate takeovers are transactions in which acquirers purchase majority shares of target firms in an effort to gain corporate control. Since change in control generally involves replacement of the target firm's managers, they often employ a variety of tactics to block the effort. Defensive tactics take many forms, including issuing contingent securities that remain harmless as long as the firm stays independent but become claims on the acquiring party when control changes hands. Enmeshed with takeovers and defensive tactics is the issue of insider trading—trading based on material, nonpublic information. Although it is illegal, insider trading prior to the public announcement of takeovers has continued over the years because of the large profits to be gained.

Since takeovers, defensive tactics, and insider trading are often intertwined, we examine them in the context of a unified framework. We begin with a discussion of incentive problems within corporate governance and demonstrate the role of corporate takeovers in mitigating managerial incentive problems. An obstacle to a successful takeover resolution may appear in the form of a defensive tactic used by the target management. We examine six categories of defensive tactics widely used by target firms. Takeover efforts are further complicated by the lingering problem of illegal insider trading. Various federal and state laws restrict takeover activities for a variety of reasons, including an objection to insider trading, which is considered rampant around takeover events. We discuss legal and financial issues related to these transactions throughout the chapter.

Part III covers financial derivatives. Chapter 15 examines the expansion of financial risk in the past two decades and presents financial derivatives as a means of hedging and redistributing risk. In the 1970s, three separate events significantly increased financial risk. First, the 1973 dismantling of the Bretton Woods Agreement, which for three decades had held foreign exchange rates stable, led to a substantial increase in volatility of exchange rates. Second, in 1974, the Organization of Petroleum Exporting Countries (OPEC), the oil cartel, doubled the price of oil, affecting the prices of a wide range of industrial goods that rely on oil as raw material. In addition, OPEC members began to use oil as a political weapon in an effort to influence the policies of industrialized nations, further increasing volatility in commodities prices. And third, the 1979 shift in the Federal Reserve policy from controlling interest rates to monitoring money supply increased the level and volatility of interest rates. In response to increased financial risk, derivatives products such as forwards, futures, swaps, and options were introduced to hedge against currency, interest-rate, and commodities price risks. As the largely unregulated over-the-counter derivatives market has expanded, major derivatives-related blowups have occurred, creating legal battles between dealers and end-users. We provide a critical review of many of the important cases—including Barings and Orange County—to draw insights into the causes of the problem and to devise ways to improve the market. The chapter concludes with an appendix of 24 recommendations for good industry practices.

While Chapter 15 sets the stage to explain the evolution of financial derivatives, Chapters 16–18 focus on pricing and hedging strategies using individual derivative products, including forwards and futures, swaps, and options. Chapter 16 examines forwards and futures. Here we describe the contractual features of forwards and present forward-based pricing and hedging strategies involving foreign currencies, interest rates (forward rate agreements), and commodities. Since forwards are over-the-counter instruments designed to the specifications of individual customers, they are generally illiquid instruments. They are also credit instruments that carry default risk. The liquidity, credit risk, and high transaction costs associated with customized forward contracts have provided the impetus for the development of futures contracts. While similar to forwards in many respects, futures are highly liquid instruments with no credit risk and low transaction costs. But futures have their shortcomings, too. In order to increase liquidity, futures have to be standardized with few underlying assets and a limited number of maturities. The chapter provides institutional details of futures markets and presents pricing and hedging strategies on currency, interest-rate, and commodity contracts.

Chapter 17 studies swaps, the newest of the derivatives products. Similar to other derivatives, swaps enable the user to redistribute risk arising from fluctuations in interest rates, exchange rates, and commodities prices. The chapter analyzes the origin and subsequent growth in the swap market, the economic rationale for its existence, and the reasons for the dominant role of commercial banks in the market. The discussion continues with market structure, pricing conventions, and hedging strategies. The chapter concludes with a look at regulatory issues surrounding the swap market.

Chapter 18 presents options as the last major tool in the building block of financial derivatives. Unlike forwards, futures, and swaps, which convey obligations to both contracting parties, options provide rights for the buyer and obligations only to the seller. Options provide unique opportunities for the financial manager to hedge against the unwanted downside risk while holding the rights to the profitable upside risk. Similar to other derivatives, options can also be written on interest-rate instruments, currencies, commodities, and equities. Pricing methods and hedging strategies are investigated for a wide variety of options.

Chapter 19 examines trends in financial intermediaries and markets. The discussion is divided into three segments, presenting the three parts of the book. First, we discuss the trends in organizational structure, product mix, and regulatory environment for the global financial intermediary industry. In the United States, the lifting of restrictions on interstate banking has already caused major market restructuring through takeovers in the financial intermediation industry similar to the market for nonfinancial firms in the 1980s. This promises a future for banking in the United States composed of fewer and larger banks. Proposals to allow mergers among commercial banking, investment banking, and insurance businesses are currently debated and may well be realized in the near future. This will lead to a universal banking environment similar to the German system, in which various banking, securities, and insurance products can be purchased from the same outlet.

In the second section of this chapter, we elaborate on changes in the global financial markets by focusing on new electronic markets that eliminate the need for specific geographic locations, reduce transaction costs, increase liquidity, and enhance efficiency among competitors. In equity markets, while the first and second markets composed of organized exchanges and the NASDAQ market have flourished over the years, problems have surfaced regarding their efficiency and fairness. The phenomenal growth of NASDAQ since its inception in 1971 has been plagued by accusations of wrongdoing and collusion, necessitating a reevaluation of its operating and organizational rules. This may also lead to further development of the electronic-based third and fourth markets such as Instinet and Posit that provide significant savings to investors in transaction costs. The success of the third and fourth markets put pressure on the first and second markets to improve their efficiency, reduce transactions costs, and increase value for customers.

In the final section, we discuss the trends in the evolution of derivatives. Despite some mishaps, derivatives have significantly increased in volume in recent years. The total volume of the over-the-counter derivatives increased from $7.3 trillion in December 1991 to $17.3 trillion by the end of the second quarter of 1995. While there are various reasons to use derivatives, their primary advantage continues to be in hedging and redistributing financial risk.

Why Do Firms Exist?

OBJECTIVES

This chapter uses the transaction cost paradigm to explain modern firms. It begins with assumptions about the behavior of the transacting parties and continues with factors that affect the choice between organizing a transaction in the market or within the firm. The choice of ownership structures, including proprietorship, partnership, and corporations, depends on which mode of organization best economizes on the transaction costs for a given line of business. Efforts to minimize the incentive problems within corporations lead to solutions in the capital and labor markets. The chapter concludes by introducing the financial intermediary as a means of mitigating an important incentive conflict within the corporation, the information asymmetry problem.

INTRODUCTION

Transaction cost analysis is based on the insight that the most fundamental unit of analysis in an economic organization is the *transaction*, which is defined as the transfer of goods or services from one individual to another. The way a transaction is organized depends on its attributes. For example, a routine transaction such as withdrawing cash from a bank account is conducted with an ATM, which reduces the costs of carrying out the withdrawal. If a transaction is unusual, such as requesting changes in the terms of a loan, then the parties have to bargain about the terms, which raises the costs of carrying out the transaction.

The choice of the organizational mode for a transaction depends on its efficiency. It is more efficient to withdraw cash from a drive-through ATM than it is to drive to a particular bank office, park your car, walk into the bank, and wait in line for a teller to execute your withdrawal. The economic notion of efficiency means that a transaction conducted in a particular way makes everyone concerned at least as well off as other ways and at least one person better off. In analyzing how organizations emerge, we pay close attention to the notion of efficiency. We do so because people in general wish to make their activities efficient rather than wasteful in both their personal lives and their business lives.

The ultimate participants in transactions are individuals whose wants and needs, interests and preferences, are of fundamental importance for understanding the organization of transactions. It is ultimately the individuals—not the organizations—who make decisions. Organizations do not exist without people who create and manage them, judge their performance, and make restructuring decisions if the performance is inadequate. Indeed, organizations are set up to serve the needs and wants of individual human beings. These needs and wants may take different forms but we concentrate here only on the economic needs. We assume that individuals are capable of choosing one situation over another if it gives them greater satisfaction. The economic goal of individuals is to maximize their welfare.

Organizational structures that facilitate transactions can take many forms. Two extreme forms of organizations are markets and firms. At the one end, all transactions could be between separate individuals in the market where the rule of market price prevails. The price system is efficient because it economizes on information demands. For example, organized stock exchanges play an essential role in the efficient allocation of resources. Organized exchanges are secondary markets where shares already issued are traded. While stock exchanges do not provide new capital to individual companies, they produce stock prices that embody all relevant information about the performance outcome of the underlying companies. All any investor needs to know are his or her own taste for risk and the prevailing stock prices. There is no need for extensive information gathering of previous prices or accounting information because the prices summarize all the relevant information. As material information arrives in the market, prices quickly react to reflect it. A detailed knowledge of a company's product lines is not necessary to achieve effective responses because prices convey all the information needed.

At the other extreme, transactions could be organized within the firms where resources are allocated by managerial direction. But if markets perform efficiently, why are there firms? What is their function? What determines which transactions should be conducted in the market and which should be organized within firms? These questions were posed for the first time by Ronald Coase in 1937. According to Coase, there are costs to conducting transactions and these transaction costs vary depending on the nature of the exchange and on the way the exchange (the transaction) is organized. A transaction occurs in the market when doing so is most efficient (i.e., when it minimizes transaction costs). A transaction is brought within a firm or some other formal organization when doing so minimizes transaction costs.

What is the primary source of *transaction costs*? Transaction costs include the "search and information costs, bargaining and decision costs, and policing and enforcement costs." [1] Before analyzing the attributes of transactions and the underlying incentive problems to determine the organizational mode, we examine behavioral assumptions about the transacting parties.

BEHAVIORAL ASSUMPTIONS

We assume that human beings are generally self-serving and rational in their conduct.[2] Moreover, they are not above behaving opportunistically. Opportunism does not necessarily imply illegal behavior, but usually involves actions with incomplete and distorted information that may intentionally mislead the

---

[1] Dahlman (1979).
[2] While the origin of the transaction cost economics lies in the pioneering work by Coase (1937, 1960, 1988), Williamson (1975, 1985) has made significant contributions to its operationalization.

other party. For example, when trading for a new car, an individual may conveniently forget to mention that the cruise control stopped working several weeks earlier. Withholding this information allows the individual to obtain a better price on the trade. This behavior is not illegal if the buyer did not specifically ask about the cruise control. Of course, not everyone has to be opportunistic. Individuals operate at varying degrees of opportunism, which means that additional resources are needed to identify various types of opportunistic behavior in the contracting process.

Opportunism can occur before ("ex ante") or after ("ex post") the transaction is consummated. Ex ante opportunism results in the adverse selection problem most vividly observed in the insurance industry. When an insurance company announces a fixed insurance premium, those with above average risk purchase the insurance while those with below average risk do not. The party that faces above average risk may opportunistically withhold information regarding the true nature of the risk and the insurer is incapable of verifying the actual risk exposure.

Ex post opportunism results in the moral hazard problem that is also observed in insurance contracts. The moral hazard problem refers to the behavior of the insured who does not take appropriate precautions to avoid adverse events because the cost of the event is borne by the insurer. For example, once one has purchased theft insurance on a laptop computer, there is little worry about leaving the office door unlocked when wandering down the hall to fetch a cup of coffee. Ex post opportunism may be mitigated or reduced by writing a contract that anticipates such behavior. A $500 deductible on a theft insurance policy is likely to make the insured more responsible about locking the door.

Some may consider the assumption of opportunism too cynical. The assumption, however, does not require everyone to be equally opportunistic. The above problems exist when a few opportunists attempt to take advantage of nonopportunists. This type of behavior creates the need for ex ante screening efforts and ex post safeguards as well as mutual restraint among parties. Even criminals believe in some kind of mutual understanding and restraint (the code of "honor among thieves" is one such example).

The assumption of rationality implies that individuals have a reasonable idea about the outcome of their actions. For example, they know that if they take course action A, the outcome will likely be X, and if they take course action B, the outcome will likely be Y. A student can generally figure out the level of effort necessary to receive a particular grade in a course. If a student provides significant effort in preparing for an exam, there is a good chance that the grade will be an A or a B. A mediocre effort will earn a grade of C. Little or no effort or not showing up for the exam will earn an F.

TRANSACTION ATTRIBUTES

Transaction costs ascertain whether activities take place in markets or within firms. The key factors determining transaction costs are asset specificity, uncertainty, and frequency of occurrence.

Asset Specificity

Asset specificity is the most important factor in determining how a transaction should be organized. Asset specificity refers to the ease with which an asset can be put to alternative uses. Assets that are easily redeployable to other uses are more flexible and, therefore, have lower asset specificity than assets that can be used only in limited activities. General-purpose buildings or vehicles, for example, can be deployed for different tasks without significant cost. In contrast, highly skilled labor such as computer programming may be focused on specific tasks in the production process and difficult to redeploy. In this example, buildings and vehicles are low in specificity while the specialized labor is high in specificity.

Uncertainty

The structure of economic organizations is also a function of the level of uncertainty. Uncertainty has two sources: (1) external sources, in which events change beyond the control of the contracting parties, and (2) opportunistic behavior of the contracting parties. If changes in external events are readily verifiable, then it would be possible to make adaptations to original contracts from problems caused by external uncertainty. For example, in the aftermath of the Midwest floods of 1993, some banks voluntarily postponed the repayment of loans for parties affected by the disaster.

However, when circumstances are not easily observable, opportunism creates incentives for contracting parties to portray a change in external factors in different ways. For example, a borrower may ask a bank for postponement of a payment because of illness. The borrower will likely consider the illness to be much more serious than does the bank. In this case, secondary uncertainty (opportunism) aggravates the impact of the primary uncertainty (illness). If the circumstances are verifiable by a third party (a doctor), the parties may agree on changes in the schedule of payment. Any remaining dispute can be resolved through court decisions.

Frequency

Frequency of occurrence also plays an important role in determining if a transaction should take place in the market or within the firm. A one-time transaction does not justify within-firm production or elaborate contracting. Conversely, frequent transactions require detailed contracting among parties to ensure that transaction costs are kept at a minimum. For example, repeat transactions play an important role in the banking business. Customers who return time and again receive services superior to nonrepeating clients because banks know it is much less costly to maintain existing accounts than to generate new ones.

GOVERNANCE STRUCTURES

If assets are specific, transactions are frequent, and there are significant uncertainties, ownership integration within the firm may be the most efficient governance structure. Conversely, if assets are nonspecific, transactions are infrequent, and there are no significant uncertainties, market governance will be least costly. If we hold uncertainty constant, highly specific assets and less frequent transactions may require a trilateral market governance structure, such as the use of an arbitrator, to provide the least costly solution. The low frequency of the activity does not justify internalizing the transaction within the firm even though assets are highly specific. Such a case may be handled at lower cost through arbitration. An arbitrator relieves the parties of the high costs of having to contract every possible outcome.

If the transaction is frequent but the asset is moderately specific, arbitration may be too costly. In this case, a bilateral governance may be sufficient if both parties can verify the event. To protect the seller, a contract can be devised that will pass through increases in the cost of producing the asset or the service to the buyer. This type of provision in the contract is generally called a *scalator provision*. To protect the buyer, provisions such as *most-favored customer (MFC)* or *meet-or-release (MOR)* clauses may solve the conflict bilaterally. In the case of most-favored customer, the seller agrees to provide to the buyer the lowest price it has offered to any other customer. In the meet-or-release clause, the seller agrees to either meet the lowest price or release the buyer from the contract. These two provisions may protect the interests of the buyer. Seller and buyer protection clauses work only when an unanticipated event is verifiable by both parties. Unverifiable events are difficult to contract bilaterally.

BOUNDARIES OF THE FIRM: WHY DO FIRMS OUTSOURCE?

Outsourcing has become big business in the 1990s. Manpower, a temporary-worker agency, was the second largest employer in the United States in 1994.[3] Electronic Data Systems (EDS), a GM-owned computer-service company, had revenues of $8.6 billion in 1993, primarily from contracting. In Britain, FI Group, an information technology firm, has 5,000 freelance associates, but only 250 full-time employees. The examples even cross national boundaries. In Britain, the most successful competitor for contracts to manage prisons is Group Four Securities, a Dutch firm. Ford plans to have Yamaha design the engines for some of its European cars.

Why do firms outsource? They do so for two reasons: (1) They can enjoy the virtues of size or economies of scale, and (2) they can reduce within-firm incentive conflicts, leading to better focus, responsiveness, and low overheads in their core business. These benefits come about not only because of actual outsourcing but also because of the threat of such action. When a division within the firm realizes that it may face dismantlement by outsourcing, it has the incentive to cut costs, resist the temptation to strike, and come up with innovative ideas. Outsourcing also provides a benchmark for cost comparison. The cost of conducting a business within the firm can always be compared to that of purchasing the service from outside.

Advantages of outsourcing are hindered by problems inherent in the market purchase. These are: (1) the danger of information leaks to competitors; (2) incentive problems of the monopoly supplier; and (3) the loss of economies of scope. This brings us to the question, What are the boundaries of the firm?

The firm internalizes every transaction with a combined production and transaction cost less than the cost of that transaction in the market. The marginal transaction included in the firm has the same total cost as one conducted in the market. This is not, however, a static arrangement. Over time, the underlying costs may change, requiring the incorporation of some new transactions and divestiture of others. The rule is that at every point the marginal transaction within the firm should have a total cost equal to that within the market. Among factors that induce change are technological advancements and globalization of the economy.

Improvements in computer technology have introduced an impressive array of products that enable management to significantly downsize their operations.[4] Large assembly lines are being replaced by smaller, more specialized production units.[5] The advances in technology have significantly reduced the costs of telecommunication and transportation.[6] The cost of air travel has declined to one-

---

[3] *The Economist*, March 5, 1994, p. 79.

[4] A 1988 survey shows that 35% of 1,000 chief executives who were interviewed had downsized their companies over the preceding year (Wattenberg 1988, p. 4A).

[5] McKenzie and Lee (1991, Chapter 3). The authors provide many examples of capital downsizing.

[6] In 1960, some 3.3 million international phone calls were made from the United States. This increased to 478 million calls by 1986. Since the cost of long distance calls is expected to decline by as much as 40% by the mid-1990s, the trend is expected to continue (*Statistical Abstract of the United States*, 1989, p. 545). For statistics on air travel, see Cooper (1986).

third of its level in the past decade. Telephone communication has increased significantly in volume due to reduced costs made possible by advanced technology. Computer-based electronic mail systems enable instantaneous transfer of large volumes of data at a very low cost. The reduced cost of communication and transportation makes the exchange of intermediate products within the market a more attractive alternative to producing them within firms. In addition, advances in technology have reduced the production levels needed to obtain economies of scale and scope, thereby leading to the downsizing of firms. Downsizing means greater reliance on market procurement.

Consider, for example, the impact of computer technology on the savings and loan industry. In recent years, the share of mortgages originated by savings and loans has fallen by about 50%. Advancements in computer technology and financial innovations have enabled other financial intermediaries to complete the information gathering required to originate a mortgage quickly and cheaply. Unlike thrift institutions, which originate and often fund their mortgages with deposits, private mortgage corporations originate mortgage loans and simultaneously sell them in the market. This amounts to splitting the origination and funding functions of the loan. Growth of private mortgage corporations in recent years indicates that these firms can reduce the cost by concentrating on the origination function and leaving the funding function to the market. As a result, they are able to offer better rates and lower closing costs than do thrifts. Financial innovation in the form of mortgage securitization eliminates the need to fund the loans with deposits. The mortgages are sold to prospective investors as collateralized mortgage obligations or mortgage-backed securities. Citicorp Mortgage accepts on-line mortgage applications and provides fast turnarounds. This has simultaneously increased choices for borrowers, improved liquidity for mortgage lenders, altered market shares, and provided new market opportunities for investors.

Globalization also plays a very important role in the reduction of transaction costs. With advancements in communication and transportation, firms have entered global markets in large numbers. The economic unification of Europe, the General Agreement on Tariffs and Trade (GATT), and the North American Free Trade Agreement (NAFTA) are a few examples of how these advances have created a much-integrated world in terms of trade and commerce. Globalization of the economy and advancement in technology intertwine and magnify the effects of one another. These elements suggest that the number of transactions that take place within the market will increase and firms will become relatively smaller. Instead of producing intermediate products within the firm, these products will be purchased within the market at lower costs. The end result is less vertically integrated firms.

TRANSACTION COSTS WITHIN THE FIRM: AN INTRODUCTION TO AGENCY THEORY

We previously discussed the relative cost of making transactions as a powerful incentive to integrate activities within the firm. A firm is set up as an entity in which various parties provide different functions. Depending on the ownership structure, capital is provided by one group or several groups, while the day-to-day operation of the firm may be handled by yet another group. For example, in corporations, capital is provided by stockholders and bondholders while management runs the organization. There are also other stakeholders in the company, such as the employees, suppliers of intermediate goods, and customers of the firm's products. These groups also have vested interests in the ongoing activities of the firm.

While ownership integration mitigates the high cost of market contracting, it introduces another category of incentive conflicts. The interests of stockholders, bondholders, and managers may diverge once the firm is formed. This creates its own set of transaction costs that need to be minimized if the firm is to survive in a competitive environment. The next section examines three types of ownership structures—proprietorships, partnerships, and corporations—and demonstrates how different organizational structures minimize different types of transaction costs and incentive conflicts.

AGENCY PROBLEMS AND OWNERSHIP STRUCTURE

Agency theory defines the firm as a "nexus" of contracts among stockholders, bondholders, and management.[7] The term "agency" refers to the fact that owners of the firm (stockholders and bondholders) delegate the responsibility of running the firm to agents (management). Without a mechanism to control inherent conflicts of interest among stockholders, bondholders, and management, the value of the firm will decline. The survival of any firm is subject to its ability to minimize the costs of such conflicts. These costs, which are referred to as agency costs (transaction costs within the firm), include (1) the cost of establishing contracts; (2) the cost of monitoring and enforcing contractual agreements; and (3) the cost of unresolved conflicts.

The various organizational structures observed in the economy (proprietorships, partnerships, and corporations) each reflect a cost-minimizing solution to a particular problem. The determining factor as to which organizational structure is employed depends on the extent to which decision-making responsibilities and risk-bearing responsibilities need to be combined or separated. We will examine each of these ownership structures to determine factors that influence their formation.[8]

Proprietorships

Proprietorships are owner-operated businesses so the decision-making and risk-bearing responsibilities are combined. The person who contributes the capital and therefore bears the risk controls the operation of the business. Ownership and control functions are integrated and there is no friction between management and the owners. A business that is organized as a proprietorship should have the following three attributes. First, the amount of capital required is small because an individual proprietor's wealth endowment is relatively limited. Second, the magnitude of specialized skills required for the business is limited. The proprietor generally has knowledge of the business and an understanding of the whole operation. Since an individual does not normally have a large number of different skills, the business has to require a simple line of expertise. Third, since the proprietor is generally an undiversified investor whose wealth is primarily committed to the business, the total risk (uncertainty) must be limited to make the proprietorship economically viable.

Partnerships

Partnerships can take several different forms. The basic partnership is developed as an outgrowth of a proprietorship that requires a larger capital investment. While a single proprietor's capital is limited, additional capital may be available

---

[7] Jensen and Meckling (1976).
[8] This section draws from Fama and Jensen (1983a and 1983b).

if a partnership is formed. Each partner has unlimited liability for the business and the partnership is dissolved if one of the partners leaves either voluntarily or due to natural causes, such as death.

A more interesting form of this ownership structure is found in professional partnerships, which arise in the areas of investment banking, accounting, and law. Professional partnerships are appropriate for lines of businesses when human capital is the main input in the production of services, and when employees have detailed knowledge of a relatively narrow subject.

Because human capital is the most important input for the production of investment, accounting, and legal services, the most efficient ownership structure is the one that minimizes the incentive problems among employees who are, to a great extent, similarly trained. Partners are the recipients of not only the outcome of their own efforts but also that of the other partners. If a partner provides less than optimal effort, the other partners' wealth can also be affected. Since partners are similarly trained, they can effectively monitor one another's performance. In addition, each partner monitors the performance of the staff. For example, in an accounting firm, the hierarchy from top to bottom includes the partner, senior manager, manager, supervisor, senior accountant, and staff accountant. A staff accountant who wants to advance in his or her career knows the steps needed to reach the partner level. Therefore, incentives exist for the staff accountant to put forth optimal effort to be eligible for the next promotion.

Incentives apply to all levels in the hierarchy. At each stage before partner, the employee must supervise the performance of those in the hierarchy below and be supervised by those in the hierarchy above. There is also a bottom-up monitoring. If a senior manager, who is looking forward to the next promotion, perceives the performance of the reporting partner to be inadequate, there is an incentive to complain to the managing partner.

Professional partnerships integrate ownership and control, thereby eliminating the typical owner-manager conflict. Mutual monitoring allows for an efficient system capable of minimizing overall incentive conflicts and related transaction costs.

Corporations

While the first two ownership structures impose varying degrees of personal liabilities on proprietors and partners, corporations limit the liabilities of stockholders to the amount they have invested in the firm. There are various types of corporations, ranging from open corporations whose stocks and bonds are publicly traded, to privately held corporations, whose securities cannot be bought or sold in open markets. Other forms of corporations include mutual corporations and not-for-profit corporations. In mutual corporations, the ownership of stockholders and bondholders is combined. Mutual insurance companies, mutual savings and loan associations, and mutual savings banks are examples of this type of corporation. Examples of not-for-profit corporations include various health and public service organizations such as the YMCA, charitable organizations such as church-affiliated concerns, and art-related endowments.

Corporate forms of ownership structure have the following attributes. First, a large number of specialized skills are required. Second, there is a significant amount of risk in the enterprise. Third, a large amount of capital is required. Fourth, the cost of mitigating incentive conflicts due to separation of ownership and control is low.

Open corporations are suitable for lines of business that require a large number of specialized skills. Corporations allow for the separation of decision-making (management) and risk-bearing (ownership) responsibilities. The limited liability feature of the corporate form reduces the risk faced by investors. Investors in an open corporation can lose only as much as they have invested in the firm. For example, at the end of the investment horizon, the value of a stockholder's investment in the firm is either zero—when the market value of the assets is less than the debt—or positive—when the market value of assets is greater than the debt.

Stockholders who own shares in more than one company bear less risk than do partners or proprietors who invest solely in one line of business. If cash flows from these companies are not perfectly positively correlated, the shareholders' total risk is reduced due to diversification. Empirical research shows that an investment strategy incorporating 15–20 randomly selected stocks eliminates the unique or firm-specific risk. Therefore, a project that may be passed over by a partnership or a proprietorship because of its high, unique risk may be undertaken by a corporation because the stockholders in the corporation are diversified.

Size can also be an important factor in choosing the corporate form of ownership. A corporation that needs additional capital can issue new stocks and/or bonds. In contrast, the original investor in a proprietorship has to provide additional capital. Similarly, in a partnership, either the original partners provide additional capital or new partners must be brought in.

Finally, open corporations are generally characterized by the separation of ownership and control. This raises a potential conflict of interest between management, who control the firm, and stockholders and bondholders, who own the firm. In addition to the management incentive problem, there are problems arising from debt financing between stockholders and bondholders. Finally, information asymmetry problems are also pervasive in corporations. We will examine each of these problems.

AGENCY PROBLEMS WITHIN CORPORATIONS

There are three general categories of agency problems observed in an open corporation[9]:

1. Conflicts of interest between management and stockholders, which lead to excessive managerial perquisite (perk) consumption;
2. Conflicts of interest between stockholders and bondholders, which can be further split into risk-incentive and investment-incentive problems and bankruptcy disputes; and
3. Conflicts of interest between old and new stockholders due to information asymmetry problems.

Management Perquisite Problem (Stockholder-Management Conflict)

Berle and Means identified the problems caused by the separation of ownership and control as early as 1932:

> Those who control the destinies of the typical modern corporation own so insignificant a fraction of the company's stock that the returns from running the corporation profitably accrue to them in only a very minor degree. The stockholders, on the other hand, to whom the profits of the corporation go, cannot be moti-

---

[9] Barnea, Haugen, and Senbet (1985) provide an excellent exposition of agency problems.

vated by those profits to a more efficient use of the property, since they have surrendered all disposition of it to those in control of the enterprise.[10]

The problem can be explained as follows. Suppose initially the manager owns all of the firm and spends $100 of the firm's money on perks. This reduces the manager's personal wealth by $100. Assume that this $100 is the manager's desired spending amount. Now suppose that the manager sells 20% of the firm's shares to outsiders. With 80% ownership remaining, every dollar the manager spends has a personal cost of only 80 cents. If the manager wants to keep the reduction in personal wealth to $100, the total perk consumption can reach $100/0.80 = $125. The extra $25 spent is due to the agency problem arising from partial ownership of the firm. Suppose that the manager sells another 30% of the firm to outsiders, retaining only 50%. Now the perk consumption can increase to $100/0.50 = $200 for a cost of $100 to the manager. The agency cost increases to $200 − $100 = $100. As ownership declines, the manager may be compelled to spend more and more because such consumption provides positive utility. When the management ownership stake declines to 0%, which is the case with a large number of publicly held firms, the perk consumption problem is at its worst state.

Perk consumption can take a monetary form through using valuable resources of the firm, such as payment of country club dues from the firm's treasury, or an indirect and nonfinancial form, such as applying less than optimal effort on the job. Other examples of managerial perk consumption are hiring friends and relatives while more qualified people are available at the same cost; using corporate funds to make charitable contributions that provide social recognition to the manager personally; providing the business of the company to an outside firm in which the manager has financial interests; and using the resources of the office in any way that will provide benefit to the manager. While these actions yield personal gains to the manager, they detract from the wealth of the firm. This cost is inversely correlated with the share of managerial ownership.

The managerial perk–consumption problem is due to the conflict of interest between management and shareholders and arises from the fact that shareholders have a residual claim on the firm's cash flows. Since bondholders carry fixed claims on the firm, they are not affected as strongly by the managerial perk-consumption problem. In fact, debt financing may be used as a means of reducing managerial incentive problems. We will return to this subject later.

Risk-Incentive Problem (Stockholder-Bondholder Conflict)

After the firm issues debt securities at terms agreeable to both stockholders and bondholders, there are incentives for stockholders to use their influence on management to change the firm's asset composition for their own interests and to the detriment of bondholders' interests. Incentive conflicts between stockholders and bondholders include risk incentives, investment incentives, and bankruptcy disputes. Stockholder-bondholder conflict is further aggravated by the presence of financial distress. Financial distress is present when a firm has difficulty servicing its debt. The likelihood of financial distress increases with an increase in the debt ratio (debt/total assets). We discuss the risk-incentive problem in this section and the others in the following two sections.

---

[10] Berle and Means (1932, pp. 8–9).

Suppose that a firm has raised $100 from issuing $60 in equity and $40 in debt due in two years. Further, assume that the firm has invested this amount on a risky asset with an investment horizon of one year. At the end of the first year the firm has lost $70 on its investment. The debt is outstanding for another year. The market value of the asset drops to $30. If the debt were due today, the bondholders, who loaned the firm $40, would lose $10. But there is a year of maturity remaining on the debt and stockholders are interested in investing the firm's remaining $30 on another project. Suppose there are two mutually exclusive projects available for investment. Both projects have an expected profit of $5. The first project has cash flows of either $0 or $10 with equal probability (expected profit = 0.5 × $0 + 0.5 × $10 = $5). At the end of the second year the value of the asset will be either 30 + 0 = $30 or 30 + 10 = $40. Bondholders may either lose $10 or receive their full claims at $40. Stockholders, however, get nothing under either outcome and their financial position will not be any better at the end of the second year than it is at the end of the first year. So if they take the first project, they are providing efforts for the potential benefit of bondholders but not for themselves.

Now consider a second project that provides the same expected profit of $5, but much more risk. The profit at the end of year two will be either –$5 or $15 with equal probability (expected profit = 0.5 × (–$5) + 0.5 × $15 = $5). The total value of the assets will be either $30 – $5 = $25 or $30 + $15 = $45. Bondholders receive either $25 (lose $15) or $40 (recoup their entire investment) with this project. Bondholders are obviously better off with the first project. For the stockholders, however, the reverse is true. The first project does not improve their financial position but the second project does, by the prospect of either $0 (the total asset value of $25 is fully paid to bondholders) or $5 (the total asset value is $45 from which $40 is paid to bondholders, leaving $5 for stockholders). While stockholders prefer the second project, the bondholders prefer the first, and the two parties clearly have conflicting interests.

Investment-Incentive Conflict (Stockholder-Bondholder Conflict)

This problem is also prevalent when the firm is in financial distress. We use an example similar to the one from the previous section to demonstrate this problem. Suppose the firm has lost $70 of its original value and is planning to invest the rest. There is a project that is available for investment that promises a profit of $5 with certainty. The return on investment of $5 along with the $30 asset value will go to bondholders, who have a total claim of $40. There is no incentive for the stockholders to invest in the project simply because they will not receive any of the benefits. Therefore, they will forgo a profitable investment. Forgoing the investment, however, denies the bondholders the extra $5 they could have recouped on their claims.

The problem gets worse when we introduce risk. Let us assume that two projects are available that have different expected profits. The first project offers $10 in profits with certainty (no risk) and the second project offers a profit of $18 or a loss of $30 with equal probabilities, so the project has an expected loss of $6 (expected loss = 0.5 × $18 + 0.5 × –$30 = –$6). If the first project is undertaken, the total value of the assets at the end of the second year will be $30 + $10 = $40, all of which will go to bondholders. If the second project is undertaken, the outcome will be either a loss of $30 or a profit of $18. If the project produces a loss of $30, the asset value will be wiped out ($30 – $30 = $0) and the bondholders will receive nothing. If the project earns a profit of $48, the assets value will be $30 + $18 = $48, of which bondholders will be entitled to $40 and the remaining $8 will go to stockholders. Faced with these two choices, stockholders would intentionally reject a profitable project that pays $10 with certainty and would undertake a project with an expected loss of $6 because it has significant risk. This is a combined case of investment-incentive and risk-incentive problems.

Bankruptcy Disputes (Stockholder-Bondholder Conflict)

Bankruptcy is a legal term referring to a case in which different security holders have varying opinions as to their claims on the assets of the corporation. Bankruptcy proceedings start when one group asks the court to temporarily suspend all distributions of cash flows to the claimants and subsequently determine the extent of each group's claim.

Filing for bankruptcy does not necessarily mean that the firm is unprofitable. A popular misconception is that bankruptcy means liquidation due to lack of profits. However, there is a major distinction between liquidation and bankruptcy. Liquidation is a capital budgeting decision whereby a firm determines that the value of its operation as an ongoing concern is less than its liquidated value. A proprietor who owns several businesses and has significant personal wealth may decide to liquidate one of the businesses because it is earning less than its opportunity cost. Bankruptcy, however, exists only if there are different claimants such as stockholders and bondholders. A 100% equity-financed firm will not face bankruptcy unless it fails to pay its workers. In that case, the workers become debtholders.

When a firm experiences financial distress, stockholders may take actions that are detrimental to the interests of the bondholders. Stockholders may decide to pay themselves large dividends before debt matures, thereby reducing cash flows available to pay off debtholders. Under these circumstances, bondholders may ask the court for protection. The court assigns a trustee to handle the affairs of the firm until a decision is made as to the claim of each party.

Bankruptcy disputes are costly. The direct costs of bankruptcy include court costs, attorney fees, accountants' expenses, and other related administrative expenses. The indirect costs of bankruptcy are lost customers, lost preferred-customer status with suppliers, and declining employee productivity.

Bankruptcy disputes and risk-incentive and investment-incentive problems constitute three aspects of agency problems related to debt financing. The higher the debt ratio, the greater the extent of agency problems between stockholders and bondholders.

Information Asymmetry Problem (Old and New Shareholder Conflict)

This problem arises when insiders to a corporation have access to information unavailable to outsiders. Suppose a firm has developed plans to invest in a positive net present value project. If financing is done with equity, the price of a new share of the stock will reflect the discounted value of the project's expected future cash flows. Suppose the project is developed with a great deal of secrecy to prevent information leaks to potential competitors. At the financing stage, the market price of the stock reflects only the publicly available information on the project. This creates a problem for the issuer. If the issuer discloses all inside information about the true nature of the project, the market price will reflect the intrinsic value of the stock. However, the release of inside information will tip off competitors, who may use the information to develop their own products. The firm ends up losing a segment of the market and a portion of the profits.

Conversely, if the firm chooses not to release its inside information, the stock price will reflect less than its intrinsic value. Suppose the firm proceeds to sell the new shares at a price below the intrinsic value. When the project is completed and the product is introduced to the market, the true nature of the project will be revealed and the share price will increase to reflect the intrinsic value. The new shareholders end up receiving a windfall profit because when the project was developed they did not own shares and therefore should not receive any of its profits. The windfall profit constitutes a transfer of wealth from old to new shareholders, causing friction between the two.

Information asymmetry is a widespread phenomenon. A new technology, a new marketing and packaging strategy, or a new product developed within a firm provide opportunities for significant profits. To realize these profits, the firm has to contain the leakage of information and protect the property rights of the new product. Patents and copyrights help to preserve property rights to some extent, but do not guarantee that the developing firm will fully realize its profits.

SOLUTIONS TO AGENCY PROBLEMS WITHIN CORPORATIONS

The problems described in the previous section create significant transaction costs that could threaten the viability of the corporation. In the long run, the surviving corporations are those that successfully mitigate these problems and avoid agency costs.

Avenues to alleviate agency problems include the following:

1. Corporate law, which provides an efficient means of contracting that reduces agency problems;
2. Corporate governance, which helps to mitigate incentive problems;
3. Capital markets, which provide solutions to incentive problems through takeovers;
4. Labor markets, which provide a mechanism to reduce management incentive problems; and
5. Signaling and financial intermediation, which provide solutions to information asymmetry problems.

Corporate Law as a Means of Efficient Contracting

Earlier, we defined a corporation as a nexus of contracts among stockholders, bondholders, and management. Explicit contracts written among these parties govern many aspects of their future relationships. For example, management compensation contracts may include payments based on stock price performance, and bond contracts (indentures) may include provisions such as limitations on dividend payments and restrictions on issuing new debt. However, it is impossible to write contracts that cover every plausible outcome. Furthermore, explicit contracts are costly to write and to monitor.

While every corporation has its own special attributes, there are general features that are common to all. If these general features were separately contracted for by every corporation, the total cost of contracting and monitoring would be astronomical. Furthermore, while some corporations would spend resources to write contracts on these general features, others could simply copy them without incurring significant costs. This phenomenon, known as the free-rider problem, may lead to inferior contracting. A cost-efficient alternative for contracting these standard features is to write one that covers all corporations. This leads to corporate law, which includes standard provisions applicable to all corporations.[11] The task of monitoring and complying with the provisions of corporate law is assigned to the Securities Exchange Commission (SEC), a government agency. Ex-

---

[11] Easterbrook and Fischel (1991).

amples of features in corporate law are limited liability of shareholders, voting rights for shareholders, establishment of a board of directors, and the fiduciary responsibilities of management and the board. We will return to corporate law and securities regulations in Chapter 14.

Corporate Governance as a Means of Mitigating Management-Incentive Problems

An important feature of corporate law is the provision that requires corporations to establish a board of directors. The board of directors is charged with the responsibility to protect shareholders' interests and to monitor the actions of management. Currently, the law requires corporations to set up a board composed of three or more individuals, whose specific roles are described in the chartering requirements of the state in which the corporation is legally established.

The board of directors represents an internal mechanism within the corporation to deal with management-incentive problems. The responsibilities in running a corporation can be divided into four functions[12]:

1. the *initiation* of new projects by management;
2. the *ratification* of some of these initiated projects by the board;
3. the *implementation* of the ratified projects by management; and
4. the *monitoring* of management's performance by the board.

The division of responsibilities between management and the board induces a monitoring process.

The board of directors may not be a fully independent body capable of evaluating and monitoring managerial activities in an unbiased fashion. The problem arises from the fact that top-level executives are not only board members themselves but are also instrumental in recruiting members from outside. To the extent that there are financial and prestige benefits in serving on the board, the outside directors are often reluctant to confront managers with whom they disagree. While the board has the legal power to hire the managers, set their compensation plans, and fire them, this power is rarely used to discipline the managers. Notable recent exceptions include replacement of the top executives at General Motors and at International Business Machines by their respective boards. These are extreme cases, however, since both companies had functioned with managerial problems for a long time before such action was finally taken.

The Capital Market Solution

If the board of directors is unable or unwilling to effectively mitigate managerial incentive problems, the stock price will decline. As the share price declines, the firm becomes an attractive target for a takeover. A successful takeover will result in the replacement of the management and an improvement in the efficiency. Actual takeovers and threats of takeovers provide a powerful means to mitigate managerial-incentive conflicts. Takeovers will be examined more fully in Chapter 14.

Capital market solutions to conflicts of interest between stockholders and bondholders can be addressed through financial unification. This involves investors buying stocks and bonds in the proportion issued by the company. In reality, this creates only one group of claimants, and the deductibility of the interest payment on bonds may be in jeopardy. A more practical way to achieve financial unification is to change the ownership structure of the firm from a stock

---

[12] These categories were suggested by Fama and Jensen (1983a and 1983b).

to a mutual corporation (e.g., mutual insurance companies). We will return to mutual ownership structure in Chapter 3.

The Labor Market Solution

The labor market may also mitigate managerial incentive problems. In an efficient labor market, salaries and wages of top executives are determined by their previous performance. Managers who have demonstrated serious incentive problems in their previous positions would find their salaries discounted in subsequent positions. This *ex post settling up*[13] can ease incentive problems for managers who are going to reenter the labor market. *Reputational capital*,[14] which managers carefully establish over the years, may also play a role in resolving managerial incentive problems.

There are impediments to labor market solutions to management incentive problems: First, the labor market is not as efficient as the capital market in incorporating managerial past performance into future wages; second, an executive who is approaching retirement does not have to face ex post settling up and may be indifferent to changes in reputational capital. For example, Roger Smith, the former chief executive officer of General Motors, held his position for more than 10 years before he retired. During this time the total domestic share of the auto market for GM declined from 44% to 32%. It is doubtful that Smith worried much about his future employment at any point during his tenure.

Signaling and Financial Intermediation as a Means of Mitigating Information Asymmetry Problems

As we discussed earlier, the viability of certain investments may be threatened by what is characterized as an information asymmetry problem. Credible *signaling* can mitigate this problem without disclosure of inside information.[15] Signaling may take the form of increased dividend payments or increased debt financing. Most companies make steady payments of dividends over time even when their earnings fluctuate. A significant shift in the dividend payment may signal the market that there is impending news concerning the firm. For example, if a company is in the process of developing a project that it believes is going to increase its long-run profits, it may signal this information by increasing its dividend payments. In the absence of such positive news, management will be reluctant to increase dividends because that may necessitate additional external financing.

An increase in the amount of debt financing is also believed to provide credible positive signals about the issuer. Consider a firm that currently operates at an optimal debt ratio of 40%, which is consistent with its operating characteristics and industry norms. After years of adhering to this ratio, the firm goes to the market and raises a significant amount of debt, increasing its debt ratio to 50%. Unless there is some positive news impending about the firm, this increased level of debt will increase the probability of financial distress. Consequently, the management is generally quite cautious in increasing the debt ratio. When such an action is taken, the market understands it as a credible positive signal. The positive signal helps to increase the price of the stock and resolves the information asymmetry problem without revealing the inside information to competitors.

---

[13] Fama (1980).
[14] Diamond (1989).
[15] Ross (1977).

Financial intermediaries also provide an important service in resolving the information asymmetry problem. Intermediaries collect, process, and produce information concerning their corporate clients. In the process of gathering data, financial intermediaries often receive inside information from their clients on a confidential basis. Since intermediaries gain access to both public and private information, they can price their loans more appropriately based on the intrinsic values of the projects being financed. The decision to make a loan, extend a previously existing credit, or issue a standby letter of credit also provides a credible signal to the market that something positive is taking place within the firm. Intermediaries, therefore, play an important role in mitigating the information asymmetry problem.

SUMMARY

The exchange of goods and services may take place in the market or within the firm, depending on the size of their transaction costs. Transactions within markets require costly contracting and monitoring. The cost of contracting depends on asset specificity, uncertainty, and frequency of transactions. Transactions involving high asset specificity, high frequency, and high uncertainty are generally organized within the firm to reduce transaction costs.

There are also transaction costs within the firm. For every type of business, there is an ownership structure that minimizes these costs. This explains the existence of proprietorships, partnerships, and corporations.

The incentive problems facing corporations are due to conflicts of interest among stockholders, bondholders, and management. The surviving corporations are those that minimize the agency costs created by these conflicts. Solutions to corporate agency problems come from explicit contracting within the firm, corporate law, corporate governance and the board of directors, the capital market, the labor market, and information signaling. Financial intermediaries provide a valuable service by producing information and resolving the information asymmetry problem.

REVIEW QUESTIONS

1. Use the three dimensions of transactions to determine whether the following activities should take place within a firm or within the market:
   a. providing daily software support and debugging for bank computers.
   b. annual transportation of crops from upper Midwest to gulf states.
   c. production of subassemblies used in one of big three auto engine manufacturers.
   d. satellite MBA programs run by small private colleges.
2. Why do firms exist? What defines their boundaries?
3. Describe conditions best suited for the corporate form of ownership structure.
4. Describe the roles of the board of directors, takeovers, and labor markets in mitigating management incentive problems.
5. Describe the effects of risk and investment incentives on a corporation in financial distress. Why would bankruptcy be invoked in this situation? Whose interests are affected?
6. Provide three examples each of the *ex ante* and *ex post* behavior predicted in a transaction with information asymmetry.
7. Realtors commonly fail to disclose to buyers the lopsided nature of their fiduciary responsibility. Often, buyers believe that real estate agents represent their interests and, therefore, volunteer all their negotiation tactics to them. But realtors are in fact obliged to work against the buyers' best interests. Suppose you are a buyer and you

know of this incentive problem. You are also aware of the information asymmetry problem that exists between you (the buyer) and the seller. How would you go about mitigating the realtor's incentive problem? What can you do to learn about things that the seller knows and you do not?

8. *Consumer Reports* does not accept ads and is fully supported by purchasers of the magazine. The information is sold directly to consumers. *Video Guide* writes about consumer electronics such as audio-video products but also accepts ads from manufacturers. Explain the differences in the incentives that these two magazines have. Under what circumstances do you think *Video Guide* may provide unbiased information?

9. We receive solicitations for auto insurance, which claims to be targeted to "responsible" (i.e., low-risk) drivers and to give them rate reductions for this. If this is true, what happens to the remaining insured population as low-risk drivers are skimmed off?

10. Many children are "bribed" annually to be "good" before Christmas in order to ensure the receipt of gifts. Needless to say, the illogic of the entire transaction does nothing to lead them to internalize "good"; instead, they are more likely to have their earliest experience of moral hazard, reverting to form the day after the gifts are opened. How can you alter this scheme?

REFERENCES

Barnea, A., R. Haugen, and L. Senbet. 1985. *Agency Problems and Financial Contracting.* Englewood Cliffs, NJ: Prentice-Hall, Inc.

Berle, A., and G. Means. 1932. *The Modern Corporation and Private Property.* New York: Macmillan Publishing.

Coase, R. 1937. "The Nature of the Firm." *Econometrica,* vol. 4 (November): 386–405.

Coase, R. 1960. "The Problem of Social Cost." *The Journal of Law and Economics* (October): 1–44.

Coase, R. 1984. "The New Institutional Economics." *Journal of Institutional and Theoretical Economics,* vol. 140 (March): 229–231.

Coase, R. 1988. *The Firm, the Market, and the Law.* Chicago, IL: The University of Chicago Press.

Cooper, R. 1986. "The United States as an Open Economy." In *How Open Is the U.S. Economy?,* edited by R. Cooper. Lexington, MA: Lexington Books: 3–24.

Dahlman, C. 1979. "The Problem of Externality." *The Journal of Law and Economics* (April).

Diamond, D. 1989. "Reputation Acquisition in Debt Markets." *Journal of Political Economy* (August): 828–862.

Easterbrook, F., and D. Fischell. 1991. *The Economic Structure of Corporate Law.* Cambridge, MA: Harvard University Press.

Fama, E. 1980. "Agency Problems and the Theory of the Firm." *Journal of Political Economy* (April): 288–307.

Fama, E., and M. Jensen. 1983a. "Separation of Ownership and Control." *Journal of Law and Economics* (June): 301–325.

Fama, E., and M. Jensen. 1983b. "Agency Problems and Residual Claims." *Journal of Law and Economics* (June): 327–349.

Jensen, M., and W. Meckling. 1976. "Theory of the Firm: Managerial Behavior, Agency Costs and Ownership Structure." *Journal of Financial Economics* (October): 305–360.

McKenzie, R., and D. Lee. 1991. *Quicksilver Capital: How the Rapid Movement of Wealth Has Changed the World.* New York: The Free Press.

Ross, S. 1977. "The Determination of Financial Structure: The Incentive Signaling Approach." *Bell Journal of Economics,* vol. 8 (Spring): 23–40.

Wattenberg, B. 1988. "CEOs Optimistic about the Future of Business." *Greenville (SC) News* (March 5), p. 4A.

Williamson, O. 1975. *Markets and Hierarchies: Analysis and Antitrust Implications.* New York: Free Press.

Williamson, O. 1985. *The Economic Institutions of Capitalism.* New York: Free Press.

C H A P T E R

3

Why Do Financial Intermediaries Exist?

OBJECTIVES

This chapter explains the economic reasons for the existence of financial intermediaries. We analyze the advantages of intermediary loans from the perspectives of both borrowers and lenders and show the unique role bank loans and commitments play in the resolution of the information asymmetry problem. The chapter concludes with a discussion of organizational efficiencies and ownership structures commonly observed among intermediaries, namely the mutual and stock corporations.

SIGNIFICANCE OF FINANCIAL INTERMEDIARIES IN THE ECONOMY

Financial intermediaries bring together borrowers and lenders. In the process, resources are allocated more efficiently. Two types of financial intermediaries exist: depository and nondepository. *Depository intermediaries* include commercial banks, savings and loan associations, mutual savings banks, and credit unions. *Nondepository intermediaries* include insurance companies, pension funds, mutual funds, finance companies, and investment banks.

Figure 3.1 demonstrates the importance of financial intermediaries in the credit market. As of December 1994 there was $17,071 billion of credit outstanding in the capital market, out of which $10,478.8 billion (61%) was held by financial intermediaries. The private domestic nonfinancial sector (e.g., households) held 15% and foreign investors held 8%. Others, including government-sponsored agencies, made up the remaining 16% of the total credit outstanding. Financial intermediaries are by far the largest single group of creditors in the capital market.[1]

Figure 3.2 provides the distribution of assets held by major financial intermediaries as of December 1994. Commercial banks held the largest share of the intermediary assets (43%), followed by mutual funds, including open- and closed-

---

[1] *Federal Reserve Bulletin*, October 1995, p. A44.

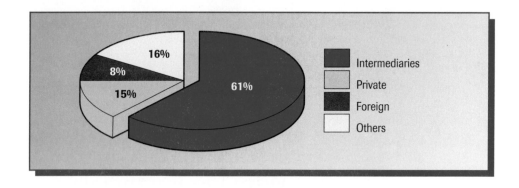

FIGURE 3.1
Credit Market Assets
by Sectors

end investment companies (23%); life insurance companies (20%); and thrift institutions, including savings and loans, savings banks, and credit unions (14%).[2]

Figure 3.3 presents sources of external financing for corporations in the United States. Despite its visibility, the stock market represents only a small fraction of the total (2.3%). This is due to a variety of factors. First, investment in corporate stock is risky. Stockholders do not have the security of a collateral or a fixed claim against future cash flows. Stockholders are residual claimants who get paid only after all other claimants have been paid. Second, investment in corporate stock involves information asymmetry. Investors often do not have access to all material information because corporations are hesitant to disclose anything that their competitors may use against them. Third, investment in corporate stock often involves conflict of interest with management. Stockholders face managerial incentive conflicts arising from separation of ownership and control. Fourth, stock issues are costly. Underwriting costs generally amount to 4% to 5% of proceeds, depending on the size of the issue. Most of the stock market activities involve buying and selling of already issued stocks, and not the financing of new investment activities.

Bond issues constitute 27.7% of the total external financing by corporations. Bondholders have a fixed claim on the cash flows of the firm. This reduces investor concern about the size of future payments. Bondholders are also less concerned with managerial incentive problems. Faced with fixed claims, management has to either make good on the promised payments or face the prospect of bankruptcy. Bankruptcy diminishes the value of management's human capital. Bondholders' fixed claim forces the management to work harder to meet its obligations. As a result, a project is financed by selling bonds only if project uncertainty is low. In contrast, financing through stocks does not require managers to meet any fixed obligations. If a project fails to produce sufficient cash flows, stockholders will not receive the expected dividends. The information asymmetry problem, however, does not entirely disappear with bond financing.

This leaves a significant portion of financing (66%) to loans from intermediaries. In the next section, we explain how intermediary loans mitigate information asymmetry, collateral, and management incentive problems.

WHY DO FINANCIAL INTERMEDIARIES EXIST?

Financial intermediaries play a unique role in producing information and in resolving the information asymmetry problem. To demonstrate, we will examine various functions of financial intermediaries that are information driven. We will

---

[2] *Mutual Fund Fact Book*, 1995, Investment Company Institute, p. 142.

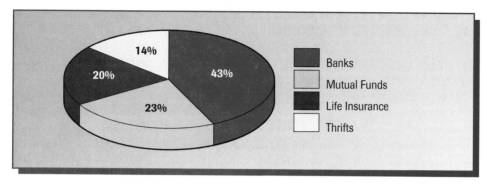

FIGURE 3.2
**Distribution of Assets
by Intermediary Type**

begin with the classic "lemons problem" to demonstrate the genesis of information production by an intermediary. As intermediaries develop repeat business with their customers, the transaction cost of information production declines, solidifying their role as efficient producers of information. Confidentiality in the intermediary-client relationship is proven to bring a speedy resolution to the information asymmetry problem. Intermediaries also effectively monitor the conduct of the management in the borrowing firm and carefully scrutinize the collateral to ensure loan repayment. The unifying theme in all these functions is information.

The Unique Role of Financial Intermediaries in Producing Information: The Lemons Problem

Akerlof (1971) made an interesting observation in the market for used cars that illuminates the problem of information asymmetry. A simple version of his story is as follows. Suppose that someone proposes to sell you a used car. You don't know much about the car other than the year it was built, its model, and some reports about its mechanical problems. You have little or no information about the driving history of the current owner, the car's maintenance schedule, and its performance record. The seller, on the other hand, knows more about the car.

Suppose there are 10 cars in the market for a particular vehicle model. Five

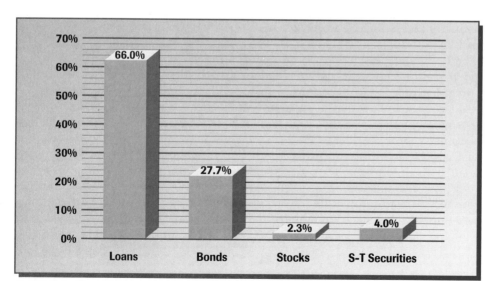

FIGURE 3.3
**Sources of External
Financing by
Instruments**

Source: Colin Mayer, "Financial Systems, Corporate Finance, and Economic Development," in Hubbard (1990), p. 312.

are good cars and the other five are bad cars, or "lemons." Since potential buyers cannot distinguish between good cars and lemons, they offer a price equal to the average price of a good car and a lemon. The average price, however, is not acceptable to the good-car owners so they are unwilling to sell. The good cars leave the market, and only lemons remain. Realizing the situation, buyers refuse to pay the average price for a used car. Once the good cars leave the market and only the bad cars are left, the price adjusts and we end up with a market for lemons only.

Suppose someone develops the expertise to distinguish between good cars and lemons. Such superior knowledge of cars is a valuable commodity and can only be attained through costly efforts. The car expert can be hired as a broker, for a fee, by potential car buyers to help them distinguish between good cars and lemons. The price the buyers are willing to pay is the price of the good car minus the fee paid to the broker. The broker's fee considers the cost of developing the expertise in car diagnosis and a profit.

Since attaining specialized skill is costly, it is possible for another person to make a false claim of having the necessary expertise to be a used-car broker. The new broker can charge a lower fee than the first broker because no resources were spent in developing the expertise. Since there is no way for the buyers of used cars to distinguish between the knowledgeable broker and the imposter, the second broker wins in the price war. The market for used cars collapses because buyers are not any better off using services of the low-priced broker than they would be in relying on their own uninformed choices.

The problem is resolved if the honest broker acts as a dealer who invests personal funds to buy used cars, and then sells them to interested buyers. Based on personal expertise, the knowledgeable dealer only purchases the good cars. The dealer's sale price reflects the price paid for the car, the opportunity cost of gaining the expertise necessary to distinguish between good cars and lemons, and a profit.

The dealer can also offer limited performance warranties to buyers. Imposters no longer pose a problem because to be a player at this stage of the game means risking one's own money. Furthermore, the imposter cannot offer warranties. In this scenario, the market for used cars survives.

Of course, this scenario assumes that the dealer has sufficient personal funds to purchase cars. This creates a wealth barrier: Only those who have the financial resources and the necessary expertise can become used-car dealers. This is obviously not a satisfactory solution. A way out of this dilemma is for the used-car expert, without personal funds, to establish a dealership intermediary in which individual investors can put their money. The dealer pools the invested funds, purchases the good cars, and proceeds to sell them for a profit. A fraction of the profit is used to cover costs, including the dealer's commission, and the rest is distributed among investors. This will be an optimal solution to the information asymmetry problem in the used-car market if investors trust the dealer. The dealer must have either sufficient reputation capital or an equity position, albeit small, in the intermediary in order to convince investors.[3]

This is also the genesis for financial intermediaries who produce the information necessary to resolve the information asymmetry problem in financial markets. Suppose that 10 entrepreneurs are seeking financing for their projects. Five

---

[3] Think of Don Dixon of Vernon S&L, who purchased the S&L on credit and not only lost the investors' money but also imposed substantial losses on the Federal Savings and Loan Insurance Corporation.

are good and the other five are bad projects, or lemons. Since individual investors cannot distinguish between good and bad projects, direct financing of good projects may not be feasible. A financial intermediary may enter the picture in which individual investors deposit their funds. The intermediary pools the deposits and lends to companies with good projects. The loan rate reflects the risk in the good project, the opportunity cost of gaining the expertise to evaluate projects, and a residual profit that is passed on to depositors and the owners.

Why don't we conduct these transactions within financial markets instead of going through intermediaries? The answer lies in transaction costs. The costs of investing in and receiving loans from an intermediary are lower than the alternatives available in the market for two reasons: First, repeat transactions within an intermediary reduces the search and information production costs; second, the intermediary can provide confidentiality to the borrower.[4]

Repeat Business Through Intermediaries Reduces Transaction Costs

When a borrower approaches an intermediary for the first time with a project to finance, the intermediary has to collect and process significant amounts of information in order to decide if the project has merit and if the borrower has the ability to complete it successfully. While the cost of initial information gathering can be quite high, the intermediary may offer the borrower a loan with provisions more attractive than market alternatives, given that there are prospects for repeat business in the future. If the project is successful and the borrower is satisfied, that intermediary will be the likely choice for the next round of project financing. In the second round, the intermediary needs little additional data to update its information file on the borrower. This is also beneficial to the borrower, who receives quick turnaround on the second loan. Often, timely financing is crucial for the successful execution of a project.

Repeat transactions can also take the form of multiple business transactions that a customer conducts with an intermediary. The customer is often simultaneously a depositor, a borrower, and a user of a variety of other bank services. The cost economies developed from multiple transactions provide the intermediary with an advantage over competitors that offer fewer services.

Confidentiality in Intermediary-Customer Relationship Reduces Transaction Costs in Producing Information

In a competitive market, the success of a project is critically dependent upon the investor's ability to keep the details of the project secret from competitors. An entrepreneur with a good investment project would like to receive a financing package consistent with the merit of the project. The nature of the project, however, may involve trade secrets that should not be disclosed publicly. If the project is financed by issuing bonds without releasing proprietary information, the uninformed investors will only offer an average price for the bonds. Under both alternatives—releasing the information and getting a good financing arrangement but losing part of the profits to competitors, or not disclosing the information but receiving an average financing deal—the entrepreneur stands to lose.

A solution is to finance the project through an intermediary. If the borrower discloses the inside information to the lender in confidence, the lender will be able to offer a loan with financing terms consistent with the merit of the project without jeopardizing the opportunity for the entrepreneur to capture its full ben-

---

[4] See also Campbell and Kracaw (1980), Diamond (1984, 1991), Ramakrishnan and Thakor (1984), Fama (1985), Sharpe (1990), and Rajan (1992).

efits. Confidentiality is one of the unique features of the intermediary-client relationship.

Financial Intermediaries Provide Superior Monitoring of the Collateral

As we have noted, stock investors face greater risk partially due to a lack of collateral. Investors in corporate bonds are only slightly better off with collateral because they have little, if any, control over the management and risk configuration of corporate assets once bonds are issued. For intermediaries, collateral plays an important role in protecting the principal of the loan. Consequently, intermediaries examine collateral very carefully before they make a loan and keep close scrutiny of its management while the loan is outstanding. Since loans are generally shorter in maturity than are corporate bonds, intermediaries have a chance to reevaluate the collateral value when the loan is considered for renewal. This provides the incentive for management to protect the value of collateral in order to meet the requirements of the loan renewal. Not every loan is successfully repaid, of course. Every intermediary has its share of problem loans for which the value of collateral is depleted. Overall, however, the value of a collateral to a particular bond issue is less closely monitored than is the value of a collateral to an intermediary loan.

Monitoring by Financial Intermediaries Reduces Managerial Incentive Problems

One of the major concerns with equity financing is the conflict of interest between management and equity holders. To the extent that managers are less than full owners of their enterprises, they have incentives to do what is best for themselves and not necessarily what is best for shareholders. While bond financing reduces managerial incentive problems, it does not fully eliminate them. Financing through bank loans further mitigates the management incentive problems because the lender closely monitors the performance of the managers.

When an intermediary makes a loan to a corporation, it receives certain assurances about the performance of the project. The manager briefs the lender periodically about the project. If the lender is involved with the financing of multiple projects for the firm, a closer monitoring of managerial performance takes place in the form of intermediary executives sitting on the board of directors of the borrowing firm. When executives from lending institutions become board members of the borrowing firm or vice versa, they have an opportunity for mutual monitoring, leading to improved efficiencies for both.[5] Interlocking board membership is a common feature among corporations. A corporate client of an intermediary is often both an investor in the intermediary and a borrower from it. They have a mutual interest in ensuring that both the firm and the intermediary operate efficiently with reduced managerial incentive problems.

THE UNIQUENESS OF INTERMEDIARY LOANS

We have discussed the reasons for lending through intermediaries from the perspective of the suppliers of loanable funds. In this section, we elaborate on the reasons for securing funding through intermediaries from the perspective of borrowers. Why do large corporations that have ready access to capital markets, through which they issue stocks, bonds, and commercial paper, often simultane-

---

[5] See Kummer, Arshadi, and Lawrence (1989).

ously seek intermediary loans? There must be something special about them that motivates even large, publicly traded corporations to seek financing through intermediaries.

An ongoing relationship with a bank is of great value to a corporate customer as well as to the bank. Over time, the bank cultivates important private information about the customer, based on which loans and commitments are extended. The transaction is profitable for the bank because it can properly price its loans and commitments by using its private information. The association with the bank is also rewarding for the customer, whose information asymmetry problem is resolved, leading to lower borrowing costs.

A bank loan or a commitment not only provides an immediate source of financing for the borrower, but also gives a credible signal to the capital market about the value of the corporate enterprise and the project for which the loan or commitment is arranged. The market uses this signal to temper its uncertainties about the borrower, enabling favorable financing for the borrower.

If intermediary loans are truly special in resolving information asymmetry problems and in providing credible signals to capital markets, we should observe changes in the stock prices of corporate borrowers upon the news of agreements. Generally, the stock price is a good gauge of the impact of a public announcement of a previously unknown event. When a publicly traded company makes an announcement that the market perceives as positive (negative), the share price increases (decreases). When corporations announce bank loan agreements, their stock prices indeed increase. Conversely, when they announce public issues of debt securities (bonds) to retire bank debt, stock prices decline.[6] Further research shows that most of the positive impact of the loan announcement is due to the news of the renewal of a previously existing loan. The strong positive reaction of the share price suggests that the market places further credence on repeat transactions. While the announcement of a first-time loan agreement between a bank and its client may indicate tacit approval of the borrower's financial credibility, a renewal sends a stronger signal based on the timely assessment of the information gathered.

The value of a binding relationship between the bank and its customer can also be examined when an economic event threatens to destroy the bank-client arrangements. One such example is when a bank becomes insolvent. This news puts the customers of the bank in a state of uncertainty. Depending on the severity of the financial difficulty faced by the bank and the level of the customer's financial dependence upon the bank, the value of the firm will be adversely affected. A case in point is the news of the financial insolvency of Continental Illinois Bank in 1984. After a series of energy and real estate loan defaults, uncertainty about the financial health of the bank caused its investors in Japan and Europe to withdraw their funds. The bank run eventually moved to the United States, and large uninsured investors here also withdrew their deposits. Finally, the Federal Deposit Insurance Corporation (FDIC) stepped in and pronounced the bank insolvent. The news created speculation concerning the bank's future. The prospects for the bank were: (1) liquidation, (2) acquisition by a healthy institution, and (3) effective nationalization through substantial capital contributions by the FDIC. While all three options looked bleak for Continental's corporate customers, the first two strongly threatened their existing agreements with the bank.

The Continental case supports the thesis concerning the bank-borrower rela-

---

[6] James (1987).

tionship.[7] Companies that had their primary banking relationships with Continental experienced a 4.2% decrease in their stock prices (adjusted to market returns) upon the public announcement of the insolvency of the bank. Subsequently, when the government announced its intention to rescue the bank and, therefore, revive it, the share price of the client firms gained 2% on average.

This suggests a cost advantage for corporate customers in conducting their banking relationship with one particular institution over time. This relationship allows a customer to receive better terms on loans from the lending bank than from financing sources that are available in the capital market. The lending bank can offer lower rates and other preferable terms to its clients who have provided a significant amount of private information on their projects. The lender not only collects the information provided by the client, but also uses data gathered across the bank's portfolio of client firms. The bank maintains confidential records on its corporate clients, including previous borrowing and repayment patterns, deposit flows, and the quality of their management. Because bank loans are primarily short-term contracts, the lender monitors the performance of the client's enterprise and encourages discarding bad projects as a condition for the renewal of existing loans.

These results provide interesting insights into economic functions of financial intermediaries in general, and banking firms in particular. While the primary functions of a banking firm are to accept deposits, make loans, and provide other transaction services, these are not unique features. Other firms can provide these functions. What is unique about a bank is that it produces material and previously unknown information about its clients and signals them to the market by entering into loan agreements. These agreements are taken by the market as credible signs of positive news about customers, leading to increases in their share prices.

THE UNIQUENESS OF INTERMEDIARY CONTINGENT CLAIMS

In addition to loans, intermediaries also provide contingent services to their customers. These services include loan agreements, standby letters of credit, banker's acceptances, and over-the-counter derivative instruments such as forwards, swaps, and options. The proliferation of these activities in the last decade has raised important questions as to their economic functions. Since these activities are contingent agreements and not actual loans, they do not show up on balance sheets. This, in turn, has made the regulatory agencies suspicious of these activities. Often the Federal Reserve and the FDIC have questioned whether such activities were for the purpose of avoiding regulatory inspection. When a loan appears on the balance sheet, its performance can be monitored by the regulatory agencies during routine bank examinations. The off-balance-sheet activities, by definition, do not appear on the balance sheet. Regulators consider this factor one of the reasons for their proliferation. This concern resulted in the 1992 adoption of the risk-based capital requirement that includes the credit equivalent of off-balance-sheet activities in computing the regulatory-required minimum capital ratios. We will explore off-balance-sheet activities and capital requirements in Chapters 5 and 7. We examine financial derivatives in Chapters 15–18. In this chapter, we focus only on the economic function of off-balance-sheet activities.

The proliferation of off-balance-sheet activities is consistent with the role of intermediaries as information producers. Most corporate customers can finance their own capital needs directly in the marketplace by issuing stocks, bonds, or

---

[7] See Slovin, Sushka, and Polonchek (1993).

commercial paper. They supplement their capital market financing with intermediary loans and commitments because these instruments provide credible signals to the market and resolve problems of information asymmetry. While bank loans traditionally have provided this service, advancements in information technology have made off-balance-sheet activities a viable alternative. This becomes clear if you consider four functions that a bank provides when it issues a loan: (1) the origination function that requires collecting and processing information to determine the creditworthiness of the borrower; (2) risk-bearing; (3) funding; and (4) servicing the loan. These functions may be separate. The bank can perform the first function by issuing contingent agreements without an immediate need to provide the loan itself. These agreements provide the customer with the necessary backing to do actual funding of the loan in the capital market. The bank may also provide risk-bearing functions by issuing forwards, swaps, or options designed to mitigate interest-rate, foreign-exchange-rate, and commodity-price risks.

BANK LOANS AND CONTINGENT AGREEMENTS PRODUCE MARKET-BASED RATINGS

Bank loans and contingent claims perform a function similar in some ways to that provided by bond-rating agencies like Moody's and Standard & Poor's. The difference between the two lies with the type of information used. The ratings issued by Moody's and Standard & Poor's rely primarily on information contained in accounting reports, which in turn reflect earlier events. In fact, most ratings changes occur in the weeks following the release of quarterly accounting statements. Since accounting reports convey old information, their release generally does not alter bond prices. This is because long before accounting reports are released, material information becomes public, altering bond prices. In contrast, bank loans and commitments are issued based on material and often confidential information that has more to do with the future prospects of the customer than past performance. Issuing loans or commitments, therefore, provides positive signals to the market about the creditworthiness of the customer. Consequently, bank signals affect the prices of the company's securities in the market.

OWNERSHIP STRUCTURE

As we saw in Chapter 2, the choice of ownership structure is a crucial factor in the viability and performance of every firm. With the exception of investment banks—which are often organized as partnerships—most financial intermediaries are set up as either stock or mutual corporations. For example, commercial banks are generally organized as stock corporations; savings and loan associations (S&Ls), savings banks (SBs), and insurance companies are often structured as mutual corporations. Credit unions (CUs) are community-owned institutions resembling the mutual form of ownership. Because of the differences in the regulation and the economics of depository and nondepository intermediaries, we discuss separately the choice between mutual and stock ownership for each of these two categories. In the next two sections, we examine ownership structures for S&Ls and insurance companies.

Stock vs. Mutual Ownership: The Case of S&Ls

A stock S&L is owned by stockholders and bondholders (depositors) and controlled by management. The incentive problems are between stockholders and management and stockholders and depositors. In contrast, a mutual S&L is owned only by one group of claimants (depositors). Because of the combined ownership in mutual S&Ls, the only conflict is between the management and depositors as residual claimants.

The choice of the most efficient form of ownership structure depends on two factors: (1) the surviving structure should minimize transaction costs arising from incentive problems; and (2) the ownership choice should allow for specific economic needs of the firm, such as adequate capitalization.

Management incentive problems in stock S&Ls are less severe than in mutual S&Ls.[8] In Chapter 2, we learned that management incentive problems in stock S&Ls may be mitigated by an internal mechanism such as monitoring by the board of directors. If the board fails to resolve the management incentive problem, labor and capital markets may provide solutions.

Mutual S&Ls suffer from more serious management incentive problems. The residual claimants in a mutual S&L have only limited ownership rights. For example, upon liquidation, a depositor receives a payment that consists of the original deposit and interest that is calculated based on either a fixed rate or a rate attached to some interest-rate index. Depositors lack significant voting rights and have no access to retained earnings. The board of directors, which is often composed of firm executives and their hand-picked members, controls the institution through perpetual proxies signed by a majority of the depositors. While these proxies are revocable, the limited number of votes allowed for a depositor, the restricted nature of disclosure requirements (including the identities of the other depositors), and the power of the board to redeem a depositor's savings account (thereby eliminating the opposition) make it virtually impossible for depositors to revolt and replace the board of directors or the management. Consequently, the board, which is heavily influenced by management, lacks sufficient independence to provide any effective monitoring of management's conduct.

Mutual S&L shares are not sold publicly. Therefore, the specter of takeovers is nonexistent. The capital market solution to management incentive problems, which has played such an important role in stock S&Ls, is ineffective for mutual S&Ls. Mutual S&L managers, who are unlikely to face serious job threats because of an ineffectual board and the lack of fear of takeover, are not sufficiently concerned about the labor market discipline. These factors aggravate managerial incentive problems within mutual S&Ls.

Mutual S&Ls can only grow through their internal resources, namely, retained earnings. Retained earnings, however, can be an insufficient financing source in a changing economy. For example, in an expanding economy where there is greater loan demand, a mutual S&L may be short of funds. Conversely, in a shrinking economy with significant loan losses, equity capital may suffer, leading to regulatory interference. When there are significant loan defaults, the write-offs reduce regulatory capital, increasing the probability of foreclosure by the FDIC.

On the positive side, the mutual ownership structure eliminates the stockholder-bondholder conflict that often plagues stock corporations. Managers are no longer induced by shareholders to take higher risks. Without pressure from shareholders, management will act conservatively because their own interests are served by accepting projects with lower risk. High-risk projects may result in losses that can jeopardize the viability of the institution and may ultimately cost managers their jobs. This is good news for the uninsured depositors and the FDIC.

---

[8] Fama and Jensen (1983a and 1983b).

Historically, the majority of S&Ls have been mutual corporations, but in recent years a significant number have converted to stock ownership. In 1955, only 10% of all S&Ls were organized as stock corporations, controlling 11% of the industry assets. By mid-1995, more than half of S&Ls were organized as stock corporations, controlling more than two-thirds of the industry assets. Clearly, there is a trend toward stock ownership in the S&L industry. The evidence on the conversion of a large number of mutual S&Ls to stock charter indicates that conversion yields organizational efficiencies resulting from the injection of new equity capital into the association and a decreased risk of insolvency.[9] The data also suggest that mutual corporations are more likely to convert to stock associations in markets that are characterized by higher growth and greater competition. Individual S&Ls that are more likely to convert from mutual to stock charter are generally larger institutions. In the postconversion period, converting institutions exhibit greater capital ratios, higher returns on capital, larger growth rates in assets, and higher loan fees.

While the mutual form of ownership was the dominant structure in the early years of the industry, changes in the economy, breakthroughs in technology, and shifts in regulatory structure have provided the impetus for the conversion of a large number of mutual corporations to stock charters. This suggests that the positive gains from increased managerial efficiency and the opportunity to respond to economic fluctuations have outweighed the negative aspects of the conflicts between stockholders and uninsured depositors and between stockholders and the FDIC.

Stock vs. Mutual Ownership: The Case of Insurance Companies

Similar to S&Ls, insurance companies are organized as either stock or mutual corporations. Stock insurance companies are subject to incentive problems among stockholders, policyholders, and management. The claims of policyholders are similar to those of bondholders. In mutual insurance companies, the ownership is combined into the claims of the policyholders. The incentive problem in a mutual insurance company is between management and the policyholders.

As we have seen, managerial incentive problems can be mitigated more easily in stock companies than in mutual corporations. As we pointed out in the previous section, management faces both internal and external disciplining mechanisms if the institution is a stock corporation. First, the internal-control system embodied in the board of directors calls for the task of hiring managers, setting their compensation plans, monitoring their performance, and firing them if their performance is not satisfactory. The market for corporate control provides an additional source of management discipline when and if the internal system fails to resolve managerial incentive problems. Stock firms that are plagued by managerial inefficiencies and show a subsequent decline in their share prices may become targets of takeover attempts. The labor market, too, imposes some degree of discipline on management. The combination of the internal- and external-control systems induces the management to perform in the best interests of the shareholders.

In mutual firms, however, management does not encounter such discipline. The control decisions—setting premium rates, offering various insurance products, and making investments—are made without the close scrutiny found in stock insurance companies. Mutual corporations have an advantage in that they

---

[9] See Masulis (1987).

combine the ownership interests in one group, eliminating the typical stockholder-policyholder conflict. This conflict arises when after issuing insurance policies, stockholders decide to change the risk configuration of the assets or simply plan to pay larger-than-expected dividends to themselves. If self-serving actions by stockholders lead to financial insolvency, policyholders may not be covered as promised in their contracts with the company.

The most efficient ownership structure in an insurance company is the one that minimizes incentive problems and their resulting transaction costs. With management incentive problems the only source of conflict, mutual insurance companies should dominate lines of insurance in which: (1) management exercises little discretion in setting insurance rates, i.e, standard actuarial tables are used to set the rates; and (2) there are fewer lines of insurance products and greater specialization. These conditions reduce managerial discretion in decision making and hence limit their self-serving conduct.

The evidence generally supports these conclusions. While there are many mutual insurance companies both in the life/health and property/liability fields, a closer scrutiny shows that mutual companies concentrate on fewer lines of insurance and specialize in policies with longer maturities. Long-term policies compel managers to stay with the stated rates and investment plans and prevent them from postcontract changes that may be detrimental to policyholders. Another distinction is that mutual insurance companies generally sell participating insurance while stock insurance companies sell nonparticipating insurance. In a participating life insurance, a policyholder receives annual dividends equal to the portion of the premium that is not needed by the company for death payments to beneficiaries, additions to reserves, and administrative expenses. In a nonparticipating life insurance, a policyholder pays a lower premium but does not receive annual dividends.

In the 1950s, mutual corporations had about two-thirds of the life insurance business in the United States. The number declined to about 40.5% by the end of 1993.[10] This drop is due mostly to the aggressive marketing of shorter-term life insurance policies and new product lines such as term insurance and universal insurance policies by stock insurance companies. In term insurance, the policyholder is covered for a limited period. The policy is generally renewable, typically at higher rates as the policyholder's age increases. Universal policies provide a diverse combination of insurance products, including separate insurance, investment, and expense elements. Mutual corporations, in turn, have concentrated primarily on long-term life insurance policies that feature savings elements as part of retirement plans. Due to the nature of their product lines, mutual life insurance companies controlled 38.9% of the assets of all U.S. life insurance companies, even though their numbers are significantly lower than stock-chartered life insurance companies. From a total of 1,840 life insurance companies at the end of 1993, only 109 were mutual corporations. Since 1970, 16 mutual life insurance companies have converted to stock companies and two stock companies have converted to mutual corporations.[11]

There were 3,346 property-casualty domestic insurance companies in the United States at the end of 1993 and about two-thirds of them were stock-chartered.[12] Mutual corporations are again very large in size and much smaller in numbers.

---

[10] *1994 Life Insurance Fact Book*, American Council of Life Insurance, Washington, DC, p. 19.
[11] *1994 Life Insurance Fact Book*, American Council of Life Insurance, pp. 108–109.
[12] *The Fact Book, 1996 Property/Casualty Insurance Facts*, Insurance Information Institute, p. 7.

Financial intermediaries play a significant role in the economy. They provide a unique function in producing material nonpublic information about their customers and in mitigating their problems of information asymmetry. Bank loans, commitments, and other off-balance-sheet activities provide credible signals to the capital market about the creditworthiness of bank customers. In the capacity of producing information and sending signals to the capital market, financial intermediaries play a role similar to that of credit-rating agencies. While Moody's and Standard & Poor's focus primarily on publicly available accounting information, financial intermediaries produce material nonpublic information. It is not surprising, therefore, that financial intermediaries play a crucial role in mitigating information asymmetry problems. This explains why when a bank loan or a commitment is publicly announced, the share price of the firm changes significantly to reflect the news, while a rating change by Moody's and Standard & Poor's generally does not affect the market price of the underlying security.

Ownership structures in financial intermediaries generally confirm the point made in Chapter 2 that for any line of business, there is one structure that is most efficient. While banks are generally set up as stock corporations and investment banking firms are often partnerships, savings and loans and insurance companies embody both stock and mutual ownerships, depending on their size and product mix. The trend in the S&L industry is toward conversion from mutual to stock charters under the new capital guidelines. In the insurance industry, the number of stock firms has increased significantly in recent years. Mutual insurance companies, while being small in number, control between one-third and one-half of the industry's assets.

REVIEW QUESTIONS

1. Briefly explain the "lemon problem." How does it relate to the existence of financial intermediaries?
2. What is "unique" about a bank loan?
3. What are some of the advantages of a bank loan over obtaining financing in the capital market?
4. What are off-balance-sheet activities? Name three and explain the benefits they offer to borrowers and to lenders.
5. Which form of corporate ownership (mutual vs. stock) offers the better solution to managerial incentive problems? Explain your choice.
6. What are the four functions of a bank loan? Briefly explain each.
7. In a stock corporation, the ownership consists of stockholders and bondholders. Who are the owners in a mutual form of corporation?
8. Why is it that the stock market, while a very important source of capital financing, provides such a small fraction of total business financing?

REFERENCES

Akerlof, G. 1970. "The Market for 'Lemons': Qualitative Uncertainty and Market Mechanism." *Quarterly Journal of Economics,* vol. 89 (August): 488–500.

Campbell, T., and W. Kracaw. 1980. "Information Production, Market Signaling, and the Theory of Financial Intermediation." *The Journal of Finance,* vol. 35 (September): 863–881.

Diamond, D. 1984. "Financial Intermediation and Delegated Monitoring." *Review of Economic Studies,* vol. 52 (July): 393–414.

Diamond, D. 1991. "Monitoring and Reputation: The Choice Between Bank Loans and Directly Placed Debt." *Journal of Political Economy,* vol. 99: 689–721.

Fama, E. 1985. "What's Different About Banks?" *Journal of Monetary Economics*, vol. 15: 29–39.

Fama, E., and M. Jensen. 1983a. "Separation of Ownership and Control." *Journal of Law and Economics,* vol. 26 (June): 301–325.

Fama, E., and M. Jensen. 1983b. "Agency Problems and Residual Claims." *Journal of Law and Economics,* vol. 26 (June): 327–349.

Hubbard, R., ed. 1990. *Asymmetric Information, Corporate Finance, and Economic Development.* Chicago: University of Chicago Press.

James, C. 1987. "Some Evidence on the Uniqueness of Bank Loans: A Comparison of Bank Borrowing, Private Placements, and Public Debt Offerings." *Journal of Financial Economics,* vol. 19: 217–235.

Kummer, D., N. Arshadi, and E. Lawrence. 1989. "Incentive Problems in Bank Insider Borrowing." *Journal of Financial Services Research,* vol. 3: 17–31.

Masulis, R. 1987. "Changes in Ownership Structure: Conversions of Mutual Savings and Loans to Stock Charter." *Journal of Financial Economics,* vol. 18: 29–60.

Rajan, R. 1992. "Insiders and Outsiders: The Choice Between Informed and Arm's Length Debt." *Journal of Finance,* vol. 47: 1367–1400.

Ramakrishnan, R., and A. Thakor. 1984. "Information Reliability and a Theory of Financial Intermediation." *Review of Economic Studies,* vol. 52: 415–432.

Sharpe, S. 1990. "Asymmetric Information, Bank Lending, and Implicit Contracts: A Stylized Model of Customer Relationships." *Journal of Finance,* vol. 45: 1069–1087.

Slovin, M., M. Sushka, and J. Polonchek. 1993. "The Value of Bank Durability: Borrowers as Bank Stakeholders." *Journal of Finance,* vol. 48: 247–266.

C H A P T E R

4

Basic Functions
of Depository Intermediaries

OBJECTIVES

The objective of this chapter is to examine the basic functions of depository financial intermediaries. We begin by defining brokerage and asset transformation functions of depository intermediaries. While the brokerage function does not require the intermediary to bear risk, the asset transformation function exposes the intermediary to liquidity, maturity, credit, and interest rate risks. We use the goldsmith analogy to demonstrate the origin of banks, the creation of the medium of payment, and the formation of the central bank. This leads us to the institutional history of depository intermediaries, including banks, savings and loans, mutual savings banks, and credit unions. The last section examines risks faced by depository intermediaries.

THE BROKERAGE FUNCTION

The brokerage function involves bringing together suppliers and users of capital without taking risk. For example, originating a loan and subsequently selling it without recourse constitutes a brokerage function. The intermediary receives an origination fee for its information-gathering service.

The value of the brokerage function depends on the observability of information, and its reusability. Suppose that a corporation is seeking a merger partner. It approaches an investment bank for advice. The investment bank deciphers a large quantity of publicly available information to determine the compatibility of corporate cultures, strategic plans, and potential for synergy. If the information were readily observable, the brokerage function could be a simple task. However, a merger decision has to be made based on a skilled interpretation of the attributes of two firms. It is the private interpretation of publicly available information that creates a niche for the investment bank in providing the brokerage function.

The reusability of information makes it economical for the investment banker to produce detailed information about various firms and industries. Since the one-time use of information does not reduce its value, and it can be reused again, intermediaries have the incentive to spend sufficient resources to produce information on firms and industries. Suppose, for example, there are seven Baby Bell companies that are interested in finding merger partners in the cable industry. Now assume that there are five cable companies with significant market shares to be considered as potential partners. If each Baby Bell and each cable company individually seeks its own merger partner and incurs $100,000 in search costs (the observability cost), the total cost will be $7 \times 5 \times \$100,000 = \$3,500,000$. However, if the investment banker produces the information on all companies, the cost will be $100,000(7 + 5) = \$1,200,000$, saving $2,300,000. Savings increase exponentially with the number of firms (potential for reusability of information) and linearly with unit search cost (observability cost). The less observable the attributes of the transactions and the greater the number of firms, the greater the potential value of a broker. It is not surprising that investment banking firms so forcefully defend their reputation and rank in their industry.

The brokerage function requires the intermediary to produce and sell information without risk-bearing. If the investment bank takes an equity position in a merger transaction, it will no longer provide just the brokerage function but will also perform the asset transformation function. Alternatively, if the bank originates a loan and subsequently sells it with recourse, it accepts risk and the transaction is then classified as asset transformation.

THE ASSET TRANSFORMATION FUNCTION

Asset transformation requires the intermediary to produce a service and bear the associated risk. Consider a 20-year mortgage loan with a prepayment option. Since a mortgage loan is often financed by short-term savings deposits, there is an exposure to interest-rate risk. The intermediary is also exposed to the borrower's credit risk. For example, a 1% across-the-board increase in market interest rates reduces the market value of a long-term mortgage more than do short-term deposits.

Financial intermediaries manage their risk exposure in the asset transformation process in one of three ways: (1) they pass it along to other parties; (2) they diversify the risk away; or (3) they accept and manage the risk. In the first case, the intermediary hedges its risk using a derivative instrument. In the second case, the intermediary reduces its total risk by mixing different loans and eliminating the unique risk of individual loans. In the third case, the intermediary may choose to bear the risk and to receive compensation accordingly.

Financial intermediaries, as both depository and nondepository entities, provide a combination of brokerage and asset transformation functions. Depository intermediaries often operate in the asset transformation capacity, even though recent product innovations have expanded their brokerage activities (see Chapter 5).

FRACTIONAL RESERVE BANKING, PAYMENT SYSTEM, AND CENTRAL BANK: THE GOLDSMITH ANALOGY

Although it has not been proven that modern banking evolved from the goldsmiths of the Middle Ages, the story works too well as an explanation of fractional reserve banking to discard for lack of authentication. The main point of the story is to show how a goldsmith could evolve from a provider of storage services to an asset transformer. We use a simple balance-sheet approach to illustrate the similarities between the goldsmith and the modern bank. In addition, we illustrate the role of a central bank or similar regulatory agency in solving the basic liquidity problem of banks. The goldsmith story is also used to show the conventional approach to money creation by depository institutions.

The original role of the goldsmith was that of a provider of security services. Individuals and merchants brought their surplus gold—gold that was not needed for immediate transactions—to the goldsmith for safekeeping. He issued a receipt that allowed the individual to obtain the gold deposit at any time in the future. The goldsmith charged a storage fee based on the amount of gold deposited.

Suppose we have a transaction in which an individual brings $1,000 of gold to the goldsmith for storage.[1] The goldsmith writes out a receipt to the individual promising to deliver $1,000 of gold at any time in the future. The changes to the balance sheet of the goldsmith and to the balance sheet of the individual can be recorded as follows:

Goldsmith			
Gold	$1,000	Receipts Outstanding	$1,000

Individual		
Gold Receipts	$1,000	
Gold	− $1,000	

Notice that no new wealth has been created. The form of wealth held by the individual has changed but the amount is still $1,000.

The goldsmith, by acting purely as a safe keeper of gold, has exactly as much gold on hand as outstanding receipts. This amounts to perfect liquidity for the goldsmith. Even if every depositor showed up at exactly the same time, there would be enough gold on hand to satisfy everyone's claim. The goldsmith earns a return for the storage service but no other reward because no risk is involved.

As the reputation of the goldsmith as a conscientious keeper of gold grows, two facts become noticeable. First, the goldsmith is able to determine how much gold is likely to be withdrawn on any given day and how much is going to be deposited on any given day. Second, depositors find that the transaction cost can be reduced by paying for commerce with the receipts of the goldsmith instead of converting the receipts to gold. So long as the goldsmith's reputation is untarnished, individuals will be willing to accept receipts for gold instead of gold itself. The goldsmith finds himself in the position of supplying the community with a commodity-based currency by making loans to customers. The goldsmith recognizes this as an opportunity to earn income in addition to the storage fees he is currently receiving. The goldsmith knows that there is little chance the gold will be demanded by the true owners because gold withdrawals are known with virtual certainty.

Suppose the goldsmith decides to loan out $100 worth of gold. A loan contract is carefully drawn up that requires the borrower to pay back the gold and a fee for the use of the gold (the cost of borrowing funds). The changes in the balance sheets of the goldsmith and the individual are recorded as follows:

---

[1] Actually gold, not dollars, was the likely unit of account in these early times and the transaction would have been recorded in terms of weight (e.g., 10 ounces of gold). For expositional ease we use dollar values in the story.

Goldsmith			
Gold	$900	Receipts Outstanding	$1,000
Loan	$100		

Borrower			
Gold	$100	Loan	$100

The goldsmith has accomplished an interesting transformation by undertaking this transaction. While the loan appears to be a simple conversion of a nonearning asset (gold) to an earning asset (loan), it has changed the nature of the goldsmith's business. The goldsmith now has on the balance sheet an asset that is mismatched with liabilities in two ways. First, there are $1,000 of gold receipts for $900 of actual gold inventory. Since holders of gold receipts have the right to redeem gold on demand but the loan is not due until some time in the future, there is a maturity mismatch. The maturity mismatch creates a potential liquidity problem because there is not enough gold on hand to pay off depositors if they all show up at the same time. Second, the loan contains an element of default risk. The goldsmith can no longer guarantee that all depositors will receive their gold under every possible circumstance. The interest rate on the loan must cover these risks as well as compensate the goldsmith for the costs of originating and servicing the loan.

This loan was transacted in gold. The amount of gold existing in the community did not change. The receipts issued by the goldsmith did not change. There is, at least in principle, exactly enough gold to cover the outstanding receipts in the economy. The goldsmith, however, has only a fraction of the gold on hand to cover all the receipts that have been issued. This represents the start of a fractional reserve banking system.

This loan does have a money-creating impact on the economy. To visualize this, think of the balance sheets of the goldsmith and the individuals in the community. Prior to the loan, all of the gold in the community was in the hands of the goldsmith. Commerce was transacted with the receipts issued by the goldsmith. The money supply, in essence, consisted of all of the outstanding receipts of the goldsmith. Once the loan was made, the borrower obtained gold worth $100 that could be spent on materials necessary to complete the planned investment project. Total capital in the community now includes the receipts outstanding plus the gold lent by the goldsmith. The loan transaction resulted in an expansion of the money supply for the community. By now you may have realized that there is no reason for the goldsmith to make the loan in the form of gold. We previously established that commerce was accomplished with receipts issued by the goldsmith. If the borrower spends the gold to purchase materials and the business receiving the gold deposits it with the goldsmith, the balance sheet of the goldsmith changes as follows:

Goldsmith			
Gold	$900 + $100 = $1,000	Receipts Outstanding $1,000 + $100 = $1,100	
Loan	$100		

At this point there is still $1,000 worth of gold but $1,100 in gold receipts issued in the economy. There is no longer enough gold to satisfy all the outstanding claims. The goldsmith has transformed the business from a warehouse to a bank. The amount of gold in the economy is only a fraction of the receipts that have been issued. The goldsmith has an incentive to keep on making loans against the gold reserve until reaching the point where there is just enough gold on hand to meet withdrawals that customers need in order to transact in another community.

Suppose the goldsmith, after many years of experience, determines that the maximum amount of gold that would ever be needed is 20% of deposits. The goldsmith can issue receipts until the gold stock is 20% of the outstanding receipts. With a gold stock of $1,000, the maximum amount of receipts that could be issued can be found as follows:

$$\$1,000 = 0.20 \times \text{receipts}$$
$$\text{Receipts} = \$1,000 \times 1/0.2$$
$$\text{Receipts} = \$5,000$$

If we define the fraction of receipts that must be held as reserves as R, then we have the following general expression:

$$\text{Receipts} = \text{reserves} \times 1/R$$

Taking the change (Δ) in both sides of the above expression we have

$$\Delta \text{ receipts} = \Delta \text{ reserves} \times 1/R \quad \text{or} \quad \Delta \text{ receipts}/\Delta \text{ reserves} = 1/R$$

where $1/R$ represents the simple deposit expansion multiplier. The interpretation of the multiplier is that an extra dollar of reserves can create $1/R$ dollars of receipts or deposits. In our example, with a reserve of 20% the goldsmith can create $1/0.2 = \$5$ of receipts with each extra dollar of gold deposited.

Modern depository intermediaries operate with constraints similar to those of the goldsmith. The official medium of exchange is not gold but currency issued by the Federal Reserve Bank. Individuals deposit currency at their local banks, savings and loans, or credit unions. These deposits are used to issue loans, similar to the asset transformation function performed by the goldsmith.

When the goldsmith engages in the lending aspect of financial intermediation, it creates a potential liquidity problem because of the balance-sheet mismatch. The goldsmith needs the ability to quickly convert the illiquid loans on the balance sheet to more liquid assets. A way to accomplish this is to hold some assets that are somewhat liquid and can be quickly converted to gold in an emergency. This provides a rationale for banks to hold a diversified (in the liquidity sense) portfolio of assets. Another way of acquiring the necessary liquidity is to have the ability to borrow on a moment's notice. A way to achieve this is to have agreements with other banks allowing a pooling of reserves when liquidity is needed by an individual goldsmith. Other private sources of borrowing can also provide liquidity.

These methods of liquidity management will not work when there is a general run on banks. In this case, a central bank is needed to provide liquidity by lending against the illiquid assets on the balance sheet. This is especially valuable if depositors know that a bank can obtain liquidity whenever needed. Customers no longer have a reason to make a run on their deposits if they believe a bank has sufficient access to funds.

A central bank is also useful for the economy in another way. Individuals probably learn very early on that it is cheaper and more convenient to transact with the goldsmith's receipts than with the gold itself. That advantage disappears once the individual leaves the local community and attempts to do commerce in areas where the reputation of the goldsmith is not established or known. The goldsmith's receipts will be discounted in a neighboring town to take account for the lack of information as to the redeemability of the deposits.

A central bank serves the purpose of coordinating the redeemability of receipts issued by different goldsmiths. It can require each goldsmith to hold clearing balances and then provide the accounting function of redeeming receipts among the different goldsmiths. To illustrate how this works, suppose an individual has received receipts of $50 issued by Goldsmith First and brought them to Goldsmith National for redemption. The receipts pass through a central bank where both First and National have reserve balances (in the form of gold). The individual banking at Goldsmith National can deposit the receipts at their face value of $50. National passes the receipts to the Central Bank knowing that it will receive credit in its clearing account. The receipts are sent back to First, their clearing account balance falls by $50, and First counts those liabilities as redeemed.

Check clearing today works in essentially the same way. The checks written on depository institutions are equivalent to the receipts issued by the goldsmiths. Instead of each bank issuing its own type of receipt (currency), the central bank issues currency. Checks are ultimately redeemable into currency of the Federal Reserve Bank.

THE INSTITUTIONAL HISTORY

Commercial Banks

The story we have told about the development of banking from the goldsmith is probably very close to the way commercial banking actually evolved. By the time America was founded, banking systems in Europe were well established and many of the early American entries into banking were patterned after their European counterparts. The prohibition on the ownership of banks by nonbank corporations presumably grew out of the English law that established the Bank of England but prohibited it from doing other types of commerce. This separation of banking and commerce was adopted for nationally chartered banks in the United States but was allowed for state-chartered banks. The Chase Manhattan Bank, for instance, grew out of a water utility company.[2]

The ongoing battle between political groups favoring a strong federal government and those favoring strong states' rights led to the development of both state and national bank charters in the United States. In the early and mid-1800s, state banks dominated the American banking industry. This dominance was due in large part to the failure of Congress to renew the charter of the Second (Central) Bank of the United States.

The First Central Bank was established by Congress in 1791 with the responsibility for regulating the money supply of the country. This bank acted as the official bank for the U.S. government with branches throughout the country. It also acted as a private bank by accepting deposits and making loans. The bank took an active role in limiting note issuance by state-chartered banks in order to provide for monetary stability. The power of this bank brought charges of unfair competition by state banks, and politicians favoring states' rights succeeded in blocking the charter from being renewed in 1811.

The history of the next central bank of the United States was much the same. It was chartered in 1816 in response to excessive note issuance by state banks. The bank was issued a 20-year charter, but its failure to stop a major inflation-recession cycle shortly thereafter led to attempts to revoke its charter. These attempts failed, but then President Andrew Jackson, a strong states' rights advocate, vetoed the bill to renew the charter. The override of the veto failed and the

---

[2] See Mester (1992) for a review of the pros and cons of combining banking and commerce.

United States operated without a central bank until the establishment of the Federal Reserve Bank in 1913.

The absence of a strong central bank led to several private attempts to handle the liquidity problems of the banking system. The Suffolk Bank of Boston started an early correspondent banking system whereby it redeemed the notes of other local banks at face value. Surrounding banks held deposits at the Suffolk Bank for clearing purposes and transactions were accomplished in the manner illustrated in the earlier section on the goldsmith bank. The relatively large Suffolk Bank forced smaller banks to join the system by threatening to amass a large amount of outstanding notes of these small banks and present them for immediate redemption. Such an action would, of course, ruin a small bank, so it was in their interest to join this private clearing system.

A system closely paralleling the Federal Deposit Insurance Corporation was developed by New York banks and the State Treasury in the 1830s. Banks paid a percentage of their capital into a safety fund that could be drawn on in case of a depositor run on the bank. The fund worked for over 10 years but then succumbed to extensive bank failures in the next decade.

The pattern of banking in the 1800s was similar to that suggested in the goldsmith story. Bank owners tended to be opportunistic and issued too many notes. Local and regional economies were highly volatile because of the periodic expansion of bank notes and the resulting panics and bank runs. Politics, not expertise or capital, played the biggest role in the issuing of bank charters. The need for greater control and the financing requirements of the Civil War gave rise to the passage of several banking acts in 1863, 1864, and 1865.

These acts formed the basis of the national bank chartering system that is in effect today. National charters could be obtained from the Office of the Comptroller of Currency provided the owners could show a need in the community, proof of sufficient capital, and evidence of the ability to manage the bank. Reserve requirements were established for national banks, asset restrictions were placed on banks to ensure sufficient liquidity, and a supervisory (auditing) system was established.

These acts also attempted to standardize the currency notes issued by banks. Notes issued by national banks had to be printed by the U.S. Treasury Department to ensure standardization. National banks had to redeem the notes of other national banks at face value. State banks were forced to be more prudent in the issuing of currency notes by a 10% annual tax on all currency notes issued. This greatly increased the cost of issuing notes and that tax, combined with changing technology, provided the impetus for the development of checking accounts. State banks avoided paying the tax but could create loans and profits by issuing checking account balances instead of currency notes. State banks were thus able to avoid the tax while the economy moved toward a standardized currency. Because state bank charters were associated with fewer regulatory costs, state banks still grew more rapidly than national banks after the banking reform of the 1860s. By the time the Federal Reserve came into existence, there were some 7,500 nationally chartered banks and 17,500 state-chartered banks.

Even with the formation of a well-regulated national bank chartering system, the U.S. economy was still subject to periods of inflationary price spirals and bank panics. A true central bank was created with the passage of the Federal Reserve Act of 1913. The primary goals of the Federal Reserve System were to: (1) provide for monetary stability by controlling the money supply; (2) provide an efficient transactions mechanism for the clearing of bank checks; and (3) provide liquidity to the banking system in times of financial distress by serving as the lender of last resort.

The Federal Reserve did not do well as the lender of last resort in the Great Depression of the 1930s. Close to one-half of the banks in the United States were closed by depositor runs. The passage of the 1933 Banking Act establishing the Federal Deposit Insurance Corporation finally provided depositors with virtually risk-free deposits. Not until the later part of the 1980s did the problem of bank closures surface again.

The Banking Act of 1933 (Glass-Steagall Act) also played a major role in the appearance of today's commercial banks. This act separated the underwriting and brokerage function (investment banking) from commercial banking. Banks offering both types of services had to choose which direction to go. Most chose to dissolve their securities business or spin off this part of the bank into an independent company.

Another aspect of U.S. commercial banking that developed in the early part of the 1900s was branch banking. Branching authority was not mentioned in the Banking Act of 1863, so it was interpreted by the courts that national banks could not branch. State banks followed the laws of their own legislatures, and these varied from state to state. Most states did not allow branching or allowed only very limited branching. The McFadden Act of 1927 gave national banks the authority to branch within their home city boundaries if the state permitted it. The Glass-Steagall Act further extended this authority by giving national banks the same branching rights as state-chartered banks.

To overcome the restrictive branching polices of national and state banks, many banks formed holding companies to achieve some type of banking network. A bank holding company acquires banks and places some type of common managerial control on the member banks. Acquired banks retained their original charter and customers could not receive bank services across charters. The consolidated balance sheet of the holding company was, however, better diversified. Significant cost savings were often achieved by cooperating in check clearing and other functions.

The role of bank holding companies was limited in 1956 and again in 1970 by restricting the activities of the nonbank subsidiaries within the holding company and by limiting the geographical expansion of holding companies. States could allow for holding-company acquisitions by out-of-state holding companies but did not do so until the late 1970s. Since that time, there have been a number of state agreements that allow for holding-company acquisitions across state lines. While the holding company cannot combine the charters of banks across state lines, improved technology and a gradual lessening of regulation have made the large bank holding companies of today look very much like interstate banks. In 1994, regulation was eased to allow interstate banking across the country.

Savings and Loan Associations

Savings and loan institutions developed from the building associations that were established throughout the country. The first of these was founded in Philadelphia in 1831. These associations were founded by groups of individuals who would pool their wealth and let one or more individuals borrow against the combined assets of the group to build a house. The association would continue to exist until all members had built or purchased homes and repaid the loans. At that time the association would be dissolved.

These associations evolved into savings and loan or thrift institutions. Thrifts were consumer-oriented financial institutions that accepted savings deposits of individuals and made residential mortgage loans. Thrift institutions were different from banks in the fundamental sense that they had no money-creating potential. Cash reserves were held at commercial banks to meet withdrawal needs, and most mortgages were of the long-term, fixed-rate variety. Savings and loans could still suffer serious liquidity problems because the deposits had an immediate maturity and the loans were longer-term and subject to default. In the Great Depression of the 1930s, more than 1,700 thrifts failed because of depositor runs.[3]

Housing supply became a national priority following World War II. This, combined with the stable interest rate policy of the Federal Reserve, allowed the savings and loan industry to grow at a rate of about 10% per year between 1940 and 1980. By the beginning of the 1980s there were approximately 4,700 savings and loans in existence. Over 600 of these institutions were uninsured. By the end of the 1980s there were about 2,200 thrifts in existence.

The 1980s saw a great many changes in the thrift industry. The large decline in the number of savings and loans was due to the high interest rate volatility in the late 1970s and early 1980s. The debacle of the savings and loan industry taught us a difficult lesson about the nature of the deposit insurance contract. This will be discussed in detail in Chapter 7.

Attempts to deal with the problems of savings and loans in this period brought about several pieces of legislation that provided thrifts with powers similar to commercial banks. The most important of these were the Depository Institutions Deregulation and Monetary Control Act of 1980 and the Garn-St. Germain Act of 1982. These acts granted federally chartered thrifts the right to make consumer and commercial loans and to issue checking accounts. Deposit insurance levels were increased, making it easier for thrifts to fund these new lending activities.

Credit Unions

Credit unions operate essentially as mutual consumer savings and lending organizations. As depository institutions, these are relatively new intermediaries. The first American credit union was started in 1909. The basic idea was similar to the buildings societies that led to the modern savings and loan. Individuals with a common bond (e.g., all the employees of a large company) would save a small amount from their paychecks each month. The deposits were then loaned back to the members of the credit union to help finance household and automobile purchases.

Credit unions were established in part because of the lack of attention paid to consumer lending by commercial banks. Commercial banks did not cater to the needs of small savers or retail customers. Business was oriented toward commercial lending. The lack of services available to consumers gave rise to the credit union movement.

Although the first credit union did not open until the early 1900s, growth was quite rapid. By the middle of the 1930s there were some 2,500 credit unions. Forty years later, the number of credit unions had increased tenfold. A great deal of consolidation has occurred in the industry since that time. The number of credit unions now stands at about 14,000.

One of the important features of a credit union is the common bond requirement. Federal law mandates that credit union membership should include a well-defined group of individuals. The well-defined group is the common bond and can be the employees of a business, individuals with the same occupation, or members of a community or even a neighborhood. Occupationally related groups make up the great majority of the common bond membership. These credit unions hold close to 90% of the assets of all credit unions.

---

[3] The movie classic *It's a Wonderful Life* vividly illustrates the function of the building association in American life and the way in which a depositor run gets started.

Like savings and loans, credit unions were prohibited from issuing checking accounts prior to the early 1980s. Since that time they have become more bank-like, with deposit products closely rivaling those of many banks. One feature of credit unions that gives them a competitive advantage over both banks and savings and loans is their tax-exempt status. Because credit unions are organized as not-for-profit organizations, they can often pay higher rates on deposits and charge lower rates on loans because no income taxes are levied on these firms. In addition, many credit unions receive subsidized or free office space from the company forming the common bond. As might be expected, banks have lobbied to have the tax status of credit unions changed as they have moved into traditional banking areas.

Mutual Savings Banks

Mutual savings banks were started in the United States in 1816 and were similar to mutual savings and loan associations. They were geared to small depositors who could borrow for consumer-related needs. A primary difference is a legal one. Depositors in a mutual savings bank are customers; in a mutual savings and loan, they are owners. Mutual savings banks were organized by a group of investors who appointed a trustee group to oversee the bank. Equity was accumulated through retained earnings. By the 1980s, these banks were also experiencing real estate loan difficulties and were allowed to convert to stock ownership, as did many mutual savings and loan associations. The distinction between mutual savings banks and savings and loans was further blurred in 1982 when federally chartered savings and loans were allowed to convert to federal savings banks.

BALANCE-SHEET ACTIVITIES OF DEPOSITORY INSTITUTIONS

The common element of commercial banks, savings and loans, mutual savings banks, and credit unions is the immediate maturity deposit. The great majority of assets of most of these intermediaries are funded by these deposits. Table 4.1 provides a breakdown of the balance sheet of these institutions. We briefly discuss the major components of these institutions and note the differences where significant.

ASSETS OF DEPOSITORY INSTITUTIONS

Cash and Reserves

The cash in a depository institution is used to meet daily liquidity needs. Liquidity needs are determined by customer deposits and withdrawals, net check clearings against the bank, and reserve requirements set by the Fed. All depository institutions must hold cash and reserves (required reserves) against their transaction deposits. For transaction deposits less than $54 million[4] the required reserve rate is 3%. For transaction deposits above the cutoff, the rate is 10%. Currently, no reserves are required against time or savings deposits, as restrictions were removed in 1991. A depository institution would need to hold at least the amount of required reserves (qualifying deposits times the required reserve ratio) in cash assets.

As can be seen in Table 4.1, banks hold about 7.6% of their assets in cash and

---

[4] The transactions deposit cutoff varies with the transaction balances in money supply. The cutoff grows by 80% of the growth of the money supply. The $54 million cutoff was effective in November 1994.

TABLE 4.1 Consolidated Balance Sheet for Depository Institutions: December 1994 (Percentage of Total Assets)

Assets	Commercial Banks	Savings and Loans	Credit Unions
Cash and Reserves	7.56	2.50	2.2
Securities	20.52	28.77	34.9
U.S. Government & Corporate	16.05	23.23	18.3
Municipal	1.93	0.19	–
Other	2.54	5.35	16.6
Federal Funds Sold and Repurchases	3.87	0.61	–
Loans	57.50	63.72	60.1
Commercial	14.69	0.98	–
Consumer	12.14	3.82	35.4
Real Estate	24.88	58.80	19.7
Other	5.79	0.12	5.0
Other Assets	10.55	4.40	2.8
Total Assets in Dollars			
(in millions of dollars)	$4,010,664	$1,008,644	$289,466
Liabilities and Net Worth			
Transactions Accounts	21.27	NA	9.8
Savings Deposits	26.12	NA	65.5
Time Deposits	21.17	NA	12.8
Foreign Deposits	3.42	–	–
Borrowed Funds	16.84	2.57	1.4
Subordinated Debt	1.02	0.24	–
Other Liabilities	2.37	13.55	0.9
Equity Capital	7.79	7.94	9.6

Source: FDIC, *Statistics on Banking*, 1994, NCUA *Yearend Statistics for Federally Insured Credit Unions*, 1994.

reserves. Savings and loans and credit unions hold a much smaller cash position of 2.5% and 2.2%, respectively. Larger depository institutions hold a higher percentage of their assets in cash and reserves because of a higher rate of reserve requirement and a larger amount of check payment than in smaller institutions.

The cash account consists of currency held by the institution in its vault and deposit balances at a Federal Reserve Bank or a correspondent bank. Deposit balances at the Fed represent the checking-account balances of the depository institutions with the central bank. Banks use this account to collect checks drawn on other banks and to pay other banks for checks that have been written against it. Instead of transferring currency between banks, check clearing is handled as a bookkeeping entry by the Fed on the reserve accounts of the banks involved. The reserve account is also used by depository institutions to wire funds between accounts and for borrowing or lending in the Federal Funds Market.

Another important type of cash asset for a depository institution is the *correspondent account*. This is a transaction account in other depository institutions. The account is used in the check-clearing process because it is sometimes cheaper to clear checks directly with another bank and because not all banks are members of the Federal Reserve System. Nonmembers, and especially thrift institutions and credit unions, clear their checks through a larger bank. The deposit balance that is kept at the clearing or correspondent bank is equivalent to the reserve balances banks hold at the Fed. Correspondent balances count as legal reserves in allowing a depository institution to meet reserve requirements.

Securities

The securities portfolio of depository intermediaries is maintained for the purpose of providing liquidity while earning interest income. The U.S. Treasury securities or securities issued by an agency of the U.S. government constitute a major part of these portfolios. Corporate bonds may also be held if they are of investment grade. Bonds issued by state and local governments are held by depository institutions because of their tax-exempt status. In 1994, securities made up 20.5%, 28.8%, and 38.9% of total assets in commercial banks, savings and loans, and credit unions, respectively. Depository intermediaries are not allowed to hold equity securities.

The securities portfolio of a depository intermediary contains both short-term and long-term securities. Short-term securities, such as Treasury bills, are risk-free marketable securities held for the purpose of increasing liquidity. Long-term Treasury securities and securities of government agencies are held because of their higher income yield. These instruments also are liquid. Tax-exempt municipal bonds are also heavily favored by banks. The interest paid on these bonds is exempt from federal income taxes and is free from state and local taxes in many cases.

Federal Funds Sold and Repurchases

Federal funds sold are excess reserves that are sold on a short-term (often overnight) basis to other depository institutions. Fed funds represent a small portion of assets because of their relatively low yield. The funds are important in an overall cash management sense because they represent a type of financial inventory account. Banks with surpluses of assets can cheaply transform them to short-term earning assets and contribute to earnings. Banks with deficiencies in cash can quickly and cheaply acquire these funds, thus reducing liquidity management problems. As might be expected, smaller institutions generally accumulate excess reserves and are the suppliers of federal funds, while larger institutions are the primary users.

Repurchase agreements consist of securities that are sold to another institution with the condition that they will be repurchased by the seller at a fixed price. Institutions with excess funds will purchase these securities and the difference between the price paid and resold price will represent earned interest. Repurchase agreements, in effect, act as "secured" federal funds transactions. In 1994, fed funds sold and repurchases made up 3.9% and 0.6% of total assets for banks and S&Ls, respectively.

Loans

The core of the balance sheet for a depository intermediary is the loan portfolio. In 1994, loans accounted for about 57.5%, 63.7%, and 60.1% of total assets in banks, S&Ls, and credit unions, respectively. Loans generate the greatest percentage of revenue for depository institutions and also create the greatest potential for problems. The credit risk in the loan portfolio requires a depository institution to spend extensive resources gathering information about borrowers. The information must be evaluated to determine the ability and willingness of the borrower to repay the loan. The bank must also continually monitor the activities of the borrower while the loan is outstanding.

The loan portfolio composition of commercial banks has changed significantly in the last decade. While commercial loans used to make up almost one-third of total assets, it now stands at about 15% (excluding commercial real estate loans). As commercial loans have declined in volume, off-balance-sheet activities, securitization, and loan sales have increased significantly. This presents a re-alignment in the commercial loan business where banks provide fee-based services that facilitate direct financing in the capital market (for more details see Chapter 5). As one would expect, real estate loans constitute the largest single asset for S&Ls, with 58.8% of total assets. The most important loan category for credit unions is consumer credit, with 35.4% of total assets.

Much commercial lending activity involves bank lines of credit established by businesses. These lines of credit are used to finance working capital needs such as inventories and accounts receivable. A maximum borrowing limit is established and the borrower draws on the line of credit as funds are needed. This drawing of funds is referred to as a "take down" and the amount of the take down, not the size of the commitment, is the loan amount recorded on the balance sheet. Besides earning interest on the amount borrowed, the bank also receives fee income for establishing the line of credit and keeping funds available for borrower use.

In addition to lines of credit, banks also make term commercial loans. These are fixed-maturity loans exceeding one year. Hybrids exist whereby a commitment will be taken down and converted into a term loan. Revolving credit is a longer-term line of credit. The maturity is greater than one year and the borrower can repay at any time over the outstanding loan. Rates on these loans can be fixed, but most often commercial loans are of the variable-rate variety. The rate will often be pegged to an agreed-upon base rate such as the prime rate or the bank's cost of funds. Savings and loans also have the authority to make commercial loans, but such loans are an insignificant proportion of thrift portfolios.

Consumer loans consist primarily of credit card and automobile loans. Credit unions also issue short-term installment loans to finance purchases of household durables. The consumer credit market is relatively new for banks. Prior to the Great Depression, banks did not actively court consumer customers. The rapid rise of credit unions caught the attention of bankers, who then saw retail customers as a potentially profitable source of business.

The most recent innovation in consumer lending has been the credit card. The first bank credit card was started in the early 1950s in New York. It was a common activity of department stores and gasoline companies but did not really catch on with banks until Bank of America introduced the first nationwide card plan in 1966. To give the card national appeal, Bank of America had to set up a nationwide system of redemption services. When a credit card is used in a store, the merchant brings the receipt to a bank where it is discounted (often 1% to 3%) and sent back to the originating bank. Bank of America was the first to set up this system with its BankAmericard. This organization has now evolved into the Visa card franchise. The main competitor is the MasterCard or MasterCharge, as it was originally known. Sears has another nationwide card service, its Discover card system.

It is widely known that the credit card business can be a highly profitable one. Interest rates on credit cards often are 10% above the prime interest rate. The spread over the cost of funds is very large but administrative costs are high and default rates are rising. Recently, public outcry over the high rates charged by financial institutions appears to have had some effect in lowering card rates.[5]

---

[5] Credit card lenders are promoting their cards as "value-enhanced" (i.e., long-distance discounts, travel and purchase insurance, identification features, etc.). The lowering of rates has come primarily in the form of variable rates or a low rate for the first six months.

Real estate loans are the primary loans of both banks and thrift institutions. These loans are used to finance new housing and commercial construction and for the purchase of existing homes. Real estate loans require that the property being purchased or constructed be used as the collateral on the loan. The buyer is required to contribute an equity position between 5% to 30% of the purchase price on a mortgage. Residential real estate mortgages have historically been of the fixed-rate variety but variable-rate mortgages became popular during the high-interest-rate era of the 1980s.[6]

One of the biggest changes in mortgage markets in recent years has been the securitization of residential mortgages. Well-developed secondary mortgage markets allow thrift institutions to originate loans and then to sell them off to mortgage pools. These mortgage pools issue mortgage-related instruments that have different cash-flow characteristics than the original instruments. For instance, a mortgage pool may issue some bonds that mature in two years against the mortgages. The new instruments are then repurchased by financial institutions to alter the maturity imbalance on the balance sheet. The originating institution may also earn fee income on the mortgages by continuing to service the amortization and escrow provisions of the mortgage.

Banks also lend for two other purposes. Agricultural loans are common in rural banks. For many small rural banks, agricultural loans make up 30% to 50% of the loan portfolio. Lending in this area requires different types of skills than does commercial lending analysis. Banks also lend to other financial institutions, such as finance companies and brokerage houses. Loans to finance companies are used to finance consumer installment lending. Brokerage houses borrow from banks in order to be able to allow their customers to borrow a certain percentage of the funds when purchasing the stock (buying on margin).

Other Assets

The other primary type of asset that all financial institutions hold is the real physical plant of the institution. These fixed assets comprise only 2% to 3% of the assets of a typical depository institution, compared with 40% to 50% for an industrial company. Other assets may also include collateral from foreclosed loans.

LIABILITIES AND EQUITY CAPITAL

Transaction Accounts

Transaction deposits include a number of different types of accounts that are payable on demand and transfer ownership of the account by check. For individuals, these checking accounts typically pay interest and are referred to as NOW (Negotiable Order of Withdrawal) accounts. These accounts are also available to not-for-profit organizations and governmental units but are prohibited for businesses. The NOW account is a relatively new deposit account and was not legally allowable at most depository institutions prior to the passage of the Depository Institutions Deregulation Act in 1980.

The commercial checking account is a transaction account that pays no interest. Here the account balances are usually kept to a minimum. This is accomplished by having daily surpluses swept into overnight, interest-earning investments. Small banks and other depository institutions also keep noninterest-earning transaction balances at commercial banks as payment for correspondent

---

[6] 0% and 3% down payment mortgages are becoming popular because mortgage interest is one of the few remaining tax deductions. Also, banks are offering 0% to 3% down payments as part of their CRA programs.

banking services. The larger bank provides check clearing, foreign exchange, and investment services to the correspondent. Income is earned by investing the proceeds of the deposits. The U.S. Treasury also holds deposit balances at most commercial banks. Treasury accounts serve as collection accounts for tax receipts and are employed to minimize fluctuation in deposits and reserves that occurs through the tax-collection process. These are called tax and loan accounts and must be secured by the pledging of U.S. Government Securities against the deposits.

As would be expected, commercial banks still are the largest supplier of transaction accounts. These deposits represent over 20% of total liabilities and net worth at commercial banks but less than half that amount for the other depository institutions. Credit unions are the next largest supplier of transaction accounts, due to their consumer orientation.

Savings Deposits

Prior to the advent of the certificate of deposit in the 1970s, savings accounts were the most common savings instrument for individuals and the most important source of funds for depository institutions. The historical savings account was the passbook account. When a passbook account was opened, the depositor was issued a small book in which to record deposits and withdrawals. These accounts paid a fixed rate of interest that was limited by regulatory authorities. Interest-rate ceilings were lifted in 1986. Today, computer technology has eliminated the need for passbooks.

Technically, a passbook savings account has a maturity of 30 days. A depository institution can legally require the depositor to wait this period after notification of withdrawal is presented to the institution. For practical purposes, this is almost never enforced and most institutions provide passbook deposits on demand. Passbook savings are associated with small savers but are valuable to depository institutions because of their low maintenance cost.

The newer type of savings account is the money market deposit account (MMDA). These accounts became available with the passage of the Garn-St. Germain Act of 1982 as a way for depository institutions to compete with the money market mutual fund accounts offered by investment banks. The money market account is a variable-interest-rate account with funds available on demand. Also, MMDAs allow three third-party checks per account per cycle (usually monthly). The rate on the account reflects the rate paid on money market instruments, such as treasury bills. Many institutions initially had restrictive minimum balances in these accounts, but these restrictions have been substantially reduced or eliminated.

Savings accounts are the most important source of funding for credit unions. The small-saver feature of the traditional passbook account makes this especially suited to their customers. Savings accounts were also the traditional source of funds for savings and loans but now play a much smaller role in thrift institutions.

Time Deposits

Time deposits are a savings type of deposit with a fixed maturity. Unlike savings accounts, which are open ended, the time deposit specifies a rate of interest for a fixed period. At maturity the deposit can be rolled over at the current market rate of interest or withdrawn and invested in another product. Technically, time deposits must be held for at least seven days, and if cashed prior to maturity a penalty must be levied. The penalty is the loss of three months' interest payment on maturities of one year or less and the loss of six months' interest for maturities greater than one year.

The most common time deposit is the certificate of deposit, or CD. CDs pay a fixed rate of interest to maturity and are issued in almost any denomination. A distinction is generally made between small (less than $100,000) CDs and large CDs. This distinction is for purposes of deposit insurance. Large CDs are only insured up to $100,000 and therefore can be very sensitive to rumors of the health of a bank. Large CDs are also negotiable and are actively traded in secondary markets.

Time deposits account for 50% of the total liabilities and net worth of thrift institutions. Many of these have maturities of less than one year. Time deposits are also the most important source of funds for banks, but account for only about 25% of liabilities and net worth. Time deposits are of little importance for credit unions.

Foreign Deposits

This source consists of funds deposited in American-owned institutions but originating in a foreign nation. The deposits are not insured and are usually very short-term in nature. These deposits are likely to arise in the course of international commerce and as a result are found only at the largest commercial banks. They represent less than 5% of total funding sources for all banks, but of course the proportion is much higher at a large bank with international branches.

Borrowed Funds

Borrowed funds are short-term, uninsured borrowing of depository institutions from the regulatory agency of the institution or in a money market such as the federal funds market. For banks and S&Ls, the federal funds market is the major source of borrowed funds. Savings and loans also borrow a significant amount from the Home Loan Bank, which at one time served as the thrift version of a central bank. Unlike other borrowed funds, advances from the Home Loan Bank can have quite long maturities (up to 20 years). This source of funds is used to reduce the maturity mismatch on the balance sheet of a thrift.

The federal funds market is a highly organized secondary market for short-term, unsecured borrowing. Financial institutions are the dominant players in this market, but participation is by no means restricted to them. Suppliers of funds are firms with short-term reserve surpluses, and users are institutions requiring short-term funds. The role of the federal funds market is described in greater detail in Chapter 12.

Another source of borrowed funds for depository institutions is the repurchase agreement, or repo market. Repurchase agreements are essentially short-term secured loans. The underlying source of collateral is typically a Treasury Security; however, it is possible to use other money-market instruments. Under a repo agreement, a borrower sells a security with a commitment to buy it back (at a higher price) within a short time. The repurchase price is stated at the time of the sale so the difference between the selling and the buying price represents the interest cost on the transaction. Repo agreements can be used by firms excluded from the federal funds market or by firms looking for a cheap source of short-term funds.

Subordinated Debt and Other Liabilities

Like industrial firms, depository institutions can issue long-term debt claims, which are uninsured and are subordinate to other debt in the bankruptcy process. Such debt can be attractive to depository institutions because it can help to overcome the typical maturity mismatch between liabilities and assets. Because subordinated debt is not insured, it tends to be an expensive way for depository institutions to raise funds; thus, it represents an insignificant portion of the balance sheet.

Equity Capital

The capital account represents the owners' stake in the institution. Equity capital consists primarily of common stock issued by the bank and nondistributed profits or retained earnings. The ratio of equity capital to total assets represents the proportion of assets funded with invested capital. As can be seen in Table 4.1, the proportion is around 8% for banks and thrifts and close to 10% for credit unions. This is quite low compared to an industrial firm, which would be more likely to have a capital ratio of 40% to 50%.

Another way to represent the capital ratio of a depository institution is to take the reciprocal of the ratio of equity capital to total assets. This ratio is referred to as the equity multiplier (EM) and is computed as:

$$EM = total\ assets\ /\ equity\ capital.$$

Depository institutions have a capital ratio of about 8% on average, so they have an equity multiplier of $1/0.08 = $12.5. This means that each dollar of equity invested in the firm can support slightly more than $12.50 of assets. The other $11.50 that are needed to fund the $12.50 of assets are obtained via deposits or purchased funds. Depository institutions in this sense are highly leveraged companies.

One reason that depository institutions can operate with so little equity capital is the nature of the business. Banks are providers of intermediation services, and individuals are willing to allow these institutions to hold their wealth as debt claims at a very low cost in exchange for transactions and savings services. As long as a bank does a good job of liquidity management, there is little need for large amounts of owners' equity.

One of the primary causes of illiquidity on the part of a depository institution is the transformation of deposits to loans. Because loans carry some credit risk, the possibility arises of nonpayment to depositors. Bank loans almost always require the borrower to pledge some type of collateral to protect the bank against nonpayment. A bank thus obtains indirect capital in the form of collateral to protect the value of assets, in addition to having some capital of its own.

Credit unions and mutual depository institutions are technically owned by the depositors and have no shareholders in the traditional sense of the term. Deposits are considered to be shares, and the return on the deposits is a dividend. For practical purposes, however, these deposits act like debt, and equity capital is obtained through operating surpluses (profits). One disadvantage of this type of ownership is that it is difficult to raise capital quickly if the need arises. The conversion from mutual to stock form of ownership for savings and loans was encouraged (and regulations were relaxed to make it easier) in the early 1980s to help the thrift industry overcome the problem of deteriorating mortgage portfolios and capital positions.

The reported value of equity capital for a depository institution (as it is for any audited company) is a book value rather than a market value. The loans and securities of a bank are recorded on the balance sheet at historical cost. The same is true for the deposit liabilities of the institution. While there is an adjustment to the loan portfolio to account for potential losses, the difference between assets and liabilities does not necessarily reflect a market determination of the value of the institution. In some cases, the market value may be much higher than the book value, while in others the market value may be lower than the book value. A recent ruling by a Financial Accounting Standards Board (FASB) committee will require banks to start reporting their securities portfolio in market-value terms. This will make equity capital on the balance sheet more of a market-value measure. The role and reporting of equity capital for financial institutions will be examined more fully when we examine the deposit insurance system.

As discussed earlier, most depository institutions are 90% to 95% leveraged. The relatively low levels of capital means that asset returns are highly magnified when transformed to equity returns. The low capital levels allow bank owners to earn competitive rates of return on their investment even though return on assets may be relatively low.

The undesirable part of high leverage is the susceptibility of depository institutions to bankruptcy. With capital at only 8% of total assets and loans at 60% of total assets, an unexpected decline in the value of the loan portfolio of only 10% wipes out almost all of the capital. Unfortunately, insured depositors have no incentive to monitor the true market value capital position of the institution, so even a technically insolvent institution is able to keep operating so long as depositors do not withdraw their funds.

THE INCOME STATEMENT OF DEPOSITORY INTERMEDIARIES

Financial intermediaries act as asset transformers or brokers. The business of depository institutions falls into both categories, and the income statement reflects that fact. The major part of the income of a bank comes from transformation services and shows up as net interest income—the difference between interest income from the asset side of the balance sheet and interest expense from the liability side of the balance sheet. Brokerage service income is represented in the form of fee income. Part of this income may not be pure brokerage income, as fees are charged for loan commitments and letters of credit, which are more transformation-type services. The calculation of net income for a depository institution is relatively simple and just equals net interest income less loan losses less operating expenses plus fee income less taxes.

The consolidated income statements of the different depository institutions provided in Table 4.2 illustrate the typical form of an income statement. Many states have reporting standards that require banks and savings and loans to publish simplified balance sheets and income statements in their local newspapers. Such reports look very similar to that depicted in Table 4.2.

Before going on to an example in which we will calculate income and profitability measures for a financial institution, we point out a couple of conventions on the income statements. As was mentioned earlier, banks hold relatively large amounts of municipal bonds. This interest is not taxable and earnings on municipal bonds are not directly comparable to earnings on taxable bonds. A common way to report municipal interest income is to gross up the yield to what is called the tax equivalent rate. If a bank has some municipal bonds that yield 5% and is in the 30% tax bracket, the tax equivalent yield on those bonds would be 7.14% ($0.05/1 - 0.3 = 0.0714$). One million dollars worth of these bonds yields $50,000 of nontaxable interest income or $71,400 of taxable interest income. The tax equivalent amount could be included on the income statement and taxes deducted to obtain the correct income figure.

The loan loss expense that is shown on the income statement is an accounting entry that reflects any increase to the loan loss reserve over the year. The loan loss reserve is calculated by classifying loans as to the likelihood of loss and then using historical data and knowledge of market conditions to assign an anticipated dollar loss to each category of loans. It is important to note that this estimate is forward looking and does not reflect what has been written off in the past as bad debt.[7]

---

[7] This is confusing because loan loss reporting for tax purposes is based on actual losses and not a reserving procedure, as is required for Call and Income Reporting statements.

TABLE 4.2 Consolidated Income Statement for Depository Institutions: December 1994 (in Millions of Dollars)

	Commercial Banks	Savings and Loan Institutions	Credit Unions
Interest Income	257,843	63,470	19,551
− Interest Expense	−111,266	−33,410	−8,516
= Net Interest Income	146,577	30,060	11,035
− Provision for Loan Losses	−10,912	−2,421	−1,325
+ Noninterest Income	+76,222	+6,238	+1,899
− Noninterest Expense	−144,196	−23,218	−8,113
+ Gain (Loss) on Sale of Assets Plus Net Extraordinary Items	(585)	(465)	(59)
= Income Before Taxes	67,106	10,194	3,437
− Taxes	−22,426	−3,781	−0
= Net Income	44,680	6,413	3,437

Source: FDIC, *Statistics on Banking,* 1994, NCUA *Yearend Statistics for Federally Insured Credit Unions,* 1994.

To illustrate how this works, suppose a bank has $101 million in loans outstanding and has calculated from past experience that it will suffer loan losses of $1 million on this portfolio. These items are carried on the balance sheet as follows:

Assets	
Gross Loans	$101,000,000
−Loan Loss Reserves	$1,000,000
Net Loans	$100,000,000

When a depository institution has loans that are charged off, the loan loss reserve account and gross loans are written down by an equal amount. Suppose, in continuing with our example, that this bank actually experienced $1,000,000 of actual loan losses. The balance sheet looks this way after the losses are charged off:

Assets	
Gross Loans	$100,000,000
−Loan Loss Reserves	0
Net Loans	$100,000,000

Any additions the bank makes to the loan loss reserve account are considered expenses to be allocated to the income statement. The charge-off of the $1,000,000 in bad loans does not, however, alter the total value of assets because that was accomplished when the loan loss reserve account was created.

Income Calculation: An Example

To illustrate the calculation of income and the impact of interest-rate changes on income we construct a simplified example. Suppose we have a depository institution with a fee income of $5 million, an operating expense of $15 million, no increases in its loan loss reserve account, and a tax rate of 20%. The balance sheet for our institution is given below:

Assets		Liabilities and Net Worth	
Securities	$500,000,000	Deposits	$1,200,000,000
Loans	$1,000,000,000	Equity	$300,000,000
Total	$1,500,000,000	Total	$1,500,000,000

Further assume that the average yield on securities of this bank is 7% while loan rates average 10%. The rate paid on deposits is 5%. The income statement of the bank is then constructed as follows:

Income Statement	
Interest Income: $500,000,000 \times 0.07 + $1,000,000,000 \times 0.10	$135,000,000
Interest Expense: $1,200,000,000 \times 0.05	−60,000,000
Net Interest Income	75,000,000
Operating Expense	−15,000,000
Fee Income	5,000,000
Income Before Taxes	65,000,000
Taxes @ 20%	13,000,000
Net Income	$52,000,000

The net income of the institution is used to compute standard profitability ratios. The most common measure is the return to owners equity or ROE. This is calculated as net income divided by equity, which in our case would equal $52,000,000 / $300,000,000 or 17%[8]. An excellent return would be in the 12% to 15% range, so this institution did well indeed.

The return on equity can be broken down into components that reflect asset quality and financial leverage. Multiplying the ratio definition of return on equity by total assets/owners equity and then rearranging yields:

$$ROE = (\text{net income}/\text{total assets}) \times (\text{total assets}/\text{owners equity})$$

The first expression in parentheses is the return on assets (ROA) and is a measure of asset quality, while the second is the equity multiplier that was discussed earlier. Calculating these ratios for the institution in our example we have:

$$ROE = (52,000,000 / 1,500,000,000) \times (1,500,000,000 / 300,000,000)$$
$$= 0.034 \times 5 = 0.17$$

This bank has a return on assets of almost 3.5%. A rule of thumb for banks is to achieve an ROA of 1%. On the other hand, this bank is not highly leveraged with an equity multiplier of 5. This translates to an equity-to-assets ratio of 20%. The average for all banks is closer to 7%. Hence, we find that our bank is highly profitable for the owners but could be even more profitable if they were to

---

[8] Often financial ratios that mix balance-sheet and income totals will use the average balance-sheet measure from the beginning to the end of the year. This is due to the fact that income variables represent a flow of payments over the course of a year, while balance-sheet numbers reflect the value at a particular point in the year. Taking the average of the beginning- and end-of-year values reflects the fact that the income was generated from equity over the entire year.

TABLE 4.3 Profitability Measures for Depository Institutions 1987 and 1994				
	ROE		ROA	
Institution	**1987**	**1994**	**1987**	**1994**
Commercial Banks	1.55%	14.30%	0.093%	1.14%
Savings and Loan Institutions	−9.92%	8.10%	−0.355%	0.636%
Credit Unions	7.74%	12.42%	0.508%	1.19%

Source: FDIC, Statistics on Banking, 1994, NCUA Yearend Statistics for Federally Insured Credit Unions, 1994.

create more financial leverage. Asset quality is extremely high, which reflects low levels of loan losses and/or very high spreads between lending and deposit rates.

The profitability of banks, thrifts, and credit unions in recent years is provided in Table 4.3. Banks were barely profitable in 1987, while savings and loans showed substantial losses. A low point for the profitability of depository institutions occurred in 1987. Loan losses were high and spreads between loans and deposits had narrowed considerably. By 1994, the outlook had changed dramatically. Profits were at record levels in the banking industry and the remaining savings and loan institutions were also doing well. The main reason for the increased profitability was sharply lower interest rates in the economy. Spreads increased as deposit rates fell faster than loan rates. In addition, many depository institutions had written off bad loans several years before and profits were buoyed by the lowering of the loan loss expense.

RISK IN DEPOSITORY INTERMEDIATION

Liquidity Risk

Liquidity risk arises through the interaction of the different services provided in the financial intermediation process. Accepting deposits with immediate maturity is the primary source of the risk. It is compounded by investing in financial claims with different maturity, size, and default risk. Liquidity risk is best defined as the possibility that the financial institution will decline in value when attempting to satisfy the claims of depositors. This could mean that a bank ends up selling loans at a deep discount in order to obtain funds to meet depositor withdrawals. Alternatively, it could mean being forced to borrow funds at a rate higher than usual to meet an unanticipated withdrawal.

A depository institution can generate liquidity from both the asset and the liability sides. Depository institutions hold a substantial amount of cash assets to meet normal liquidity needs. Most also use their security portfolio as a source of liquid funds. Untapped sources of borrowing and new deposits are also sources of liquidity.

A common measure of the liquidity needs of a depository institution is a forecast of cash outflows relative to cash inflows. This is defined as the liquidity gap. A positive liquidity gap indicates more cash will leave the institution than will flow in over a predetermined time period. With a positive liquidity gap, a bank must decide on a method for funding the mismatch between outflow and inflow. With a negative liquidity gap, a depository institution will experience a surplus of cash funds and must decide on an appropriate investment. The liquidity gap is computed this way:

Liquidity gap = new loans and security purchases + deposit withdrawals −
loan repayments and maturing securities − new deposits

Suppose we use the information from the balance sheet in the example used to calculate net income. Assume that 25% of the loans will be repaid over the forthcoming year and 10% of the securities will mature. Suppose that normally 5% of deposits leave the bank over the course of the year, and this bank anticipates raising $150 million in new deposits next year. Previous experience with loan commitments indicates that take downs will amount to $400 million in the next year, and the bank wants to maintain the same dollar value of its security portfolio. Because $50 million will be maturing, the bank needs to spend that much on the purchase of new securities. Using this information, we calculate the liquidity gap (in millions):

$$\text{Liquidity gap} = \$400 + \$50 + \$60 - \$250 - \$50 - \$150 = \$60 \text{ million}$$

Over the coming year this bank anticipates it will need to raise $60 million of funds from available sources to meet net liquidity demands. Note that this calculation is a forecast and is subject to error. Changes in market conditions or customer preferences may dramatically alter the liquidity needs of the institution from the estimated levels.

Most financial institutions undertake this type of liquidity analysis on a monthly, weekly, or even daily basis. The management of funds is a central concern for most institutions. One can get an understanding of the importance of the Federal Funds market in liquidity management by noting that the construction of the liquidity gap measure is very much like a money inventory measure. If this analysis is undertaken on a daily basis, then any positive liquidity gap can be managed by borrowing in the Federal Funds market. Any negative liquidity gap can be managed by selling off the excess funds through the Federal Funds market.

A financial institution must also take a long-term view of liquidity management and carefully plan the balance sheet to meet liquidity needs. A standard way of meeting longer-term liquidity problems would be to hold highly marketable securities that could be sold very quickly to meet unanticipated withdrawals or loan demand. Another way is to make sure that funding sources are available to the bank. It would be unwise to make a habit of borrowing federal funds because additional borrowing cannot be relied upon. Depository institutions keep the liability side of the balance sheet well diversified in order to have funding sources readily available in the event of liquidity needs. The large number of savings products and the appeal to a broad customer base is a way of diversifying some of the liquidity risk faced by a depository institution. Diversification also occurs on the asset side by holding a combination of assets, some of which are highly liquid and some of which are not.

One last aspect of liquidity management that has been alluded to in the discussion of the goldsmith is the role of a central bank. The likelihood of massive deposit withdrawals is reduced if depositors know that the central bank is a lender of last resort, willing to lend to an institution in the case of a liquidity crisis. That may not be sufficient to end all depositor runs (deposit insurance is also needed), but it does provide more stability for the banking system.

The presence of a lender of last resort is a two-edged sword in liquidity management. On the one hand, it provides for stability by giving depositors a sense of security. However, it also creates a moral hazard problem between the depository institution and the central bank. Once the central bank announces that it will provide lender of last resort services, the depository institution knows it will now have a convenient and perhaps cheap source of liquidity. Management of existing liquidity risk can now be relaxed because of this new funding source. An institution may thus respond by holding fewer cash assets or by obtaining more deposits from specific sources instead of maintaining a well-diversified portfolio of deposit customers. The central bank may therefore place restrictions on depository institutions to limit the moral hazard problem.

Credit Risk

Credit or default risk arises from the fact that the borrower may not fully comply with the terms of the loan agreement. Ultimately this means that a depository institution receives less than the full value of future cash flows that were promised by the borrower. Managing this risk requires an extensive investment in information gathering and monitoring.

The sources of credit risk are twofold. First, natural risk—such as fire, machine breakdown, and economic downturns—provides an element of uncertainty to the repayment schedule that is, to a large degree, outside the control of both the bank and the borrower. The second type of risk is the moral hazard problem a bank faces when it provides funds to the borrower. After receiving the loan, an opportunistic borrower may increase the payoff potential on an investment project by increasing the amount of risk.

The measurement of credit risk is difficult for banks, regulators, and investors in bank stocks. On the portfolio level, one can monitor the rate of defaults as a measure of credit risk. Financial ratios, such as nonperforming loans to total loans or charge-offs to total loans, provide information on the past and current performance of the loan portfolio. As explained earlier, the loan loss reserve is supposed to be a forward-looking measure of loan losses so the ratio of the level of the loan loss reserve to total loans may indicate anticipated credit risk.[9] This assumes, of course, that management is doing its job and can forecast changes in future loss rates.

On an overall basis, credit risk is measured and managed to some extent by diversification of the loan portfolio and by diversification of loans and other assets. Institutions that choose to have a loan-to-asset ratio of 75% are likely to be carrying more credit risk than institutions with a loan-to-asset ratio of 50%. The overall risk also depends on how well the loan portfolio itself is diversified. A bank that has a loan-to-asset ratio of 50% may be more risky than one with a 75% ratio if the loans consist entirely of credit card receivables.

On an individual loan basis, the management of credit risk is accomplished by a careful analysis of the creditworthiness of the borrower and the monitoring provided once the loan has been granted. The typical analysis of creditworthiness revolves around the five C's of credit analysis. These characteristics are: (1) Conditions, (2) Capacity, (3) Collateral, (4) Capital, and (5) Character. Conditions refers to the general state of the economy and, in particular, the ability of the borrower to withstand a downturn in the economy. Capacity is the borrower's ability to repay the loan from the cash flows associated with the project or the cash flows from other income sources. Collateral is the assets that are used to support the principal value of the loan. Collateral is forfeited to the lender in the event of a default. Capital refers to the part of the project that will come from the wealth of the borrower. A home mortgage, for instance, typically requires a 20% capital contribution (down payment) by the borrower or some form of private default insurance. Finally, character refers to the willingness of the borrower to repay.

The first four factors require the gathering and analysis of financial information. Statistical scoring models are often used to determine the creditworthiness of individual borrowers. These models provide a score based on employment

---

[9] Currently, domestic loan loss reserves account for 200–300% of nonperforming loans.

history, income, savings, and other factors that can legally be used to discriminate between safe and unsafe borrowers. The factors are given weights and a score is obtained via some predetermined statistical function. Those below a certain level would not normally be considered for the loan.

Commercial lending requires greater attention to financial information. A commercial borrower must typically provide several years of balance sheet and income information that the bank uses to determine creditworthiness. An analysis of key financial ratios is usually prepared in spreadsheet format and the information is compared to peer group or industry averages. Deviations from the averages or dramatic changes in the ratios over time are carefully analyzed to determine the reasons for the deviations or changes. Pro forma cash flow, balance sheet, and income statements are prepared to determine the capacity of the borrower.

When collateral is involved in the loan (and it almost always is), a bank must carefully appraise its worth and file all of the necessary paperwork so the property can be easily recovered in the event of a foreclosure. A collateralized loan means that the project belongs to the lender and not to the borrower. In a simple car loan, for instance, the ownership title remains in the hands of the bank until the loan is paid off. The bank will require the borrower to obtain collision insurance on the vehicle, with payment made to the bank if the vehicle is totally damaged.

The fact that the project actually belongs to the lender suggests that the borrower has obtained an agreement allowing ownership if and when the principal balance is paid off (an option). This option agreement creates a moral hazard problem between the borrower and the lender. Once the funding has been obtained, there is an incentive to increase utility at the expense of the lender. Not maintaining a car is a simple example.

The default risk introduced by the moral hazard problem requires more information analysis by the lender. One of the first lines of defense against the moral hazard is the evaluation of the character of the borrower. Loan officers often spend large amounts of time with existing and potential borrowers in order to evaluate the willingness to repay. Lunches, golf outings, and visits to the business all can play a role in this evaluation. It is this aspect of credit analysis that keeps loan officers from being replaced by computers.

In addition to character evaluation, lenders also construct loan agreements to minimize the opportunistic behavior of the borrower. Equity contributions, restrictions on dividends, maintenance of key financial ratios, and regular disclosure of financial information are all examples of covenants in a loan that act to minimize the moral hazard problem. In addition, continual monitoring of the collateral and the financial information of the borrower is needed to manage this aspect of credit risk.

Interest Rate Risk

To illustrate interest rate risk or the risk of maturity intermediation, we continue with the balance sheet and income statement example introduced earlier in the chapter. In that example, the bank had loans of $1,000 million, securities of $500 million and deposits of $1,200 million. The interest rates on those financial instruments were 10%, 7%, and 5%, respectively. As shown in the example, net interest income was $75 million. Suppose that all of the loans are of the fixed-rate variety with maturities exceeding one year. Suppose all of the securities and deposits will come due immediately and will be repurchased with one-year maturities. If all market interest rates were to rise by 1%, the net interest income of the bank in the forthcoming year would be affected in the following way:

1. Interest income on loans would be unchanged because the contractual rate would not change when the market rate changed,
2. Interest income on securities would rise by $5 million (500 × 0.01) because the rate received on the new securities would be 1% higher than the rate received on the old securities,
3. Interest expense on deposits would rise by $12 million (1,200 × .01) because the rate paid on the new deposits would be 1% higher than the rate paid on the old deposits.

The sum of all these changes is a decline in net interest income of $7 million. Net interest income declines in this case because interest rates rose and the bank had more liabilities that needed to be repriced than it had assets that could be repriced. If interest rates had fallen by 1%, net interest income would have risen by the same $7 million.[10]

A rate-sensitive asset (RSA) is defined as one that will be repriced or will have a new interest rate associated with it over the forthcoming planning period. Short-term securities and variable-rate loans are both examples of rate-sensitive assets. A rate-sensitive liability (RSL) is one that will be repriced over the forthcoming planning period. Money market deposit accounts and variable-rate certificates of deposit are examples of a rate-sensitive liability.

From the above example, it is clear that the change in net interest income is due solely to the impact of unanticipated interest-rate changes on rate-sensitive assets and rate-sensitive liabilities. Thus, we can measure one part of interest-rate risk (reinvestment risk) of a depository institution by calculating a dollar measure of the difference between rate-sensitive assets and rate-sensitive liabilities. This measure is referred to as the repricing gap (RGAP) and is calculated:

$$RGAP = RSAs - RSLs$$

The repricing gap (also referred to as the maturity or funding gap) can be measured over any time period. Often an institution will use time intervals of less than one month, one month to three months, three months to six months, six months to one year, and over one year. These intervals are referred to as "time buckets" and the gap is computed with each time bucket as well as an accumulation of all of the previous time buckets.

Our example assumes that none of the loans was to be repriced over the forthcoming year, but all of the securities and all of the deposits were to be repriced. The repricing gap would then be calculated (in millions):

$$RGAP = \$500 - \$1,200 = -\$700$$

Remember that the repricing gap measure is a net value of the assets and liabilities to be repriced over the planning period. The gap does not measure the interest income or interest expense of the repriced instruments.

Our example also revealed that the change in net interest income depended on the relative amounts of assets and liabilities that were to be repriced. Noting that assets and liabilities that will not be repriced cannot cause any change in net interest income over the time period, we can write the relationship between the change in net interest income and the rate sensitivity of assets and liabilities:

$$\Delta NII = \Delta r \, (RSAs - RSLs)$$

---

[10] When rates start to fall, borrowers often refinance their loans at lower rates. Our example does not consider refinancing.

where NII is net interest income and Δr is the change in market rates of interest (assumed to be the same for all financial instruments). The term in parentheses is just the definition of the repricing gap, so we can rewrite this equation:

$$\Delta NII = \Delta r \, (RGAP)$$

Using the numbers from our example of a 1% increase in interest rates and a negative $700 million funding gap, we have:

$$\Delta NII = +0.01 \times (-\$700) = -\$7 \text{ million,}$$

which is exactly the amount we computed earlier.

This is essentially what happened to savings and loan institutions in the late 1970s and early 1980s. As rates started to rise, net interest margins were squeezed because of the large maturity imbalance. Eventually, the yield curve shifted up to the point where the spreads for savings and loans turned negative. The result was the failure of almost one-half of all savings and loans in the United States.

Of course risk has an upside to it as well. If interest rates had fallen in our example, net interest income would have increased. The relationship among the repricing gap, interest-rate changes, and net interest income are summarized below:

Repricing Gap	Δ%	Δ in Income	Δ in Expense	Δ in Net Income
+	↑	+	+	+
+	↓	−	−	−
−	↑	+	+	−
−	↓	−	−	+
0	↑	+	+	0
0	↓	−	−	0

Setting the repricing gap to zero immunizes the institution against the reinvestment component of interest rate risk. If the gap is zero, a change in market interest rates will have no impact on net interest income.

The above discussion has implicitly assumed that changes in interest rates have no impact on the volume or mix of assets and liabilities. A sharp decline in interest rate may actually cause interest expense to rise if many savings depositors withdraw their funds and invest them in equity mutual funds. A depository institution would need to find different and perhaps more expensive sources of funding (a change in the mix of liabilities), which could lead to different levels of interest expense. In addition, market interest rate changes affect the immediate market value of assets and liabilities. This is another component of interest rate risk. We will examine interest rate risk management in Part III.

SUMMARY

Depository institutions are unique among financial firms because they have customers on both sides of the balance sheet. The customers on the liability side are the depositors who have a strong desire for liquidity. In fact, most deposits have immediate maturity, allowing these types of liabilities to serve as a medium of exchange in an economy.

The most common type of depository institution is the commercial bank. As the name implies, commercial banks have for years concentrated on the business sector of the economy. Competition from nonbank financial institutions in recent years has changed the focus of commercial banking toward real estate and consumer lending, but commercial lending remains an integral function of most banks.

Savings and loans have for many years dominated the residential mortgage segment of the loan market. The number of savings and loans has greatly decreased in the last ten years because of problem loans. The remaining thrift institutions have had their powers extended to provide services more like commercial banks but remain heavily invested in mortgages and mortgage-related products. Credit unions have historically focused on consumer lending. Regulatory changes have also allowed credit unions to compete directly with banks in some areas of commercial lending and with demand and savings deposits. The unique aspect of credit unions is their tax-exempt status. This allows them to deal with the high fixed costs of making small loans and servicing small deposit accounts.

The depository institution has its historical roots in the service activities of goldsmiths. The safekeeping function eventually led to the development of fractional reserve banking and the attendant liquidity problems. The motivating force in the development of modern banking was the attempt to reduce transactions costs. Customers found it was much cheaper to transact with the receipts of the goldsmith than with the gold itself. Goldsmiths were willing to supply receipts by taking deposits and eventually making loans. A problem that arose was keeping the supply of receipts limited to make sure value was retained.

The use of bank receipts and eventually checking accounts to transact encouraged the development of a central clearing system and a system of deposit insurance. These functions were initially provided by a coalition of banks, but history shows a coalition is not strong enough to withstand the most serious economic recessions. These functions have now been taken over by the federal government with a slightly better track record.

The primary way a depository institution earns a profit has not changed much over the years. Deposits are collected and transformed into assets such as loans and debt securities. The spread on assets over the cost of funds is the major component of the income statement of a depository institution. In recent years, more attention has been devoted to fee income. Fee income is earned for brokerage services, information and accounting services, and safekeeping services. As spreads have declined from increased competition, depository institutions have become more innovative in earning fee income.

The transformation function provides the most difficult management problems for depository institutions. Liquidity risk arises from the mismatch in maturities between assets and deposits. It is also due in part to the credit risk in the loans held by depository institutions. Failure to obtain loan repayments can result in the inability of an institution to meet all of the demands of its depositors. In addition to liquidity and credit risk, banks must also manage interest rate risk. This is the risk that arises from the fact that interest rate changes on assets and liabilities are not synchronized. If rates on deposits change faster than rates on assets, then profits will decline (increase) in a rising (falling) interest rate environment. If, instead, assets are more rate sensitive than liabilities, profits will rise (fall) in a rising (declining) interest rate environment.

The inherent risks in banking can be dealt with in three ways. As in all finance theory, diversification is a proven method of managing risk. Depository institutions diversify the loan portfolio to reduce interest rate risk as well as credit risk. Deposits are gathered from many sources to diversify away liquidity risk and to help match up asset maturities. Risk can also be managed by passing it along to a third party. This is accomplished by hedging techniques and by selling and securitizing assets. Finally, risk can simply be accepted and monitored. This aspect of dealing with risk allows a financial institution to earn something other than a risk-free rate of return.

REVIEW QUESTIONS

1. Who are the customers of a depository institution? What is the difference between a bondholder and a depositor in a financial institution? Between a bondholder and a stockholder?
2. Why are banks and other depository institutions prohibited from holding equity securities on the balance sheet? What are the advantages of this prohibition? The disadvantages?
3. Use simple T-accounts to post the changes to the balance sheet of a depository institution from the following transactions:
   a. Withdrawal of $100 from a checking account.
   b. The repayment of a $1,000 automobile loan.
   c. The purchase of $1 million in currency by a bank from the Fed.
   d. The purchase of a $10,000 bond from a security broker with an account at the bank.
   e. The purchase of a $10,000 bond from a security broker with an account at a bank in another state.
4. Determine the impact on total, required, and excess reserves for each of the above transactions assuming the required reserve ratio is 3%.
5. What is the asset transformation function provided by depository institutions? How does asset transformation differ from brokerage? Are these two functions always independent of one another?

6. Consider the simple balance sheets for two depository institutions at the bottom of the page. Suppose current interest rates on variable-rate loans are 10% while they are 11% on the 30-year mortgage (fixed rate). Money market deposits are currently priced at 7% while long-term certificates of deposits are at 8%. If the noninterest income of each of these banks is $10 and noninterest expense is $20, calculate the return on equity, return on assets, and the net interest income assuming a tax rate of 30%.
7. Which of the above banks has more interest rate risk exposure? Calculate the repricing gap for each bank. Show what will happen to the net interest income of each bank if market interest rates decline by 2%; increase by 2%.
8. How does a bank measure credit risk? What are the ways in which a bank can deal with credit risk? Do depository institutions have some natural advantage in the handling of credit risk?
9. Where does liquidity risk stem from in a depository institution? How is liquidity risk related to interest rate risk? To credit risk?
10. How do banks account for potential loan losses on their balance sheet? How does this transfer to the income statement? Why is the loan loss reserve not counted as equity capital?

Bank A			
Cash	100	L-T CDs	900
Variable rate loans	900	Equity	100

Bank B			
Cash	100	Money market deposits	900
30-year mortgage	900	Equity	100

REFERENCES

James, C. 1987. "Some Evidence on the Uniqueness of Bank Loans." *Journal of Financial Economics*: 217–235.

Mester, L. 1992. "Banking and Commerce: A Dangerous Liaison?" Federal Reserve Bank of Philadelphia, *Business Review* (May/June): 17–29.

Morgan, D. 1993. "Bank Monitoring Mitigates Agency Problems: New Evidence Using the Financial Covenants in Bank Loan Commitments," Research Working Paper, Federal Reserve Bank of Kansas City (December).

5

Modern Functions of Depository Intermediaries: Off-Balance-Sheet, Loan Sale, and Securitization Activities

OBJECTIVES

This chapter examines a set of fast-growing businesses for depository intermediaries: off-balance-sheet, loan sale, and securitization activities. We provide economic reasons for this recent growth and discuss the regulatory ramifications of these activities. From the perspective of a borrower, a traditional depository institution loan provides four distinct functions: (1) origination, (2) risk-bearing, (3) funding, and (4) servicing. The activities described in this chapter involve some of these four functions but not all of them. We explain the reasons for customer demand and intermediary supply of these products.

OFF-BALANCE-SHEET, LOAN SALE, AND SECURITIZATION ACTIVITIES AS ALTERNATIVES TO TRADITIONAL LOANS

The traditional asset transformation function of depository intermediaries involves gathering deposits and investing in loans and securities. These activities are known as balance-sheet items because they are recorded on the balance sheet. Depository intermediaries, especially commercial banks, engage in a host of other endeavors that are off-balance-sheet activities designed to generate fee income. Table 5.1 shows the increasing reliance of banks on fee income. Fee income is more important for large banks than for small banks because of the specialized resources of large banks. All banks, however, are placing greater emphasis on fee income these days. For example, NationsBank's goal for fee income is for it to account for 50% of its total income in the near future.

What is interesting about these new fee-generating activities is that they embody some but not all of the functions of traditional loans. One can think of a bank loan providing four functions: origination, risk-bearing, funding, and servicing. There is no reason that a depository intermediary must perform all of

TABLE 5.1 Non-Interest Income as a Percent of Operating Income for Commercial Banks	
Year	Non-Interest Income / Operating Income
1960	14.67%
1970	12.11
1980	7.03
1982	7.81
1984	9.58
1986	13.11
1988	14.17
1990	14.62
1992	20.45
1994	22.82

Source: FDIC, *Statistics on Banking*, various issues.

these functions. The origination function involves information gathering and processing. Origination requires a knowledge of the laws regarding perfection of collateral, filing of forms, and proper documentation of the supporting materials in the loan file. Banks have traditionally specialized in the origination of commercial loans, savings and loans in the origination of mortgage loans, and credit unions in the origination of consumer loans. Depository intermediaries capitalize on their expertise and cost advantage in information production to originate loans and subsequently sell them to other parties. Loan sales embody the origination function but not the other three components of a traditional loan. Making a bank loan constitutes an asset transformation function; selling the loan without recourse constitutes a brokerage function. The asset transformation function requires risk-bearing. In the context of a bank loan, the risk element can be described by the following equation:

$$\text{Risky loan} = \text{risk-free loan} + \text{default risk}$$

A risky loan can be made free of default risk by purchasing insurance on the loan that pays off in the event of a default. Clearly, the provider of the insurance must be able to evaluate the extent of the default risk in order to profitably provide the insurance. Depository intermediaries with expertise in the origination function are also equipped with the necessary skill in credit-risk evaluation and are therefore likely candidates to provide risk-bearing services as well. Depository intermediaries provide a combination of the origination and risk-bearing functions through off-balance-sheet activities such as loan commitments, standby letters of credit, commercial letters of credit, and derivatives. These instruments are designed to insure the borrower against future uncertainties in interest rates, foreign exchange rates, or commodities prices. With these guarantees, a borrower can secure loans in capital markets at nearly risk-free rates. The depository intermediary receives fees for its origination and risk-bearing services without an immediate need for funding or servicing.

The third component of lending is the funding function. If loans are to be carried on the balance sheet of the originating intermediary, they must be funded. The cost of funds to an intermediary includes the interest paid on the deposits, the regulatory tax through reserve and capital requirements, and deposit insurance premiums. The cost of a bank loan is generally higher than the cost of issuing commercial paper in the market. Commercial paper is a short-term, negotiable security sold by corporations in the financial market. For a well-known corporation, it is less expensive to issue commercial paper than to obtain a bank loan. Since commercial paper is an unsecured instrument, corporations obtain a standby letter of credit from a bank that guarantees the repayment on maturity. Standby letters embody the origination and risk-bearing functions produced by the bank for a fee.

The final component of a loan is the servicing function. This function involves the administrative detail in recording loan payments and in handling customer services in the amortization of the loan. For example, in mortgage lending, the servicing function involves the management of escrow accounts for real estate taxes and hazard insurance. Escrow accounts are trustee accounts created to ensure that real estate taxes and hazard insurance payments are made on time. The payments into escrow accounts are included in the monthly payment, and the disbursement of funds is handled by the intermediary. Even when a loan is sold or securitized, the intermediary may continue to perform the servicing function for a fee.

OFF-BALANCE-SHEET ACTIVITIES

Off-balance-sheet activities include loan commitments, standby letters of credit, commercial letters of credit, and derivatives.

Loan Commitments

A loan commitment is essentially a forward contract that provides the customer the right to borrow up to a prespecified amount during the contract period. The terms of the commitment comprise the maximum amount of borrowing, the length of time the agreement is in effect, the maturity of the loan if the commitment is utilized, and the interest rate charged on the funds used. Over half of all commercial lending at depository intermediaries is in the form of loan commitments. For example, a bank enters into an agreement with a battery manufacturer to provide a line of credit to finance the inventory. The manufacturer can borrow up to a predetermined amount such as $1 million. The inventory serves as collateral for the amount borrowed. The loan is paid off as the batteries are produced and sold.

A loan commitment generally earns fees for the bank in addition to the interest charged on the borrowed amount. A commitment fee is levied on the dollar amount of the credit line. In addition, the customer may be charged a percentage fee on the unused portion of the credit line. For instance, a customer arranges for a $1 million line of credit (a loan commitment) that charges a 2% commitment fee on the total credit line and a 1/2% (50 basis points) fee on the unutilized portion. The customer owes $20,000 in fees immediately. If the customer utilizes 80% of the commitment, another $1,000 ($200,000 × 0.005) in fees is charged when the commitment is terminated.

In addition to commitment fees, the bank also earns income by requiring the customer to hold a compensating balance in its bank account. A compensating balance is a percentage of the commitment or a percentage of the borrowed amount that is kept in the customer's account. The compensating balance either earns no interest or earns a below-market rate. The customer, in effect, uses part of the loan proceeds to meet the compensation balance requirement.

The combination of commitment fees and compensating balances provides the bank a yield on the loan commitment well in excess of the quoted rate of interest on the loan.[1] The extent to which a customer is willing to hold a compen-

---

[1] For a description of the pricing of loan commitments, see Karels and Prakash (1988).

sating balance and pay commitment fees depends on the degree of competition in the loan market. With the increasingly competitive lending environment, compensating balances are quickly disappearing from many loan commitment contracts.

In addition to loan commitments in commercial lending, commitments are also used in the real estate lending market. The typical time to originate a residential mortgage is one to three months. Mortgage rates may fluctuate during a three-month period. For a fee, an intermediary may offer a commitment to guarantee the interest rate on the mortgage. This type of commitment is prevalent on mortgages that are not expected to be completed for at least two months. For shorter time periods, there is often no extra charge on a guaranteed mortgage rate. In addition to guaranteeing the rate, the lender is implicitly guaranteeing that the loan amount will be available at closing if the borrower meets the necessary credit standards.

A modern credit card is also a loan commitment. This commitment differs from most commercial loan commitments in two ways. First, the line of credit on a credit card is usually for a longer period of time, perhaps three to five years, whereas the line of credit for a commercial commitment is often one year or less. Second, credit cards are unsecured loans, whereas commercial loans are collateralized. Losses in the credit card business are compensated by close monitoring of the payments, high interest rates, and fees on the accounts.

It is not surprising that much of the commercial lending done by banks is accommodated through loan commitments. Banks are heavily regulated relative to many other financial intermediaries, and commitments provide a way around some of the regulation. One of the major advantages of a loan commitment is that funds are not needed until the line of credit is actually utilized. This provides a way to avoid the costs of reserve requirements and insurance premiums because the commitment is not posted on the balance sheet until it is taken down. In the meantime, the commitment earns substantial fee income for the bank. Another reason for the popularity of loan commitments is the desire of commercial customers to ensure the availability of funds for inventory in the event of a credit crunch.

A loan commitment provides the borrower with a right to borrow in the future, often at a prespecified rate. This is a valuable option and the fees paid are commensurate with such an option. While loan commitments provide flexibility for customers and additional income for intermediaries, they create complications in the conduct of monetary policy. Loan commitments diminish the ability of the Federal Reserve Bank to control the supply of money and credit in the economy. If firms enter into commitments to hedge against a credit crunch, then a tightening of credit by the Federal Reserve Bank will have little effect on the availability of credit. This creates a delay in the effects of a tight credit policy until outstanding commitments expire. Widespread use of loan commitments has reduced the power of the Federal Reserve Bank to control the economy.

Loan commitments subject the issuing bank to interest-rate risk and credit risk. However, the level of loan commitments is inversely related to the overall bank risk and directly related to bank profitability.[2] This implies that before issuing commitments, banks carefully examine the credit risk of the customer to minimize future problems. By issuing a loan commitment, a bank also creates a valuable binding relationship with its customer, who will then use the bank's services as long as the commitment is outstanding.

---

[2] Avery and Berger (1991).

Standby Letters of Credit

Standby letters of credit are third-party guarantees in which a depository intermediary substitutes its credit rating for that of the customer. A common use for a standby letter of credit is to back an issue of commercial paper. Commercial paper is an unsecured debt with a maturity less than 270 days. Because commercial paper is an unsecured debt, it is issued only by highly rated firms. Because of the short-term maturity of commercial paper, firms issue a new commercial paper to retire the old one at its maturity. A successful payoff of the old commercial paper is, therefore, subject to the ability of the issuing firm to sell new paper. If the issuer is unable to sell the new paper either because of market conditions or due to worsening of the issuing firm's credit standing, the maturing commercial paper holders may not receive their payments. To mitigate this uncertainty, the issuing firm often obtains a standby letter of credit from a bank that guarantees payment to investors if the issuer fails to sell the new paper. The yield on commercial paper backed by a standby letter of credit issued by a reputable bank is therefore near the risk-free rate. The bank that issues the standby letter of credit bears the credit risk.

In addition, standby letters of credit are used in conjunction with municipal bond offerings, construction loans, and mergers and acquisitions. For the standby letter of credit to be beneficial to the borrower, the credit reputation of the bank must be better than that of the borrower. A standby letter of credit issued by a financially distressed intermediary or by an unknown entity would not reduce the risk premium in the commercial paper market. For this reason, standby letters of credit are generally issued by the largest and most well-known depository intermediaries with good credit ratings. The use of standby letters of credit has grown dramatically in the past 20 years. In 1970 there were only about $5 billion of letters outstanding at commercial banks. By the mid-1990s, the volume of commercial paper exceeded the $200 billion level.

Commercial Letters of Credit

Commercial letters of credit are issued in conjunction with the import-export business. They are generally used when the seller is uncertain about the creditworthiness of the buyer. Suppose that Kobelco America, an American-based distribution company, wants to import backhoe loaders from Fermec Holdings, a Manchester, England-based construction equipment company. Kobelco offers to pay for the shipments of the backhoe loaders within 90 days but Fermec is uncertain about the credit-standing of Kobelco.

To assure Fermec about the payment, Kobelco turns to its bank, First National Bank of Chicago, for help. First National Bank of Chicago issues a commercial letter for the total cost of the 100 machines ordered by Kobelco and sends it to Fermec in Manchester. Upon receipt of the letter, Fermec ships the loaders. Within 90 days, Kobelco will pay for the shipment. If Kobelco is unable to make the payment, First National Bank of Chicago will make the payment to Fermec and will book the amount as a loan to Kobelco. Most often, importers pay on time and their banks are relieved of their obligations. Through issuing commercial letters of credit, banks provide origination and risk-bearing functions.

The holder of a letter of credit (the exporter) may present it to the importer's bank for acceptance. Upon stamping the letter ACCEPTED, a new instrument is created, known as a "bankers acceptance." The exporter can subsequently sell the instrument in the secondary market at a discount, the size of which is determined by the credit risk of the issuing bank and the maturity of the instrument. Bankers acceptances carry low risk because the commitment made by the importer is backed by the bank. When a commercial letter of credit is converted to a bankers acceptance, the instrument's status changes from an off-balance-sheet item to a balance-sheet figure. Bankers acceptances are highly liquid, short-term securities.

Derivatives

One of the most intriguing and fastest-growing activities of large depository intermediaries in recent years has been in the derivatives business. Derivatives are instruments whose performance depends upon (or are derived from) the performance of some other asset. In their basic design, derivatives include forward, futures, swap, and option contracts. Corporations, municipalities, individual investors, and institutional investors use derivatives to mitigate risk arising from fluctuations in interest rates, foreign exchange rates, and commodities prices. Financial intermediaries, and especially large commercial banks, are mainly active in interest-rate and currency instruments and less active in commodity derivatives. Commodity derivatives such as grain futures have been available for decades in organized exchanges. Part III of this book will discuss the pricing schemes and hedging strategies (ways of reducing risk) for derivatives. In this section, we describe these instruments briefly in the context of intermediary products and their economic and regulatory ramifications.

A forward contract on foreign currencies is an agreement between two parties to exchange two currencies at a prespecified exchange rate on a predetermined future date. Suppose that your company, an American-based manufacturing firm, is planning to sell its products to a company in England. You expect to receive £1 million in one year. You read the exchange rates reported in the *Financial Times:* The spot $/£ price (number of dollars needed to buy one pound) is 1.5036; and the one-year forward exchange rate is 1.4811. You are concerned that the exchange rate may drop further in the next year. For example, if the actual exchange rate drops to 1.40 one year from today, your £1 million will be worth $1.4 million. A way to avoid this risk is to get into a forward contract to lock in an exchange rate of 1.4811 today, which will provide you with $1.4811 million in one year with certainty ($81,100 more than what you will get without the contract if the exchange rate drops to 1.40). If the exchange rate goes up, of course, you would have been better off without the forward contract.

A futures contract is similar to a forward contract, but with a few exceptions. While a forward contract is a customized, over-the-counter product purchased from a financial intermediary, a futures contract is a standardized product traded on an organized exchange. In addition, a forward contract is less liquid and more risky than a futures contract. With its customized feature, a forward contract is designed to the specific need of a customer, whereas a futures contract is a standardized instrument that may not fully protect a customer against the underlying risk. A forward contract is settled at the expiration date. A futures contract is settled daily (marked to market). Parties to a futures contract are required to maintain a margin account that can be increased or decreased according to daily changes in the price of the underlying instrument.

A swap is an agreement between two parties to exchange a series of cash flows over a period of time specified now. The frequency of the exchange and the size of cash flows are contract-specific. There are at least three different sets of swaps. One set is the single currency swap and includes fixed-to-floating swaps, in which one party receives payments based on a fixed interest rate in return for payments based on a floating-rate index, and floating-to-floating swaps, in which one party makes payments based on one index (e.g., six-month LIBOR[3]) in ex-

---

[3] London Interbank Order Rate is an interbank rate in the Eurocurrency market. Common maturities include one month, three months, and six months.

change for payments based on another index (e.g., three-month commercial paper rate). Another set, called cross-currency swaps, includes fixed-to-fixed currency swaps, in which two parties make payments based on fixed rates in two currencies; fixed-to-floating currency swaps, in which one party pays in reference to a fixed rate in one currency while the other party pays based on a floating-rate index in the other currency; and floating-to-floating currency swaps, in which two parties make payments in reference to floating-rate indices in two different currencies. The final set involves commodities and equity swaps, in which two parties agree to exchange a certain quantity of one asset in exchange for a pre-specified amount of cash or another asset.

The following is an example of a single currency fixed-to-floating swap. Suppose that Netscape plans to borrow $200 million per year in each of the next four years. The uncertainty of future interest rates compels Netscape to enter into a swap agreement with its bank, Citicorp, in which Netscape will pay based on a fixed rate of 5% and Citicorp will pay based on LIBOR. The payment dates are 12/19/96, 12/19/97, 12/19/98, and 12/19/99 (we assume all these dates are working business days). The $200 million is called the notional amount, which is a measure of the size of the swap based on which payments are calculated. In the next two years, if interest rates increase, the cost of the loan for Netscape will increase but this increase will be offset by an increase in the swap cash inflows. If rates decline, the cost of the loan will decline but the swap cash inflows will also decline. In either case, the cost of the fund remains at 5% and Netscape is hedged.

To illustrate this point, suppose the rates are 5.5%, 6.5%, 5%, and 4.5% in each of the future settlement dates. This will provide the following cash flows to Netscape:

12/19/96	Netscape pays 5% and receives 5.5% of $200 million = +$1,000,000
12/19/97	Netscape pays 5% and receives 6.5% of $200 million = +$3,000,000
12/19/98	Netscape pays 5% and receives 5.0% of $20 million = +$0
12/19/99	Netscape pays 5% and receives 4.5% of $20 million = –$1,000,000.

At the first two settlement dates, Netscape receives $1,000,000 and $3,000,000; at the third settlement date, there is no exchange of cash flows; and at the final settlement date, Netscape pays $1,000,000. The cost of the loan will increase or decrease by exactly the same amount as the gain or loss in the swap contract. This leaves the cost of the fund at a flat rate of 5%. While this example is simplistic, it provides the essence of hedging using a single currency fixed-to-floating swap.

While forward, futures, and swap contracts are obligations for both contracting parties, an option is a right for the buyer and an obligation only to the seller of the contract. Since the buyer of an option acquires a right, there is a premium that the buyer has to pay to the seller. For example, suppose you buy an option to purchase £1 million for $1.50 million within the next 12 months at a premium of 1 cent per pound. If the pound appreciates within this period to $/£ = $1.55, you will have an incentive to exercise the option to purchase pounds at $1.50. This will yield a net profit of ($1.55 − $1.50 − $.01) × £1,000,000 = $40,000. However, if the pound depreciates to $1.45, then you will let your option expire because you are better off purchasing pounds at the market rate of $/£ = 1.45, and ending up with a total cost of $1.46 per pound, including the option premium.

For the seller, if the exchange rate increases to $1.55, then the option seller will lose 1.55 − 1.50 + 0.01= \$0.04 per pound or \$0.04 × 1,000,000 = \$40,000. If the exchange rate stays below \$1.50, the holder will have no incentive to exercise the option; therefore, the seller will keep the premium of \$0.01 × £1,000,000 = \$10,000 as a net profit.

The Economic Reasons for the Growth of Derivatives Supplied by Financial Intermediaries

The financial environment in the 1990s is characterized by fluctuations in interest rates, foreign exchange rates, and commodities prices. The sources of these variations are found in three seemingly separate but inherently interdependent events of the 1970s. In 1973, three decades of fixed exchange rates came to an end, setting the scene for today's volatile currency rates. Shortly thereafter, the Organization of Oil Producing Countries (OPEC) raised the price of oil from \$12 to \$30 per barrel, substantially increasing commodities prices. On October 6, 1979, the Fed changed its monetary policy from the control of interest rates to the control of the monetary base, leading to a period of high and volatile interest rates. An example of the effect of the interest rate rise is seen in the Savings and Loan industry. The S&L industry had historically raised more than 80% of its funds from short-term savings accounts and had invested a similar amount in long-term, fixed-rate mortgages. When interest rates increased substantially in the 1979–1982 period, the values of S&L asset portfolios, comprising long-term assets, declined significantly more than the values of their short-term liabilities, resulting in the failure of 1,500 intermediaries, or one-third of the entire industry.

In the post-1970s era, double-digit inflation and economic recession forced many corporations in various industrial nations into insolvency. Having operated for a long time in an environment of stable interest rates, fixed foreign exchange rates, and relatively steady prices, these corporations were not prepared to endure the effects of these external shocks. Those that survived had to develop a series of strategies to combat the uncertainties of the new environment. This was the genesis of the rise in demand for instruments of financial risk-hedging. Off-balance-sheet items in general and derivative securities in particular are devices to mitigate financial risk.

From the beginning, depository intermediaries have been in the forefront of innovations in instruments of risk-hedging for two reasons: (1) their corporate customers demanded the products, and (2) their own asset portfolios required risk-hedging. With hindsight, had the failed S&Ls been able to hedge their interest-rate risk, a majority of them may have survived.

A LOOK AT THE OFF-BALANCE-SHEET ACTIVITIES OF U.S. COMMERCIAL BANKS

Table 5.2 presents the components of off-balance-sheet activities in commercial banks grouped by asset size at the end of June 1995. The level of off-balance-sheet activities is highest for the largest banks. Banks with assets greater than \$1 billion had close to six times their assets in off-balance-sheet activities. In contrast, banks with assets between \$100 million and \$1 billion and banks with assets of less than \$100 million had off-balance-sheet-to-asset ratios of 36% and 14%, respectively. Overall, all banks combined had 4.5 times as much in their off-balance-sheet activities as they had in their booked assets. Among off-balance-sheet activities, the largest category belonged to derivatives, which made up 88% of off-balance-sheet activities for all banks. This figure, however, is influenced strongly by derivative activities of large banks. While the ratio of derivatives to

TABLE 5.2   Components of Off-Balance-Sheet Activities in Commercial Banks Grouped by Asset Size June 1995 ($ Millions)

Off-Balance-Sheet Item	$1 Billion or More	$100 Million to $1 Billion	Less than $100 Million	All Banks
Commitments	$1,570,199	$163,991	43,058	$1,777,248
Letters of Credit	200,630	6,674	1,263	208,567
Acceptances	152,241	2,602	179	155,022
Derivatives	15,943,734	72,153	926	16,016,813
Total Off-Balance-Sheet	17,866,804	245,420	45,426	18,157,650
Total Assets	3,011,706	683,019	315,939	4,010,664
Off-Balance-Sheet as a Percentage of Total Assets	593%	36%	14%	453%

Source: Call Report, Schedule RC-L, June 1995.

off-balance-sheet activities for banks with assets greater than $1 billion exceeded 89%, for banks with assets between $100 million and $1 billion and banks with assets of less than $100 million the ratios were only 29% and 2%, respectively.

Tables 5.3 and 5.4 present derivative activities of banks by contract type and by the underlying risk for 1991–1995. In terms of total volume, the notional amount of bank derivatives increased from $7.3 trillion in 1991 to $17.4 trillion in 1995. This is a substantial growth. Forward and futures contracts had the largest segment of derivatives, followed by swaps and options. In 1995, interest-rate instruments made up the largest segment of derivatives with more than 65% of total, followed by foreign exchange instruments, 33%, and other derivatives with 2%.

Table 5.5 demonstrates the concentration of derivatives among the largest banks in 1995. The top nine banks comprised 94% of total derivative activities. The remaining 581 banks with derivative activities accounted for only 6% of the total volume. For all banks with derivatives, futures and forward contracts made up more than 46%, whereas swaps and options comprised 33% and 21% of total derivatives.

Table 5.6 presents notional amounts of derivatives in 25 banks and trust companies with the largest volume of activities in 1995. This table provides information on individual players in the derivatives market. Chemical Bank had the largest notional amount of derivatives with more than $3.5 trillion. Chemical Bank, Morgan Guaranty, Citibank, Bankers Trust, and Bank of America were the banks with the most derivative activities in 1995.

TABLE 5.3   Derivative Activities of Banks by Contract Type 1991–1995 ($ Billions)

Contract	Dec. 1991	Dec. 1992	Dec. 1993	Dec. 1994	June 1995
Futures and Forwards	3,876	4,780	6,229	8,109	8,065
Swaps	2,071	2,417	3,260	4,823	5,697
Options	1,393	1,568	2,384	2,841	3,632
Total	7,340	8,765	11,873	15,773	17,394

Source: Call Report, Schedule RC-L, June 1995.

TABLE 5.4 Derivative Activities of Banks by Underlying Risk 1991–1995 ($ Billions)

Underlying Risk	Dec. 1991	Dec. 1992	Dec. 1993	Dec. 1994	June 1995
Interest Rate	3,837	4,872	7,210	9,926	11,385
Foreign Exchange	3,394	3,789	4,484	5,605	5,664
Other Derivatives	109	104	179	242	345
Total	7,340	8,765	11,873	15,773	17,394

Source: Call Report, Schedule RC-L, June 1995.

While notional amounts are useful in depicting the level and the trend in derivative activities, they are misleading as indicators of risk exposure. For example, in interest-rate swaps, the notional amounts never change hands. Instead, fixed and floating payments are calculated by multiplying the respective rates by the notional amount. At each settlement date, a difference check is written by the losing party. To examine the actual risk exposure, we present credit equivalents of notional amounts in Table 5.7. These figures are better representatives of the actual risk exposure than the gross notional amounts. For the top 25 banks involved in derivatives, the percentage of credit exposure to risk-based capital was 111%. For the same 25 banks, the percentage of total assets to risk-based capital was 663%.

Table 5.8 groups the 1995 derivative activities of the top nine banks under trading and hedging categories. Trading activities, including both customer transactions and proprietary positions, are restricted to the very large banks. Hedging activities involve using derivatives for the purpose of risk management of the bank itself. Smaller banks confine themselves to using derivatives to manage their own risk exposure. As Table 5.8 demonstrates, 95% of derivative activities of the top nine banks involved trading, primarily customer services, while only 5% involved hedging. In contrast, for the remaining 582 banks with derivatives, trading made up only 40% of derivative activities, whereas hedging comprised the remaining 60%. These figures indicate that the largest banks hold derivatives primarily for the purpose of trading, while smaller banks use derivatives for the purpose of risk management.

Table 5.9 presents gross positive and negative values for the top nine banks in 1995. Gross positive values are tied to market values of contracts where counterparties owe money to the bank. This represents the maximum amount the

TABLE 5.5 Concentration of Derivatives Among Large Banks June 1995 ($ Billions)

Contract	($) 9 Banks	(%) Total Derivatives	($) 581 Banks	(%) Total Derivatives	($) All Banks	(%) Total Derivatives
Futures and Forwards	$7,694	44.2%	$371	2.1%	$8,065	46.3%
Swaps	$5,232	30.1%	$465	2.7%	$5,697	32.8%
Options	$3,363	19.3%	$269	1.5%	$3,632	20.8%
Total	$16,289	93.7%	$1,105	6.3%	$17,394	100%

Source: Call Report, Schedule RC-L, June 1995.

TABLE 5.6 Notional Amounts of Derivatives in 25 Banks and Trust Companies with Largest Volume of Derivatives June 1995 ($ Millions)

Rank	Bank Name	Total Assets	Total Derivatives	Futures (Exch. TR)	Options (Exch. TR)	Forwards (OTC)	Swaps (OTC)	Options (OTC)
1	Chemical Bank (NY)	142,023	3,586,350	422,725	102,020	1,361,045	1,499,387	201,173
2	Morgan Guaranty (NY)	137,784	3,041,464	155,400	403,239	651,588	1,308,394	522,844
3	Citibank (NY)	217,107	2,698,898	247,757	106,398	1,464,713	496,982	383,048
4	Bankers Trust (NY)	80,877	1,877,986	151,219	200,077	520,647	713,529	292,514
5	Bank of America (CA)	162,577	1,726,388	108,355	24,958	983,135	468,879	141,061
6	Chase Manhattan (NY)	97,821	1,476,473	60,031	20,511	740,902	390,859	264,170
7	NationsBank (NC)	50,060	922,634	240,094	277,032	83,834	121,191	200,483
8	First NB of Chicago (IL)	49,326	691,709	38,144	30,349	317,737	181,978	123,501
9	Republic NB of NY (NY)	32,662	266,612	26,555	1,777	120,356	50,093	67,831
10	First NB of Boston (MA)	37,893	88,458	24,448	923	38,094	11,793	13,200
11	Bank of New York (NY)	43,511	69,806	3,237	10,152	35,824	11,704	8,889
12	First Union NBNC (NC)	24,664	59,011	11,402	16,992	4,367	17,128	9,121
13	Natwest BK NA (NJ)	28,420	50,422	11,233	15,899	8,689	12,607	1,994
14	State Street B&TC (MA)	25,201	48,890	839	1,059	44,453	2,107	433
15	Seattle-First NB (WA)	16,397	40,876	20,763	0	4,390	15,502	221
16	Mellon BK NA (PA)	34,577	34,653	895	750	11,490	15,684	5,835
17	Wells Fargo BK NA (CA)	49,726	31,619	5,723	3	1,051	5,479	19,362
18	PNC BK NA (PA)	44,566	28,068	875	50	83	17,680	9,381
19	Bank One (OH)	6,701	27,526	0	0	1,178	20,733	5,615
20	Bank of America (IL)	17,165	24,147	8,003	0	372	13,573	2,199
21	Citibank SD NA (SD)	10,136	24,050	1,500	8,000	0	6,912	7,638
22	Citibank NV NA (NV)	10,007	20,196	1,500	8,000	1	4,935	5,760
23	National City BK (OH)	9,988	19,122	1,796	800	596	9,628	6,303
24	Boston Safe Deposit (MA)	5,192	17,814	0	0	15,552	2,160	103
25	Harris T&SB (IL)	12,079	16,913	5	100	10,062	1,475	5,271
	Total Top 25 Banks	1,346,458	16,890,083	1,542,499	1,229,087	6,420,156	5,400,392	2,297,948
	Other 565 Banks with Derivatives	1,767,807	504,394	39,000	12,159	63,107	297,392	92,736
	Total 590 Banks with Derivatives	3,114,264	17,394,477	1,581,499	1,241,246	6,483,264	5,697,784	2,390,684

Source: Call Report, Schedule RC–L, June 1995.

TABLE 5.7 Credit Equivalent Exposure and Distribution of Derivatives in 25 Banks and Trust Companies with Largest Volume of Derivatives June 1995 ($ Millions; Ratio in Percent)

Rank	Bank Name	$ Credit Exposure	% Credit Exposure to Capital	% Exchange-Traded	% OTC Contracts	% Interest Rate Contracts	% Foreign Exchange Contracts	% Other Contracts
1	Chemical Bank (NY)	$32,276	268%	14.6%	85.4%	75.1%	24.7%	0.2%
2	Morgan Guaranty (NY)	$55,371	563%	18.4%	81.6%	73.3%	22.6%	4.1%
3	Citibank (NY)	$38,672	171%	13.1%	86.9%	53.1%	45.8%	1.1%
4	Bankers Trust (NY)	$29,514	523%	18.7%	81.3%	65.4%	30.4%	4.2%
5	Bank of America (CA)	$21,063	139%	7.7%	92.3%	50.9%	49.1%	0.0%
6	Chase Manhattan (NY)	$19,789	192%	5.5%	94.5%	53.7%	45.0%	1.3%
7	NationsBank (NC)	$5,396	155%	56.0%	44.0%	85.2%	9.9%	4.9%
8	First NB of Chicago (IL)	$12,092	273%	9.9%	90.1%	50.5%	46.9%	2.6%
9	Republic NB of NY (NY)	$4,375	137%	10.6%	89.4%	35.5%	58.6%	5.9%
10	First NB of Boston (MA)	$717	19%	28.7%	71.3%	76.2%	23.6%	0.2%
11	Bank of New York (NY)	$1,253	26%	19.2%	80.8%	44.4%	55.5%	0.0%
12	First Union NBNC (NC)	$457	20%	48.1%	51.9%	93.7%	6.3%	0.0%
13	Natwest BK NA (NJ)	$379	15%	53.8%	46.2%	91.7%	8.3%	0.0%
14	State Street B&TC (MA)	$1,069	76%	3.9%	96.1%	4.8%	95.2%	0.0%
15	Seattle-First NB (WA)	$157	9%	50.8%	49.2%	99.1%	0.9%	0.0%
16	Mellon BK NA (PA)	$483	14%	4.7%	95.3%	67.6%	32.4%	0.0%
17	Wells Fargo BK NA (CA)	$433	9%	18.1%	81.9%	96.6%	3.4%	0.0%
18	PNC BK NA (PA)	$113	3%	3.3%	96.7%	97.0%	3.0%	0.0%
19	Bank One (OH)	$203	24%	0.0%	100%	99.4%	0.6%	0.0%
20	Bank of America (IL)	$463	17%	33.1%	66.9%	97.9%	2.1%	0.0%
21	Citibank SD NA (SD)	$180	13%	39.5%	60.5%	100%	0.0%	0.0%
22	Citibank NV NA (NV)	$138	12%	47.0%	53.0%	100%	0.0%	0.0%
23	National City BK (OH)	$206	23%	13.6%	86.4%	98.0%	2.0%	0.0%
24	Boston Safe Deposit (MA)	$292	53%	0.0%	100%	12.7%	87.3%	0.0%
25	Harris T&SB (IL)	$277	25%	0.6%	99.4%	32.9%	67.1%	0.0%
	Total Top 25 Banks	$225,390	111%	15.9%	81.2%	62.8%	32.3%	2.0%
	Other 565 Banks with Derivatives	$5,407	n/a	0.3%	2.6%	2.6%	0.3%	0.0%
	Total 590 Banks with Derivatives	$230,797	6.6%	16.2%	83.8%	65.5%	32.6%	2.0%

Source: Call Report, Schedule RC-L, June 1995.

81

TABLE 5.8 Trading vs. Hedging Components of Derivatives in Nine Banks with the Largest Volume of Derivatives June 1995

Rank	Bank Name	% Held for Trading	% Held for Hedging
1	Chemical Bank (NY)	95%	5%
2	Morgan Guaranty (NY)	90%	10%
3	Citibank (NY)	95%	5%
4	Bankers Trust (NY)	98%	2%
5	Bank of America (CA)	97%	3%
6	Chase Manhattan (NY)	97%	3%
7	NationsBank (NC)	97%	3%
8	First NB of Chicago (IL)	99%	1%
9	Republic NB of NY (NY)	97%	3%
	Total Top Nine Banks	95%	5%
	Other 581 Banks with Derivatives	40%	60%
	Total 590 Banks with Derivatives	92%	8%

Source: Call Report, Schedule RC-L, June 1995.

bank will lose if the counterparties default. Gross negative values are tied to market values of contracts where the bank owes money to its counterparties. This represents the maximum amount counterparties will lose if the bank defaults. In both trading and nontrading (hedging) accounts, banks maintained relatively balanced books where the value of accounts with gains is not significantly different from the value of accounts with losses. The same scenario applies to end-users who hold derivatives for risk-management purposes. This is a further indication that, while the size of derivative activities in notional terms is very large, the actual risk exposure of banks is relatively small.

Table 5.9 also presents derivative trading revenues. The revenue data is useful not only to portray the profitability of derivative transactions but also as a gauge in evaluating trends. For the first half of 1995, revenues generated from derivatives reached $1.4 billion for the top nine banks.[4] For all banks involved in derivatives, the revenues reached $1.6 billion.

REGULATORY RAMIFICATIONS OF OFF-BALANCE-SHEET ACTIVITIES

There is a strong economic incentive for corporations and investors to purchase insurance in the form of derivatives or other off-balance-sheet contingencies. Regulators have been concerned that the rapid growth in the supply of these instruments may be motivated by a lack of sufficient regulatory control. This concern was partially responsible for the changes made in the computation of capital requirements for insured banks. Since 1992, regulatory agencies have incorporated off-balance-sheet activities in the computation of risk-based capital ratios for the purpose of granting deposit insurance coverage. In addition, the explo-

---

[4] During the same period, the net interest income for the nine banks was about $12 billion.

Source: Call Report, Schedule RC-L, June 1995.

TABLE 5.9 Positive vs. Negative Value Positions, and Profitability of Derivatives in Nine Banks with Largest Volume of Derivatives June 1995 ($ Millions)

Rank	Bank Name	Traded (MTM) Gross Positive Value	Traded (MTM) Gross Negative Value	Non-Traded Gross Positive Value	Non-Traded Gross Negative Value	Derivative Trading Revenues
1	Chemical Bank (NY)	$41,625	$43,599	$785	$718	$163
2	Morgan Guaranty (NY)	$48,570	$47,956	$3,634	$3,019	$304
3	Citibank (NY)	$35,017	$34,229	$840	$559	$479
4	Bankers Trust (NY)	$35,664	$35,302	$217	$232	$105
5	Bank of America (CA)	$22,187	$22,799	$466	$629	$44
6	Chase Manhattan (NY)	$21,116	$21,945	$692	$488	$138
7	NationsBank (NC)	$5,481	$5,408	$140	$266	$39
8	First NB of Chicago (IL)	$12,106	$11,785	$74	$19	$19
9	Republic NB of NY (NY)	$3,042	$3,111	$171	$165	$63
	Total Top Nine Banks	$224,808	$226,134	$7,019	$6,095	$1,354
	Other 581 Banks with Derivatives	$5,059	$4,838	$4,476	$4,564	$277
	Total 590 Banks with Derivatives	$229,867	$230,972	$11,495	$10,660	$1,631

83

sive growth in the derivative activities of large banks has prompted legislators to examine whether further restrictions are necessary.

What seems troublesome to legislators is that derivatives are highly complex instruments and their payment schedules are contingent upon future changes that are difficult to predict. But the fact that the instruments are complex does not mean that they will induce more risk than do traditional banking activities. In fact, there is little empirical evidence to date to support this view. While the General Accounting Office, an arm of Congress, has called for vastly expanded regulation of the dealers and users of derivatives, the current chairman of the Federal Reserve Board, Alan Greenspan, has disagreed with such a conclusion. According to Greenspan, "There is no presumption that the major thrust of derivatives is any riskier, indeed it may very well be less risky, than commercial lending." [5] In the same statement, Greenspan argued that additional government regulation was not necessary because of "private regulation" by investors, credit rating agencies, and customers who insist on financial soundness in those with whom they do business.

An alternative explanation for the growth in off-balance-sheet activities lies with increased customer demand. Customers have found that they can secure credit in the market at a lower cost than that of a bank loan. To facilitate their credit market financing, customers need banks' credit approval in the form of an off-balance-sheet product. This is consistent with the observation that bank loan balances have decreased in recent years while their off-balance-sheet activities have increased.

LOAN SALES

An increasingly important way of obtaining fee income and reducing regulatory costs is to sell loans once they have been originated. This may involve direct sales to a third party or packaging loans and selling pieces of the pool to different investors. Sales of the first type are referred to as loan sales; those of the second type are called loan securitization.

In a loan sale, the depository institution is acting as a broker by originating the loan and then selling it to an investor at a premium. The premium represents fee income to compensate for the administrative costs of the loan origination process. A common example of a loan sale is the transfer of a mortgage from a savings and loan to an insurance company. The savings and loan originates the mortgage just as if the mortgage will be kept on the books of the company. Application and origination fees are charged and all necessary forms are filed by the savings and loan. Immediately upon loan closing, the loan is handed over to the insurance company and the customer is notified that loan payments are to be made to that company.

It is not necessary that the loan or mortgage be immediately sold to a third party, nor is it always the case that the payments are sent directly to the new owner of the loan. In many cases the originating institution will continue to service the loan (collect loan payments and perform the necessary bookkeeping) for a fee. The servicing fees represent another source of income for a depository institution. While mortgage sales have been common, sales of other types of loans have increased in recent years: Now many business loans are sold off by originating banks, and automobile and credit card loans also have been sold.

For a loan actually to be considered sold and removed from the asset side of

---

[5] *The New York Times*, May 26, 1994, pp. C1 and C5.

the balance sheet of a depository institution, the loan must be sold without recourse. This means that in the event of a loan default, the new owner of the loan, and not the originator of the loan, must absorb the loss. When a loan is sold with recourse, it remains on the balance sheet of the depository institution. While the loan does not have to be funded in the normal sense, it is still subject to capital regulation. Because of this added cost, most loans are sold without recourse.

Loan sales are likely to involve agency problems. Because the final owner of the loan is not the originator, there is always the danger of the lemons problem. That is, a bank may be most interested in selling the loans that are the poorest investment. The good loans will be held on the balance sheet and fee income earned on the bad loans. Of course, the purchaser of the loans wants to guard against this. One way to police this potential problem is to set strict underwriting standards and require selling banks to meet these standards. This may lead to less variety in the types of loans offered to consumers, but it provides a means of protection for the purchaser of the loan. A second way to overcome the agency problem is to purchase less than 100% of the loan. By forcing the originating bank to retain part of the loan, the purchaser is requiring some equity participation in the investment. Loan participation is common in international banking and in correspondent banking relationships.

SECURITIZATION

Securitization involves issuing debt claims based on a pool of loans where the principal and interest from the underlying loans are used to pay the security holders. Securitization allows a financial intermediary to focus on originating a loan and often servicing the loan without funding it. Depending on the nature of securitization, a financial intermediary may also provide the risk-bearing function by issuing securities with recourse. Securitization in effect substitutes market funding for intermediary funding. Market funding is less expensive because regulatory tax in the form of reserve and capital requirements and deposit insurance premiums increase the cost of intermediary funding.

While securitization may involve a variety of loan pools, mortgage-related securitization is the most prominent in terms of the size of the market. The market for securities collateralized by mortgage pools has grown tremendously since its inception in 1970. The volume of these securities increased from $114 billion in 1989 to $1.5 trillion in June 1995.[6] Securities collateralized by credit card loans, automobile loans, truck loans, equipment leases, and even boat loans are also available.[7] We now examine a variety of asset-backed securities, including pass-through securities, asset-backed bonds, and collateralized mortgage obligations and real estate mortgage investment conduits.

Pass-Through Securities

Securitization began in 1970 when the Government National Mortgage Association (GNMA or "Ginnie Mae") developed a pass-through security collateralized by mortgages. The majority of Ginnie Mae pass-throughs are collateralized by single-family mortgages, which are loans for one-to-four-family primary residences. Other mortgages used as collateral are graduated-payment mortgages, growing equity mortgages, and mobile-home loans insured by the Federal Housing Administration (FHA), the Veterans Administration (VA), or the Farmers Home Administration. The security is called a *mortgage-backed security (MBS)*

---

[6] *Flow of Funds Accounts: Flows and Outstandings*, Second Quarter 1995, pp. 81–82.
[7] Even Mexican toll-road receivables are being securitized.

and classified as a *pass-through* because interest and principal payments on mortgages are distributed among security holders. GNMA guarantees payment of principal and interest when due, even if some mortgagors fail to make their monthly payments. This type of security is called a *fully modified pass-through*. Since Ginnie Mae is a government agency, its pass-throughs are guaranteed by the full faith and credit of the U.S. government. Consequently, these pass-throughs are free of default risk.

Ginnie Mae has two pass-through programs: *GNMA I* (established in 1970) and *GNMA II* (established in 1983). GNMA I is collateralized by the qualifying fixed-rate mortgages; GNMA II is backed by adjustable-payment mortgages. GNMA does not hold mortgages or pass-through securities. It simply provides insurance services to security holders.

In 1971, the Federal Home Loan Mortgage Corporation (FHLMC, or "Freddie Mac"), a publicly held corporation, developed a pass-through security called a *participation certificate (PC).* Despite its public ownership, Freddie Mac carries a line of credit from the U.S. Treasury should it need funds in an emergency. Consequently, the market treats Freddie Mac as a quasi-governmental agency with little default risk.

Freddie Mac has two PC programs, the *cash program* and the *guarantor/swap program*. In the cash program, Freddie Mac buys mortgages from the originators, then pools them to back the PCs. In the guarantor/swap program, the originators swap pools of mortgages for PCs in the same pools.

In the fall of 1990, Freddie Mac introduced the *gold PC*, which has stronger guarantees. Gold PCs, which are issued in both programs, will be the only type of PCs issued in the future. Gold PCs are all fully modified pass-throughs similar to those issued by Ginnie Mae. Almost all nongold PCs guarantee only the timely payment of interest. The principal is passed through as collected; Freddie Mac guarantees only that the scheduled payment will be made no later than one year after it is due. Securities with these provisions are called *modified pass-throughs*. PCs are backed by a wide variety of loan pools, including fixed-rate level-paying mortgages, adjustable-rate mortgages, and balloon mortgages.

The Federal National Mortgage Association (FNMA, or "Fannie Mae") developed the mortgage-backed securities (MBSs) in 1981. Similar to Freddie Mac, Fannie Mae is a publicly held corporation with a line of credit from the U.S. Treasury. Fannie Mae also has both a cash and a swap program. All Fannie Mae MBSs are fully modified pass-throughs, with Fannie Mae guaranteeing timely interest and principal payments.

The private sector securitization began when Bank of America issued a security backed by conventional mortgages in 1977. The issuer purchases insurance on the entire portfolio of mortgage pools. Diversification reduces the risk and enables the issuer to buy this insurance at a lower cost than that of obtaining insurance individually for each mortgage.

A pass-through security is created based on a pool of qualifying loans. The pool is then passed to a trustee agency and securities are issued against the underlying pool. Each security represents a share of ownership in the entire pool. All the principal and interest payments are passed along to security holders in proportion to total ownership. The interest received by the investors is less than the original interest on the mortgages because of the fees paid for credit insurance and servicing costs.

Pass-through securities have a number of characteristics that account for their popularity. The sale of pass-throughs against the underlying pool of mortgages is treated as the sale of the mortgages themselves. This allows financial intermediaries to take these assets off their balance sheets. In addition, these securities are more liquid than the underlying mortgages because they are issued in large denominations and are insured. This makes them attractive to institutional investors.

Pass-through securities also have shortcomings. Pass-throughs are subject to prepayment risk. For example, suppose that an investor buys an 8% coupon Ginnie Mae pass-through when mortgage rates are at 8%. If mortgage rates decline to 5%, the mortgagors will refinance their loans. When the original mortgages are prepaid, the investor in the pass-through has to reinvest the prepaid funds at a lower rate. If mortgage rates increase to 10%, the market price of the pass-through will decline. The rate of prepayments will also decline, denying an opportunity for the investor to invest additional funds at a higher rate. Prepayment risk in pass-through securities, therefore, makes the size of payments to investors unpredictable.

Pass-through securities subject their investors to monthly cash flows; other corporate and government bonds provide semiannual cash flows. The greater frequency of cash flows may subject the investor to higher transaction costs in reinvesting the funds. The uncertainties about size and timing of the cash flows in pass-throughs led to the development of asset-backed bonds and collateralized mortgage obligations.

Mortgage pass-throughs make up the largest segment of the market, but other loans may also be used as collateral. For example, automobile loans are packaged as pass-throughs in Certificates of Automobile Receivables (CARs). Credit card receivables are packaged as pass-throughs in Certificates of Amortizing Revolving Debts (CARDs). Both automobile and credit card loans have stable repayment rates, so prepayment risk with these asset-backed securities is not as great as it is with mortgage-backed securities.

Asset-Backed Bonds

Asset-backed bonds were developed in response to problems faced by pass-through securities. While asset-backed bonds are also collateralized by the underlying pool of assets, the cash flows from assets are not passed directly to investors. The bonds therefore can have different cash-flow frequencies than the underlying assets. For example, while the underlying pool may have monthly payments, the asset-backed bond can have semiannual payments.

Unlike pass-through securities, the investor in an asset-backed bond does not have an ownership claim on the underlying pool of assets. The assets remain on the books of the issuing institution, and the bonds they support are simply a liability of the institution. The general setup of an asset-backed bond is similar to that of a pass-through. The accounting treatment complicates the asset-backed bond. Because cash flows are not dedicated to the investors, the underlying mortgages must be first sold off to a subsidiary of the originating institution so the bond issue can be underwritten. While the mortgages may leave the books of a particular bank or savings and loan, they are still on the consolidated balance sheet of the holding company. The lack of direct dedication of the mortgage payments to the bonds also means that the bonds themselves are not insured even though the underlying mortgages may be insured. To protect against this risk, asset-backed bonds are over-collateralized. This protects investors against declines in the market value of the underlying mortgages. The result is that asset-backed bonds are typically an expensive way of raising funds. Not surprisingly, they make up a very small percentage of the overall asset-backed securities market.

Collateralized Mortgage Obligations (CMOs) and Real Estate Mortgage Investment Conduits (REMICs)

A third category of asset-backed securities is collateralized mortgage obligation (CMO). CMOs have characteristics of both pass-through securities and mortgaged-backed bonds. Like pass-throughs, cash flows from the underlying pool of loans are directly dedicated to CMOs. As a result, the administrative cost is less than that of asset-backed bonds. Like asset-backed bonds, investors in CMOs are not the owners of the underlying loans, so the loans remain on the books of the issuer. In addition, while the loans themselves may be insured, CMOs are not.

The first CMO was issued by Freddie Mac in June 1983. Each CMO issue was divided into three maturity classes, or tranches. Tranches were prioritized so that bondholders in the first class received all of the principal payments before bondholders in the next class received any principal payments. This process continued until all classes of bondholders were paid off. Bondholders in all classes received semiannual interest payments. The original CMO was set up as such that the first class of bondholders were paid off in 5 years, the second class were paid off within 12 years, and the third class were paid off within 20 years. The purpose of different tranches is to reduce prepayment risk to investors. Although prepayment risk still exists, bondholders can be reasonably certain of the rate of prepayment. In this sense, CMOs are an improvement over pass-throughs.

A wide variety of CMOs have been issued, with the number of tranches ranging from three to six. Most CMOs have four tranches—three regular tranches and one residual tranche, called Z class (because it is similar to a zero-coupon bond). While the first three classes receive regular interest, bondholders in the Z class do not. The interest that would have been paid to the Z class is used to speed up pay-down of the principal balance in earlier tranches. After the three regular classes receive their principal payments, the Z class receives the principal as well as the compounded value of the accrued interest.[8]

CMOs are issued by thrifts, investment banks, insurance companies, and federal agencies, among others. The popularity of CMOs lies in their usefulness in reducing not only the prepayment risk but also the interest-rate risk. For example, an intermediary with long-term mortgage loans financed with short-term deposits is susceptible to such risk, but it can be reduced by swapping some of the mortgages with CMOs with shorter maturities.

The trust created to distribute interest and principal payments is considered a taxable entity unless it meets conditions specified in a provision of the Tax Reform Act of 1986, which authorizes Real Estate Mortgage Investment Conduits (REMICs). REMICs are similar to CMOs with one major distinction—tax treatment. Unlike CMOs, REMICs qualify as asset sales for tax purposes if the following two conditions hold. First, a REMIC must contain at least one regular tranche and no more than one residual class. Second, the collateral for a REMIC should include either "qualified mortgages" or "permitted investments." Qualified mortgages include single- and multifamily mortgages, commercial mortgages, and mortgage-backed securities. Permitted investments include investments in short-term interest-bearing securities made only for the purpose of investing cash flows of mortgages until they are paid to the REMIC investors. Another permitted investment is in qualified reserve funds, which are composed of long-term investments set aside for the explicit purpose of funding operating expenses of a REMIC. Permitted investments do not need to be mortgage-related.[9]

The advantages of securitization have been noted throughout our discussion. Briefly, securitization allows for specialization in the lending function and the opportunity for depository intermediaries to earn fee income. From an investor perspective, the newly created instruments have more manageable cash flow

---

[8] Fabozzi (1996), Chapter 12.
[9] Pavel (1989) pp. 67–68; Baldwin and Stotts (1990), Chapter 9.

characteristics that can be used to control the interest-rate risk of an institution. In addition, asset-backed securities are more liquid than the assets that collateralize them, thereby increasing liquidity for investors. These characteristics are so important that many banks and savings and loans originate mortgages but hold mostly mortgage-backed securities in their investment portfolios.

All of the financial instruments described in this chapter are complicated compared to a treasury bond or a car loan. The complexity suggests that intermediaries need to invest in specialized resources in order to make sound decisions as to their use. As suggested earlier larger banks are better able to afford the specialized resources needed to deal with these instruments. Smaller intermediaries will either refrain from these activities or merge with larger intermediaries to acquire needed resources.

SUMMARY

Depository intermediaries have increased their off-balance-sheet, loan sale, and securitization activities substantially in recent years. Expansion of products in these areas have coincided with a decline in the traditional lending arena. A traditional bank loan provides four distinct functions: origination, risk-bearing, funding, and servicing. Depository intermediaries can specialize in some of these functions and provide products that their customers need. For example, the origination function is provided when a loan is originated and then sold without recourse. A combination of the origination and risk-bearing functions occurs when depository intermediaries engage in off-balance-sheet activities. Securitization allows depository intermediaries to avoid the funding function while performing the other three.

The economic basis for the rapid growth in off-balance-sheet activities lies in the increased financial risk that corporations face today. This increased risk is due to three events of the 1970s that made interest rates and foreign currencies flexible while commodities prices increased. Derivative securities are instruments to hedge financial risk, in demand by corporate customers. Regulatory concerns over these instruments are generally due to their complexity and their recent rapid growth. Further, the off-balance-sheet nature of these instruments makes their monitoring especially difficult for regulators. So far, there is no evidence to suggest that these instruments unduly increase the riskiness of depository intermediaries.

Loan sale and securitization improve liquidity by allowing depository intermediaries to originate loans and subsequently package and sell them in the capital market. This frees depository intermediaries from the funding function and reduces the cost of borrowing. Depository intermediaries concentrate on areas in which they have a cost advantage, such as origination, risk-bearing, and servicing, while forgoing the funding function.

A pass-through constitutes the sale of a pool of loans by an intermediary. The pool of loans is transferred to a trustee, who oversees the collection and distribution of interest and principal payments to investors. The ownership of the pool of loans is transferred to investors and its income is taxed at the investor level. Since a pass-through often provides monthly cash flows, investors may face high transaction costs in reinvesting these funds. In addition, investors in pass-throughs face prepayment risk when borrowers decide to refinance their loans when interest rates decline. To avoid these problems, asset-backed bonds and collateralized mortgage obligations are issued. While asset-backed bonds are backed by a pool of loans, payments to bondholders do not have to match the frequency of the loan payments. As it is often the case, asset-backed bonds make semiannual payments to bondholders, whereas mortgagors pay interest and principal payments on a monthly basis. Asset-backed bonds are issued by a subsidiary of the intermediary who owns the loan pool. Therefore, the issue of asset-backed bonds does not constitute asset sale. The loan pool therefore stays as an asset in the consolidated financial statement and the asset-backed bonds constitute a new debt.

CMOs reduce prepayment risk by creating classes of claimants who receive interest income regularly but receive the principal payments in a particular order. Bondholders in the first class receive all their principal claims before any principal payments are made to the second class, and so on.

REVIEW QUESTIONS

1. What are the four functions of a traditional depository institution loan?
2. Cite examples of depository institution products that provide some of these functions without being a loan.
3. Define off-balance-sheet activities, loan commitments, standby letters of credit, and commercial letters of credit.
4. Explain how a line of credit is different from an actual loan. Why do business firms prefer to borrow using lines of credit rather than regular loans?
5. Under what circumstances does a commercial letter of credit become a bankers acceptance?
6. What are derivative securities? Define forward, futures, options, and swaps. Explain their differences.
7. Discuss three different sets of swap contracts.
8. What are the economic reasons for the rapid growth of derivative securities in recent years?
9. Why are large depository intermediaries more active in the derivative securities business than small depository intermediaries?
10. What are the regulatory concerns over the rapid growth of derivatives?
11. Explain the process of loan sales.
12. What are the differences between loan sale and securitization?
13. Explain the functions of GNMA, FNMA, and FHLMC.
14. Explain the differences among a pass-through security, an asset-backed bond, and a collateralized mortgage obligation. Which of these mortgage-backed securities is subject to the most interest-rate risk? Explain.
15. Why should banks and other depository intermediaries worry about their declining market share of financial assets? In what ways might this decline be overstated?

REFERENCES

Avery, R. B., and A. N. Berger. 1991. "Loan Commitments and Bank Risk Exposure." *Journal of Banking and Finance*, vol. 15: 173–192.

Baldwin, E., and S. Stotts. 1990. *Mortgage-Backed Securities.* Chicago: Probus Publishing Company.

Fabozzi, F. J. 1996. *Bond Markets, Analysis and Strategies.* Upper Saddle River, NJ: Prentice Hall, Third Edition.

Karels, G. V., and A. J. Prakash. 1989. "Loan Pricing and Loan Yields on Commercial Line of Credit." *Review of Banking and Finance* (Spring): 29–39.

Pavel, C. A. 1989. *Securitization.* Chicago: Probus Publishing Company.

6

Regulation of Depository Intermediaries

OBJECTIVES

This chapter examines the theoretical and structural issues in the regulation of depository intermediaries. The discussion begins with the fundamental question of why depository intermediaries are regulated. We present four theories of regulation and explain the underlying incentives. The goals in regulating depository intermediaries are: safety and soundness, consumer and investor protection, fairness, and information disclosures. The regulatory structure for depository intermediaries is an intricate system of overlapping responsibilities. The Federal Reserve System, the Office of Comptroller of the Currency, the Federal Deposit Insurance Corporation (FDIC), the Securities Exchange Commission (SEC), the Justice Department and state banking authorities enforce a complex set of laws that have governed the industry since the turn of this century. Most laws currently applied to the industry were enacted in the aftermath of the Great Depression of the 1930s. While technological advance and the globalization of the economy have significantly altered the parameters of the business, many restrictive features of the early regulation remain. This explains the conflicting policies that appear to pervade the financial services industry. Often, regulation leads to a reallocation of resources from one segment of the economy to another. In the process, compliance with the regulatory framework creates significant costs. We conclude the chapter with an appendix that covers all of the major laws that affect the operation of depository intermediaries.

WHY ARE DEPOSITORY FINANCIAL INTERMEDIARIES REGULATED?

Although depository intermediaries operate as ordinary profit-seeking businesses, they face strict rules regarding the identity of their owners, the location of their operations, and the mix of their products. There are two distinct but interrelated aspects to the regulation of depository financial intermediaries. First, the liabilities of depository intermediaries serve as a major source of the money supply. In order to control the money supply, regulators seek to influence the operation of depository intermediaries. Second, the liabilities of depository intermediaries represent a major portion of the nation's financial wealth. Accordingly, protecting deposits is an overriding concern for regulators.

An environment conducive to economic growth and prosperity requires stability in the monetary system, which in turn depends upon public trust in the payment system and the safety of depository intermediaries.[1] Without public trust, even a slight rumor about an intermediary's financial difficulty can create disruptive bank runs. Providing excessive protection to depositors, however, removes the policing role of debt financing. With no incentive for depositors to monitor the safety of their own funds, depository intermediaries are freer to take excessive risk, from society's point of view.

The regulation of the financial services industry is also targeted at intermediary products. Financial products such as loans, securities, and deposits are complex contracts filled with legal rights and responsibilities that are not always easily understood by borrowers or lenders. A substantial portion of regulation involves releasing information to customers to enable them to make informed decisions.

Viewed in this context, depository intermediaries are regulated because of their impact on macroeconomic performance. Long-term growth and price stability require market intervention when informational problems threaten economic stability. The highly informational nature of financial industry products makes them susceptible to rumors and public panics. Consequently, regulators monitor closely the types and amounts of financial products offered by depository intermediaries.

While depositor safety is a primary concern, the safety of each and every institution is not a goal of financial regulation. It would be unwise to keep every financial institution from failing under the guise of depositor safety and monetary stability. This would clearly amount to unwarranted protection of owners and managers instead of depositors. Some institutions fail because of bad investment decisions, and the proper allocation of scarce resources suggests that these mistakes should not be subsidized. Failure to allow individual institutions to go under would provide the wrong incentives for future decisions.

Effective regulation requires supervision and monitoring. Too much, however, may also cause problems. Targeting specific intermediaries, customers, or areas of the economy for differential treatment can distort the resource-allocation process. The savings and loan debacle showed how encouraging home ownership led to misguided protectionism and ended with a $200 billion taxpayer bailout. Similarly, regulatory failure in understanding financial innovations could lead to costly distortions. Regulation should not constrain management to the point where the only available alternatives are regulated choices. When this occurs, the regulators and not the managers are running the intermediary. Consequently, regulated industries may be disadvantaged in the market for new products.

THE THEORY OF REGULATION

The rationale for the regulation of depository financial intermediaries has been advanced in the following theories:

- public interest theory
- many interest theory
- special interest or capture theory
- public choice theory

---

[1] See Spong (1992a and 1992b).

Regulation in the financial services industry stems, in large part, from its impact on overall macroeconomic performance. The public interest theory argues that regulation is supplied on demand from the general public to control potential and actual market failures. This theory is a sort of "big brother" view of government. There are certain conditions under which markets may not allocate goods and services in a socially optimal way. When there are externalities or natural monopolies, the socially optimal allocation can only be achieved through regulatory intervention in the marketplace.

Markets may fail in their optimal resource allocation due to externalities, the most common of which relates to air pollution. A steel factory located close to a residential area may pollute the air significantly, lowering the value of homes in the neighborhood. The market for homes would work correctly if the effect of the external factor (i.e., air pollution) could be removed by regulating the production process and charging the polluter a fee commensurate with the reduced value of the homes.

The externality does not have to be negative. The decision to locate an exclusive golf course next to an existing residential area may have a beneficial impact on housing values in the neighborhood. No market exists that allows the builders of the golf course to price and capture the increased value of the homes.

Solutions to these types of problems are almost always handled through a regulatory zoning board. Decisions as to where to build a steel plant are closely regulated to minimize the negative impact on homeowners. Decisions regarding where to build a golf course are also regulated, although the objective may not be clear from the ruling issued by the zoning board.

Externalities and information problems are the driving forces behind regulation in the financial services industry. The link between macroeconomic performance and the money supply is used to justify regulatory control over financial institutions whose deposits constitute money. The control of the money supply also requires supervising and monitoring, and depends on detailed and precise information. Depository financial intermediaries are therefore required to file standardized financial reports on a quarterly, semiannual, and annual basis with the FDIC, the Fed, and the SEC, among others. Truth-in-lending regulations are another example of standardized reporting requirements. Lending companies of all types must report finance charges in the standard form of annual percentage rates (APR) so that borrowers can compare rates across various lenders.

Deposit insurance is probably the best example of regulation deemed to be in the public interest. The numerous bank failures of the 1930s no doubt contributed to the length and magnitude of the Great Depression. The result was a public outcry for a safe and stable banking system. This was satisfied by setting up a federal deposit insurance system that appeared to work effectively. Six decades after its inception, however, deposit insurance regulation has become one of the most intrusive regulatory powers in the depository institutions industry. In addition, deposit insurance regulation created incentive problems that encouraged excessive risk-taking. Because of the importance of this regulatory area, the next chapter is devoted entirely to this subject.

Many Interest Theory

Public interest theory is used to justify much of the regulation in the financial services industry, whether or not it is really in the public interest. One of the problems with a pervasive regulatory structure, however, is the possibility that a regulatory system can be exploited by special interest groups acting in their own behalf. This is the basic premise of the many interest theory.

A major impact of regulation in any market is to change the allocation of goods and services. A vested interest group can change the current allocation in the market to one with a more favorable outcome for itself. It is similar to having Congress impose a tax on one group and redistribute the proceeds to another. For example, mortgage borrowers are one of the biggest beneficiaries of financial regulation. Regulations allow savings and loans to receive special tax breaks if their asset portfolios exceed a threshold in residential mortgage holdings. This provides an incentive to issue more mortgages, which may be accomplished by lower mortgage rates. Home owners also benefit through the tax deductibility of mortgage interest. This is not to say that regulations of this sort are necessarily bad or socially suboptimal. There has been a conscious choice in the United States to promote single-family housing through regulation and tax incentives. As a result, Americans live in spacious and well-equipped homes. In addition, the United States has the highest rate of home ownership among industrialized countries.[2]

An implication of the many interest theory of regulation is a fragmented regulatory policy. Regulations that benefit one group may detract from another. Regulations that limit interest rates charged to borrowers may benefit some consumers when credit is scarce but prohibit high-risk borrowers' access to legal credit markets. The development of loansharking, with its very high interest rates and unorthodox collection methods, can be viewed as a result of such interest-rate restrictions.

Special Interest or Capture Theory

If regulation can benefit many diverse groups, as suggested by the many interest theory, it can also provide potential monopoly profits to a group that uses the regulatory structure to eliminate competition. This is the essence of the capture theory. There exists a strong incentive for those firms that are regulated to cooperate with the regulators in order to earn monopoly rents. Viewed from this perspective, regulation exists for the benefit of the regulated as opposed to consumers. For example, a community sets up a regulatory board to review and restrict the pricing and customer policies of a cable television company. The technology of stringing wires or burying cable makes it efficient for only one cable operator to serve a community (i.e., a natural monopoly). The regulatory board, therefore, grants an exclusive franchise to the company with the condition that the rates and channel offerings be approved by the board. The cable company is allowed to earn a "fair rate of return" on its investment and all is well in the world.

If technology were static, such regulatory arrangements could work. Suppose, however, a new technology allows for transmitting digital television signals through telephone lines. The cable company would ask the regulators to exclude the competition because a superior technology with cheaper rates would destroy its monopoly. If the regulatory board disallows the phone company entry, consumers will lose. However, if the board allows the entry, cable company shareholders and employees will lose. If the cable company is forced out of business, the phone company becomes the new monopolist until an even more advanced technology developed by a third party starts the battle all over again.[3]

---

[2] See, for example, Metzler (1974).

[3] Such arguments have been made recently. A solution that seems plausible is the merger of the telephone and cable companies. So far, however, such efforts have not succeeded due to regulatory problems with the FCC. A potentially powerful competition for cable is RCA's 18½-inch dish that transmits digital signals.

There are also cases where regulations that were intended to protect public interest against certain industries end up doing exactly the opposite. Consider, for instance, state laws in Nebraska regulating intrastate moving charges. Moving companies must all charge exactly the same price per 100 pounds. The only dimension movers can compete on is service reputation. This is done in the name of consumer protection so moving companies do not purposely quote low prices to capture business and then do a poor job.

One of the interesting features of this particular regulation is that intrastate moving rates are regulated while interstate rates are not.[4] Clever moving companies have discovered that they can price compete in cities located close to state borders, such as Omaha, by first moving the furniture to Iowa for a few minutes and then back into Nebraska. The moving companies, therefore, circumvent the intrastate restrictions whenever it is to their benefit to do so.

Such efforts to avoid regulation have also existed in the financial services industry. For many years, regulators prohibited interest payments on checking accounts and limited the maximum interest rates on savings accounts. While bankers occasionally bemoaned these regulations, they generally profited from the resulting low-cost funds during periods of economic stability. To attract new customers and deposits, the regulations were skirted by offering free gifts (toasters were popular) on deposits. These regulations were repealed only when depository intermediaries lost substantial market share to money market mutual funds.

Public Choice Theory

According to public choice theory, regulators realize value in the power they exert over the regulated and seek to maintain and expand the scope of their control. At the extreme, this view suggests that regulators use their positions to gain monetary and nonmonetary benefits from the regulated. The theory also predicts that regulatory agencies will be unwilling to share or surrender their power because doing so will diminish its potential benefits.

This view is consistent with the policies of the Federal Savings and Loan Insurance Corporation (FSLIC) in the 1980s. Instead of admitting the magnitude of the industry's losses and its insurance fund deficit, regulators systemically understated the problem in order to preserve their power base. It was not until 1989 that the depleted FSLIC was stripped of its power and merged with the FDIC. This delay, however, came with an estimated $100–$200 billion price tag in the form of an industry bailout.

One of the latest proposals to change the regulatory structure of depository intermediaries has met the kind of opposition predicted by the public choice theory. The Fed proposed to take over regulation of all state-chartered banks. This plan was immediately opposed by the Treasury Department (home of the Office of Thrift Supervision, the Resolution Trust Corporation, and the Comptroller of Currency) on the grounds that such action would be confusing and counterproductive.

The Fed plan was itself in response to a proposal by the Secretary of the Treasury on behalf of the Clinton administration to combine the regulatory functions of four agencies into a single Federal Banking Commission.[5] The new commission would have combined the Office of the Comptroller of the Currency, which regulates about 3,600 national banks, and the Office of Thrift Supervision, which regulates some 1,800 savings and loans. In addition, the regulatory banking func-

---

[4] Prior to 1980, interstate rates were also determined by regulators instead of the market.
[5] *The Wall Street Journal*, November 24, 1993, p. A2.

tions of the Fed, which regulates about 1,000 state banks and 6,300 bank holding companies, and the FDIC, which supervises 7,500 state-chartered banks, would have been transferred into the new commission. Such a reorganization would have greatly diminished the power and stature of the Federal Reserve. Needless to say, the Fed immediately attacked the proposal on the grounds that it needed a hands-on role in banking supervision in order to carry out its responsibilities for the stability of the financial system. The Fed then proposed a counterplan that would have enhanced rather than reduced its power.

THE REGULATORY CYCLE

The theories discussed above are not mutually exclusive in their descriptions of regulatory behavior. The public interest theory may explain the initial intent of the regulators. As regulation takes hold, those who are adversely affected try to circumvent the burden by introducing innovative products. The new products often avoid the strict interpretations of the law. As regulatory circumvention becomes widespread in the industry, the original regulation is neutralized. The cycle starts all over again as regulators see the opportunity to expand their power over new products. Politicians, on behalf of special interest groups, also reign in the regulatory process. An endless cycle of regulation-circumvention-reregulation increases the volume of regulation, expands the regulatory power of the supervisory agencies, and leads to the formation of the political action committees that represent special interest groups.[6]

OBJECTIVES OF FINANCIAL REGULATION

There are four broad objectives in regulating depository intermediaries:

- safety and soundness
- consumer and investor protection
- fairness
- information disclosure

Safety and Soundness

The main focus of safety and soundness is to prevent disruptions in the payments system and to avoid a systemwide collapse of financial intermediaries. There are three basic methods used in promoting safety and soundness. First, monetary policy is conducted so as to influence the level of prices, output, and employment. Second, a framework is established to maintain a stable payment system. Third, depository intermediaries are closely monitored to prevent general financial failure.

The first of these methods is accomplished with a combination of monetary and fiscal policy. The Fed is responsible for the conduct of monetary policy by means of monitoring depository reserves and controlling short-term interest rates. If the Fed perceives economic growth to be greater than is desirable, it will increase short-term interest rates in order to slow the rate of growth. If the Fed does not do this, the demand for goods will exceed the supply, and prices will rise. For example, from February 1994 through February 1995, the Fed raised the discount rate and the federal funds rate seven times, doubling the federal funds rate to 6% and increasing the discount rate from 3% to 5.25%. On the other hand, when the economy is operating significantly below its capacity, the Fed may decrease short-term interest rates in order to stimulate economic growth.

---

[6] See, for example, Hester (1981) and Kane (1981).

The framework for ensuring a stable payments system is maintained through a network of clearing systems. The Fed operates the oldest of the check-clearing systems. Through a system of local and regional banks, checks are cleared quickly and payments are transferred from one part of the country to another. Global central banks also cooperate to promote the smooth clearing of international checks. In addition to the Fed system, several private clearing networks also provide efficient clearing services. Currently, electronic transactions account for a progressively larger portion of all payments and receipts. This amplifies the importance of financial intermediaries in the operation of the payment system, since the focus is no longer on just banks. Other financial intermediaries also play an increasingly important role in the payment system.

The third method of promoting safety and soundness is through supervising depository intermediaries. This entails protecting depository intermediaries on the one hand and restricting their activities on the other. The protection comes in the form of the Fed's role as the lender of last resort and the FDIC's role as the provider of deposit insurance. The restriction involves limitations on the asset composition of depository intermediaries.

Depository intermediary assets are generally less liquid than are their liabilities. If depositors as a group decide to withdraw their funds on short notice because of the financial distress of an intermediary (or a simple rumor to that effect), the intermediary will be forced to make sudden and costly adjustments to its illiquid asset portfolio. Depending on the size of the intermediary and the pervasiveness of the problem in the industry, a bank run may cause a serious interruption in economic activity. To address the liquidity problem, the Fed acts as lender of last resort by providing temporary liquidity assistance to financial intermediaries in the form of discount loans. To avoid bank runs, the FDIC provides deposit insurance.[7] However, if depository intermediaries believe that emergency funding through the Fed will always be available in case they get into trouble, they will have incentives for excessive risk-taking. The problem is further exacerbated by depositor apathy in the presence of FDIC insurance. These types of incentive problems are referred to as "moral hazard" problems. Regulatory agencies closely scrutinize depository intermediaries in order to limit their exposure to risk. Depository intermediaries are currently prohibited from investing in common stocks and low-grade corporate bonds that are deemed too risky.

Consumer and Investor Protection

Financial instruments are complex legal contracts. Accordingly, regulators are concerned about the ability of an average person to comprehend the risk-return trade-off in these instruments. Regulations of this sort require standardized and simple reporting of the necessary information. In addition, insider transactions and potentially fraudulent schemes are closely monitored in the name of consumer and investor protection.[8]

An important example of this provision is truth-in-lending regulation. The law requires a common reporting of interest costs in the form of an Annual Percentage Rate (APR). In addition to the APR, financial intermediaries are required to provide documentation on all other finance charges and payments. The goal is to provide standardized, easily comparable data to prospective borrowers. Such requirements are in effect for almost all types of loans. Similar reporting requirements also exist for deposit accounts, due to recently enacted "truth-in-savings" legislation.

---

[7] See Diamond and Dybvig (1983).
[8] See, for example, Kummer, Arshadi, and Lawrence (1989).

In addition to consumer protection legislation, much attention is also given to investor protection. Insider trading regulations and the more broadly defined antifraud provisions of the Securities Exchange Act of 1934 represent attempts to ensure equity among investors.[9]

One of the difficulties with consumer protection regulation is that it does not target the average investor; instead, it assumes an investor has little or no knowledge of financial markets and intermediaries. The target borrower, according to the truth-in-lending provision, is a person who cannot independently gather any relevant information. The law, therefore, requires intermediaries to disclose extensive details of each loan or deposit to their customers and subsequently to solicit their signatures. Failure to do so may subject the intermediary to legal penalties. This is a substantial burden on financial intermediaries, and its usefulness is suspect.

Fairness

A market-based system will allocate its goods and services to those who are willing to pay the highest price. While unimpeded markets grant efficiency, they do not satisfy all of society's objectives. Moreover, when markets do not operate with full information, allocation may no longer be efficient. Consequently, regulators intervene in markets to obtain a more desirable allocation of resources.

One of the major reallocation schemes in the U.S. economy involves mortgage credit. This reallocation policy is accomplished through tax subsidies to both borrowers and lenders. First, thrift institutions receive a tax subsidy if they hold a certain portion of their assets in mortgage-related instruments. This is a strong incentive to supply more mortgage loans. Second, borrowers receive tax deductions for their mortgage interest expenses. This reduces their cost of borrowing, and, consequently, increases their demand for mortgage loans. Tax subsidies to borrowers and lenders encourage a greater flow of funds into the housing industry.

Preferential tax treatment also plays a role in the consumer credit market. Credit unions have long been exempt from income taxes. Thus, they can pay higher rates on their deposits and charge lower rates on their loans. This tax-exempt status increases the flow of funds into credit unions, resulting in a greater supply of consumer loans.

Fairness also entails nondiscriminatory lending practices. Customers should be treated equally when applying for a loan or conducting other financial transactions regardless of their race, sex, or national origin. Thus, practices that restrict lending in certain areas of a city or to certain groups of people are specifically prohibited.

Another example of fairness legislation is the Community Reinvestment Act (CRA). CRA requires lenders to document carefully all loans to ensure that funds are being reinvested in the community from which deposits are gathered. Because the guidelines regarding allocation requirements are ambiguous, compliance costs tend to be high. Loan applications must be carefully screened and a long paper trail must be produced to provide evidence of compliance. Fortunately, the law is being revised to emphasize performance as opposed to procedure.

Fairness is also sought through efforts to preserve competition. Antitrust laws have been used to prohibit monopoly power. Corporate restructuring efforts involving mergers and acquisitions are often scrutinized by the Justice

---

[9] See, for example, Arshadi and Eyssell (1993).

Department to prevent anticompetitive ventures. Similarly, holding company acquisitions are carefully examined by the Fed. Expansion of depository intermediaries through branching is still partially restricted, despite 1994 legislation liberalizing the practice. Realizing an optimal level of competition is difficult because too little competition hurts consumers and too much competition harms safety and soundness.

Information Disclosure

The final regulatory objective is to ensure the disclosure of an adequate amount of information so that investors can make educated decisions in their borrowing and lending. Moreover, information disclosure is crucial in preventing fraud. Without regulation, information disclosure is generally uneven and difficult to compare. While some intermediaries may attempt to develop a reporting system best suited for their shareholders and customers, they are unlikely to succeed in the long run, because a one-time development of an information disclosure system and its subsequent refinement is both costly and inefficient. There will also be a free-rider problem: Since efforts to produce optimal reports are costly, some intermediaries may wait for others to spend their resources to develop such reports, and then simply try to copy them. In a competitive market, such cost shifting will put those who make the effort at a cost disadvantage. Consequently, the development of an optimal reporting system may be deterred simply because no one is willing to spend sufficient resources to accomplish it. A government agency, acting on behalf of all intermediaries, can develop standardized scheme and impose it universally on all participants. This will guarantee that optimal resources are spent on developing the reporting plan, and since it is developed only once for everyone, it would be cost efficient.

Disclosure rules rely exclusively on historical accounting data. Critics of historical accounting disclosure argue that past information is relevant only to the current stock price and has no value in determining future stock prices. Only future events and soft information about management strategies will affect future performance and thus the performance of the investor's portfolio.[10] The proponents of historical cost disclosure (e.g., Easterbrook and Fischel, 1991) have provided three reasons in support of historical accounting. First, historical accounting provides objective and uniform information, facilitating intraindustry comparisons. Without such uniformity in reporting, intermediaries might only disclose unusual developments, making any comparisons difficult. Second, uniform disclosure of historical data makes legal enforcement of disclosure rules more effective. It also reduces litigation costs through class-action suits because everyone is exposed to the same set of information and is affected similarly. Third, standardized disclosure is a federal law. This mitigates incentive problems in state disclosure requirements and fraud rules that might favor residents of one state over another.

Disclosure rules have two basic objectives: first, to inform investors, and, second, to prevent fraud. Call reports filed by depository intermediaries provide detailed financial information to both customers and regulators. The Fed and the FDIC, among others, use the information to determine the overall soundness of the intermediary. Information on interest payments to depositors is used by the

---

[10] Historical cost accounting has contributed to major losses to federal deposit insurance funds. The problem arises when an insolvent bank conceals its bad loans in the balance sheet without posting sufficient loan loss reserves. If the bank writes off its bad loans or takes large loan loss reserves, its capital may decline below the minimum required level, alarming the regulators, who may then close it down.

IRS to monitor the accuracy of tax returns of individuals and businesses. A similar type of regulation requires depository intermediaries to keep track of all currency transactions in excess of $10,000. This regulation was passed to assist law enforcement in monitoring drug trafficking and money laundering.

Disclosure requirements also provide opportunities for trade and academic research into intermediary compliance with regulations. These efforts strengthen regulatory monitoring. Bank examiners, for example, were not alarmed by the pervasiveness of insider borrowing practices until they required disclosure of such information in the Call Reports in December 1983. Although Regulation O, which limited insider borrowing, was in place at the time, a large number of banks had violated the rule without regulators' knowledge. Shortly after the disclosure of this information in the Call Reports, research in this area revealed major abuses, drawing the attention of regulators and legislators. By 1991, Regulation O was refined and its enforcement was strengthened.[11]

There is an extensive list of regulations affecting depository financial intermediaries. They are presented in the Appendix to this chapter with a brief discussion of their purposes.

REGULATORY CONFLICTS

The complex tapestry of regulation often creates internal conflicts.[12] For example, how should regulators simultaneously promote safety, soundness, and competition? Safety and soundness regulation often involves restricting the activities of the regulated. Such restrictions, however, place regulated intermediaries at a competitive disadvantage compared with unregulated intermediaries. In another area of regulation, the Fed promotes growth in the economy and stability in prices. Again, these two objectives are often in conflict. The federal deposit insurance system, which was established to limit deposit risk, has contributed to excessive risk-taking because depositors no longer monitor the intermediary's level of risk. What is safe for individual depositors is not safe for the system as a whole.

Safety and Soundness vs. Competition

The objectives of promoting safety and soundness on the one hand and competition on the other often collide at the implementation stage. A good example of this conflict can be seen in the process of applying for a new bank charter. When a bank applies for a charter, the chartering agency[13] must evaluate, among other things, whether there is enough demand for intermediary services in the market[14] to warrant a new bank entry. However, study of new-bank performance indicates that the performance of a newly chartered bank is determined by internal factors such as efficiency in the cost and pricing of its products.[15] This performance level seems to be unrelated to external factors, including existing banks in the market. These results obviously contradict the long-standing policy of the chartering agencies, which attempt to balance increased competition due to new-bank entry against a perceived reduction in safety for both new and existing banks.

---

[11] See Lawrence, Kummer, and Arshadi (1987); Kummer, Arshadi, and Lawrence (1989); and Federal Register, Vol. 56, No. 153 (August 8, 1991, pp. 37,673–37,686).

[12] See, for example, Peterson (1985).

[13] If the charter is for a national bank, the chartering agency is the OCC; if the charter is for a state bank, the state banking commission is responsible for evaluating the charter proposal.

[14] The market is defined as either the Standard Metropolitan Statistical Area (SMSA) or the non-SMSA county where the new bank is located.

[15] See Arshadi and Lawrence (1987).

Conflicts also arise between safety and soundness and competition in branching policies. For years, interstate branching was prohibited on the grounds that it would reduce competition in local markets. On September 29, 1994, President Clinton signed into law a bill that allows both American and foreign banks to launch takeovers across state borders beginning in September 1995. Beginning in June 1997, banks are permitted to branch across state lines.

States will be allowed to opt out of de novo branches even if they permit interstate branching. The new law will enable bank customers to conduct a full range of transactions anywhere their bank retains a branch, regardless of whether it is in the state in which they work or live.[16] This will help banks to diversify their operations across regions and to use their profits from one region to cover losses in another. The result will be fewer bank failures and less frequent calls on the deposit insurance fund. Critics of the new law argue that it may accelerate bank mergers and acquisitions, reduce competition, and make it harder for local businesses and home owners to get loans at competitive rates. Again, the conflict is between increased safety and its cost in terms of reduced competition.

Competition is also restricted in the name of safety and soundness through balance sheet regulation. Savings and loans, for instance, were not allowed to issue and hold commercial and some types of consumer loans until the early 1980s. With most of their assets in long-term fixed payment mortgages, they could not survive the soaring interest rates of 1979–1982. During this period, about 1,500 S&Ls (one-third of the entire industry) failed, due primarily to lack of diversification and the absence of any risk-hedging strategies. Depository intermediaries are also restricted from holding noninvestment-grade bonds.

Conflict also exists in the area of permissible activities. The most famous example is the Glass-Steagall Act, which separated commercial and investment banking activity. Banks were forced to choose between underwriting and lending activities.

Restrictions on activities also extend to sales of insurance, mutual funds, and other products that are handled by universal banks in other parts of the world. Bank holding companies were established in part because of these restrictions. Bank holding companies have an ownership form that controls one or more depository institutions along with other related companies. The holding company acts as the common owner although each subsidiary is, in theory, financially independent.

One of the commonly explored issues regarding bank holding companies is whether nonbank activities increase or decrease the overall risk of depository intermediaries. Are banks in a holding company sufficiently insulated from losses in the nonbank entities within that holding company? In recent years, an increasingly permissive approach to holding company acquisitions and nonbank activities by holding companies suggests that regulators view these companies more favorably than they did in the past.

Restrictions on bank activities, along with rate ceilings, were traditionally made in the name of safety and soundness. By limiting assets, liabilities, and the cost of funds, regulators hoped to reduce competition and the level of risk in depository intermediaries, thereby enhancing the safety and soundness of the banking system. The cost to customers was a limited choice of products and generally lower yields on savings.

---

[16] For many years ATMs located across states and in various countries have allowed customers to withdraw limited amounts of cash or check on their account balances. However, they could not use ATMs to make deposits or to conduct other banking business.

Monetary Policy Conflicts

The Fed pursues two main objectives in its conduct of monetary policy: an expansionary economy and stable prices. These goals are often difficult to pursue simultaneously. For example, during 1994 the U.S. economy grew 4% while the Fed was more comfortable with a growth rate of only 3%. Accordingly, the Fed increased short-term interest rates several times to slow growth and prevent an increase in the inflation rate.

Another conflict in the pursuit of monetary goals arises from the role of the Fed as the lender of last resort. In this capacity, the Fed stands ready to provide emergency loans to depository intermediaries in the event of liquidity crises. The knowledge of this source of liquidity makes banks less concerned about liquidity risk in their assets. Thus, what was intended as a safety and soundness measure can result in excessive risk-taking by banks, which is a moral hazard problem.

The Fed accomplishes monetary policy primarily by acting on loanable bank reserves. Again, there is a conflict between greater economic growth and the control of credit quality. The problem of poor credit quality was exacerbated during the economic expansion of the 1980s. This led regulators to require that banks establish greater loan loss reserves, which increased the cost of lending to the intermediaries. Default premiums increased and regulatory monitoring costs rose. Consequently, intermediaries became reluctant to lend, stifling growth by the late 1980s.

Deposit Insurance Conflicts

No area of regulation has received more attention in the last two decades than that of federal deposit insurance. This is due in large part to the colossal failure of the savings and loan insurance fund. Paradoxically, the basic conflict in the implementation of deposit insurance concerns safety and soundness even though the purpose of deposit insurance is to promote those qualities. The problem is that deposit insurance is designed for the safety and soundness of the depositor, and not of the deposit insurance system. What is good for one is not necessarily good for all.

Deposit insurance removes any incentive for depositors to monitor the safety of an individual bank, or to scrutinize the investment decisions of the depository intermediary. In the absence of depositor monitoring, there is an advantage to be had in investing in risky assets. If the risk pays off, the intermediary captures the benefits. If it does not, then the insurance fund is responsible for paying off the depositors. The availability of federal deposit insurance has provided opportunities for depository intermediaries to increase their leverage and to expand the overall risk of their assets.

The failure of an increasing number of depository intermediaries further alarmed regulators, who responded by further restricting the choice of assets (e.g., high-risk bonds) and liabilities (e.g., brokered deposits) to prevent additional failures. A risk-based capital ratio has been adopted to incorporate asset risk in determining minimum capital requirement. A risk-based deposit insurance premium system has replaced the fixed premium system of the past, to mitigate the moral hazard of excessive risk-taking.

REGULATORY STRUCTURE

Depository intermediaries are regulated by several state and federal agencies. For example, commercial banks are regulated by the Fed, the FDIC, the OCC (or a state banking commission), and in some cases by the SEC. Table 6.1 presents depository intermediaries and their designated supervisory agencies. For the

TABLE 6.1 Federal and State Regulatory and Insurance Agencies	
Commercial Banks	Federal Reserve System
	Federal Deposit Insurance Corp.
	Comptroller of the Currency
	Bank Insurance Fund
	State Banking Commissions
Thrift Institutions (Includes Mutual Savings Banks and Savings and Loan Associations)	Federal Deposit Insurance Corp.
	Office of Thrift Supervision
	Savings Association Insurance Fund
	Bank Insurance Fund
	Resolution Trust Corporation
	State Banking Commissions
Mutual Funds	Securities and Exchange Commission
Bank Holding Companies	Federal Reserve System
	State Banking Commission
Credit Unions	National Credit Union Administration Board
	National Credit Union Share Insurance Fund
Finance Companies	State Banking Commissions
Life Insurance Companies	State Insurance Commissions
Investment Banks	Securities and Exchange Commission
	Security Investor Protection Corp.
Private Pension Funds	Pension Benefit Guarantee Corp.
	Department of Labor
Options Market	Securities and Exchange Commission
	Commodity Futures Trading Commission
Futures Market	Commodity Futures Trading Commission

purpose of comparison, the table also displays agencies that oversee nondepository financial intermediaries. It is clear that depository intermediaries such as commercial banks and thrift institutions are regulated by a greater number of agencies than are nondepository intermediaries. The operation of organized options and futures markets is also narrowly regulated by the SEC and the Commodity Futures Trading Commission. While regulatory objectives in supervising nondepository intermediaries focus on providing information to investors and preventing fraud, the regulation of depository intermediaries goes far beyond that, by addressing the safety and soundness of the financial system, and the fairness of resource allocations.

Supervisory Agencies for Depository Intermediaries: The OCC, the Fed, the FDIC, and Others

Depository intermediaries face regulatory directives from the chartering agency (the OCC or a state banking commission), the lender of last resort (the Fed), and the deposit insurance provider (the FDIC).

The history of bank regulation in the United States has long been divided be-

TABLE 6.2   Number and Total Assets of Insured Commercial Banks by Charter December 31, 1994 ($ Millions)

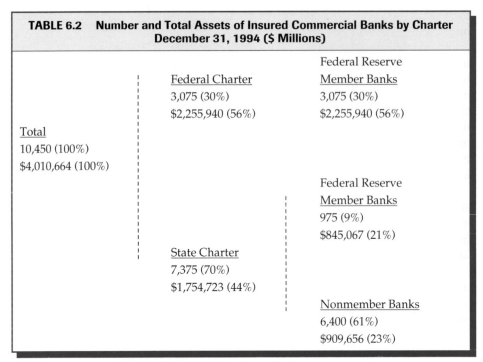

Total
10,450 (100%)
$4,010,664 (100%)

Federal Charter
3,075 (30%)
$2,255,940 (56%)

Federal Reserve
Member Banks
3,075 (30%)
$2,255,940 (56%)

State Charter
7,375 (70%)
$1,754,723 (44%)

Federal Reserve
Member Banks
975 (9%)
$845,067 (21%)

Nonmember Banks
6,400 (61%)
$909,656 (23%)

Source: Federal Deposit Insurance Corporation, *Statistics on Banking,* 1994.

tween state and federal control. Table 6.2 demonstrates that while state-chartered banks outnumber federally chartered banks, the largest banks tend to be nationally chartered. The National Banking Act of 1863 established uniform chartering rules, which set the stage for establishing national banks.

In order to obtain a national charter, the applicant must document

- the general character of the proposed management
- the earnings potential of the bank
- adequate capital
- the need for the bank in the community

The list of requirements suggests that an overriding concern for the chartering agency is the ability of the bank to remain solvent. This is evident from the importance placed on earnings, capital, and community needs. In addition, the chartering agency evaluates the market for a new bank and whether competition from a new-bank entry may jeopardize the financial strength of existing banks.

Applications for national bank charters are filed with the OCC. This agency is part of the Department of the Treasury. In addition to issuing national bank charters, the OCC contributes to balance-sheet regulation and conducts annual examinations of national banks. Nationally chartered banks must be members of the Fed. The membership requires the banks to purchase stock in the Fed and in essence to become shareholders of federal reserve banks. Since, technically, the Fed's ownership is private, the operating expenses of the federal reserve banks are not paid by the federal government.

We pointed out earlier that the primary function of the Fed is to implement monetary policy. The Fed is also involved in regulating the nation's payment system, implementing consumer protection regulations such as truth-in-lending and mortgage disclosure rules, and regulating foreign banking operations in the United States. In conjunction with the regulation of depository intermediaries, the Fed is responsible for the approval of the formation of bank holding companies and any subsequent acquisitions and expansion of their activities.

While Fed membership is mandatory for nationally chartered banks, it is voluntary for state-chartered banks. Most smaller state-chartered banks choose not to join the Fed because of regulatory costs. However, most large state-chartered banks do join the Fed. As Table 6.2 demonstrates, 30% of all banks are nationally chartered while 70% are state chartered. Since national banks tend to be larger, they control about 60% of industry assets even though they make up less than one-third of all banks. All national banks (30% of the total) and some state banks (9% of the total) are members of the Fed. Member banks control about 77% of the total assets of the industry.

Banks that are not chartered by the OCC are chartered by their respective state banking commissions. Like the OCC, the state commissions influence the balance-sheet composition of state banks and, more importantly, exercise auditing powers. While chartering requirements differ from state to state, they all follow OCC standards.

The FDIC is the one regulatory agency with control over both state and nationally chartered banks. The FDIC provides deposit insurance at a premium to all banks. The requirements for obtaining and maintaining FDIC deposit insurance are similar to those for obtaining a national bank charter. As a result, even state banks are regulated in similar fashion to national banks.

The FDIC has broad examining power over banks. As an insurance agency, the FDIC is vitally concerned with its own financial stability and that of the insured banks. Accordingly, the FDIC closely monitors their activities.

In addition to insuring commercial banks, the FDIC is also responsible for insuring deposits in savings and loan associations. The collapse of the FSLIC in the late 1980s led to the merger of the S&L insurance fund with the FDIC. Separate accounting is maintained between the bank (BIF) and the savings association (SAIF) insurance funds, but the FDIC applies the same basic standards to both.

While the FDIC provides deposit insurance to thrifts, the primary regulator of federally chartered savings and loans is the Office of Thrift Supervision (OTS). The OTS is to thrifts what the OCC is to commercial banks. It is the federal chartering agency for thrifts. Like the OCC, the OTS is part of the Department of the Treasury. The OTS was created in 1989 as a part of the legislative package that bailed out the thrift industry. The OTS replaced the former federal thrift regulatory agency, the Federal Home Loan Bank Board (FHLBB). The FHLBB had served in several capacities: Besides being the primary federal regulator of thrifts, the FHLBB also acted as a central bank of sorts for thrifts and as an advocate for the thrift industry. The conflicting roles of the Federal Home Loan Bank Board probably hastened its demise.

The Federal Home Loan Bank system continues to operate today, but not in a regulatory capacity. It acts as a quasi-central bank for thrifts by providing both short- and long-term sources of funds. Even commercial banks can borrow from the Federal Home Loan Bank. The primary focus of this system is to help the housing industry in the United States. It is especially interested in providing housing opportunities for low-income families.

The credit union industry is organized in a manner similar to that of the thrift industry before its reorganization in the 1980s. All federally chartered credit unions are regulated by the National Credit Union Administration (NCUA). As with commercial banks and thrifts, state-chartered credit unions are regulated by state agencies. All are subject to reserve requirements set by the Fed. Deposit insurance is provided to credit unions by the National Credit Union Share Insurance Fund (NCUSIF). This is part of the NCUA; thus, the chartering and insurance functions are not entirely independent. All federally chartered credit unions (about 60% of all credit unions) must obtain deposit insurance, but not all state-chartered credit unions are required to do so. Those who choose to belong to the NCUSIF are subject to the regulations of the NCUA. Approximately 40% of state-chartered credit unions do not belong to the NCUSIF.

THE COST OF REGULATION

So far, we have focused on the regulation, supervision, and taxation of depository intermediaries without explicitly considering the cost of government control. The regulation of depository intermediaries' activities through mandatory reserve requirements, minimum capital requirements, restrictions on entry and merger, and limits on the level of each activity creates a rigid structure within which depository intermediaries are allowed to function. Supervision of depository intermediaries adds further to the rigidity of their operating environment through extensive disclosure requirements, on-site examinations, and the close scrutiny of top management. The tax-exempt status of credit unions and the preferential taxation of mortgage lending also influence the structure of financial intermediation.

Government intervention may be justified at the outset of regulation on the basis of externalities and market imperfections—without intervention, certain products may not be supplied or may be supplied inadequately. However, government regulations tend to be static, unable to adjust to advancing technology and global competition. With advances in telecommunications technology, many restrictions have become obsolete, even though their compliance costs continue to burden the regulated industry. The growth of mutual funds and mortgage banks outside the domain of the regulators placed depository intermediaries at a competitive disadvantage. It was only after a prolonged protest by the industry and significant losses to the deposit insurance fund that regulatory change occurred. Examples of this phenomenon are numerous, including the Depository Institutions and Deregulation and Monetary Control Act of 1980 (DIDMCA), which expanded bank activities to include money market accounts, and the Garn-St. Germain Act of 1982, which expanded the permissible asset activities of thrift institutions. Interstate branching restrictions were finally eased in 1994, but only after bank-holding-company expansions had made them virtually obsolete.

There is also the argument that regulators' self-interest calls for the expansion of their powers, leading to overregulation, which inhibits economic development.[17] Others, however, are not so cynical.[18] Either way, regulation and supervision may not achieve the intended results, or the costs may exceed the benefits.

The cost of regulation can be separated into three areas. First, regulation causes a reallocation of resources with a potential for negative side effects. Second, moral hazard problems may arise when regulatory agencies act as the lender of last resort and the provider of deposit insurance. Third, compliance with disclosure requirements is generally costly.

The reallocation effects can be seen in the restrictions on asset holdings that tend to reduce the competition and price for some assets. For example, restric-

---

[17] See, for example, Shaw (1973) and McKinnon (1973).
[18] See, for example, Kareken (1981, 1984) and Diamond and Dybvig (1983).

tions on holding noninvestment-grade (junk) bonds reduce the demand for them and hence decrease their liquidity in the secondary market. Alternatively, regulation may increase the demand for certain assets (e.g., real estate).

Reallocation may also arise from subjecting different groups of intermediaries to varying levels of regulation. For example, commercial banks are regulated more strictly than are credit unions or finance companies, although many of their functions are comparable. Consequently, similar products may be priced differently. Too, international banks operating in the U.S. are subjected to less restrictive rules than are domestic banks. All else being equal, these differing rules may hinder the ability of one segment of the intermediation industry to compete effectively in certain product lines.

The lender of last resort and deposit insurance functions of the regulatory agencies may create moral hazards in the sense that depository intermediaries may take on excessive risk (from society's point of view) if they feel sufficiently assured that they will be bailed out in case of financial distress. What regulators intended was to reduce the risk and improve the stability of the financial system. What they found, however, was excessive risk-taking by depository intermediaries with a potential for huge losses to the insurance fund.

Compliance costs include expenses incurred in preparing financial reports, personnel expenditures due to on-site examinations, and the expenses of training and supervision. The total industry compliance cost is an estimated $10.7 billion annually.[19] The cost components are as follows:

Salaries and benefits of compliance management staff	15%
Compliance training materials	7%
Compliance employee training	10%
Outside compliance support (e.g., consultants, attorneys)	13%
Indirect compliance costs (e.g., compliance-related hardware/software costs, costs of noncompliance staff time devoted to compliance such as tellers and loan officers, printing costs, postage, telephone expenses, etc.)	55%

A comparison of the compliance costs to the total net income of the industry underscores their magnitude. In 1991, net income for the industry was $18.0 billion, and compliance costs were $10.7 billion. In addition to that $10.7 billion, the cost of forgone interest on Fed reserves and the cost of deposit insurance premiums were $1.6 billion and $5.2 billion, respectively, bringing the total regulatory cost to the industry to $17.5 billion.

As we observed above, indirect compliance cost comprised 55% of the total compliance cost. In this figure, the noncompliance staff time accounts for a major portion of the cost. Tellers and loan officers allocate their compliance time in the following categories of regulation:

Community Reinvestment Act	10%
Truth in Lending	24%
Bank Secrecy Act/CTR	35%
Expedited Funds	15%
Other	16%

---

[19] American Bankers Association, "Survey of Regulatory Burden," June 1992. For a historical review of regulatory burden, see American Bankers Association, *The Burden of Bank Regulation*, 1989.

The results of the ABA survey also suggest the following points: First, compliance costs are not only large, but they are also growing. Second, regulatory costs are similar for banks of all sizes. While economies of scale do exist, large banks face costs roughly proportional to small banks because they are more heavily regulated. Third, bank managers and owners report the most costly regulation is changing regulation. A substantial proportion of compliance costs are incurred in trying to keep up with new regulations.

Regulating the Regulators

If regulators are subject to incentive problems, then who regulates the regulators? Efforts to control excessive disclosure requirements have been made with mixed results. The burden of excessive paperwork was first recognized in 1942 with the Federal Reports Act, which explicitly required information obtained by government agencies be collected with a minimum burden on companies. The act attempted to control reporting requirements by centralizing all requirements affecting ten or more persons under the Bureau of the Budget, the predecessor to the OMB. This was largely unsuccessful because tax-related reports and those deemed necessary in supervising the credit system were exempt from the act. The 1970s witnessed another effort to control the paperwork called for by the federal government. President Carter issued an executive order to reduce paperwork by formulating simplified regulations, adopting less burdensome regulations wherever possible, and periodic review of the outdated requirements.

In 1980, the Paperwork Reduction Act was passed to control the cost of regulatory compliance. This act requires every federal agency to report to the OMB the burden created by necessary paperwork. These costs comprise the "Information Collection Budget," and are targeted for reduction. New forms and revisions of existing forms require approval by the OMB.

The Regulatory Flexibility Act forces federal agencies to reduce the burden of the new rules on small institutions. While depository intermediaries smaller than $100 million in total assets file relatively simple financial information with the regulatory agencies, the difference is not substantial. These intermediaries have continued to demand further reporting reductions from Congress.

SUMMARY

Depository intermediaries are highly regulated because of their crucial role in the economy. Individuals amass most of their wealth in the form of financial assets, which are complex legal contracts that are not easily understood. Consequently, regulations are designed to protect the public from deceptive practices and the risk of ruin. In addition, depository institutions as providers of transactions services are subject to greater regulation because of their important role in the payments system.

Various theories of regulation contribute to our understanding of the regulatory structure. Many of the directives are issued in the name of public interest and consumer protection. Regulation serves diverse interests in the economy. The demand for regulation by various interest groups leads to a reallocation of resources. Regulators' self-interest is also served by expanding the scope of regulation.

As regulations become effective in restricting activities, incentives develop to circumvent them by designing new contracts and new products. Regulators then try to design new restrictions to cover the new circumstances. Those regulated may try again for some other way to avoid the new restrictions and the regulator may follow up with another round of rules. Each party attempts to stay one step ahead of the other. This is in the nature of regulation.

There are four goals in regulation: (1) safety and soundness of the financial system; (2) consumer and investor protection; (3) fairness; and (4) information disclosure. These objectives have led to a maze of regulations (see the Appendix) from asset restrictions to the reporting of interest income to the IRS. While largely successful in the sense of providing a stable monetary system and a growing economy, regulations are also costly. Estimates of compliance costs in the banking industry alone are in the billions of dollars.

REVIEW QUESTIONS

1. Describe briefly four theories of regulation.
2. Explain the differences among the public interest, the many interest, and the special interest theories. Provide examples for each.
3. According to the public choice theory, regulators seek power and attempt to maintain their control over intermediaries. Provide an example.
4. Explain the process of regulation-circumvention-reregulation.
5. What are the four objectives of regulation?
6. Provide examples of safety and soundness, consumer and investor protection, fairness, and information disclosure objectives.
7. Discuss the provisions of the Truth in Lending Act and the Community Reinvestment Act.
8. Describe examples of these regulatory conflicts
   safety and soundness vs. competition
   price stability vs. economic growth depositor
   safety vs. deposit insurance fund soundness.
9. Examine the moral hazard problem created by the lender of last resort and deposit insurance functions of the Fed and the FDIC.
10. Briefly describe the functions of the following regulatory agencies: the OCC, the Fed, the FDIC, the OTS, the RTC, NCUA, and NCUSIF.
11. What are the costs of regulation?
12. How does one regulate the regulator?

REFERENCES

American Bankers Association. 1989. *The Burden of Bank Regulation*. Washington, DC.

American Bankers Association. 1992. "Survey of Regulatory Burden" (June).

Arshadi, N., and E. C. Lawrence. 1987. "An Empirical Investigation of New Bank Performance." *Journal of Banking and Finance*, vol. 11: 33–48.

Arshadi, N., and T. H. Eyssell. 1993. *The Law and Finance of Corporate Insider Trading: Theory and Evidence*. Boston: Kluwer Academic Publishers.

Diamond, D., and P. Dybvig. "Bank Runs, Deposit Insurance, and Liquidity." *Journal of Political Economy*, vol. 91: 401–419.

Easterbrook, F. H., and D. Fischel. 1991. *The Economic Structure of Corporate Law*. Cambridge, MA: Harvard University Press.

Hester, D. D. 1981. "Innovations and Monetary Control." *Brookings Papers on Economic Activity*, vol. 1: 141–189.

Kane, E. J. 1981. "Accelerating Inflation, Technological Innovation and the Decreasing Effectiveness of Banking Regulation." *Journal of Finance*, vol. 36 (May): 355–367.

Kareken, J. H. 1981. "Deregulating Commercial Banks: The Watchword Should Be Caution." *Federal Reserve Bank of Minneapolis Quarterly Review*, vol. 5 (Spring-Summer): 1–5.

Kareken, J. H. 1984. "Bank Regulation and the Effectiveness of Open Market Operations." *Brookings Papers on Economic Activity*, vol. 2: 405–444.

Kummer, D. R., N. Arshadi, and E. C. Lawrence. 1989. "Incentive Problems in Bank Insider Borrowing." *Journal of Financial Services Research*, vol. 3: 17–31.

Lawrence, E., D. Kummer, and N. Arshadi. 1987. "Insider Borrowing Practices of Commercial Banks." *Issues in Bank Regulation*: 28–32.

McKinnon, R. I. 1973. *Money and Capital in Economic Development*. Washington, DC: Brookings Institute.

Metzler, A. H. 1974. "Credit Availability and Economic Decisions: Some Evidence from the Mortgage and Housing Markets." *Journal of Finance*, vol. 14, no. 3 (June): 763–777.

Peterson, M. O. 1985. "Regulatory Objectives and Conflicts" in *Handbook for Banking Strategies*, edited by Aspinwall and Eisenbeis. New York: John Wiley and Sons: 317–346.

Shaw, E. S. 1973. *Financial Deepening in Economic Development*. New York: Oxford University Press.

Spong, K. 1992. "History of Banking Regulation" in *Bank Management and Regulation*, edited by Anthony Saunders, Gregory F. Udell, and Lawrence J. White. Mountain View, CA: Mayfield Publishing Company.

Spong, K. 1992. "Why Regulate Banks" in *Bank Management and Regulation*, edited by Anthony Saunders, Gregory F. Udell, and Lawrence J. White. Mountain View, CA: Mayfield Publishing Company.

APPENDIX

INTRODUCTION

Following are all of the important regulations pertaining to depository intermediaries discussed in this chapter. Consistent with the structure of our discussion in the text, we have categorized these regulations into four groups: safety and soundness, consumer and investor protection, fairness, and information disclosure. If an act has a narrow focus, we place it in one of the four groups. However, if an act has a broad focus, we catalog individual provisions of the act separately. We begin with a content list and then discuss each regulation briefly.

THE LIST OF REGULATIONS PERTAINING TO DEPOSITORY INTERMEDIARIES

Safety and Soundness

National Currency and Bank Acts of 1863–1864
Federal Reserve Act of 1913
Reserve Requirements (Regulation D; A Part of the Federal Reserve Act, 1913)
Banking Act of 1933 (also known as Glass-Steagall Act)
Transactions with Affiliates: Sections 23A and 23B Restrictions (A Part of the 1933 Act)
Credit Issued by Banks for Purchasing / Carrying Margin Stock (A Part of the SEA of 1934)
Bank Holding Company Act of 1956
Restrictions on Insider Loans (Regulation O, 1978)
Depository Institutions Management Interlocks Act of 1978
Change in Bank Control Act of 1978
Depository Institutions Deregulation and Monetary Control Act of 1980 (DIDMCA)
Garn-St. Germain Depository Institutions Act of 1982
Capital Adequacy Requirements (standardized in 1983 and revised in 1992)
Competitive Equality in Banking Act of 1987
Financial Institutions Reform, Recovery, and Enforcement Act of 1989
The Federal Deposit Insurance Corporation Improvement Act of 1991 (FDICIA)
The Riegle-Neal Interstate Banking and Branching Efficiency Act of 1994

Consumer and Investor Protection

Interest on Deposits (A Part of the Banking Act of 1933)
Truth in Lending: (Regulation Z, 1969)
Truth in Lending: Fair Credit and Charge Card Disclosure Act of 1988
Truth in Lending: Home Equity Lines of Credit Disclosure of 1989
Truth in Saving: 1991
Consumer Leasing (Regulation M, 1969)
Electronic Funds Transfer Act (Regulation E, 1980)
The Expedited Funds Availability Act (Regulation CC, 1988)
The Truth in Savings Act of 1991 (a part of FDICIA)

Fairness

Fair Housing Act of 1968
Fair Credit Reporting Act of 1971
Equal Credit Opportunity Act (Regulation B, 1975)
Community Reinvestment Act of 1977
Community-Development Banking Act of 1994

Information Disclosure

Call Reports (Reports of Condition and Income, In Conjunction with Deposit Insurance, 1933)
Interest Information Reporting, 1962
Bank Secrecy Act of 1970: Currency Recordkeeping and Reporting Act
Individual Retirement Account (IRA) Reporting (A part of the Employee Retirement Income Security Act of 1974 or ERISA)
International Investment Survey (A Part of the International Banking Act of 1978)
Broker and Real Estate Transaction Reporting, 1982
Mortgage Interest Reporting, 1984
IRS Levies on Customer Accounts
ESCHEAT

DESCRIPTION OF REGULATIONS PERTAINING TO DEPOSITORY INTERMEDIARIES

SAFETY AND SOUNDNESS

National Currency and Bank Acts of 1863–1864   These acts were the first major federal banking laws in the United States. They created the Comptroller of the Currency, which charters, examines, and approves applications of new branch offices, mergers, and bank holding companies involving national banks.

Federal Reserve Act of 1913   This act established the Federal Reserve System. It was initially established to provide liquidity to the banking system, functioning as a lender of last resort, and to provide a nationwide system for check clearing. The system of twelve Federal Reserve Banks helps control the supply of money and credit, as well as supervising state-chartered member banks and bank holding companies.

Reserve Requirements (Regulation D, Part of the Federal Reserve Act of 1913)
Reserve requirements, initiated in 1913, applied only to member banks. The Garn-St. Germain Depository Institutions Act of 1982 made reserve requirements applicable to all depository institutions, including foreign branches in the United States. Historically reserves were required to maintain liquidity. Their purpose today, however, is to enable the Federal Reserve Bank to manage monetary policy. A varying percentage of deposits, depending on the deposit type, must be deposited with the central bank. No interest is paid on reserves. Reports of deposits are required, as of every second Monday and/or quarterly, depending on the size of the institution. These forms include the series FR 2910, 2910a, and 2910q.

The Banking Act of 1933 (The Glass-Steagall Act)   This act legally separated commercial and investment banking. It prohibited banks from engaging in investment banking on most private-issue securities, particularly underwriting new issues of corporate bonds and stocks. It also established the FDIC. The act was intended to prevent excessive risk-taking, bank failures, and conflict-of-interest. In addition, the act allowed national banks to branch statewide, if the state in which they resided granted similar powers to its own state-chartered banks. Interstate branching was finally allowed in 1994.

Transactions with Affiliates: Sections 23A and 23B Restrictions (Part of the 1933 Act) Sections 23A and 23B are restrictions on transactions with bank affiliates and currently apply to all federally insured banks and thrifts. Section 23A, passed as part of the Banking Act of 1933 for member banks, became applicable to all FDIC-insured banks in 1966 and to all S&Ls through the FIRREA in 1989. These restrictions have been eased in some areas and strengthened in others by the Banking Affiliates Act of 1982 (a portion of the Garn-St. Germain Depository Institutions Act of 1982). This act prohibits a bank from extending credit to an affiliate greater than 10% of capital and surplus and limits a bank's total loans to all affiliates to 20% of capital and surplus. Section 23B was enacted in 1987 and applied to all S&Ls by FIRREA in 1989. It requires all loans and other transactions (sales, leases, fee services, etc.) with affiliates to be on equivalent terms and conditions as with the public.

Credit Issued by Banks for Purchasing/Carrying Margin Stock (Part of the SEA of 1934) Regulation U originated in the Securities Exchange Act of 1934 and became effective in 1936. It prohibits banks from extending credit, secured directly or indirectly by margin stock, that exceeds the maximum loan value of the collateral securing the credit. If the bank lends more than $100,000, the bank must submit form FR U-1.

The Bank Holding Company Act of 1956 Under the 1956 act as amended in 1970, the Fed is the principal regulatory authority overseeing the creation and subsequent expansion of bank holding company activities. Bank holding companies are defined as entities that own or control one or more banks. An ownership of 25% or more is deemed to be sufficient for control, even though an even lower percentage may be considered controlling ownership if the Fed concludes that the bank has controlling influence. Less than 5% ownership is considered noncontrolling. Bank holding companies have to seek the approval of the Fed not only for their initial creation but also for their subsequent efforts to acquire a bank as a subsidiary, to acquire more than 5% of the stock in a bank, to acquire assets of another bank, or to merge with another bank holding company. The expansion of bank holding companies is attributed to restrictions on branching. Bank holding companies must register when they acquire control of a bank and subsequently must file both annual and quarterly reports on activities and financial conditions.

Restrictions on Insider Loans (Regulation O, 1978) Regulation O, initiated by the Financial Institutions Regulatory and Interest Rate Control Act of 1978, was extended to thrifts by FIRREA in 1989. It prohibits banks and thrifts from extending credit to executive officers, directors, and principal shareholders, except as specified. Credit must be extended on the same terms and with the same risks as persons not covered by the regulation. Advance approval by the board of any loan exceeding $25,000 or 5% of capital and surplus is required. Despite the restrictive nature of the 1978 Act, there were significant abuses in insider loans. The extent of the problem became apparent after the FDIC required the disclosure of insider loans in the Call Reports for the first time in December 1983. The Federal Deposit Insurance Corporation Improvement Act of 1991 further refined the restrictions of regulation O. Extensive documentation is required to ensure compliance. Every bank has to report the number, the total dollar amount, and the range of interest charged on insider loans. The information on insider loans is contained in Schedule RC-M of the Call Reports.

Depository Institution Management Interlocks Act of 1978 (Regulation L)
This regulation prohibits the management official of a depository institution or depository holding company from serving as a management official for another depository institution or depository holding company if the organizations are not affiliated and are very large or are located in the same local area. The 1978 act was amended in 1988 to provide exemptions for diversified S&L holding companies and in failing institutions and again in 1989 by FIRREA to provide exceptions for certain qualified stock issuances. The act applies to certain commercial banks, savings and loans, and credit unions. The regulation further establishes prohibitions relating to metropolitan statistical areas and assets of the institutions involved. There are several instances in which the statute permits interlocking relationships and exceptions are also permitted by order of the regulatory agency involved.

Change in Bank Control Act   Beginning in 1978, acquisitions by any person or corporation of more than 25% of the voting power of any depository institution must be approved by the applicable regulators. Individual acquisitions of 10% or more, if no other party owns a larger percentage, also require agency approval. This policy is applicable to the acquisition of any FDIC-insured depository institution and includes bank holding companies. In 1989 FIRREA extended these requirements to thrift institutions. An application for change of control, business history, and identity information must be filed with the primary regulator.

Depository Institutions Deregulation and Monetary Control Act of 1980   The DIDMCA (1980) was the first major legislation deregulating some elements of bank activities. It authorized NOW accounts, phased out legally mandated federal interest-rate ceilings on deposits (Regulation Q), and increased FDIC insurance coverage to $100,000. It attempted to resolve the problem of eroding Fed membership by imposing reserve requirements on all depository institutions. This act and the subsequent act in 1982 were partially in response to competitive pressures from the money market mutual fund industry. Disintermediation, or the loss of deposits in depository intermediaries, was rampant in the 1970s due to federal Regulation Q. High inflation and the availability of high interest rates in nondepository institutions such as money market mutual funds combined to threaten the source of funds for all regulated depository institutions.

The Garn-St. Germain Depository Institutions Act of 1982   In response to the 1980–1982 nationwide crisis in the savings and loan industry resulting from disintermediation (reduced deposits), this act authorized depository institutions to offer a deposit account fully competitive with those offered by the money market mutual fund industry. Subsequently, money market deposit accounts were offered. The remaining interest-rate restrictions on specific accounts were eliminated and savings institutions were allowed to offer commercial loans subject to a limit on loans to a single borrower of 10% of total assets. Consumer loans were allowed with a limit of 30% of total assets. Savings and loan holding companies were allowed to acquire insurance underwriting, while such powers remained unavailable to bank holding companies. This act also took a step toward relaxing branching restrictions. Interstate restrictions that were otherwise illegal under the Bank Holding Company Act were now permitted with the following priorities in merger partners: first, between depository institutions of the same type and within the same state; second, between depository institutions of the same type in different states; third, between depository institutions of different types in the same state; and fourth, between depository institutions of different types in different states. As deteriorations in the savings and loan industry continued, mergers of all sorts occurred after 1982, including those between banks on the one coast and S&Ls on the other.

Capital Adequacy Requirements   Capital adequacy regulations establish minimum levels of bank capital that serve as a source of strength for the institution and provide a buffer between the institution and the insurance fund. Uniform standards among the three bank regulatory agencies (OCC, FDIC, and Federal Reserve) have been in effect since 1985. In 1987, the three agencies proposed risk-based capital adequacy requirements. Assets, including off-balance-sheet items, are grouped into one of four risk categories and each risk category is assigned a weight of 0%, 20%, 50% or 100%, with higher risks receiving higher weights. The sum of these products results in risk-adjusted assets. Total capital is defined as the sum of Tier 1 capital and Tier 2 capital. Tier 1 capital, which includes common equity and perpetual preferred stock, must account for at least 4% of risk-adjusted assets. Tier 2 capital includes other types of preferred stock, subordinated debt, loan loss reserves up to 1.2% of risk-adjusted assets, and mandatory convertible debt. As of December 31, 1992, the sum of Tier 1 and Tier 2 capital must equal at least 8% of total risk-adjusted assets.

Competitive Equality in Banking Act of 1987   In response to the increasing number of bank failures during the 1980s, Congress passed a law authorizing emergency interstate bank acquisitions and allowing the FDIC to take over and operate failing banks. This act also commissioned the recapitalization of the FSLIC. Additionally, the FDIC received the right to establish bridge banks, which are new national banks created to take over the assets and liabilities of failed banks, and which are run by the FDIC for a limited period of time.

Financial Institutions Reform, Recovery, and Enforcement Act of 1989
FIRREA was formed primarily in response to the large number of failed savings and loans. It reformed the regulatory structure of S&Ls, replacing the Federal Home Loan Bank Board with the Office of Thrift Supervision; restructured the FDIC, dividing the insurance fund into a Bank Insurance Fund and a Savings Insurance Fund; and established the Resolution Trust Corporation, which is responsible for disposing of the assets of failed S&Ls. In addition, the law restricted certain S&L activities including investments in junk bonds, the amount of investment in equity, the size of loans made to a single borrower, and the use of brokered deposits for institutions with insufficient capital. The law also attempted to return the S&Ls to housing-related investments by subjecting their access to advances from FHLBs to the condition that they hold more than 70% of their asset portfolios in housing-related investments. Finally, the act authorized regulators to move swiftly to close a failing institution and recover losses from other institutions owned by the parent of the failing S&L.

The Federal Deposit Insurance Corporation Improvement Act (FDICIA) of 1991   The law increases the authority of the FDIC in examining depository institutions and requires more frequent examinations. All depository institutions, with the exception of small, well-capitalized institutions with no prior problems, are subjected to on-site examinations every twelve months. In addition, the law requires the inclusion of interest-rate risk and credit concentration exposure in computing risk-based capital ratios. FDICIA and FIRREA effectively reversed the regulatory liberalization trend initiated by the Garn-St. Germain Depository Institutions Act of 1982.

The Riegle-Neal Interstate Banking and Branching Efficiency Act of 1994
This act promises to be one of the most influential of legislative banking reforms. It allows American and foreign banks to launch cross-border takeovers and to merge their operations into seamless national networks. While in the past two decades all states except Hawaii allowed out-of-state banks to do business within their borders, they often required separate subsidiaries within each state. The act makes interstate branching less costly by brushing aside subsidiary requirements.

CONSUMER AND INVESTOR PROTECTION LAWS

Interest on Deposits   Various restrictions on interest on deposits date back to the 1930s. The actions of the Depository Institutions Deregulation Committee during 1980–1986 resulted in significant amendments to this regulation. The new regulations relate to restrictions on the advertisement of interest on deposits. Formerly this regulation restricted the interest rate payable on savings instruments issued by banks and thrifts. Current requirements include a statement of the annual rate of simple interest, notice of penalty for early withdrawal, restrictions on percentage yields due to compounding interest, a written notice of all automatically renewable time deposits, and accuracy in advertising.

Truth in Lending: Regulation Z, 1969   Regulation Z became effective June 1, 1969. Due to its complexity, it was simplified by Congress in 1980, resulting in the Truth in Lending Simplification and Reform Act. This regulation has subsequently been updated annually. It applies to banks, savings institutions, credit unions, finance companies, and federal land banks. It provides consumers with information on the terms and costs of consumer credit, gives consumers the right to cancel certain credit transactions secured by a principal dwelling, regulates specific credit card transactions, and provides for the resolution of credit-billing disputes. Specific disclosure requirements are mandated for both closed-end and open-end credit. Generally, disclosures are required before consummation of the transaction. Among other items, they include amount financed, itemization of amount financed, finance charge, APR, payment schedule, prepayment rebate or penalty, late payment fees, security interest, insurance, default, and the right to accelerate the maturity of the obligation. In the case where a security interest is retained in the consumer's principal dwelling, two right of rescission notices must be provided to the consumer. These must disclose the retention or acquisition of a security interest, the consumer's right to rescind the transaction, the method used to rescind, the effects of rescission, and the date the rescission period expires.

Truth in Lending: Fair Credit and Charge Card Disclosure Act of 1988   This regulation applies to banks and other institutions that issue credit and charge cards. The legislation was passed in 1988 and became effective August 31, 1989. It requires additional disclosures on or with credit card applications. Regulation Z was amended to implement this act on April 6, 1989. Credit card applications must include annual percentage rate, annual fee or periodic fee, minimum fixed charge, transaction fees, length of grace period, name of balance computation method, over-the-limit fees, cash advance fees, and late payment fees.

Truth in Lending: Home Equity Lines of Credit Disclosure Act of 1989   This legislation, effective November 7, 1989, applies to banks, savings institutions, finance companies, and credit unions regarding all open-end consumer credit plans secured by a consumer's principal dwelling. Its purpose is to educate consumers on the nature of home equity products. Home equity loans are also subject to the requirements of Regulation Z. Specific disclosure requirements must be met at both the time the application is provided and the time of closing. Information required includes how minimum payments are determined and the timing of these payments; limits on the number of extensions or total amount of credit; the length of time a consumer can submit an application and receive the stated terms; how the APR is determined, the frequency of changes in the APR and the maximum APR; conditions that allow the creditor to take certain actions, such as termination of the plan; the length of the draw period and any repayment period; and a statement that the creditor will receive a security interest in the consumer's dwelling and that loss of the dwelling may occur in the event of default.

Consumer Leasing (Regulation M, 1969)   The regulation of consumer leasing was first implemented in 1969 by Regulation Z, and was reissued as Regulation M in 1981. Its purpose is to ensure that those leasing personal property are provided with disclosures regarding lease terms. Businesses covered are banks, savings institutions, credit unions, federal land banks, and all other lessors. Disclosures required prior to consummation of the lease agreement are description of leased property; total amount of any payment; number, amount, and due dates of payments; total amount to be paid; identification of insurance, warranties, guarantees, and maintenance responsibilities; description of any security interest held by the lessor; amount of or method of determining any penalties; and statements of conditions to terminate the lease prior to the end of its term.

Electronic Funds Transfer Act (Regulation E, 1980)   Regulation E is applicable to all financial institutions or persons that directly or indirectly offer electronic funds transfer services. It establishes the rights, liabilities, and responsibilities of those participating in EFT systems. The regulations are updated on an annual basis. This regulation requires both initial disclosures at the time a consumer contracts for an EFT device or prior to the first transaction, and periodic statements and terminal receipts. Required information includes details regarding the participant's liability for unauthorized transactions; information on error resolution; monthly or quarterly periodic statements, including the amount, type, date, and location of transfer; terminal receipts provided at the time of the transaction; and a notice of any change in terms.

The Expedited Funds Availability Act (Regulation CC, 1988)   This regulation applies to all banks, savings institutions, and credit unions. Regulation CC requires banks to make funds from deposited checks available in a timely manner and to expedite the return of checks. This legislation requires covered institutions to disclose their funds' availability policies through initial disclosures to new customers, posted policies at offices, and notices on deposit slips and ATMs. An immediate notice of availability date is required when checks are held beyond the posted schedule.

The Truth in Savings Act of 1991   This act went into effect in June 1993. The objective of TIS is to improve the ability of customers to make informed deposit decisions. TIS requires uniform disclosure of the terms and conditions of deposit interests paid and fees charged. TIS also seeks to promote competition among depository intermediaries through pricing of their deposits. The act applies to all banks and thrifts regardless of their insurance status. While credit unions are not explicitly named in the act, the National Credit Union Administration (NCUA) is required to adopt similar rules.

FAIRNESS

The Fair Housing Act of 1968 This legislation is applicable to all housing lenders. It prohibits discrimination on the basis of race, color, religion, national origin, marital status, or sex in extending credit for the purpose of purchasing, constructing, improving, repairing, or maintaining a dwelling. In 1988, the FDIC amended the definition of home loan to eliminate home improvements, repair and maintenance loans, and home equity loans from coverage.

The Fair Credit Reporting Act of 1971 This legislation requires consumer reporting agencies to provide accurate information to banks and other users of information in a fair and equitable manner. Those who use reported information are required to disclose that fact. Any bank, credit union, savings and loan institution, or user of credit information collected by an external source is covered by this regulation. If a consumer has been denied credit, insurance, or employment based on a consumer reporting agency's information, the financial institution must report the name and address of that agency.

Equal Credit Opportunity Act (Regulation B, 1975) Regulation B was enacted to prevent discrimination in the availability of credit to consumer or commercial borrowers. It requires creditors to notify applicants of action taken and reasons for any adverse action. The legislation applies to all persons who are creditors, including banks, savings institutions, credit unions, federal land banks, and investment and finance companies. Regulation B requires banks to notify the applicants, within 30 days of application, of the action taken on their request. It requires banks to collect information regarding the applicant's race, sex, marital status, and age when the credit is for the purchase or refinancing of the applicant's principal residence, and requires that the applicant be informed that this information is for government monitoring purposes. Written notice must be provided to business credit applicants explaining their right to receive a written statement regarding the denial of credit. Creditors must keep records of business credit applications for at least one year.

Community Reinvestment Act (CRA) of 1977 The CRA applies to all federally insured depository institutions. It requires that institutions be able to demonstrate that they serve their communities' credit needs, particularly with regard to housing in low- and moderate-income neighborhoods. Each Board of Directors must adopt a CRA policy identifying its communities' credit needs and adjust loan programs to serve those needs. All banking and thrift federal regulatory agencies must evaluate their banks for CRA compliance and factor it into any relocation, branching, merger, or insurance coverage applications.

Community-Development Banking Act of 1994 This legislation provides subsidies to a fledgling network of lenders in low-income areas.

INFORMATION DISCLOSURE

Call Reports The requirement to disclose call reports was established in conjunction with the establishment of the FDIC in 1933. Call reports provide balance-sheet and income-statement information as well as off-balance-sheet data. The intent of these requirements is to provide the public and shareholders with information regarding financial status, safety, and soundness.

Interest Information Reporting Act of 1962   This legislation applies to all payers of interest. It requires institutions to report the payment of interest of $10 or more to any person during a calendar year.

Bank Secrecy Act of 1970: Currency Recordkeeping and Reporting Act   This regulation, as amended in 1982, 1986, and 1988, applies to commercial banks, savings and loans, credit unions, casinos, the Postal Service, broker-dealers, currency dealers, and exchanges and telegraph companies. It requires that financial institutions report monetary transactions that may concern tax evasion, money laundering, or other criminal activity.

International Investment Survey   The intent of this act is to provide comprehensive data regarding foreign investment in the United States and U.S. investment abroad. It requires that banks and brokers provide information on capital flows for the purpose of analyzing the balance of payments and international investment position of the United States.

Broker and Real Estate Transaction Reporting   Enacted in 1982, this legislation requires the gross proceeds from the sale of securities to be reported. In the case of real estate, a seller must report any gain or loss resulting from the sale of real estate on his tax return. The legislation is applicable to middlemen, including banks, in all transfers and redemptions of securities and real estate. Brokers are required to make an information return on the gross proceeds from each sale of securities, commodities, tax-exempt obligations, and regulated futures and forward contracts. Banks that redeem or return stock or securities for their customers, or which regularly issue or retire their own notes, are required to file. Real estate brokers must report the sale or exchange of one- to four-unit residential real estate.

Mortgage Interest Reporting   The purpose of this legislation is to assist the IRS in verifying claimed mortgage interest deductions. It was enacted in 1984 and applies to all mortgage lenders that receive $600 or more of interest on real estate secured loans. Banks must report the receipt of $600 or more of mortgage interest received from an individual, including banks servicing loans originated by other institutions and collection agents. All obligations secured by real property must be reported, even if the loan can be classified as something other than real estate. Interest received after 1987 on any mortgage in the form of a line of credit or credit card obligation must be reported.

Individual Retirement Account (IRA) Reporting   This legislation was enacted to assist the IRS in verifying the accuracy of claimed IRA contributions and distributions. IRA reporting applies to trustees of all IRA accounts, of which a majority are at banks. Banks must report the fair market value of an IRA on an annual basis. Banks that make distributions from IRAs and other retirement products must withhold federal income tax on the distribution unless the customer elects not to have withholding apply. Banks must report the amount of contributions and rollover contributions to the IRA annually. Prior to the first distribution, the bank must provide the customer with an election form and instructions and must provide annual reminder notices of the right to make an election.

IRS Levies on Customer Accounts   This act was intended to assist the IRS in investigating persons who may be liable to pay internal revenue tax. It applies to third parties, including financial institutions, that hold property or rights to property or discharge obligations. The IRS has the authority to ask the taxpayer's bank to surrender a portion of the taxpayer-customer's property, if an assessed tax is not paid within 10 days of assessment. The bank is obligated to "freeze" the property up to the amount assessed for 21 days, upon receipt of the Levy Notice. The bank must pay interest on the funds during the 21-day hold if interest is normally paid. The IRS may request the bank to exhibit the records concerning the customer's property immediately prior to or after a levy has been effected.

ESCHEAT   This regulation requires that all "abandoned" property be turned over to the government within a specific time. It includes lost or forgotten bank accounts, cashier's checks, and other credits. It applies to all depository institutions.

C H A P T E R

7

The Deposit Insurance System

OBJECTIVES

This chapter presents a detailed discussion of the deposit insurance system. We provide a brief history of deposit insurance in the United States and examine the circumstances that led to the establishment of the federal deposit insurance system in 1933. We discuss the savings and loan crisis of the 1980s, leading to a critical analysis of the moral hazard problem in the federal deposit insurance system. We examine regulatory reforms designed to address these problems, including the risk-based premium system and risk-based capital requirements. The chapter concludes with an exploration of alternative solutions and the outlook for depository intermediaries and their insurance fund.

AN OVERVIEW OF DEPOSIT INSURANCE PROBLEMS

Established in 1933, the federal deposit insurance system has been credited with increasing the stability of the financial system, reducing bank failures, and eliminating bank panics. However, the view has not always been so positive. The failure of almost half of all savings and loan associations in the 1980s led to the demise of their insurer, the Federal Savings and Loan Insurance Corporation. Increases in bank failures during that period significantly diminished the bank insurance fund. However, reforms adopted in the late 1980s seem to have reversed this course; as of the mid-1990s, the financial position of depository intermediaries and their deposit insurance fund is significantly improved.

No topic in the analysis of financial institutions has generated as much controversy as the proper role of government-sponsored deposit insurance. The discussion ranges from attempts to determine the correct level of supervision of the financial services industry to questions of whether we should even have deposit insurance.

In its current form deposit insurance insures depositors for up to $100,000 in the event of a bank failure. The amount of coverage has been increased several times since the inception of deposit insurance; in addition, it has always been possible to increase coverage through the use of joint or multiple accounts. Historically, banks were required to pay a fixed insurance premium, which depended only on the amount of qualifying deposits. The system worked well until the 1980s, when the savings and loan crisis and the insolvency of the FSLIC forced regulators to rethink the role of deposit insurance.

The problem with the historical, fixed-rate deposit insurance system was the issue of moral hazard. The theoretical basis for this problem is as follows. Deposit insurance allows banks to borrow funds (obtain deposits) at virtually risk-free rates, with no monitoring from depositors. The managers of depository institutions recognize this lack of monitoring, and the fact that payoffs from risky investments are shared unequally. Projects that succeed directly benefit owners and managers, while projects that fail will ultimately be covered by the deposit insurance agency. Therefore, projects that would have been rejected as too risky by debt holders exposed to actual losses are accepted in the presence of deposit insurance. Thus, the moral hazard problem leads to excessive risk-taking by management.

The incentives that favor excessive risk-taking are threefold. First, deposit insurance increases bank financial risk by lowering the relative cost of debt financing. Insuring deposits removes the threat of bankruptcy to investors and allows debt to be raised cheaply. As a result, depository institutions tend to substitute deposit insurance protection for equity capital. With relatively low equity capital participation by owners, the likelihood of bank failure increases because there is a very small buffer to cover unanticipated losses. Second, deposit insurance also creates an incentive for financially distressed intermediaries to increase overall asset risk. Banks that are in financial distress have an incentive to take on high-payoff investments even if the probability of success is low. Insured depositors will not monitor how funds are invested, making it easy for the bank to engage in high-payoff, low-probability investments. Third, healthy depository institutions also have an incentive to increase the overall level of risk in their assets because of deposit insurance. The moral hazard suggests that shareholder value can be increased through increasingly risky investments because of the asymmetry in the payoffs on investment projects. Owners will get to keep the rewards but the deposit insurance fund will absorb the losses.

Given the inherent moral hazard problem, one may question why we choose to offer government-sponsored deposit insurance. The answer is partly economic and partly political. From an economic perspective, it is widely accepted that some form of deposit protection is needed to insure the soundness of the financial system. Other alternatives to deposit insurance exist but have not been shown to be superior to government-sponsored insurance; these will be discussed later in the chapter. As a political matter, it is difficult to change the existing system because the industry is now accustomed to operating with deposit insurance. Any drastic change in deposit insurance would likely be opposed by both depository intermediaries and their customers.

THE HISTORY OF DEPOSIT INSURANCE

Bank Runs and Bank Panics

The importance of deposit insurance stems from its ability to help control the safety and soundness of the financial system. Safety and soundness have always been major concerns of state and federal governments. From a banking perspective, this implies that the control of both the amount and the value of money has precedence over other economic issues.

The money supply has two major components: currency and demand deposits. The ability to redeem bank deposits into currency (or some expensive mineral such as gold) presents a potentially serious liquidity problem. If a large number of depositors at a single bank attempt to redeem their deposits for cur-

TABLE 7.1	Bank Panics in the United States	
NBER Business Cycle Dates[a]	Panic Date	Severity of Economic Downturn[b]
October 1873–March 1879	September 1873	Severe
March 1882–May 1885	June 1884	Severe
March 1887–April 1888	No Panic	Mild
July 1890–May 1891	November 1890	Severe
January 1893–June 1894	May 1893	Severe
December 1895–June 1897	October 1896	Mild
June 1899–December 1900	No Panic	Mild
September 1902–August 1904	No Panic	Mild
May 1907–June 1908	October 1907	Severe
January 1910–January 1912	No Panic	Severe
January 1913–December 1914	August 1914	Severe
August 1918–March 1919	No Panic	Severe
January 1920–July 1921	No Panic	Severe
May 1923–July 1924	No Panic	Mild
October 1926–November 1927	No Panic	Mild
August 1929–March 1933	October 1930 March 1931 January 1933	Severe

[a] Measured from peak to trough of the business cycle
[b] Mild downturn defined as a reduction in economic output (proxied by pig iron production of less than 10% increase severe greater than 10%). This measure is used through 1914. After 1914, a severe downturn was negative GNP growth.

Source: Gorton (1988), pp. 751–781.

rency, a bank run is said to occur. If a large number of depositors at all banks in the country attempt to redeem their deposits for currency, a bank panic is said to occur.

The distinction between a bank run and a bank panic is an important one. Obviously, the demise of a single bank in a system of many banks will not do irreparable damage to the economy. The failure of the banking system will, however, significantly worsen and/or lengthen any recessionary period in the economy.

An important aspect of bank runs is their potential to lead to bank panics. A bank run that leads to other bank runs is said to have a contagion effect. Regulators fear the failure of a single bank will cause depositors at other banks to change their behavior and to withdraw their funds even when there is no evidence that their bank is in financial difficulty. Preventing runs on individual banks is thus fundamental to preventing bank panics.

The history of the United States includes a large number of bank panics. Gorton (1988) has chronicled bank panics in this country from the 1860s through the Great Depression. The period from 1860 to 1914 is referred to as the National Banking Era. National bank chartering was instituted in the mid-1860s, but no central bank existed until the Federal Reserve System was created in 1914.

As shown in Table 7.1, there were 11 swings in the business cycle over that time period. Bank panics occurred in seven of these business cycle swings. Three of the four no-panic periods occurred in very mild recessions. However, the no-panic period of 1910–1912 occurred during a severe recession; in contrast, several other business cycles with bank panics were accompanied by little change in economic output.

The creation of the Federal Reserve System had significant impact on bank panics. From 1914 to 1934 there were five business cycle periods. No panics appeared until the Great Depression, and then three separate bank panics occurred in the same business cycle. Federal deposit insurance was instituted in 1933, and no bank panic has occurred since.

Early Deposit Insurance Schemes

Deposit insurance had been tried in a number of states prior to the adoption of the federal system. The most famous of these is the New York State plan, which was in force between 1829 and 1866. The historical record for most plans has been less than impressive. States that adopted deposit insurance plans had higher failure rates than did states without plans, and the insurance appeared to create greater losses than would have been incurred without it.

The states that attempted to institute deposit insurance are listed in Table 7.2. As we can see, six states instituted deposit insurance plans before the Civil War. The Michigan system was a monumental failure. It went into effect just prior to the Bank Panic of 1837 and as a result had no time to accumulate reserves before claims started to pour in. The plan was terminated without paying off any of the depositors of the failed banks. In contrast, the deposit insurance systems of Indiana, Ohio, and Iowa were quite successful. Depositors in those states did not lose any money as a result of bank closings. The success of these insurance plans is attributed to the nature of their guarantee system. In these plans, insured banks could be assessed any premium necessary to cover the outstanding obligations of the insurance fund. Payouts were not limited to the reserves of the fund. Deposits of a failing bank were essentially guaranteed by the surviving member banks.

TABLE 7.2	State-Sponsored Deposit Insurance Plans	
State	**Years in Existence**	**Participation by Banks in the Plan**
New York	1829–1866	Voluntary
Iowa	1858–1865	Voluntary
Vermont	1831–1866	Voluntary
Ohio	1845–1866	Voluntary
Michigan	1836–1842	Voluntary
Indiana	1834–1866	Voluntary
Oklahoma	1908–1921	Mandatory
Kansas	1909–1926	Voluntary
Nebraska	1911–1930	Mandatory
South Dakota	1915–1925	Mandatory
Texas	1910–1925	Voluntary*
Mississippi	1914–1930	Mandatory
North Dakota	1917–1929	Mandatory
Washington	1917–1921	Voluntary

* State banks could opt out of the plan by purchasing a private bond to guarantee their deposits.

Source: Wheelock (1993), pp. 10–14.

Following a large number of bank failures in 1907, eight states instituted deposit insurance plans for state-chartered banks. All these state deposit insurance funds ultimately failed. Federally chartered banks were prohibited from joining state insurance funds, and state banks that were required to join were able to switch to a federal charter to avoid participation.

Voluntary deposit insurance plans tended to attract certain types of banks. As suggested earlier, deposit insurance allows banks to take on more risk by engaging in more speculative lending activity and by substituting insured deposits for equity funding. A study of the Kansas deposit insurance system by Wheelock (1993) found that membership in the deposit insurance fund was a good predictor of bank failure. The more risky banks tended to join the Kansas system. In Wheelock's study, banks that had deposit insurance had lower capital-to-asset ratios than did banks that were not in the system.

The lessons learned from the state deposit insurance funds were to some degree incorporated into federal deposit insurance. Since the voluntary nature of previous plans had led to a deposit fund including only the riskiest banks, participation was made mandatory. Ultimately, the success of a deposit insurance fund depends on its credibility. Depositors must believe it is capable of meeting the needs of depositors in a bank panic. Since any private insurance fund would always be suspect, in regard to its ability to cover large losses, the decision to operate deposit insurance in the public sector was probably for the best.

THE FEDERAL DEPOSIT INSURANCE CORPORATION

The Banking Act of 1933 created the current deposit insurance system. This act provided wide-ranging changes in the banking industry by separating commercial and investment banking activities, restricting the assets that commercial banks could own, restricting the payment of interest on demand deposit accounts, and establishing the Federal Deposit Insurance Corporation. The legislation was passed in the midst of the greatest banking crisis in history. As mentioned earlier, the Great Depression was witness to three separate bank panics. During the period 1930–1933, over 40% of the banks in the United States (9,096 banks) failed. The country was mired in a deep and prolonged recession and was on the verge of financial collapse.

The overriding purpose of the deposit insurance portion of the 1933 Banking Act was to stop the bank runs that continued to sweep the country. It attempted to do so in two main ways: by providing a timely procedure for handling failed banks, and by protecting depositors. The original provisions of the act called for deposits to be insured up to $2,500. This coverage was put into effect in 1933 and was raised to $5,000 by the beginning of 1934.

Table 7.3 provides historical background regarding the amount of coverage provided to depositors. Insurance coverage remained at $5,000 until the beginning of the 1950s, when it was raised to $10,000 per account. Around half of commercial bank deposits were covered by deposit insurance throughout this period. Coverage remained at the $10,000 level until 1966, when it was increased to $15,000 per account. It was then raised again to $20,000 in 1969. Within five years, deposit insurance coverage was doubled once again and in 1980 coverage was increased to the current $100,000 level.

The percentage of deposits in the banking system covered by deposit insurance increased fairly constantly through the years. When first instituted, only 45% of bank deposits were insured by the FDIC. At the end of 1994, 77% of bank deposits were FDIC insured. Note that the amount of deposits covered has not increased in proportion to the level of coverage. The maximum coverage has increased by a factor of 20 while the percent of deposits covered has increased by a factor less than 2. This suggests that many depositors do not have accounts that exceed the coverage limits.

Table 7.3 also provides the cost of deposit insurance to banks since its inception. When deposit insurance was first instituted, banks paid an insurance premium of 0.0833%. This translated to a cost to the bank of 83.3 cents per $1,000 dollars of qualifying deposits. For a bank with $100 million of insured deposits, total annual premiums amounted to $83,300.

An important aspect of deposit insurance premiums was their insensitivity to bank risk. All banks paid exactly the same premium for exactly the same cov-

TABLE 7.3 Insured Deposits, Coverage, and Premiums of the FDIC				
Year	Total Deposits in Insured Banks ($M)	Percentage of Deposits Insured	Insurance Coverage	Effective Premiums Assessment (Rate)
1934	40,060	45.1	5,000[a]	NA
1935	45,125	44.7	5,000	0.0833%
1949	156,786	48.8	5,000	0.0833
1950	167,818	54.4	10,000	0.0370
1965	377,400	55.6	10,000	0.0323
1966	401,096	58.4	15,000	0.0323
1968	491,513	60.2	15,000	0.0333
1969	495,858	63.1	20,000	0.0333
1973	766,509	60.7	20,000	0.0385
1974	833,277	62.5	40,000	0.0435
1979	1,226,943	65.9	40,000	0.0333
1980	1,324,463	71.6	100,000	0.0370
1981	1,409,322	70.2	100,000	0.0714
1982	1,544,697	73.4	100,000	0.0769
1983	1,690,576	75.0	100,000	0.0714
1984	1,806,520	76.9	100,000	0.0800
1985	1,974,512	76.1	100,000	0.0833
1986	2,167,596	75.4	100,000	0.0833
1987	2,201,549	75.3	100,000	0.0833
1988	2,330,768	75.1	100,000	0.0833
1989	2,465,922	76.0	100,000	0.0833
1990	2,540,930	75.9	100,000	0.1200
1991	2,520,074	77.7	100,000	0.2125
1992	2,512,278	77.4	100,000	0.2300
1993	2,493,636	76.5	100,000	0.2440
1994	2,463,813	77.0	100,000	0.2360
June 1995	NA	NA	NA	0.0043

[a] Coverage was $2,500 for the first six months the FDIC was in existence.

Source: Federal Deposit Insurance Corporation, 1994 Annual Report and FDIC News Release, PR-70-95, November 14, 1995.

erage.[1] In this sense, the plan was social insurance with equal treatment for all banks. This aspect of the plan also created a situation in which the safest banks in effect subsidized the riskiest banks.

The premium amount was unchanged between 1933 and 1950. Beginning in 1950, however, the FDIC provided assessment credits to banks that effectively lowered the rate to less than half of the original levy (0.0370%). This practice continued until 1985, when the effective rate was again raised to 0.0833%. Bank failures encountered in the 1980s caused premiums to increase almost every year during the decade. By the beginning of the 1990s the insurance trust fund had a negative balance and premium assessments had risen to 0.23%.

Because of improvements in the state of the economy and the banking system, financial positions of a majority of depository intermediaries improved significantly in 1994–1995. These improvements compelled the FDIC to reduce the average assessment rate on banks to 0.43 cents per $100 (effective 1996), the lowest average assessment rate in more than the FDIC's 60-year history. The lowest average assessment rate for banks previously was 3.13 cents per $100, in 1962–1963. It is estimated that this reduction in insurance premium will save the banking industry about $946 million a year.[2]

The size of insurance premiums depends on the number of bank failures and the size of the insurance reserves. Table 7.4 documents the level of the insurance fund since the start of deposit insurance coverage. The deposit insurance fund grew steadily until 1987, reaching its maximum value of more than $18 billion in 1987. Beginning in 1988, the insurance fund declined in value because of a large number of bank failures. In 1992, the Bank Insurance Fund (BIF) had more than a $7 billion deficit. As the economy became stronger and the banking industry became healthier, the BIF reserves also improved. As of June 30, 1995, the BIF reserve fund surpassed $25 billion, increasing the ratio of the insurance fund as a percentage of insured deposits to 1.30%. The statutory requirement is to maintain the BIF reserve ratio at the target rate of 1.25%. Since the reserve ratio by mid-1995 was 1.29 and was expected to increase in the near future, the FDIC decided to reduce its insurance premiums for the healthiest banks, which account for 92% of all banks, to 0%. All banks combined are assessed 0.43 cents per $100 deposits.

THE DISPOSITION OF FAILED BANKS

One of the original purposes of the establishment of the FDIC was to provide a method for quickly disposing of failed banks. In practice, failed banks can be closed in a variety of ways. A bank may be closed by its chartering agency, the Office of the Comptroller of Currency for national banks or a state banking office for state-chartered banks, or, through recent legislation, by the FDIC if it is deemed insolvent. Besides technical insolvency, a bank can also be closed if it fails to meet minimum capital standards or when it is deemed to threaten the safety and soundness of the banking system.

Once a bank has been identified as an impending failure, the Division of Resolution of the FDIC attempts to determine the best way to handle the failure. As soon as the bank is closed and the FDIC is named the receiver, it then decides

---

[1] A notable exception was the "too big to fail" doctrine. Under this plan, the FDIC would not allow the largest money-center banks to fail because of the potential collapse of the entire monetary system. Large banks were therefore fully insured even though they paid premiums only on qualifying deposits.
[2] *FDIC News Release*, PR-70-95, November 14, 1995.

TABLE 7.4 Financial Condition of the FDIC for Selected Years				
Year	Total Income ($M)	Total Expense ($M)	Deposit Insurance Fund ($M)	Insurance Fund as a % of Insured Deposits
1935	20.8	11.3	306.0	1.52
1940	55.9	12.9	496.0	1.86
1945	121.0	9.4	929.2	1.39
1950	84.8	7.8	1,243.9	1.36
1955	105.7	9.0	1,639.6	1.41
1960	144.6	12.5	2,222.2	1.48
1965	214.6	22.9	3,036.3	1.45
1970	382.7	46.0	4,379.6	1.25
1975	689.3	97.5	6,716.0	1.18
1980	1,310.4	83.6	11,019.5	1.16
1985	3,385.4	1,957.9	17,956.9	1.19
1986	3,260.1	2,963.7	18,253.3	1.12
1987	3,319.4	3,270.9	18,301.8	1.10
1988	3,347.7	7,588.4	14,061.1	0.80
1989	3,494.6	4,346.2	13,209.5	0.70
1990	3,838.3	13,003.3	4,044.5	0.21
1991	5,789.9	16,862.3	(7,027.9)	(0.36)
1992	6,310.5	(625.8)	(100.6)	(0.01)
1993	6,430.8	(6,791.4)	13,121.6	0.69
1994	6,467.0	(2,259.1)	21,847.8	1.15
June 1995	NA	NA	25,000.0	1.29

Source: Federal Deposit Insurance Corporation, *1994 Annual Report* and *FDIC News Release*, PR-70-95, November 14, 1995.

how best to settle the bank's estate. The overriding principle in settling the estate is the minimization of cost to the FDIC.

There are three ways the FDIC can dispose of a failed bank. The most common is through deposit assumption. Through this method, prospective purchasers pay a premium to acquire a bank's deposits (franchise) along with certain assets. Historically, all deposits of the failed institution—not just the insured deposits—are transferred to the acquiring institution in a deposit assumption.

The deposit payoff method requires the FDIC to pay off the depositors of the bank and liquidate the assets of the failed institution. All insured deposits are covered by the FDIC and no insured depositor has ever lost money as a result of a bank failure. Uninsured deposits are a different story. The FDIC is not responsible for losses to uninsured deposits. From a practical standpoint, the FDIC attempts whenever possible to cover all the deposits of a failed institution. The FDIC has an explicit policy of "too big to fail" whereby the largest banks in the United States are deemed too important to be allowed to fail and all depositors are in essence insured.

Prior to 1991, uninsured deposits were often redeemed in full through the sale of the failed institution to another bank, as long as this was cheaper than a payout of insured deposits and the liquidation of assets. The FDIC is currently required to pursue the least costly among all alternatives. This includes the possibility of accepting proposals to assume only the insured deposits of a failed institution as well as proposals that would accept all of the deposits of an institution.

TABLE 7.5	Bank Failures, FDIC Disbursements, and Disposition of Failures for Selected Years				
Year	Total # of Bank Failures	Deposit Payoff	Deposit Assumption	Assisting Transaction	Disbursement in Thousands of $s
1934–1971	496	293	202	1	681,319
1972–1975	26	7	17	2	3,186,750
1976–1980	51	10	39	2	1,417,321
1981	10	2	5	3	888,999
1982	42	7	26	9	2,275,149
1983	48	9	36	3	3,766,884
1984	80	16	62	2	7,696,212
1985	120	29	87	4	2,917,550
1986	145	40	98	7	4,717,666
1987	203	51	133	19	5,037,650
1988	221	36	164	21	12,183,632
1989	207	32	174	1	11,444,554
1990	169	20	148	1	10,807,651
1991	127	21	103	3	20,611,900
1992	122	24	96	2	12,843,085
1993	41	5	36	0	1,755,358
1994	13	0	13	0	1,249,352

Source: Federal Deposit Insurance Corporation, *1994 Annual Report.*

In 1992, when this requirement was in effect, over 50% of bank failures (66 out of 122) resulted in uninsured depositors receiving less than 100 cents on each dollar of uninsured deposit. This contrasts with uninsured losses in only 20% of the bank failures in 1991.

The third method of handling a bank failure is through an assistance transaction. In this case, a bank on the verge of failure is kept open through financial assistance provided by the FDIC. This method is rarely used because it is difficult for a proposal of assistance to be judged the least costly alternative, since the bank is on the verge of failure.

The closing of failed institutions is not quite as simple as the above description of methods of resolution indicates. In many cases, a purchaser for a failed institution cannot be found immediately. In such cases a bridge bank is formed by the FDIC to continue to provide service to customers until an orderly closure can be organized.

Table 7.5 provides information on the number of bank failures since the formation of the FDIC as well as the method by which closures were handled. The total number of bank failures from 1934 to 1994 is 2,121, with most of these failures occurring in recent years. While in the first five decades of its operations the FDIC resolved only 753 failures (36%), in the decade of 1985–1994 it resolved 1,368 bank failures or 64% of the total. In addition, this same period accounts for over 80% of the total disbursements of the FDIC in handling bank failures. This indicates that both the number of failures and the size of bank failures have been disproportionately large in recent years.

The deposit assumption method is by far the most common way of handling bank closures; over two-thirds of bank failures have been handled in this manner since the beginning of the FDIC, and more than 75% of the failures since 1985 have been resolved this way. It is interesting to note that deposit assumption cases account for about 60% of the total disbursements of the FDIC, which is less than the proportion of failures handled with this method. This, of course, makes sense if it is the least costly alternative in closing a failed bank.

Deposit payoffs have accounted for slightly less than 30% of all cases and open assistance has been provided in less than 4% of the cases that have been handled by the FDIC. Since 1985, deposit payoffs have been used in about 20% of the cases and open assistance has been provided in the remaining 5%. Perhaps not surprisingly, open assistance is the most expensive way to resolve bank failures. Total disbursements in these cases account for almost 20% of total FDIC disbursements, while representing only 5% of all cases.

THE SAVINGS AND LOAN CRISIS

The crisis with the FDIC insurance fund in the early 1990s was preceded by an even bigger crisis in the savings and loan industry some 10 years earlier. As mentioned earlier, deposit insurance for the thrift industry originated at almost the same time as the FDIC, with identical coverage and premiums. The insurance fund was administered by the Federal Savings and Loan Insurance Corporation (FSLIC). By 1983, the FSLIC insurance trust fund was technically insolvent. Emergency funding from Congress and some regulatory accounting changes allowed the FSLIC to remain in operation until 1987, when it was finally put to rest. The story behind the demise of the FSLIC is an interesting one, showing that good intentions do not necessarily lead to good policy.

To understand the nature of the crisis in the S&L industry and the failure of the FSLIC insurance fund it is necessary to understand the history and regulatory environment of the industry. Savings and loans started in this country as building associations. These organizations represented a pooling of savings by a group of connected individuals such as neighborhood groups or company employees. The pooled funds were used to build the homes of members. The repayment of outstanding loans allowed others in the association to build their homes. The organization continued until all initial contributors had their homes built. The order of building was often established by a lottery system.

The first savings and loan was the Oxford Provident Building Association, established in 1831 in Philadelphia. The industry grew fairly rapidly over the next 100 years, but was badly damaged during the Great Depression. Over 1,700 savings and loans failed during the 1930s.

During the 45 years immediately following the Great Depression, the thrift industry had few problems. The return on equity for thrifts was comparable to that of commercial banks. Default rates on mortgages were very low, which meant there were few failures. In addition, interest rates were stable for a number of years after the Depression, minimizing any concern with interest-rate risk.

Following World War II, housing became a national priority in the United States. The result was unparalleled growth for the thrift industry. During the 35-year period following World War II, assets of the savings and loan industry grew at a rate exceeding 10% per year.

The primary asset on the balance sheet of savings and loans was fixed-rate residential mortgages. This was the case for a number of reasons. The primary reason for the establishment of S&Ls was to fund housing, so it was natural to hold a portfolio consisting almost exclusively of mortgages. Savings and loans also received tax breaks if a substantial portion (70% to 80%) of their portfolio was invested in mortgages. Mortgages therefore dominated the other investment opportunities of savings and loans. Fixed-rate mortgages were encouraged in order to keep payments stable for borrowers. In fact, federally chartered savings and loans and many state-chartered thrifts were explicitly prohibited from issuing variable-rate mortgages.

Restrictions on the types of mortgages were not offset by restrictions on funding. No regulations encouraged long-term deposits to balance the serious maturity mismatch between the assets and liabilities of thrifts. Their primary funding source was the common savings account, which had an almost immediate maturity.

The first signs of trouble in the thrift industry emerged in 1965. Interest rates rose substantially and thrifts were squeezed as interest rates on deposits were raised to keep deposits from leaving the industry. The regulatory response was to impose rate ceilings on savings and loan deposits. Previously, rate ceilings had applied only to commercial banks.

Rate ceilings on deposits can be effective only if no alternatives are available for savers. To insure a lack of substitutes, the Department of the Treasury increased the minimum denomination on Treasury Bills from $1,000 to $10,000. Competition for deposits was thus severely restricted and limited to giveaways (toasters and the like), and the establishment of branches close to customers.

The industry remained healthy until the late 1970s. At this time interest rates rose sharply; savers now had an attractive alternative to thrifts in the form of money market mutual funds, which were not subject to rate ceilings. The result was large deposit outflows from thrifts and a substantial increase in the cost of funds to thrifts. Losses accumulated as interest costs continued to rise and interest revenue remained fixed because of the fixed-rate mortgages dominating thrift portfolios.

To understand the magnitude of the problem, note that capital ratio (book value of equity to book value of assets) for the industry as a whole was a rather comfortable 5% in early 1980. By 1982, the capital ratio for the thrift industry was less than 1%. Nearly every thrift in the United States was in danger of failure.

The regulatory response came in the form of two significant pieces of legislation in the early 1980s. The Depository Institutions Deregulation and Monetary Control Act of 1980 (DIDMCA) and the Garn-St. Germain Act of 1982 provided a number of actions designed to improve the profitability of thrifts. Briefly, there were five main actions:

1. Federally chartered thrifts were given the right to make commercial, consumer, and commercial real estate loans. Direct equity investments were allowed in commercial real estate.
2. Regulation Q, which limited the rate banks and thrifts could pay on savings accounts, was eliminated to allow thrifts to compete with money market mutual funds.
3. Thrifts were allowed to compete for checking account balances by offering NOW accounts.
4. Thrifts were allowed to issue adjustable- or variable-rate mortgages.
5. Deposit insurance coverage was increased to $100,000.

Thrifts now had new opportunities to earn profits, although in many cases the risks were correspondingly higher. New funding sources were also available to enable thrifts to take advantage of these opportunities. Several other factors set the thrift industry up for its eventual losses. First, the deterioration of equity position in the thrift industry made risky investments more attractive than they once were. Second, a tax law change in 1981 made commercial real estate a reasonable tax shelter. This significantly increased building activity for such real estate and increased the demand for commercial real estate funding. Finally, oil prices collapsed in the early 1980s, leading to a significant recession in the southwestern part of the United States.

The results of the regulatory reform were somewhat predictable. The growth rate in the thrift industry had slowed considerably in 1981–1982 to 7.1%. During the period 1983–1984, the growth rate skyrocketed to an incredible 19.1% per year. By 1985, the risky nature of its new investments caught up with the thrift industry. Failures increased in both number and magnitude as the recession in the Southwest—and defaults on residential mortgages throughout the country—increased.

In 1979 there were 4,684 savings and loans, of which 645 were uninsured. By 1987 this number had been reduced to 3,147, of which 313 were still uninsured. The FSLIC had long since become insolvent, but was kept operating by a series of Congressional actions that provided funding.

The politics of the crisis created even greater troubles for the industry. As mentioned, nearly every thrift was operating with negative or barely positive capital positions. Because the FSLIC could not afford to close a large number of institutions that were technically in default, it instead merged them with healthier institutions or created phantom capital to avoid having to shut them down. Poorly capitalized thrifts continued to operate and took bigger and bigger gambles to pull themselves out of their financial dilemma. As a result, losses in the industry continued to mount.

Table 7.6 indicates the number of FSLIC-insured thrifts and their earnings and resolutions through the 1980s. As indicated in the table, the crisis came in two stages. The first was in the early 1980s when interest-rate risk resulted in large negative earnings for the industry. The second came in the late 1980s, when many of the investments made by thrifts with newly expanded powers turned sour.

Many of the thrifts that disappeared in the 1980s did so through mergers. This occurred because the FSLIC actively encouraged such arrangements as a way to conserve the FSLIC insurance fund. The FSLIC finally acknowledged in 1985 that the problem was too big for the agency to handle. A $15 billion capital infusion was requested by the FSLIC from Congress to handle the insolvency problem. When the legislation was finally passed in 1987, the FSLIC was provided with $10.8 billion. By that time, the FSLIC estimated the size of the problem at $50 billion.

TABLE 7.6   FSLIC-Insured Thrifts and Their Earnings and Resolutions

Year	Number of FSLIC-Insured Savings and Loans	Industry Return on Assets	FSLIC Liquidation
1981	4,002	−0.71%	1
1982	3,779	−0.61%	1
1983	3,343	0.24%	6
1984	3,183	0.16%	9
1985	3,246	0.39%	26
1986	3,220	0.01%	40
1987	3,147	−0.56%	49
1988	2,949	−0.87%	160
1989	2,878	−1.66%	124*

* Includes RTC Liquidations.

Source: Office of Thrift Supervision.

The entire period of the 1980s could be best described as one of regulatory forbearance. Instead of closing failed institutions, new accounting rules were adopted that allowed institutions to give the appearance of positive capital, or institutions were folded into other thrifts so that the combined thrift appeared to have positive capital. This provided these institutions with a strong incentive to take on greater risk in the hopes of bailing themselves out independently. In addition, the lack of close supervision created a tremendous potential for fraud, which was a factor in the closing of several thrift institutions.

One of the most publicized examples of incentive problems and fraud in thrift institutions was the Lincoln Savings and Loan of Irvine, California. Lincoln was purchased in 1984 for $51 million by American Continental, a Phoenix-based real estate development company controlled by Charles H. Keating Jr. Using Lincoln, Keating raised hundreds of millions of dollars in insured deposits to finance real estate developments, including those of American Continental, and to invest in junk bonds. By the time that Lincoln was closed down in 1989, the cost to taxpayers had risen to $2.5 billion. The cost of this bailout would have been $1 billion had regulators closed Lincoln in 1987. Keating was sentenced to 10 years in prison for fraud.

Major legislation was enacted in 1989 to deal with the savings and loan crisis. The Financial Institutions Reform, Recovery, and Enforcement Act (FIRREA) was passed with the intent of reforming, recapitalizing, and reorganizing deposit insurance. To accomplish this, the act dissolved the FSLIC and placed the control of deposit insurance for thrifts with the FDIC. The FDIC was to administer two funds: BIF, the Bank Insurance Fund, and SAIF, the Savings Association Insurance Fund. FIRREA also created the FSLIC Resolution Fund (FRF) to liquidate the assets and obligations of the FSLIC.

The FRF was assigned responsibility for thrifts that failed before January 1, 1989, or were assisted before August 9, 1989. This agency receives income from the disposition of assets, liquidating dividends from receiverships and excess SAIF assessments. Shortfalls in funding are covered by appropriations from the Treasury.

The Resolution Trust Corporation (RTC) was established by FIRREA to manage and resolve thrifts previously insured by the FSLIC, and that failed after January 1, 1989. From its inception through September 1995, RTC closed 747 institutions and resolved more than 25 million deposit accounts. The recoveries in assets amounted to $393 billion, which represents 87% of the book value of the assets.

The healthy thrifts are insured by SAIF. The number of SAIF-insured S&Ls was 1,847 at the end of 1994. With the general improvement in the state of financial services industry, S&Ls have also improved their performance. For 1994, SAIF-insured S&Ls had an average return on assets of 0.64 percent.[3]

While BIF reduced its average insurance premium significantly in 1995, SAIF premium remained at the average rate of 23.7 cents per $100 of deposits. SAIF-insured institutions continue to pay higher premiums because SAIF remains seriously undercapitalized. At the end of the second quarter of 1995, SAIF had a balance of $2.6 billion in reserves, or 37 cents for $100 of deposits. In order to bring the reserves up to the level of the statutory requirement, an additional $6.27 billion is needed.[4]

---

[3] *Flow of Funds Accounts, Flows and Outstandings, Second Quarter 1995.*
[4] *FDIC News Release*, PR-70-95, November 14, 1995. At the time of this writing, Congress is working on legislation to address the SAIF's problems. Among alternatives considered is a one-time assessment and the elimination of the penalty imposed on thrifts that want to convert their charters to banks.

It is quite clear from the discussion to this point that something went terribly wrong with the federal government's deposit insurance scheme in the 1980s. The large number of failures in both the savings and loan and the banking industry suggests a need to look at the incentives offered to depository intermediary managers under a fixed premium scheme. Ex post, it is obvious that deposit insurance was not correctly priced.

In this section we examine the pricing of deposit insurance from an incentive standpoint. We first discuss the value of deposit insurance to a subscribing institution and then look at ways that value enhancement incentives are affected with deposit insurance. We begin this analysis with a simple example of insurance in a nonbank institution. Specifically, we examine the value of insurance as seen in the provision of guaranteed loans to the Chrysler Corporation in the late 1970s. These loan guarantees are almost identical to deposit insurance guarantees, offering an easy way to estimate the value of such insurance to a company.

The Value of Government Loan Guarantees:
The Chrysler Corporation Case

A host of bad business decisions led Chrysler to the verge of bankruptcy in the late 1970s. Chrysler had been losing money steadily, and by the beginning of 1980 was in the midst of a severe cash crunch. Following an enormous political debate, the U.S. government agreed to guarantee up to $1.5 billion in new loans to the Chrysler Corporation. The terms of the agreement required Chrysler to pay fees equal to 1% of the guaranteed loans and to provide warrants for 14.4 million shares of Chrysler stock exercisable at $13 per share until 1990. The government was also given first lien on the assets of Chrysler Corporation (estimated value: $2.5 billion) and banks participating in the loans were given warrants for 13.286 million shares with the same strike price and maturity as the federal government.

At the time that Chrysler was seeking the loan guarantee, its stock was selling for $7.50 per share. The warrants thus represented a claim allowing participating banks and the federal government to buy stock at $13 per share from the corporate treasury when the current market value was only $7.50. Clearly these warrants would only be valuable if the loan guarantee succeeded in reviving the company and increasing the value of the stock.

The loan guarantees allowed Chrysler to borrow at near risk-free rates. Interest rates were at historically high levels at the time Chrysler sought the loan guarantees. Rates on U.S. Treasury 10-year bonds in early 1980 were at 11%. At the same time, current yields on existing Chrysler debt were in excess of 20%. Chrysler actually used $1.2 of the $1.5 billion loan guarantee. In June 1980, $500 million in notes was issued at 10.35%. Another $300 million in notes was issued later in the year at 11.4%, with a final $400 million issued in February 1981 at 14.9%.

The price of Chrysler stock remained in the $4–$8-per-share range until early 1982. At that point the fortunes of the company quickly turned around. By January 1983, Chrysler stock was selling for about $18. By July 1983 the price was over $30 per share. On July 13, Chrysler repaid the guaranteed loans in their entirety.

One can think of the value of the loan guarantee (and hence deposit insurance) in a couple of different ways. An ex post valuation would view the guarantee simply as the actual value of the interest savings to the company. We can calculate the present value of the interest savings as the difference between the rate

Chrysler would have paid without the loan guarantees and the rate actually paid multiplied by the amount actually borrowed.

We know that the initial $500 million in borrowing was outstanding for 3.1 years, the next $300 million was outstanding for about 2.8 years, and the final $400 million for 2.4 years. The initial interest-rate differential between Chrysler debt and U.S. Treasury bonds was about 10%. Assuming this spread was the same for each of the three issues, we can discount the interest savings on $1.2 billion of debt for 2.4 years, the saving on $800 million for another 0.4 years, and the savings on $500 million for another 0.3 years.

The present value of these savings is therefore:

$$PV = \frac{120}{(1+0.20)^1} + \frac{120}{(1+0.20)^2} + \frac{120 \times 0.40}{(1+0.20)^{2.4}}$$

$$+ \frac{80 \times 0.40}{(1+0.20)^{2.8}} + \frac{50 \times 0.30}{(1+0.20)^{3.1}} = \$242.05 \text{ million}$$

Rather than looking at the actual interest savings, we could also value the guarantee by assuming the full amount would be borrowed for the full 10 years. Assuming the appropriate discount rate for the entire period is the 20% used above, the present value of the interest savings is:

$$PV = \frac{150}{(1+0.20)^1} + \frac{150}{(1+0.20)^2} + \cdots + \frac{150}{(1+0.20)^{10}} = \$628.87 \text{ million}$$

Both of these calculations are naive in that the real value of the guarantees is their worth in helping Chrysler recover from its economic difficulties. The reason the actual interest savings are less than the total potential savings is that the guarantees in fact helped Chrysler overcome its difficulties and thus were no longer needed. Their true value would seem likely to lie somewhere between the two values calculated above.

A third way to think of the value of Chrysler's loan guarantees is in the economic sense of how important the guarantees were in helping Chrysler achieve a recovery. What the government was really offering to Chrysler was the chance to borrow money at the risk-free rate to invest in the firm. If the investments paid off, the loans could be repaid and Chrysler could go on with business as usual. If the investments did not work out, Chrysler would simply let the government pay off the loans.

Chrysler thus had the option of selling the assets from the loans (the investments that were made with the funds) back to the government at a price of $1.5 billion. The proceeds would then be used to pay off the loans. Of course, if the investments were worth more than $1.5 billion Chrysler would want to keep them, and would pay off the loans themselves. The above payoff scheme represents the granting of a put option to Chrysler by the government.[5] Using an options pricing model, one would calculate the value of this option to Chrysler at approximately $400 million.

When thought of in this manner, deposit insurance is similar to collision insurance on an automobile. When you purchase this insurance you have the option of selling your car to the insurance company at fair market value if you should happen to total the car in an accident. You would obviously exercise this option if such an event occurred so that you could pay off your outstanding loan

---

[5] A put option is the right to sell an asset at a prespecified price over a prespecified period of time. We will cover options in detail in Part III.

balance on the vehicle and purchase a new one. The price you pay for the insurance represents the value of this option.

The cost of automobile insurance is risk-adjusted—the option will cost you more if you have a history of speeding tickets or other blemishes on your driving record. The greater your perceived risk to the insurance company, the higher the premium or cost of insurance. Deposit insurance, as described earlier, had no such pricing mechanism. All banks paid the same premium regardless of their financial condition or the risk of their assets. It is hardly surprising that we encountered a crisis in the depository institutions industry, given the pricing structure that was employed.

Deposit Insurance and Capital Adequacy

At the beginning of this chapter we discussed two types of risk associated with deposit insurance. The first was financial risk or the risk of excessive leverage. It is easy to see that deposit insurance that guarantees 100% coverage up to $100,000 makes it possible for financial institutions to issue almost as much debt as they would like. Depositors have no need to monitor the status of the firm because the deposit insurance guarantor will settle all insured claims in the event of a default.

This lack of monitoring by debt holders (depositors) means the depository intermediary has the opportunity to substitute debt for equity because there are no bankruptcy costs to its depositors. In the absence of deposit insurance, debt holders (depositors) would require a firm to put up some equity to align the incentives of debt and equity holders. Without this requirement, debt is strictly preferred to equity because of its tax advantage.

The evidence is consistent with this incentive effect of deposit insurance. Table 7.7 illustrates aggregate capital ratio (equity to total assets) for banks in the United States since 1935. It is clear that the trend has been toward increased leverage since the inception of deposit insurance. Capital ratios declined until the early 1980s, when a number of regulatory agencies mandated common capital requirements. Since that time the amount of required capital has been slowly increasing.

In addition to the incentive to take on excessive leverage, a fixed premium deposit insurance system encourages depository institutions to take excessive risk. With a fixed-premium insurance system, both financially distressed and healthy firms have risk-incentive problems.

Risk-Incentive Problems: The Case of Financial Distress

Consider a depository institution that has anticipated severe loan losses and is in fact operating with a negative book value of equity. We presume a balance sheet that looks as follows:

Assets		Liabilities and Net Worth	
Cash	100	Demand Deposits	500
Securities	400	Time Deposits	500
Gross Loans	500		
Loan Loss Reserves	(200)	Net Worth	(200)
Total Assets	800	Total Liabilities and Net Worth	800

The negative book value of equity stems from the large allocation to the loan loss reserve account. Technically, this institution is insolvent, but recent history has

TABLE 7.7 Capital Ratios for Insured Commercial Banks	
Year	Total Capital/Total Assets
1994	7.78%
1993	8.00
1992	7.52
1991	6.75
1990	6.45
1989	6.21
1988	6.28
1987	6.02
1986	6.19
1985	6.19
1984	6.14
1983	6.00
1982	5.87
1981	5.83
1980	5.80
1979	5.75
1978	5.80
1977	5.92
1976	6.11
1975	5.88
1970	7.12
1965	7.53
1960	8.05
1955	7.16
1950	6.75
1945	5.48
1944	9.44
1935	12.19

Source: FDIC, Statistics on Banking, various issues.

many examples of institutions that are insolvent and yet allowed to operate because regulators lack the funds necessary to close the company and pay off the depositors.

If the institution were closed, depositors would be paid off in full and the FDIC would have a shortfall of $200, assuming the assets could be sold at the recorded values. Suppose that while the managers of the institution are awaiting closure by the appropriate regulatory institution, the following investment opportunity presents itself to the bank. The bank can invest $500 now and earn profits of $300 with a probability of 10% and a loss of $100 with a probability of 90%.

The expected profit on such an investment is:

$$E(\text{profit}) = 300 \times .1 + -100 \times .9 = -\$60$$

This means that the bank will raise $500 and will receive gross cash flows of either $800 or $400. Ignoring time value of money considerations, this yields a negative expected profit. A rational investor would not accept this project.

Limited liability plays a crucial role in determining the value of this investment project to the equity holders. Suppose we consider this project as a loan of $500 and assume that after it is made the loss occurs, and the bank realizes that it will not be fully repaid. The bank allocates $100 to the loan loss reserve account to cover the loss. In addition, suppose the loan was funded with time deposits. The new balance sheet would look like this:

Assets		Liabilities and Net Worth	
Cash	100	Demand Deposits	500
Securities	400	Time Deposits	1,000
Gross Loans	1,000		
Loan Loss Res	(300)	Net Worth	(300)
Total Assets	1,200	Total Liabilities and Net Worth	1,200

The bank is still technically insolvent but net worth has decreased another $100. Equity holders are no worse off, however. The maximum that stockholders stand to lose is their original investment. This amount was lost before this loan was made, so the cost of the bad loan is effectively shifted to the FDIC.

Suppose, instead, that the investment earns a profit and the loan is now worth $800. The balance sheet will now look like this:

Assets		Liabilities and Net Worth	
Cash	100	Demand Deposits	500
Securities	400	Time Deposits	1,000
Gross Loans	1,300		
Loan Loss Res	(200)	Net Worth	100
Total Assets	1,600	Total Liabilities and Net Worth	1,600

The bank is now solvent, as net worth has turned positive and managers now have some hope that the bank will be allowed to remain open. Limited liability truncates any losses to the owners so that what would normally be an unwise investment turns out to be a potentially profitable one. Managers know that any losses will be absorbed by the insurance fund and therefore have an incentive to invest in high-risk projects.

One can see that this type of behavior must be monitored very carefully by the deposit insurance agency, or it will end up with exorbitant losses. To some extent this is exactly what happened to the FSLIC insurance fund. Because the size of the fund was insufficient to close all of the technically insolvent thrifts, regulators used accounting gimmicks to increase book capital and allowed these thrifts to remain open. Owners and managers recognized that the only way they could earn their way out of insolvency was to take on extremely risky projects. Thrifts purchased junk bonds and invested heavily in commercial real estate projects (sometimes taking equity positions) as ways to generate sufficient earnings to create positive net worth positions. These high-risk strategies failed in most cases, and ended up increasing the liabilities of the deposit insurance fund significantly. A valuable lesson was learned by regulators. Current regulations require that depository institutions be closed before capital levels become negative. The age of regulatory forbearance appears to be behind us.

Risk-Incentive Problem: The Case of Healthy Firms

In the previous section we suggested that excessive risk-taking was due to the limited liability created by deposit insurance. But there is another force at work that allows banks and thrifts to engage in excessive risk-taking behavior. This force is the lack of market discipline commonly associated with debt financing. With deposit insurance guarantees, depositors are not concerned with the default risk in investment projects (loans).

This lack of market discipline, when coupled with the fixed-rate premium system, creates subsidies for depository intermediaries. The deposit insurance fund charges a fixed premium, p, and the depositors are willing to lend funds to the bank at the risk-free rate, r_f, because deposits are insured. The cost of borrowing, ignoring the administrative costs of the account, is therefore $r_f + p$. If this cost is less than the rate a bank would have to pay for uninsured funds, then the bank is receiving a deposit insurance subsidy. To see how this situation can create excessive risk-taking by banks, consider an investment project that will pay $10,000 per year forever with an initial cost of $110,000. In the absence of deposit insurance, the riskiness of this project would dictate a cost of capital of 10%. The net present value of this project would therefore equal:

$$NPV = \$10,000/.10 - \$110,000 = -\$10,000$$

As with the previous example, a rational investor would not take on this project. Limited liability will not help in this case, because it is assumed that this is a healthy institution with positive capital levels. Any losses on the project would therefore be taken out of equity and not covered by the deposit insurance fund.

Suppose the risk-free interest rate (the cost of deposits to this bank) is 4.75% and the deposit insurance premium is 0.25%. The cost of funds to this bank for investing in this project is therefore 5%. Notice that depositors are willing to lend money to the bank at 4.75% even though the risk on the project was assumed to require a discount rate of 10%.

Suppose that the bank borrows the entire $110,000 to undertake the project. The savings provided by the deposit insurance is 5% of $110,000 or $5,500 per year. The appropriate discount rate for this subsidy is the cost of unsubsidized borrowing. Assuming that the unsubsidized cost of borrowing is the 10% used earlier, the present value of the subsidy is therefore

$$PV = 5,500/0.10 = \$55,000$$

The value of the investment project to the bank is the net present value of the unsubsidized project plus the present value of the subsidy. This is referred to as the adjusted present value of the project and is equal in this case to

$$APV = -\$10,000 + \$55,000 = \$45,000$$

The project is one that should be undertaken because the adjusted present value is positive.

The effect of the deposit insurance subsidy is twofold. First, it allows a project to be accepted that normally would have been rejected because the project was too risky relative to the cash flows. (A discount rate less than 9.09% would have made the original NPV positive.) Second, the subsidy increases the size of a bank because projects that otherwise would have been deemed unprofitable are now acceptable. The deposit insurance subsidy thus provides an incentive to increase the overall size of banks as well as to increase the overall risk of the assets.

Another way to think about the deposit insurance subsidy is in terms of the option value of the loan guarantees, as was discussed with the Chrysler example. The FDIC essentially provides loan guarantees to banks. The equity holders have the option to sell the assets to the FDIC at the value of the insured deposits. This option will be worth more the greater the risk of the assets. Maximizing the value of the deposit subsidy thus implies that the risk of the assets be increased in order to increase the option value of the loan guarantees.

CONTROLLING RISK INCENTIVES

We have seen that a combination of factors has led to the problems in the deposit insurance industry. Owner-managers have an incentive under fixed-rate deposit insurance to capture the subsidy inherent in such a rate structure. Regulators may have been forced to keep open technically insolvent thrifts, thereby increasing the incentive to invest in high-risk assets. Finally, the implicit policy of encouraging deposit assumptions, which typically protected both insured and uninsured depositors, eliminated the incentive for depositors to monitor the riskiness of their intermediary. This last problem was further aggravated by a regulatory policy, announced at the onset of the Continental Illinois bailout in 1984, that some banks were simply "too big to fail" and that for those banks the FDIC would insure all deposits. Regulators were concerned about the contagion effects of a money-center bank failure on other banks and the financial system. A study by O'Hara and Shaw (1990) indicates that the announcement of the "too big to fail" policy increased the equity values of the money-center banks, commensurate with the subsidies afforded to them by the FDIC. Conversely, those banks that were not perceived as money-center banks experienced a decline in their equity prices. The "too big to fail" policy further reduced the monitoring power of intermediary debt.

A great deal of debate has taken place over the appropriate direction of regulatory efforts. As might be expected, most of the recent changes in deposit insurance policy have been directed toward correctly pricing deposit insurance. The main change has been a move to link the risk of the assets of an institution with the price of explicit and implicit deposit insurance premiums.

The pricing of risk has taken two forms. First, deposit insurance premiums have been explicitly adjusted for risk by charging higher premiums to intermediaries with greater risk. Second, risk has been implicitly priced by requiring differing levels of capital (self-insurance), depending on the risk of the intermediary. The mechanics of these risk-adjusted policies will be discussed in turn.

Risk-Adjusted Deposit Insurance Premiums

One of the distinguishing features of federal deposit insurance was the lack of a risk-based premium structure. Under the old fixed-rate system, depository intermediaries paid the same premium per dollar of qualifying (domestic) deposits regardless of what the deposits were used to fund. Thus, a thrift that used insured deposits to purchase Treasury bills paid the same cost of funds (interest plus insurance premium) as a thrift that lent insured deposits to a commercial real estate venture.

The flat deposit insurance structure meant that safe banks were subsidizing risky banks. The extent of the subsidies captured by an intermediary was determined by the degree of its asset risk. This led banks to accept projects that otherwise would have been rejected as too risky, and to hold larger portfolios of risky assets than they would have in the absence of the subsidy.

The FDIC moved to a system of risk-based deposit insurance premiums in 1993. The measurement of the underlying risk of the intermediary is one of the practical problems in implementing risk-based deposit insurance. The determinants of the risk groups are the risk-based capital ratio and a supervisory measure of the intermediary's health. The higher the capital and the healthier the intermediary, the lower the insurance premium. Conversely, the lower the capital and less healthy the institution, the higher the premium.

The 1996 risk-based premium structure adopted by the FDIC is presented in Table 7.8. The system is fairly simple in terms of groupings, and the differences in premium rates are not very drastic. Banks are considered to be well capitalized, adequately capitalized, or undercapitalized. The overall health of a bank is similarly judged as falling into one of three groups: healthy, one to be concerned about, or one to be substantially concerned about.

The measures of health are somewhat subjective. Healthy institutions are said to have few weaknesses in the eyes of bank regulators. Banks in the concern group have weaknesses that could result in significant risk to the insurance fund if not corrected. Those banks deemed to be of substantial concern could cause substantial losses to the fund if not corrected.

The groupings for capitalization are not nearly so subjective. Banks must meet minimum capital standards based on the new risk-adjusted standards to be discussed shortly. It is interesting to note the symmetry in the risk-based deposit schedule. Banks judged to be healthy but undercapitalized are treated in the same manner as banks judged as adequately capitalized but of concern to regulators. The lowest premium charged is zero for well-capitalized and healthy banks. This category includes 9,723 banks (92% of all banks). These banks

**TABLE 7.8   Assessment Rate Schedules BIF–Insured Institutions Effective 1996
(Rates in Cents per $100)**

Panel A

Capital Category	Healthy	Concern	Substantial Concern
Well	0	3	17
Adequate	3	10	24
Under	10	24	27

Average Annual Assessment Rate: 0.43; subject to the statutory minimum of $2,000 per institution per year.

**Panel B
Distribution Among Insurance Groups BIF-Insured Institutions**

Capital Group	Number and Base	Healthy	Concern	Substantial Concern
Well	Number	9,723 (92.0%)	552 (5.2%)	133 (1.3%)
	Base ($B)	$2,256.6 (94.6%)	$52.8 (2.2%)	$16.4 (0.7%)
Adequate	Number	70 (0.7%)	24 (0.2%)	33 (0.3%)
	Base ($B)	$42.6 (1.8%)	$10.0 (0.4%)	$3.7 (0.2%)
Under	Number	6 (0.1%)	4 (0.04%)	23 (0.2%)
	Base ($B)	$1.0 (.04%)	$1.0 (0.04%)	$12.3 (0.1%)

Based on June 30, 1995, data.

**TABLE 7.9   Assessment Rate Schedules SAIF-Insured Institutions Effective 1996
(Rates in Cents per $100)**

Panel A

Capital Category	Healthy	Concern	Substantial Concern
Well	23	26	29
Adequate	26	29	30
Under	29	30	31

Average Annual Assessment Rate: 23.7.

Panel B
Distribution Among Insurance Groups SAIF-Insured Institutions

Capital Group	Number and Base	Healthy	Concern	Substantial Concern
Well	Number	1,529 (86.1%)	137 (7.7%)	24 (1.4%)
	Base ($B)	$611.1 (83.6%)	$58.4 (8.8%)	$17.0 (2.3%)
Adequate	Number	22 (1.2%)	30 (1.7%)	26 (1.5%)
	Base ($B)	$16.6 (2.3%)	$18.3 (2.5%)	$6.8 (0.9%)
Under	Number	0 (0.0%)	0 (0.0%)	7 (0.4%)
	Base ($B)	$0.2 (0.0%)	$0.0 (0.0%)	$2.1 (0.3%)

Based on June 30, 1995, data.

have to pay the statutory annual minimum of $2,000 for FDIC insurance. The highest premium charged is 27 cents per $100 of deposits for banks that the regulators consider to be of substantial risk and with undercapitalized position. There were only 23 banks (0.2%) in this category. The average premium charged for all BIF-insured banks is 0.43 cents per $100 of total deposits. The new premium schedule is estimated to save the banking industry close to $1 billion per year.

A similar set of information is provided for SAIF-insured institutions in Table 7.9. These institutions pay premiums ranging from 23 cents per $100 of deposits in healthy, well-capitalized institutions to 31 cents per $100 of deposits in risky, undercapitalized institutions. A total of 1,529 savings institutions (86.1%) were considered healthy and well capitalized whereas 7 institutions (0.4%) were considered high-risk, undercapitalized institutions.

The difference in the premiums charged against healthy, well-capitalized savings institutions and risky and undercapitalized institutions is only 8 cents per $100 of deposits. A savings institution with $100 million in deposits and falling into the lowest premium category would pay a total premium of $230,000. An institution with the same level of deposits but falling into the riskiest category would pay a total premium of $310,000. It is not clear that the $80,000 difference in deposit premiums would be a significant deterrent to risk-taking for a savings institution of this size. Notice also that the premium differential would also be adjusted by the tax rate on the bank, as deposit insurance premiums are tax-deductible expenses.

The newly implemented structure has a much greater premium differential for banks. In essence, the new structure rewards banks in the best categories and retains the high premiums for potential problem banks. Now a $100 million bank operating in the lowest premium bracket would pay just $2,000 of premiums while the most risky banks would still pay $270,000.

One of the improvements in the current system is that premiums are applied to all deposits even though some are not insured. In the previous fixed-premium system, premiums were calculated based on domestic deposits, excluding foreign deposits. The emphasis on domestic deposits at the time the FDIC was established was of little concern, because few institutions held substantial amounts in foreign deposits. With the globalization of financial intermediation in recent years , some money-center banks have raised more than half of their funds from foreign deposits. Since deposit insurance premiums were not assessed on foreign deposits, a bank with a high ratio of foreign to total deposits could reduce its premiums significantly.

Some have argued against including foreign deposits in insurance assessments because they were not covered. But this is not quite true, since, as we discussed earlier, regulators have extended insurance coverage to all deposits, including foreign deposits, for money-center banks under the "too big to fail" policy. Needless to say, money-center banks are the most active participants in the market for foreign deposits.[6]

Risk-Adjusted Capital Requirements

A complement to the risk-based insurance premium system is the risk-adjusted capital requirement. This system, in place in the United States and eleven other industrialized countries, stems from a document known as the Basle Accord. This was an agreement implemented in stages beginning in 1988 to level the playing field in international banking by subjecting all banks to similar minimum capital requirements. The minimum would depend on the riskiness of the assets on and off the balance sheet of the intermediary.

Table 7.10 provides a list of risk categories and the weights that are used in calculating risk-adjusted assets. The first step in calculating risk-adjusted capital requires that banks categorize each asset and off-balance-sheet item according to these guidelines. The off-balance-sheet items are then converted to credit equivalent values by using the conversion factors shown in Table 7.11. Once all qualifying items have been converted, all assets and off-balance-sheet items are multiplied by the weights in Table 7.10. Totaling these dollar amounts produces the risk-adjusted assets of the institution.

The capital requirements of an institution are now stated in terms of qualifying capital as a percent of risk-adjusted assets. Table 7.12 provides a list of qualifying capital. Core capital or Tier 1 capital consists primarily of stockholders' equity. Tier 2 capital consists primarily of loan loss reserves, preferred stock, and subordinated debt. Total capital is the sum of Tier 1 and Tier 2 capital.

Banks are required to hold at least $4 of core capital for every $100 of risk-adjusted assets (4%). Total capital must be at least 8% of risk-adjusted assets. In addition, bank regulators require depository institutions to hold at least 3% capital relative to unadjusted total assets.

The idea behind risk-adjusted capital is simple. The greater the risk of a bank's assets, the more capital it must hold. The more capital a bank holds, the greater the self-insurance of the institution. Because equity is more expensive than debt, this implies that the cost of funding riskier assets is more expensive than with risk-free assets, so less of a deposit insurance subsidy can be captured by a bank.

To see the difference this might make in the asset choice of a bank, consider the capital requirements of two equally sized banks with different levels of asset

---

[6] For more information, see Lawrence and Arshadi (1988) and Arshadi (1989b).

TABLE 7.10   Risk Categories and Risk Weights for Balance-Sheet Items

Category 1:   0%

1. Cash.
2. Balances due from, and claims on, Federal Reserve banks.
3. Securities issued by the U.S. government or its agencies.
4. Federal Reserve bank stock.

Category 2:   20%

1. All claims on domestic depository institutions.
2. Claims on foreign banks with an original maturity of one year or less.
3. Claims guaranteed by, or backed by, the full faith and credit of domestic depository institutions.
4. Local currency claims on foreign central governments to the extent the bank has local currency liabilities in the foreign country.
5. Cash items in the process of collection.
6. Securities and other claims on, or guaranteed by, U.S. government-sponsored agencies.
7. Portions of loans and other assets collateralized by securities issued by, or guaranteed by, U.S. government-sponsored agencies.
8. General obligation claims on, and claims guaranteed by, U.S., state, and local governments that are secured by the full faith and credit of the state or local taxing authority.
9. Claims on official multilateral lending institutions or regional development institutions in which the U.S. government is a shareholder or contributing member.
10. Securities and other claims guaranteed by the U.S. government or its agencies.
11. Portions of loans and other assets collateralized by securities issued by, or guaranteed by, the U.S. government and its agencies or by cash on deposit at the lending institution.

Category 3:   50%

1. Revenue bonds or similar obligations, including loans and leases, that are obligations of U.S., state, or local governments, but for which the government entity is committed to repay the debt only out of revenues from the facilities financed.
2. Credit equivalent amounts of interest rate and foreign exchange rate related contracts, except for those assigned to a lower risk category.

Category 4:   100%

1. All other claims on private obligers.
2. Claims on foreign banks with an original maturity exceeding one year.
3. Claims on foreign central governments that are not included in item 4 of Category 2.
4. Obligations issued by state or local governments repayable solely by a private party or enterprise.
5. Premises, plant, and equipment, other fixed assets, and other real estate owned.
6. Investments in any unconsolidated subsidiaries, joint ventures, or associated companies, if not deducted from capital.
7. Instruments issued by other banking organizations that qualify as capital.
8. All other assets.

TABLE 7.11   Credit Conversion Factors for Off-Balance-Sheet Items

100% Conversion Factor

1. Direct credit substitutes (general guarantees of indebtedness and guarantee-type instruments including standby letters of credit serving as financial guarantees for, or supporting, loans and securities).
2. Acquisitions of risk participation in banker's acceptances and participation in direct credit substitutes.
3. Sale and repurchase agreements and asset sales with recourse, if not already included on the balance sheet.
4. Forward agreements to purchase assets, including financing facilities with certain drawdown.

50% Conversion Factor

1. Transaction-related contingencies (such as bid bonds, performance bonds, warranties, and standby letters of credit related to a particular transaction).
2. Unused commitments with an original maturity exceeding one year, including underwriting commitments and commercial credit lines.
3. Revolving underwriting facilities (RUFs), note issuance facilities (NIFs), and other similar arrangements.

20% Conversion Factor

1. Short-term, self-liquidating, and trade-related contingencies, including commercial lines of credit.

0% Conversion Factor

1. Unused commitments with an original maturity of one year or less or which are unconditionally cancelable at any time.

Credit Conversion for Interest-Rate and Foreign Exchange Contracts

The total replacement cost of contracts (obtained by summing the positive marked-to-market values of contracts) are added to a measure of future potential increases in credit exposure. This future potential exposure measure would be calculated by multiplying the total value of contracts by one of the following credit conversion factors.

Remaining Maturity	Interest Rate Contracts	Exchange Rate Contracts
Less than one year	0%	1.0%
One year and over	0.5%	5.0%

No potential exposure would be calculated for single currency floating/floating interest-rate contracts. The credit exposure on these contracts would be evaluated solely on the basis of their marked-to-market value. Exchange rate contracts with an original maturity of seven days or less are excluded. Also, instruments traded on exchanges that require daily payment of variation margin would be excluded.

TABLE 7.12 Definitions of Qualifying Capital	
Types of Capital	**Minimum Requirements and Limitations**
Core Capital (Tier 1)	Must equal or exceed 4% of risk-weighted assets
Common stockholders' equity	No limit
Minority interest in common equity accounts of consolidated subsidiaries	No limit
Less goodwill and other disallowed tangibles	
Supplementary Capital (Tier 2)	Limited to 100% of Tier 1
Allowance for loan and lease losses	Limited to 1.25% of risk-weighted assets
Perpetual and long-term (maturity of 20 years or more) preferred stock	No limit within Tier 2, long-term preferred is amortized for capital purposes
Hybrid capital instruments (including perpetual debt and mandatory convertible securities)	No limit within Tier 2
Subordinated debt and intermediate-term (maturity of seven years or more) preferred stock	Limited to 50% of Tier 1, intermediate-term preferred is amortized for capital purposes
Revaluation reserves	Not included
Deductions (from sum of Tier 1 and Tier 2)	
Investments in unconsolidated banking subsidiaries	
Reciprocal holdings of bank-issued capital securities	
Other deductions as determined by supervisory authority	
Total Capital (Tier 1 + Tier 2 − Deductions)	Must equal or exceed 8% of risk-weighted assets

risk. Suppose that Bank A has only two assets on the balance sheet: Treasury securities of $100 million, and mortgages of $300 million. Bank B has Treasury securities of $50 million and commercial loans of $350 million. The risk-adjusted assets of each institution, according to the weights in Table 7.9, would be

Bank A: risk-adjusted assets $= 0 \times 100 + .5 \times 300 = \$150$ million
Bank B: risk-adjusted assets $= 0 \times 50\ \ + 1 \times 350 = \$350$ million

The minimum core capital Bank A would need to hold would be $6 million (0.04 × 150), while Bank B would need $14 million (0.04 × 350). Total capital requirements (Tier 1 + Tier 2) would be double those amounts.

The choice of assets and off-balance-sheet items now has a substantial impact on profitability. Riskier projects have to be judged more on the underlying cash flows than the potential deposit insurance subsidy. Arshadi (1989a) and Eyssell and Arshadi (1990) show that upon the adoption of the risk-based capital requirements, the stock prices of publicly traded banks declined, signifying the reduction in insurance subsidies. In another study, Haubrich and Wachtel (1993) suggest that risk-adjusted capital requirements are having a significant effect on the asset choices of depository intermediaries. Commercial banks of all sizes have shifted their portfolios. Banks now hold more securities, particularly Treasury securities, than they did in 1990. In addition, banks hold less of all types of loans relative to total assets with the exception of mortgage loans.

This is exactly the type of reaction that would be expected given the weighting scheme employed by regulators. Because most securities carry a zero weight, a bank would continue to purchase them so long as the spread between the yield and the cost of deposits (including administrative expense) was positive. This part of a bank could be funded totally with debt. Mortgage loans would be preferred to all other types of loans because the equity required is exactly one-half that required for other types of loans.

The portfolio changes that occurred were probably along the lines desired by bank regulators. The changes are not without some consequence, however. Reduced commercial lending has been cited as one of the major reasons for the prolonged recession of the early 1990s. The purchase of relatively low-yielding Treasury securities has held deposit rates down to enable banks to obtain a positive spread. As a result, many customers have left banks for mutual funds and other substitutes paying higher rates, but carrying greater risk.

THE OUTLOOK FOR DEPOSIT INSURANCE

Depositors have benefited greatly from the deposit insurance system of the past 60 years. The presence of such insurance reduces the need to gather information about the potential safety of deposits. From this standpoint, the social savings have been enormous. Deposit insurance has also been instrumental in eliminating bank panics. The disruption of the economy from instability in the financial sector is a thing of the past. The U.S. economy has grown tremendously as a result of its financial stability.

The collapse of the Federal Savings and Loan Insurance Corporation in the 1980s has taught us that these benefits do not come without costs. The change in the interest-rate environment during and after the 1970s brought to the forefront the embedded risk in many financial intermediaries. Because interest rates had changed so infrequently in past years, many banks and thrifts were ill equipped to deal with interest-rate risk. This situation was coupled with a major recession and a period of deflation in the housing industry of a magnitude that had not been experienced since the Great Depression.

The outlook for depository intermediaries and the deposit insurance system looks brighter in the 1990s. Bank failures have been drastically reduced and the thrift industry is thriving. The deposit insurance fund is on solid footing and has met its mandated target of at least 1.25% of insured deposits much earlier than expected. Premium rates have fallen since the target has been reached, thereby increasing intermediary profits.

Concern still exists about the safety of the deposit insurance fund because financial innovation continues. It seems clear that we are headed toward interstate banking and perhaps universal banking. The impact of those changes will have to be weighed by bank regulators.

There have been a number of suggestions besides risk-based insurance and capital requirements as potential solutions for deposit insurance problems. One of the simplest is the requirement of a deductible on deposit insurance coverage. Deposits would be fully insured up to some minimum amount such as $10,000 with additional deposits insured at 90% of their face value. This would force greater market discipline as depositors would now have an incentive to monitor the financial health of their bank.

Another idea that has been widely discussed is placing a greater number of asset restrictions on banks that choose to fund assets with insured deposits. This would create "narrow banks" in the sense that institutions that chose to have insured transactions and savings deposits could only hold limited types of earning assets, such as government securities and perhaps short-term mortgage-related instruments. With relatively safe assets, the possibility of a failure would be greatly diminished, thereby eliminating any danger of a deposit insurance crisis.

One of the difficulties with the narrow bank concept is the maintenance of a firewall between the insured and the uninsured activities of an institution. Regulatory supervision would need to be much enhanced to make sure that insured deposits were not implicitly funding prohibited activities. If banks could not fund any type of commercial lending activities with insured deposits, many smaller communities would be likely to suffer disproportionately. The small size of many markets may not justify separate loan companies, yet many individuals prefer one-stop shopping for deposits and loans. The firewall problem is already apparent, with many banks now offering stock mutual fund products in an effort to maintain customers. The OCC has issued guidelines for the sale of such products so that customers will not get the impression that these investments carry deposit insurance. The guidelines basically suggest that sales of such investments be done in an area different (preferably on a different floor) from the sale of insured CDs and other insured accounts!

SUMMARY

One of the most widely discussed banking issues of the 1980s has been the appropriate role of government-sponsored deposit insurance. The crisis in the savings and loan industry brought to a head the moral hazards prevalent under a fixed-rate premium system. Depository institutions appear to have reduced their capital levels and increased their level of asset risk in response to the advent of deposit insurance. The eventual resulting losses to the FSLIC and FDIC insurance funds generated heated debates on the proper role of government in the provision of deposit insurance.

Several observations emerge from the history of deposit insurance. The overall economy has benefited from the reduction in monitoring costs to individuals. Insurance has allowed funds to be raised cheaply and has provided for the expansion of the commercial and housing sectors. Deposit insurance has contributed to the stability of the payment system and has reduced bank failures. There have been a few bank failures and bank runs, but no bank panics.

At the same time, all the costs of deposit insurance have not been paid through the premiums assessed against financial intermediaries. The bailout of the thrift industry has already cost taxpayers an estimated $150–$200 billion.

The current outlook for the FDIC has very much improved over the past five years. Bank and thrift failures have fallen dramatically. The deposit insurance trust fund is fully supplied. The conversion to risk-adjusted capital requirements and a risk-based premium system has changed the incentive structure so that riskier assets are now more expensive to fund.

REVIEW QUESTIONS

1. Explain the economic rationale in offering a government-sponsored deposit insurance.
2. What are the unintended side effects of deposit insurance?
3. Examine the moral hazard problem in a fixed-rate insurance premium system.
4. Describe briefly the savings and loan crisis and explain how moral hazards contributed to the crisis.
5. Discuss briefly the provisions of the new risk-based premium system.
6. Explain briefly how the risk-based capital ratio is calculated.
7. Define Tier 1 and Tier 2 capital. What are the regulatory minimum requirements on each of these two categories?
8. What is the evidence on the effectiveness of the risk-based capital requirement?
9. Explain the risk-based premium schedule based on the risk-based capital ratio and the intermediary health.
10. What are the unresolved issues in the deposit insurance system?

REFERENCES

Arshadi, N. 1989. "Capital Structure, Agency Problems, and Deposit Insurance in Banking Firms." *The Financial Review*, vol. 24, no. 1 (February): 31–52.

Arshadi, N. 1989. "Exclusion of Foreign Deposits from the Deposit Insurance Assessments." *Issues in Bank Regulation* (Summer): 29–32.

Eyssell, T.H., and N. Arshadi. 1990. "The Wealth Effects of the Risk-Based Capital Requirement in Banking." *Journal of Banking and Finance*, vol. 14, no. 1 (March): 179–197.

Federal Deposit Insurance Corporation 1992 Annual Report.

Gorton, G. 1988. "Banking Panics and Business Cycles." *Oxford Economic Papers*, vol. 40: 751–781.

Haubrich, J.G., and P. Wachtel. 1993. "Capital Requirements and Shifts in Commercial Bank Portfolios." *Economic Review*, Federal Reserve Bank of Cleveland, vol. 29, no. 3: 2–15.

Lawrence, E.C., and N. Arshadi. 1988. "The Distributional Impact of Foreign Deposits on Federal Deposit Insurance Premia." *Journal of Banking and Finance*, vol. 12, no. 1 (March): 105–115.

O'Hara, M., and W. Shaw. 1990. "Deposit Insurance and Wealth Effects: The Value of Being 'Too Big to Fail'." *The Journal of Finance*, vol. 45, no. 5 (December): 1587–1600.

Wheelock, D.C. 1993. "What Have We Learned About Deposit Insurance from the Historical Record." *Economic Review*, Federal Reserve Bank of St. Louis (January/February): 10–14.

White, L.J. 1992. "What Should Banks Really Do?" *Contemporary Policy Issues* (July): 104–112.

C H A P T E R

8

Nondepository Financial
Intermediaries: Insurance Companies

OBJECTIVES

This is the first of two chapters that examine nondepository financial intermediaries. As the name suggests, these institutions do not raise their funds through traditional deposits. Notwithstanding this difference, nondepository intermediaries offer many of the same services that their depository counterparts provide. Despite regulatory restrictions, there is a trend toward the convergence of these two types of intermediaries. Our discussion of nondepository intermediaries includes the following:

Insurance

> Life insurance
> Annuities
> Health insurance
> Property-casualty insurance
> Lloyd's of London

Pension Funds
Investment Companies

> Open-end investment companies (mutual funds)
> Closed-end investment companies

Investment Banks
Finance Companies

After a preliminary discussion of nondepository intermediaries, we will examine the insurance business. In the next chapter, we will look at pension funds, mutual funds, investment banks, and finance companies.

RECENT TRENDS IN THE FINANCIAL ACTIVITIES
OF NONDEPOSITORY FINANCIAL INTERMEDIARIES

Banks provide two basic services for their customers: They take customer excess funds in the form of insured deposits (bank liabilities), and they make loans from the pool of deposits (bank assets). In providing these services, banks face strong competition from nondepository intermediaries. For example, mutual funds have successfully convinced many bank customers to switch their deposit accounts to mutual fund shares. Mutual fund shares often provide check-writing privileges similar to those of bank accounts. Convenience, coupled with the promise of higher returns, makes mutual funds formidable competitors to banks. Mutual fund shares totaled $2.16 trillion in 1994, compared with $2.46 trillion in bank deposits.[1]

In 1970, bank loans accounted for about two-thirds of the total short-term borrowing of nonfinancial U.S. companies, and this bank share had dropped to about one-third by 1995. In today's market, corporations often issue their own commercial papers instead of borrowing from a bank. These papers, in turn, are purchased by mutual funds, insurance companies, and pension funds. Nondepository financial intermediaries are credible alternatives to banks in providing investment and financing services to customers.

The importance of nondepository financial intermediaries is apparent in their asset size. Table 8.1 presents the assets of both depository and nondepository intermediaries. In 1994, depository intermediaries held only one-third of the total assets of financial intermediaries, while nondepository intermediaries controlled the remaining two-thirds. Insurance companies, pension funds, and investment companies held 16.1%, 24.5%, and 26.2% of total intermediary assets, respectively.

As with depository intermediaries, nondepository financial firms are also in the business of collecting, processing, and producing information. For example, insurance companies develop expertise in gathering information to assess the risk of underwriting insurance contracts. They receive premiums commensurate with the size of the risk. They pool the premiums and invest them in securities. For a sound investment decision, insurance companies develop relationships with the issuer of the securities similar to bank-customer relationships. Known as institutional investors, insurance companies, mutual funds, pension funds, and finance companies carry significant power in their investment decisions. As major blockholders of corporate securities, these intermediaries actively participate in important corporate decisions such as mergers, acquisitions, and restructuring.

THE ECONOMIC PRINCIPLES OF INSURANCE

Insurance is a financial contract whereby one party (the insurer) agrees to compensate another party (the insured) for losses in exchange for a prepaid fee (insurance premium). The insurer provides for losses from the pool of insurance premiums. Insurance in effect transfers the potential losses from individuals to an insurance pool. This pool combines the potential losses and redistributes the actual losses among its members.

Suppose there are 1,000 houses that face the risk of fire. While the probability of fire is small for each house, its occurrence among 1,000 houses can be predicted with reasonable accuracy. Based on historical experience, we expect 5 houses out of the 1,000 houses to burn each year. We further assume that the losses due to fire will be $150,000 per house, resulting in total losses of $5 \times \$150,000 = \$750,000$. We can create an insurance pool to provide insurance for

---

[1] *Mutual Fund, 1995 Fact Book*, Investment Company Institute, p. 9.

TABLE 8.1   Assets of Financial Intermediaries (Billions of Dollars)

	$ 1992	$ 1993	$ 1994[a]	% 1994
Depository Intermediaries				
Commercial Banks	$3,657.0	$3,896.1	$4,161.7	25.3%
Savings Institutions	1,078.8	1,029.5	1,013.1	6.1
Credit Unions	263.9	280.9	294.6	1.8
Nondepository Intermediaries				
Insurance Companies:				
Life Insurance Companies	1,664.5	1,839.1	1,942.3	11.8
Property and Casualty				
Companies	637.3	671.5	704.6	4.3
Pension Funds:[b]				
Private Non-Life Insurance				
Company	2,144.5	2,342.1	2,356.4	14.3
Government-Administered Plans	1,509.5	1,587.2	1,673.5	10.2
Investment Companies:				
Mutual Funds	1,646.3	2,075.4	2,161.5	13.1
Closed-End Investment				
Companies	94.3	110.9	116.0	.7
Bank-Administered Trusts	1,791.5	2,050.1	NA	12.4
Total Assets of Intermediaries	$14,487.6	$15,882.8	$16,473.8	100%

[a]For those categories for which the 1994 data was not available, the 1993 figures were used in
  calculating total assets and respective percentages.
[b]Excluding pension funds held by life insurance companies.

Source: Mutual Fund Fact Book, 1995, p. 142; *Property/Casualty Insurance Fact Book, 1996,* p. 16; and *1994
Life Insurance Fact Book, 1995,* pp. 21, 42.

home owners at an annual premium of $750,000 ÷ 1,000 houses = $750. Each home owner pays $750 to the pool in return for a contract that provides fire insurance on each house.

This example is a simplified version of an insurance contract. We can make it more realistic by considering a series of provisions. We have assumed that each house has the same value and suffers the same amount of loss if there is a fire. This does not have to be the case. To solve for this problem we can calculate the premium charged for $100 of coverage, ($750 ÷ $150,000) × 100 = $0.50. The premium is 50 cents for every $100 of coverage. A premium of $0.50 does not consider the operating cost of running an insurance pool. Suppose that operating cost amounts to another $0.15 for every $100 of coverage. The total premium now is $0.50 + $0.15 = $0.65. Since the pool has an expected loss of 0.5% of its value, it is prudent to set up a reserve for unexpected losses. Assume that we require another $0.05 for this purpose. This brings the premium to $0.65 + $0.05 = $0.70. If insured parties pay their premiums on January 1, and, on average, losses are paid on July 1, the insurer can invest the premiums and earn 6% a year, which amounts to 3% for six months. This 3% is earned on $0.50 (the cost of paying for losses) + $0.05 (loss reserves) = $0.55, and amounts to 3% × $0.55 = $0.0165. The premium cost is reduced by the investment income, and the actual premium charged per $100 of coverage is therefore calculated as follows:

Premium = cost of paying for losses + operating costs
$$+ \text{ loss reserves} - \text{investment income}$$
Premium = $0.50 + $0.15 + $0.05 − $0.0165 = $0.6835.

The actual premium per year for $150,000 of coverage is ($150,000 ÷ 100) × 0.6835 = $1,025.

What are the benefits and costs of insurance? There are several benefits. Insurance reduces uncertainty and allows families to maintain their standard of living after a loss. Insurance also provides benefits to businesses. With insurance, losses due to death or property damage do not threaten to destroy a business. Therefore, creditors can deal with the business without undue concern for such losses. Without insurance, only large businesses could afford losses. Small businesses could not secure credit without insurance because they are limited in resources to cover large losses. Generally, the cost of capital for an insured business is lower than the cost for an uninsured business.

Insurance also creates social costs. For example, the operating expenses and losses due to insurance fraud are social costs of insurance. Overall, however, insurance plays a socially desirable role, where benefits outweigh costs. We now examine each line of insurance.

LIFE INSURANCE COMPANIES

People purchase life insurance for two primary reasons. First, it provides financial security for a family if the main wage earner dies unexpectedly. Second, depending on the type of policy, life insurance may serve as a saving vehicle.

There are four general categories of life insurance: ordinary, group, industrial, and credit life. Table 8.2 presents the amount of life insurance outstanding for each of these categories in 1970, 1980, and 1994. Ordinary life insurance is the largest product; group life insurance is the second largest on the list. Industrial and credit life insurance are significantly smaller, with the former declining in 1994.

Ordinary Life Insurance

Depending on the type of protection one seeks, ordinary life insurance can be written as whole life, term, universal, variable, and variable-universal life insurance. We examine each in turn.

Whole Life Insurance　Whole life insurance is effective for the life of the policyholder and includes financial protection against untimely death in the form of a savings plan. The policy requires a fixed premium payment per year. This pay-

TABLE 8.2　Life Insurance Products in U.S. Life Insurance Companies (Billions of Dollars)			
	1970	**1980**	**1994**
Ordinary Life Insurance	777.2	2,086.6	6,835.2
Group Life Insurance	593.7	1,719.3	4,608.7
Industrial Life Insurance	39.2	40.0	20.1
Credit Life Insurance	96.4	210.0	209.5
Total	1,506.5	4,055.9	11,673.5

Source: Life Insurance Fact Book Update, 1995, American Council of Life Insurance, p. 4, and earlier issues.

ment is higher than the actuarially determined cost of insurance for early years when the insured is younger and has a lower probability of death, and lower than the cost in later years when the insured is older and has a higher probability of death. In early years, when the fixed premium payment is higher than the cost, the difference is invested by the insurance company. The cash value of the overpayment in early years plus the interest earned constitute embedded savings, against which the policyholder can borrow. The interest earned is tax deferred. A policyholder who decides to give up the protection can receive its cash value.

Term Insurance Term insurance is a simple life insurance policy with no savings involved. As the name implies, it has a prespecified coverage period—typically from 1 to 10 years. If the insured dies during the period the policy is in effect, the beneficiaries receive the insurance benefit. If the policy runs out while the insured is still alive, there will be no benefit payments. Because of its pure insurance coverage without any savings elements and its limited period of coverage, the premiums of term insurance policies are generally lower than those of whole life insurance. With term insurance, the insurer has the opportunity to reevaluate the risk of the insured periodically. If the insured is at a risk category acceptable to the insured, the term insurance is renewed.

In recent years, new versions of term insurance have been introduced that are more flexible. While under *level term* policy the death benefits remain constant over the term, in *decreasing term* the benefits decline over the term of the policy. Decreasing term insurance is more appropriate for those who need more protection in earlier years. The *increasing term* adjusts for the effects of inflation by increasing the benefits over the term of the policy. A *renewable term* policy allows for continued coverage up to a specified age regardless of the health of the insured. The renewed policy generally requires a higher premium. Suppose a 35-year-old person purchases a five-year renewable term policy at a premium of $3 for each $1,000 coverage. At the age of 40, the premium for another five-year renewable term policy is likely to increase to $3.50 per $1,000. Although a renewable term policy tends to get expensive over time, it has the advantage of providing continuous insurance.

A *convertible term* policy allows the insured to switch from a term policy to a whole life insurance policy at the end of the term. This feature is desirable for a person who expects a substantial increase in income over time and wants to take advantage of the savings plan available with a whole life insurance policy. The premium goes up when the policy is converted to whole life. A *reentry term* policy provides for a two-track system in which the insured has to go through a medical examination at the time of policy renewal. If the insured passes the medical test, the policy is renewed at a given premium level. However, if the person fails the medical test, the policy is renewed at a higher premium. The difference between the two premiums is small while the insured is still young (less than 35 years old) and significantly large when the insured is over age 35. This allows for a competitive premium system and prevents an otherwise cross subsidy between high-risk and low-risk insured parties. A person may also choose to have a combination policy. For example, it is possible to acquire a five-year, renewable, level, convertible term policy.

In the late 1970s, whole life insurance became less desirable because high inflation caused a decline in the purchasing power of death benefits and savings. Consequently, new products were offered to counter the impact of inflation. Table 8.3 presents information on these "inflation-proof" products including variable, universal, and variable-universal life insurance.

TABLE 8.3 Variable, Universal, and Variable-Universal Life Insurance (Billions of Dollars)		
	1990	**1994**
Universal Life Insurance	1,518.7	2,114.0
Variable Life Insurance	52.1	102.0
Variable-Universal Life Insurance	114.0	338.6

Source: Life Insurance Fact Book Update, 1995, American Council of Life Insurance, p. 12.

Universal Life Insurance   Universal life insurance was introduced in 1979 during the height of inflation as an "inflation-proof" alternative. Under a universal plan, the size of the premium and the frequency of the payments are flexible within limits. The minimum premium is equal to an amount necessary to provide for term insurance. The maximum premium is dictated by the IRS, which sets the limit on the amount allowed under the tax-free status of policy loans. The payments in excess of the minimum are invested in a portfolio of securities whose returns are claimed to be inflation-hedged. Overall, the advantage of this policy over a whole life insurance policy lies within the relative flexibility of its premiums.

Variable Life Insurance   Variable life insurance is another "inflation-era" alternative where premiums paid are invested in equity-type securities. The death benefits fluctuate depending on the market value of the underlying assets with a guaranteed minimum.

Variable-Universal Life Insurance   Depending on the performance of the underlying assets, variable-universal life insurance combines the flexible premium feature of universal life insurance and the fluctuating death benefit of variable life insurance.

Group Life Insurance

Group life insurance constitutes 40% of the total life insurance in the United States. Group term life insurance constitutes more than 99% of total group life insurance. The remaining 1% includes survivor income benefit insurance and group accidental death and dismemberment insurance. The former pays monthly income benefits to eligible dependents if the insured is deceased, and the latter pays additional benefits if the employee dies in an accident or incurs bodily injuries.

Group term life insurance provides a low-cost, yearly renewable term insurance to the members of a well-defined group who are associated for some purpose other than purchasing life insurance. The eligible groups include employees of corporations or universities, and members of professional associations or labor unions. Depository financial intermediaries provide group term life insurance to their borrowers. If the borrower dies before full payment of the loan, the policy covers the outstanding loan balance.

The group term life insurance benefit typically amounts to one or two times the employee's annual salary. The policy is in place as long as the employee is a group member. If the employee leaves the group either by voluntary resignation or due to company reorganization, the cash value of the policy can be converted to an individual term insurance policy within 31 days. However, this right is rarely used by anyone other than those who are otherwise uninsurable. Since the conversion takes place at a premium consistent with the age of the insured, the cost may be too high. If the employee joins another organization, the cost of the new group term life insurance is generally cheaper than that of the converted policy. If the person remains unemployed, the cost may be unaffordable.

The lower cost of group term life insurance is due to the following factors. First, coverage of many persons under one contract provides administrative efficiencies. For example, premiums for employees of a corporation are collected from the employer, who either fully pays for the coverage or shares the charges with employees through payroll deductions. Second, group term insurance covers people whose average age does not change much over time. As some employees get older and retire, new and younger employees are brought into the plan. Premiums remain stable over time because the average age of the employees stays relatively unchanged. Third, since insurance is incidental to the group, there is less of an adverse selection problem. Potential employees may consider insurance benefits as one of several factors in joining an organization but not as an overriding reason.

Group term life insurance is generally used as a supplementary policy in conjunction with social security and individual life insurance. There are several reasons why group term life insurance may be inadequate as the only life insurance policy. First, group term life insurance is generally issued without any attention given to the individual needs of an employee. Second, if employment is terminated or if the plan is discontinued due to bankruptcy or some other type of organizational restructuring, the employee may be left without life insurance coverage. Finally, group term life insurance does not include savings, which may be of interest to the employee.

Industrial Life Insurance

Industrial life insurance is designed to meet the needs of low-income workers who have no other life insurance plan. It is generally for a small amount, $1,000 or less. The premiums are collected by insurance agents at the home of the insured on a weekly basis, which coincides with the workers' weekly paychecks.

Industrial life insurance is generally more expensive than others because people with low incomes often have higher risk of an early death than does the average person in the population. There have been abusive practices in the marketing of this plan wherein multiple policies have been sold to an individual. However, with greater expansion of other life insurance alternatives such as group plans, the total number and the amount of industrial life insurance contracts have declined in recent years.

Credit Life Insurance

Credit life insurance is designed to protect lenders against borrowers' death prior to repayment of a loan. The face value of insurance is typically set equal to the outstanding principal and interest on the loan. Mortgage loans and car loans are examples of loans that carry credit life insurance.

The Balance Sheet and Income Statement of Life Insurance Companies

Table 8.4 presents the consolidated balance sheet of U.S. insurance companies in 1970, 1980, and 1994. The combined assets of the industry reached $1.94 trillion in 1994. Since 1970, there has been a sharp change in the asset composition of the industry, most notably in mortgage holdings. Mortgages comprised 35.9% of the assets in 1970 but declined to 11.1% by 1994. This was partially caused by high interest rates in the late 1970s and early 1980s, which reduced the market value of mortgages and hence diminished their investment appeal. Additionally, interest

TABLE 8.4 U.S. Life Insurance Companies Balance-Sheet Composition						
	1970		1980		1994	
	$Billion	%	$Billion	%	$Billion	%
Assets						
Government Securities	$11.1	5.4%	$33.0	6.9%	$395.6	20.4%
Corporate Bonds	73.1	35.3	179.6	37.5	790.6	40.7
Corporate Stocks	15.4	7.4	47.4	9.9	281.8	14.5
Mortgages	74.4	35.9	131.1	27.4	215.3	11.1
Real Estate	6.3	3.0	15.0	3.1	53.8	2.8
Policy Loans	16.1	7.8	41.4	8.6	85.5	4.4
Other Assets	10.9	5.2	31.7	6.6	119.7	6.1
Total Assets	**$207.3**	**100%**	**$479.2**	**100%**	**$1,942.3**	**100%**
Liabilities and Net Worth						
Life Insurance Reserves	$115.4	55.7%	$197.9	41.3%	$468.5	24.1%
Health Insurance Reserves	3.5	1.7	11.0	2.3	58.0	3.0
Annuities	41.0	19.8	172.0	35.9	1,094.6	56.4
Supplementary Contracts	7.9	3.8	9.5	2.0	23.0	1.2
Other	19.9	9.6	48.0	10.0	129.5	6.6
Capital*	19.6	9.4	40.8	8.5	168.7	8.7
Total Liab. & Net Worth	**$207.3**	**100%**	**$479.2**	**100%**	**$1,942.3**	**100%**

*Capital = Mandatory securities or asset valuation reserves + interest maintenance reserves + surplus funds + capital (stock companies).

Source: Computed from *Life Insurance Fact Book Update*, American Council of Life Insurance, Washington, DC, 1995, pp. 41–42.

rates have become more volatile since the late 1970s, making mortgage portfolios especially vulnerable. As of December 1994, more than 75% of life insurance company assets were in government and corporate securities, from which about 60% were in fixed income securities and the rest were in corporate stocks.

On the liability and net worth side, life insurance reserves comprised 55.7% of the total in 1970, declining to 24.1% by 1994. Annuities increased from 19.8% to 56.4% during the same period. We will discuss annuities in detail in a later section.

Table 8.5 presents the 1994 income statement for the industry. Premiums and annuity considerations totaled $250.1 billion and benefit payments and operating expenses reached $451.9 billion, resulting in underwriting losses of $201.8 billion. Investment and other income produced $126.0 billion and $28.5 billion, respectively, generating pretax profits of $28.9 billion for the industry. This demonstrates the importance of investment income to the life insurance industry.

A Global Perspective on Life Insurance

Life insurance used in various countries may provide interesting information about similarities and differences in the standards of living and cultural factors across international communities. A comparison of the amounts of life insurance

TABLE 8.5 U.S. Life Insurance Companies Income Statement, 1994 (Billions of Dollars)	
Income	
Life Insurance Premiums	$96.3
Annuity Considerations	153.8
Health Insurance Premiums	76.2
Investment Income	126.0
Other Income	28.5
Total Income	**$480.8**
Expenses	
Benefit Payments	276.5
Additions to Policy Reserve Funds	121.6
Operating Expenses:	
Commissions to Agents	21.6
Home and Field Office Expenses	32.2
Total Expenses	**$451.9**
Income Before Taxes	**$28.9**
Taxes	13.9
Dividends	6.3
Total Taxes and Dividends	**$20.2**
Additions to Special Reserves and Surplus Funds	**$8.7**

Source: Computed from *Life Insurance Fact Book Update*, American Council of Life Insurance, Washington, DC, 1995, pp. 31 and 37.

utilized, however, may be inadequate since there are major differences in economic conditions, health standards, personal income levels, and other circumstances. A more useful measure is the ratio of life insurance to national income. Table 8.6 provides information on this ratio for several countries. It is interesting to note that Japan and South Korea have the first and second largest ratios, with 494% and 308%. Other countries with large ratios include South Africa, Canada, and Ireland. Countries that have life insurance amounts equal to or greater than their national income include Australia, France, the Netherlands, Norway, Sweden, the United States, and the United Kingdom.

ANNUITIES

While a life insurance policy provides financial protection to survivors against early death, an annuity provides financial protection to the insured (the annuitant) against a long life. This does not sound like a risk that a person would have to protect against, but living to old age without sufficient financial means is no small problem. An annuity provides a series of periodic payments that often will supplement other sources of income such as Social Security.

An annuitant may convert the cash value of a life insurance policy into an annuity upon reaching an age when the risk of early death is no longer an issue. Alternatively, an annuitant may invest a lump sum amount to start an annuity

TABLE 8.6			Ratio of Life Insurance in Force to National Income in Various Countries		
Country	**1988**	**1993**	**Country**	**1988**	**1993**
Australia	124%	170%	Japan	381%	494%
Austria	43	50	Korea	156	308
Belgium	68	76	Netherlands	182	217
Canada	192	239	Norway	97	137
Denmark	77	96	Pakistan	18	17
Fiji	56	75	Philippines	23	31
France	126	149	South Africa	194	249
Germany	77	96	Spain	50	81
Honduras	42	62	Sweden	125	152
Iceland	30	42	Thailand	15	19
India	22	32	Tunisia	5	6
Indonesia	6	11	U.K.	117**	131***
Ireland	210	224	U.S.	183	196
Italy	13	17*	Zambia	7	1

Note: National income data is on a "market prices" basis. In general, the figures represent life insurance in force on the lives of residents of the country with both domestic and foreign private companies. In a few cases, annuities are included; in other cases, the figures represent the total business of domestic companies of the country and/or insurance that has been issued by government organizations. *1991 data; **1987 data; ***1992 data.

Source: Life Insurance Fact Book Update, American Council of Life Insurance, Washington, DC, 1995, p. 59.

either immediately (single-premium immediate annuity) or on a deferred basis (single-premium deferred annuity).

Annuities have grown significantly in the last two decades. Annuities comprised only about 20% of the life insurance industry's liabilities in 1970 but increased to 56% by 1994. Some annuities guarantee fixed retirement income for life (fixed-dollar benefit plans). Others make flexible payments depending on the performance of the underlying portfolio (variable-dollar plans).

Fixed-Dollar Benefit Annuities

This type of annuity provides fixed periodic payments. For example, a benefit payment of $700 a month remains $700 a month for the contractual period. The following types of annuities are included in this category:

- Single-premium immediate annuity
- Level-premium annuity
- Single-premium deferred annuity
- Flexible-premium deferred annuity
- Period-certain life-income annuities
- Cash-refund annuity
- Installment-refund annuity
- Single-life annuity
- Joint-life annuity, including joint-and-survivor annuity and joint-and-one-half survivor annuity

A *single-premium immediate annuity* requires a lump sum payment and delivers a series of periodic payments immediately thereafter. For example, upon retirement, an individual invests $100,000 in a single-premium annuity with a life insurance company. Using a mortality table, the insurance company calculates the life expectancy of the annuitant and determines annuity payments of $700 per month. When the annuitant dies, the insurance company either discontinues the payments or transfers them to the survivors, depending on the specifications of the contract. Instead of investing a lump sum, a retired individual may convert a life insurance policy with accumulated cash benefits into a single-premium immediate annuity.

A *level-premium deferred annuity* allows for premiums to be paid over time and for benefits to begin at some later date. For example, a person may want to make a series of equal monthly payments of $400, beginning at age 50 and continuing until the age of 65. Thereafter, the insurance company will pay $700 a month for the rest of the annuitant's life.

In a *single-premium deferred annuity*, the premium payment is made at a certain date while the benefit payments begin at some later date. The annuitant may pay $47,000 at the age of 50 and start receiving $700 per month at age 65.

The annuities we have discussed require a fixed premium with a minimum of $5,000. Alternatively, one can purchase a *flexible-premium deferred annuity* that allows for uneven contributions of as little as $25 per month. This flexibility generates higher administrative expenses that are either deducted from each premium payment (a front-end load) or treated as a surrender charge (a back-end load).

The annuities previously described provide benefits as long as the annuitant lives. If the annuitant dies soon after benefits begin, payments will stop. If the annuitant lives longer than the average life expectancy for the age group, the payment will continue. An annuity insurance operation, therefore, transfers funds from those who die early to those who die late. Some annuitants receive more than they have contributed, while others receive less. Overall, the annuitants' benefits come from liquidated premiums, earned interest, and residual funds from early deaths. These annuities are called pure or straight-life annuities.

If an annuitant is unhappy with the prospect of losing a significant portion of the benefits due to a premature death, the insurance company may guarantee a minimum payment to the annuitant or a beneficiary. The guarantee includes either a minimum benefit period or a refund to the survivors in the case of early death.

A *period-certain life-income annuity* calls for payments for a certain number of years or until the annuitant dies, whichever occurs last. For example, a 10-year certain annuity guarantees a minimum of 10 years of benefit payments. If the annuitant dies in less than 10 years, a beneficiary will receive the balance of the payments. If the annuitant lives more than 10 years, the insurer has to continue the payments beyond the 10-year period. The premium is higher as the period-certain becomes longer.

A refund is also possible. A *cash-refund annuity* guarantees that if the annuitant dies before receiving benefits equal to premiums paid, a beneficiary will receive the balance of the premiums at the time of the annuitant's death. Another variation of the refund guarantee is the *installment-refund annuity*, which continues benefit payments to a beneficiary after the death of the annuitant until benefits equal the premiums paid.

Annuities are also structured either as a *single-life annuity*, covering only one life, or a *joint-life annuity*, covering two lives. Payments stop at the death of either annuitant with a joint-life annuity. Another variation of this type of annuity is called a *joint-and-survivor annuity*, wherein payments continue to the surviving partner either in full or in some fraction. For example, a *joint-and-*

one-half survivor annuity provides one-half of the benefits to the surviving partner.

Variable-Dollar Benefit Annuities

Variable annuities were developed in the late 1980s to mitigate the impact of inflation on the purchasing power of annuitants. A variable annuitant receives shares in equity and bond mutual funds. Accordingly, the size of benefits received depends on the performance of the mutual fund shares.

Similar to fixed-dollar benefit annuities, variable-dollar benefit annuities provide the annuitant with a tax-sheltered investment. During the period that premiums are paid (the accumulation period) there are no tax payments. The benefits paid to the annuitant after the age of 59½ are taxed only on the interest portion of the payments. For example, if the annuitant has contributed a total of $50,000 to a fund that provides for a series of benefit payments with a present value of $75,000, the annuitant has to pay taxes only on one-third of each payment (($75,000 − $50,000) ÷ $75,000 = ⅓). Suppose the monthly benefit payment is $600. From this amount one-third or $200 is taxable. If the annuitant is in the 28% marginal tax bracket, the tax liability is $200 × 0.28 = $56. However, if the annuitant withdraws before the age of 59½, there is a 10% penalty on top of the 28% tax on the income, which increases the tax liability to $200 × 0.38 = $76, a penalty of $20.

In recent years, insurance companies and other intermediaries have been advocating the use of variable annuities in IRA accounts. However, tax-deferred variable annuities in tax-deferred IRA accounts seem to have one tax-shelter wrapper too many. In a study of this phenomenon, Arthur Anderson concludes that "the variable annuity is not an appropriate vehicle for an IRA." [2] The problem lies with the high cost of investing in variable annuities and placing them in IRAs. The insurance cost of a variable annuity is about 1.25% of the assets annually. There is also an extra 0.92% fee to manage the stock or bond portfolio. The combined cost is 2.17%. Alternatively, the investor can place shares of a mutual fund into an IRA at a cost of 1.40%. Both are tax-sheltered but the former is more expensive. Suppose there are two investors, a mutual fund investor and a variable annuity investor who each roll $10,000 into IRAs. Further assume that both investments provide a return of 10% per year for 20 years. At the end of this period, the accumulated investments after paying taxes at 35% are $33,846 for the mutual fund investor and $29,357 for the variable annuity investor.

HEALTH INSURANCE

Prior to the Great Depression, health care services in the United States were purchased like other services by individuals paying for doctors, hospitals, and medication expenses out of their own pockets. In 1929, Baylor Hospital began to offer a prepaid hospital coverage plan for a group of 1,200 teachers, thus starting an insurance system that is known today as Blue Cross. The dramatic increase in health insurance occurred during World War II. The cause of this expansion may be traced back to a provision in the tax code adopted in 1913. According to this code, an employer's payment of employee fringe benefits was not taxable at the individual level, but was tax deductible for the employer. During World War II, when wages were frozen, companies started offering more generous fringe benefits to attract the best employees. In the post-war period, the wage freeze was eliminated, but the practice of offering health care as a fringe benefit continued.

---

[2] *The Wall Street Journal*, June 2, 1994, pp. C1 and C6.

By 1943, forty-three Blue Cross plans were operating across the nation. *Blue Cross* covers hospital expenses, and its companion, *Blue Shield*, covers doctors' fees and other outpatient expenses. Blue Cross and Blue Shield are operated as not-for-profit organizations.

The government's involvement in the health care system goes back to the enactment of Medicare and Medicaid by Congress in 1965. *Medicare* provides health care coverage for the elderly, while *Medicaid* covers the poor. This was a conscious effort to ensure that no American was denied health care due to old age and/or economic status.

Incentive Problems in the Health Care System

The purchase of health care services is different from the purchase of any other services in the economy in one crucial way. While consumers pay for the entire cost of other services, about 78% of the cost of health care is paid by a third party. The third party is either the government or an insurer who is hired by an employer to provide health care services. Even though ultimately the individual consumer pays for the health care costs through higher taxes and/or wage adjustments at the workplace, the amount of health care used at the individual level does not affect the person's direct contribution to the pool. This contributes to the overuse of health care services and rising health care cost.

A second incentive problem that contributes to more expensive health care is the increase in the practice of *defensive medicine*, a practice wherein physicians order excessive tests and procedures to reduce the likelihood of facing medical malpractice suits. Defensive medicine has become more common in recent years. In 1992 claims per 100 doctors reached 14.1.[3] Claims alleging failure to diagnose, improper treatment, and complications in surgery accounted for 81% of total claims. The most frequent and costly area of medical malpractice claims is in improper birth-related treatments. A 1992 survey conducted by the American College of Obstetricians and Gynecologists showed that 80% of these doctors were sued, a 71% increase over the previous five years. Of those sued, 25% were sued four or more times. The average medical malpractice jury award is over $1 million. During 1982–1992, there were 3,554 medical malpractice verdicts, and 944, or 26.6%, of medical malpractice verdicts were million-dollar judgments.

A third incentive problem in the health care system is one of adverse selection. The problem goes back to early experiences with Blue Cross. Originally, Blue Cross based its premiums on the cost of insuring a specific geographic area *(community-rated premium)*, with each resident paying an equal amount. This system, however, started an adverse selection problem where those with poor health or chronic illnesses bought insurance, and those with good health did not purchase insurance because of its high premiums. Over time, this system forced out healthy people.[4] To solve this problem, an experience-rated premium system was introduced that determined individual premiums based on age, sex, and health status. While an experience-rated premium system brought the healthy group back into the market by offering them actuarially determined premiums, it also created a problem wherein elderly people and those with preexisting conditions were effectively priced out of the system. Medicare provides insurance for the elderly, but others may remain without insurance coverage.

The incentive problems described here have contributed to the problems of (1) rising health care costs and (2) the lack of universal health insurance.

---

[3] *The Property/Casualty Insurance Fact Book*, Insurance Information Institute, New York, 1994, p. 64.

[4] New York State adopted a community-rate premium system in 1993. In less than one year, premiums increased by about one-third while the percentage of the uninsured increased substantially.

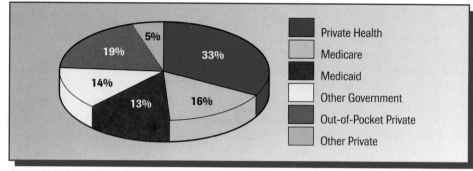

FIGURE 8.1
Composition of Health Care Providers

Source: Health Care Financing Administration, Office of Actuary; data from the Office of National Costs Estimates.

The Rising Cost of Health Care Insurance

When Congress enacted Medicare and Medicaid in 1965, the cost of health care was 5.9% of the nation's total output. This cost had increased to 14% in 1992 and is estimated to reach 19% in the year 2000 if the current system is not reformed.[5]

Americans paid $751.8 billion for health care in 1991, 12.8% more than they paid in 1990. This has been the trend over the past three decades, during which health care costs have grown at a rate significantly higher than the overall economy. Figure 8.1 presents the composition of health care providers in 1991. Government-sponsored health insurance programs (e.g., Medicare, Medicaid, Veterans Affairs, and others) covered 43%, and the private sector health insurance covered 33% of the insured population. The remaining 24% include out-of-pocket contributions and other private plans.

Using the data from 1991, Figure 8.2 shows where the insurance dollars go. Hospital costs amount to 38% of total health care costs, an increase of 11.8% over the 1990 figure. Physician services accounted for 19% of total costs. Professional services including physician services, dental services, and services of other professionals increased 11% over the 1990 cost. The pattern of increasing costs at a rate of 3–4 times that of the rate of inflation and the rate of economic growth are major sources of concern and important reasons for a demand for reform in the health care system.

Universal Health Insurance

Despite the fact that federal and state governments spent more than $328 billion in 1995 to provide medical care for the poor and the elderly through Medicaid and Medicare,[6] approximately 15% of the population—40 million people—still lack medical insurance. A significant portion of this group are employees of small businesses who do not have work-related insurance plans or people who are self-employed and unable to pay high premiums on an individual basis. Others may have lost their jobs due to economic cycles and have not yet found new jobs with health insurance coverage. The lack of universal coverage has been crit-

---

[5] See *Projections of National Health Expenditures,* Congressional Budget Office (CBO) study, October 1992, p. ix; and *Managed Competition and Its Potential to Reduce Health Spending,* CBO study, May 1993, p. ix.

[6] The cost projection for Medicare and Medicaid is as follows (Burner and Waldo, 1995):

Year	Medicare	Medicaid	Total
1995	$190.0 billion	$138.4 billion	$328.4 billion
2000	$293.5	$314.5	$608.0
2005	$450.9	$333.4	$784.3

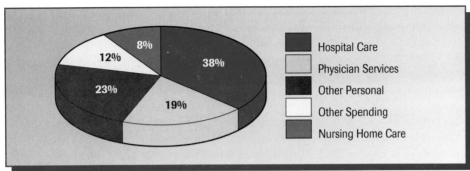

FIGURE 8.2
**Composition of Health
Insurance Costs**

Source: Health Care Financing Administration, Office of Actuary; data from the Office of National Costs Estimates.

icized on three grounds. First, some argue that this country, with all its rich resources, should take care of those who cannot provide health insurance for themselves. The proponents of this view argue that all other industrialized nations such as Canada and Japan provide universal health care and question why the United States does not. Second, those who do not have insurance still may use expensive emergency room services without being able to pay for them. In 1989, 6% of hospital costs were not reimbursed due to uncompensated care.[7] Hospitals then recover their uncompensated bills with higher charges levied against private providers or those paying out-of-pocket. Due to this cost shifting, individuals who have health insurance and those who pay out-of-pocket end up paying higher premiums and spending more on health care expenses. Third, the lack of universal coverage causes job-lock situations wherein people do not look for better jobs because they fear losing their health care coverage. Job-lock situations create economic inefficiencies by reducing the mobility of human capital toward the most efficient use in the market.

Opponents of universal coverage argue that in order to have universal access, the employers in small businesses must be forced to pay for insurance premiums. Many have stated that some small businesses may not be able to afford to pay the premiums, and this may force them either to close down their businesses or to hire fewer employees. Neither alternative is acceptable for this group. Small businesses also feel such a requirement is an infringement on the rights of private enterprise and is another sign of government intervention that is bad for business.

Market Initiatives to Resolve Health Insurance Problems

There have been some market initiatives to reduce health care expenses and to enable more people to have access to health care in the long run. Health maintenance organizations (HMOs) and preferred provider organizations (PPOs) have been developed to reduce the costs of health care.

HMOs operate in limited geographic areas, charge a set fee or capitation payment, and cover a broad range of health care services including physicians' charges, hospital costs, prescriptions, lab tests and procedures, and emergency care. The capitation payment does not change by usage, and the member pays a small fee of $5–$10 upon visiting a physician or filling a prescription in order to reduce the incentive for overuse of health services.

HMOs are private enterprises that strive for cost efficiency. They do so by

---

[7] See "Responses to Uncompensated Care and Public-Program Controls on Spending: Do Hospitals Cost Shift?" CBO paper, May 1993, Table B-2, p. 34.

several means. First, they provide periodic physical examinations and engage in preventive health care. Preventive health care reduces future costs of illnesses and hospitalizations. This is very different from not-for-profit operations such as Blue Cross and Blue Shield that generally do not cover preventive physical exams. Second, they reduce the cost of physicians' services by either hiring their own physicians or contracting with physicians with whom they pay a fixed amount per visit. HMOs are either group practice HMOs or individual practice association HMOs. With the former, physicians are hired to work for the HMO exclusively. With the latter, physicians may join several HMOs and charge them a prespecified fee for each visit. Both alternatives reduce the cost of physicians' fees and, perhaps more importantly, the costs of defensive medicine. Third, HMOs further reduce the amount of money spent on health care by limiting visits to specialists. A patient has to get permission from the assigned primary care physician prior to visiting a specialist. A study by the Congressional Budget Office (CBO) shows HMOs that have fully integrated their financing and delivery systems reduce hospital usage by about 20%.[8]

PPOs are associations of cooperating physicians and hospitals that contract with employers to provide health care services to employees at reduced rates. PPOs are different from HMOs in three areas. First, PPOs charge per number of visits while HMOs charge regardless of the frequency of usage. Second, PPOs do not require their members to use only the facilities of given physicians. If members choose to use other physicians not in the plan, the employer will pay 60% of the cost. If members choose to use physicians associated with the plan, the employer will pay 80% of the cost. With HMOs, the patient has to choose from a group of physicians and hospitals that have joined the plan. Third, PPOs may not cover annual physical exams, while HMOs do cover them. Studies show PPOs reduce hospital usage by about 8%.[9]

Government Initiatives to Reduce the Cost of Health Care

In recent years, Medicare and Medicaid costs have increased more than any other program in the health industry. In order to slow the growth of these costs, the Omnibus Budget Reconciliation Act of 1981 allowed states to pay reimbursements based on the expenses of an "economically and efficiently operated hospital."[10] A result of this change in policy is that some hospitals end up receiving less than their full costs in treating Medicare and Medicaid patients. In 1991, 88% of hospitals' Medicare costs and 82% of their Medicaid costs were reimbursed.

The CBO study also shows that an unintended side effect of a government cost control policy is that in 1991, 25% of U.S. physicians refused to treat Medicaid patients. This rate rises to 45% for reproductive-related services. Hospitals have also discouraged physicians from admitting Medicaid patients, which, in turn, encourages those patients to use emergency room facilities at even higher costs. Another side effect of paying a fixed rate for hospitals and doctors for the treatment of Medicare and Medicaid patients is cost-shifting. When a hospital does not receive the full fee for a patient, it shifts the costs in terms of higher fees to those with private insurance plans and those who pay out-of-pocket for health care expenses. While in 1985 the unreimbursed Medicare and Medicaid costs to hospitals was 0.6%, the figure increased to 5% in 1989.[11]

---

[8] "Rising Health Care Costs: Causes, Implications, and Strategies," CBO study, April 1991, p. 34.
[9] Ibid.
[10] Ibid., p. 42.
[11] See "Responses to Uncompensated Care and Public-Program Controls on Spending: Do Hospitals Cost Shift?" CBO paper, May 1993, Table B-2, p. 34.

Government plans, as shown earlier, provide 43% of total health care coverage in the United States. Double-digit increases in the costs of Medicare and Medicaid and the lack of insurance coverage for 40 million Americans have created a strong demand for health care reform.

Demand for Health Care Reform

Rising costs, lack of universal coverage, and a growing consensus that without reform the health care system will soon face major crises have propelled the public to demand health care reform. When President Clinton was running for office in 1992, one of his main campaign promises was to reform the health care system. Shortly after taking office in 1993, his administration sent a health care proposal to Congress that asked for universal coverage and an employer mandate to pay for employees' insurance. Since a large number of uninsured people were employed in small businesses, the employer mandate required them to purchase insurance for their employees. The conservative members of Congress opposed the bill on the grounds that it was too costly for small businesses and it required too much government involvement in health care. The bill was defeated.

What will happen if there is no health care reform? Some believe that without health care reform the percent of uninsured and the percent of government share of the health care cost will increase substantially in the near future.[12] This argument relies on the premise that large corporations are voluntarily paying high premiums to purchase health care coverage for their employees. Part of the high premiums collected from these employers are spent to cover the unreimbursed cost of the care provided to the uninsured. This pattern, however, is changing.

With rising health care costs, large employers have begun to trim their costs by requiring their employees to take blood, drug, and urine tests, as well as a physical exam. In some cases the employees are also required to provide information about family histories of heart disease, cancer, and genetic disorders. Some other employers also inquire about personal characteristics such as whether the employee rides a motorcycle, wears a seat belt, participates in sports, or has a happy marriage. Lockheed Aeronautical Systems Co., a subsidiary of Lockheed Corp., recently announced it would not hire smokers. Turner Broadcasting System Inc. in Atlanta has not hired any smokers since 1986. Employers use this information to determine preexisting conditions.

As the percent of self-insured employers increases (currently at 75%), employers realize that every dollar saved in health care cost is a dollar earned. These employers use their screening devices to hire and retain a healthier workforce. Often they hire a health care provider to provide health care services on their behalf and only purchase catastrophic insurance from insurance companies. As large corporations succeed in cutting their health care costs and negotiating lower premiums, insurance companies will no longer be able to shift costs of uninsured and underreimbursed patient care to large employers. As Medicare and Medicaid payments often fall below the costs incurred, the balance is covered from privately purchased insurance premiums paid by the large corporations. To the extent that large employers are successful in reducing their health care costs, the cost to the government will go up. This will also increase premiums to small businesses that currently provide health care coverage for their employees, and may force some small businesses to discontinue the coverage, increasing the number of uninsured.

---

[12] Wessel (1994), p. 1.

In 1996, limited health care legislation was passed, which would make health insurance portable for many people who switch or leave their jobs. While this health reform is not comprehensive, it is a step in that direction. The following are highlights of this legislation:

- It guarantees that people with employer-sponsored health plans will be able to obtain health insurance after switching or losing their jobs. Coverage cannot be denied because of existing medical problems.
- It guarantees coverage for those who leave an employer-sponsored plan, but does not set Federal limits on the premiums, leaving regulation to states.
- It assists employers and individuals in forming private, voluntary coalitions to obtain health insurance.
- It requires insurers to offer group health plans to all employers in markets where they operate.
- It forbids employer-sponsored health plans from denying coverage or charging higher premiums to individual employees because of their health problems.
- It gradually increases the tax deductions for health insurance purchased by the self-employed from the current 30% to 80%.
- It provides new tax breaks for people who purchase nursing home care or insurance to cover the cost of long-term care.
- It allows for accelerated tax-free payments of life insurance benefits to people who are terminally ill.

PROPERTY-CASUALTY INSURANCE

The property-casualty segment of the insurance business provides coverage for individual and commercial property and liability risks. At the end of 1994, the property-casualty insurance industry had a total of $704.6 billion in assets. Total premiums collected in the property-casualty insurance business amounted to $250.7 billion in 1994.[13]

There were 3,300 property-casualty insurance companies operating in the United States in 1994. While the largest 900 companies wrote most of the policies, no single company had more than 15% of the market. The 10 largest companies had a combined market share of 45%.[14]

Property-Casualty Insurance Products

Table 8.7 presents various property-casualty insurance lines and their definitions. Table 8.8 provides information about the relative importance of each line of insurance and its profitability. The biggest single line of insurance is that of automobile insurance, which constituted 45.2% of total premiums collected in 1994. Within the realm of automobile insurance, 38.6 percent was from the private passenger auto business and the balance was from commercial auto insurance. Automobile insurance has generally been a profitable line for the industry. The probability of occurrence and the size of losses attributed to automobile accidents can be predicted with relative accuracy. This makes it possible for insurers to charge premiums that accurately reflect expected losses.

A widely used profitability measure in property/casualty insurance is the *combined ratio,* a ratio of losses incurred plus the expenses due to loss adjustments and commissions divided by the premiums charged minus any dividends paid to policyholders as a proportion of premiums collected. If the ratio is less

---

[13] *Property/Casualty Insurance Fact Book*, Insurance Information Institute, New York, 1996, p. 5.
[14] Ibid.

TABLE 8.7   Definition of Major Property-Casualty Insurance Products

Private Passenger and Commercial Automobile	Provides liability, collision, and comprehensive coverage for owning and operating automobiles.
Non-Auto Liability	Covers medical, product, and general liability for damages caused by a policyholder to a third party.
Homeowners Multiple Peril	It combines features of both property and liability insurance to protect against multiple hazards to personal dwelling and to cover legal liability to a third person.
Commercial Multiple Peril	Similar to homeowners insurance but applied to commercial property.
Marine Insurance (Ocean and Inland)	Marine insurance covers risks associated with transportation. The ocean marine covers ships and their cargoes, while the inland marine covers air, rail, truck shipments, bridges, tunnels, pipelines, and radio and TV communication equipment.
Workers' Compensation	Protects against work-related injury and illness.
Surety Bonds	Insures against nonexecution of a contract. For example, a film studio requires a production company to purchase a guarantee from a surety that it will complete a motion picture on budget and on time. Building construction bids also require surety guarantees.
Fidelity Bonds	Common in financial intermediaries, they protect the employer against embezzlement, fraud, and theft by an employee who works with cash and marketable securities.

than 100%, then premiums are sufficient to cover the incurred losses. If the ratio exceeds 100%, the premiums are not sufficient and the extra losses need to be covered by the investment income and capital gains generated by assets of the insurance companies.

In 1994, collision and comprehensive automobile insurance were profitable, but liability insurance was not. Non-auto liability insurance had a total of 9.4% of premiums, including medical malpractice, general liability, and product liability insurance. Unlike automobile insurance, liability insurance losses are difficult to predict. The probability of occurrence and the size of the losses are difficult to determine with any degree of accuracy. In recent years the cost of liability insurance has increased significantly. The combined ratios in 1992 for the three lines of non-auto liability insurance were 94.2 (medical malpractice), 125.1 (general liability), and 130.8 (product liability).

Losses due to liability insurance have increased significantly in recent years because juries have had the tendency to award large punitive damages. Liabil-

TABLE 8.8   Composition and Profitability of Property-Casualty Insurance Products, 1994

	% of Total Premiums[a]	Combined Ratio[b]
Private Passenger Auto		
Liability	24.7	104.9
Collision & Comprehensive	13.9	92.6
Total Private Passenger Auto	38.6	
Commercial Auto		
Liability	4.8	108.2
Collision & Comprehensive	1.8	93.0
Total Commercial Auto	6.6	
Total Automobile	45.2	
Non-Auto Liability		
Medical Malpractice	1.9	94.2
General Liability	6.7	125.1
Product Liability	0.8	130.8
Total Non-Auto Liability	9.4	
Fire/Allied Lines	3.5	106.4/112.5
Homeowners Multiple Peril	9.0	118.0
Farm Owners Multiple Peril	0.5	108.2
Commercial Multiple Peril	7.1	118.7
Workers' Compensation	11.5	95.1
Inland Marine	2.0	100.6
Ocean Marine	0.7	107.8
Surety/Fidelity	1.3	90.9/75.4
Financial Guaranty	0.9	
Burglary and Theft	0.0	59.3
Boiler and Machinery	0.3	93.9
Glass	0.0	105.4
Aircraft	0.3	
Accident and Health	2.9	
Other Lines	5.4	
Total, All Lines	100%	107.1

[a]Net premiums for each line of insurance as a percentage of total premiums received in 1994.
[b]The combined ratio is a measure of profitability. It is the ratio of claims paid plus expenses divided by total premiums received. If the number is less than 100, it means the premiums received were sufficient to cover the costs, thus, the line is profitable. If the ratio is greater than 100, the premiums received were less than the sum of claims and expenses and the difference constitutes underwriting losses.

Source: Property/Casualty Insurance Fact Book, Insurance Information Institute, New York, 1996, pp. 13–14, 22–31.

ity insurance compensates the claimant for the injury incurred and the cost of defending the policyholder in court. From 1986 to 1994 all but seven states passed liability reform laws. For example, Michigan has enacted legislation that caps noneconomic damages at either $200,000 or $500,000, depending on the severity of the injury. Arizona enacted a law that allows the jury to learn whether a plaintiff had been compensated for the injury by another source and provides for periodic payments for future medical expenses instead of lump-sum payments. North Dakota passed a medical malpractice reform law that limits punitive damages to $250,000 or double compensatory damages, whichever is larger. Texas passed a new product liability law that, among other things, allows for immunity for manufacturers from liability 15 years after a product is sold. Mississippi established a clear standard for punitive damages. Several other states are also currently considering liability reform laws.

The homeowners multiple peril and commercial multiple peril generated more than 16% of the net premiums collected in 1994. Approximately 95% of the nation's home owners carry household insurance. The combined ratios for homeowner and commercial multiple peril were 118.0 and 118.7, respectively. Although a major improvement over the combined ratio of 158 in 1992—the year of Hurricanes Andrew and Iniki—the Northridge earthquake and severe winter weather caused considerable damage in 1994. Hurricane Andrew caused a total loss of $15.5 billion, Hurricane Iniki caused a loss of $1.6 billion, and the Northridge earthquake brought an estimated loss of $12.5 billion. Other losses of recent years include the Los Angeles civil disorder of April 29–May 4, 1992, that cost $775 million.

Overall, the combined ratio for all lines of insurance was 107.1 in 1994. For every $1 received in premiums, there were $1.07 in losses and other payments. Despite tremendous losses experienced by property-casualty insurance companies in recent years, the industry remains relatively healthy. This is because the industry has earned substantial investment income over those years.

Balance Sheet and Income Statement of the U.S. Property-Casualty Insurance Industry

Tables 8.9 and 8.10 present the balance sheet and the income statement for the property-casualty insurance industry in 1994. More than 62% of assets are invested in government and corporate bonds and another 14% are invested in corporate equity. Thus, the securities portfolio of the industry constitutes more than 76% of its assets. The investment income and capital gains from these investments provide further coverage for incurred losses.

The profit (loss) statement shows a $22.2 billion underwriting loss for 1994. The investment income of $33.7 billion and realized capital gains of $1.7 billion were more than sufficient to cover the underwriting losses. The securities portfolios of the insurance companies have enjoyed healthy returns in recent years due to the decline in interest rates and improvements in the general state of the economy. Despite losses in the underwriting business, the industry had a net income of $10.9 billion in 1994.

LLOYD'S OF LONDON[15]

Lloyd's of London is not an insurance company; rather, it is the oldest and most famous insurance market. Having traded for some 300 years, it has grown to a size where collectively it generates more than £11 billion annually in premiums. It earns the majority of its income in U.S. dollars and trades in many countries in

---

[15] The information about Lloyd's operation is derived from *Lloyd's Global Results, Membership: The Issues, Statutory Statement of Business and Statistics Relating to Lloyd's,* all published by the Corporation of Lloyd's. Further data was obtained from Insurance Research published by UBS Global Research. Our visits and conversations with the following Lloyd's directors provided us with valuable insights: Tim Holbech and Emma Royds, Directors; Christie Brockbank Shipton Limited (members' agents); David Ambrose, Managing Director; Clarkson Bain Limited (international brokers); and N. S. Foden-Pattinson, Director, J. H. Minet Reinsurance Brokers Limited. Many thanks for their insights and kindness.

TABLE 8.9   Balance-Sheet Composition of U.S. Property-Casualty Insurance Companies, 1994

	$ Billion	% of Total Assets
Assets		
Bonds:		
U.S. Government Bonds	$133.0	18.9%
Other Government Bonds	6.1	0.9
State, Municipal Bonds	72.0	10.2
Special Revenue Bonds	132.1	18.7
Others	99.0	14.1
Total Bonds	**$442.2**	**62.8%**
Common Stock	100.4	14.2
Preferred Stock	11.7	1.7
Mortgages	3.8	0.5
Collateral Loans	0.1	0.0
Other Assets	146.4	20.8
Total Assets	**$704.6**	**100%**
Liabilities & Net Worth		
Policy Liabilities	511.3	72.6
Capital Surplus	193.3	27.4
Total Liabilities & Net Worth	**$704.6**	**100%**

Source: Computed from *Property/Casualty Insurance Fact Book,* Insurance Information Institute, New York, 1996, p. 20.

virtually every part of the world. Lloyd's is known for underwriting an extensive array of insurance policies.

The History of Lloyd's of London

In the late 17th century, Edward Lloyd, who ran a coffeehouse in London, encouraged people with seagoing trade to meet in his establishment and to share in

TABLE 8.10   Profit (Loss) in the U.S. Property-Casualty Insurance Business, 1994 (Billions of Dollars)

Earned Premiums	$244.3
Incurred Loss (Including Loss Adjustment Expense)	(198.1)
Underwriting Expenses	(65.3)
Policyholder Dividends	(3.1)
Underwriting Loss	(22.2)
Investment Income	33.7
Other Items	0.1
Operating Gain	11.6
Realized Capital Gains	1.7
Income Before Taxes	13.3
Income Taxes	(2.4)
Net After-Tax Income	$10.9

Source: Computed from *Property/Casualty Insurance Fact Book,* Insurance Information Institute, New York, 1996, p. 6.

the risks encountered by vessels. They did this by writing their names under the wordings of insurance policies, thereby initiating the terminology of an "Underwriter" and a "Name." These individuals, or Names, had substantial wealth that enabled them to pay claims as they arose, ensuring the reputation for the security of Lloyd's policy. The Names later organized themselves into a group, or "syndicate," in which one person became the known leader through whom the others underwrote the risk.

Lloyd's initially engaged in marine insurance and Edward Lloyd was instrumental in providing shipping information. This information-gathering became an important part of Lloyd's business; in fact, in 1734 a newspaper was founded, *Lloyd's List*, which is now Britain's oldest newspaper.

Nonmarine insurance was developed during the 19th century. Today, Lloyd's is involved in four general categories of insurance: marine, nonmarine, aviation, and motor. Each of these categories includes a wide variety of different risks. For example, Lloyd's has issued policies for risks inherent in the launch and operation of satellites; the failure of a sovereign government to honor its contractual obligations; the loss of aircraft to terrorist attacks; and the reinsurance of insurance companies underwriting natural disasters such as earthquakes, hurricanes, and floods. More specialized policies issued by Lloyd's include a concert pianist's hands, the legs of a racehorse, the kidnapping of a wealthy individual, and protection for a major art exhibit.

Market Structure

Lloyd's is a marketplace situated in the Lloyd's building currently located at No. 1 Lime Street, London. Lloyd's is a collective name for all the underwriters who trade in "the Room," although this name refers to five floors in the Lloyd's building. Policies issued under the name of Lloyd's are actually underwritten by syndicates on behalf of the Names. The marketplace consists of four sets of separate but interdependent trading groups: (1) the broker, (2) the underwriter, (3) the Name, and (4) the underwriting agency.

The Broker The insurance broker is the intermediary between a client who wishes to insure certain risk and the insurance underwriter. The underwriter does not generally have any contacts with the client and conducts all business with the broker. Once the underwriter accepts the risk, the broker handles all of the paperwork and any claims that may subsequently arise. The broker receives a percentage of the insurance premium known as brokerage.

The Underwriter The underwriter of insurance is a professional trader who is employed on behalf of a group of Names, collectively known as a Lloyd's syndicate. The underwriter has complete discretion on the type of risk being covered and on its terms and conditions. While the underwriter is employed by a managing agency, the ultimate responsibility is given to the Names on whose behalf policies are issued. To ensure prudence, the underwriter is a Name on the syndicate who personally takes the largest portion of the risk underwritten, and is also generally a specialist in a certain type of insurance.

The Name The Name is a private individual who pledges all personal assets to support the insurance policy issued by an underwriter on the Name's behalf. The total amount of premium income the underwriter or underwriters accept on behalf of a Name depends on the amount of assets held in trust by Lloyd's on behalf of the Name. To diversify risk, a Name generally underwrites through a number of syndicates specializing in a variety of risks. The size of the Name's overall portfolio starts at £250,000 per year and increases to £3 million. With the advise of the Members' Agency and based on the Name's wealth, the amount of exposure, known as the Name's "Overall Premium Limit" (OPL), is agreed upon annually and split among the syndicates. The Name is required to have "Funds at Lloyd's" in the form of security deposits at the Members' Agency and the Corporation of Lloyd's equal to 30% of the OPL. It is important to note that regardless of the size of the overall portfolio, the line of risk, or "Funds at Lloyd's," a Name has unlimited liability. When a loss occurs on a particular syndicate, the Name is responsible solely for the loss proportionate to the Name's share in the syndicate. If another Name in that same syndicate is unable to fulfill the loss obligation, other Names on the syndicate have no liability for the failure to pay by that Name. The obligation of the Name who is unable to pay is paid for by a General Guarantee Fund to which All Names subscribe and pay 0.6% of their respective annual premium limit. There are currently more than 22,000 Names in Lloyd's of London.

The Underwriting Agency   These agencies fall into two categories: the Managing Agency and the Members' Agency. The Managing Agency recruits the underwriters and managers for one or more syndicates. The Members' Agency represents the Names on all aspects of Lloyd's membership, most significantly in the area of choosing the annual portfolio of syndicates. The decision as to which Members' Agency a Name should join is critical. Every Members' Agency is required to provide the prospective members with its business philosophy, policies, and practices for placement of members in syndicates. Some Members' Agencies are owned by Managing Agencies and are known as combined Managing/Members' Agencies, while others are owned by Brokers. There are also Members' Agencies that are independent.

Regulation of Lloyd's

Lloyd's activities are regulated by various Acts of British Parliament from 1871 to 1982. These acts have enabled Lloyd's to draw up a set of self-regulatory rules for the conduct of its operations "in accordance with both present-day requirements and practice in the interests of Lloyd's policy-holders." The acts have established the Council of Lloyd's and have empowered it with the responsibilities for all of the legislative and disciplinary functions of the market. This includes the regulation of the insurance business at Lloyd's; the election of new underwriting members, agents, and brokers; the establishment of an effective disciplinary process for offenders against the policies; and continuous review of all governing rules of Lloyd's.

The council is composed of Names who work at Lloyd's; Names who do not work at Lloyd's; and persons nominated by the Bank of England, the British central bank. The council delegates its powers to the Committee of Lloyd's for various matters. The Committee of Lloyd's, which is composed of the working Names of the council, handles the day-to-day operation of the market.

The Lloyd's Corporation, which consists of a large central support staff, manages the details of self-regulation and market coordination. This task, however, does not involve an active underwriting of risks. Lloyd's charges an annual 0.5% subscription fee of the allocated premiums, which goes toward covering the costs of operating the Corporation of Lloyd's.

Ownership Structure and Incentive Conflicts in Lloyd's of London

As we explained earlier, some Members' Agencies are owned by Managing Agencies and are known as combined Managing/Members' Agencies, some are owned by Brokers, and others are independent. There is the potential for con-flicts of interest within each group.

An independent Members' Agency has no managed syndicates and therefore it may be able to take an independent view of the syndicates with which it has arrangements. A typical independent Members' Agency[16] charges an annual fee of 0.675% of a Name's allocated premium limit and a commission of 7.5% on the Name's overall profit. Since an independent Members' Agency earns the bulk of its income when a Name earns large profits, we expect them to do their best to that end.

Members' Agencies associated with Lloyd's Brokers are generally in the same position as independent Members' Agencies, except that they usually have more contacts in the underwriting community through their brokerage connections. The incentives in these agencies should be similar to those in independent ones.

A combined Managing/Members' Agency can offer places to a Name on syndicates it manages and it can also exchange places on other combined agen-cies' syndicates. This possible advantage has to be weighed against the impartial view of syndicates that an independent Members' Agency can provide.

Conflicts of interest may develop when a combined Managing/Members' Agency places a Name on its managed syndicate although the risk in that syndi-cate may be unacceptable to the Name. On the surface, this should not happen because a combined agency is required to disclose the type and size of syndicates it manages before a Name joins its membership. However, there have been cases where a Name has requested to be placed on a conservative portfolio of low-risk syndicates and has instead been allocated to high-risk ones.

In 1993, a group of Names brought litigation against their Members' Agency involving losses of over £3 billion ($4.5 billion). In a landmark case, a British High Court judge made an unprecedented ruling that a Members' Agency was li-able for losses incurred by two Names.[17] Separately, the House of Lords rejected an appeal from 71 Members' Agents who claimed they were not liable for negli-gence. This cleared the way for legal cases seeking damages. On October 31, 1995, the court ruled in favor of some 2,000 Names who had claimed damages for negligence from their agents, underwriters, and auditors. For the first time, an auditing firm (Ernst & Young) was found negligent in a Lloyd's case. The total claim against Ernst & Young amounted to £1.5 billion.[18]

Profitability and Financial Position of Lloyd's of London

With over 300 years of continuous trading, Lloyd's has recorded only seven years of overall losses[19], including the most recent four years for which financial data exist. The total loss for 1988–1991 amounted to £8.5 billion. Table 8.11 pro-vides the details.[20]

To provide more detail on how these profitability figures are calculated, we present the full financial statement for 1990 in Table 8.12.

---

[16] Christie Brockbank Shipton Limited.

[17] *Financial Times*, April 14, 1994, p. 1. In a later ruling on October 4, 1994, the High Court ordered record compensation for losses incurred by Names in the now-defunct Gooda Walker agency. The judgment provided encouragement for other groups of Names taking action against Lloyd's agencies. See *Financial Times*, October 5, 1994, p. 1.

[18] *The Economist*, November 4, 1995, p. 84. At the time of this writing, Lloyd's is trying to persuade the 17,000-odd Names who are suing agents, auditors, and Lloyd's itself for negligence to drop their liti-gation and settle at about £2.8 billion. Names are asking for £4 billion. See *The Economist*, November 18, 1995, p. 83.

[19] This includes actual results through 1990 and projected results for 1991. Because of the three-year ac-counting method used by Lloyd's, the actual financial results for 1991 become available in June 1994.

[20] Lloyd's financial data are published with several years of lag.

TABLE 8.11 The Overall Profitability (Loss) for Lloyd's of London, 1984–1991 (£ Millions)		
Year	Profit (Loss) to Names Before Tax	$/£
1984	290	1.48
1985	196	1.88
1986	649	1.81
1987	509	1.61
1988	(510)	1.93
1989	(2,063)	1.87
1990	(2,915)	1.51
1991	(3,000)*	1.50

*Estimated loss reported in the *Financial Times*, April 6, 1994, p. 8.

Source: Global Results 1992, Corporation of Lloyd's.

The figures in Tables 8.11 and 8.12 reflect the aggregate results of 431 syndicates at Lloyd's with open accounts as of December 31, 1992.

Recent losses at Lloyd's reflect unusually high numbers of natural disasters. In the next section we examine the performance patterns of Lloyd's and the insurance companies in the United States and the United Kingdom.

TABLE 8.12 Profitability Computation for Lloyd's of London, 1990 (£000)	
Premiums	
Gross premiums	9,325,817
Premiums in respect of reinsurance ceded	(4,045,318)
Reinsurance premiums received from previous accounts	9,060,143
Total premiums available	**14,340,642**
Claims	
Gross claims	16,722,073
Reinsurance recoveries	(10,817,870)
Reinsurance premiums paid to close the account	10,854,091
Total claims	**16,758,294**
Underwriting Results	
Total Premiums—Total Claims	**(2,417,652)**
Investment Income	
Gross investment income	590,612
Gross investment appreciation	155,414
Loss on currency exchange	(90,013)
Net investment results	**656,013**
Expenses	
Syndicate expenses	696,408
Names' expenses: annual subscription; agents' fees; commissions	456,845
Total expenses	**(1,153,253)**
Loss attributable to Names before tax	**(2,914,892)**

Source: Global Results 1992, Corporation of Lloyd's.

A COMPARISON OF THE PROFITABILITY OF UNITED STATES AND UNITED KINGDOM INSURANCE COMPANIES WITH THAT OF LLOYD'S

Comparisons of the performance of insurance companies in the United States and the United Kingdom with that of Lloyd's require a careful selection of variables. There are at least two problems that must be addressed. First, insurance companies hold their shareholders' capital whereas Lloyd's syndicates do not. For insurance companies, profitability can be measured as returns on capital. A comparable measure for Lloyd's would require not only the reserves and deposits of Names at Lloyd's but also their personal wealth. This stems from the fact that Names have unlimited liability on the policies that are underwritten on their behalf. The second problem arises from differences in accounting methods. Taxes are also different, so we need to concentrate on some pretax figures. The performance measure with the least problem is the ratio of profits to net written premiums. For Lloyd's the profit (loss) figure used is that attributable to Names before tax, as shown in the last two tables. Two adjustments need to be made to Lloyd's premiums. First, the "reinsurance to close" must be excluded. This refers to the procedure at Lloyd's whereby an account is normally closed at the end of the third year by the payment of "reinsurance to close" to the successor syndicate. Second, since Lloyd's premium income is net of brokerage, the amount is "grossed up" to be comparable to those figures for insurance companies. For the U.S. insurance industry, stock companies are included. With these adjustments made, the results are presented in Table 8.13.

The results indicate that Lloyd's outperformed both U.S. and U.K. insurers from 1978 to 1987. Lloyd's best performance was in 1986 with returns of 13.6%.

TABLE 8.13 Comparative Insurance Profits as Percentage of Net Written Premiums U.S., U.K., and Lloyd's Insurance: 1978–1992

Year	U.S. Insurers	U.K. Composites	Lloyd's
	%	%	%
1978	9.1	8.7	11.1
1979	7.3	6.3	9.4
1980	5.3	5.3	11.8
1981	4.1	3.9	6.4
1982	1.3	0.4	3.3
1983	−1.9	−0.1	2.8
1984	−8.6	−4.0	7.6
1985	−8.9	−4.4	5.0
1986	0.4	3.5	13.6
1987	5.4	4.0	9.3
1988	6.5	6.6	−10.3
1989	3.2	2.1	−39.4
1990	3.0	−9.8	−45.5
1991	3.5	−13.1	−43.2
1992	−1.5	−4.5	NA

Sources: U.S. (A.M. Best Company Inc.), U.K. (UBS Research Limited), Lloyd's (*Lloyd's Global Results, Lloyd's Business Plan, Statutory Statement of Business and Statistics Relating to Lloyd's,* all published by Corporation of Lloyd's). Certain adjustments were made as described in the text.

However, since 1988 Lloyd's has incurred tremendous losses. The 1988–1991 period has provided the worst results in Lloyd's history. The Piper Alpha oil platform incident in 1988, Hurricane Hugo in 1989, and Hurricane Andrew in 1992 are the main causes of the reported losses in recent years. Because of the differences in accounting procedures, we should not assume that all of the losses from an event are presented in the same year. For example, Lloyd's results show a −10.3% for 1988, while those for the U.K. did not fully capture their 1988 losses until 1990.

The business of these three groups of insurers are, of course, quite different. Lloyd's underwrites in large international risks with an emphasis on marine and international reinsurance, which are generally riskier than other lines of insurance. The overall pattern seems to be that Lloyd's does particularly well when insurance is very profitable, which is associated with an increase in insurance rates and a decrease in the number of natural disasters. Conversely, Lloyd's does significantly worse than its competitors when the insurance market is faced with large-scale losses. The U.S. and U.K. insurers face a more cyclical market. In recent years U.S. insurers have performed relatively well despite the losses due to Hurricanes Hugo and Andrew. It appears that a higher proportion of Hurricane Andrew's loss was retained in the U.S. market than was the case with Hurricane Hugo. Overall, Lloyd's has higher risk in its insurance portfolio than U.S. and U.K. insurance companies.

SUMMARY

Nondepository financial intermediaries play an increasingly important role in the market for financial services. This is evident from the phenomenal increase in their market shares vis-à-vis a corresponding decline in the shares of depository financial intermediaries. The major categories of nondepository financial intermediaries are insurance companies, pension funds, mutual funds, and finance companies. We have examined in detail various types of insurance companies including life, health, and property and casualty insurance. The next chapter continues our discussion of nondepository financial intermediaries by analyzing pension funds, mutual funds, and finance companies.

Total assets for life-health insurance companies amounted to $1.9 trillion in 1994. More than 75% of life insurance assets are invested in corporate and government bonds and equities. Mortgage holdings that comprised 36% of total assets in 1970 declined to about 11% by 1994. On the liability side, the most important single item consisted of annuities with 56%. Life insurance reserves amounted to another 24%. It is interesting to note that in 1970, life insurance reserves comprised 56% while annuities totaled 20%. Within two decades, life insurance companies have almost tripled their annuities while their traditional life insurance reserves have declined to less than half by 1994. The underwriting and annuity business of life insurance companies lost $201.8 billion in 1994 but their investment portfolios earned $154.5 billion, resulting in an overall pretax profit of $28.9 billion in 1994.

Health insurance entered the center of the political debate in the United States during the presidential election of 1992. When Mr. Clinton was elected, one of the first campaign promises he tried to fulfill was that of health care reform. A bill was produced and debated in Congress during the 1993–1994 session. The main features of the health care bill were universal coverage and employer mandates to pay for premiums of their employees. The bill did not pass.

The demand for reform arises from two interrelated problems—increasing costs and the lack of insurance coverage for some 40 million Americans. Americans paid $751 billion for health care in 1991, 13% more than they paid the previous year. In fact, this has been the trend in the last three decades, where health care costs have grown at a rate significantly higher than that of the overall economy.

Health care insurance is offered by both the government and private sectors. Government-sponsored health care plans include Medicare and Medicaid, which cover 43%; private plans cover 33% of the insured. The cost of health care is increasing in both sectors.

Property-casualty insurance companies cover individual and commercial property and liability risk. At the end of 1994, the property-casualty insurance industry had a total of $704.6 billion in assets. There were 3,300 companies in the industry, from which the 900 largest companies wrote most of the policies. The 10 largest companies had a combined market share of 45%. From an array of insurance products, auto insurance underwriting has been profitable. However, other areas, such as property insurance and medical, product, and general liability underwriting, have lost significant amounts of money in recent years. Property losses due to natural disasters such as Hurricane Andrew in Florida and Louisiana, Hurricane Iniki in Hawaii, and the Midwest flood, among others, have been substantial. Despite efforts to reinsure some of the natural disaster risks with Lloyd's of London, property insurance underwriting has lost money for the industry. Operating losses amounted to $22.2 billion in 1994. As with life insurance companies, the investment portfolios of property-casualty insurance companies performed quite well, bringing in $35.4 billion in profit, which produced an overall pretax profit of $13.2 billion for the industry.

Lloyd's of London is a unique operation in the insurance business. Lloyd's is not an insurance company; it is an insurance market. Having traded for 300 years, it has grown to a size where it generates more than £11 billion in annual premiums. Lloyd's underwrites an extensive array of insurance policies and is an important underwriter in the reinsurance business. Partially due to reinsurance losses associated with natural disasters including Piper Alpha in the North Sea, and Hurricanes Hugo and Andrew, Lloyd's has lost money in recent years. The total losses for 1988–1991 amounted to £8.5 billion.

REVIEW QUESTIONS

1. Define nondepository financial intermediaries and compare them with depository financial intermediaries.
2. The share of nondepository financial intermediaries in the financial services market has increased in recent years while the share of depository financial intermediaries has decreased. Explain the reasons.
3. Briefly explain the economic principles of insurance. Explain how an insurance pool provides a socially desirable function in risk coverage.
4. Define the four major categories of life insurance products: ordinary, group, industrial, and credit life insurance.
5. Compare and contrast whole life, term, and universal life insurance.
6. What are the three reasons for lower cost in group life insurance?
7. If life and property-casualty insurance companies have been losing money in their underwriting functions, how do they stay in business?
8. Define fixed-dollar benefit annuities in general and provide a brief definition for each of the following categories:
   - single-premium immediate annuity
   - level-premium annuity
   - single-premium deferred annuity
   - flexible-premium deferred annuity

- period-certain life-income annuity
- cash-refund annuity
- installment-refund annuity
- single-life annuity
- joint-life annuity

9. Define variable-dollar benefit annuities. Provide some examples.
10. What are two major problems in the health care system?
11. What are the reasons for increasing costs of health care in the United States?
12. What are the incentive problems in the health care system?
13. Define major government-sponsored health plans. What percentage of total health insurance is provided by these plans?
14. Discuss the relationship between the increasing cost of health care and the lack of universal health insurance coverage.
15. Describe the important issues in the health care reform.
16. Explain the risks that property-casualty companies underwrite.
17. Briefly explain the following property-casualty insurance products and indicate if they have been profitable in recent years:

- private passenger and commercial automobile
- non-auto liability
- homeowners multiple peril
- commercial multiple peril
- marine insurance (ocean and inland)
- workers' compensation
- surety bonds
- fidelity bonds

18. What is a combination ratio? What is the range of combination ratios for a profitable insurance product?
19. Briefly explain the functions of Lloyd's of London. What distinguishes Lloyd's from other insurance entities?
20. What are the major risks that Lloyd's of London underwrites?
21. Discuss the market structure of Lloyd's of London and define four trading groups that comprise Lloyd's.
22. Who are ultimate risk bearers in Lloyd's? Who are Lloyd's "Names"?
23. What are the incentive problems in the operation of Lloyd's of London?

REFERENCES

Burner, S. T., and D. R. Waldo. 1995. "National Health Expenditure Projections: 1994–2005." *Health Care Financing Review* (Summer): 221–242.

Life Insurance Fact Book. 1995. Washington, DC: American Council of Life Insurance.

Lloyd's Global Results 1992. 1993. London: Corporation Lloyd's.

Lloyd's of London: A Comparative Analysis. 1993. London: UBS Global Research (May).

"Managed Competition and Its Potential to Reduce Health Spending." 1993. CBO study (May).

Membership: The Issues. 1993. London: Corporation of Lloyd's.

Mutual Fund 1995 Fact Book, Washington, DC: Investment Company Institute.

Planning for Profit: A Business Plan for Lloyd's of London. 1993. London: Corporation of Lloyd's (April).

"Projections of National Health Expenditures." 1992. CBO study (October).

Property/Casualty Insurance Fact Book. 1996. New York: Insurance Information Institute.

"Rising Health Care Costs: Causes, Implications, and Strategies." 1991. Washington, DC: CBO study (April).

Statutory Statement of Business and Statistics Relating to Lloyd's. 1993. London: Corporation of Lloyd's.

"Responses to Uncompensated Care and Public-Program Controls on Spending: Do Hospitals Cost Shift?" 1993. CBO paper (May).

"Trends in Health Spending: An Update." 1993. CBO study (June).

Wessel, D. 1994. "Health-Care Inaction Can Carry a High Cost." *The Wall Street Journal* (June 27): 1.

C H A P T E R

9

Nondepository Financial Intermediaries: Pension Funds, Mutual Funds, Investment Banks, and Finance Companies

OBJECTIVES

This chapter continues the examination of nondepository financial intermediaries by addressing pension funds, mutual funds, investment banks, and finance companies. Our discussion of pension funds covers funds set up by employers and other privately purchased annuities. We examine open-end investment companies (mutual funds) and closed-end investment companies. Finally, we present investment banks and finance companies.

PENSION FUNDS

In this section we look at intermediaries that provide retirement income. In the United States, retirement income comes in the form of Social Security, which is often supplemented by employer-funded pension plans. A pension plan is an agreement to provide retirement income to its participants. A pension fund is the intermediary that collects the pension contributions, invests the proceeds, manages the assets, and pays the benefits.

A Historical Perspective on Retirement Funds

"The relationship between a civilization's socio-economic structure and its culture is perhaps the most complicated of all problems. . . ." [1] In 19th-century tradition, elderly people lived with their adult sons and daughters and were provided for during retirement years. There were few worries about being old and poor, since the culture demanded that families take care of their aged members. The advanced capitalist system has brought its own distinct culture, character-

---

[1] Bell (1978), p. 33.

ized by individualism and self-reliance. This culture has absolved the children of the aged of direct responsibility for their parents. Thus, during their years of economic productivity, individuals are expected to plan for their own retirement savings or pension plans.

The first major pension plan in the United States was established in the late 19th century by the railroad, the nation's largest employer at the time. Employers often used pension plans as a disciplinary device on their employees. An employee who did not perform well faced both unemployment and the loss of his pension. In objecting to the disciplinary component of employer-initiated pensions, labor unions offered their own pension plans. Many of the pension plans of this period were significantly underfunded and their viability depended on the survival of the underwriting companies.

The most serious economic problem in this country occurred during the Great Depression of 1929–1932. Many people experienced its impact through unemployment and loss of investment income. Underfunded pension plans also failed in large numbers. In response to the problem, President Franklin D. Roosevelt announced his New Deal program, which included, among other things, the Social Security Act, which in turn included the Federal Insurance Contributions Act (FICA). Formally stated as the Old-Age, Survivors, Disability and Hospital Insurance Program, it was passed in 1935 and became effective in 1937. The act applied the principles of insurance to provide economic security to the public.

Social Security is a social insurance program operated by the federal government. It provides coverage toward premature death, disability, and medical care and living income for the aged. Currently, Social Security is on a pay-as-you-go basis, where benefits for the retired are paid from contributions of those still working. Those who are working today pay for Social Security and in turn are promised benefit payments in the future from the next generation's contributions. As of this writing, employers and employees each pay 7.65% of earnings up to $61,200 for 1995 and $62,700 for 1996 to fund the program. Any wages in excess of this amount are only subject to a 1.45% charge for the Medicare component.

The adequacy of retirement income is generally measured by a replacement ratio, which is the ratio of retirement benefits to preretirement income. Currently, the replacement ratio provided by Social Security ranges from 24% for a person with annual taxable earnings of $53,400 to 49% for a person with earnings of $15,000. In other industrialized nations, government-sponsored retirement plans generally support a higher replacement ratio. For example, France provides 50% to 100% (depending on the age of the retiree), Germany offers 60%, and Japan pays 50% of preretirement income. Obviously, such generosity has a price in the form of higher social security tax rates.

What is an adequate retirement income? A replacement ratio of 70% may provide a standard of living comparable to that of the preretirement period presumably because during retirement years one does not incur work-related expenses such as transportation costs and does not pay Social Security tax. If 70% is the desired replacement ratio, why do our Social Security benefits amount to only 24% to 49%? The reason is that Social Security is designed to provide some but not all of the benefits. In addition to Social Security benefits, individuals must plan for their own retirement using private pension plans.

Private pension plans grew significantly during World War II as a result of a government-imposed wage control. Since employers were prevented from offering high salaries, they used pension plans to attract better employees. Table 9.1 presents information on the number of persons covered by various retirement plans spanning the 1940–1994 period. The number of people covered by private

TABLE 9.1 Number of Persons Covered by Major Pension and Retirement Programs, in the United States (000 omitted)

| Year | Private Plans | | Government-Administered Plans | | | |
	With Life Insurance Companies	Other Private Plans	Railroad Retirement	Federal Civilian Employees[a]	State and Local Employees	OASI[b]
1940	695	3,565	1,349	745	1,552	22,900
1945	1,470	5,240	1,846	2,928	2,008	41,070
1950	2,755	7,500	1,881	1,872	2,894	61,506
1955	4,105	12,290	1,876	2,333	3,927	74,887
1960	5,475	17,540	1,654	2,703	5,160	91,496
1965	7,040	21,060	1,661	3,114	6,780	103,827
1970	10,580	25,520	1,633	3,624	8,591	120,014
1975	15,190	30,300*	1,564	4,171	11,230	135,744
1976	16,965	NA	1,572	4,210	12,290	138,633
1977	19,205	NA	1,567	4,292	13,124	141,596
1978	21,165	NA	1,580	4,380	13,400*	144,260
1979	23,310	NA	1,567	4,398	13,680*	147,178
1980	26,185	NA	1,533	4,460	13,950*	153,634
1981	27,665	NA	1,483	4,566	14,230*	157,569
1982	31,010	NA	1,404	4,610	14,504	160,611
1983	32,680	NA	1,383	4,683	14,464	161,836
1984	35,570	NA	1,362	4,791	14,788	161,986
1985	39,620	NA	1,309	4,887	15,235	162,881
1986	45,895	NA	1,271	4,938	15,426	164,438
1987	51,015	NA	1,243	5,065	15,460	167,077
1988	54,000	NA	1,229	5,281	15,864	169,270
1989	59,185	NA	1,212	5,499	17,086	171,801
1990	61,990	NA	1,184	5,447	16,857	174,143
1991	59,255	NA	1,157	5,506	17,502	176,615
1992	58,290	NA	1,133	5,475	18,320	179,839
1993	60,680	NA	1,107	5,330	NA	181,630
1994	64,385	NA	1,084	5,340	NA	182,179

Notes: Some data are revised. It is not possible to obtain a total for number of persons covered by pension plans by adding together the figures shown by year. Each series has been derived separately and there are differences in amount of duplication within each series and among the various series and also differences in definition of 'coverage' among the series.

Private plans with life insurance companies include persons covered by Keogh plans, tax deferred annuities, and, after 1974, IRA plans.

Data for 'Other Private Plans,' compiled by the Social Security Administration, exclude plans for the self-employed, those having vested benefits but not presently employed at the firm where benefits were accrued, and also exclude an estimated number who have vested benefits from employment other than from their current employment.

These data represent various dates during the year, since the fiscal years of the plans are not necessarily the same. Trends from year to year within each series are not affected. The number of persons covered include survivors or dependents of deceased workers and beneficiaries as well as retired workers. Retirement arrangements for members of the armed forces, and provisions for veterans' pensions, are not included.

NA—Not Available.
* Estimated.
[a]Includes members of the U.S. Civil Service Retirement System, the Tennessee Valley Authority Retirement System, the Foreign Service Retirement System, and the Federal Reserve Employee Retirement System (Board and Bank plans).
[b]Includes living workers insured for retirement and/or survivors' benefits, including the self-employed, plus dependents of retired workers and survivors of deceased workers who are receiving periodic benefits.

Source: 1995 Life Insurance Fact Book Update, American Council of Life Insurance, p. 20.

TABLE 9.2	Defined-Contribution and Defined-Benefit Plans	
	Defined Contribution	Defined Benefit
Number of Plans	584,066	146,041
Number of Participants	37,401,000	40,494,000
Assets	$608.4 billion	$906.6 billion

Source: Turner and Beller (1992).

plans was 4.3 million in 1940. By 1950 this number increased to 10.2 million. In 1994 more than 64 million people were covered under private pension plans. Various government-sponsored plans covered more than 206 million people, some 182 million under Social Security, 18 million under state and local government plans, 5 million under the federal civilian plan, and 1 million under the railroad plan. There is substantial duplication due to people being covered by more than one plan.

There are two major types of private pension plans—defined-contribution and defined-benefit plans. Table 9.2 provides comparative information on these two plans.

Defined-Contribution Plans

The employer, and sometimes the employee, makes regular contributions into a trust account with defined-contribution plans. Contributions are stipulated as a predetermined fraction of each employee's salary, although the fraction may change during the course of an employee's career. Pension contributions are tax deductible for both parties. Additionally, taxes on investment income are deferred. The employee often has some choice among investment opportunities, which amounts to selecting from various stock, bond, and money market funds.

At retirement the employee receives a lump sum or an annuity, the size of which depends on the amount accumulated in the account from contributions and investment earnings. The plan is fully funded and the employee bears the risk of the investment choice. The employer has no responsibility other than periodic contributions.

In addition to basic defined-contribution plans, there are other variations including 401(k) plans, 403(b) plans, Employee Stock Ownership Plans (ESOPs), Individual Retirement Accounts (IRAs), and Keogh Plans.

401(k) Plans Named after the section of the Internal Revenue Code that authorizes and regulates them, 401(k)s allow for a portion of an employee's compensation to be contributed to a tax-sheltered plan. Contributions to 401(k) plans are tax-deferred and are often matched by contributions from the employer. The current tax laws limit the 401(k) contributions to $9,500 per year in 1996, indexed to inflation. Once an amount is placed in a 401(k) plan, it remains there until the employee reaches the age of 59½, after which the employee can withdraw money after paying ordinary income taxes. Any withdrawal before this age subjects the employee to an additional 10% tax penalty, unless it is due to the employee's death, disability, or hardship.

403(b) Plans 403(b) plans are designed for employees of not-for-profit institutions such as schools, hospitals, museums, and charitable organizations. A special section of the Internal Revenue Code is devoted to 403(b) plans because not-for-profit employers do not have the same tax incentives that taxpaying employers have in providing employee pension plans. Originally, the law allowed for employees of the specified not-for-profit institutions to allocate part of their income to tax-sheltered deferred annuities. Later, the law was amended to include contributions to mutual funds. There are limits on how much an employee may contribute to this fund and there is also a 10% penalty for withdrawals before the age of 59½.

Employee Stock Ownership Plans (ESOPs) Instead of contributing a set amount to each participant's account, a sponsoring company may contribute a portion of its profits either in the form of cash (a profit-sharing plan) or in the form of company stock (ESOP). ESOPs are useful in mitigating employee-incentive problems. Stock ownership aligns the interests of employees and shareholders, thus encouraging them to be efficient and productive. ESOPs are also tax deductible, providing a means of reducing tax liability for the employer. A drawback of ESOPs is that they create an undiversified retirement plan wherein both the current income and the future retirement fund of an employee depend upon the performance of the sponsoring company. In other pension plans, the employee has more flexibility with diversification.

Individual Retirement Accounts (IRAs) Any wage earner under the age of 70½ may contribute up to $2,000 per year to an IRA. Contributions to an IRA may be fully deductible, partially deductible, or not deductible. However, the interest earned on the investment in all three cases is tax-deferred. An IRA contribution is fully deductible if the employee does not belong to an employer-sponsored or a union-sponsored pension plan. An IRA contribution by an employee whose salary is less than $25,000 ($40,000 for married couples, filing jointly) is also fully deductible even if the employee is covered by an employer retirement plan. An employee who is covered by an employer pension plan with an adjusted gross income of $25,000–$35,000 annually ($40,000–$50,000 for married couples) may take a partial deduction for his contribution to an IRA. The partial deduction is calculated using the following formula:

 Partial deduction = [($10,000 − excess adjusted gross income) / $10,000] × $2,000

For example, suppose an employee's annual adjusted gross income is $30,000. The excess adjusted gross income is $30,000 − $25,000 = $5,000 and the partial deduction is:

Partial deduction = [($10,000 − $5,000) / $10,000] × $2,000 = $1,000

This indicates that an employee who is covered by an employer pension plan with $30,000 in adjusted gross income may contribute a maximum of $1,000, fully deductible, to an IRA. Of course, this employee may contribute another $1,000 to an IRA with no deduction. Employees with annual income of greater than $35,000 ($50,000 for couples) may also contribute a maximum of $2,000 nondeductible to an IRA. The accumulated contributions earn tax-deferred investment income.

   If an IRA holder makes a withdrawal after the age of 59½, there is an ordinary income tax assessment on both the contributions that were deductible and the interest income. The portion of the contributions that was not deductible is not taxed, since it has already been taxed. If the withdrawal is before the age of 59½, there is a penalty tax of 10% in addition to the ordinary income tax, unless withdrawal is due to death or disability. An IRA holder is required by the IRS to begin taking distributions no later than April 1 of the year following the year she turns 70½. Distributions must be taken each subsequent year thereafter and taxed accordingly.

Keogh Plans   Named after the sponsoring legislator, Keogh plans are designed to provide retirement savings for the self-employed (sole proprietors and partners). Contributions may be as high as 20% of profits up to a maximum of $30,000 per year. These contributions are tax deductible and their investment income is tax-deferred. Upon withdrawal, Keogh plans have tax assessments similar to IRAs.

Keogh plans, along with IRAs, are primarily employee-initiated private pension plans, differentiated from employer-initiated plans such as 401(k)s, ESOPs, and, to a lesser extent, 403(b)s.

Defined-Benefit Plans

In defined-benefit plans, the pension benefits are calculated based on a formula that takes into account the length of service and the salary of the employee. For example, suppose an employee works at the same corporation for 40 years. Further, assume the preretirement annual salary of the employee is $60,000. A defined benefit plan provided by the employer may calculate the retirement benefit by taking 1.5% of the last year's salary times the number of years of employee service: $60,000 × 1.5% × 40 = $36,000. This plan will pay a minimum of $36,000 or 60% of the employee's last salary as annual benefits.

The annuity promised to employees is the liability of the corporation. This liability is insured by the Pension Benefit Guaranty Corporation (PBGC), a federal government agency. The employer has to pay an insurance premium to the PBGC based on the number of employees in its defined-benefit plan and the level of its funding. The plan's assets serve as collateral for the liabilities of the benefits plan.

The guaranteed minimum amount derived from a defined-benefit plan does not explicitly adjust for cost-of-living increases. The minimum benefit implicitly adjusts to the cost-of-living increases only if the employee remains at the same job, receives annual raises equal to or better than the inflation rate, and the employer continues to maintain the same plan. This adjustment is partial at best because, unlike Social Security benefits in which starting value is indexed to a general index of wages, defined-benefit-plan payments remain the same after retirement.

In order to offset the cost-of-living adjustment problem, large corporations often provide a defined-benefit plan supplemented by a defined-contribution plan in the form of profit-sharing or ESOP. Some sponsors also occasionally increase their benefits to their retired employees depending on the financial condition of the firm and the increase in the cost of living.[2] This may be interpreted as an implicit pledge by the employer to adjust the benefits to increases in the cost of living.[3] The increase in benefits may not be permanent, however. Corporations that face financial difficulties or face outside hostile takeover threats may decide to terminate their overfunded pension plans and give employees the legal guaranteed minimum.[4] This is also consistent with both the Financial Accounting Standards Board (FASB) Statement 87 and the Omnibus Budget Reconciliation Act passed by the U.S. Congress in 1987. Accordingly, the liability of the sponsor is equal to the present value of pension benefits owed to employees under the

---

[2] Bodie (1990).
[3] Cohn and Modigliani (1985) and Ippolito (1986).
[4] VanDerhei and Harrington (1989).

plan's benefit formula. This is the amount that the sponsor has to report in its corporate balance sheet as pension liability.

Management of Retirement Assets and Pension Funds

Private pension plans are established for employees by private agencies including industrial, financial, labor, and not-for-profit institutions. Additionally, private plans are initiated by individuals in the form of IRAs and Keogh plans. The management of these funds falls into two categories—government-administered funds and privately managed funds. Private pension plans are managed by financial intermediaries. Most large businesses choose defined-benefit plans under which contributions are put into a trust managed by an intermediary. Small businesses generally choose defined contribution plans and often leave the management of the plan to life insurance companies.

Table 9.3 presents assets and reserves of major retirement funds. Life insurance companies managed $878 billion in retirement funds in 1994. Other private pension funds managed $2.4 trillion. Total assets managed by private pension funds amounted to $3.2 trillion. Government-administered plans amounted to a total of $1.6 trillion.

Table 9.4 presents outstanding amounts of IRAs and Keogh plans managed by selected financial intermediaries for 1993–1994. The total of IRAs and Keogh plans amounted to $75.6 billion and $84.8 billion in 1993–1994, respectively. Various depository and nondepository financial intermediaries are involved in the management of these funds. Depository intermediaries including commercial banks, savings and loans, savings banks, and credit unions managed a combined 28.3% of the total assets in 1994, a decline from 30.6% in 1993. The share of mutual funds reached 31.8% in 1994. Life insurance companies with 8.4% of the total in 1994 had a slight increase in their share of private pension plans. Self-directed accounts, including IRAs not included in other categories, had an increase from 28.5% in 1993 to 31.5% in 1994.

Table 9.5 provides asset distribution of noninsured private pension funds for the 1952–1994 period. Private pension funds grew from $10.7 billion in assets in 1952 to $2.4 trillion four decades later. Fixed income securities, including government and corporate bonds, constituted 29% while corporate equities comprised 51% of total assets.

What criteria do pension fund managers consider in choosing their asset portfolios? The first factor for a pension fund manager to consider is the financial risk of pension assets. Since the sponsor bears the risk in defined-benefit plans, a conservative strategy would be to invest in a series of zero coupon bonds with a payoff schedule similar to those of planned-benefit payments. This will virtually eliminate the risk exposure of the sponsor.

Investment in corporate equities is generally more risky than investing in fixed-income securities. If this is the case, then why do pension funds invest such a high portion of their portfolios in equity? The reason is that investment in equity has a higher expected return than investment in fixed-income securities. Do corporate sponsors share in the benefits of upside risk? The answer is yes. If a pension fund portfolio performs well, and, in the process, greatly exceeds its obligations, the sponsor may reduce its contributions in later years or use one of several methods to revert the excess assets back to the corporation. The reversion of excess assets may take place in the event of a corporate merger, plant shutdown, or benefit restructuring.[5] How about the downside risk? The government-

---

[5] Alderson and VanDerhei (1992).

TABLE 9.3 Assets and Reserves of Major Pension and Retirement Programs in the United States (000,000 omitted)

Year	Private Plans		Government-Administered Plans			
	With Life Insurance Companies	Other Private Plans	Railroad Retirement	Federal Civilian Employees*	State and Local Employees	Old-Age, Survivors, and Disability Insurance**
1950	$5,600	NA	$2,553	$4,344	$5,154	$13,721
1960	18,850	$38,148	3,740	10,790	19,600	22,613
1965	27,350	74,367	3,946	16,516	33,100	19,841
1970	41,175	112,028	4,398	23,922	58,200	38,068
1975	72,210	225,012	3,100	39,248	103,700	44,342
1976	88,990	251,894	3,065	44,089	117,300	41,133
1977	101,520	271,700	2,584	50,832	130,800	35,861
1978	116,555	326,200	2,787	57,677	142,573	31,746
1979	138,515	386,100	2,611	65,914	161,649	30,291
1980	166,850	469,600	2,086	75,802	185,226	26,453
1981	193,210	486,700	1,126	86,867	209,444	24,539
1982	233,790	675,900	460	99,462	245,252	24,778
1983	269,425	811,200	601	114,219	289,731	24,867
1984	313,215	880,200	3,712	129,787	324,369	31,075
1985	373,475	1,038,400	5,109	148,166	373,932	42,163
1986	441,390	1,198,400	6,365	167,606	437,229	46,861
1987	495,420	1,216,400	6,860	185,946	512,854	68,807
1988	562,155	1,313,100	8,031	205,145	577,621	109,762
1989	624,290	1,536,000	8,906	225,963	634,978	162,968
1990	695,700	1,505,800	9,891	247,513	720,803	225,277
1991	745,950	2,179,500	10,655	272,765	783,234	280,747
1992	768,215	2,349,400	11,746	300,555	866,131	331,473
1993	825,375	2,342,100	12,047	330,701	NA	378,285
1994	878,460	2,356,400	12,929	358,012	NA	436,385

Note: Some data are revised. These data are as of various dates during the year, since the fiscal years of the plans are not necessarily the same. Trends from year to year are not affected.

NA—Not Available.

*Includes the U.S. Civil Service Retirement System, the Tennessee Valley Retirement System, the Foreign Service Retirement System, and the Federal Reserve Employee Retirement System (Board and Bank plans).

**Beginning in 1957, assets of Disability Insurance Trust Funds are included. Hospital and Supplementary Medical Insurance is not included.

Includes funds borrowed from the Hospital Insurance Fund.

Source: 1995 Life Insurance Fact Book Update, American Council of Life Insurance, p. 21.

sponsored Pension Benefit Guaranty Corporation (PBGC or "Penny Benny") provides defined-benefit insurance in the event that a plan defaults or is terminated.

In defined-contribution plans, the participants have some influence in the choice of their asset portfolios from a group of stock or bond funds. They also bear the investment risk of their portfolios. Since they are exposed to both the upside and the downside of their investment risk, they make their choices based on their overall risk preference. This generally leads participants to an investment strategy that includes both equity and fixed-income securities.

TABLE 9.4   Outstanding Amounts in IRAs and Keogh Plans with Selected Financial Institutions, Year-End ($ Millions)

Institution	IRA/Keogh 1993	IRA/Keogh 1994	% of Total 1993	% of Total 1994
Life Insurance Co.	$75,615	$84,775	7.9%	8.4%
Mutual Funds	314,335	320,098	33.0	31.8
U.S. Treasury Retirement*	89	85	**	**
Commercial Banks	144,200	143,300	15.1	14.2
Mutual Savings Banks	20,521	20,454	2.2	2.0
Savings and Loans	94,079	91,146	9.9	9.0
Credit Unions	32,445	31,216	3.4	3.1
Self-Directed Accounts	271,000	317,500	28.5	31.5
Total	$952,284	$1,008,574	100%	100%

*These bonds are no longer issued.
** Less than .05%.

Sources: 1995 Life Insurance Fact Book Update, American Council of Life Insurance, p. 23.

Regulation of Pension Funds

Prior to 1974, the regulation of pension funds was minimal, but in 1974 Congress passed the Employee Retirement Income Security Act (ERISA). This act has five main features:

1. The act established the Pension Benefit Guaranty Corporation (PBGC) to provide insurance for participants of pension plans.
2. All defined-benefit plans have to purchase PBGC insurance.
3. Pension rights must be fully vested within 10 years.
4. No more than 10% of a pension fund portfolio can be invested in the sponsor's securities.
5. Trustees of pension funds have fiduciary duties toward plan participants. Thus, they are legally bound to make investment decisions to benefit solely their participants.

Another important piece of legislation that affected pension plans is the Tax Reform Act of 1986. Prior to the 1986 act, pension plans provided a tax-sheltered opportunity for sponsors through overfunding. An overfunded plan served as a reserve for the future. If the sponsor needed extra funds, it could revert the excess funds back to the company by terminating the original plan and establishing a new one with assets equal to the minimum level of the obligations. The 1986 act reduced the incentives for overfunding by creating a ceiling where deductible funding was limited to 150% of the liabilities of the plan. ERISA covers only defined-benefit plans. Defined-contribution plans are minimally regulated by the Department of Labor.

The government-sponsored plans are not regulated in any meaningful way. For example, trustees of government-sponsored plans make investment decisions that are often influenced by the politics of their sponsors. It is well known that government-sponsored plans invest heavily in the securities of their sponsoring state and local governments. Some government sponsors have employed a more subtle approach by using their pension funds to guarantee issues of their municipal bonds. While there is generally a fee charged for this guarantee, in all likelihood it is underpriced.

TABLE 9.5 Distribution of Assets of Noninsured Private Pension Funds ($ Millions)

Calendar Year	U.S. Government Securities	Corporate and Foreign Bonds	Corporate Equities	Mortgages	Open Market Paper*	Time Deposits	Demand Deposits and Currency	Miscellaneous	Total
1952	2,500	4,600	1,800	200	—	400	300	900	10,700
1955	3,000	7,900	6,100	300	—	700	400	1,300	19,600
1960	2,700	15,700	16,600	1,300	—	1,400	600	2,800	40,900
1965	3,000	22,700	41,200	3,400	—	2,900	900	6,200	80,200
1970	3,000	29,400	67,900	4,200	—	6,300	1,100	11,900	123,900
1975	17,900	41,900	110,800	2,400	9,100	14,500	4,400	43,500	244,300
1976	24,200	40,200	129,000	2,400	11,000	16,700	4,500	47,400	275,300
1977	29,800	44,600	127,300	2,500	11,400	19,700	4,800	57,200	297,300
1978	31,900	53,000	154,000	2,700	11,600	23,700	5,200	69,400	351,300
1979	38,600	63,700	180,500	3,100	16,600	27,900	5,100	77,700	413,100
1980	50,500	77,700	230,600	3,600	22,100	31,900	4,200	83,800	504,400
1981	66,900	83,300	222,600	3,900	31,100	36,500	3,400	82,600	530,200
1982	105,800	95,200	288,700	9,100	19,900	49,400	2,300	87,000	659,400
1983	132,700	107,900	357,200	9,900	23,100	60,900	2,700	106,000	800,500
1984	153,900	123,400	366,900	10,000	26,500	68,000	3,300	109,000	861,100
1985	191,100	155,100	475,200	12,500	29,000	90,000	4,000	136,300	1,093,000
1986	224,300	178,300	564,900	15,500	39,200	109,400	4,300	155,100	1,290,800
1987	242,600	190,100	567,900	13,500	46,600	126,700	5,000	174,800	1,367,000
1988	251,200	203,900	640,700	17,700	51,100	151,300	4,600	101,300	1,421,800
1989	312,600	226,100	776,300	25,100	44,100	188,000	5,800	127,600	1,705,600
1990	323,100	235,500	703,000	23,800	42,700	175,600	5,800	119,600	1,629,100
1991	364,300	275,700	952,900	32,200	39,600	229,100	4,700	157,300	2,055,900
1992	385,300	292,100	1,048,500	35,200	38,200	238,600	4,600	171,600	2,213,800
1993	403,000	309,400	1,216,800	39,000	43,500	244,600	4,600	189,000	2,449,800
1994	380,100	294,500	1,189,200	38,400	41,100	218,700	3,500	185,400	2,350,900

Note: Some data are revised. Details may not add to totals due to rounding.
*Includes Money Market Fund shares.

Source: 1995 Life Insurance Fact Book Update, American Council of Life Insurance, p. 24.

The Pension Benefit Guaranty Corporation (PBGC)

189

Nondepository Financial
Intermediaries: Pension Funds,
Mutual Funds, Investment Banks,
and Finance Companies

In many respects, the PBGC functions like the FDIC. The PBGC charges pension funds a premium for the insurance it provides. The level of premium charged is a function of how well funded the plan is. Companies currently pay $19 per employee as a base assessment for the insurance. In addition, a company must pay a sliding-scale charge based on the extent of underfunding up to another $53 per employee. These fees are up substantially from the initial $1-per-employee assessment at the inception of the PBGC.

The increased cost of pension insurance is due to underfunding. Companies are not required by law to fund their plans fully. Since there is no legal obligation to do so, employers decide on their level of funding based on three factors. First, the presence of the PBGC creates moral-hazard problems for pension fund sponsors, similar to those of the FDIC. Accordingly, a sponsor in financial distress may underfund the plan and invest the funds in excessively risky projects. If the risk pays off on the upside, the sponsor receives the benefits. If it pays on the downside, the business may liquidate and the burden of the underfunded plan would be left to the PBGC. To avoid the arbitrage against its fund, the PBGC monitors pension plans. If a pension plan is considered to be inadequately funded, the PBGC can terminate the plan and take it over. In the case of a pension plan takeover, the PBGC can seize up to 30% of the net worth of the sponsor to support an underfunded plan.

The second factor in determining the funding level is related to employee incentives. When a plan is fully funded, the employee receives the pension at retirement, regardless of the level of productivity. To mitigate the employee incentive in sabotaging the firm, the sponsor will offer a lower funding level. By underfunding its pension plan, the firm will encourage the employee to work harder, in part to ensure the survival of the firm and the full payment of the pension.[6] This makes the employee a long-term bondholder in the firm. Unionized workers are good examples of this incentive problem. Since work hours and pensions are among negotiated items in labor bargaining, an underfunded pension plan affords greater leverage to the firm.

The third factor affecting the level of pension funding is the tax incentive. Since pension contributions are deductible, the sponsor has the incentive to increase its contribution within the IRS-mandated limit. If the tax incentive is the overriding concern, pension plans will be fully funded. This, however, does not seem to be the case in a substantial number of cases. The presence of the PBGC itself suggests that the tax incentive for full funding has not succeeded.

Table 9.6 provides evidence consistent with the second argument. Industrial corporations with large unionized workforces have the largest underfunded plans. The company with the greatest dollar amount of underfunding is General Motors Corporation. In 1992, the present value of GM's pension liabilities totaled $59.75 billion and its assets amounted to $39.57, producing a deficit of $20.18 billion. The underfunding represented 34% of GM's total pension liability.

While GM has the largest dollar amount of underfunding among U.S. corporations, it ranks 19th in the percent of underfunding. The highest percent of underfunding belongs to Ravensworth Aluminum with 89% underfunding (a $95 million underfunding out of a total pension liability of $106 million). The total underfunding at the end of 1992 was close to $40 billion. The PBGC would be liable for about $32 billion of this amount. The PBGC fund is currently running a deficit of $3 billion. The potential for another insurance crisis is clearly there with the current structure of the PBGC.

---

[6] Ippolito (1985) and Fowler and Rumsey (1994).

TABLE 9.6	Companies with the Greatest Underfunded Pension Liabilities December 1992		
Company	Amount Underfunded ($M)	Total Pension Liability ($M)	% Underfunded
General Motors	$20,182	$59,754	34%
Bethlehem Steel	2,431	5,857	42%
LTV	2,102	3,375	62%
Chrysler	1,360	9,692	14%
Westinghouse	1,271	5,189	24%
American National Can	546	2,614	21%
Navistar	544	2,614	21%
Uniroyal Goodrich Tire	501	1,018	49%
New Valley	429	698	61%
Rockwell International	380	842	45%

Source: USA Today, November 23, 1993.

MUTUAL FUNDS

A mutual fund is a nondepository financial intermediary that issues and sells its shares and uses the proceeds to invest in equity, debt, taxable, and tax-exempt securities. A mutual fund provides two distinct functions—diversification and reduced transaction costs. A portfolio is diversified when it contains at least 20 different securities. A fully diversified portfolio effectively eliminates the unique risk of each security included in the portfolio. Since securities are generally sold in multiples of 100, creating a diversified portfolio by an individual may require tens or even hundreds of thousands of dollars, an amount that is not available to most investors. In addition, purchasing a large number of different securities involves high transaction costs. Mutual funds resolve the wealth constraint problem by selling their shares at prices as low as $1,000 and sometimes even lower. Subsequently, they pool the financial resources of thousands of shareholders, each with a different amount to invest. The proceeds are invested in as many as 50 to 200 or more different securities to achieve full diversification. Since the purchase size of each security is large, the transaction cost incurred by each shareholder is significantly lower than when the purchase is handled by each investor.

Each fund sets an investment objective, which is important both to the fund manager and to the investor. The fund manager uses it as a guide in investment decisions. The investor uses it to choose a fund that provides the desired risk-return trade-off. A mutual fund is also called an open-end investment company. There are also investment companies that are called closed-end companies. While the main focus in this chapter is on open-end funds, it is important to understand the differences between the two types of funds.

Open-End vs. Closed-End Funds

The distinction between these two categories of investment companies lies primarily in the way they issue their shares. In an open-end company or a mutual fund, the company stands ready to sell new shares every day as the demand arises. It also stands ready to buy back its shares if investors decide to sell off their holdings. The price of a share in an open-end company is determined at the end of each business day by adding up the value of all securities in the portfolio, subtracting the expenses, and dividing it by the number of shares outstanding. This computation provides the Net Asset Value (NAV). The value of a shareholder's investment is determined each day by multiplying the number of shares the investor holds by the NAV. Unlike a traditional corporation, an open-end company can issue an unlimited number of shares. The shareholders can also redeem all or part of their shares in any business day.

In contrast to an open-end fund, a closed-end company issues a fixed number of shares, which are traded publicly. Each share of a closed-end fund has two prices—the NAV and the fund's stock price, which fluctuates either above (a "premium") or below (a "discount") the NAV. Closed-end funds generally do not buy their shares back from investors who choose to liquidate their holdings. Instead, closed-end shares trade on a stock exchange.

Similar to open-end funds, closed-end companies invest in securities. As of December 1994, there were 539 closed-end funds with combined assets of $116 billion, or roughly 5% of the total assets of open-end and closed-end funds. There were 5,357 open-end funds with total assets of $2.16 trillion, or 95% of the total assets of open-end and closed-end funds.[7] Since open-end companies clearly dominate this market, they will be the focus of the rest of this discussion.

The Historical Background of Mutual Funds

Mutual funds originated in 19th-century England. After the American Civil War, a group of English and Scottish investment companies contributed to the financing of the American economy through their investments in farm mortgages, railroads, and other industries.[8] In the United States the first mutual fund was organized in Boston in 1924.

Shortly after the first mutual fund was organized, the U.S. economy experienced the market crash of 1929 and the beginning of the Great Depression. Despite this major setback, the mutual fund industry survived. As part of the government's post-Depression plan, the Securities Exchange Commission (SEC) was established as mandated by the Securities Exchange Act of 1934. Among other things, the SEC examined the operation of investment companies, which culminated in the Investment Company Act of 1940. The 1940 act was the result of a study the SEC undertook with the help of industry professionals. In the aftermath of the legislation, these professionals formed a permanent organization, the National Committee of Investment Companies, to cooperate with the SEC in the formulation of rules and regulations to implement the new law. The committee changed its name a few times and evolved into an influential self-regulating body for the industry, known today as the Investment Company Institute.

Mutual funds had total assets of $448 million in 296,000 shareholder accounts in 1940. Total assets surpassed $1 billion in 1945, and there were more than 1 million shareholder accounts by 1951. By the early 1970s there were 400 different funds with total assets of more than $50 billion. At the end of 1994, there were 5,357 funds with total assets of more than $2.16 trillion. Today, mutual funds are the second largest group of financial intermediaries in terms of total assets, with commercial banks being the largest.

The Evolution of Mutual Funds

Table 9.7 provides information on the growth of mutual funds for the years 1970 to 1994. First established in the 1920s, mutual funds grew steadily but at a slow

---

[7] *Mutual Fund Fact Book*, 1995. Investment Company Institute, Washington, DC, pp. 29 and 142.
[8] In Great Britain today, open-end companies are called unit trusts and closed-end companies are called investment trusts.

TABLE 9.7	Mutual Fund Industry Net Assets 1970–1994 (Billions of Dollars)				
Year	Equity Funds	Bond & Income Funds	Taxable Money Market Funds	Tax-Exempt Money Market Funds	Total
1970	$38.5	$9.1	—	—	$47.6
1971	44.5	10.5	—	—	55.0
1972	48.6	11.2	—	—	59.8
1973	36.9	9.6	—	—	46.5
1974	26.3	7.8	$1.7	—	35.8
1975	32.4	9.8	3.7	—	45.9
1976	34.3	13.3	3.7	—	51.3
1977	30.0	15.0	3.9	—	48.9
1978	29.0	16.0	10.9	—	55.9
1979	32.5	16.5	45.2	$0.3	94.5
1980	41.0	17.4	74.5	1.9	134.8
1981	38.4	16.8	181.9	4.3	241.4
1982	50.6	26.3	206.6	13.2	296.7
1983	73.9	39.7	162.6	16.8	293.0
1984	83.1	54.0	209.7	23.8	370.6
1985	116.9	134.8	207.5	36.3	495.5
1986	161.5	262.6	228.3	63.8	716.2
1987	180.7	273.1	254.7	61.4	769.9
1988	194.8	277.5	272.3	65.7	810.3
1989	249.1	304.8	358.7	69.4	982.0
1990	245.8	322.7	414.7	83.6	1,066.8
1991	411.6	441.4	452.6	89.9	1,395.5
1992	522.8	577.3	451.4	94.8	1,646.3
1993	749.0	761.1	461.9	103.4	2,075.4
1994	866.5	684.0	500.4	110.6	2,161.5

Source: Mutual Fund Fact Book, Washington, DC: Investment Company Institute, 1995, p. 101.

rate in the following five decades. By 1970 industry assets had grown to $47.6 billion. During the 1970s the same pattern persisted. High interest rates at the end of the decade brought major changes. Until the late 1970s most individuals had kept their savings at depository institutions, which paid the maximum regulatory-determined rate of 5¼% to 5½% per year. The high inflation of the late 1970s pushed interest rates to double digits. Although large investors could take advantage of less-regulated bank negotiable CDs that paid market rates, small depositors were effectively kept out of these markets due to denominations that often exceeded $10,000. This created a strong demand for investment vehicles that would pay market rates on small investments.

While mutual funds were in existence for more than half a century, they had primarily focused on equity and long-term debt funds until the mid-1970s, when short-term funds such as taxable money market funds were introduced for the first time. By 1977 there was only $3.9 billion in short-term fund accounts. High interest rates and an effective advertising campaign by mutual funds enticed small savers to switch to mutual funds. Money market mutual funds were quickly accepted by many depositors as superior alternatives to bank accounts. During this period, most of the new investments in mutual funds came from withdrawals from depository financial intermediaries, a process called disintermediation.

The phenomenal growth of money market mutual funds had other side effects. During the first five decades of mutual fund history, the industry was serving primarily the institutional investors and a few wealthy individuals. When small savers joined mutual funds in the late 1970s, they discovered not only money market mutual funds but also other investment categories such as equity and long-term debt funds. Additionally, the expanded market sparked new products including tax-exempt money market funds in 1979, government income, and Ginnie Mae funds in the early 1980s. Index funds, adjustable-rate mortgage funds, and international funds have also been recently introduced.

By mid-1982 interest rates started to decline and the stock and bond markets began an upside swing that continued through the third quarter of 1987. The decline in interest rates made money market funds less attractive. As a result, investors shifted their attention from short-term money market funds to long-term equity and bond and income funds. By the end of 1994, equity funds and bond and income funds managed assets in the amount of $866.5 and $684.0 billions, respectively. Taxable money market funds totaled $500.4 billion and tax-exempt money market funds reached the $110.6 billion level.

Table 9.8 provides information on the growth of mutual funds' shareholder accounts. In 1978 there were only 8.7 million accounts managed by mutual funds, primarily as equity funds. Taxable money market mutual funds grew substantially during the 1980s, reaching 20 million by the end of the decade. The equity funds increased from 5.8 million in 1980 to 59.1 million in 1994. Bond and income funds constituted the second largest category of the funds with 30.5 million accounts by the end of 1994. Tax-exempt money funds comprised only 2 million ac-

TABLE 9.8	Number of Mutual Fund Shareholder Accounts (Millions)				
Year	Equity Funds	Bond & Income Funds	Taxable Money Market Funds	Tax-Exempt Money Market Funds	Total
1978	6.8	1.4	0.5	—	8.7
1979	6.1	1.4	2.3	—	9.8
1980	5.8	1.5	4.8	—	12.1
1981	5.7	1.5	10.3	—	17.5
1982	6.2	2.0	13.1	0.1	21.4
1983	8.9	3.2	12.3	0.2	24.6
1984	10.0	4.4	13.6	0.3	28.3
1985	11.5	8.3	14.4	0.5	34.7
1986	16.6	13.2	15.6	0.7	46.1
1987	21.4	15.5	16.8	0.8	54.5
1988	20.6	15.6	17.6	0.9	54.7
1989	21.5	15.4	20.2	1.1	58.2
1990	23.0	16.6	21.6	1.4	62.6
1991	26.1	18.9	21.9	1.7	68.6
1992	33.2	23.4	21.8	1.9	80.3
1993	42.5	27.5	21.6	2.0	93.6
1994	59.1	30.5	23.3	2.0	114.9

Source: *Mutual Fund Fact Book,* Washington, DC: Investment Company Institute, 1995, p. 102.

counts at the end of 1994. The total number of mutual fund shareholder accounts reached 114.9 million in the United States at the end of 1994.

Types of Mutual Funds

The investment objective set forth by a mutual fund is important for both the investor and the manager of the fund. By law, a mutual fund has to stay within its stated objective in selecting securities. The investor chooses a fund based on its risk and return attributes while the manager follows the stated objective of the fund as a guideline in selecting securities.

Mutual funds provide investment opportunities in a relatively small number of fully diversified portfolios with well-defined risk characteristics. A typical mutual fund investor is a person who is either unwilling or unable to choose from thousands of securities that are available in the securities market. A small investor with no particular knowledge about securities who puts $1,000 in a fund receives the same yield per share as a busy person with a degree in finance who invests $100,000.

We have already introduced four categories of funds—equity funds; bond and income funds, which involve long-term securities; taxable money market funds; and tax-exempt money market mutual funds, which focus on short-term instruments. In each of these four categories there are several alternatives. The Investment Company Institute classifies mutual funds into 21 major groups that are presented in Table 9.9. Out of 21 different alternatives, there are 7 equity funds, 11 bond and income funds, 1 taxable money market fund, and 2 tax-exempt money market funds.

Organization of Mutual Funds

The ownership structure of a mutual fund is similar to that of other mutual organizations, including mutual savings and loans, mutual saving banks, and mutual insurance companies. A mutual fund is owned by hundreds or thousands of its shareholders. A board of directors elected by the shareholders is ultimately responsible for carrying out the fund's investment objectives. The board is charged with the responsibility of appointing officers to manage the daily operation of the fund or to delegate that function to a management company.

The management company, which is often the entity that created the fund, may offer anywhere from one to a dozen or more mutual funds, each with a different investment objective. The management company often serves as the fund's investment adviser. The investment adviser or the money manager is responsibile for selecting the portfolio of securities and managing the fund. The investment adviser receives a management fee that is based on the total value of the assets being managed. The management fee is generally around one half of 1% of total assets annually. Other operating expenses are usually in the same range, bringing the total costs of the operation to 1% of total assets.

There are three parties other than the investment adviser who provide for the orderly operation of a mutual fund: a custodian, a transfer agent, and a principal underwriter. The custodian, which is generally a bank, safeguards the securities owned by the fund, makes the payments when new securities are purchased, and receives the proceeds when securities are sold. The transfer agent provides the record-keeping function such as issuing new shares, canceling redeemed shares, and distributing dividends and capital gains to shareholders. Finally, the principal underwriter distributes mutual fund shares to the investing public.

How Does One Invest in a Mutual Fund?

Mutual fund shares are distributed publicly through one of two channels. First, a fund may distribute its shares directly to the public. Second, a fund may sell its

TABLE 9.9 Types of Mutual Funds

195

EQUITY FUNDS

Aggressive Growth Funds Seek maximum capital gains as their investment objective. Current income is not a significant factor. Some may invest in stocks of businesses that are somewhat out of the mainstream, such as fledgling companies, new industries, companies fallen on hard times, or industries temporarily out of favor. Some may also use specialized investments such as option writing or short-term trading.

Global Equity Funds Seek growth in the value of their investments by investing in securities traded worldwide, including the United States. Compared to direct investments, global funds offer an easier avenue to investing abroad. The funds' professional money managers handle the trading and record-keeping details and deal with differences in currencies, languages, time zones, laws and regulations, and business customs and practices. In addition to another layer of diversification, global funds add another layer of risk—exchange-rate risk.

Growth and Income Funds Invest mainly in the common stock of companies that have had increasing share value but also a solid record of paying dividends. This type of fund attempts to combine long-term capital growth with a steady stream of income.

Growth Funds Invest in the common stock of well-established companies. Their primary aim is to produce an increase in the value of their investments (capital gains) rather than a flow of dividends. Investors who buy growth funds are more interested in seeing the funds' share price rise than in receiving income from dividends.

Income-Equity Funds Seek a high level of current income by investing in high-dividend equities.

International Funds Seek growth in the value of their investments by investing in equity securities of companies located outside the United States. Two thirds of their portfolios must be so invested at all times to be categorized here.

Precious Metals/Gold Funds Seek an increase in the value of their investments by investing at least two-thirds of their portfolios in securities associated with gold, silver, and other precious metals.

BOND AND INCOME FUNDS

Corporate Bond Funds Seek a high level of income by purchasing bonds of corporations for the majority of the fund's portfolio. The rest of the portfolio may be in U.S. Treasury bonds or bonds issued by a federal agency.

Ginnie Mae or GNMA Funds Seek a high level of income by investing in mortgage securities backed by the Government Mortgage Association (GNMA). To qualify for this category, the majority must always be invested in mortgage-backed securities.

TABLE 9.9   Types of Mutual Funds (Continued)

Global Bond Funds   Seek a high level of current income by investing in the debt securities of companies and countries worldwide, including the United States.

High-Yield Bond Funds   Maintain at least two-thirds of their portfolios in lower-rated corporate bonds (Baa or lower by Moody's rating service and BBB or lower by Standard & Poor's rating service). In return for a generally higher yield, investors must bear a greater degree of risk than for higher-rated bonds.

Income-Bond Funds   Seek a high level of current income by investing at all times in a mix of corporate and government bonds.

National Municipal Bond Funds—Long Term   Invest in bonds issued by states and municipalities to finance schools, highways, hospitals, airports, bridges, water and sewer works, and other public projects. In most cases, income earned on these securities is not taxed by the federal government, but may be taxed under state and local laws. For some taxpayers, portions of income earned on these securities may be subject to the federal alternative minimum tax.

State Municipal Bond Funds—Long Term   Work just like national municipal bond funds except their portfolios contain the issues of only one state. A resident of that state has the advantage of receiving income free of both federal and state tax. For some taxpayers, portions of income from these securities may be subject to the federal alternative minimum tax.

U.S. Government Income Fund   Seek current income by investing in a variety of government securities, including U.S. Treasury bonds, federally guaranteed mortgage-backed securities, and other government notes.

Balanced Funds   Generally have a three-part investment objective: (1) to conserve investors' initial principal; (2) to pay current income; and (3) to promote long-term growth of both principal and income. Balanced funds have a portfolio mix of bonds, preferred stocks, and common stocks.

Flexible Portfolio Funds   May be 100% invested in stocks or bonds or money market instruments, depending on market conditions. These funds give the money managers the greatest flexibility in anticipating or responding to economic changes.

Income-Mixed Funds   Seek a high level of current income by investing in income-producing securities, including both equities and debt instruments.

TAXABLE MONEY MARKET FUNDS

Taxable Money Market Mutual Funds   Seek to maintain a stable net asset value by investing in the short-term, high-grade securities sold in the money market. These are generally the safest, most stable securities available and include Treasury Bills, certificates of deposit of large banks, and commercial paper (the short-term IOUs of large U.S. corporations). Money market funds limit the average maturity of their portfolio to 90 days or less.

TABLE 9.9   Types of Mutual Funds (Continued)

TAX-EXEMPT MONEY MARKET FUNDS

Tax-Exempt Money Market Funds—National   Invest in municipal securities with relatively short maturities. Investors who use these funds seek investments with minimum risk. For some taxpayers, portions of income from certain securities may be subject to the federal alternative minimum tax.

Tax-Exempt Money Market Funds—State   Work just like other tax-exempt money market funds except their portfolios contain the issues of only one state. A resident of that state has the advantage of receiving income free of both federal and state tax. For some taxpayers, portions of income from these securities may be subject to the federal alternative minimum tax.

Source: *Mutual Fund Fact Book*, Washington, DC: Investment Company Institute, 1995, pp. 17–18.

shares through another intermediary such as a brokerage house, a bank, an insurance company, or a financial planning firm. The direct sale to the public takes place through advertisements and direct mail to potential investors. The indirect sale takes place through an intermediary. The sales commission under direct sale is generally lower than those under indirect sale.

At the end of 1994, there were 5,357 mutual funds offering 21 different investment categories. The minimum investment requirements vary among funds. Some funds have no minimum requirement, while others, such as institutional funds, may have a minimum requirement of $1 million or more. Figure 9.1 presents the distribution of minimum investment requirements in mutual funds. More than two-thirds of all mutual funds require $1,000 or less as a minimum investment.

Mutual funds have made many convenient options available for shareholders to make their investments. An investor may sign up for a payroll deduction option to make regular contributions. Alternatively, one may authorize the mu-

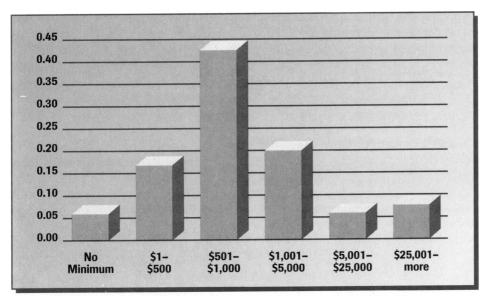

Source: *Mutual Fund Fact Book*, Washington, DC: Investment Company Institute, 1995, p. 32.

FIGURE 9.1
Minimum Investment Requirements in Mutual Funds

tual fund to withdraw regularly a specified amount from a personal bank account. Mutual funds also offer automatic reinvestment plans in which dividends, interest income, and capital gains earned by a shareholder can be used automatically to purchase new shares.

Convenient options are also available for withdrawals from a mutual fund. A shareholder may make an arrangement with the fund to receive checks at regular intervals from earnings or the principal of its investments. Arrangements may be made for someone else to receive the payments. A shareholder may also write checks against a mutual fund account, although in some cases there is a minimum check amount of $250 or $500. A shareholder may also use the checking privilege in redeeming shares immediately. By law, given proper notification, a mutual fund has to be ready to redeem any or all shares on any given business day.

A mutual fund shareholder may choose to switch from one fund to another within the family of funds offered by the management company. Mutual funds often provide exchange privileges several times a year for either no fee or a low fee per exchange. A shareholder may even exchange funds by telephone. In the event of an exchange, the writing of a check, or any additional investments, a shareholder will receive a confirmation statement from the mutual fund. The shareholder also receives account updates on a monthly, quarterly, or annual basis, depending on the fund.

Institutional Investors in Mutual Funds

Institutional investors account for a significant portion of the business for mutual funds. In 1993, retirement plans, nonprofit organizations, personal trusts, and business organizations accounted for $898 billion or 42% of total mutual fund assets. Institutional investors' accounts totaled 15 million in 1994. Table 9.10 provides the details.

The fiduciary category includes two groups—bank trusts and individuals serving as trustees, guardians, and administrators. Bank trusts generally invest in money market mutual funds, and individual trusts mainly invest in all other types of funds. Fiduciary accounts with mutual funds reached $351.6 billion at the end of 1994. The business organizations category had the largest share of institutional investors in mutual funds with a total of $473.8 billion. Retirement funds had the largest share of the business organizations with $248.9 billion, and insurance companies and other financial intermediaries had the second largest share with $139.9 billion. The not-for-profit group had a total of $17.8 billion invested in mutual funds, from which 70% is invested in equity and income and bond funds and the rest is invested in taxable money market funds. By virtue of their tax-exempt status, these institutions have little interest in tax-exempt funds.

A Global Perspective on Mutual Funds

As global economies move toward free markets, privatization, and lower trade barriers, further resources are required to finance the new investment opportunities. As financial intermediaries, mutual funds play an important role in pooling the resources of individuals and institutions and investing them in new business ventures. The same basic economic reasons that induced investors in the United States to join mutual funds—namely, diversification and a reduction in transaction costs—also apply to investors in other countries. Table 9.11 presents information on the asset growth of mutual funds for 26 countries, including the United States. The combined assets of mutual funds in these countries grew from $2.4 trillion in 1990 to $4.5 trillion in 1994. U.S. mutual funds had the largest percentage of growth with a 19% average annual compound rate. Excluding the

TABLE 9.10 Assets of Institutional Investors in Mutual Funds, 1994
(Billions of Dollars)

	Equity and Bond & Income Funds	Taxable Money Market Funds	Tax-Exempt Money Market Funds	Total
Fiduciaries[a]	$200.9	$125.5	$25.2	$351.6
Business Corporations	31.1	45.8	6.4	83.3
Retirement Plans	213.0	35.2	0.7	248.9
Insurance Companies and Other Financial Inst.	115.8	22.6	1.5	139.9
Unions	0.9	0.2	0.6	1.7
Total Business Organizations	**$360.8**	**$103.8**	**$9.2**	**$473.8**
Churches & Religious Organizations	4.1	1.6	0.1	5.8
Fraternal, Welfare, and Other Public Associations	2.7	1.3	0.0	4.0
Hospitals, Sanitariums, Orphanages, etc.	1.1	0.8	0.0	1.9
Schools and Colleges	2.0	0.9	0.0	2.9
Foundations	2.6	0.6	0.0	3.2
Total Not-for-Profit	**$12.5**	**$5.2**	**$0.1**	**$17.8**
Other Institutional Investors[b]	$32.9	$18.9	$3.2	$55.0
Total	$607.1	$253.4	$37.7	$898.2

[a]Fiduciaries include bank trusts and individuals serving as trustees, guardians, and administrators.
[b]Institutional investors that do not fall into any of the categories mentioned above.

Source: *Mutual Fund Fact Book,* Washington, DC: Investment Company Institute, 1995, pp. 135, 139, and 141.

United States, the average annual compound rate of growth for the remaining 25 countries was 16%. We now take a closer look at growth trends in various parts of the global market.

The European Union (EU) The Treaty of the European Union was signed in Maastricht, the Netherlands, on December 10, 1991, and, after some delay, went into effect on November 1, 1993. As of 1995, the European Union (EU) comprised 15 countries: Austria, Belgium, Denmark, Finland, France, Germany, Greece, Ireland, Italy, Luxembourg, the Netherlands, Portugal, Spain, Sweden, and the United Kingdom. The EU expands on the previous close cooperation that existed under the EC agreement. Pertinent to our discussion here, in October 1989, the EC issued a directive known as Undertakings for Collective Investment in Transferable Securities (UCITS). This directive facilitates the cross-border marketing of mutual fund shares within the EU by allowing a fund registered in one EU country to be marketed in other EU countries without need for further registrations. A common regulatory framework is designed that covers investment policies, disclosure rules, and the structure of investment funds. While this has helped in the expansion of mutual funds, there are still some remaining problems that need to

TABLE 9.11 Global Activities in Mutual Funds (Millions of U.S. Dollars)		
Non-U.S. Countries	1990	1994
Australia*	$29,125	$44,050
Austria	14,324	23,464
Belgium	4,538	19,725
Canada*	21,483	97,631
Denmark	3,614	5,406
Finland	NA	1,155
France	378,826	531,085
Germany	145,495	253,436
Greece	936	6,111
Hong Kong	NA	32,540
India	7,645	11,033
Ireland	6,977	7,056
Italy	41,924	86,344
Japan	353,528	466,892
Korea	33,806	78,190
Luxembourg	94,559	289,033
Netherlands	24,308	49,306
New Zealand	NA	2,397
Norway	NA	5,214
Portugal	2,848	11,711
South Africa	NA	6,855
Spain	11,996	90,175
Sweden	21,113	26,465
Switzerland	NA	39,941
United Kingdom	91,530	135,197
Total Non-U.S.	1,288,575	2,320,412
Total U.S.	1,066,892	2,161,400
Total World	$2,355,467	$4,481,812

*Includes real estate funds.

Source: *Mutual Fund Fact Book*, Washington, DC: Investment Company Institute, 1995, p. 65.

be sorted out. For example, there are still major differences among EU countries as to the tax ramifications of mutual fund investments. There are also differences in marketing and distribution practices in various countries. These obstacles are believed to be temporary, however, and are expected to be resolved as competition intensifies.

The EU, with a population of close to 400 million in 1995, is a continent with advanced economies and substantial wealth. It is no surprise, therefore, that mutual funds have grown significantly in these countries, which have many differences among them. For example, in the United Kingdom, mutual funds (called unit trusts) invest over 90% of their funds in equity funds, indicating a higher tolerance for risk. In Germany, mutual funds invest nearly 80% of their assets in debt funds. In France, over 50% of mutual fund assets are invested in money market funds and 30% are invested in debt funds. Concerning distribution channels, EU countries are also very diverse. In Germany and France, mutual fund shares are primarily sold through banks. In the UK, distribution channels are similar to those of the United States, where a mix of company representatives and independent intermediaries sell unit trust shares side by side.

Canada and Mexico in the Post-NAFTA Era   The North American Free Trade Agreement (NAFTA) among the United States, Mexico, and Canada, which was ratified by the U.S. Congress in November 1993, substantially increased trade opportunities among these countries. It is expected that this agreement will facilitate the growth of mutual funds in Canada and Mexico. As of 1994, Canada had $97.6 billion (U.S. dollars) in mutual fund assets and Mexico had $20 billion (1993 figure). NAFTA permits the United States to register mutual funds as investment counselors/portfolio managers in Canada without establishing a Canadian subsidiary. Under NAFTA, U.S. mutual funds are permitted to sponsor and distribute Mexican mutual funds. In the post-NAFTA era it is expected that mutual funds will grow rapidly in Mexico. Canada, because of its common language with and cultural similarity to the United States, has sales and distribution channels similar to those here. NAFTA will further expand this cooperation.

Japan and Other Pacific Rim Countries   The Pacific Rim countries are among the fastest growing economies in the world. Despite the economic challenges of the early 1990s, the foundation of the Japanese economy is strong and its population is well known for high savings rates. Mutual funds in Japan had total assets of $466.9 billion in 1994, second only to France. Currently, foreign entry into the Japanese mutual fund market is difficult due to licensing and distribution problems.

Regulation and Taxation of Mutual Funds

Regulation   Mutual funds are the most heavily regulated entities under the federal securities laws. The Securities Act of 1933 established the first set of regulatory rules for mutual funds. The 1933 act requires all mutual funds to provide to investors a detailed prospectus that contains information on the fund's management and its investment policies and objectives. The act also regulates the type and the content of advertisements by mutual funds. As with all other securities, the purchase and sale of mutual fund shares are subject to the antifraud provisions of the Securities Exchange Act of 1934. In addition, the distribution of mutual fund shares is subject to regulation by the SEC and the National Association of Securities Dealers (NASD), a self-regulatory entity for securities brokers.

The Investment Company Act of 1940 requires mutual funds to register with the SEC. This act also includes provisions that prohibit self-dealing and conflict of interest. It requires the funds to maintain the integrity of their assets and limits the amount of fees and commissions charged against shareholders' accounts. The regulated fee structure is an important factor in the choice of mutual funds by investors.

There are basically two types of distribution channels for mutual funds. Those that are sold through brokers, financial planners, and insurance companies charge the investor a sales commission in the range of 3% to 8.5%. These funds are called load funds. The load funds may be front-end loads, which charge a commission at the time of purchase, or back-end loads, which charge a fee when the shares are redeemed. Often, with back-end load funds, the commission charge declines as the investor holding period increases. Mutual funds that are sold directly by funds through advertising, direct mail, 800 numbers, and sales staff often do not have sales commission but charge an annual management fee based on the size of the assets managed. These funds are called no-load funds. Under SEC rule 12b-1, fees cannot exceed 0.75% of a fund's average net assets. An additional fee of 0.25% may be added if services of other brokers or professionals are used to assist shareholders. Effective July 1, 1993, the SEC has set a maximum of 8.5% on the total of all fees, including front-end and back-end loads and advertising expenses.

The Investment Advisers Act of 1940 regulates the functions of investment advisers to mutual funds. Another securities law that affects the operation of mutual funds is the Insider Trading and Securities Act of 1988, which requires investment advisers of mutual funds and brokers and dealers to develop and enforce procedures to prohibit insider trading. Finally, there is the Market Reform Act of 1990, enacted in response to the market crash of 1987, that gives the SEC emergency authority to halt trading activities in organized exchanges in the time of high market volatility.

Taxation   Mutual funds that meet the requirements of Subchapter M of the Internal Revenue Code do not have to pay taxes themselves, but their shareholders have to pay taxes as if they directly owned a proportion of the fund's securities. To qualify for Subchapter M, a mutual fund has to distribute 90% of its taxable income each year and follow certain rules of asset diversification. Furthermore, mutual funds must satisfy certain rules about sources of income and comply with stated restrictions on certain short-term gains.

Payments to shareholders take the form of interest and dividends and capital gains. Interest income and dividend income are taxed at the ordinary income tax rates, while long-term capital gains are taxed at the current capital gains tax rate of 28% percent. Tax-exempt mutual funds' income is obviously exempt from tax at the shareholder level. For tax purposes, shareholders receive an end-of-the-year statement from their mutual funds indicating the ordinary income and capital gains portions of their earnings for the year.

INVESTMENT BANKS

The primary business of investment banks is to facilitate corporate financing by issuing long-term debt and equity. In addition, investment banks trade securities after they have been issued and provide other services including advice on mergers and acquisitions and portfolio management to both corporate and individual customers.

The investment banking business in the United States has evolved differently in the rest of the world. In most industrialized countries, the business of commercial banking and investment banking is combined into a single entity that is known as a universal bank. In the United States, these two lines of businesses were separated by the Glass-Steagall Act passed by Congress in 1933.

Prior to the Glass-Steagall Act, many commercial banks functioned as brokers, dealers, and underwriters of securities in addition to their deposit-gathering and lending functions. During the Great Depression of 1929–1933, nearly 10,000 banks or 40% of all commercial banks in the United States failed. This large-scale failure was partially blamed on the risk involved in securities-related transactions. The separation of commercial and investment banking was an effort to insulate commercial banks from the risk of the securities business. Another possible reason for separating commercial and investment banking was to mitigate conflicts of interest in lending to a corporation whose securities the bank owned and traded.

The separation of commercial and investment banking in the United States has contributed to increased specialization and competition in both industries. In terms of liquidity and transaction costs, the U.S. securities markets are among the most efficient in the world. U.S. commercial banks have outperformed their universal banking competitors in other countries. We will provide more detail on these comparisons in Chapters 10 and 13.

Advancements in banking technology and global competition may have dispelled the early concerns that led to the separation of commercial and investment banking in the United States. We expect in the near future that Congress will dismantle the Glass-Steagall Act and will allow for commercial and investment banking functions to be combined.

Primary Functions of Investment Banks

Investment banks are divided into two categories: members of the New York Stock Exchange (NYSE) and nonmember firms. NYSE members are prohibited from making a market (holding an inventory) in NYSE-listed stocks. The NYSE is an auction system wherein all securities listed are brought to a single specialist for pricing and reporting. The organized exchange market is referred to as the first market.

Nonmember investment banks provide both brokerage and dealer functions in unlisted or over-the-counter (OTC) securities, which are traded on the National Association of Securities Dealers Automatic Quotation (NASDAQ) system. NASDAQ is a computer-linked network of dealers, brokers, and customers who trade in OTC securities without a centralized location. Most member firms are also active dealers in NASDAQ.

There are three levels of subscribers to NASDAQ:

- *Level 3* subscribers are dealers or market makers in OTC securities. Market makers maintain inventories of a security and stand ready to buy and sell shares from or to the public and earn a profit in the form of bid-ask spreads. These subscribers enter the bid-ask prices of the securities that they are willing to buy or sell in the computer network.
- *Level 2* subscribers are brokers who execute trades for their customers but do not hold an inventory of the underlying securities. In order to execute a trade, a Level 2 broker calls a Level 1 market maker with the best quoted price.
- *Level 1* subscribers are investors who are not actively buying or selling securities but want information on current prices. The market in OTC securities is called the second market.

The third market is composed of nonmember firms who trade exchange-listed securities in the OTC market. The third market enables large traders to benefit from cost economies in large trades. In May 1975, the fixed commission system was abolished and commissions on all NYSE orders became negotiable. The fourth market refers to direct trading of exchange-listed securities without the benefit of a broker. Large institutional investors, who want to avoid going through a broker or an exchange, trade directly with each other with the benefit of electronic networks such as Instinet or Posit.

The number of member and nonmember investment banks had increased over the years until the market crash of 1987, after which the number declined significantly. Table 9.12 presents the data on the size of the industry.

The major activities in investment banking include the following:

- Underwriting
- Trading and Brokerage

TABLE 9.12	Number of Investment Banks in the United States		
Year	NYSE Member Firms Dealing with Public	NYSE Member Firms Total	NASD Total
1981	390	604	3,265
1982	387	617	3,697
1983	412	639	4,885
1984	393	628	5,726
1985	381	599	6,307
1986	417	611	6,658
1987	392	596	6,722
1988	363	555	6,432
1989	353	535	6,148
1990	327	516	5,827
1994	311	501	5,400

Source: New York Stock Exchange Fact Book, 1994 Data, p. 86, and Securities Industry Association.

- Research
- Private Placements
- Mergers and Acquisitions
- Funds Management

The financial statements for member banks are presented in Tables 9.13 and 9.14.[9]

Underwriting

An investment bank underwrites a new issue by purchasing the entire debt or equity issue at one price and then reselling it to the public at a higher price. The investment bank assumes the risk that the securities can be sold for at least their cost. In order to minimize the risk and help to sell the issue, investment banks form an underwriting *syndicate* to share the risk. One firm serves as the lead manager with the responsibility for all aspects of the issue, and others in the syndicate help to sell the issue.

The difference between the investment bank's purchase price and the offering price is called the *spread* or *discount*. The spread is the compensation for the investment bank for its efforts. In addition to the spread, the investment bank may receive warrants (rights to purchase shares) or stock in the issuing company. The maximum spread permitted by the SEC is 10% of the offered price. Equity issue spreads normally range from 4% to 8%, whereas debt issue spreads range from 0.5% to 2.5%, depending on the size and quality of the issue. Table 9.15 lists the 1994 volume of the underwriting activities by the top 10 U.S. investment banks and their reported fees from new issues.[10]

The underwriting procedure previously discussed is known as *firm commitment*, in which the investment bank bears the risk by buying the entire issue. An investment bank may also enter into a *best effort* agreement without bearing the risk of buying the entire issue. In the best effort method of issuing securities, the investment bank serves as an agent who provides best effort to sell the securities at the offering price in exchange for a commission for each share sold. Best effort

---

[9] *New York Stock Exchange Fact Book, 1994 Data*, pp. 86–88.
[10] *The Wall Street Journal*, January 2, 1995.

TABLE 9.13   Income Statement for NYSE Member Firms Doing Business with Public, 1994

Item	$ Million	% of Total
Securities commissions	$13,510	18.9%
Trading and investment	13,342	18.7
Interest on customers' debit balances	4,527	6.3
Underwriting	5,854	8.2
Mutual fund sales	3,193	4.5
Commodity revenues	1,952	2.7
Other income related to securities	24,234	34
Other income unrelated to securities	4,757	6.7
Gross income	**$71,369**	**100%**
Registered representatives' compensation	10,897	15.3
Commissions and fees to others	2,625	3.7
Clerical and administrative	14,593	20.4
Communications	2,714	3.8
Occupancy and equipment	3,168	4.4
Promotional	1,297	1.8
Interest	23,731	33.3
Service bureaus and data processing	1,205	1.7
Bad debts, errors, and nonrecurring costs	455	0.6
Other	9,518	13.3
Total expenses	**$70,203**	**98.4%**
Net profit before federal taxes	$1,166	1.6%
Estimated federal tax	408	0.9
Net profit	**$758**	**1.0%**

offerings are generally used in the context of small initial public offerings (IPOs) whereas firm commitments are used in seasoned new issues and large IPOs.[11]

Trading and Brokerage

After newly issued securities are sold in the primary market, they become available to be bought and sold in the aftermarket. An investment bank involved in aftermarket trading may function as either a broker by executing customer orders or a dealer by trading for its own account. The Glass-Steagall Act prohibits commercial banks from holding an inventory of securities as dealers. While the act does not preclude commercial banks from providing brokerage services in securities to their customers, many have abstained from securities brokerage except for servicing some large clients in their trust departments.

Other trading activities of investment banks include pure arbitrage, risk arbitrage, and trading in government bonds and derivatives. A pure arbitrage trading refers to simultaneous purchase and sale of a security in two different mar-

---

[11] Seasoned new issues include new securities issued by companies that are already public, whereas IPOs encompass new securities issued by companies that are going public for the first time. See Ritter (1987).

TABLE 9.14 Balance Sheet of NYSE Firms, 1994		
Assets	**$ Millions**	**% of Total**
Bank balances, cash, and other deposits	$9,596	1.1%
Receivables from other brokers and lenders	252,376	29.7
Receivables from customers and partners	63,796	7.5
Long positions in securities and commodities	494,153	58.3
Secured demand notes	383	0.1
Exchange memberships	300	0.0
Land and other fixed assets	3,375	0.4
Other assets	24,727	2.9
Total Assets	**$848,706**	**100%**
Liabilities and Capital		
Money borrowed	$401,974	47.4%
Payable to other brokers and dealers	99,527	11.7
Payable to customers and partners	86,222	10.2
Short positions in securities and commodities	131,758	15.5
Other accrued expenses and accounts payable	72,376	8.5
Total liabilities	$791,857	93.3%
Total capital	$56,849	6.7
Total Liabilities and Capital	**$848,706**	**100%**

kets to take advantage of price differential. A risk arbitrage transaction takes place in the context of corporate mergers wherein the investment bank purchases shares in the potential target firm and sells shares short[12] in the acquiring firm. For example, suppose there is a merger negotiation between Company A and Company T where A offers one share in exchange for two shares of T. The share prices are $40 and $15 for A and T, respectively. The investment bank purchases 100,000 shares of T at the cost of $1,500,000 and sells short 50,000 shares of A for $2,000,000. If the merger goes through, the investment bank will receive 50,000 shares of A in exchange for its inventory of 100,000 shares of T. The investment bank will settle its short position by returning the 50,000 shares of A and earn a risk arbitrage profit of $2,000,000 − $1,500,000 = $500,000. If the merger does not go through for legal reasons or because of opposition by the target firm, share prices may move in unpredictable ways, causing considerable loss.

Investment banks also trade in government bonds in a separate trading department. Since the Glass-Steagall Act did not prohibit commercial banks from underwriting and trading in government bonds, they are strong competitors of investment banks in this business. Some investment and commercial banks are official U.S. government bond dealers who are authorized to bid for new issues auctioned periodically and to trade directly with the Federal Reserve Bank of New York. (More to come on government bond dealers in Chapter 13.) Finally, investment banks are involved in the design and sale of derivatives, an area we will cover in detail in Part III.

---

[12] Short-selling stock involves borrowing shares from a dealer and selling them in the market. The short seller has to buy the shares later and return them to the dealer.

TABLE 9.15	Top Underwriters of U.S. Debt and Equity Issues and Their Disclosed Fee Income			
Underwriter/Manager	**Amount ($ Billion)**	**% Market Share**	**Fees ($ Million)**	**% Market Share**
Merrill Lynch	$117.0	16.5%	$944.2	16.9%
Lehman Brothers	78.7	11.1	361.1	6.5
CS First Boston	73.5	10.4	329.7	5.9
Goldman Sachs	64.4	9.1	666.3	12.0
Morgan Stanley	58.7	8.3	564.6	10.1
Salomon Brothers	57.2	8.1	331.2	5.9
Kidder Peabody	48.8	6.9	192.3	3.5
Bear, Stearns	34.0	4.8	145.2	2.6
J.P. Morgan	26.5	3.7	NA	NA
Donaldson, Lufkin & Jenrette	23.1	3.3	277.7	5.0
Top 10	$581.9	82.0%	$3,812.3	68.4%
Industry total	$709.8	100%	$5,571.5	100%

Research

Research departments in investment banks are cost centers in which information on various companies and securities is gathered and processed. The data produced in research departments are used by various departments including trading and brokerage, mergers and acquisitions, and risk arbitrage. Prior to May 1, 1975, when commissions were fixed, investment banks used to compete with other firms by the quality of their research. With the negotiable commission system in place, investment banks now compete directly on price basis. The expansion of the discount brokerage firms (e.g., Charles Schwab & Co.), which offer no investment advice, has reduced the importance of what is called sell-side research. Part of the research activities has moved to institutional investors who conduct their own research for their own investment purposes. This type of research is called buy-side research.

Private Placements

For many firms, public issue of securities may not be feasible. The alternative to a public issue is the private placement of the issue with individual or institutional investors. Investment banks play an important role in the design and the placement of these issues. The reasons for private placements include: (1) the small size of the issue, (2) a need for a speedy process, (3) the problem of information asymmetry, and (4) the complexity and nonstandard nature of the securities. Institutional investors such as insurance companies, pension funds, and trusts are main customers for privately placed securities. For the investment bank, private placements provide business when public issues are in decline due to low historical prices in securities markets.

Mergers and Acquisitions

The decade of the 1980s was characterized by major corporate restructuring in the United States. These restructuring efforts were made possible by friendly and hostile takeover transactions. By the end of the 1980s, the wave of corporate restructuring seemed to have abated. The impact of corporate restructuring on the state of the economy was seen shortly thereafter. When the United States and other industrialized nations entered into a recession in 1991, the U.S. economy was able to emerge from the recession quickly by mid-1992. The economic efficiency brought about by corporate restructuring has been credited for the quick recovery of the U.S. economy. In contrast, the Japanese economy, which had avoided corporate restructuring, remained sluggish for many years. By the mid-1990s, another wave of merger activities was under way involving banking, communications, computer technology, health care, and the pharmaceutical industries.

Investment banks perform various functions in the mergers and acquisitions process. They provide investment advice to acquiring firms by finding and pricing suitable acquisition targets. They also provide professional services to target firms by helping to negotiate a fair price for the company or by designing defensive tactics to repel unwanted takeover efforts.

As merger activities continue in this economy, investment banks continue to earn substantial revenues from retainer fees, a percentage of the transaction, or both. In the capacity of investment advisers to acquiring and target firms, investment banks have access to material nonpublic information. This access has tempted many professionals in the investment banking community to engage in illegal insider trading. We will discuss in more detail mergers and acquisitions, defensive tactics, and insider trading in Chapter 14.

Funds Management

In this section we examine investment banking activities in funds management including merchant banking, portfolio management, and mutual fund management. Merchant banking involves investing the capital of the bank's partners in the debt and equity securities of customers. The practice is common more in the United Kingdom than it is in the United States. Commercial banks in the United States are explicitly prohibited from this practice. Merchant banking often relates to mergers and acquisitions activities of the investment bank. In some cases, the only way to bring a merger to successful fruition is for the investment bank to invest its funds as part of the financing. In this capacity, the practice of the investment bank is similar to holding an inventory of securities to support the trading desk.

The portfolio management activity of an investment bank is a fee-based fiduciary function provided to individual and institutional investors. In this capacity, the investment bank has discretionary investment powers similar to those of commercial banks in handling their trust departments. Investment banks are also involved in mutual funds activities. As mutual funds have gone through a period of explosive growth, investment banks have been able to reap lucrative profits from this business.

FINANCE COMPANIES

Finance companies are distinguished from banks and other depository financial intermediaries in that they finance their loans not by deposits but by issuing liabilities held directly as investments by households and businesses. Since they do not issue deposits, they are not regulated the way depository intermediaries are regulated. This gives them flexibility in their pursuit of new and profitable opportunities.

Finance companies are organized as either independent financial firms or as subsidiaries of manufacturing firms. In either case, they finance their assets by issuing commercial paper and long-term bonds and by borrowing from banks and from their parent companies. Often, they seek lines of credit from banks to facilitate selling their commercial paper and other securities in the financial markets.

TABLE 9.16 Balance Sheet for U.S. Finance Companies, 1993–1995 (Billions of Dollars, Not Seasonally Adjusted)			
	1993	**1994**	**1995 (2nd Q)**
Assets			
Consumer loans	$116.5	$134.8	$141.7
Business loans	294.6	337.6	361.8
Real estate loans	71.7	78.5	83.4
Less:			
Reserves for unearned income	−50.7	−55.0	−62.2
Reserves for losses	−11.2	−12.4	−13.7
All other assets	170.9	183.4	198.0
Total Assets	**$591.8**	**$666.9**	**$709.0**
Liabilities and Capital			
Bank loans	25.3	21.2	21.5
Commercial paper	159.2	184.6	181.3
Owed to parent	42.7	51.0	57.5
Not elsewhere classified	206.0	235.0	264.1
All other liabilities	87.1	99.4	102.1
Capital and surplus	71.4	75.7	82.5
Total Liabilities and Capital	**$591.8**	**$666.9**	**$709.0**

Source: Federal Reserve Bulletin, November 1995, p. A36.

Banks earn a fee on lines of credit and finance companies earn their revenues from loans. A major difference between finance companies and depository inter-mediaries is the size-intermediation function. Depository intermediaries collect small deposits from a large number of customers and make large loans. Finance companies raise large sums through commercial paper issues and lend in smaller amounts to borrowers.

General Electric's GE Capital is a large commercial lender, competing with banks on a wide range of business loans. GE Capital, which started as a small lender to help people purchase its parent company's refrigerators, now makes an annual profit of nearly $2 billion.[13] Ford Motor Company owns Ford Financial Services, Ford Motor Credit and United States Leasing, and First Nationwide Bank. Ford Financial is one of the top 10 issuers of credit cards in the United States and one of the biggest originators of mortgages. More than half of the company's receivables come from its financial activities. General Motors' GMAC is a multi-service finance company. It distributes credit cards and owns GMAC Mortgage and GM Capital Corporation, which issues industrial loans.

The Balance Sheet of Finance Companies

The balance sheet for U.S. finance companies is presented in Table 9.16. Finance company loans include consumer, business, and real estate loans. Their con-sumer loans include automobile and other consumer durable product loans, is-sued often in conjunction with the sale of their parent companies' products. Real estate loans include home mortgage and equity loans. Business loans of finance companies include retail, wholesale, and leasing of motor vehicles and equip-

---

[13] *The Economist,* April 30, 1994, p. 13 of the survey.

ment. Consumer, business, and real estate loans comprised 24%, 62%, and 14% of finance company loans in 1995.

Liabilities of finance companies totaled $626.6 billion, or 88% of total assets, in 1995. Bank loans provided 3% of financing, and parent companies on average contributed 11% of the debt. Commercial papers comprised 29% of the debt while the remaining 57% included other securities issued by finance companies.

Finance companies on average are better capitalized than depository financial intermediaries. For example, in 1995, the capital/asset ratio of finance companies as a whole was 12.10%, almost twice as high as that of depository firms. Of course, this should not be a surprise since finance companies' debt securities do not carry federal deposit insurance, and, therefore, they have to maintain a larger capital base to assure their capital market creditors.

SUMMARY
································

This chapter continues the discussion on nondepository financial intermediaries by examining pension funds, mutual funds, investment banks, and finance companies. Pension funds are broadly defined to include all retirement accounts including Social Security, other government-sponsored funds, and private pension plans. In the United States, the first major pension plan was established in the late 19th century by the railroad, the nation's largest employer at the time. Other private plans followed. During the Great Depression a large number of businesses failed, and employees lost their jobs and pension plans. President Roosevelt initiated the Social Security Act, which was passed in 1935 and went into effect two years later. Social Security provides 24% to 49% of preretirement income to individuals upon their retirement. In order to maintain one's preretirement standard of living, a replacement ratio of at least 70% is required. This means that individuals need to establish their own pension plans in addition to Social Security benefits.

There are two general categories of pension plans—defined contribution and defined benefit. In a defined-contribution plan the employer, and sometimes the employee, makes regular tax-deferred contributions into a trust account. The money accumulated in the trust account is invested in a portfolio of stock, bond, and money market funds. At retirement the employee receives a lump sum or an annuity, the size of which depends on the amount accumulated in the employee's account from contributions and investment earnings. The plan is fully funded and the employee bears the risk in the investment choice. The employer has no responsibility other than periodic contributions.

In addition to basic defined-contribution plans, there are other variations including 401(k) plans, 403(b) plans, Employee Stock Ownership plans (ESOPs), Individual Retirement Accounts (IRAs), and Keogh plans. In defined-benefit plans, pension benefits are calculated based on a formula that takes into account the length of service and the salary of the employee. This amount is paid to the employee as an annuity upon retirement. The annuity promised to employees is the liability of the corporation. This liability is insured by the Pension Benefit Guaranty Corporation, a federal agency. The employer has to pay an insurance premium based on the number of employees in the plan and the level of its funding. The plan's assets serve as collateral. Since neither Social Security nor employee pension plans are that secure, an individual should have an additional personal retirement plan.

Mutual funds are nondepository intermediaries that issue shares and invest in equity, debt, taxable, and tax-exempt securities. Mutual funds provide risk diversification to small savers. In addition, mutual funds reduce transaction costs. Technically, mutual funds are open-end investment companies. In an open-end investment company, the company stands ready to sell new shares every day. The company also stands ready to redeem shareholders' holdings if they decide to liquidate all or part of their investment. However, closed-end investment companies issue a fixed number of shares. Closed-end investment companies generally do not buy their own shares back from investors. Instead, closed-end shares are traded on a stock exchange. About 94% of assets in investment companies are in open-end funds and the remaining 6% are in closed-end companies.

Investment banks have developed independent of commercial banks because of the passage of the Glass-Steagall Act in 1933, which separated commercial and investment banking businesses. The primary function of investment banks involves underwriting new securities for corporations. Investment banks are also involved in the aftermarket trading both as brokers and as dealers. Other activities of investment banks include research, private placements of debt securities, investment advice on mergers and acquisitions, portfolio and mutual fund management.

Finance companies are distinguished from banks and other depository financial intermediaries in that they finance their loans not by deposits but by issuing liabilities held directly as investments by households and businesses. Since they do not issue deposits, they are not regulated as strictly as are depository institutions.

Finance companies are organized either as independent companies or as subsidiaries of manufacturing firms. They raise their funds by issuing commercial papers and long-term bonds and by borrowing from banks and parent companies. Often, they seek lines of credit from commercial banks before selling commercial papers in the capital market.

Finance companies issue consumer, business, and real estate loans. In 1995, finance companies controlled $709.1 billion in assets. Finance companies on average have 12.10% in capital, significantly larger than those of depository intermediaries. The remaining amount is raised through various debt instruments.

Nondepository Financial Intermediaries: Pension Funds, Mutual Funds, Investment Banks, and Finance Companies

REVIEW QUESTIONS

1. Describe the first major retirement fund established in the United States.

2. What were the circumstances under which the Social Security Act was passed?

3. What is the "replacement ratio"? What is the range of replacement ratio provided by Social Security? How does the replacement ratio provided by U.S. Social Security compare with that of France and Germany? What is the cause of this difference?

4. Describe the major private and public retirement funds. What percent of retirement funds are operated by private funds and what percent by government-sponsored plans?

5. Explain defined-benefit and defined-contribution plans. What are their similarities and differences? Who bears the risk under each of these plans?

6. Describe various types of defined-contribution plans including 401(k), 403(k), ESOP, IRA, and Keogh plans.

7. Suppose you are a single employee with an annual income of $28,000. How much can you contribute to an IRA under the partial deduction formula? You have an employer-sponsored pension plan as well.

8. Assume that you are married with a joint income of $45,000. How much can you contribute to an IRA under the partial deduction formula? You have an employer-sponsored pension plan as well.

9. Suppose you have a defined-benefit plan and you expect to have a preretirement annual salary of $120,000. The defined-benefit plan provided by your employer calculates the retirement benefit by taking 1.25% of your last salary

before retirement times years of service. With 35 years of service, how much will you receive in annual benefits? What will be the replacement ratio? If your Social Security offers a replacement ratio of 15%, what will be your overall replacement ratio? Is your overall replacement ratio adequate to maintain your pre-retirement standard of living?

10. Describe the incentives in underfunding and overfunding pension plans.
11. What are the incentives for industrial firms to underfund their pension plans?
12. What are the similarities and differences between the PBGC and the FDIC?
13. Define open-end and closed-end investment funds.
14. What is the NAV?
15. Explain the reasons for the rapid growth of mutual funds in the late 1970s and 1980s.
16. Describe four major categories of mutual funds and identify the natural clientele for each group.
17. Who are the institutional investors and what portion of mutual fund shares are owned by institutional investors?
18. What are the minimum investment requirements in mutual funds?
19. The economic rationale for the existence of mutual funds revolve around two basic functions. Discuss.
20. Discuss the international dimension of mutual fund activities.
21. What is the role of the Investment Company Institute in the operation of mutual funds?
22. What is an investment bank? How is it different from a commercial bank? In which areas may a commercial bank and an investment bank compete?
23. What was the original rationale for separating commercial and investment banking firms?
24. What is underwriting? What is the difference between a "firm commitment" and a "best effort" method of issuing securities?
25. What is the difference between public issues and private placements of securities?
26. Discuss the significance of mergers and acquisitions for investment banking.
27. Discuss the similarities and differences between finance companies and commercial banks.

REFERENCES

Alderson, M., and J. VanDerhei. 1992. "Pension Asset Reversions." in *Trends in Pensions 1992*, edited by John Turner and Daniel Beller. Washington, DC: U.S. Government Printing Office.

Bell, D. 1978. *The Cultural Contradictions of Capitalism.* New York: Basic Books, Inc., Publishers.

Bodie, Z. 1990. "Pension Funds and Financial Innovation." *Financial Management*, vol. 19, no. 3 (Autumn): 11–22.

Cohn, R.A., and F. Modigliani. 1985. "Inflation and Corporate Financial Management," in *Recent Advances in Corporate Finance*, edited by Altman and Subrahmanyan. Homewood, IL: Richard D. Irwin.

Fowler, D., and J. Rumsey. 1994. "Why Are Some Pension Plans Partially Funded?" *Journal of Economics and Business*, vol. 46: 207–213.

Ippolito, R. 1986. "The Economic Burden of Corporate Pension Liabilities." *Financial Analyst Journal*, vol. 42, (January/February): 23–34.

Ippolito, R. 1985. "The Economic Function of Underfunded Pension Plans." *Journal of Law and Economics*, vol. 28: 611–651.

Mutual Fund Fact Book. 1995. Washington, DC: Investment Company Institute.

Ritter, J. 1987. "The Costs of Going Public." *Journal of Financial Economics*, vol. 19.

Turner, J., and D. Beller (eds.). 1992. *Trends in Pensions 1992*. Washington, DC: U.S. Government Printing Office.

VanDerhei, J., and S. Harrington. 1989. "Pension Asset Reversions." in *Trends in Pensions 1989*, edited by John Turner and Daniel Beller. Washington, DC: U.S. Government Printing Office.

C H A P T E R

10

Global Financial Intermediation

OBJECTIVES

In our discussions in the previous chapters we have included global issues whenever feasible. If there were no regulatory, monetary, cultural, or language differences among countries, there would be no need for a separate chapter on global intermediation. With divergent systems, however, there are significant obstacles to true global markets where goods and services can be bought and sold in every corner of the world. Despite these obstacles, many intermediaries readily trade their financial instruments beyond their national boundaries. Differences in the regulatory structures of various countries have simultaneously restricted global transactions and provided the impetus for innovations designed to escape such restrictions. This chapter examines global financial intermediaries including offshore, multinational, foreign, and universal banking. The discussion includes the economic reasons for the growth of global financial intermediation, the distinct functions of various intermediaries, and the regulatory issues affecting the market.

GLOBALIZATION OF FINANCIAL INTERMEDIATION AND MARKETS[1]

The growth of global intermediation and markets is attributed to rapid growth in global trade, advances in communications and computer technology, and divergence in regulatory restrictions across nations. While international banking in support of trade has a long history, a major expansion of global intermediation occurred in the 1950s and 1960s when U.S. banks established foreign branch banks to serve international U.S. corporations. These banks have been credited with a considerable role in diffusing financial innovations to other nations, including the development of "wholesale" banking in 1950s London.[2] Prior to this expansion, the financing of international trade was often handled through corre-

---

[1] Nasser Arshadi would like to acknowledge the significant contributions made to this chapter by Anne Lewis.
[2] Lewis and Davis (1987).

spondent banking relationships between banks in the respective countries. Correspondent banks maintain interbank deposits in one or both currencies to facilitate trade transactions. Trade services provided by such banks include letters of credit, bankers' acceptances, short-term lending for trade finance, and foreign exchange services.

Technology has been a major contributor to the globalization of financial intermediation and markets. The expansion of telecommunications and computerized data processing has had an enormous role in decreasing transaction costs and the "economic distance" between countries. Screen trading has made location increasingly irrelevant. Access, liquidity, and efficiency are all powerfully affected by communications technology, and financial intermediaries have been positioned to take early advantage of these developments.

Differing national banking regulations have played a significant and continuing role in the development of international finance. U.S. restrictions on deposit interest and reserves requirements had a substantial role in the growth of offshore banking and the Eurocurrency market. International transactions have in turn fueled the demand for risk management through foreign exchange derivatives contracts. The international risk-based capital requirement imposed by the Basle Committee is contributing to a realignment in bank portfolios with a shift from traditional bank loans to fee-based products.

GLOBAL FINANCIAL INTERMEDIATION

Some Definitions

After World War II, international lending (as distinct from postwar assistance programs such as the Marshall Plan) was largely done to support trade and/or corporate expansion abroad. Virtually all loans to foreign borrowers were made in the currency of the lender, which meant that banks resident in capital-exporting countries had a competitive advantage in the international banking market. In addition, the exported dollars of the postwar assistance programs and the dollar reserves provisions of the Bretton Woods agreement increased the international role of the U.S. dollar, which became the dominant international currency of exchange by the 1950s. This posed a challenge to the long-established international hegemony of British banks.

Due to legal restrictions on branching, U.S. banks had long used a combination of correspondent bank and Fed Funds transactions to maintain reserves, to clear checks, and to meet liquidity needs. British banks adopted this networking approach from U.S. banks in London in the 1950s and applied it to a growing segment of their own banking industry, which was characterized by relatively few but very large transactions, often in nondomestic currencies. This development marked the beginning of *wholesale* finance in Britain, which from the outset was closely allied with international finance. Because wholesale banking involved a small number of very large transactions, retail banking techniques for managing liquidity and risk (the "law of large numbers" and diversification) did not apply. Instead, British wholesale banking of the 1950s used a growing network of international wholesale banking relationships to manage liquidity through interbank funds transfers. Risk management also involved a "systems" approach, with large transactions parceled out through interbank relationships and syndication. Asset and liability management techniques that were wholesale banking innovations in the 1950s and 1960s have become standard in the banking industry at all levels since then. These include the use of term loans or rollover credits with variable interest rates pegged to benchmarks like LIBOR or the U.S. prime rate, and large interest-bearing time deposits now known as jumbo CDs.

The "systems" approach to risk-bearing characterizes the global financial market to this day. For decades, about 70% of the dollar volume of offshore and Eurocurrency transactions has consisted of interbank transfers, revealing the liquidity and brokerage functions of this market as well.

With the development of a large pool of expatriated dollars in the 1950s and 1960s, the link between lending and the currency of the lender began to weaken, primarily through the dollar-based international transactions of London bankers. Various restrictive regulations in the United States accelerated the expatriation of dollar-based transactions. When these dollar deposits were joined with other currencies in the 1960s and later, the result was the creation of the financial *Euromarket*, which is defined by the separation of the currency of the transaction from that of the host country. The Euromarket is limited to wholesale transactions and is a truly global financial market, which exists primarily as an electronic network linking large multinational banks: There is no separate set of "Eurobanks." The Euromarket has both lending and capital market segments, which are described below.

Before continuing, however, we should clarify the meaning of some terms. The basis for the distinctions among international, multinational, Eurocurrency, and offshore banking lies in the residency of the financial institution (where it is domiciled), the foreign or domestic identity of the customer, the currency of the transaction, and the scale (wholesale or retail) of the transaction. Traditional *international banking*, for example, has involved a bank making loans to a foreign borrower in the bank's home currency. *Multinational banking* is defined as the establishment of bank branches and subsidiaries outside of the parent bank's home country—which does not necessarily involve a multinational bank in offshore or Eurodollar transactions, since these branches could confine themselves to dealing in the local currencies where they are located. Traditional international banking, including trade support transactions, had typically involved a commercial loan to a nonbank customer, but could also involve transactions on a retail level; multinational banks often do retail banking in their branches' local economies. In contrast, *offshore* and *Eurocurrency banking* involve transactions in a foreign currency relative to the host country and the customer can be foreign or domestic. Both are strictly wholesale transactions, frequently inter- or even intrabank.

There is considerable overlap between offshore and Eurocurrency banking, but a distinction can be drawn along functional lines. Offshore banking predominantly involves transactions carried out by the foreign branches of large banks in the currency of the parent bank. Therefore, while there is a difference between the host country currency and that of the offshore transaction (thus qualifying the transaction as Eurocurrency business), there is no such difference between the currency of the transaction and that of the parent bank. Typical examples would be New York banks transacting in dollars through their own branches in the Caribbean, or German banks transacting in marks through their branches in Luxembourg. The specific intent here is the avoidance of banking regulations in the home country of the parent bank; offshore banking is driven by the avoidance of domestic regulations. Eurocurrency banking is strictly defined as banking in any location in a currency other than that of the host country. Obviously, offshore and Eurocurrency banking are often one and the same. Eurocurrency shares with offshore banking a high degree of exemption from domestic regulations of all kinds; however, the historic focus and driving force in Eurocurrency banking has been in its role in foreign currency intermediation. In the absence of a goal of "regulatory arbitrage," there is no particular reason to expect that Eurocurrency banking done by the foreign branch of a parent bank will be in the same currency as the parent bank.

Offshore Banking

"Offshore" banking occurs in financial centers as diverse as London, Luxembourg, the Netherlands Antilles, Hong Kong, Singapore, and the Caribbean centers that serve New York banks. Offshore centers vary from "functional" centers, where all types of transactions are originated, to "shell" or "booking" centers, which are little more than postal addresses and wholly subordinate to the home offices of the offshore banks. While the common explanation for the development of offshore banking centers is "regulatory arbitrage," the financial regulations applicable to offshore financial centers vary considerably, from relatively high-tax but otherwise hospitable London to truly minimal regulatory environments, such as the Caribbean. Banks in countries with reserves requirements, such as the United States and Germany, use offshore sites to avoid them. Likewise, banks in countries that restrict banking activities, such as the United States and Japan, become involved in offshore banking in order to expand into businesses that are prohibited in their domestic markets. In particular, U.S. regulations limiting interest on deposits, requiring reserves, and restricting branching are credited with a major role in the development of offshore banking centers. Although many of the U.S. regulations that originally spurred offshore banking were subsequently repealed, it was not until "onshore offshore banking" was instituted in 1981 that significant portions of this business were repatriated to the United States. In other countries where banks are less regulated, such as the United Kingdom, the distinctions between traditional foreign banking and offshore or Eurocurrency banking are increasingly blurred; for such countries, the role of offshore sites may be confined to minimizing taxes. Typically, the transactions and the currency denominations used by offshore banks have little or no relation to the offshore site. Thus, offshore banking, like the Euromarket, is sometimes described as "stateless" finance.

U.S. Multinational Banking

The growth of traditional multinational banking accelerated in the 1970s, as U.S. banks vied aggressively with European and Japanese rivals for market shares. When the success of the OPEC oil cartel led to a buildup of petrodollars in the mid-1970s, cartel members displayed a strong inclination to deposit their new wealth at large European and U.S. banks. The banks recycled most of these deposits in the form of loans to "less developed countries" (LDCs) whose economies were variously affected by the OPEC price increases. Preexisting correspondent bank relationships sometimes functioned as the channels for this expansion from trade-related to foreign corporate and sovereign lending.

The rapid growth of LDC lending by U.S. banks in the 1970s has been linked to numerous factors, apart from the enormous disequilibrium created by the OPEC deposits at the outset. Banks lent with scant apparent concern for risk. Contributing factors to this practice may have included: (1) the risk incentives inherent in deposit insurance, which were conducive to increasing asset risk; (2) a push for growth, which was a U.S. banking industry response to deregulation in the early 1980s (the scale of foreign lending provided dramatic increases in asset size); (3) an underestimation of the credit, currency, and exchange control risks in "sovereign" lending; (4) overestimation of the adequacy of the information provided by new technology, and the relative risk reduction provided by loan syndication; and (5) an intense competition with Japanese banks, among others, for international market shares, with success measured more by size than by profits. Additional factors may have included the relative absence of domestic investment opportunities, due to recession, and continuing business losses due to disintermediation, as corporate borrowers resorted to commercial paper, and depositors decamped for money market mutual funds.

Foreign lending by U.S. and European banks increased until 1982, when Mexico declared a suspension of principal repayments on its debt. The ensuing negotiations, which frequently involved the International Monetary Fund as well as the banks and their foreign borrowers, revealed a peculiar form of moral hazard in sovereign lending. Loans to sovereign borrowers were frequently made for projects designed to generate national income, such as port facilities or hydroelectric dams. If the borrower consumed the loan at a pace that exceeded any possibility that national income would be increased by the time the loan was gone, the lender had an incentive to lend more, in the hope of salvaging the project and the previous loan. In addition, if the borrowing country failed to implement policies designed to reduce its current account deficit, it might also be unable to repay loans because its currency reserves were exhausted. Bank loans to "LDCs" were "restructured" (extended) for both reasons; banks had little or no control in either case. Thus, an initial foreign loan could lead to an obligation to throw good money after bad. To avoid this situation, many banks eventually ceased their sovereign lending, drastically contracting the market by the end of the decade.

U.S. banks also found themselves in a regulatory version of this trap, caught between the exhortations of the IMF and U.S. Treasury Secretary James Baker to continue lending and restructuring, and the urging of bank regulators to improve the quality of their balance sheets. With the exception of the largest money center banks, most U.S. banks wrote off and otherwise disposed of these loans during the late 1980s, and exited the multinational banking market with a concerted effort that rivaled the speed of their entrance some 10 years earlier. As a result, very few U.S. banks are now active in multinational banking—the most notable exception being Citibank, which earns over half of its income from overseas. However, this pattern may be changing once again, at least in the case of Mexico.

In the aftermath of the passage of NAFTA, various U.S. and other foreign investors were attracted to the Mexican economy, which was seen as an untapped growth market. Following a presidential election and political unrest in the southern region of the country, Mexico faced serious economic troubles, which led to its decision to devalue its currency, the peso, on December 20, 1994. The economic and political uncertainties surrounding Mexico caused a free fall in the peso and the Mexican stock market. On February 21, 1995, U.S. and Mexican government officials announced a financial aid package to Mexico totaling $50 billion. The U.S. government provided $20 billion from its discretionary funds and the IMF and the World Bank provided the rest of the rescue package. For its share of the assistance package, the U.S. charged a fee of 2¼ percentage points or more over T-bill rates to discourage Mexico from leaning too heavily on the guarantees.[3] The receipts of Mexico's state-owned oil company, Pemex, were used as collateral.

Foreign Banking in the United States

Foreign banks have operated in the United States since the middle of the 18th century. British banks have been present since colonial times; Canadian banks appeared in California by the mid-19th century. The growth of foreign banking operations in the United States accelerated in the late 1970s, with foreign banking

[3] *The Economist*, February 25, 1995, p. 79.

	U.S.-Owned Banks		Foreign Banking Offices	
Year	**Number**	**Total Assets (Billions)**	**Number**	**Total Assets (Billions)**
1980	14,015	$1,688.8	441	$252.0
1985	14,058	2,502.9	621	485.8
1990	12,221	3,198.1	700	822.4
1991	11,742	3,200.6	726	910.3
1992	11,307	3,249.9	686	946.1
1993	10,827	3,429.7	660	933.1
1994	10,583	3,620.3	652	951.9

TABLE 10.1   The Number and Assets of Foreign Banking Offices in the United States and U.S.-Owned Banks

1994 figures are drawn from second-quarter data.

Source: Board of Governors of the Federal Reserve System.

offices doubling between 1975 and 1980. Foreign banks operating in the U.S. market did not contract their operations in the late 1980s, as U.S. banks were doing relative to their own foreign lending. As a result, data on foreign bank operations in the United States reveal a continuing expansion, slowed somewhat by recession in the early 1990s.

Foreign banks operate in the United States in the form of an agency, a branch, or a subsidiary. A foreign bank agency is a separate office of a foreign-domiciled parent bank, which provides full banking services with the exception of taking deposits from U.S. citizens,[4] selling CDs, and offering trust services. A foreign branch bank is a separate office of a foreign-domiciled parent bank, which provides full banking services including taking deposits. A foreign subsidiary is a U.S. subsidiary of a foreign bank with 25% or greater foreign ownership, which offers a complete set of banking services. We use "foreign banking offices" as a generic term encompassing foreign banking agencies, branches, and subsidiaries.

The number of foreign banking offices grew significantly in the last two decades: from 50 in 1970 to 652 in 1994. Table 10.1 presents the extent of foreign bank growth in the United States for 1980–1994. In 1980, there were 441 foreign banking offices in the United States with combined assets of $252 billion, while there were 14,015 U.S.-owned banks with combined assets of more than $1,688.8 billion. The number of foreign banking offices peaked at 726 in 1991 and then declined to 652 by 1994. The decline in offices was not unique to foreign banks: In recent years, U.S.-owned banks have also declined in numbers, from 14,015 in 1980 to 10,583 in 1994.

Table 10.2 provides further information on the significance of foreign banking operations in the United States. In terms of total assets, foreign banking offices held 13% of total U.S. bank assets in 1980. This figure grew to 20.8% by 1994. Growth was even more substantial in some categories of banking operations: For example, foreign banking offices held 30.3% of commercial and industrial (C&I) loans in 1994.

---

[4] Unless related to international activities.

TABLE 10.2	Market Share of Foreign Banking Offices in the United States					
	Assets (Billions)	Market Share %	Total Loans (Billions)	Market Share %	C&I Loans (Billions)	Market Share %
1980	$252.0	13.0%	$148.9	14.1%	NA	NA
1985	485.8	16.3	265.4	15.1	$115.3	19.7%
1990	822.4	20.5	408.1	17.1	198.8	27.6
1991	910.3	22.1	426.8	18.2	212.1	30.9
1992	946.1	22.5	435.8	18.7	215.9	32.2
1993	933.1	21.4	416.1	17.2	205.9	31.0
1994	951.9	20.8	412.0	16.6	210.0	30.3
1994 figures are drawn from second-quarter data.						

Source: Board of Governors of the Federal Reserve System.

Table 10.3 presents loan portfolios of major foreign participants in the U.S. banking market for 1985 and 1994. Japan ranked first in both years with $65.1 and $141.9 billions in total loans, respectively. Real estate (R/E) loans as a percent of total loans comprised only 0.4% of Japanese bank assets in the United States in 1985, but increased to 21.3% by 1994. C&I loans constituted more than 50% of the total loans for Japanese banks in both years. Italy ranked second in terms of total loans in 1985 with $22.7 billion, no R/E loans and 28.5% in C&I loans. Italy's total loan amount ranked only fifth in 1994 with $15.6 billion, below Japan, Switzerland, Canada, and France.

Universal Banking

U.S. banks have long complained that the cost of domestic regulation renders them uncompetitive; they have aspired to the relatively unregulated "universal" status of European banks. Universal banks are unrestricted with regard to their activities, branching, and investments: They can sell securities and insurance, and take equity positions in the industrial corporations they lend to. As a result,

TABLE 10.3	Major Foreign Participants in the U.S. Banking Market					
	1985			1994		
	Total Loans (Billions)	R/E Loans (%)	C&I Loans (%)	Total Loans (Billions)	R/E Loans (%)	C&I Loans (%)
Japan	$65.1	0.4%	50.5%	$141.9	21.3%	58.0%
Italy	22.7	0.0	28.5	15.6	1.3	31.9
Canada	15.8	24.6	61.7	20.3	12.0	72.6
Switzerland	12.6	0.4	26.8	23.8	4.7	58.6
France	10.0	2.0	39.4	17.7	5.5	69.6
United Kingdom	9.3	2.7	51.0	11.7	10.7	32.8
Germany	5.8	0.2	34.7	10.6	9.8	37.6
Netherlands	2.3	14.5	11.8	9.8	3.1	82.5
1994 figures are drawn from second-quarter data.						

Source: Board of Governors of the Federal Reserve System.

European banks—many of them with a history of state ownership—have tended to be few in number and very large in size, with extensive branch networks. These banks have become nationally entrenched, able to ward off would-be competitors through price wars subsidized by their own diverse operations, or even through the help of their national regulators. Because these European banks offer all financial services under one roof, the proliferation of nonbank competition (investment banks, insurance and finance companies) that is typical of the United States has not developed in Europe. Disintermediation has been much slower than in the United States, with the universal banks retaining a much higher proportion of total domestic financial assets than is the case here. As of early 1994, relatively little cross-border bank expansion has occurred in the EC, despite the liberalization of access at the end of 1992.[5] There has been no unleashing of cross-border competition and innovation, and such consolidation as has occurred has been mainly in-country.

European capital markets remain generally much less developed than in the United States. There is relatively little recourse to securitization, although the use of commercial paper by industrial firms—despite the close embrace of their banks—is increasing. As U.S. banks specialize and innovate in their struggle for survival, European banks are likely to find it difficult to emulate them. It has been estimated that European banks throw away one-fifth of their profits each year because of their failure to properly manage their asset and liability positions, using techniques that are already in wide use in the United States.[6]

Due to their huge size and diversified activities, European universal banks are more like conglomerates than the increasingly cost-efficient specialists that are expected to dominate U.S. banking. A telling comparison can be made, for instance, between the cost-to-income ratios for top U.S. and European banks.[7] Table 10.4 presents the performance rankings of the top 100 banks in the world using profitability, cost-efficiency, pricing, and analysts' ratings for 1993–1994.[8] In the United States, three top-rated retail banks—Banc One, Wachovia, and Fifth Third Bankcorp—had cost-to-income ratios of 63%, 59%, and 49%, respectively. In contrast, Deutsche Bank, the Swiss Bank Corporation, and Credit Suisse Group had ratios of 79%, 82%, and 77%. This means that costs consumed between less than one-half to under two-thirds of income for the U.S. banks; for the Europeans, they were consistently over three-fourths. Return on equity (ROE) for the same three U.S. banks was more than 16%; for the European banks, ROE was no higher than 10.7%. Ironically, the case can thus be made that European banks' "universal" status may have offered them too much protection. A 1992 study of retail banking productivity in the United States, the United Kingdom, and Germany found that American banks had a productivity advantage of nearly 50% over their German or British peers.[9]

---

[5] *The Economist*, April 30, 1994, p. 32 of the survey.

[6] *The Economist*, May 2, 1992, p. 3 of the survey.

[7] "The World's 100 Best Banks," *Euromoney*, August 1994, pp. 68–72.

[8] In this ranking, banks with over $1 billion in equity are included. Scoring is out of 100 and allocated as follows: return on equity, 15 points; return on assets, 10 points; cost-to-income ratio, 10 points; net interest margin, 10 points; total net income, 15 points; credit ratings, 15 points; analysts' ratings, 25 points. For more detail, see Ibid.

[9] *The Economist*, April 30, 1994, p. 39 of the survey.

The post–World War II regulations that erected economic fences around national borders were the outcome of a cooperative international effort intent on supporting international trade while preserving the economic autonomy of the trading nations. The gradual removal of these barriers, or **deregulation**, is credited with a large role in the expansion of trade and international finance in recent decades. In contrast, the imposition of banking regulation in a single country, the United States—specifically, reserve requirements, deposit insurance, capital movement restrictions, and interest ceilings—is also "credited" with a decisive role in the creation of the Eurocurrency markets, which have proven extremely resistant to all attempts at nonmarket-based controls. Thus, international deregulation has played a large role in increasing cross-border banking, while certain restrictive national regulations have had a major role in the development of offshore banking. Eurocurrency markets have not been problem-free—the Herstatt crisis and the Banco Ambrosiano collapse both exposed systemic problems (see below). However, on a purely national level, the banking regulations of most Western countries have de facto favored international transactions because of the "hands-off" approach taken toward them—if less clearly defined and protected, international transactions have also been much less burdened with regulation.

International Banking Regulation in the United States

The U.S. regulation of international banking dates from the creation of the Federal Reserve system in 1913. The national banks created by this act were allowed to conduct international banking, and this permission was extended to state-chartered banks and corporations in 1916, provided they agreed to be subject to Federal Reserve control (hence "Agreement Corporations"). There was no rush by national or state banks to develop international banking until the "Edge Act" amendment of 1919, which permitted banks to invest in nonbank businesses, and most Edge Act corporations were set up initially for this purpose. Currently, Edge Act corporations require a minimum of $2 million in capital and 10% in reserves; before 1978, only U.S. citizens could act as directors (none of these requirements applies to Agreement corporations). Although located in the United States, Edge Act corporations have traditionally been allowed the full range of activities that are permitted in the foreign countries with which they do business.

Prior to the International Banking Act (IBA) of 1978, the agencies and branches of foreign banks in the United States enjoyed a substantial competitive advantage relative to U.S.-chartered banks. Because they were licensed and supervised by individual states, they (1) could establish full-service branches in multiple states; (2) were not required to hold reserves with the Federal Reserve system; (3) were not subject to activity restrictions (unless operating U.S. subsidiaries), and could thus operate both securities companies and deposit-taking branches in the United States.[10] Generally, the "national treatment" of foreign banks is considered a relatively liberal policy, in that foreign banks, instead of being singled out for protective restrictions, are accorded the same powers and range of activities as domestic banks. In the case of the IBA, however, the imposition of "national treatment" on foreign banks served to correct what had been a de facto advantage held by foreign banks relative to their U.S. counterparts. After passage of the IBA, foreign banks were required to declare a single "home" state, with the activities of all nonhome-state branches or agencies limited to those allowed for Edge Act corporations—i.e., international transactions. At the same time, Edge

---

[10] Hall (1993), p. 261, note 26.

1994	1993	Bank Name—Country	Total Score	Share-holders' Equity ($B)	Return on Equity (%)	Score	Return on Assets
		TABLE 10.4 The World's 100 Best Banks					
1	1	JP Morgan—*U.S.*	69.52	9.86	16.09	9.27	1.18
2	6	Banc One Corporation—*U.S.*	69.22	7.03	16.21	9.29	1.43
3	3	Union Bank of Switzerland Group—*Switzerland*	67.93	14.06	10.84	8.39	0.73
4	2	Banco Popular Espanol—*Spain*	67.90	1.85	21.89	10.24	2.03
5	11	Wachovia Corporation—*U.S.*	67.85	3.02	16.31	9.30	1.60
6	16	Norwest Corp—*U.S.*	66.00	3.57	18.32	9.64	1.29
7	—	HSBC Holdings—*U.K.*	65.80	16.10	18.98	9.75	1.00
8	8	Lloyd's Bank Group—*U.K.*	64.78	5.33	19.25	9.80	0.97
9	4	Deutsche Bank—*Germany*	64.37	12.09	10.67	8.36	0.40
10	—	Fifth Third Bancorp—*U.S.*	63.21	1.20	16.40	9.32	1.64
11	15	Swiss Bank Corporation—*Switzerland*	62.87	9.34	9.82	8.21	0.66
12	9	BankAmerica Corporation—*U.S.*	62.72	17.14	11.40	8.48	1.05
13	12	Credit Suisse Group—*Switzerland*	62.62	9.48	10.35	8.30	0.63
14	—	Citicorp—*U.S.*	62.41	13.95	15.90	9.24	1.02
15	19	Credit Agricole Group—*France*	62.29	15.05	6.18	7.60	0.33
16	14	Suntrust Banks—*U.S.*	61.68	3.61	13.12	8.77	1.16
17	24	Halifax Building Society—*U.S.*	61.32	5.50	145.74	9.21	0.86
18	13	Bankers Trust New York Corp—*U.S.*	61.27	4.15	23.97	10.59	1.16
19	18	Babobank—*Netherlands*	61.14	7.89	7.31	7.79	0.44
20	22	NBD Bancorp—*U.S.*	60.90	3.25	14.95	9.08	1.20
21	21	National Australia Bank—*Australia*	60.88	5.84	12.61	8.68	0.97
22	17	Republic New York Corp—*U.S.*	60.82	2.75	10.96	8.41	0.79
23	5	Banco Santander—*Spain*	60.71	3.61	15.07	9.10	0.75
24	—	Northern Trust Corporation—*U.S.*	60.61	1.15	14.58	9.01	0.99
25	50	Keycorp—*U.S.*	60.55	4.39	16.16	9.28	1.19
26	27	Generale Bank—*Belgium*	60.53	3.03	10.55	8.34	0.31
27	—	Huntington Banc-shares—*U.S.*	60.48	1.22	19.48	9.84	1.41
28	33	ABN Amro—*Netherlands*	60.40	9.83	10.58	8.34	0.41
29	52	First Bank System—*U.S.*	59.96	2.25	13.27	8.79	1.13
30	—	Firstar Corporation—*U.S.*	59.92	1.16	17.67	9.53	1.48

Score	Cost to Income (%)	Score	Net Interest Margin (%)	Score	Net Profit ($M)	Score	Credit Rating	Score	Analysts' Rating	Score
4.63	57.09	7.97	1.32	1.15	1,586.00	9.66	9.7	14.55	8.12	22.30
5.00	62.96	7.76	5.12	4.46	1,139.98	8.04	7.3	10.95	8.63	23.72
3.93	52.11	8.14	1.17	1.02	1,523.64	9.43	10	15.00	8.02	22.20
5.92	41.65	8.52	5.70	4.97	405.21	5.37	8	12.00	7.60	20.88
5.27	59.18	7.89	4.18	3.65	492.10	5.69	7.7	11.55	8.92	24.50
4.78	71.90	7.44	4.74	4.14	653.60	6.28	6.7	10.05	8.62	23.67
4.35	69.22	7.53	2.15	1.88	3,056.95	15.00	5	7.50	7.20	19.78
4.29	62.07	7.79	2.95	2.57	1,025.39	7.62	8	12.00	7.53	20.70
3.43	78.79	7.19	2.11	1.84	1,289.95	8.59	10	15.00	7.27	19.96
5.33	48.78	8.26	3.65	3.18	196.45	4.62	5	7.50	9.10	25.00
3.82	81.82	7.09	1.51	1.32	917.01	7.23	9.7	14.55	7.52	20.65
4.41	63.88	7.72	3.98	3.47	1,954.00	11.00	5.3	7.95	7.17	19.69
3.77	76.83	7.26	1.19	1.04	980.83	7.46	10	15.00	7.20	19.78
4.38	66.03	7.65	3.55	3.10	2,219.00	11.96	5	7.50	6.77	18.59
3.31	58.69	7.91	3.07	2.68	929.73	7.28	9	13.50	7.28	20.01
4.59	66.78	7.62	3.39	2.96	473.73	5.62	6.3	9.45	8.25	22.66
4.12	54.02	8.08	2.25	1.96	865.26	7.04	8.7	13.05	6.50	17.86
4.59	63.76	7.73	1.63	1.42	995.00	7.51	6.7	10.05	7.05	19.37
3.49	79.10	7.18	2.29	2.00	576.66	6.00	10	15.00	7.17	19.69
4.64	66.32	7.64	3.91	3.41	485.79	5.67	6.3	9.45	7.65	21.02
4.30	70.32	7.50	3.50	3.05	735.92	6.57	7.7	11.55	7.00	19.23
4.01	54.21	8.07	2.02	1.76	301.21	5.00	7.7	11.55	8.02	22.02
3.95	56.74	7.98	2.32	2.03	544.58	5.88	8	12.00	7.20	19.78
4.33	73.46	7.38	1.95	1.70	167.90	4.51	7	10.50	8.43	23.17
4.64	64.80	7.69	4.49	3.92	709.93	6.48	5	7.50	7.66	21.04
3.29	56.41	7.99	1.89	1.65	319.66	5.06	8	12.00	8.08	22.20
4.97	59.16	7.89	4.79	4.18	236.91	4.76	5	7.50	7.77	21.34
3.44	77.61	7.24	1.80	1.57	1,039.32	7.68	8.3	12.45	7.17	19.69
4.54	63.98	7.72	4.36	3.80	298.00	4.98	5	7.50	8.23	22.62
5.08	64.56	7.70	4.12	3.59	204.29	4.64	4.5	6.75	8.23	22.62

1994	1993	Bank Name–Country	Total Score	Share-holders' Equity ($B)	Return on Equity (%)	Score	Return on Assets
31	30	Dresdner Bank—*Germany*	59.86	7.34	8.35	7.97	0.28
32	94	Nationsbank Corporation—*U.S.*	59.70	9.98	15.04	9.09	0.95
33	—	Golden West Financial Corporation—*U.S.*	59.53	2.07	13.26	8.79	0.95
34	7	Abbey National—*U.K.*	59.36	5.00	11.52	8.50	0.47
35	—	Chemical Banking Corporation—*U.S.*	59.22	11.16	14.37	8.98	1.07
36	36	Kredietbank—*Belgium*	59.16	2.33	13.55	8.84	0.46
37	—	Wells Fargo & Company—*U.S.*	59.13	4.32	14.18	8.95	1.17
38	—	First Interstate Bancorp—*U.S.*	59.09	3.55	20.76	10.05	1.43
39	86	ING Bank—*Netherlands*	58.97	4.09	10.30	8.29	0.40
40	42	PNC Bank Corporation—*U.S.*	58.94	4.33	16.79	9.39	1.17
41	44	Société Générale—*France*	58.93	8.18	8.04	7.92	0.25
42	61	Bank of Nova Scotia—*Canada*	58.63	4.43	12.09	8.60	0.69
43	84	First Union Corporation—*U.S.*	58.58	5.21	15.70	9.20	1.15
44	34	Crédit Communal de Belgique—*Belgium*	58.40	1.76	10.04	8.25	0.22
45	—	TC Ziraat Bankasi—*Turkey*	58.36	1.41	40.37	13.35	4.68
46	32	Caja de Madrid—*Spain*	58.34	2.06	10.71	8.36	0.72
47	29	Bank of Montreal—*Canada*	58.25	4.32	12.30	8.63	0.61
48	84	National Westminster Bank—*U.K.*	58.18	8.71	10.91	8.40	0.42
49	10	Banco Bilbao Vizcaya—*Spain*	57.99	5.18	11.72	8.53	0.75
50	87	First Fidelity Bancorp—*U.S.*	57.90	2.74	14.48	9.00	1.17
51	—	Bank of New York Company—*U.S.*	57.70	4.07	13.73	8.87	1.23
52	—	Standard Chartered Bank—*U.K.*	57.48	1.98	17.12	9.44	0.72
53	—	Meridian Bancorp—*U.S.*	57.56	1.19	13.31	8.80	1.12
54	64	Bayerische Vereinsbank—*Germany*	57.44	4.39	7.65	7.85	0.20
55	—	Amsouth Bancorp—*U.S.*	57.42	1.09	13.42	8.82	1.17
56	40	Corestates Financial Corp—*U.S.*	57.38	2.03	10.41	8.31	0.82
57	65	Leeds Permanent Building Society—*U.K.*	57.33	1.47	12.95	8.74	0.65
58	31	Cassa di Risparmio delle Provincie Lombarde—*Italy*	57.20	6.08	3.06	7.08	0.26
59	26	Argentaria (Corporacion Bancaria de España)—*Spain*	57.18	5.15	11.41	8.48	0.71
60	58	National City Corp—*U.S.*	56.90	2.76	14.62	9.02	1.30

TABLE 10.4   The World's 100 Best Banks (Continued)

Score	Cost to Income (%)	Score	Net Interest Margin (%)	Score	Net Profit ($M)	Score	Credit Rating	Score	Ana-lysts' Rating	Score
3.24	33.53	8.81	1.65	1.44	612.71	6.13	9.5	14.25	6.57	18.04
4.27	63.37	7.74	2.94	2.57	1,501.00	9.35	5	7.50	6.98	19.18
4.27	34.20	8.78	2.54	2.22	273.90	4.90	5	7.50	8.40	23.08
3.52	58.93	7.90	1.60	1.39	576.23	5.99	8	12.00	7.30	20.05
4.45	61.12	7.82	3.09	2.70	1,604.00	9.73	5	7.50	6.57	18.04
3.51	57.14	7.96	1.78	1.56	315.02	5.05	7.3	10.95	7.75	21.29
4.60	57.62	7.95	5.06	4.42	612.00	6.12	4.3	6.45	7.52	20.65
5.01	67.16	7.61	4.03	3.51	736.72	6.58	4	6.00	7.40	20.33
3.42	70.89	7.47	2.52	2.20	421.07	5.43	8	12.00	7.33	20.15
4.60	56.58	7.98	2.62	2.28	726.00	6.54	5.3	7.95	7.35	20.19
3.20	69.49	7.52	1.51	1.31	657.64	6.29	8.7	13.05	7.15	19.64
3.86	58.36	7.92	2.80	2.44	535.21	5.85	7	10.50	7.08	19.46
4.58	63.61	7.73	3.91	3.41	817.52	6.87	4.7	7.05	7.18	19.73
3.14	84.32	7.00	1.26	1.10	176.24	4.54	9	13.50	7.60	20.88
10.00	67.76	7.59	11.46	10.00	570.73	5.97	—	0.00	4.17	11.45
3.91	58.02	7.93	3.57	3.12	221.09	4.70	8	12.00	6.67	18.32
3.74	60.84	7.83	2.75	2.40	531.47	5.83	7	10.50	7.03	19.32
3.45	65.59	7.66	2.41	2.10	950.03	7.35	8.3	12.45	6.10	16.76
3.95	63.68	7.73	2.69	2.35	606.66	6.10	7.7	11.55	6.47	17.77
4.61	58.41	7.92	4.01	3.50	396.46	5.34	4.5	6.75	7.57	20.79
4.69	58.45	7.92	3.29	2.87	559.00	5.93	4.7	7.05	7.42	20.38
3.91	63.34	7.74	2.98	2.60	338.35	5.13	5	7.50	7.70	21.15
4.53	17.06	9.39	4.54	3.96	157.80	4.48	3.5	5.25	7.70	21.15
3.12	63.48	7.74	1.28	1.12	336.05	5.12	9.5	14.25	6.64	18.25
4.60	65.90	7.65	3.53	3.08	146.23	4.43	5	7.50	7.77	21.34
4.07	69.37	7.53	4.73	4.12	211.75	4.67	5.7	8.55	7.33	20.12
3.81	40.99	8.54	2.20	1.92	190.14	4.59	7	10.50	7.00	19.23
3.20	34.07	8.79	2.40	2.09	186.14	4.58	8	12.00	7.08	19.46
3.90	53.51	8.09	2.17	1.90	587.80	6.04	7	10.50	6.65	18.27
4.80	66.99	7.61	3.86	3.37	404.00	5.37	5.7	8.55	6.62	18.18

1994	1993	Bank Name–Country	Total Score	Share-holders' Equity ($B)	Return on Equity (%)	Score	Return on Assets
61	—	SouthTrust Corporation—U.S.	56.88	1.05	14.31	8.97	1.02
62	—	First Chicago Corp—U.S.	56.65	4.26	18.86	9.73	1.53
63	—	State Street Boston Corporation—U.S.	56.78	1.10	16.27	9.30	0.96
64	56	Boatmen's Bancshares—U.S.	56.59	2.13	14.88	9.06	1.19
65	60	Allied Irish Banks—Ireland	56.42	1.77	11.54	8.50	0.69
66	—	Barnett Banks—U.S.	56.06	2.87	14.65	9.03	1.10
67	—	Deutsche Pfand-brief-und Hypothekenbank—Germany	55.95	1.13	6.33	7.63	0.11
68	—	Fleet Financial Group—U.S.	55.87	3.64	13.41	8.82	1.02
69	—	IMI-Istituto Mobiliare Italiano—Italy	55.86	4.27	6.97	7.74	0.66
70	47	Sanwa Bank—Japan	55.86	17.83	4.65	7.35	0.18
71	41	Toronto-Dominion Bank—Canada	55.62	3.78	5.48	7.49	0.32
72	81	Bank Burssels Lambert—Belgium	55.57	1.91	9.73	8.20	0.26
73	85	Den Danske Bank—Denmark	55.54	2.95	11.99	8.58	0.67
74	67	Cheltenham & Gloucester Building Society—U.K.	55.49	1.28	15.26	9.13	0.75
75	73	CA Banking Group—Austria	55.45	2.45	6.86	7.72	0.28
76	62	Bank Austria Banking Group—Austria	55.43	2.29	5.26	7.45	0.25
77	—	Schroders—U.K.	55.37	1.01	20.88	10.07	1.83
78	25	Bayerische Landesbank Girozentrale—Germany	55.28	3.02	5.61	7.51	0.12
79	83	Shizuoka Bank—Japan	55.14	3.51	5.43	7.48	0.28
80	80	Barclays Bank—U.K.	55.13	7.85	5.89	7.55	0.19
81	—	Bank of Ireland—Ireland	54.95	1.36	20.27	9.97	1.07
82	20	Commonwealth Bank of Australia—Australia	54.91	3.75	8.04	7.92	0.50
83	75	Bank of Scotland—U.K.	54.85	1.79	6.22	7.61	0.27
84	—	Chase Manhattan Corporation—U.S.	54.66	8.12	11.89	8.56	0.95
85	—	Kreditanstalt für Wiederaufbau—Germany	54.63	2.62	7.49	7.82	0.18
86	93	Mellon Bank Corp—U.S.	54.44	3.31	10.90	8.40	1.00
87	23	Landeskreditbank Baden-Würtemberg—Germany	54.16	1.83	3.96	7.23	0.27
88	89	Royal Bank of Scotland Group—U.K.	54.15	2.72	10.15	8.27	0.51
89	—	Canadian Imperial Bank of Commerce—Canada	53.96	5.96	9.13	8.11	0.54
90	55	Nationwide Building Society—U.K.	53.87	2.50	8.15	7.93	0.37

TABLE 10.4 The World's 100 Best Banks (Continued)

Score	Cost to Income (%)	Score	Net Interest Margin (%)	Score	Net Profit ($M)	Score	Credit Rating	Score	Analysts' Rating	Score
4.38	60.23	7.85	3.72	3.25	150.54	4.45	4	6.00	8.00	21.98
5.16	54.20	8.07	2.33	2.03	804.00	6.82	4.7	7.05	6.48	17.79
4.28	75.66	7.31	1.64	1.43	179.83	4.56	7	10.50	7.07	19.41
4.64	64.44	7.70	3.68	3.21	317.42	5.05	5	7.50	7.07	19.41
3.86	76.41	7.28	3.95	3.44	204.33	4.64	6	9.00	7.17	19.69
4.49	66.71	7.62	4.31	3.76	421.00	5.43	4.7	7.05	6.80	18.68
2.98	44.76	8.41	0.53	0.46	71.54	4.16	7.5	11.25	7.67	21.06
4.37	68.94	7.54	4.28	3.73	488.00	5.67	4.3	6.45	7.02	19.28
3.82	39.58	8.59	0.00	0.00	297.89	4.98	8	12.00	6.82	18.73
3.09	78.76	7.19	1.20	1.05	828.57	6.91	7.3	10.95	7.03	19.32
3.30	83.43	7.03	1.89	1.64	207.46	4.66	8	12.00	7.10	19.51
3.20	64.58	7.70	1.70	1.48	185.77	4.58	7	10.50	7.25	19.92
3.84	64.62	7.70	2.57	2.24	353.68	5.19	6.3	9.45	6.75	18.54
3.95	48.19	8.28	1.87	1.63	194.88	4.61	6.5	9.75	6.60	18.13
3.24	38.90	8.61	3.73	.325	168.18	4.51	6.5	9.75	6.68	18.36
3.19	90.52	6.78	2.13	1.86	120.28	4.34	9	13.50	6.67	18.32
5.62	60.17	7.86	1.15	1.01	211.28	4.67	4	6.00	7.33	20.15
2.99	75.84	7.30	0.65	0.57	169.35	4.52	10	15.00	6.33	17.40
3.24	70.29	7.50	1.57	1.37	190.43	4.59	7	10.50	7.45	20.47
3.09	65.29	7.67	2.36	2.06	462.46	5.58	8	12.00	6.25	17.17
4.45	71.57	7.45	3.77	3.29	276.21	4.91	5.3	7.95	6.17	16.94
3.57	82.60	7.06	3.32	2.90	301.34	5.00	8.3	12.45	5.83	16.03
3.22	51.83	8.15	2.36	2.06	111.19	4.31	7	10.50	6.92	19.00
4.26	66.35	7.64	3.78	3.30	966.00	7.41	4.7	7.05	5.98	16.44
3.08	65.33	7.67	0.47	0.41	196.11	4.61	10	15.00	5.83	16.03
4.34	71.65	7.45	3.64	3.18	361.00	5.21	4.3	6.45	7.07	19.41
3.23	56.89	7.97	1.66	1.44	72.78	4.17	10	15.00	5.50	15.11
3.59	81.76	7.09	2.31	2.01	275.71	4.90	6.7	10.05	6.64	18.25
3.64	62.50	7.77	2.79	2.43	547.21	5.89	7	10.50	5.68	15.61
3.37	48.08	8.29	2.40	2.10	204.15	4.64	7	10.50	6.20	17.03

				Share-holders'	Return on		Return on
1994	**1993**	**Bank Name–Country**	**Total Score**	**Equity ($B)**	**Equity (%)**	**Score**	**Assets**
91	—	Crestar Financial Corp—*U.S.*	53.65	1.06	13.22	8.79	1.06
92	—	Cera Bank—*Belgium*	53.64	1.44	16.71	9.37	0.93
93	28	Svenska Handelsbanken—*Sweden*	53.51	2.58	7.90	7.89	0.43
94	51	US Bancorp—*U.S.*	53.32	1.82	14.18	8.95	1.20
95	78	Gruppo Bancario Credito Romagnolo—*Italy*	53.22	1.45	6.78	7.70	0.47
96	54	Caja de Ahorros y Pensiones de Barcelona—*Spain*	53.15	2.47	13.53	8.84	0.61
97	—	Banca CRT—*Italy*	53.08	1.46	3.79	7.20	0.25
98	92	Woolwich Building Society—*U.K.*	53.07	1.94	10.63	8.35	0.54
99	—	Westdeutsche Landesbank Girozentrale—*Germany*	52.76	6.68	4.14	7.26	0.14
100	77	Royal Bank of Canada—*Canada*	52.67	5.94	3.78	7.20	0.19

TABLE 10.4   The World's 100 Best Banks (Continued)

Score	Cost to Income (%)	Score	Net Interest Margin (%)	Score	Net Profit ($M)	Score	Credit Rating	Score	Analysts' Rating	Score
4.43	73.75	7.37	3.97	3.46	140.49	4.41	3.3	4.95	7.37	20.24
4.24	65.23	7.68	1.87	1.63	241.03	4.78	6	9.00	6.17	16.94
3.46	87.27	6.89	2.48	2.16	203.80	4.64	6	9.00	7.08	19.46
4.66	65.75	7.66	4.50	3.92	257.90	4.84	5	7.50	5.75	15.80
3.53	81.10	7.11	3.26	2.84	98.49	4.26	6	9.00	6.83	18.77
3.74	74.18	7.36	2.74	2.39	333.93	5.11	6	9.00	6.08	16.71
3.20	35.04	8.75	2.61	2.28	55.39	4.10	6	9.00	6.75	18.54
3.64	67.64	7.59	1.96	1.71	206.49	4.65	6	9.00	6.60	18.13
3.03	66.00	7.65	0.98	0.86	276.62	4.91	9.3	13.95	5.50	15.11
3.10	68.04	7.58	2.77	2.42	224.88	4.72	7.3	10.95	6.08	16.7

Act corporations were exempted from the branching limitations imposed by the McFadden Act, and foreign majority ownership of Edge Act corporations was permitted. These measures increased the popularity of Edge Act corporations with foreign banks.

"International Banking Facilities" (IBFs) were created in 1981 in an attempt to bring offshore banking back onshore. IBF legislation exempted these facilities from local taxes and federal reserve requirements; minimum deposit and loan sizes were set in order to ensure that IBFs confined their business to the wholesale banking market. IBFs can only transact with foreign nonbank residents, foreign banks, and the foreign offices of U.S. banks. Physically, IBFs are usually just a separate set of records housed within a U.S. bank or Edge Act corporation. By 1992, nearly 500 IBFs had opened, with nearly half (representing 80% of the deposits) doing business in the New York area. However, IBFs have not replaced Caribbean banks because they are not permitted to offer overnight deposits. In 1986, Japan legislated a comparable facility for its banks (the Japan Offshore Market, or JOM), which has proved popular with smaller Japanese banks that had previously had no access to the Eurodollar markets.

The 1991 Foreign Bank Supervision Enhancement Act, also known as the BCCI Act, was a response to the Bank of Credit and Commerce International (BCCI) scandal. Blocked by U.S. regulators from entering the country, BCCI illegally acquired several U.S. banks that became enmeshed in the fraud and corruption endemic to the parent bank. When BCCI was shut down in 1991, it had worldwide depositors whose total losses were estimated at around $5 billion. Both the United States and the Basle Committee responded to the collapse of the bank with strengthened supervisory regulations. Designed to block loopholes exploited by BCCI, the U.S. regulations require that the Federal Reserve: (1) approve any federal or state branch and/or subsidiary established by a foreign bank; (2) examine such banks annually, and close down any foreign branch or agency where the Federal Reserve examiners are convinced that home country supervision is inadequate; and (3) approve any foreign bank's purchase of 5% or greater equity in a U.S. bank. In addition, any foreign bank that accepts deposits must be a separately capitalized subsidiary (i.e., it cannot lend on the basis of consolidated equity). As might be expected, there was a cost for reducing the risk of another BCCI—the U.S. market as a whole became less attractive to foreign banks, which now had increased incentives to operate offshore. Foreign banks' competitive status in the United States has thus changed from a state of relatively deregulated advantage, to "national treatment" in 1978, to supervisory disadvantage in 1991.

As with so many other cases, the BCCI regulations reveal the continuing trade-off between reducing systemic risk through regulation and losing business to more efficient arrangements elsewhere. This conflict was evident in a 1992 Federal Reserve study that documented the continuing success of offshore banking as a supplier of loans to U.S. corporations and industries.[11] The study demonstrated the ability of financial intermediaries to finesse differences in funding costs caused by the interaction of interest-rate changes and regulation. In this case, the applicable regulation required 3% reserves of U.S. banks, whether on- or offshore, a 3% reserves of foreign banks only if onshore. Offshore foreign bank loans escaped these reserve requirements. The authors of the study documented a rise in offshore foreign lending to U.S. corporate borrowers during the 1980s, which slowed only when the differential reserve requirement was lifted in 1990.

---

[11] McCauley and Seth (1992)..

They concluded that the volume of foreign lending to U.S. corporations was much greater than previously estimated, supplying about 45% of corporate borrowing in 1992, vs. a prior estimate of around 30%. Because of the undercounting of offshore foreign lending, the authors also concluded that recent claims about the rising significance of securitized corporate borrowing (i.e., commercial paper) in the United States were exaggerated.

The International Regulation of International Banking

Given that unilateral changes in banking regulation seem to do little more than produce another wrinkle in the Eurocurrency system, the need for some form of collective action to address systemic problems in international banking seems inescapable. The most prominent agent of collective international regulation is the Basle Committee on Banking Supervision. Some of the recent developments in major international system "safety" issues relate to market entry, capital adequacy, permitted activities, foreign exchange exposure, country risk, payment systems, bank supervision, and deposit insurance. Below, we describe each briefly.

Market Entry   In the United States, federal legislation authorized interstate banking in 1995. In Europe, the provisions of the Second Banking Directive commit the 15 nations of the European Community to permit the banks in any member country to operate in any other EC country after 1992. This access is also available to banks outside the EC, provided their home country grants free access to EC banks (a "reciprocity" policy). Coupled with the removal of all trade barriers and the development of a common currency, these changes are expected to go a long way toward the integration of the EC financial system.

Capital Adequacy   The development of new capital adequacy ratios by the Basle Committee on Banking Supervision has been discussed in Chapter 7. The international adoption of these standards is widely credited with changes in bank lending practices. The standards have been criticized for being too indiscriminate within their weight categories (i.e., a loan to Wang would receive the same risk weight as a loan to Microsoft), and for being limited to considerations of credit risk. Recently, efforts have been made to expand the risk-based weights of the ratios to include the market (price) risk and possibly interest-rate risk.

Permitted Activities   In the United States, three separate proposals were made in early 1995 by the Clinton administration and both houses of Congress to remove the Glass-Steagall prohibitions on securities activities. Most foreign operations of U.S. banks are already exempted from them, and bank holding companies have long been permitted to engage in limited securities operations. Japanese banks tend to emulate U.S. regulation in this area, although they are allowed to take equity positions in the firms they lend to. Some European "universal" banks have very few restrictions on their activities. The trend, both in the United States and internationally, is to reduce the restrictions placed on bank activities.

Foreign Exchange Exposure   U.S. banks' foreign exchange positions are monitored, although there are no regulatory limits. When other countries do set limits for their banks, they are usually expressed as a percentage of bank capital. In the case of Barings Bank, discussed in detail in Chapter 15, the Bank of England failed to uncover the reasons behind the transfer of billions of pounds to Barings Securities in Singapore prior to the collapse of the bank due to losses in derivatives trading.

Country Risk The United States has rather detailed assessments of country risk on a worldwide consolidated basis. An Inter-Agency Country Exposure Review Committee (IACERC) determines "allocated transfer risk reserves" that have to be held against country exposures. In addition, loans to foreign governments are subject to a loans-to-one-borrower limit. Countries are classified as "strong," "moderately strong," or "weak" using various current account ratios. Most other industrial countries do not apply aggregate country risk limits, although they also give considerable priority to the measurement of country risk.

Payment Systems The 1974 failure of the German Bankhaus Herstatt was a defining event for payment systems issues. First, because the failure interrupted the completion of numerous, very large wire transfers, it shook confidence in the electronic funds transfer system (CHIPS, the Clearing House Interbank Payments System), and raised questions about the jurisdiction of remedial action for such failures.[12] Second, because Bankhaus Herstatt was involved in large-scale OPEC Eurodollar transactions, it precipitated an OPEC "run" on non-U.S. Eurodollar banks. The new recipients of the OPEC Eurodollar deposits, large U.S. Eurodollar banks, averted a liquidity crisis by lending the deposits back to the European banks. The Herstatt crisis led to the development of the "Basle Concordat," an agreement that each central bank should assume responsibility for the foreign branches and subsidiaries of its own banks. While this principle is viable within a single currency, it becomes problematic in a Eurocurrency context, since the availability of reserves in the required currency may be limited. Eurocurrency banks set up their own "Lender of Last Resort" arrangements after Herstatt, however, by establishing dollar-denominated lines of credit with U.S. banks, often in exchange for equivalent credit lines in their own currency.

Bank Supervision Both the Banco Ambrosiano and the BCCI crises focused attention on the issue of international bank supervision. In both cases, the Basle Committee responded with international regulatory policies. The 1983 Banco Ambrosiano failure involved a Luxembourg Eurodollar subsidiary of an Italian bank that failed due to insider loans. Although the parent bank was supported by its national banking system, the subsidiary was not, on the basis that it was not a bank (it was a financial holding company). The resulting anxiety in the Eurocurrency markets was one of the factors that led the Basle Committee to propose new international capital standards for all banks.

The BCCI scandal raised another issue, that of the home vs. host country supervision of banks. The Basle Committee issued new guidelines in 1992 for a "dual key" approach, in which both the home and host country regulators of an international bank assess each other's supervisory standards. If, in the view of either party, the other side's supervision is inadequate, the "dual key" policy dictates that the bank should be excluded from the host country if home country regulations are too lax, or (if host country supervision is lax) discouraged from expanding there. This represented a modification of the Basle Concordat of 1975, and was designed to ensure that no foreign-owned banking operation would escape adequate supervision, as judged by both host and parent authorities.

The effectiveness of the "dual key" approach to bank supervision was tested in the Japanese Daiwa Bank scandal. The case involved a bond trader in Daiwa's New York office, Toshihide Iguchi, who had lost $1.1 billion in bond trading spanning several years. He had concealed his losses for a long time by selling

---

12 Bryant (1985), p. 130.

client bonds, which were still recorded on the bank's books. The case seriously tested the ability and willingness of the host country supervisors (New York Fed) and those of the home country (Japanese Finance Ministry) in monitoring foreign bank activities. The New York Fed had examined Daiwa Bank in 1993, and despite its concerns about Iguchi's trading activities, failed to uncover the depth of his illegal activities.[13] On the Japanese side, despite the fact that Iguchi had notified senior Daiwa officials in Tokyo about his activities in July 1995, they failed to share the information with the New York Fed (Daiwa's regulator in New York) for several weeks. As if that were not bad enough, Daiwa's senior officials in Tokyo ordered Iguchi to continue concealing his losses by selling bonds on three occasions to meet interest payments to clients whose bonds Iguchi had sold, but which were still recorded on the bank's books. Despite the good intentions in the "dual key" approach to bank supervision, cultural and nationalistic tendencies became impediments to the standard of good industry practice in the Daiwa Bank case.

Deposit Insurance   Virtually all industrialized economies have banking safety nets of some sort. These range from a simple reliance on the central bank as the lender of last resort, to the type of formalized deposit insurance employed in the United States. As the Japanese banking industry faced losses of $500–$800 billion in 1995, the government vowed to bail out a large number of failing banks in order to protect depositors.[14] Within the United States, the recent introduction of market discipline into the deposit insurance program through risk-based premiums was accompanied by proposals for further increases in market discipline, including a debate about the advisability of continuing the insurance program at all.

SUMMARY

Global financial intermediation has expanded dramatically since World War II. The primary causes include: (1) the expansion of "real sector" global activities, such as trade and multinational corporate operations; (2) the enormous impact of technological change in decreasing transactions cost and the economic distance between countries; (3) regulation—both its presence (providing the incentive to move offshore) and its removal (eliminating policy-imposed barriers to the global movement of goods and capital); and (4) risk reduction through diversification.

Many of the techniques and characteristics of present-day global banking can be traced to the development of "wholesale" banking in 1950s London. The use of large-scale term loans with variable rates, time deposits (CDs), and a "systems" approach to the management of liquidity and risk all continue to characterize offshore and Eurocurrency banking. Traditional foreign or international banking is conducted in the currency of the lender; multinational banking is often conducted in the various currencies of the local branches of the parent bank. Both types of banking can involve wholesale or retail transactions. In contrast,

---

[13] Iguchi pleaded guilty in New York on six counts of fraud, including money laundering, falsifying bank documents, embezzling, and misappropriating funds.

[14] The Japanese economy entered into a recession in 1991 along with most of the industrialized countries. While the U.S. economy emerged from the recession by 1992, the Japanese economy remained sluggish. The Japanese economic growth for 1996 is estimated to be less than 1%. By 1995, even though the Japanese government has reduced the short-term interest rate to ½ of 1%, the outlook for the economy in general and the banking industry in particular remained gloomy. The banking industry losses are attributed to a general malaise in the economy and huge losses in the real estate business. It has been argued that the only way for the Japanese economy to emerge from its current predicament is a systematic deregulation of its economy.

offshore and Eurocurrency banking involve only wholesale transactions in which the currency used is not that of the host country. Offshore financial centers have developed primarily to serve banks seeking to avoid domestic regulations, whereas Eurocurrency transactions have been linked to foreign exchange markets and cross-currency intermediation.

The recent history of U.S. multinational banking has been marked by rapid expansion, fueled by OPEC deposits in the 1970s, followed by rapid contraction due to massive losses on loans to LDCs in the late 1980s. As a result, very few U.S. banks are truly multinational in the 1990s, with the exception of Citibank. Foreign banks operating in the United States, in contrast, have not abandoned their expansion plans, although there has been some slowing due to recession in the early 1990s.

As the recent history of international banking shows, banks prefer to avoid regulation when they can. U.S. banks have long aspired to the "universal" status of many European banks, which are very lightly regulated in comparison to U.S. banks. European universal banks are not restricted in the scope of their activities, or in their branching. The result is a very concentrated banking system with many financial activities under one organization. There is some movement in the United States to reduce or eliminate domestic restrictions on bank activities (branching is already deregulated). Recent studies of European banking have shown it to be considerably less efficient than U.S. banking, possibly due to the reduced competition in a universal banking system.

International banking regulation varies considerably by country. In the United States, the supervision of international banking activities has been divided between the Federal Reserve (Edge Acts, foreign branches of U.S. banks) and states (Agreement Corporations; until recently, foreign banks in the United States). The International Banking Act of 1978 imposed "national treatment" on foreign banks in the United States, while the creation of International Banking Facilities (IBFs) in 1981 attempted to move "offshore banking" back onshore. The Foreign Bank Supervision Enhancement Act of 1991 (the "BCCI" Act) imposed Federal Reserve supervision on all foreign banks in the United States. To date, recent attempts to reduce U.S. bank regulation have been rejected by Congress, with the exception of interstate branching, which is permitted as of 1995.

The international regulation of international banking has largely become the province of the Basle Committee on Banking Supervision, which has issued a series of influential recommendations since the 1970s. The best known of these has dealt with international responsibility for bank supervision and support (in response to the Herstatt and BCCI problems), payment systems (Herstatt), and risk-based measures of capital adequacy (in response to the Banco Ambrosiano crisis). Regulations concerning market entry, permitted activities, foreign exchange, country exposure, and deposit insurance continue to vary widely by country.

REVIEW QUESTIONS

1. What are some of the major differences between retail and wholesale banking? Between international (cross-border) and offshore banking? What role has banking regulation (or deregulation) had in the post–World War II development of international and offshore banking?

2. As international financial transactions, what are some of the major differences between international bank lending, as practiced in the 1970s and 1980s, and Eurocurrency finance (e.g., Eurobonds or Euronotes), as practiced in the 1990s?

3. Which supervisory body oversees the following international banking organizations? Edge Act Corp., Agreement Corp., foreign branches of

U.S. banks, foreign subsidiaries of U.S. banks, foreign banks in the U.S., International Banking Facilities (all: per U.S. law); any foreign branch of any bank (per: Basle Committee).

4. What are the major U.S. regulations concerning permitted activities for banks? Why were these regulations implemented? What would have to be changed in order for U.S. banks to become "universal banks"?

5. What was the problem with the Banco Ambrosiano? What was its regulatory policy outcome?

6. What was the problem with the Bankhaus Herstatt? What was its regulatory policy outcome? How does the BCCI case relate to this?

7. What are some of the payments-system issues raised by Herstatt? How does this relate to the systemic risk problems posed by rapid growth in the volume of international transactions? What are some of the proposed remedies?

REFERENCES

Bryant, R. 1985. *International Financial Intermediation*. Washington, DC: The Brookings Institution.

Hall, M. 1993. *Banking Regulation and Supervision: A Comparative Study of the UK, USA, and Japan*. U.K.: Edward Elgar Publishing Ltd.

Lewis, M., and K. Davis. 1987. *Domestic and International Banking*, Cambridge, MA: MIT Press.

McCauley, R., and R. Seth. 1992. "Foreign Bank Credit to U.S. Corporations: The Implications of Offshore Loans." *Federal Reserve Bank of New York Quarterly Review* (Spring): 52–65.

C H A P T E R
11

Market Efficiency and Asset Pricing

OBJECTIVES

This chapter examines asset pricing in money and capital markets. All asset pricing theories assume that markets are efficient. Consequently, we begin with a discussion of market efficiency. Next we discuss asset pricing in a risk-free environment and apply the concept to price financial assets. We then relax the assumption of certainty and examine asset pricing with risk, including the Capital Asset Pricing Model and the Arbitrage Pricing Theory.

MARKET EFFICIENCY

The basic premise of market efficiency is that asset prices reflect all relevant information. If this premise is accepted, all asset prices should reflect their fundamental values. The notion of fundamental value holds that there is an implicit value to each asset and, depending on the amount of information available on that asset, the market price would represent that intrinsic value.

Empirical tests on market efficiency have been conducted in the past three decades and the results have been debated. Fama (1970) categorized market efficiency into three testable hypotheses: weak, semi-strong, and strong forms. *Weak-form market efficiency* states that all past price information is reflected in the current price. If the market is believed to be weak-form efficient, there will be no benefit in checking historical price patterns to identify overvalued or undervalued assets. This form of market efficiency refutes *technical analysts* or *chartists*, who use the past price information to identify the future price pattern.

Semi-strong-form market efficiency states that asset prices reflect not only the past price information but also all other information publicly available, including balance-sheet composition, income statement figures, earnings forecasts, product lines, quality of management, patents, and accounting methods. If semi-strong-form market efficiency holds, there will not be any benefit in collecting and processing publicly available information to identify overvalued or undervalued assets. All are fairly priced. This form of market efficiency refutes *fundamental analysts*, who rely on such information to make buy and sell recommendations to the investing public.

Strong-form market efficiency states that market prices reflect all information relevant to the asset, including not only public information but also private information held by company insiders. The implication of this form of market efficiency is that even insider trading will not help investors earn abnormal returns.

Fama (1991) reclassified the three categories of market efficiency as return predictability, event studies, and private information. *Return predictability* explores whether future returns (or prices) can be predicted based on the current information. If the market is efficient, future returns will not be predictable. *Event studies* refer to a particular methodology of testing whether asset prices reflect efficiently the information being released. If the market is efficient, asset prices will quickly reflect the newly released information. *Private information* ponders whether investors with access to inside information beat the market. If the market is efficient, trading based on private information will not yield abnormal profits.

Empirical Evidence on Return Predictability

The early studies of weak-form market efficiency tested whether past stock returns could be used to forecast future stock price movements. For markets to be weak-form efficient, rates of returns should be uncorrelated over time. Early tests conducted in the 1960s and 1970s concluded that equity returns followed a random walk with very low correlation for short-time horizons.[1]

While studies of short-time horizon returns have shown minor positive serial correlation in stock prices, more recent empirical tests of long-time horizon returns (e.g., a few years) have found significant negative serial correlation. Some have argued that the observed negative correlation in stock prices over long-time horizons can be explained by "fads hypothesis."[2] According to this hypothesis, stock prices may overreact to relevant news, leading to positive serial correlation in returns over short-time horizons. A run of positive returns due to overreactions to short-term fads or bubbles will tend to be followed by negative returns over longer horizons. Since asset prices drift away from their fundamental values slowly, there is little correlation observed over a short-time horizon. Over a long-time horizon, however, asset prices revert to their fundamental values, exhibiting strong negative serial correlation. If one believes in the theory of fads and bubbles, the market will be inefficient because there is indeed an element of correlation in returns.

Fads and bubbles should be limited to individual securities or markets. The evidence, however, suggests that this phenomenon is not unique to individual securities; rather, it is related to various business cycles affecting both the equity market and the bond market. In addition, the evidence from international markets also shows similar findings. In light of these findings, another explanation of the observed patterns in expected returns has surfaced that relies on the notion of time variation in expected returns.[3]

The efficient market hypothesis does not depend on constant expected returns on assets over time. Indeed, a perceived predictability of return that can be explained by a rational change in market expectations is consistent with the notion of market efficiency. The observed correlation in returns that is explained by time variation in expected returns is consistent with the notion of market efficiency. This time variation in expected returns can be predicted by the level of in-

---

[1] See, for example, Fama (1970).
[2] Summers (1986); Shiller (1989); and Cutler, Poterba, and Summers (1991).
[3] Fama (1991).

terest rates, the term structure of interest rates, dividend yields, and default risk premiums.[4]

Another group of researchers have tried to establish other anomalies or seasonalities in the behavior of asset prices. This includes the day-of-the-week effect, turn-of-the-month effect, holiday effect, January effect, and intraday effect.[5] The *day-of-the-week* effect shows negative returns occur on Mondays in many national stock markets. The *turn-of-the-month effect* states that returns tend to be larger on the last trading day of the month. The *holiday effect* implies that returns tend to be higher the day before a holiday. The *January effect* indicates that monthly returns are higher in January than in other months of the year. *Intraday effect* means that most of the daily returns come at the beginning and end of the day. Anomalies, however, cannot be exploited to make profits because the profit potential is smaller than bid-ask spreads. Thus, market efficiency holds out despite the anomalies.

Empirical Evidence from Event Studies

Event studies provide an opportunity to test market efficiency directly in light of all publicly available information. Companies often make announcements about their investment decisions, dividend changes, changes in capital structure, and corporate control transactions. Market efficiency states that share prices should react quickly and significantly to such news. Event studies of takeover announcements show that target firm stock prices react quickly to the announcement.[6] Studies of other corporate events similarly indicate that prices adjust efficiently to firm-specific information.

Empirical Evidence on Private Information

A direct test of the third category of market efficiency involves insider trading. If access to inside information enables the investor to earn abnormal returns, we would conclude that the market is strong-form inefficient. Insider trading has been tested extensively in the past 30 years. The results show that insider trading provides large abnormal returns despite rigorous enforcement efforts of anti-insider trading laws.[7]

In addition to the insider trading test of private information, the impact of other forms of private information on stock prices has also been tested. For example, a study of *The Wall Street Journal* column "Heard on the Street," which often provides material nonpublic information about companies, shows that stock prices change on average by 1.7% on the day of publication.[8] The overall conclusion is that trading based on private information indeed provides abnormal returns. Thus, markets are inefficient with regard to private information.

How Efficient Is the Market?

From the preceding discussion we can conclude that markets are efficient in the weak and semi-strong forms but are not efficient in the strong form. Similarly, research on earnings predictability suggests that over a long-time horizon, correlations in expected returns are explained by time variation, which is consistent with the notion of market efficiency. Also, an extensive body of event study literature suggests that equity markets react quickly and efficiently to the public release of new information, further substantiating market efficiency as it relates to publicly

---

[4] Harvey (1991) and Hawawini and Keim (1994).

[5] Agrawal and Tandon (1994).

[6] See, for example, Jensen and Ruback (1983) and Jarrell, Brickley, and Netter (1988). For further examples of event studies see Chapter 14.

[7] For a detailed review of empirical evidence on insider trading see Arshadi and Eyssell (1993), Chapter 4. Also see Chapter 14 in this book.

[8] Liu, Smith, and Syed (1990).

available information. The only aspect of market efficiency that does not seem to live up to empirical testing is trading that is based on private information. The results of insider trading and other research involving private information suggest that trading that is based on private information indeed provides abnormal returns.

ASSET PRICING WITHOUT RISK

If markets are efficient, asset prices will be determined as a function of their cash flows and discount rates. Asset pricing without risk assumes that we know with certainty the amount of cash flows to accrue in the future. The discount rate used will be a risk-free rate. This section examines asset pricing under certainty. The next section will address the issue of risk and its impact on asset pricing.

The current price of an asset is the sum of the discounted values of all its future cash flows. The future price of an asset is the sum of the compounded cash flows at some future date. The link between the present price and the future price is the interest rate.

Present Value and Future Value of a Sum

Suppose that you invest $1,000 today for one year in an account that pays 11.87% interest. At the end of the year you will have

$$\$1,000\ (1 + 0.1187) = \$1,187$$

If you leave your investment in that account for three years, the accumulated future value of your investment will be

$$\text{Accumulated value} = \$1,000\ (1 + 0.1187)^3 = \$1,400$$

If we call your initial investment the present value and your accumulated value the future value, the relationship can be stated as

$$FV = PV\ (1 + r)^t$$

where

$$FV = \text{future value}$$
$$PV = \text{present value}$$
$$r = \text{interest rate}$$
$$t = \text{number of periods}$$

We can state the equation in PV terms as

$$PV = \frac{FV}{(1+r)^t}$$

In these equations, we assume that the interest rate is compounded annually. In our numerical example, the future value of your investment three years from today is calculated as the sum of: (1) the principal amount; (2) the first year's interest on principal; (3) the second year's interest on the principal and the first year's interest; and (4) the third year's interest on the principal and first two years' interest. Annual compounding provides interest once a year, which is added to the principal amount. At the end of the second year, the interest is calculated based not only on the principal but also on the first year's interest, and so on. If compounding is more than once a year, the previous equations need to be adjusted to reflect the intrayear compounding:

$$FV = PV\left(1 + \frac{r}{m}\right)^{t \times m}$$

$$PV = \frac{FV}{\left(1 + \dfrac{r}{m}\right)^{t \times m}}$$

where m is the number of intrayear compounding. In this example, if we assume semiannual compounding, the future value will be

$$FV = \$1,000\left(1+\frac{0.1187}{2}\right)^{3\times 2} = \$1,413.31$$

The semiannually compounded future value is greater than the annually compounded future value because there is greater interest on interest income. Accordingly, the effective yield, I, can be calculated as

$$I = \left(1+\frac{r}{m}\right)^{m}-1 = \left(1+\frac{0.1187}{2}\right)^{2}-1 = 0.1222 = 12.22\%$$

Semiannual compounding increased the effective yield by 35 basis points, with one basis point equaling $1/100$ of 1%. With daily compounding, the effective yield will be

$$I = \left(1+\frac{0.1187}{365}\right)^{365}-1 = 0.12601 = 12.601\%$$

Daily compounding increased the effective yield by 73 basis points over annual compounding and 38 basis points over semiannual compounding. At the limit, when compounding is continuous, the equation will be

$$FV = PV\,e^{rt}, \quad PV = \frac{FV}{e^{rt}}, \quad \text{where } e = 2.718$$

In the previous example, if compounding is continuous, the future value of \$1,000 invested over three years at an 11.87% continuously compounded rate will be

$$FV = \$1,000\,e^{0.1187\times 3} = \$1,427.75$$

The effective annual yield will be

$$I = e^{0.1187} - 1 = 0.12603 \text{ or } 12.603\%$$

In order to compare rates on various investment opportunities, one has to convert different reported rates into their effective rate equivalents. For example, consider the reporting of loan rates under the Truth in Lending Act. A car loan rate is reported as having an 8% APR (annual percentage rate). The payments are monthly. The bank divides 8% by 12 to get a monthly rate of 0.667%. But this method of computing the monthly rate results in a higher effective rate

$$I = (1 + 0.08/12)^{12} - 1 = 0.083 = 8.30\%$$

It is obviously advantageous for the bank to advertise its loan rate at 8% while it effectively charges 8.30% per year.

Rates reported on many money market instruments also use varying calculation techniques. For example, Treasury bill yields are calculated based on 360 days on a bank discount basis:

$$Y_d = \frac{F-P}{F} \times \frac{360}{t}$$

where

Y_d = annualized yield on a bank discount basis
F = face value
P = price
$F - P$ = dollar discount
t = number of days remaining to maturity

For example, on November 20, 1995, the U.S. Treasury auctioned 13-week (91-day) T-bills with the face value of \$10,000 at a discount price of \$9,867. The yield quoted was

$$Y_d = \frac{10,000 - 9,867.29}{10,000} \times \frac{360}{91} = 0.0525 = 5.25\%$$

But the quoted rate on a bank discount basis is not a true measure of the return on a T-bill for two reasons. First, the yield is annualized according to a 360-day instead of a 365-day year. Second, the yield is calculated based on the face value (denominator in the first term of the equation) instead of the investment amount. If we adjust for these two elements, the effective yield will be

$$I = \left(1 + \frac{10,000 - 9,867.29}{9,867.29}\right)^{365/91} - 1 = 0.055 = 5.5\%$$

Other money market instruments such as commercial paper, repurchase agreements, and banker's acceptances also use a 360-day year to calculate a money market–equivalent yield (also called a CD-equivalent yield). The difference between a money market–equivalent yield and a T-bill yield is that the former measure is based on the actual dollar amount invested (the price) instead of the face value. Thus, the money market–equivalent yield is closer in value to our effective yield:

$$Y_{mm} = \frac{F - P}{P} \times \frac{360}{t} = \frac{10,000 - 9,867.29}{9,867.29} \times \frac{360}{91} = 0.0532 = 5.32\%$$

Perpetuities

An infinite stream of identical cash flows constitutes a **perpetuity**. Assuming annual payments, the present value of a perpetuity is calculated as

$$PV = \frac{C}{r}$$

where C is the annual level cash flows and r is the annual discount rate. For example, a cash flow of $100 a year forever at an annual discount rate of 7% will have a present value of

$$PV = 100/0.07 = \$1,429$$

If cash flows are received more than once a year, the present value of the perpetuity is calculated by using periodic cash flows and the discount rate. In the above example, if cash flows accrue semiannually, the present value of perpetuity will be

$$PV = 50/0.035 = \$1,429$$

If cash flows accrue continuously, the continuous rate equivalent of annual rate is used:

$$1 + r = e^{r'}$$
$$1.07 = e^{r'}$$
$$r' = \ln 1.07 = .0676$$
$$PV = 100/.0676 = \$1,479$$

Present Value and Future Value of an Annuity

Annuities are similar to perpetuities except that cash flows do not last forever. *The present value of an annuity (PV)* is calculated as the difference between two perpetuities starting on two different dates. For example, the present value of a three-year annuity with $100 per year is equal to the present value of a $100-per-year perpetuity starting today minus the present value of a $100-per-year perpetuity starting in three years. Assuming a 5% discount rate, the PV of annuity is calculated as

PV(today of a $100-per-year perpetuity starting next year) =
$$100/0.05 = \$2,000$$
PV(in year three of a $100-per-year perpetuity starting in year four) =
$$100/0.05 = \$2,000$$
PV(today of perpetuity starting in year four) =
$$\$2,000/(1+.05)^3 = \$1,727.68$$
PV(today of a 3-year annuity of $100 per year starting next year) =
$$\$2,000 - \$1,727.68 = \$272.32$$

The general equation for calculating the present value of an annuity of C dollars per year for t years at a discount rate of r percent is

$$PV = C\left[\frac{1}{r} - \frac{1}{r(1+r)^t}\right]$$

Using this equation, we recalculate the present value in the preceding example:

$$PV = 100\left[\frac{1}{0.05} - \frac{1}{0.05(1+0.05)^3}\right] = \$272.32$$

The computation of the present value of an annuity with intrayear compounding involves adjusting the equation to reflect the periodic cash flows, the discount rate, and the number of periods:

$$PV = C/m\left[\frac{1}{r/m} - \frac{1}{r/m(1+r/m)^{t \times m}}\right]$$

For example, the present value of $300 per month (C/m = $300) for five years ($t = 5$) at 12% ($r = 12$%) is calculated as

$$PV = 300\left[\frac{1}{0.12/12} - \frac{1}{0.12/12(1+0.12/12)^{5 \times 12}}\right] = \$13,486.51$$

Monthly annuities such as the one illustrated here are common in consumer and real estate installment loans. Suppose that the previous example was for a car loan of $13,486.51 over a five-year period at an annual rate of 12% and monthly payments of $300. The effective rate of the loan is

$$I = (1 + 0.12/12)^{12} - 1 = 0.01268 = 12.68\%$$

The *future value of an annuity (FV)* is simply the present value of an annuity multiplied by $(1+r)^t$

$$FV = C\left[\frac{1}{r} - \frac{1}{r(1+r)^t}\right](1+r)^t$$

Bond Pricing

The most common type of bond is a coupon bond that makes semiannual coupon payments and redeems the principal at maturity. For example, a five-year bond with a coupon rate of 8% (paid semiannually), a face value of $1,000, and a yield to maturity of 8% is priced as

$$PV = 80/2\left[\frac{1}{(1+0.08/2)} - \frac{1}{0.08/2(1+0.08/2)^{5 \times 2}}\right] + \frac{\$1,000}{(1+0.08/2)^{5 \times 2}} = \$1,000$$

Coupon payments are calculated by multiplying the coupon rate by the face value of the bond, which amounts to $80. Since the bond makes semiannual coupon payments, each payment will be $40. The yield to maturity, which is the average rate of return earned on the bond, is also adjusted for semiannual payments. The price of the bond is calculated by finding the present value of an annuity of $40 coupon payments per every six months plus the present value of the face value of the bond due at maturity. The price of the bond is equal to the face value of the bond because the coupon rate is equal to the yield to maturity.

When the price of the bond is equal to its face value, the bond is called a *par bond*.

Suppose that immediately after the bond is issued, the interest rate on the bond decreases to 6%. The price of the bond will increase to

$$PV = 80/2 \left[\frac{1}{(1+0.06/2)} - \frac{1}{0.06/2(1+0.06/2)^{5 \times 2}} \right] + \frac{\$1,000}{(1+0.06/2)^{5 \times 2}} = \$1,085.30$$

The price of the bond is greater than the face value of the bond because the coupon rate is greater than the yield to maturity of the bond. This bond is called a *premium bond*.

If the yield to maturity of the bond had increased to 10% instead of decreasing, the price of the bond would have declined to

$$PV = 80/2 \left[\frac{1}{(1+0.10/2)} - \frac{1}{0.10/2(1+0.10/2)^{5 \times 2}} \right] + \frac{\$1,000}{(1+0.10/2)^{5 \times 2}} = \$922.78$$

Since the price of the bond is less than its face value, it is called a *discount bond*.

A simpler version of a coupon bond is a *zero coupon bond*, which makes no coupon payments and is sold at a discount. For example, a five-year, $1,000 face value zero coupon bond with a yield to maturity of 6% is priced as

$$PV = \frac{\$1,000}{(1+0.06)^5} = \$747.26$$

The inverse relationship between interest rates and bond prices is easily seen in the zero coupon bond pricing equation. As rates increase, the prices of all fixed-income securities such as zero coupon bonds decrease.

Pricing Treasury and Corporate Securities

In addition to Treasury bills, the U.S. Treasury also issues Treasury notes and bonds. Treasury notes are issued with maturities of three, five, or seven years. Treasury bonds are issued with maturities of 10 or 30 years. Both notes and bonds have semiannual coupon payments. In addition to Treasury securities, agencies of the federal government such as the Farm Credit Bank System and the Federal Home Loan Bank System also issue debt securities. Discount securities like T-bills have maturities less than one year, and coupon securities are issued with maturities of two years and higher.

Both Treasury and agency securities trade actively in the primary and secondary markets. The price quotation method is much different for coupon securities and discount bonds. Instead of quoting in terms of a discount yield, coupon instruments are quoted in terms of the percentage value per $100 of par value. The smallest unit of measure is 1/64 of 1% and the common unit of measure is 1/32 of 1% of par value. A quote of 90–16 would mean 90 and 16/32 per $100 of par value. If the price is quoted with a + at the end, it means add 1/64 to the price. Thus a quote of 90–16+ would mean a price that is 90 and 33/64% (90.515625%) of par value. For a bond with a face value of $100,000, the quoted price would equal $905,156.25 ($100,000 × 0.90515625).

When bond prices are *quoted* it is assumed that the purchase price is exactly on the coupon payment date so that the bond pricing equation holds exactly. The quoted price is often referred to as the *clean price*. When a bond is purchased between coupon dates, the investor must compensate the seller of the bond for the interest accrued to that point. The clean price plus the accrued interest is equal to the invoice price. This invoice price is also referred to as the *actual price* or the *dirty price*. The accrued interest in Treasury coupon securities is calculated as the semiannual coupon amount times the proportion of days that have passed in the next coupon payment. This proportion is calculated as the actual number of days since the last coupon settlement date divided by the actual number of days in the coupon period.

Suppose, for instance, you purchased a bond that had a $100,000 face value and an annual coupon rate of 8%. It has been 100 days since that last coupon was paid and there are 182 days in this coupon period. The bond price was quoted as 90–16+. The invoice price of this bond (noting that this is the same quote used above in the determination of the quoted price) would equal

$$\text{Invoice price} = 905{,}156.25 + 0.08/2 \times \$100{,}000 \times 100/182 = \$907{,}354.05$$

The dirty price is the clean price agreed upon by the buyer and seller plus the accrued interest that is paid by the buyer to the seller.

Accrued interest is computed somewhat differently for corporate coupon securities. Corporate bonds accrue interest based on a 360-day year and a 30-day month. A 12% corporate bond with a face value of $1,000 would thus accumulate $10 of interest per month (1/12 of $120). A bond purchased 3½ months into the year would therefore have $35 of accrued interest that would have to be added to the clean price to obtain the invoice or dirty price on a corporate bond.

Holding Period Return

The yield to maturity is the return that is earned on the investment if it is held to maturity and all intermediate cash flows are invested at the same rate. It is rare, however, for interest rates to stay stable to warrant such an overall return. More often, the realized return over the holding period is different from the yield to maturity. Thus, the realized return can only be known at the end of the investment horizon.

To numerically calculate the holding period return, one determines the future value of all the intermediate cash flows to the point where the investment was terminated. The percentage change between that value and the initial investment is then calculated. This is the return over the entire holding period. This return is then annualized by calculating the compound annual growth rate to obtain the (annualized) holding period return.

Consider a $1,000 face value, five-year zero coupon bond with a yield to maturity of 6%. From our earlier discussion, we know the price of this bond is $747.26. Suppose that after three years the bond is sold for $875. The holding period return is calculated as

$$\text{3-year dollar return} = 875 - 747.26 = 127.74$$
$$\text{3-year percentage return} = 127.74 / 747.26 = 0.1709$$
$$\text{Holding period return} = (1 + .1709)^{.33} - 1 = .0534 = 5.34\%$$

which is less than the original yield to maturity of 6%.

The problem becomes more complicated when coupon payments are involved. Consider a $1,000, 10-year corporate bond with a 5% coupon (paid semiannually) and a 5% yield to maturity, purchased at par. Assume that the bond is sold after two years for $980 and the coupons are reinvested at a rate of 7%. The value of the cash flows on this bond at the end of year two consists of the future value of the four $25 coupon payments received at six months, one year, 18 months, and two years plus the capital loss on the sale. The dollar return is calculated by finding the future value of the four coupon payments and then subtracting out the capital loss:

$$\text{2-year dollar return} = 25(1 + 0.07/2)^3 + 25(1 + 0.07/2)^2 + 25(1 + 0.07)^1$$
$$+ 25 + (980 - \$1{,}000)$$
$$= 105.38 - 20 = \$85.38$$
$$\text{2-year percentage return} = 85.38 / \$1{,}000 = .0854$$
$$\text{Holding period return} = (1 + .0854)^{1/2} - 1 = .0418 = 4.18\%$$

The holding period return, 4.18%, is less than the initial yield to maturity of 5%. An increase in interest rates decreased the market price of the bond from its initial value of $1,000 to $980, resulting in a capital loss of $20. The capital loss is partially offset by the gain in the reinvestment income. The gain in the reinvestment income comes from investing periodic coupon payments at 7% rather than the original 5%. If the bond had been held longer, the holding period return would have been higher because of higher reinvested income. At some point before the bond matures, the holding period return would equal the original yield to maturity. The time it takes for the holding period return to equal the yield to maturity is referred to as the *duration of the bond*. We will return to duration in Chapter 16.

Stock Pricing

Similar to other assets, the value of a share of stock is equal to the present value of all its future cash flows. Since stockholders receive cash flows in the form of dividends, stock valuation models use dividends as the source of periodic cash flows. We also need a discount rate for our valuation model. Various models exist to calculate the appropriate discount rate including the capital asset pricing model and the arbitrage pricing model. We will fully develop these models in the section on asset valuation with risk. At this point, we take the appropriate discount rate as given and focus our attention on cash flows.

The price of a share of stock should equal the sum of the discounted values of all its future dividend payments. Since the stock price at a given time embodies all future dividends, we can write a basic stock valuation model as follows:

$$P_0 = \frac{D_1}{(1+r)^1} + \frac{D_2}{(1+r)^2} + \cdots + \frac{D_n}{(1+r)^n}$$

where

$$P_0 = \text{current stock price}$$
$$D_t = \text{dividend at time t}$$
$$r = \text{appropriate discount rate}$$

If there is no growth, $D_1 = D_2 = \ldots = D_n = D$, and the valuation model turns out to be a simple equation for a stream of level and perpetual cash flows:

$$P_0 = \frac{D}{r}$$

For example, a stock that pays a constant dividend of $2 per year and has a discount rate of 10% will have a price of

$$P_0 = \frac{2}{0.10} = \$20$$

If the stock has a constant growth of g% a year, the pricing model will adjust to the following:

$$P_0 = \frac{D_1}{r-g}$$

In the previous example, if we assume a growth rate of 6%, the price will be

$$P_0 = \frac{2}{0.10 - 0.06} = \$50$$

The price of the stock increased from $20 to $50 with a growth of 6%. For a constant growth stock, we can divide the stock price into two segments:

$$P_0 = \text{PV}(\textit{existing assets}) + \text{PV}(\textit{growth opportunities})$$
$$P_0 = \frac{EPS_1}{r} + PVGO$$

where

EPS_1 = earnings per share next period
$PVGO$ = present value of growth opportunities

EPS_1/r reflects the value of the asset if there is no growth. This term is similar to D/r for a no-growth stock. Obviously, when there is no growth, the company can pay out all of its earnings as dividends and EPS_1 will equal D_1. $PVGO$ reflects the present value of future growth opportunities. In this example, when we introduce the growth rate of 6%, the price of the stock increases from $20 to $50, an increase of $30. The $30 constitutes the present value of growth opportunities.

ASSET VALUATION WITH RISK

Risk and Return for a Single Asset

The real world is plagued with uncertainty and we need to work the notion of risk into our valuation models. If we invest I dollars in a project right now and it pays W dollars at the end of one period, we can calculate the rate of return, r (the holding period return), as

$$r = \frac{W - I}{I}$$
$$W = I(1 + r)$$
$$I = \frac{W}{1 + r}$$

Of course the last two equations are the same as our FV and PV equations introduced earlier in the chapter:

$$FV = PV(1 + r)$$
$$PV = \frac{FV}{1 + r}$$

The point we would like to make is that prices and rates tell us basically the same story. If we have one, we can easily calculate the other. With risk we must talk about expected prices, as we cannot be sure of future cash flows.

While we can discuss risk and return in the context of any asset, for simplicity we use stocks as our asset of choice. Suppose you have purchased a share of a particular company's stock for $40. You plan to sell your stock in one year, during which time there will be no dividend payment. You do not know what the price is going to be in a year, but you have some hunches as to various possibilities depending on economic and firm-specific factors. For each scenario you assign a probability and an expected price, as in the accompanying table.

(1) Probabilities (Prob$_i$)	(2) Price (P_i)	(3) Return (r_i)	(4) (1) × (2)	(5) (1) × (3)
0.10	30	−25%	3	−2.5%
0.20	40	0	8	0
0.40	45	12.5	18	5
0.20	50	25	10	5
0.10	60	50	6	5
			$E(P) = \$45$	$E(r) = 12.5\%$

In column (1) we present probabilities and in column (2) the corresponding prices. For each of the prices we calculate the corresponding returns. For example, if the price drops to $30 from $40, the return will be $[(30 - 40) / 40]$ or -25%. We then calculate the expected price or mean by multiplying each price by its probability. The sum of column (4), $45, represents the expected price:

$$E(P) = \Sigma (\text{Prob}_i \times P_i) = 45$$

This price is our best estimate of what the price is going to be when we consider the element of uncertainty. If we take the price of the stock to be $45 at the end of one year, then the expected return on our investment is $[(45 - 40) / 40]$ or 12.5%. Note that we could calculate the expected return directly by multiplying probabilities (column 1) by corresponding returns (column 3) and summing them (column 5).

Expected price is a good starting point but it does not tell us exactly what the price is going to be. The actual price may be higher or lower than $45. To find out how much the actual price may vary around the expected price, we need to calculate the variance. Variance is the measure of dispersion around the mean. The following formula provides the variance:

$$\sigma_p^2 = \Sigma[\text{Prob}_i\,(P_i - E(P))^2]$$

Using our example, the variance of the price is

$$\sigma_p^2 = 0.10(30 - 45)^2 + 0.20(40 - 45)^2 + 0.40(45 - 45)^2 + 0.20(50 - 45)^2 + 0.10(60 - 45)^2$$
$$= 55$$

The variance is 55 squared dollars. Since squared dollars do not make intuitive sense we find the square root of the variance and call it the standard deviation:

$$\sigma_p = (55)^{1/2} = \$7.42$$

Standard deviation provides better intuition on the range of prices that we expect to see:

At the 99% confidence level, price at time one will be between
$$= \$45 \pm 3\ (\$7.42) = \$22.74 - \$67.26$$
At the 95% confidence level, price at time one will be between
$$= \$45 \pm 2\ (\$7.42) = \$30.16 - \$59.84$$
At the 66% confidence level, price at time one will be between
$$= \$45 \pm 1\ (\$7.42) = \$37.58 - \$52.42$$

The size of the standard deviation relative to the mean indicates the level of uncertainty. Therefore, low-risk stocks will have a lower standard deviation than will high-risk stocks. Since most people are risk averse, we expect investors to prefer lowest risk for a given stock return or highest return for a given risk. In other words, there is a trade-off between risk and return.

A similar computation for variance and standard deviation of returns is as follows:

$$\sigma_r^2 = 0.10\,(-25 - 12.5)^2 + 0.20\,(0 - 12.5)^2 + 0.40\,(12.5 - 12.5)^2 + 0.20\,(25 - 12.5)^2$$
$$+ 0.10\,(50 - 12.5)^2$$

$$\sigma_r^2 = 343.75$$
$$\sigma_r = (343.75)^{1/2} = 18.54\%$$

We could have calculated the variance of the returns directly from the variance of the price using the following formula:

$$\sigma_r^2 = \sigma_p^2 / P_0^2 = 55 / 40^2 = 0.0344$$
$$\sigma_r = (0.0344)^{1/2} = 0.1854 \text{ or } 18.54\%$$

The range of returns is as follows:

At 99% confidence level, return at time one will be between
$$= 12.5\% \pm 3(18.54\%) = -43.12\% - 68.12\%$$
At 95% confidence level, return at time one will be between
$$= 12.5\% \pm 2(18.54\%) = -24.58\% - 49.58\%$$
At 66% confidence level, return at time one will be between
$$= 12.5\% \pm 1(18.54\%) = -6.04\% - 31.04\%$$

Thus far we have examined risk and return for an individual stock. In the next section we discuss ways of calculating expected return and risk for a portfolio of multiple stocks. Since we have already made the point that prices and returns are simply two sides of the same coin, we proceed with the rest of this discussion by focusing only on returns; but keep in mind that at every point, computing the price is a simple task given the return.

Risk and Return for a Portfolio of Assets

Investors tend to hold multiple stocks, which are referred to as a *stock portfolio*. We calculate expected returns for a portfolio of stocks by multiplying expected returns of individual stocks, as we showed in the previous section, by their respective weights in the portfolio and then summing them. The weights are just the proportion of the total value of the portfolio a particular stock comprises. Therefore,

$$E(r_p) = \bar{r}_p = \Sigma \, W_i \, \bar{r}_I \text{ where } \Sigma \, W_i = 1$$

Suppose we have two stocks A and B. The expected return for these two stocks will be

$$E(r_p) = W_a \bar{r}_a + W_b \bar{r}_b \text{ where } W_a + W_b = 1$$

If stock A has an expected return of 10% and stock B has an expected return of 15% and you have decided to invest 40% in stock A and 60% in stock B, your expected return will be

$$E(r_p) = 0.40 \, (10\%) + 0.60 \, (15\%) = 13\% \quad \Sigma W_i = .40 + .60 = 1$$

The formula to calculate variance and standard deviation is as follows:

$$\sigma^2_p = W_a^2 \, \sigma_a^2 + W_b^2 \, \sigma_b^2 + 2W_a W_b \sigma_{ab}$$

σ_{ab} refers to the covariance between stock A and stock B. Covariance indicates how the returns on the two assets are correlated. The covariance term can also be stated as

$$\sigma_{ab} = \rho_{ab} \sigma_a \sigma_b,$$

where ρ_{ab} refers to correlation coefficient between stock A and stock B. Correlation coefficient represents the same notion as covariance except that its value ranges from –1 to +1 ($-1 < \rho_{ab} < +1$). Correlation coefficient makes better intuitive sense than does covariance. For example, a correlation coefficient of –1 indicates that if stock A goes up by 10%, then stock B will go down by 10%—they are perfectly negatively correlated. A correlation coefficient of + 1 implies that if stock A goes up by 5%, then stock B will also go up by 5%—they are perfectly positively correlated. Of course, a correlation coefficient of 0 indicates no correlation between the two.

For extreme values of the correlation coefficient, the formula for portfolio risk can be significantly simplified. Substituting $\rho_{ab} \, \sigma_a \sigma_b$ for σ_{ab} in the portfolio risk equation we have:

$$\sigma^2_p = W_a^2 \, \sigma_a^2 + W_b^2 \, \sigma_b^2 + 2W_a W_b \, \rho_{ab} \, \sigma_a \sigma_b$$
If $\rho_{ab} = -1$ then $\sigma^2_p = (W_a \, \sigma_a - W_b \, \sigma_b)^2$ and $\sigma_p = (W_a \, \sigma_a - W_b \, \sigma_b)$
If $\rho_{ab} = +1$ then $\sigma^2_p = (W_a \, \sigma_a + W_b \, \sigma_b)^2$ and $\sigma_p = (W_a \, \sigma_a + W_b \, \sigma_b)$
If $\rho_{ab} = 0$ then $\sigma^2_p = (W_a^2 \, \sigma_a^2 + W_b^2 \, \sigma_b^2)$

(Remember from your basic math course equations, $(a - b)^2 = a^2 + b^2 - 2ab$ and $(a + b)^2 = a^2 + b^2 + 2ab$.)

In reality, most stocks go up and down in the same direction, albeit not at the same magnitude. Using the same two stocks A and B in our expected return example, suppose stock A has a standard deviation of 8% and stock B has a standard deviation of 12%. With 40% of our money invested in stock A and the remaining 60% in stock B, we can calculate the risk of our portfolio, assuming that the correlation coefficient between A and B is 0.5:

$$\sigma^2_p = 0.40^2 \times 0.08^2 + 0.60^2 \times 0.12^2 + 2 \times 0.40 \times 0.60 \times 0.08 \times 0.12 \times 0.5 = 0.0085$$
$$\sigma_p = 0.0922 = 9.22\%$$

Now let us calculate the risk assuming correlation coefficients of 0 and –0.5:

$$\text{If } \rho_{ab} = 0, \text{ then } \sigma^2_p = 0.0062 \text{ and } \sigma_p = 0.0787 \text{ or } 7.87\%$$
$$\text{If } \rho_{ab} = -0.5, \text{ then } \sigma^2_p = 0.0039 \text{ and } \sigma_p = .0624 \text{ or } 6.24\%$$

As you can see, the standard deviation drops from 9.22% to 7.87% to 6.24% as we decrease the correlation coefficient from +0.5 to 0 to –0.5. This indicates that the risk of the portfolio is smallest when the correlation coefficient is –1 and largest when it is +1. However, as we mentioned earlier, most stocks are positively correlated and their correlation coefficient is somewhere between 0 and +1.

While computing variance and standard deviation for a portfolio of two stocks is relatively simple, it becomes very complicated when the number of stocks in the portfolio increases. In the preceding example using two stocks, we had two variance terms and two covariance terms. Generally speaking, the total number of items we need to calculate the variance is N^2, assuming that N is the number of stocks in the portfolio. For a portfolio of 10 stocks we need to calculate $10^2 = 100$ items, out of which 10 are variances of individual stocks and 90 are covariances between pairs of stocks. In other words, for a portfolio of N stocks, there are N variances and $N^2 - N$ covariances. As you can see, computing this many items will be a difficult task. Of course, some portfolios may be much larger. For example, for a portfolio of 100 stocks, we need 10,000 computations.

Capital Asset Pricing Model

The complicating factor in the preceding discussion is all of the pairwise covariance computations. The development of the *Capital Asset Pricing Model (CAPM)* in the mid-1960s solved this problem by showing that portfolio risk can be measured in a more straightforward manner.

CAPM starts by recognizing that there are two types of risk. First, *market risk* or *systematic risk* is due to macroeconomic factors such as uncertainty about interest rates, federal reserve policy, or other issues that are generally out of the control of individual corporations. These uncertainties, however, affect the bottom-line performance of the corporations. The second source of risk is called *unique risk* or *unsystematic risk,* which involves uncertainties about individual companies. For example, a company may face a labor strike or may be subject to a lawsuit. While individual stocks are subject to both market and unique risks, when we incorporate them in a portfolio of 15–20 stocks the unique risk cancels out. The reason unique risk of individual stocks cancels out is that when one stock faces an unexpected negative outcome, another stock may have the fortune of facing an unexpected positive outcome. Both cases are unexpected, but one is on the downside while the other is on the upside of the uncertainty. Empirical research shows that when we increase the number of stocks within a portfolio to 15–20 shares, almost all of the unique risk disappears and what remains is the market risk. This phenomenon is called *diversification.*

Rational investors will choose a diversified portfolio that contains only market risk because diversification is costless. Given this, computing the risk of a portfolio amounts to calculating its market risk. To calculate market risk we first choose a market index to use as a base measure. For example, the S&P 500 is an index of 500 different stocks for which price information is reported on a daily basis in *The Wall Street Journal*. Obviously, this market index is a fully diversified portfolio that contains only market risk.

If we measure the risk of other stocks or portfolios against the market portfolio, we can index the risk of the market portfolio as 1. The risk of all other stocks can be measured relative to 1. If the risk of a stock portfolio or individual stock is only half that of the market, it should have a risk measure of 0.5. If a portfolio has twice the nondiversifiable risk as the market portfolio, its risk measure will be 2. This risk measure is referred to as the stock or portfolio *beta* (β). The market beta is 1 and other stocks and portfolios of stocks will have betas greater, equal to, or less than 1 depending on how risky they are relative to the market portfolio.

To determine beta risk in calculating expected returns, we note that a risk-free portfolio must have a beta of 0 and should earn the risk-free rate R_f. The market portfolio must have a beta of 1 and would be expected to earn the overall market return R_m. Combining these two facts, we can derive the security market line, which will provide an estimate of the returns on any risky asset as

$$E(R_a) = R_f + (R_m - R_f)\beta_a$$

The term $(R_m - R_f)$ is referred to as the market risk premium. Statistically, beta is the ratio of the covariance between the returns on the portfolio and the market divided by the variance of the market returns. We will show you a fairly easy method to calculate the beta for an individual stock.

To use this pricing equation, suppose we want to know the expected return on a stock that has a beta of 2 when the risk-free interest rate is 5% and the expected market return is 12%. From the previous equation we have

$$E(R_a) = 0.05 + (0.12 - 0.05)2 = 0.19 = 19\%$$

This stock is twice as risky as the market so it will earn twice the market risk premium $(0.12 - 0.05)2 = 14\%$ plus the risk-free rate of 5%. Any cash flows originating from this stock (such as dividends) would need to be discounted at this interest rate to determine their present value.

For a portfolio of assets, beta equals the individual betas multiplied by the respective proportion of wealth the asset contributes to the portfolio. That is,

$$\beta_p = \Sigma\, W_i\, \beta_i$$

which means that the beta of the portfolio equals the summation of the weights of individual stocks multiplied by their respective betas. For example, suppose we have three stocks, A, B, and C. We have invested $3,000 in stock A, $2,000 in stock B, and $5,000 in stock C. Further, assume betas for these three stocks are 1.5, 2, and 0.5. The beta of the portfolio, therefore, will be

$$\beta_p = \Sigma\, W_i\beta_i = (3{,}000 / 10{,}000) \times 1.5 + (2{,}000 / 10{,}000) \times 2$$
$$+ (5{,}000 / 10{,}000) \times 0.5 = 1.10$$

If the standard deviation for market index is 8%, then the standard deviation for our portfolio can be easily computed. Remember that beta measures the nondiversifiable risk remaining in the portfolio, so multiplying the market standard deviation by the portfolio beta yields the portfolio standard deviation. That is,

$$\sigma_p = 8\% \times 1.10 = 8.8\%$$

Note that the only information we need to have about each stock is its beta and the weight if we want to calculate the risk as a standard deviation measure.

CAPM is also called a one-factor model—a model that says price or return depends only upon market risk. In recent years, a more general model has been developed that utilizes not only the market factor (as in CAPM) but also a set of other factors. This model is called Arbitrage Pricing Theory (APT). We briefly explain this model next.

Arbitrage Pricing Theory (APT)

Depending on the type of stock, factors other than market index may also affect stock returns. For example, returns on stocks that are sensitive to external factors such as price volatility of certain commodities (e.g., oil) may be better predicted if we include not only the market factor but also a factor depicting the volatility of oil prices. Other factors may be at work as well. In general, a multifactor model predicts expected returns in the following manner:

$$ER_j = R_f + (ER_{j1} - R_f)\beta_{j1} + (ER_{j2} - R_f)\beta_{j2} + \ldots + (ER_{jk} - R_f)\beta_{jk}$$

Of course APT is a general model that can lend itself to a single-factor model such as CAPM if we are comfortable with the predictive power of a market index. For example, in the preceding equation if we assume that the first factor is the market index and other factors are not relevant (all other betas are 0), we return to our original CAPM.

Empirical tests of CAPM and APT have provided support for both models, albeit to varying degrees. CAPM, as the older of the two, has been tested over time and is generally supported by the evidence. There are anomalies, however. What makes CAPM so appealing is its relative simplicity and widespread use in practice. While debate over CAPM and APT continues, CAPM provides an intuitive and useful framework to understand the notion of risk and return.

CAPM in the Context of the Corporate Balance Sheet

The usefulness of CAPM is also evident in the context of the corporate balance sheet. Assets of a company have their betas, and the weighted sum of those betas produces the overall asset beta. If we have the overall asset beta, we can calculate the cost of capital for a company's assets using the CAPM. Beta of the assets also relates to betas of debt and equity on the right-hand side of the balance sheet:

$$\beta_{assets} = \Sigma\, W_i\, \beta_i \text{ for } i = 1 \ldots N,$$

which represents the N assets on the balance sheet.

The balance sheet-identity, assets = debt + equity, also implies that

$$\beta_{assets} = W_d\beta_d + W_e\beta_e = (D/(D+E))\beta_d + (E/(D+E))\beta_e$$

where β_d is the beta on debt and β_e is the equity beta. Suppose that a firm has two assets, A and B. Asset A has a beta of 2 and asset B has a beta of 0.5. Further assume that asset A will generate $100,000 a year for 10 years while asset B will generate $150,000 a year forever. If the risk-free rate is 5%, the market rate of return is 10%, the equity beta is 1.33, and the debt of the firm is risk-free, we can calculate the market values of assets A and B and also the values of the debt and equity for this firm.

Using the betas for assets A and B, we can calculate their expected returns as

$$Er_a = 0.05 + (0.10 - 0.05)2 = 0.150$$
$$Er_b = 0.05 + (0.10 - 0.05)0.5 = 0.075$$

Now we can calculate values of assets A and B:

$$V_a = \$100,000\,[(1/0.15) - (1/(0.15(1+0.15)^{10})] = \$501,877$$
$$V_b = \$150,000/0.075 = \$2,000,000$$
$$\text{Total assets} = V_a + V_b = \$501,877 + \$2,000,000 = \$2,501,877$$

The weights of assets A and B are

$$W_a = 501{,}877 \: / \: (501{,}877 + 2{,}000{,}000) = 0.20$$
$$W_b = 2{,}000{,}000 \: / \: (501{,}877 + 2{,}000{,}000) = 0.80$$

Therefore, the overall asset beta of the company is

$$\beta_{assets} = 0.20 \: (2) + 0.80 \: (0.5) = .80$$

The weights in debt and equity can be calculated as

$$\beta_{assets} = 0.80 = W_d \: \beta_d + W_e \beta_e = (D \: /(D + E))\beta_d + (E \: /(D + E))\beta_e$$
$$0.80 = W_d \: (0) + (1 - W_d)(\: 1.33)$$
$$W_d = 0.40$$
$$W_e = 0.60$$

We can calculate the values of D and E by multiplying their respective weights by the total values of assets

$$V_a + V_b = 501{,}877 + 2{,}000{,}000 = 2{,}501{,}877 = D + E$$

where

$$D = 0.40 \: (2{,}501{,}877) = 1{,}000{,}751$$
$$E = 0.60 \: (2{,}501{,}877) = 1{,}501{,}126$$

How Do We Calculate Stock Betas?

Now that we have shown how betas can be useful in a variety of ways, the question is how do we calculate them? We limit ourselves to calculating the equity beta and note that one needs to use the equation for the asset beta that was discussed earlier to calculate the whole company beta. There are three types of companies that create circumstances that we need to take account of: first, those companies that are expected to continue a path in the future that is similar to that of their past with similar product lines and no significant change in their operations; second, those companies that are getting into a brand new line of business that they were not involved in before but is similar to lines other companies have had similar products in; third, those companies that are starting a brand new product that nobody else has produced before.

If a company is publicly traded, the easiest way to calculate its equity beta is by using its past price information. Merrill Lynch's beta book publishes betas for a large number of companies using their past price information. More specifically, the procedure involves collecting five years of monthly stock information for each stock and the same information for a market index such as the S&P 500. Then parameters are calculated using the following regression model:

$$\Delta P_i = \alpha_i + \beta_i \Delta P_m + \varepsilon_i$$

where

ΔP_i = monthly changes in the price of stock
α_i = the intercept in the regression model
β_i = the slope of the regression model
ΔP_m = monthly price change for the market index
ε_i = the error term in the regression model

Five years of monthly data provides 60 observations (5×12) that are used to estimate the parameters of the regression model, including α_i, β_i, and ε_i. In this regression model, β corresponds to the beta in our discussion.

This computation implicitly assumes that the future path of the company will be similar to its past. If the company is planning to enter a significantly different line of business, then it is inappropriate to use just the historical beta.

If the new line of business a company is entering into is similar to another company's product line, then it is appropriate to use the beta of the firm producing that product for that part of the business. For example, suppose the historical beta of company A is 2, and the company is planning to invest 30% of its assets in a new product line that will produce high-quality laser disks. We identify another company, Z, that is in the business of producing laser disks and nothing else. Suppose further that both companies are 100% equity financed (so we avoid the effect of leverage). If company Z has a published beta of 1.5, then the new beta for company A will be the weighted average of its historical beta and the beta of its new product line:

$$\beta_a = 0.70(2) + 0.30(1.5) = 1.85$$

The reason we can use the beta of another company, Z, for company A's new product line is because it is a similar product line. Note that beta is the measure of market risk, which depends on factors that affect the demand for the product. It is realistic that the demand for both companies' laser disks are affected by the same set of external factors; hence, they have similar betas.

Finally, in those rare occasions when a company introduces a brand new product that was not previously available anywhere else, we have to make some predictions about various scenarios and assign probabilities to each. Under each scenario, we need to estimate the rate of return on the project and corresponding return for a market index. Then we can calculate the beta using the following formula:

$$\beta_a = \sigma_{am} / \sigma_m^2 = \rho_{am}\sigma_a\sigma_m / \sigma_m^2$$

where

β_a = beta of product A
σ_{am} = covariance of asset A's returns with market returns
σ_m^2 = variance of market returns
ρ_{am} = correlation coefficient between asset A and market portfolio
σ_a = standard deviation of asset A
σ_m = standard deviation of the market index

The accompanying table provides hypothetical information to calculate beta for A.

(1) Proba- bilities	(2) R_a	(3) R_m	(4) (1)(2)	(5) (1)(3)	(6) $R_a - R_a$	(7) $R_m - R_m$	(8) (1)(6)(7)
0.10	0.05	0.08	0.005	0.008	−0.062	−0.046	0.0003
0.20	0.08	0.10	0.016	0.020	−0.032	−0.026	0.0002
0.40	0.12	0.13	0.048	0.052	0.008	0.004	0.0000
0.20	0.14	0.15	0.028	0.030	0.028	0.024	0.0001
0.10	0.15	0.16	0.015	0.016	0.038	0.034	0.0001
			$E(R_a) = 0.112$	$E(R)_m = 0.126$			$\sigma_{am} = 0.0007$

Before we can calculate beta for A, we need variance for the market.

$$\sigma_m^2 = 0.10\ (-.046)^2 + 0.20\ (-0.026)^2 + 0.40\ (0.004)^2 + 0.20\ (0.024)^2$$
$$+ 0.10\ (0.034)^2 = 0.0002$$

Finally, beta for A is calculated as

$$\beta_a = \sigma_{am} / \sigma_m^2 = 0.0007 / 0.0002 = 3.5$$

The beta for asset A is therefore 3.5.

Financial markets allow for the exchange of financial assets at very low transaction costs. Financial markets accomplish this by providing liquidity to owners of financial assets and providing information that is crucial in determining value. Ultimately, financial markets provide a mechanism for price discovery whereby owners of financial assets can easily determine value.

One of the real economic advantages of financial markets is their overall efficiency. This means that prices are determined in those markets and reflect all available information. Because of this, financial assets are "correctly" priced and are distributed to their most highly valued use.

From a practical point of view, market efficiency implies that asset prices are determined by the present value of expected future cash flows. As a result, the time value of money is of primary importance in understanding the workings of financial markets.

Future cash flows can be certain or uncertain. When values are known with complete certainty, the assets are said to be risk-free. When the amount or timing of future cash flows is not known with certainty, financial assets are said to be risky. Time value of money properties applies to both risky and risk-free assets. The difference lies in the determination of the discount rate. The discount rate for risk-free assets is, of course, the risk-free rate of interest.

The general method for calculating the price of any asset is to discount each future cash flow by the discount rate appropriate to the risk of the cash flow. The general form is

$$PV = CF_1 / (1 + r_1) + CF_2 / (1 + r_2) + \ldots$$

This formula can be used to find the price of any financial asset, stock or bond, regardless of the risk and the nature of the cash flows. Obviously the discount rate must reflect the underlying risk of the cash flows.

Simplified formulas for annuities and perpetuities were presented and applied to both stock and bond pricing. In addition, we examined the relationship between the pricing formula and the different yield measures. The yield to maturity is a forward-looking rate that solves the pricing equation given the market price, the cash flows, and an assumption that the instrument will be held until maturity. The holding period return is a backward-looking rate that makes use of the cash flows actually received and the rates at which those cash flows were reinvested. We also examined some pricing conventions such as the bank discount yield, the money market–equivalent yield, and clean vs. dirty bond quotes.

The pricing of equity stock differs little from the pricing of fixed income securities from a pure calculation standpoint. Investor expectations of future growth opportunities were shown to be major determinants of stock prices, and changes in these expectations can cause major movements in stock prices. The analysis was extended to the pricing of companies. The methods that are used to price traded financial assets may be applied to nontraded financial assets as well.

Determination of the discount rate for risky assets requires the use of a theoretical pricing model. The simplest and most common pricing model in finance is the Capital Asset Pricing Model. This model suggests the discount rate reflects only nondiversifiable risk. In addition, the amount of this risk relative to the overall risk in the economy is the crucial component in discounting risky cash flows.

REVIEW QUESTIONS

1. Calculate the price of a U.S. Treasury security that has 30 years to maturity, semiannual coupon payments, a coupon rate of 6%, and a face value of $100,000 when the market rate of interest is 7%.

2. Calculate the effective yield on a T-bill (zero coupon bond) that has a face value of $10,000 with six months to maturity and currently sells for $9,775.

3. What generates a higher yield for investors: a CD paying 6% compounded semiannually, or one paying 5.75% compounded monthly?

4. A bank has a fixed-rate mortgage on its books that has 20 years remaining to maturity and has monthly payments of $1,000. If the interest rate on the mortgage is 8%, calculate the current book value of the mortgage.

5. Suppose that the 8% rate in Problem 4 represents the rate that prevailed at the time the mortgage was issued. If in the interim period interest rates have risen to 10%, what is the market value of the mortgage?

6. If the 8% rate in the mortgage represents the annual percentage rate, what is the effective yield on the mortgage?

7. What is the price of a 30-year zero coupon bond if the face value is $1,000 and the interest rate is 5%?

8. What is the face value on a 10-year zero coupon bond with a price of $5,000 and a current interest rate of 7%?

9. What is the yield to maturity on a five-year zero coupon bond with a face value of $20,000 and a current price of $12,000?

10. Suppose you purchased a zero coupon bond four years ago for $700. If the current selling price is $850, what is your holding period return on such a bond?

11. Norwest Bank is offering a new double-up CD where the annual coupon payment doubles each year. Suppose the first coupon payment is $50, the face value is $500, and the maturity is five years. If the yield to maturity is 7%, calculate the price of such a CD.

12. Suppose you sell the above CD after three years for $900. Determine the holding period return assuming all the coupon payments were reinvested at 5%.

13. There is 30% chance that the price of IBM's stock will increase by 50% and a 70% chance that it will decline by 20%. Calculate expected return and variance and standard deviation for IBM stock.

14. Suppose expected returns for Citicorp are 12% and Nine West are 18% and their standard deviations are 8% and 14%. If the correlation coefficient between Citicorp and Nine West is 0.6, calculate the variance and standard deviation of a portfolio of these two stocks with the assumption that 40% of your money is invested in Citicorp and the rest in Nine West. Recalculate variance of the portfolio with correlation coefficients of 0 and −0.8. Explain the reason for the changes in risk.

15. Microsoft's beta of equity is 2. It promises a return of 20%. If the risk-free rate is 5% and rate of return for market index is 10%, would you invest in Microsoft?

REFERENCES

Agrawal, A., and K. Tandon. 1994. "Anomalies or Illusions? Evidence from Stock Markets in Eighteen Countries." *Journal of International Money and Finance* (February).

Arshadi, N., and T. Eyssell. 1993. *The Law and Finance of Corporate Insider Trading: Theory and Evidence*. Boston: Kluwer Academic Publishers.

Cutler, D. M., J. Poterba, and L.H. Summers. 1991. "Speculative Dynamics." *Review of Economic Studies* (May).

Fama, E. 1970. "Efficient Capital Markets: A Review of Theory and Empirical Work." *Journal of Finance* (May): 383–417.

Fama, E. 1991. "Efficient Capital Markets II." *Journal of Finance* (December).

Harvey, C. 1991. "The World Price of Covariance Risk." *Journal of Finance* (March): 111–158.

Hawawini, G., and D. Keim. 1994. "On the Predictability of Common Stock Returns: World-wide Evidence," in *Handbook in Operations Research and Management Science: Finance Volume*, edited by R.A. Jarrow, V. Maksimovic, and W.T. Ziemba. Amsterdam: North Holland.

Jarrell, G., J. Brickley, and G. Netter. 1988. "The Market for Corporate Control: The Empirical Evidence Since 1980." *Journal of Economic Perspectives*. 49–68.

Jensen, M., and R.S. Ruback. 1983. "The Market for Corporate Control: The Scientific Evidence." *Journal of Financial Economics*. 5–50.

Liu, P., S.D. Smith, and A.A. Syed. 1990. "Stock Price Reactions to the Wall Street Journal Securities Recommendations." *Journal of Financial and Quantitative Analysis* (June): 399–410.

Poterba, J., and L. Summers. 1988. "Mean Reversion in Stock Prices: Evidence and Implications." *Journal of Financial Economics* (October): 27–59.

Shiller, R. 1989. *Market Volatility*. Cambridge, MA: MIT Press.

Summers, L. H. 1986. "Does the Stock Market Rationality Reflect Fundamental Values?" *Journal of Finance* (July): 591–600.

12

The Level and Structure
of Interest Rates

OBJECTIVES

This chapter examines the economic determinants of the level and structure of interest rates. We discuss the loanable fund and liquidity preference theories of interest rates and proceed to examine the policies of the Federal Reserve System affecting interest rates. Theories of term structure, including pure expectations, liquidity premium, preferred habitat, and market segmentation, describe how bonds with identical risk, liquidity, and tax attributes may have different interest rates because the time remaining to maturity is different.

DETERMINANTS OF INTEREST RATES

An *interest rate* is the cost of credit. The level of interest charged depends on risk, liquidity, term to maturity, and tax characteristics of the issue. Competitive conditions also affect interest rates. As with other commodities, the price performs an allocative function. When interest rates are relatively high, individuals use less credit by changing their consumption and increasing their savings. When interest rates are relatively low, individuals find investment yields unattractive and choose consumption over saving. In either case, the interest rate affects the level of credit used.

The Loanable Funds Theory of Interest Rates

The *loanable funds theory of interest rates* uses the building blocks of supply and demand to explain interest-rate levels and movements. Households, businesses, and governments supply credit or loanable funds by saving and use credit by borrowing. Surplus funds move between borrowers and savers indirectly through financial intermediaries or directly through financial markets. The joint actions of borrowers and savers determine the market (equilibrium) interest rate.

The demand for loanable funds originates by the deficit spending entities in the economy. Households, business, and government entities all tend to be gross borrowers of funds (even though households are savers in net, households still

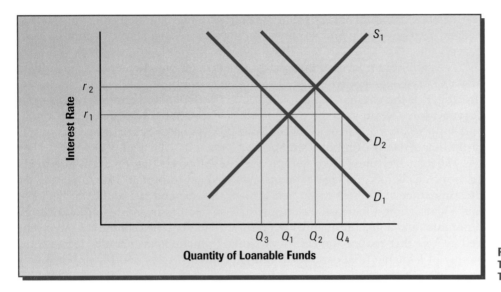

FIGURE 12.1
The Loanable Funds
Theory of Interest Rates

borrow large sums in credit markets). The combined borrowing of these groups determines overall demand for funds.[1]

The demand for funds is influenced by a variety of economic factors. Foremost, the interest rate negatively affects the quantity of funds demanded. The higher the rate, the lower the quantity demanded so the demand curve for funds is a downward-sloping function of the interest rate. In addition, factors such as expected profitability and earnings potential directly impact the demand for loanable funds. If businesses expect higher earnings, cash flows will improve and more funds will be demanded at every level of the interest rate. All noninterest factors that affect the demand for loanable funds will cause a shift of the entire curve as opposed to movement along the curve.

Demand curves for loanable funds are depicted in Figure 12.1. Demand curve D_1 is the initial demand curve. Demand curve D_2 indicates a change in demand as the result of some economic event (such as higher earnings expectations) that makes market participants willing to borrow more at every level of the interest rate. Movements along a demand curve reflect the amount of desired borrowing at different interest rates. In the figure, more funds are demanded at interest rate r_1 than at r_2 along the original demand curve D_1 (Q_1 vs. Q_3) because of the lower interest rate. Similarly, at the same interest rate r_1, the quantity of funds demanded is greater on demand curve D_2 than demand curve D_1 (Q_4 vs. Q_1) because the second demand curve was drawn under the assumption that economic agents were willing to borrow more funds at all interest rates.

A supply curve for loanable funds is also depicted in Figure 12.1. The curve is upward sloping, reflecting the fact that savers (suppliers of funds) are willing to defer greater amounts of consumption if they are paid more to do so. This is represented by the movement along the supply curve S_1 from interest rate r_1 and quantity Q_1 to interest rate r_2 and quantity Q_2. Higher interest rates bring

---

[1] The mirror image of the loanable funds market is the securities market. While supply and demand for loanable funds determine the interest rates, supply and demand for securities determine their prices. As explained in Chapter 11, interest rates and prices are mirror images of one another. Thus, parties who form the demand for loanable funds have similar functions to those who issue (supply) securities.

forth greater amounts of funds into the market. Other noninterest factors such as Federal Reserve policy and society's willingness to save shift the entire supply curve.

The equilibrium level of the interest rate is determined where the quantity of loanable funds demanded is just equal to the quantity of funds supplied. In Figure 12.1, r_1 is the equilibrium level associated with demand curve D_1 and supply curve S_1. Interest rate r_2 is the equilibrium rate associated with demand curve D_2 and supply curve S_1. Changes in the level of rates occur when either the supply or the demand curve (or both) shifts.

The loanable funds theory of interest rates suggests that financial intermediaries such as banks and credit unions may have an important role to play in the determination of interest rates. Fed actions that expand the ability of banks to make loans should increase the supply of loanable funds and result in lower interest rates and a greater quantity of credit extended in the economy. Conversely, Fed actions that reduce the ability of banks to make loans should decrease the supply of loanable funds and lead to higher interest rates and lower borrowing levels in the economy.

The effects of a Federal Reserve action that increases bank reserves is illustrated in Figure 12.2. The action increases the supply of loanable funds, shifting the supply curve from S_1 to S_2. The result is a decrease in market interest rates along with an increase in total borrowing in the economy. Increased bank lending is part of the reason economic activity increases. This lending activity suggests a credit channel in the transmission of monetary policy.

The credit channel idea implies that banks play a special role in the conduct of monetary policy. Because Fed policies directly impact bank lending under this theory, it is possible that monetary policy may have a major influence on the economy without large changes in interest rates. The policy action depicted above caused banks to directly increase the supply of loans, which allows businesses to increase their spending. The impact on the economy is immediate and significant.

FIGURE 12.2
The Loanable Funds Theory with a Federal Reserve Monetary Increase

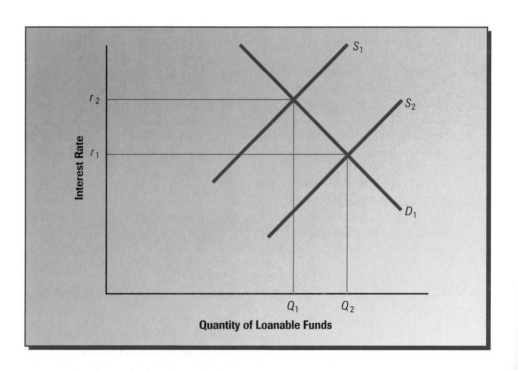

The Liquidity Preference Theory of Interest Rates

The *liquidity preference theory* explains interest rates by the preference of individuals to hold money balances as opposed to spending or investing them. Money, as the most liquid of assets, has value in that it can quickly and easily be converted to consumption or investment purposes (it has low transactions cost associated with it). It is so valuable, in fact, that individuals hold relatively large quantities of money in the form of currency and checking accounts. Individuals with higher incomes tend to hold more money than individuals with lower incomes, so the demand for money balances is directly related to income in the economy.

Holding money balances can be an expensive proposition. Wealth held as money could alternatively be invested in interest-bearing securities. These securities would pay the holder a rate of return, whereas pure money balances do not. This is the opportunity cost of holding money. The opportunity cost increases as interest rates increase. The quantity of money demanded is therefore inversely related to the rate of interest.

Money supply, as will be discussed later, is determined by Fed policy. This is accomplished in large part by security sales that influence the amount of reserves in the financial system. The Fed increases the money supply by buying securities from banks and other agents in the private sector. Conversely, the Fed decreases the money supply by selling securities to banks and the public, thereby reducing reserves in the financial system.

Interest rates are determined within the liquidity preference theory by the interaction of supply and demand forces just like in the loanable funds theory of interest rates. The difference is that the interest rate is determined in the money as opposed to credit markets. Interest-rate determination within the liquidity preference theory is illustrated in Figure 12.3. The demand for money balances is presented by demand curve D_1. Money demand depends inversely on the interest rate (hence is downward-sloping) and directly on the level of income in the

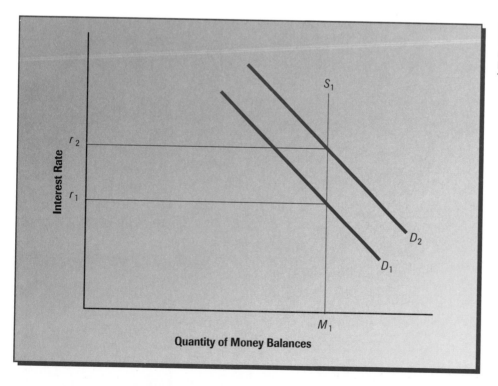

FIGURE 12.3
Interest Rate Determination within the Liquidity Preference Theory

economy. The supply curve is given by S_1 and has a vertical shape because the Fed exercises control over the level of the money supply. This means that the quantity of money supplied will not change as the interest rate changes.

The equilibrium interest rate is determined by supply and demand for money balances. Figure 12.3 depicts the equilibrium at the interest rate of r_1 and the money balances of M_1. Interest rates will change because of changes in the demand for money balances or because of a policy change by the Fed that leads to a change in the money supply.

Notice the role that the Fed plays in interest-rate determination in the liquidity preference theory. Suppose income in the economy rises because of improved business conditions. According to this model of interest-rate determination, economic agents will increase their demand of money balances at all interest rates because of the increased spending in the economy. This is represented by an outward shift of the demand curve to D_2. The interest rate rises to r_2 but the amount of money balances in the economy remains the same. In essence, rates are rising because the Fed is not accommodating the higher level of economic activity with increased liquidity in the economy. The higher rates will reduce investment and spending, thereby slowing the rate of growth in the economy.

The Fed can also intervene directly to set interest rates by controlling money balances through reserve policy. If the Fed increases money balances through an open market purchase of bonds, the result is a reduction in the equilibrium interest rate. This is illustrated in Figure 12.4. The Fed action results in an outward shift of the money supply curve to S_2. With the fixed demand for money, additional money balances are absorbed in the economy only through lower interest rates. The rate therefore declines to r_2.

One can associate the decline in interest rates to the presence of the Fed in securities markets. In order to increase money balances, the Fed purchases bonds in the open market. The holders of such securities must be offered higher bond prices to induce a sale. Higher bond prices are equivalent to lower interest rates. Thus, rates decline because of the upward pressure on bond prices. Economic

FIGURE 12.4
The Liquid Preference Theory with a Federal Reserve Monetary Increase

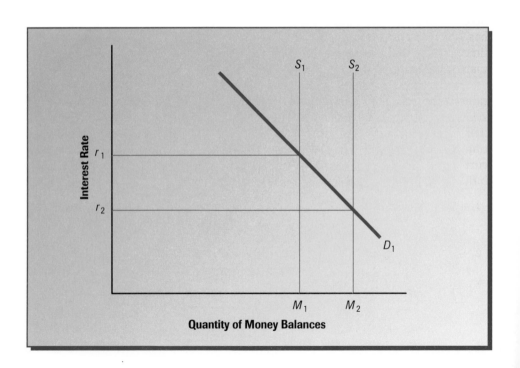

agents are willing to hold greater money balances because the opportunity cost of holding them (the interest rate) has decreased.

There is nothing in the preceding scenario of interest-rate changes that directly involves bank loans. Banks presumably end up holding more deposits. These additional funds can be invested in either securities or loans. The interest rate falls to the same level regardless of the proportion of loans or securities held by the banking sector.

The economy is impacted in this case by a monetary transmission mechanism. The importance of credit is diminished because interest rates and monetary changes influence output directly through spending changes by business and individuals. In this view, Fed actions do not really constrain bank activities, so Fed policy is not transmitted through bank lending.

There is some evidence that bank lending declines when monetary policy is tightened. This is consistent with a credit channel for monetary policy. However, much of the decline is in real estate lending and not in business lending as would be expected. In fact, there is some evidence that loans to manufacturing firms actually increase when monetary policy is tightened. There is also little evidence that the terms of lending (other than interest rates) change significantly when monetary policy is tightened. These facts would lend more support to a monetary channel. In practice, there is likely some truth to both views of the transmission of monetary policy. To the extent that monetary policy constrains some borrowers, credit channels are important.

THE ROLE OF THE FEDERAL RESERVE IN THE DETERMINATION OF INTEREST RATES

It is clear, from this discussion, that the Federal Reserve, in the conduct of monetary policy, plays a key role in the determination of interest rates regardless of the channel of monetary policy. The Fed exercises control over interest rates by managing bank reserves in the economy. This management influences both the level of interest rates and the supply of money. As will be seen, money supply determination is not independent of interest-rate determination. In fact, the Fed has shifted its focus between interest rates and the money supply targets several times in the last 20 years. (See the Appendix to this chapter for background information on the Fed.)

The Fed has several ways to influence the money supply and, hence, interest rates in the economy. To understand how the Fed influences the money supply, it is necessary to understand the role of money in the economy and the technical definitions. The main measure of the money supply, M_1, consists primarily of the transactions deposits of banks, savings and loans, and credit unions, along with currency in the hands of the public. There are three key tools the Fed can use to influence the level of the money supply:

1. **Open-Market Operations.** This is the buying and selling of government securities through the trading desk of the Fed for the purpose of changing bank reserves.
2. **The Discount and Federal Funds Rates.** These are the rates that banks pay to borrow reserves on a very short-term basis.
3. **The Required Reserve Ratio.** This is the percentage of deposits that must be held in the form of cash or deposits at the Federal Reserve Bank.

Changes in the discount and federal funds rates are the most noticeable way of observing changes in monetary policy, while open market operations are the most widely used. Changes in the required reserve ratio are rarely used to influence the money supply and will be largely ignored here. We begin by examining the effect of open-market operations on bank reserves and the money supply and then tie that to changes in the discount and federal funds rate.

Conduct of Monetary Policy Through Open-Market Operations

To examine how the Fed uses open market operations, let us first examine hypothetical balance sheets of the aggregate commercial banking system and the Federal Reserve.

Commercial Banking System				Federal Reserve Banks			
Cash	500	T. Deposits	9,000	Govt.		Bank De-	
Fed De-		Fed Bor-		Bonds	5,500	posits	500
posits	500	rowing	500	Loans to		Currency	5,000
Govt.		Equity	500	Banks	500	Govt. De-	
Bonds	4,000					posits	500
Loans	5,000						
	10,000		10,000		6,000		6,000

Briefly reviewing the balance sheets, we recall from the discussion in Chapter 4 that the primary assets of banks are loans and government securities. The remaining two assets on the commercial bank balance sheet are the nonearning assets used to provide for daily operations of the bank. Vault cash is used to provide cash directly to customers and for use in automatic teller machines. Fed Deposits are checking account balances kept at the Fed to aid in the clearing of checks through the Federal Reserve System. Banks that do not belong to the Fed will clear checks by using correspondent balances at nearby commercial banks.

The liabilities of the commercial banking system have been purposely simplified here and consist only of transactions account balances. Banks also hold other deposits, including savings and time deposits. Commercial banks also hold nondeposit liabilities in the form of Federal Reserve borrowing. These are short-term loans obtained from the Fed. These loans are liabilities for the commercial banking system but are assets to the Fed.

The primary asset of the Fed consists of U.S. government bonds. These are purchased in the conduct of monetary policy. In practice, the Fed also has small amounts of other assets, including gold and foreign currencies, but the primary earning assets are government bonds. The liabilities of the Fed consist of the deposits of the commercial banks that show up as an offsetting asset on the commercial bank balance sheet. The government deposits on the balance sheet of the Fed consist of checking account balances of the U.S. Treasury. The Treasury also has balances at commercial banks throughout the country but uses the Fed as its primary banker.

The major liability of the Fed is the currency it issues. The currency we carry in our wallets is the noninterest-bearing debt of the Federal Reserve Banks. The federal government has declared this to be legal tender and it must be accepted as legal payment for goods and services in this country. Given that the primary liability of the Fed is noninterest bearing while the major asset is interest earning, it should not be surprising that the Fed earns a great deal of profit each year. In recent years the Fed has earned $15–$20 billion. Because of the nature of the Federal Reserve banks, the profits do not go back to the owners (fixed dividends are paid on the stock) or to the employees. Instead, the profits are turned over to the U.S. Treasury and represent a revenue source to the federal government.

Several pieces of information can be deduced from an examination of the two balance sheets. First, the Fed issues the currency; according to the balance sheet, it has issued $5,000. Of that, $500 is in the banks, which means that $4,500 must be in the hands of the general public. According to the definition of the M_1 money supply, the amount of money in the economy must be $4,500 plus the transactions deposits of $9,000 for a total of $13,500.

Inspection of the balance sheet of the commercial banks reveals that $1,000 of assets are held in the form of vault cash ($500) and commercial bank deposits at the Federal Reserve ($500). The two assets constitute total or legal reserves for a commercial bank. The amount of total reserves a bank must hold is determined by the required reserve ratio. Suppose the Fed has set that rate at 10% of transactions deposits (the rate is currently 3% on deposits up to $50 million and 8% on deposits above that amount). The banking system must then hold at least $900 ($9,000 × 0.10) of assets in the form of cash and deposits at the Fed. This is referred to as the amount of required reserves. Total reserves held above the amount of required reserves are defined as excess reserves. The banking system thus has $100 of excess reserves. These reserves are assets that are available to be loaned out or used to purchase securities (both of these are interest-earning assets as opposed to the zero interest earned on cash and deposits at the Fed).

Summarizing the discussion, we have the following three reserves:

1. **Total or Legal Reserves.** These are assets of commercial banks, S&Ls, and credit unions that must be held as vault cash, Fed deposits, or correspondent balances that legally meet the required reserve obligation. (In our case, $500 + $500 = $1,000.)
2. **Required Reserves.** These are the amount of assets that must be held in the form of cash and Fed deposits (or qualifying correspondent deposits). The amount depends on the level of transactions deposits and the required reserve ratio. Required reserves are calculated as qualifying transactions deposits times the required reserve ratio. (In our case, $9,000 × 0.10 = $900.)
3. **Excess Reserves.** These are the total reserves of the banking system held over and above the amount of required reserves. This is calculated simply as total reserves minus required reserves. (In our case, $1,000 − $900 = $100.)

Remember that the Fed itself is not subject to reserve requirements; rather, it sets the requirements that are then applied to financial intermediaries that provide transactions accounts. Also remember that in the pursuit of profits, commercial banks will not want to hold excess reserves. It is more profitable to convert these noninterest-earning assets to loans or invest in government securities.

Suppose the Fed is worried that the excess reserves in our example will lead to new lending by banks, which will increase spending and lead to inflationary pressure in the economy. To prevent this, the Fed decides to sell $100 of its government securities to the banking system and reduce aggregate bank reserves. When it undertakes this transaction, purchasing banks will pay by having funds deducted from their accounts at the Fed and securities will be transferred to the banks. The changes to the balance sheets would look as follows:

Commercial Banking System		Federal Reserve System			
Fed Deposits	−100	Govt.		Bank	
Govt. Bonds	+100	Bonds	−100	Deposits	−100

This action has no immediate impact on the money supply because neither the amount of currency in the hands of the public nor the amount of transactions deposits changed. Because deposits did not change, the amount of required reserves did not change, but the total reserves of the banking system fell by $100 because banks now hold $100 fewer deposits at the Federal Reserve. By definition, excess reserves of the banking system declined by $100 and are now equal to zero.

The banking system is no longer in a position to make new loans. The restricted lending ability would be expected to drive up loan rates, thereby limiting spending and inflationary pressure in the economy. Another way to think about why this action would put upward pressure on interest rates is to think in terms of the price of government bonds. Before the Fed action, banks held $4,000 of government bonds. In order to entice them to hold more bonds, they would have to be given a good deal; the price would need to be lowered to get them to buy, which would drive up the yield on the bonds.

In this example, it was assumed that the trading desk was dealing directly with commercial banks. In practice, the trading desk deals with bond dealers that may or may not be commercial banks. The bond dealers could be acting on behalf of individuals or companies. In such a case, the transaction would be more complicated to record on the balance sheets but the results would have been essentially the same.

Let us suppose, for simplicity, that individuals deal directly with the Fed. When individuals pay for the bonds, they write checks on their bank accounts payable to the Fed. This lowers the amount of transactions deposits in the economy and reduces the amount of total reserves (Fed deposits) when the checks clear.

The changes in the balance sheets when the bonds are purchased by individuals instead of commercial banks are illustrated below.

Commercial Banking System		Federal Reserve System	
Fed Deposits −100	T. Deposits −100	Govt. Bonds −100	Bank Deposits −100

Individuals have given up a nonearning asset (a checking account balance) for a government bond. The check is written to the Fed, which passes it back to the commercial bank and reduces the amount of money banks have on deposit. The commercial bank notes the reduction by reducing its reserve asset by $100 and simultaneously reducing the account balance of the individual who wrote the check by $100.

In this case, the money supply declines by $100 because there are $100 fewer transaction deposits in the economy. The reduction in transaction deposits reduces the amount of required reserves by $10 ($100 \times 0.10$). Total reserves again decline by $100, so excess reserves decline by $90 ($100 - 10$). The qualitative result is still the same—reserves in the banking system decline, putting upward pressure on interest rates.

As can be seen from this example, Fed sales of government securities reflect a tightening of monetary policy by reducing bank reserves and the money supply (actual deposit balances or potential balances that would have been created with increased lending). When the Fed acts to increase the money supply, the trading desk buys rather than sells government bonds.

Open-market purchases work exactly the opposite of open-market sales. If the bonds were purchased directly from commercial banks, the resulting changes in the balance sheets would be the same as those shown for the sale of securities except that signs on the dollar changes would be reversed.

For example, suppose the Fed wants to expand bank reserves and decides to purchase $400 worth of government securities from commercial banks. The changes in the balance sheets would look as follows:

Commercial Banking System		Federal Reserve System		
Fed deposits	+400	Govt.	Bank	
Govt. bonds	−400	bonds +400	deposits +400	

Commercial banks give up interest-earning assets (bonds) for nonearning assets (Fed deposits). Total reserves increase by $400 but required reserves do not change because transactions deposits have not increased. Excess reserves increase by the amount of the increase in total reserves or $400. Downward pressure would be exerted on interest rates as banks attempted to loan out the excess reserves. The purchase of the bonds by the Fed also puts downward pressure on interest rates because higher prices would have to have been offered to the banks to induce them to sell.

The same qualitative results would be obtained if the bonds were instead purchased from individuals. The bond purchases would increase the amount of bank reserves and money in the economy. This would increase the supply of loanable funds and the money supply, putting downward pressure on interest rates. Hence, open-market operations act to impact bank reserves, which in turn influence the quantity of loanable funds and the money supply, which in turn influence the level of interest rates.

Conduct of Monetary Policy Through Changes in the Discount and Federal Funds Rates

A much more public way for the Fed to set the course of monetary policy is to change the level of the discount rate and/or the federal funds rate. The *discount rate* is the rate that the Fed charges financial institutions when they borrow funds from a Federal Reserve Bank. Until 1980, only member banks were able to borrow from the Fed. The Fed is now required to lend to all financial institutions offering transactions accounts. The borrowing is said to occur at the discount window and the interest rate set by the Fed on these loans is referred to as the discount rate.

The discount rate is set in response to changing economic conditions. When the Fed is concerned about inflationary pressure, the discount rate is raised to induce banks to borrow fewer reserves, to make fewer loans, and to reduce spending in the economy. When the Fed wants to expand the economy, just the opposite occurs. The discount rate is lowered and banks are induced to borrow more reserves and make more loans, and spending will ultimately increase.

The Fed adjusts the discount rate on an as-needed basis. As suggested, the primary reason for banks to borrow money from the Fed is to meet temporary liquidity needs regarding reserve management. Banks expecting to make loans will increase transactions deposits and required reserves and will need to borrow funds. The Fed treats such borrowing as a right and not a privilege. As a result, banks must apply to the Fed to borrow, and if they have appropriate collateral their loan request will be granted. Appropriate collateral takes the form of low-risk securities such as U.S. government bills, notes, and bonds.

To illustrate the mechanics of discount window borrowing, assume that the Fed has lowered the discount rate and banks collectively decide to increase discount window borrowing by $100. The changes to the commercial banking system and Federal Reserve balance sheets are as follows:

Commercial Banking System			Federal Reserve Banks		
Fed De- posits	+100	Fed Bor- rowing +100	Loans	+100	Bank Depos- its +100

The transaction is very similar to customer borrowing at a commercial bank where the loan proceeds are deposited in the customer's checking account. A bank official informs the discount window of the need for funds and the assets available for collateral. The discount window officer approves the loan and the bank is notified that its clearing deposits with the Fed have increased by the amount of the loan. The bank records a liability in the form of Federal Reserve borrowing and the Fed records an asset in the form of a discount loan to a bank.

The impact on bank reserves is identical to an open-market purchase of government securities from banks. Total reserves increase by $100 while required reserves remain unchanged because transactions deposits are unaffected. Excess reserves increase by $100, and these reserves are now available to increase commercial banks' lending. Notice that the lowering of the discount rate increases loanable funds and is ultimately expected to increase the money supply. This puts downward pressure on interest rates in the economy.

The Fed also provides other seasonal lending to banks that can demonstrate predictable swings in borrowing and deposits (agricultural banks have very seasonal needs). The Fed also, as mentioned earlier, is the lender of last resort in the economy and provides extended credit to financial institutions with major liquidity problems that have the potential to cause damaging effects on the entire financial system. Neither of these types of loans is related to monetary policy and interest-rate determination. The discount window for short-term (usually one day) borrowing is the primary interest-rate tool used to influence monetary policy.

The discount window allows banks to adjust reserves when unexpected loan demand or deposit withdrawals leave banks with negative reserve positions. While some banks have negative reserve positions, others are likely to find themselves in the opposite situation. Banks with positive excess reserves will want to invest funds for very short periods of time in instruments that have little default risk. The federal funds market serves this role.

The *federal funds market* is a market where banks with excess reserves can lend to banks with deficit reserves. In practice, the federal funds market is broader than that. Any institution that holds large balances at the Federal Reserve Banks or at depository institutions can trade fed funds. Thus banks, thrifts, credit unions, foreign and domestic governments, and the U.S. Treasury all trade fed funds.

The technical definition of a federal funds transaction is a one-day loan that is settled with *immediately available funds*. Immediately available funds must satisfy one of two requirements: (1) they must be deposits held at a Federal Reserve Bank and (2) they must be liabilities that can be transferred by Fed wire during a business day. These liabilities consist of items such as deposits at the Fed and deposit balances at correspondent banks.

Fed funds borrowing is very similar to discount window borrowing in that it can be used to increase total reserves. Unlike discount window borrowing, however, fed funds borrowing is unsecured. This means that only the most creditworthy of institutions can make use of the fed funds market.

For some banks, especially large banks with a top credit rating, fed funds represent a cheap and readily available source of funding for loan expansion and deposit creation. These banks borrow regularly and react to changes in the fed

TABLE 12.1 Recent Federal Reserve Targets for the Federal Funds Rate	
Date	**Percent**
July 6, 1995	5.75
Feb. 1, 1995	6.00
Nov. 15, 1994	5.50
Aug. 16, 1994	4.75
May 17, 1994	4.25
April 18, 1994	3.75
March 22, 1994	3.50
Feb. 4, 1994	3.25
Sept. 4, 1992	3.00
July 2, 1992	3.25
April 9, 1992	3.75
Dec. 20, 1991	4.00
Dec. 6, 1991	4.50
Nov. 6, 1991	4.75
Oct. 30, 1991	5.00
Sept. 13, 1991	5.25
Aug. 6, 1991	5.50
April 30, 1991	5.75
March 8, 1991	6.00
Feb. 1, 1991	6.25
Jan. 8, 1991	6.75
Dec. 19, 1990	7.00
Dec. 7, 1990	7.25
Nov. 16, 1990	7.50
Oct. 29, 1990	7.75
July 13, 1990	8.00
Dec. 20, 1989	8.25
Nov. 6, 1989	8.50
Oct. 16, 1989	8.75
July 27, 1989	9.00
July 7, 1989	9.25
June 6, 1989	9.50
Feb. 23, 1989	9.75

funds rate in the same fashion as outlined in the discussion regarding the discount rate. Decreases in the fed funds rate encourage borrowing and hence encourage lending by banks. Higher fed funds rates raise the cost of funding new loans and signal tighter credit.

The Fed can intervene in the fed funds market by controlling the supply of reserves in the banking system. In recent years the Fed has taken to using the fed funds rate to be a major tool of monetary policy. The Fed announces targets for the fed funds rate and then acts with open market operations to ensure those targets are achieved. Table 12.1 provides the targets for the federal funds rate as announced by the Federal Reserve for 1989–1995.

The announcement of the target fed funds rate acts as a guide for commercial banks in the setting of commercial loan rates. Very often, banks will tie their prime lending rate to the federal funds rate. For instance, when the Fed announced on July 6, 1995, a lowering of the federal funds target rate from 6% to 5.75%, it was immediately followed by an announcement from Bank of America, Bank One, and Harris Trust and Savings Bank of a reduction in their prime lending rate from 9% to 8.75%. In the days that followed the announcement, banks throughout the country lowered their prime and mortgage rates.

The fed funds rate and the discount rate do not necessarily move in concert with one another. For instance, the discount rate was left unchanged in the July 6, 1995, announcement of the lowering of the target fed funds rate. Because the Fed can control the amount of borrowing through the discount window, the Fed allows a divergence between the two rates. The Fed does prohibit any arbitrage that could occur when the discount rate is below the fed funds rate. When the discount rate is below the fed funds rate, the Fed expects discount window borrowing to increase and can limit the amount of borrowing by banks.

The Fed, Interest Rates, and Inflation

Milton Friedman, the Nobel prize–winning economist, long ago declared inflation to be always and everywhere a monetary phenomenon.[2] This means that prices can continue to increase only when there is a sufficient amount of money in the economy to allow it. In essence, the Fed must allow the money supply to grow; otherwise, price increases will eventually come to a halt.

The relationship between the growth in the money supply and inflation is described by the equation of exchange. In its simplest form, where the velocity of money remains unchanged, the equation of exchange says that the growth rate in the money supply is just equal to the inflation rate plus the growth rate in the real economy. This can be written as

$$\%\Delta M = \%\Delta P + \%\Delta Q$$

where M represents the money supply, P the price level in the economy, and Q the real output in the economy. The equation is read as the percentage change in the money supply is equal to the percentage change in the price level plus the percentage change in real economic output.

To see how this implies that inflation is a monetary phenomenon, consider the case in which the economy is growing at a real rate of 3% per year. If the Fed allows the money supply to grow by 10% over that same period, then the equation of exchange will hold only if the inflation rate is 7% per year. Hence, monetary growth in excess of the growth rate in the economy causes inflation. If the Fed had instead grown the money supply at a 3% rate, then inflation would have been 0 for the equation to hold.

If the real world were this simple, one could simply set the growth rate in the money supply equal to the growth rate in the economy. Unfortunately, this relationship is one that tends to hold in the long run but not at every point along the way. Many economists believe it is desirable to smooth short-term interest-rate fluctuations that arise in the economy because of liquidity changes. In addition, technological improvements cause constant changes in the velocity of money and make it difficult for the Fed to accurately measure the money supply. As a result, the Fed chooses to intervene in the economy by using interest-rate changes to conduct monetary policy.

---

[2] Friedman (1968).

The Fisher Effect

While the Fed has the ability to target the money supply and interest rates, it cannot do this independent of the rate of inflation. Interest rates are influenced by investor expectations of future inflation. To understand this, consider an investor interested in purchasing a one-year zero coupon bond with a face value of $1,000. Suppose at present there is no inflation in the economy and bonds of similar risk have a yield of 5%. From the pricing formula developed in Chapter 11, this bond should sell for:

$$\text{Price} = 1,000 / 1.05 = \$952.38$$

Now suppose that the investor receives new information that indicates the general price level will increase by 10% over the next year. This means that the $1,000 the investor will receive in a year is only worth $909.09 in today's dollars ($1,000 / (1 + 0.10)$). In other words, the investor is only going to receive $909.09 worth of purchasing power when the bond matures.

A rational investor will not purchase a bond for $952.38 if the bond is only going to purchase $909.09 of goods and services when it matures. Instead, the investor will discount the price of the bond because of the inflation. The price the investor is willing to pay for the bond should be the discounted value of the real purchasing power of the promised $1,000. The bond should thus sell for

$$\text{Price} = 909.09 / (1 + 0.05) = 1,000 / (1 + 0.10) / (1 + 0.05)$$
$$= 1,000 / (1 + 0.10)(1 + 0.05) = \$865.80$$

This price takes into account the interest rate in the absence of inflation and the expected rate of inflation.

A bond that sells for $865.80 and promises to pay $1,000 at maturity in one year is going to have a yield to maturity of 15.5% ($1,000/865.8 - 1$). The marketplace will anticipate the rate of inflation and include it in the price of the bond and hence the yield to maturity. Market interest rates thus have two components—a *real rate* (the interest rate in the absence of inflation) and an *expected rate of inflation*.

The market rate is referred to as the nominal rate of interest, r, and can be determined as follows. From our example the price of the bond could be written as

$$\$865.80 = 1,000 / (1 + r)$$

In addition, we showed that the price actually had two components: a real interest rate p and an expected rate of inflation π^e. The price was shown to be equal alternatively to

$$\$865.80 = 1,000 / (1 + p)(1 + \pi^e)$$

Setting these two equations equal to one another and doing a little algebra results in the expression that is termed the *Fisher equation* (after the economist Irving Fisher):

$$r = p + \pi^e + p\pi^e$$

From this example we have a real rate of 5% and an expected rate of inflation of 10%. According to the Fisher equation, the nominal rate of interest r should equal

$$r = 0.05 + 0.10 + 0.05 \times 0.10 = .155 = 15.5\%$$

As should be the case, this is the same result as when the yield to maturity was calculated.

The more common way of writing the Fisher equation is a simplified version, in which the last term in this equation is dropped off because the term is very close to zero for low levels of expected inflation. The simplified version of the Fisher equation is given as

$$r = p + \pi^e$$

For our example, the nominal rate would be 15% (5% + 10%).

There are two important characteristics associated with the Fisher equation that need to be emphasized. First, the equation uses the expected rate of inflation and not the actual rate of inflation. This is due to the fact that the nominal rate of interest is used to discount future cash flows and an inflation rate associated with future cash flows is required. Second, the real rate of interest is defined as the interest rate in the economy in the absence of inflation. The real rate is not actually observable and neither is the exact number for the expected rate of inflation. Rather, we can make inferences about the real rate and expected rate of inflation from changes in nominal interest rates.

Realized Real Rates

According to the Fisher equation, the nominal rate of interest depends on the real rate and the expected rate of inflation. The real rate is not directly observable but we can compute an ex post real rate of interest by comparing the nominal rate of interest to the actual rate of inflation. By rearranging the simplified Fisher equation and substituting the actual for the expected rate of inflation, the *realized real rate* is equal to

$$p_a = r - \pi^a$$

where π^a is the actual rate of inflation, r is the nominal rate of interest, and p_a is the realized real rate of interest.

The realized real rate tells an investor of the yield on an instrument after inflation is considered. Consider the investor who purchased a one-year T-bill with a nominal interest rate of 5.5%. If the rate of inflation turned out to be 4% over the investment horizon, the investor has realized a real yield of 1.5% (5.5% − 4.0%). Realized real rates for one-year Treasury bills over the past 15 years are provided in Table 12.2.

In the Fisher equation, the real rate of interest would never be negative as investors would always want to earn a positive return on their investment in the

	TABLE 12.2 Nominal Rates and Realized Real Returns on One-Year Treasury Securities		
Year	**Nominal Rate**	**Inflation Rate**	**Realized Real Rate**
1980	10.8	13.5	−2.7
1981	13.3	10.4	2.9
1982	11.5	6.1	5.4
1983	8.2	3.2	5.0
1984	9.2	4.3	4.9
1985	8.4	3.6	4.8
1986	7.1	1.9	5.2
1987	5.6	3.6	2.0
1988	6.7	4.1	2.6
1989	8.5	4.8	3.7
1990	7.1	5.4	1.7
1991	6.6	4.2	2.4
1992	4.2	3.0	1.2
1993	3.6	3.0	0.6
1994	3.5	2.6	0.9

Source: Federal Reserve Bulletin, various issues.

absence of inflation. The nominal rate of interest reflects this time preference and is adjusted upward or downward depending on inflationary expectations. Unfortunately, very few expectations are actually realized. If investors expect inflation to be 10% and have a time preference for a real return of 5%, then the nominal rate will be 15%. If the inflation rate turns out to be 15%, then the realized real return is 0 (15 − 15). There is nothing to prevent the realized return from becoming negative. As shown in the table, realized real returns were negative in 1980.

If investors underestimate the rate of inflation, the real return on an investment will be negative and the borrower will receive an unanticipated windfall. If borrowers and lenders overestimate the actual rate of inflation, lenders will receive higher realized real yields than planned. Although there have been periods when real short-term yields have been negative, there is no evidence that borrowers or lenders can outdo one another and earn consistent windfalls.

The Fed in Practice

As mentioned earlier, the Fed conducts monetary policy by supplying reserves to the banking system through open-market operations in conjunction with discount and fed funds rate announcements. In the 1970s, the Fed conducted monetary policy by targeting interest rates. As rates increased, more reserves were supplied to the banking system in an effort to increase the supply of loanable funds and drive down interest rates. Unfortunately, this also caused the money supply to increase and prices to rise (as would be predicted by the equation of exchange). This had the effect of increasing inflationary expectations and eventually driving up interest rates.

As inflation exceeded 10% in the late 1970s, the Fed announced a change in policy from interest-rate targeting to reserve and money supply targeting. The policy action proved to be very successful and inflation was quickly lowered to 4%. The Fed still publishes targets for monetary and credit aggregates and reports its targets to Congress each year.

Changing technology in the financial services industry in the late 1980s led to difficulty in measuring monetary aggregates as computer technology allowed customers to move monetary assets quickly and easily. As a result, the Fed now appears to have moved back to an era of interest-rate targeting and the fed funds rate is the key rate for the Fed in the conduct of monetary policy.

To determine the appropriate direction for fed funds rate changes, the Fed examines a variety of economic indicators. Among the measures the Fed carefully watches are resource utilization in the economy as measured by capacity utilization and unemployment rates; the difference between actual and potential gross domestic product; consumer and corporate debt burdens; total reserves in the banking system; growth in private and public debt, and the realized federal funds rate (fed funds rate minus inflation). Basic economic sense guides the Fed as it monitors these measures of economic performance. For instance, the rate of growth in total debt slowed in 1994 and debt burdens of both consumers and corporations eased slightly. These results were part of the rationale for the move by the Fed to reduce the federal funds rate on July 6, 1995, after seven rate increases between February 1994 and February 1995.

The primary concern of the Fed in conducting monetary policy is inflation. Note, however, that it is somewhat inconsistent to believe that inflation will decline when fed funds rates are increased because the Fisher equation suggests that a higher nominal interest rate is associated with higher inflation expectations (assuming a constant real rate). The Fed uses changes in the fed funds rate to signal its intention about inflationary beliefs and actions. A lowering of the fed funds rate can be taken as a signal that the Fed sees little chance of prices rising in the future. The long-term view is lower inflation, and rates can fall even though monetary policy has been eased. Similarly, raising the fed funds rate signals that the Fed is worried about future price increases, and investors should revise inflationary expectations upward. By announcing its intention to maintain price stability, the Fed can target interest rates to signal investors as to its view of inflationary expectations.

Conducting monetary policy by setting short-term interest rates is no simple matter, as the Fed learned in early 1994. The Fed raised the fed funds rate in hopes that a strong anti-inflationary signal would lower long-term interest rates. The unexpected move set a mini panic in financial markets when several speculators suffered huge losses because of the rate increase. The final result was that long-term rates increased substantially instead of falling.

TERM STRUCTURE OF INTEREST RATES

Until this point we have talked about interest rates as though only one rate existed in the economy. Risk, liquidity, and tax considerations influence interest rates. In addition, term to maturity affects interest rates. Bonds with similar risk, liquidity, and tax attributes may have different interest rates if their terms to maturity are different. The relationship of the yields on bonds with similar risk, liquidity, and tax attributes but different terms to maturity is referred to as the *term structure relationship* and its plot is called a *yield curve*. We will discuss the impact of risk, liquidity, and tax considerations on interest rates in Chapter 13. Here we discuss various theories of term structure of interest rates.

A recent article by John Campbell provides a comprehensive discussion of the impact of maturity differentials on bond yields.[3] A humorous aspect of his article was his reference to a paper by noted financial economist Ed Kane that criticized the economics profession for the quality of research in this area. According to Kane, "It is generally agreed that, ceteris paribus, the fertility of a field is roughly proportional to the quantity of manure that has been dumped on it in the recent past. By this standard, the term structure of interest rates has become . . . an extraordinarily fertile field indeed."[4] Much research effort has gone into the exploration of yield differences based on maturity—much of the earlier research of poor quality, according to Kane. Fortunately, the quality of the research has improved in the last 25 years and we now have a better understanding of the relationship between yield and maturity.

The upward-sloping curve in Figure 12.5 is the most common term structure relationship and is referred to as a *normal yield curve*. This means that the longer the maturity, the greater the yield to maturity. There is nothing necessarily sacred about this configuration but it is the most common. A downward-sloping yield curve is one in which the yield to maturity is higher for short-term than for long-term bonds. This relationship is often referred to as an *inverted yield curve*. When the yield to maturity is constant for all maturities, this is referred to as a *flat yield curve*. A "humped" yield curve has also been observed at various times.

The flat yield curve is virtually unseen in reality but is very common in textbook applications in finance. Recall in the previous chapter that the interest rate was the same every period when calculating the present value of the longer-term cash flows. Such an assumption is equivalent to a flat yield curve. To be totally accurate when computing present values, each cash flow should be discounted

---

[3] Campbell (1995).
[4] Kane (1970).

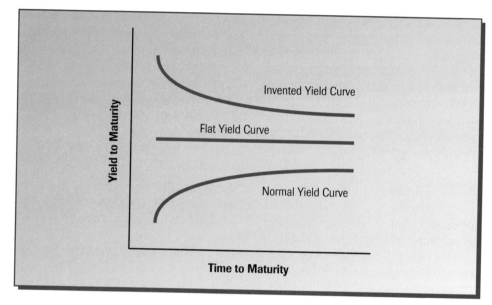

FIGURE 12.5
Common Yield Curve
Relationships

with the rate from the yield curve (adjusted, of course, for the risk in the cash flows).

There are four theories of term structure of interest rates that attempt to explain the observed shapes of the yield curve: pure expectation, liquidity premium, preferred habitat, and market segmentation.

Pure Expectation Theory

According to the *pure expectation theory*, bonds of different maturities are considered perfect substitutes for one another. In addition, the pure expectations theory assumes that the forward rates represent the expected futures rates. Under this theory, an upward-sloping yield curve implies that the market expects future short-term rates to rise. Similarly, a downward-sloping yield curve indicates that the market expects future short-term rates to decline. A flat yield curve means no change in short-term rates throughout the future periods.

To understand the expectations model, consider an investor who wants to invest for a two-year period. The only investments available are a one-year zero coupon bond with a yield to maturity of 5% and a two-year zero coupon bond with a yield to maturity of 5.995%. The investor is only concerned about maximizing the yield over the two-year period and will want to invest in the bond that provides the maximum return.

While it is tempting to think the investor should just go ahead and purchase the two-year bond, this approach ignores what the investor can do with her money in the second year after the one-year bond matures. Suppose that interest rates rise unexpectedly to 10%. If the initial investment was $1,000, she would have $1,050 after the first year (1,000 × 1.05) and $1,155 after two years (1,050 × 1.10). The holding period return for the two years would equal

$$\text{2-year holding period return} = (1,155 - 1,000) / 1,000 = 0.155$$

Annualizing this return we have

$$\text{Annual holding period return} = (1 + 0.155)^{1/2} - 1 = 0.0747 = 7.47\%$$

Clearly the investor would have been better off if she had purchased the one-year bond and rolled it over at the end of the year.

Although interest rates were chosen to go up in the second year of this example, they could just as easily have gone down or remained unchanged. If they had remained unchanged, the annual holding period return would have been 5% and the two-year bond with a yield of 5.992% would have been the superior investment. Investor expectations as to what will happen to rates in the second year will determine which investment strategy to follow.

We can solve for the interest rate on a one-year bond one year into the future; such an approach would make the investor indifferent between either investment strategy. This rate out in the future is referred to as a *forward rate.* In our example, the one-year forward rate on the one-year bond can be calculated as

$$(1 + 0.05992)^2 = (1 + 0.05)(1 + f)$$

where f is the forward rate. This equation states that the total return on the two-year investment (the left-hand side of the equation) must equal the return on an investment strategy wherein the one-year bond is purchased and then reinvested for another year (the right-hand side of the equation).

The forward rate that makes the investor indifferent between these two investment strategies can be solved as follows:

$$1 + f = (1 + 0.05992)^2 / (1 + .05) \text{ or } 1 + f = 1.07$$
$$f = 1.07 - 1 = 0.07 \text{ or } 7\%$$

This states that a two-year investment strategy of two one-year bonds with rates of 5% and 7% is identical to a two-year investment strategy of a two-year bond with a rate of 5.992%. The risk neutral investor should be indifferent between the two strategies.

In the pure expectations theory, future interest rates are expected to move in a way that makes the yields on the two investment strategies identical. In other words, forward rates are perfect predictors of future interest rates. When the yield curve is upward sloping as in our two-year example, the forward rate on the one-year bond was higher than the current market rate on the one-year bond. Thus, the expectations theory predicts that an upward-sloping yield curve implies higher future interest rates because the forward rates are the predictors of future interest rates. Similarly, a downward-sloping yield curve would lead to forward rates lower than current rates, thus predicting falling interest rates.

As the number of maturities are lengthened, the number of possible forward rates that can be determined also increases. Consider the adding on of another year to our example and suppose that the current market rate on a three-year zero coupon bond is 8%. We can now solve for a forward rate on a one-year bond two years out, and a two-year bond one year out in addition to the forward rate on a one-year bond that was already determined. To solve for the forward rate on the two-year bond one year out, we note that the expectations theory says a strategy of buying a one-year bond and rolling it over into a two-year bond after one year should provide the same expected yield as the current three-year bond. Thus, we have

$$(1 + 0.08)^3 = (1 + 0.05)(1 + f)^2$$
$$(1 + f)^2 = (1 + 0.08)^3 / (1 + 0.05)$$
$$f = 0.0953$$

Similarly, the forward rate on a one-year bond two years out can be determined by using a strategy of buying three one-year bonds and making use of the earlier determined forward rate on the one-year bond one year out. The expectations theory thus implies the following:

$$(1 + 0.08)^3 = (1 + 0.05)(1 + 0.07)(1 + f)$$
$$(1 + f) = (1 + 0.08)^3 / 1.1235$$
$$f = 0.1212$$

Because the yield curve is upward sloping, the forward rates predict higher rates in the future.

In order to generalize the forward rate equation we will use R for the observable market interest rates (spot rates) and f for forward rates in the following relationship:

$$(1 + {}_0R_n)^n = (1 + {}_0R_1)(1 + {}_1f_2)(1 + {}_2f_3) \ \ldots \ (1 + {}_{n-1}f_n)$$

This equation means that the total compounded yield on an n-period bond is just the product of the rates on one-period bonds over that same time interval.

We do not have to restrict ourselves to one-period bonds when using future rates because any investment strategy must provide the same yield over the same time horizon. Hence, the equation could be written many ways, including

$$(1 + {}_0R_{n+k})^{n+k} = (1 + {}_0R_n)^n (1 + {}_nf_{n+k})^k$$

This can be interpreted as the return on a strategy of holding an $n + k$-period bond is the same as investing in an n-period bond today, letting it mature, and then investing in a k-period bond. The forward rate, therefore, can be calculated as

$$ {}_nf_{n+k} = \left[\frac{(1 + {}_0R_{n+k})^{n+k}}{(1 + {}_0R_n)^n} \right]^{1/k} - 1 $$

Suppose for illustration we have a downward-sloping yield curve with the yields and maturities reflected as follows:

Maturity	Yield
1 year	0.10
2 year	0.09
3 year	0.08
4 year	0.07

Using this information we will calculate forward rates on a two-year bond two years from now and a three-year bond one year from now. The investment strategy of purchasing a four-year bond and holding it to maturity must yield the same when compared to a strategy of buying a two-year bond now, and then buying another two-year bond. Similarly, the strategy of purchasing a four-year bond and holding it to maturity must yield the same when compared to a strategy of buying a one-year bond today, and then buying a three-year bond one-year from now. Using the above equation we can write this as

$$ {}_2f_{2+2} = \left[\frac{(1 + {}_0R_{2+2})^{2+2}}{(1 + {}_0R_2)^2} \right]^{1/2} - 1 $$

$$ {}_2f_4 = \left[\frac{(1 + 0.07)^4}{(1 + 0.09)^2} \right]^{1/2} - 1 $$

$$ {}_2f_4 = 0.0504 $$

$$ {}_1f_{1+3} = \left[\frac{(1 + {}_0R_{1+3})^{1+3}}{(1 + {}_0R_1)^1} \right]^{1/3} - 1 $$

$$ {}_1f_4 = \left[\frac{(1 + 0.07)^4}{(1 + 0.10)^1} \right]^{1/3} - 1 $$

$$ {}_1f_4 = 0.0602 $$

These results tell us that the predicted rate on a two-year bond two years from now is 5.04% vs. the current rate of 9%. In addition, the rate on a three-year bond is predicted to be 6.02% in a year vs. the current 8% rate.

The forward rate formulas used here can also be adjusted for intrayear compounding by using the periodic interest rate (e.g., the six-month rate) and then finding the yield over the total number of compounding periods. These forward rates can also be calculated independent of the pure expectations hypothesis. The pure expectations hypothesis says, however, that the calculated forward rates are perfect predictors of future interest rates.

Liquidity Premium Theory

The *liquidity premium theory* of term structure recognizes that the pure expectations hypothesis treats bonds of different maturity as perfect substitutes even though longer maturity bonds have more risk. The risk increases as maturity increases because maturity and price volatility are directly related. Because bonds of different maturities have different risks, they should not be perfect substitutes and the forward rates that can be calculated are not perfect or unbiased predictors of future interest rates. Each maturity should also have a term or liquidity premium associated with it in addition to an expectation component. This premium should be an increasing function of the maturity; hence, an upward-sloping yield curve does not necessarily imply future interest rates will rise. Forward rates could be flat or even fall but they have a sufficiently large liquidity premium that produces an upward-sloping yield curve.

Preferred Habitat Theory

In the *preferred habitat theory*, individuals have a preference (a preferred habitat) for bonds of one maturity over another.[5] To convince investors to buy bonds that do not have their preferred maturity, a somewhat higher rate has to be offered. Investors are aware of the expected return on bonds with a maturity different from their preferred maturity and they will not allow the expected return on one bond to get too far out of line from bonds with other maturities. They will be induced to shift away from preferred habitats if the yield difference between maturities becomes sufficiently large. Thus, bonds of different maturities are somewhat substitutable, so that supply and demand considerations in one market will affect rates in other maturity markets. All possible shapes of the yield curve are still possible.

There are two major differences between the liquidity premium and the preferred habitat theories. First, in the liquidity premium theory the premium is an increasing function of the term remaining to maturity, whereas in the preferred habitat theory the size of the premium depends on the supply and demand in each maturity market. Second, in the liquidity premium theory borrowers prefer to borrow with long maturities and lenders prefer to lend with short maturities, whereas in the preferred habitat theory borrowers and lenders are risk-averse and, depending on their preferred habitats, they may require premiums to lend with long or short maturities.

Market Segmentation Theory

The simplest of the theories of yield curve determination, *market segmentation theory* assumes that investors have preferred maturities and operate only within those preferred maturities.[6] For instance, many small banks have a securities portfolio plan that commits the bank to maturities of three years or less. Similarly, some individuals may refuse to borrow for any maturity longer than five years. In this theory, neither borrowers nor lenders are willing to shift from their

---

[5] Modigliani and Sutch (1966).
[6] Culbertson (1957).

preferred maturity sectors to others. In essence, there is no substitution between bonds of different maturities.

This lack of substitutability means that interest rates for different maturities are determined by the supply and demand conditions in the market for those maturities alone. If, for instance, there is an unexpectedly high demand for 30-year fixed-rate mortgages, the supply and demand considerations in that market alone will determine the rate of interest. The level of rates on variable-rate mortgages or 15-year mortgages will not have any impact on the rate of 30-year mortgages.

The market segmentation theory allows for any shape in the yield curve depending on relative supply and demand consideration. This does not explain why the yield curve normally slopes upward, only that it is not inconsistent with the theory. The lack of substitutability between instruments is indicative of absolute risk aversion. No yield difference between maturities will induce investors from one maturity market to another. This is obviously an extreme assumption that is at odds with much of the empirical evidence.

TERM STRUCTURE IMPLICATIONS

Various theories of term structure are concerned with the ability of the market to forecast future short-term interest rates. Evidence suggests that the market is efficient, and to some extent we know that current spot rates do provide some understanding of the expected future rates. The market segmentation theory does not adequately represent the reality of today's market where borrowers and lenders get in and out of various maturity markets. Overall, the evidence supports liquidity premium theory over the expectations theory.

One of the practical implications is the shape of the yield curve in relation to business conditions. The behavior of short- and long-term interest rates over time is illustrated in Figure 12.6. We know that long-term bond prices are more volatile than are short-term bond prices, and it follows that short-term interest rates are more volatile than are long-term rates. We also know that rates tend to be highest at times of strong economic expansion because of both increased loan demand and inflationary expectations. Similarly, rates are lowest in periods of economic recession because of low loan demand and reduced inflationary expec-

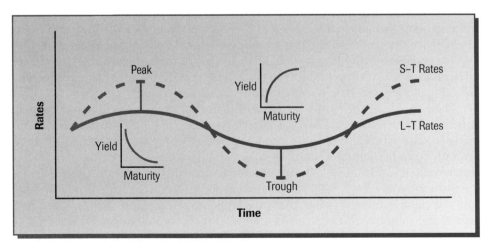

FIGURE 12.6
**The Behavior of Short-
and Long-Term Interest
Rates in Relation to
Term Structure**

At peak periods in the economy, short-term rates exceed long-term rates, resulting in an inverted yield curve. At the trough of the business cycle, long-term rates exceed short-term rates, producing a normal yield curve.

tations. Combining these notions suggests that the shape of the yield curve can provide an indication as to the state of the economy.

As illustrated in Figure 12.6, short-term rates tend to be higher than long-term rates when rates are high in general. This results in an inverted yield curve. The normal course of events would be for the economy to enter a recessionary phase to reduce inflationary expectations. The inverted yield curve is thus often associated with an impending recession. The yield curve was highly inverted in the early 1980s, for instance, and we experienced a major recession shortly thereafter.

Similarly, the yield curve will tend to be in a normal position when interest rates are low in general. This occurs in a recessionary period because inflationary expectations have declined. Once the economy is relieved of those expectations, business activity picks up as we move toward a more robust economy. The upward-sloping yield curve is therefore often indicative of an expansionary period in the economy. The yield curve has been upward sloping since the early 1990s and we have enjoyed one of the longest periods of economic prosperity in our history.

This is not to say that the yield curve is a perfect predictor of future economic activity. It does make sense that interest rates should contain some predictive content because of the inflationary expectations embedded in interest rates. Financial institutions such as banks and savings and loans are especially interested in the shape of the yield curve. As discussed in Chapter 4, the typical balance sheet contains assets that are longer in maturity than most of the liabilities. An upward-sloping yield curve thus produces a positive spread between interest-earning assets and interest-bearing liabilities. This is the maturity intermediation service that such institutions provide and are rewarded for. Sudden shifts in the yield curve can create tremendous losses for financial institutions as occurred in the S&L industry in the early 1980s. This risk has received much more attention from regulators in recent years and banks now have hedging instruments available to reduce such risks. These instruments are the subject of the discussion in Part Three.

SUMMARY

Interest-rate determination ultimately depends on supply and demand considerations in money and bond markets. The loanable funds theory of interest-rate determination presumes that supply and demand considerations in loan and bond markets are the key determinants of interest rates. The liquidity preference theory suggests that supply and demand considerations in money markets determine interest-rate levels. It is clear in either case that the Federal Reserve has considerable influence in both markets through monetary policy.

The Fed acts as the banker's bank or the central bank in the U.S. economy. It is responsible for the conduct of a monetary policy that helps to achieve stable prices and an efficient financial system. Monetary policy is conducted primarily through open-market operations in conjunction with the announcement of discount and fed funds rate levels. By selling government bonds in the open market, the Fed can reduce bank reserves, the money supply, and loanable funds. The result is a tight monetary policy that puts upward pressure on interest rates and signals the intent of the Fed to reduce inflationary expectations. This often follows the announcement of higher fed funds and/or a discount rate.

Similarly, a lowering of the fed funds or discount rate signals an easing of monetary policy. This is used in conjunction with open-market purchases of government securities, which provide reserves and money balances to the banking system and the economy. This action puts downward pressure on interest rates and induces banks to make more loans and individuals to increase spending. Fed policy can be transmitted through a credit channel (impact on lending activity) and/or a monetary channel (direct impact on money balances and spending).

Inflationary expectations play a key role in the conduct of Fed policy and the level of interest rates. The Fisher equation shows that nominal interest rates contain both a real and an inflationary expectations component. Higher expectations of inflation will drive up interest rates if real rates remain unchanged. Lower expectations put downward pressure on interest rates. Fed policy can affect nominal rates by changing inflationary expectations.

Maturity differences affect interest yields on financial instruments. The direction of influence is difficult to discern as the relationship between yield to maturity and term to maturity (called the term structure or yield curve) can take on a number of shapes. A normal yield curve is upward sloping where the long-term rates exceed the short-term rates. An inverted yield curve is downward sloping where the long-term rates are lower than the short-term rates. The yield curve can also be flat or even humped.

Several theories explain the term structure of interest rates. The market segmentation theory suggests a lack of substitutability among bonds of differing maturities so that supply and demand considerations in that maturity market alone determine the interest rate. At the other end of the spectrum, the expectations hypothesis postulates that different maturity bonds are perfect substitutes and the implied forward rates calculated from the yield curve are unbiased predictors of future rates. Somewhere in between these theories are the liquidity premium and preferred habitat theories, which postulate that implied forward rates are biased predictors because they do not include a term or liquidity premium. Overall, the liquidity premium theory seems to predict future short rates better than others.

REVIEW QUESTIONS

1. Show the impact on the supply and demand for loanable funds and the equilibrium interest rate from the following:
   a. New economic information indicates the prospects for future corporate earnings are now lower.
   b. Individuals suddenly decide the national savings rate is too low and now change their spending habits to increase savings.
   c. A Fed announcement reduces the discount rate.
2. Explain why credit card balances should not count as money balances.
3. Define the real rate of interest. What determines the level of the real rate?
4. What real interest rate is consistent with a 7% nominal interest rate and an expected rate of inflation of 3%?
5. Suppose the actual rate of inflation turned out to be 8% when the expected rate of inflation was 10%. If promised yield to maturity is 12%, what is the relationship between the expected real rate and the realized real rate of interest?
6. Show the changes that would occur on the balance sheets of the Fed and the commercial banking systems from each of the following:
   a. A $500 purchase of currency by commercial banks from the Fed.
   b. The repayment of a $200 discount loan from the Fed by a commercial bank.
   c. The payment of $300 in taxes by an individual to the U.S. government (by check deposited in the Treasury account at the Fed).
   d. The purchase of $400 in securities by the Fed from individuals.
   e. The sale of $700 of securities by the Fed to commercial banks.
   f. A $900 loan to an individual by a commercial bank.
7. For each of the items above, determine the impact on total reserves, required reserves, excess reserves, and the M1 definition of the money

supply. Assume the required reserve ratio is 5%.

8. What is the federal funds rate? How does it differ from the discount rate? Can banks profit when the discount rate is lower than the federal funds rate? When the federal funds rate is lower than the discount rate? Explain.

9. Under what type of economic conditions will the Fed increase the target fed funds or discount rate? What economic measures would the Fed be guided by in making this decision?

10. What are the components of total reserves? Suppose the Fed lowered the required reserve ratio to zero, would banks still hold total reserves? Why?

11. What shape is implied for the yield curve by the market segmentation theory? The expectations theory? The term premium theory?

12. Suppose the yield curve is highly inverted with a one-year rate of 30% and a two-year rate of 10%. Is this plausible if one can either borrow or lend at rates on the yield curve? Explain.

13. You have just purchased a two-year zero coupon bond with a yield of 12%. The yield on one-year zero coupon bonds is 8%. Assuming the real rate of interest is fixed at 4%, what is the forecasted inflation rate one year out? (Hint: Calculate the forward rate and apply the Fisher equation.)

REFERENCES

Campbell, J.Y. 1995. "Some Lessons from the Yield Curve." *Journal of Economic Perspectives*, vol. 9, no. 3, (Summer): 129–152.

Culbertson, J.M. 1957. "The Term Structure of Interest Rates." *Quarterly Journal of Economics* (November): 489–504.

Friedman, M. 1968. "Inflation: Causes and Consequences." in *Dollars and Deficits*. Englewood Cliffs, NJ: Prentice Hall.

Kane, E.J. 1970. "The Term Structure of Interest Rates: An Attempt to Reconcile Teaching with Practice." *Journal of Finance*, vol. 25 (May): 361–374.

Modigliani, F., and R. Sutch. 1966. "Innovations in Interest Rate Policy." *American Economic Review* (May): 178–197.

APPENDIX

THE FEDERAL RESERVE SYSTEM

The Federal Reserve System was created in 1913 in response to the lack of stability in the financial sector of the economy in the mid- to late 1800s and the early 1900s. The banking panics in the later part of the 1800s and another major banking crisis in 1907 led to calls for the establishment of a central bank. Although the creation of the Office of the Comptroller of Currency had done much to increase the soundness of the banking system, continuing bank runs convinced Congress of the need to create the Federal Reserve System.

The Federal Reserve System is the central bank of the United States. The system consists of 12 regional banks along with 25 branches of the regional banks and over 24,000 employees. The Federal Reserve Banks and branches are actually owned by the banks with membership in the Federal Reserve System. To join the system, commercial banks must purchase stock in the Federal Reserve for which they receive, in addition to services provided by the Fed, a dividend of 6% on their stock. The Fed operates for the benefit of the general public and is referred to as a quasi-public institution. This means that, although the Fed is privately owned, it operates more like a government agency.

The Federal Reserve's policies are overseen by the Board of Governors. This Federal Reserve Board consists of seven members appointed by the President of the United States and confirmed by the Senate. The members serve staggered 14-

year terms that are not renewable. One of the board members serves as the Fed Chairman. The term of the chair is only four years, but this can be renewed. The chair is also a presidential appointment.

The Board of Governors is responsible for regulating commercial banks and the operations of the 12 district banks. This includes approving bank holding company formations, acquisitions, and mergers. In addition, the board is responsible for establishing rules and regulations relating to consumer credit.

The Federal Open Market Committee is an extension of the Board of Governors and is responsible for conducting monetary policy. Membership consists of the members of the Board of Governors plus the president of New York Fed and four other regional Fed presidents. The decisions of the committee are forwarded to the New York Fed and operationalized by what is termed the "trading or open market desk." New York Fed engages in the buying and selling of government securities to influence the level of the money supply.

The committee meets monthly to set the course of monetary policy in the country. A good deal of time is spent by bond traders and other financial market participants trying to determine the nature of forthcoming announcements by the Fed regarding the course of the money supply and interest rates. Lately, these announcements have taken the form of changes in the interest rate in the Federal Funds market—the rate of interest on overnight borrowing among financial institutions. Rate increases are implemented to slow down the rate of expansion and price increases in the economy while rate decreases are implemented to promote economic expansion.

Commercial banks can obtain membership in the Federal Reserve through charter status or join on a voluntary basis. Nationally chartered banks are required to be members of the Fed. State-chartered banks can join on a voluntary basis. Less than 50% percent of banks in the country are members of the Fed but these banks control nearly three-fourths of the deposits in the country. Nonmember banks can and do obtain the services of the Fed through correspondent relationships with member banks or, in some instances, may purchase these directly from the Fed.

The Fed performs a number of functions in the pursuit of financial stability. The major functions of the Fed are as follows:

- To serve as the monetary authority of the country
- To enhance bank supervision
- To provide for an efficient transacting mechanism by clearing member bank checks and providing money wire transfer services
- To serve as a lender of last resort
- To serve as the banker for the U.S. Treasury

All of these functions are important to a sound and safe monetary system. Of the functions listed, the least critical is, perhaps, the supervision function. While important, there is considerable overlap in the supervision of banks and other financial institutions among the various banking agencies of the federal and state government. The Fed has taken a more active regulatory role in recent years, in large part because of the prominence of bank holding companies.

Perhaps the most critical of the functions is the lender of last resort role. While this has been used infrequently, it is the last safeguard to prevent a financial meltdown in the economy. The Fed played a prominent role in this area in the stock market crash of 1987. The financial system in the United States and many parts of the world came very close to a meltdown during the week of October 19. The stock market fell by more than 500 points (about 20% of its value) on a very long Monday. There was grave concern than several brokerage firms

TABLE 12A.1 The Use of Financial Instruments in Exchange Transactions		
	Volume (Percent)	Value (Percent)
Nonelectronic		
Cash	83.42	0.41
Checks	14.07	16.30
Credit cards	1.53	0.09
Traveler's checks	0.40	0.01
Money orders	0.24	0.02
Electronic		
Automated clearinghouse	0.28	1.05
Wire transfers	0.03	82.11
Point of sale	0.02	0.00
Automated teller machine	0.01	0.00

Sources: *The U.S. Payments System: Efficiency, Risk, and the Role of the Federal Reserve.* Boston: Kluwer Academic Publishers, 1990; and Bank for International Settlements, *Payment Systems in the Group of Ten Countries.* Basle: BIS, December 1993.

would fail because of the large losses suffered by investors. This in turn could cause the failure of several large banks with loans to the brokerage firms. The banking collapse could affect smaller banks with investments in the larger banks and create a systemwide panic.

The Fed provided stability to financial markets on Tuesday by announcing that it stood ready to provide whatever liquidity was needed to allow financial markets to function in a normal fashion. In essence, it assured market participants that it would entertain sufficient bank borrowing to allow short-term liquidity problems to be resolved. The Fed kept close watch on bank deposits to guard against bank runs and closely monitored the credit relationships between banks and brokerage houses. The Fed effectively eased the fears of many market participants; as a result, there was a quick return to normal operations in the financial markets.

While one may not judge the remaining functions to be as critical as the lender of last resort role, they encompass the largest component of the Fed's work. The transactions function is especially important on a day-to-day basis. While the vast majority of transactions in this country are accomplished by cash (about 85%) the dollar amount is less than 1% of the total dollar value of all transactions. Check transactions constitute 14% of the number of transactions and account for 16% of the total dollar value of transactions. Wire transfers, which are facilitated by the Federal Reserve System, constituted a measly 3/100 of 1% of total transactions in 1987 but constituted over 80% of the total dollar value of transactions. The volume percentage for wire service transfers has increased to over 90%. The use of financial instruments in exchange transactions is provided in Table 12A.1.

In addition to handling almost all of the dollar value of transactions in the economy, the Fed is also responsible for setting monetary policy. As mentioned earlier, this consists mainly of controlling bank reserves, but such policies impact not only the level of the money supply but also the level of interest rates. The tools used to influence monetary policy are now discussed.

CHAPTER
13

Money and Capital Markets

OBJECTIVES

This chapter examines financial markets, including money and capital markets. Short-term securities with less than one year to maturity are money market instruments. Securities with longer than one year to maturity are capital market instruments. The discussion begins by examining the general characteristics of financial markets and proceeds with describing domestic, international, and global money and capital market instruments. In discussing global financial instruments, attention is focused on the degree of market efficiency in various global markets. Equity markets in industrialized countries are examined to draw inferences about factors that affect liquidity. Risks and returns in emerging equity markets are also evaluated to determine the merit of global investment. The chapter ends with a discussion of the benefits of global portfolio diversification.

AN OVERVIEW OF FINANCIAL MARKETS

The general characteristics of financial markets including maturity of financial instruments, nature of financial claim, scope of the market, type of delivery, and market organization are summarized in Table 13.1. In terms of maturity, assets are classified as *money market* (short-term) or *capital market* (long-term) instruments. Financial assets with immediate maturities are referred to as currencies.

Financial instruments are classified as either fixed or residual claims. *Fixed-income securities* promise a predetermined set of cash flows to their holders. *Residual-income securities*, such as equity shares in publicly held corporations, provide their shareholders rights to dividends and capital gains. The size of dividends and the magnitude of capital gains depend on the performance of the firm and cannot be determined in advance.

The market for financial instruments may take a domestic, an international (Euro), or a global scope. An instrument that is issued and traded only in the country of its currency has a *domestic market*. A small publicly held company's stock listed on the American Stock Exchange is likely to be traded only in the U.S. domestic market. An instrument that is issued and traded outside the country of its currency has a *Euro market*. A Eurodollar bond, for instance, is a dollar-denominated fixed-income security issued outside the United States. A financial

TABLE 13.1 General Characteristics of Financial Markets

Characteristics	Market
Maturity	
Immediate	Currency
Short-term	Money
Long-term	Capital
Nature of Claim	
Fixed	Debt
Residual	Equity
Scope	
Host Country	Domestic
Foreign	International
Host & Foreign	Global
Delivery	
Immediate	Spot or Cash
Future	Forwards, Futures, Swaps
Contingent	Options
Organization	
Centralized	Exchanges
Network of Brokers and Dealers	OTC
Sealed Bid	Auction

instrument that is traded in several countries in addition to the country of its currency is known as a *global instrument*. A large, well-known company's stock that is listed on several countries' exchanges has a global market.

A financial transaction may specify an immediate, future, or contingent delivery plan (an option). A transaction that requires an immediate delivery has a *spot* or a *cash market*. If the delivery is to take place at some prespecified future date, the transaction has a *futures*, a *forward*, or a *swap market*. An option provides the owner the right, but not the obligation, for delivery of the underlying asset. Depending upon the exercise price of the option and the market price of the underlying asset at the expiration date, the option holder has two choices: (1) either exercise the option, which may result in an actual delivery of the asset,[1] or (2) leave the option unexercised.

Financial markets are organized in a variety of ways. A market with a central location is called an *exchange*. The New York Stock Exchange and the Toronto Stock Exchange are examples of centrally located markets. A network of security dealers and brokers is referred to as an *over-the-counter (OTC) market*. For example, the National Association of Securities Dealers Automated Quotation (NASDAQ) is a network of dispersed dealers, brokers, and traders who transact with one another using computer terminals. An instrument may also be traded in

---

[1] Depending upon the type of the option, the exercise may or may not involve an actual delivery of the asset. For example, exercising a stock option will result in the actual delivery of the underlying stock while exercise of an index option (e.g., S&P 500) will result in a cash settlement. For more detail, see Chapter 18.

**TABLE 13.2 Net Financial Position of Major Sectors of the Economy
June 30, 1995 ($ in Billions)**

Sector	Financial Assets	Financial Liabilities	Net Financial Assets
Households[a]	19,613	4,960	14,653
Nonfinancial business	3,510	5,884	(2,374)
State/local government	538	959	(421)
Federal government	472	4,037	(3,565)
Federal credit agencies[b]	827	812	15
Foreign	2,904	1,754	1,150
Commercial banks	4,339	4,169	170
Thrift Institutions[c]	1,325	1,282	43
Insurance companies	2,697	2,356	341
Pension funds	3,927	3,927	—
Finance companies	785	702	83
Mutual funds[d]	2,431	2,431	—
Real Estate Investment Trusts (REITs)	25	52	(27)
Security Brokers and Dealers	475	440	35
Issuers of Asset-Backed Securities (ABS)	570	570	—
Total	$44,438	$34,335	$10,103

[a] Households, personal trusts and nonprofit organizations
[b] Federally sponsored credit agencies
[c] Savings and loan associations, mutual savings banks, and credit unions
[d] Money and other mutual funds

Source: Board of Governors, Federal Reserve System, *Flow of Funds Accounts, Flows and Outstandings*, Second Quarter 1995.

an *auction*. In an auction, investors submit sealed bids, which are filled from the highest to the lowest bid until the supply is exhausted. U.S. Treasury securities are initially sold to investors through an auction. Some countries (e.g., France) also auction the initial public offerings of their stocks.

Financial instruments issued by government agencies and firms in the economy are purchased by other government agencies, firms, and individuals. If an economic agent issues more financial instruments than it owns, it will have a net deficit position (e.g., the U.S. government). Conversely, if an economic agent owns more financial instruments than it issues, it will have a net surplus position (e.g., households). Table 13.2 presents the net positions of major economic agents. The U.S. government, with assets of $472 billion and liabilities of $4,037 billion, has the largest net deficit position with $3,565 billion. The federal government's deficit is financed by issuing Treasury securities. Treasury securities are generally considered default-free instruments. In addition to the federal government, nonfinancial firms and state and local governments are also in net deficit positions.

Households have the largest net surplus position in the economy at $14,653 billion. Financial intermediaries also hold surplus positions. Among financial intermediaries, the net positions of pension funds and mutual funds are zero because investors in these intermediaries have proportional ownership of the

TABLE 13.3 Capital Market Instruments Outstanding ($ in Billions)					
Instruments	1980	1985	1990	1995[a]	Average Annual Growth Rate 1980–95
Treasury debt	730	1,587	2,466	3,557	11%
Federal agency debt	278	630	1,446	2,272	15
Municipal bonds	365	745	1,040	1,165	8
Corporate/foreign bonds	508	883	1,696	2,569	11
Corporate equities	1,535	2,360	3,530	7,393	11
Mortgages	1,460	2,312	3,763	4,527	8
Mutual fund shares	62	240	602	1,747	24
Total	$4,938	$8,757	$14,543	$23,230	11%

[a] Second quarter 1995.

Source: Board of Governors, Federal Reserve System, Flow of Funds Accounts, Flows and Outstandings, Second Quarter 1995.

funds, making their assets and liabilities equal. Ultimately, all assets are owned by households, which provide the savings for the economy by purchasing corporate stocks and bonds or, indirectly, by investing in financial intermediaries that pool the invested funds and channel them back to the economy.

Table 13.3 presents the outstanding dollar values for major capital market instruments for the years 1980–1995. Total capitalization increased from under $5 trillion in 1980 to over $23 trillion in the second quarter of 1995, a growth rate of almost 11% per year. The average annual rate of growth for mutual fund shares was the largest at 24%. As discussed in Chapter 9, mutual fund shares have grown substantially since the late 1970s. Double-digit inflation and interest-rate ceilings on bank deposits induced depositors to move their funds into money market mutual funds. As small investors learned more about mutual funds, they increased their investments in other types of mutual funds, including stock and bond funds. Federal agency debt had the second largest growth rate at 15%. Treasury debt, corporate and foreign bonds, and corporate stocks grew at an average rate of 11% per year. The growth in the equity value has more to do with a substantial rise in the prices of outstanding stocks than with new issues. Municipal bonds and mortgages had the lowest average annual growth rate of 8%. The 1986 Tax Reform Act changed the tax treatment of municipal bonds, thus reducing the demand for these instruments. Mortgages are sensitive to the level and structure of interest rates and the rate of economic growth.

Given this overview of financial markets, we now proceed with a detailed analysis of money and capital market instruments. The analysis includes the institutional detail, market size, and risk of each instrument.

MONEY MARKETS

Money markets encompass short-term instruments with less than one year to maturity. Our discussion includes Treasury bills, commercial paper, commercial letters of credit and banker's acceptances, Eurocurrencies, Euronotes, and Euro-commercial paper.

Treasury Bills

Treasury bills are zero coupon instruments sold at a discount from their face value. In terms of oustanding volume, T-bills are the most important type of money market instruments in the United States. T-bills are available in denominations as low as $10,000 and up to $1 million in weekly or monthly auctions. The maturity of T-bills ranges from three months to one year. All T-bills with the same maturity have the same price regardless of when they were issued.

The market for Treasury instruments has grown significantly since the 1980s. Treasury bills along with Treasury notes and bonds constitute the primary sources of financing of the U.S. government debt. In 1995, the U.S. Treasury debt reached almost $5 trillion and is expected to continue to increase in the near future.

U.S. Treasury bills are purchased by individuals, corporations, and financial intermediaries across the globe. Japanese investors, for example, purchase and hold a significant amount of U.S. Treasury bills. The primary market for Treasury bills is organized as an auction. The U.S. Department of the Treasury auctions T-bills on a weekly basis. The Treasury Department decides in advance the volume of its weekly sale. Two types of bids are submitted to the auction: first, *competitive bids*, which specify the volume and the price at which the bidders are willing to purchase the instrument. If the bid price is high, the bidder is assured of securing the purchase. If the bid is low, the bidder may not get the order filled. The second type is noncompetitive bids, which require no specific bid price. *Noncompetitive bidders* offer to buy a specific volume of T-bills at the average price in that auction. There is a maximum limit on the size of noncompetitive bids. The auction procedure involves the Treasury first accepting all noncompetitive bids and then filling the competitive bids from highest to lowest bid until all the T-bills are sold. The average price of competitive bids is then calculated and applied to the order of the noncompetitive bids.

The secondary market for Treasury bills is an over-the-counter market in which government securities dealers who purchase T-bills in the primary market offer to trade them on an ongoing basis. Trading may take place between dealers or between dealer and nondealer customers. Since the mid-1970s, the secondary market in Treasury securities has been conducted through two automated quotation systems. The first system includes the interdealer market where bid and ask prices are quoted and trade executions take place on the screen. The second system includes trades between dealer and nondealer customers where only bid and ask prices are posted. A customer who is interested in a trade based on the posted price on the billboard would then call the dealer to conduct the trade.

Currently there are 39 primary dealers recognized by the Federal Reserve Bank of New York, whose primary responsibility is the sale of Treasury securities.[2] The four key criteria used by the New York Fed to choose primary dealers are: (1) a minimum capital of $50 million; (2) a reasonable profitability record and good internal controls; (3) a willingness to provide the Fed with information on its financial position; and (4) an ability to make markets in the full range of U.S. government securities. Dealers earn their profits from bid-ask spreads. They also profit when interest rates decline, causing their security holdings to appreciate in value. Dealers often hedge their interest-rate risk exposure using Treasury futures.

---

[2] The New York Fed conducts the sale of Treasury securities on behalf of the Federal Reserve System, which, in turn, serves as the bank for the Treasury.

Problems have surfaced in the current system of auctioning Treasury securities. In May 1991, Salomon Brothers, one of the largest primary dealers, cornered the market[3] by purchasing up to 85% of a $12.26 billion issue of Treasury notes. This was a clear violation of the rule that limits the purchase of each dealer to a maximum of 35% of the issue.[4] Dealers often trade in what is known as the "when-issued" market where they buy and sell new securities prior to auction. A dealer who has committed to sell the issue must purchase an appropriate quantity of the new security when it is issued. By acquiring 85% of the issue, Salomon was able to create a "short squeeze" in the market as short sellers scrambled to cover their positions. Consequently, the price of the issue increased from 99 29/32 on May 22 to 100 29/32 on May 30. This increased the value of the entire issue by $30.65 million and gave Salomon a handsome profit of more than $26 million.

When the scandal was discovered, Salomon initially blamed the misdeed on certain traders. Later, when it was revealed that upper management knew about the transaction, Salomon's chairman, John Gutfreund, and several other officers of the firm were forced to resign.

This was not the only case of a short squeeze in the Treasury securities market. In 1986, some Japanese investors had profited from a similar scheme. However, since they were not primary dealers, they did not technically violate the rules. This incident shows how the system still remains vulnerable to abuses.

Commercial Paper

Commercial paper is an unsecured short-term instrument issued by financial intermediaries and nonfinancial corporations. Commercial paper has maturities up to 270 days in order to avoid regulation by the Securities Exchange Commission (SEC). Publicly issued securities with maturities longer than 270 days must register with the SEC—a costly process that would increase the issuer's cost of funds. As discussed in Chapter 9, finance companies often raise funds by issuing commercial paper. In addition, large nonfinancial companies also raise short-term funds by issuing commercial paper.

The commercial paper market began to grow in the early 1970s as a substitute for short-term bank loans. In 1970, the Penn Central Railroad defaulted on an $82 million issue of commercial paper and the market looked for a way to reduce investor uncertainty. The remedy came in the form of standby letters of credit issued by commercial banks guaranteeing payments to investors in the event that the issuer defaulted. The volume of the U.S. domestic commercial paper grew rapidly after that innovation and reached $649 billion by the second quarter of 1995. In that quarter, 72% of the commercial paper was issued by financial intermediaries and 28% was issued by nonfinancial companies.[5]

Commercial Letters of Credit and Bankers Acceptances

Commercial letters of credit are commitments by an importer's bank to pay an exporter upon presentation of shipping documents. *Bankers acceptances* are highly liquid, short-term securities that are created in conjunction with commercial letters of credit: The bank "accepts" the importer's postdated draft on its account with the bank, which is to be paid to the exporter on a future date. The

---

[3] If a dealer purchases a substantial portion of the actual notes issued and subsequently drives the price up, it is said that the market is cornered.

[4] A dealer may purchase Treasury securities for its own account directly or for the accounts of others indirectly. This enabled Salomon initially to conceal its share of the purchase.

[5] *Federal Reserve Bulletin*, October 1995, p. A24.

stamping of "Accepted" converts the commercial letter of credit into a bankers acceptance. The exporter can sell the bankers acceptance in the secondary market at a discount below its face value. The magnitude of this discount depends on the credit risks of the borrower and the bank and the time to maturity. The volume of bankers acceptances outstanding reached $30 billion by the end of 1994.[6]

With commercial letters of credit and bankers acceptances, the bank assumes the credit risk for the importer and is paid a fee for this service. Since the value of this service depends on the soundness and reputation of the issuing bank, commercial letters of credit and bankers acceptances are generally only issued by the largest banks.

Eurocurrencies

The Eurocurrency market is traced to a 1950s episode in which the Soviet Union, concerned that its reserve dollars might be frozen by the U.S. government, had them removed from U.S. banks and redeposited in European banks. This initiated a market in short-term dollar deposits that was soon joined by the European branches of U.S. banks and was subsequently expanded to include other major currencies. The emergence of the U.S. dollar as the primary international currency (eclipsing the British pound) strongly contributed to these developments. During the 1960s, overseas deposits by U.S. corporations increased as international inflation drove up foreign interest rates, increasing the attractiveness of foreign CDs. At the same time, the Federal Reserve Board, concerned with inflation and the U.S. balance of payments deficit, imposed limits on U.S. investments abroad while refusing to raise the ceiling on interest rates for domestic CDs. In response, U.S. banks routed their corporate deposits to their foreign branches, contributing to an expanding London-based pool of Eurodollars. These Eurodollar deposits escaped U.S. foreign investment regulations and deposit interest-rate ceilings. Despite the subsequent elimination of both regulations in the 1970s, Eurodollar banking by U.S. banks continued to grow.

The Eurocurrency market developed out of the Eurodollar market. It functions today as an interbank market, which is closely linked to foreign exchange markets—a sort of international "Fed funds." Deposits and loans in any location that are not denominated in the host country currency qualify as **Eurocurrency**. The U.S. dollar no longer dominates the Eurocurrency market. The minimum transaction size in the Eurocurrency market is around $1 million. Access is limited to top-rated institutions due to the huge size of fund transfers. The "ask" rates for Eurocurrency deposits are more or less synonymous with the London Interbank Offered Rate, or LIBOR. Currently, Eurocurrency deposits account for more than 80% of the foreign-owned deposits in U.S. banks. The attractiveness of the Eurocurrency market to world banks is similar to that of the Eurodollar markets for U.S. banks: It is relatively unregulated and is likely to remain so, since regulation imposed on any single player simply disadvantages that player, without affecting the market.

Euronotes and Eurocommercial Paper

The Euromarket for short-term debt has been active since the 1970s. The most important instruments in this market are *Euronotes* and *Eurocommercial paper*. Euronotes are placed by *Note Issuance Facilities (NIFs)*, with or without underwriting. Eurocommercial paper is placed without being backed by an underwriting facility—that is, without the commitment by a group of banks to provide

---

[6] Ibid.

funding in the event that the borrower is unable to roll over its Eurocommercial paper.

NIFs were developed in the early 1970s. These facilities are usually three- to five-year arrangements between a group of underwriting banks and a borrower. Under this arrangement, the borrower can issue short-term Euronotes, usually with a 3- to 6-month maturity, in its own name. The underwriters are committed either to purchase any or all of the unsold Euronotes or to provide standby credit, both at a predetermined spread relative to a reference rate such as LIBOR. The underwriters, in turn, receive commitment fees. By purchasing this commitment, the borrower in effect buys an insurance policy that guarantees its ability to raise short-term financing. Consequently, this commitment is like a put option purchased by the borrower at a premium equal to the commitment fee. An example will clarify the mechanics of NIFs.

Suppose that Lucas Industries, the U.K. automotive and aerospace group, intends to issue £300 million in Euronotes ranging between "LIBOR − 0.30%" and "LIBOR − 0.20%." To ensure the success of the sale of its Euronotes, Lucas pays 10 basis points to underwrite the NIF for the right to sell them the Euronotes at "LIBOR + 0.05" if the auction of the notes is not fully successful. The 10 basis points can be treated as the insurance premium or the price of a put. If Lucas is successful in selling the Euronotes at "LIBOR − 0.30%," the total cost will be "LIBOR − 0.20%." However, if the auction is not successful, the notes can be sold to underwriters at a total cost of "LIBOR + 0.15%."

In addition to the underwriters, NIFs also include another group of bankers, referred to as the "tender panel members." Tender panel members promise to attend the auction of the Euronotes with a priority in purchase right. The tender panel has no strict obligation to purchase the notes, but it has to make good-faith bids in order to be invited back to future panels. The tender panel members may purchase the Euronotes if they believe they could subsequently sell the notes at a slightly higher price.

Eurocommercial paper has some of the same features of domestic commercial paper. Like its U.S. counterpart, Eurocommercial paper consists of unsecured promissory notes, with the difference that Eurocommercial paper is issued and placed outside of the jurisdiction of the underlying currency. Eurocommercial paper was introduced in the early 1970s when U.S. restrictions on capital transfer compelled U.S. corporations to raise funds abroad. In the 1980s, foreign issuers of commercial paper were also allowed into the U.S. market.

Over the years, the U.S. commercial paper market has evolved differently from the Eurocommercial paper market. For example, while both instruments are short term, Eurocommercial paper often has twice the maturity of its U.S. counterpart. There is a simple reason for this pattern. In the United States, instruments with maturities greater than 270 days fall under a greater regulatory scrutiny by the SEC than do those with shorter maturities. Hence, the maturities of U.S. commercial paper are usually less than 270 days. Since the Euromarket is not subject to such regulation, the maturities of Eurocommercial paper are longer than those of the United States.

From the perspective of the investors in commercial paper, a foreign issuer of commercial paper in the United States has to offer a higher rate than a similarly rated domestic issuer. Similarly, a U.S. investor usually expects a higher return from Eurocommercial paper than from domestic commercial paper with the same rating. As a result, U.S. corporations find domestic commercial paper cheaper to use than the Eurocommercial equivalent, and foreign issuers find Eurocommercial paper cheaper to issue than domestic.

Similar to U.S. commercial paper, Euronotes and Eurocommercial paper are priced on a discount basis. Interest is calculated as 100 minus the product of the discount rate and the ratio of days to maturity divided by 360. For example, suppose that Citibank sells you Lucas Eurocommercial paper maturing in 55 days at a rate of 7%. The price of this paper will be quoted as: Eurocommercial paper price = 100 − (7 × 55 / 360) = 98.93. Both Euronotes and Eurocommercial paper offer the usual advantages of securitization: increased liquidity and increased access for outside investors.

CAPITAL MARKETS

Capital markets encompass instruments with maturities greater than one year. In this section, we examine Treasury notes and bonds, agency debt securities, municipal bonds, corporate bonds, hybrid bonds, junk bonds, Eurobonds, foreign bonds, and Euro-floating-rate notes. We also discuss global equity markets.

Treasury Notes and Bonds

Treasury notes have initial maturities of 1 to 10 years. *Treasury bonds* have initial maturities of seven years and longer. In contrast to Treasury bills, which carry no coupon payments, Treasury notes and bonds make coupon payments. At mid-year 1995, Treasury securities totaled $3.2 trillion outstanding, with Treasury bills, notes, and bonds making up 23%, 61%, and 16% of the total, respectively. In addition to Treasury securities, the U.S. Treasury also issues savings bonds and other nontraded instruments. As of mid-1995, the total federal debt, including Treasury securities and nontraded instruments, reached $5 trillion.[7]

Treasury notes and bonds are traded in primary and secondary markets similar to Treasury bills. Treasury notes with two-year and five-year maturities are auctioned every month. Treasury bonds are auctioned semiannually. Secondary markets for these instruments are highly liquid. In addition to domestic demand for these securities, there is a growing global demand for U.S. Treasury securities. In order to accommodate global investors, overnight trading is allowed, which has led to off-hours trading in related derivative instruments in Chicago, London, and Tokyo.

With the availability of the U.S. Treasury securities to foreign investors, other governments have been forced to make their markets more efficient to compete with the U.S. Treasury issues. For example, France has abandoned its old system of placing its bonds through a syndicate in favor of monthly auctions for its *Obligations Assimilables du Trésor* (OATS). Belgium, Italy, and Switzerland have all also moved to an auction system. Germany, Japan, and Britain market their bonds through a mix of syndicates and auctions.

Agency Debt Securities

In issuing Treasury securities, the U.S. Treasury borrows to finance deficit spending by the federal government. In issuing agency debt securities, the federal government acts as an intermediary, borrowing funds to relend to others. Examples include mortgage loans to low-income families, veterans, and farmers; commercial loans to farmers; and educational loans to students. Government-sponsored agencies were created under federal law so as to serve these explicit objectives. These agencies issue their own securities. The following is a list of federally sponsored agencies and their functions:

---

[7] *Federal Reserve Bulletin*, October 1995.

- **Farm Credit System (FCS)**. Facilitates credit to the agricultural sector of the economy. It is composed of three entities: the Federal Land Banks, Federal Intermediate Credit Banks, and Banks for Cooperatives. The financing for the Farm Credit System is handled by the Federal Farm Credit Banks Funding Corporation. The regulatory agency in charge of monitoring the Farm Credit System is the Farm Credit Administration.
- **Federal Home Loan Banks (FHLB)**. Provides credit to member thrift institutions for the purpose of mortgage lending.
- **Federal Home Loan Mortgage Corporation (FHLMC)**. Known as "Freddie Mac," it provides funds to the mortgage market by purchasing conventional and government-insured mortgages in the secondary market.
- **Federal National Mortgage Association (FNMA)**. Known as "Fannie Mae," this is a private corporation authorized by Congress to provide funds to the mortgage market by buying mortgages in the secondary market.
- **Student Loan Marketing Association (SLMA)**. Known as "Sallie Mae," it provides liquidity for private lenders participating in the Federal Guaranteed Student Loan Program, the Health Education Assistance Loan Program, and the PLUS loan program (which provides loans for parents of undergraduate students). Sallie Mae acts as an intermediary in dealing with investors who want to buy or sell participation in student loans.

While securities issued by federally sponsored agencies are not backed by the full faith and credit of the U.S. government as is the case with Treasury securities, there is a perception in the market that the federal government would not allow these entities to default on their securities.

Municipal Bonds

State and local governments also issue their own bonds, known as *municipal bonds* or *munis*. Municipal bonds consist of two categories: general obligation bonds and revenue bonds. *General obligation bonds* are repaid out of the general tax revenue of the issuing authority. *Revenue bonds* are repaid from the income of a specific municipal project such as a municipal airport.

Municipal bonds differ from federal government bonds in that the interest paid to investors is exempt from federal taxes. In addition, the interest paid on municipal bonds is often exempt from state and local taxes. The tax-exempt status of municipal bonds has reduced the cost of borrowing for the issuing states and municipalities and has been a major reason for growth in bond issuance over the years. Major investors in municipal bonds include commercial banks, corporations, and individuals in higher tax brackets. For a tax-paying investor, the interest paid on a municipal bond relates to the interest paid on an equally risky corporate bond through the equation

$$r_m = r_c (1 - T)$$

where

r_m = rate on a municipal bond
r_c = rate on a corporate bond with the same risk
T = tax rate of the investor

Suppose that a corporate bond offers a 10% yield to maturity and a municipal bond with the same maturity and risk offers 7%. The tax rate for the marginal investor in municipal bond is calculated as

$$T = 1 - \frac{r_m}{r_c} = 1 - \frac{0.07}{0.10} = 0.30$$

Investors with marginal tax rates greater than 30% will benefit from investing in municipal bonds vs. corporate bonds of similar maturity and risk.

The tax-exempt status of municipal bonds has created incentive problems for issuing entities. The volume of industrial revenue bonds increased significantly when states recognized that they could use a relatively inexpensive source of funds to finance projects that were not essential for state and local governments. In an effort to attract corporations to their areas, states and local governments issued municipal bonds to fund private ventures. This reduced the cost of funds for corporations and increased their incentive to move to communities that provided such tax breaks. In addition, some states began to issue low-cost municipal bonds only for the purpose of investing the proceeds in higher-yield instruments. While a prospectus on the bond issue must disclose "use of proceeds," it is difficult to trace where the proceeds of a bond issue are directed.

The U.S. Congress decided to limit the abuses in the municipal bond market by restricting the purposes for which such instruments could be issued. The Tax Reform Act of 1986 defined the following four categories for municipal bonds:

1. **Public-Purpose Bonds**. To be issued for the purpose of meeting essential government functions such as school financing and highway construction. These bonds retain their tax-exempt status.
2. **Nongovernmental Projects**. Bonds issued for the purpose of financing housing-related projects or student loans carry a ceiling on their amounts. Investors who purchase this category of municipal bonds have to declare the interest earned on them as a preference item in their tax returns. If the taxpayer is liable for the minimum tax mandated in the law, the interest earned on this category has to be added to taxable income.
3. **Nonessential Projects**. Projects such as upgrading pollution-control facilities or building a stadium are deemed to be nonessential and the tax exemption on these bonds is restricted.
4. **Bonds Issued Prior to August 7, 1986**. These bonds continue to carry their tax-exempt status.

The Tax Reform Act of 1986 also eliminated an extra tax break that previously existed for banks investing in municipal bonds.[8] This provision had allowed banks to deduct from their taxable income the interest paid on funds used to acquire municipal bonds. Elimination of this tax break made municipal bonds less attractive to banks, and their holdings of munis declined significantly. In 1985, there was a rush to issue nonessential revenue bonds that increased the total new issues to $280 billion. The volume of the new munis declined significantly to $185 billion in 1986 and $125 billion in 1987. The volume of new issues of municipal bonds in recent years is depicted in Table 13.4.[9]

The market surged after 1991 for several reasons. The demand for municipal bonds increased when the maximum corporate tax rate was raised from 31% to 39.6% in 1993, making tax-exempt municipal bonds more attractive than government and corporate bonds. In addition, state and local governments borrowed more to pay for renovations in deteriorating infrastructures, including roads and bridges.

Many securities laws that govern corporations including full disclosure of relevant financial information to investors also apply to municipal finance. Failure to fully disclose financial information may compel the SEC to bring legal

---

[8] Banks can still invest in "bank qualified" bonds and deduct 80% of the interest carry cost.
[9] *Federal Reserve Bulletin*, October 1995, p. A34.

TABLE 13.4 New Municipal Bonds Issues (Billions of Dollars)			
	1992	**1993**	**1994**	**2nd Quarter '95**
All Issues	$226.8	$279.9	$153.9	$65.2

charges against the offenders. A list of companies and individuals who, according to the SEC, have violated securities laws applicable to municipal finance are presented in Table 13.5.

Corporate Bonds

As the name implies, *corporate bonds* are issued by corporations. There are four classes of issuers: (1) *utilities* (electric power, gas distribution, water, and telecommunication); (2) *transportations* (airlines, railroads, and trucking); (3) *industrials* (manufacturing, merchandising, and service); and (4) *banking and finance* (financial intermediaries). Depending on the type of property used as security, corporate bonds may be classified in one of the following four categories:

1. **Mortgage Bonds**. These provide the bondholders a lien against the pledged assets. A lien is a legal right to sell the pledged property to cover the unpaid obligations. In other words, mortgage bonds are secured by property and equipment of the issuer.
2. **Debentures**. These provide the claim of general creditors on all assets that are not pledged specifically to secure other debt. Even the pledged assets may be used to cover debentures if their values exceed the obligations to secured bondholders.
3. **Subordinated Debentures**. These provide a claim ranked in security behind mortgage bonds, debentures, and after some general creditors.
4. **Guaranteed Bonds**. These provide guarantees of another entity to meet the obligations, often the parent company of the issuer.

The yields on mortgage bonds are lowest, followed by debentures, and then subordinated bonds. The yield on guaranteed bonds depends on the financial status of the guarantor.

Unlike Treasury securities, which are default-risk-free, corporate bonds carry credit risk. While large institutional investors and investment banking firms rely on their own credit analysis departments, others rely on the ratings issued by credit rating agencies. The two well-known credit rating agencies are Moody's Investor Service and Standard & Poor's. The ratings categories used by these two agencies are presented in Table 13.6.

Moody's and Standard & Poor's ratings rely primarily on accounting information. It is, therefore, no surprise that most rating changes occur within two weeks following the release of quarterly accounting reports. Since accounting numbers reflect dated information, ratings changes generally do not affect the market prices of the underlying securities. What purpose, if any, does a rating system based on old information serve? Bond ratings based on accounting information cannot help the investor to identify mispriced securities, but they summarize accounting numbers in a single rating that can be used to identify the risk category of a security. Bond ratings also present an unbiased third-party risk evaluation of a security. This mitigates potential legal problems arising from disputes in the execution of legal contracts. For example, a trustee may be instructed to limit the risk in a trust account to a certain level. If this level of risk is subject to

TABLE 13.5   SEC's Cases Against Municipal Finance Wrongdoing

Target	Charge	Outcome
Stifel, Nicolaus & Company	Stifel employees master-minded a scheme where brokers paid Stifel millions of dollars in kickbacks to participate in Oklahoma bond issues underwritten by Stifel.	Stifel paid $1.4 million to settle with the SEC without admitting or denying guilt. Criminal charges pending against three officers. Oklahoma operation was later sold.
Merrill Lynch & Company, Lazard Frères & Company, and former Lazard partner Mark Ferber	Merrill and Lazard failed to disclose a secret deal to split fees, in which Merrill paid almost $6 million to Lazard for steering business its way.	Merrill and Lazard paid $24 million to the SEC and several municipalities without admitting or denying guilt. Mark Ferber was charged with 63 criminal counts.
Louis Bethune, Charles Howard, and John Jackson	John Jackson, mayor of White Hall, Alabama (pop. 814), and the other two defendants printed White Hall municipal bonds with a face value of $45.9 billion and tried to sell them.	At this time the case is pending in Federal District Court in Alabama.
Nicholas Rudi, Joseph Salema, and Public Capital Advisors Inc.	Rudi and Salema received $300,000 in kickbacks from underwriters wanting to do business in New Jersey. Salema was a senior aide to former Gov. James Florio.	Salema agreed to disgorge more than $300,000 without admitting or denying guilt. Litigation against others is still pending.
Terry Busbee and Preston Bynum	Bynum, a former employee of Stephens Inc., a public finance firm in Little Rock, Ark., paid Busbee, a former member of the Escambia County (Fla.) Utilities Board, more than $30,000 so that his firm would be selected as the underwriter for Escambia utility bonds.	Busbee and Bynum received 27-month and 24-month prison terms, respectively. They both still face federal securities fraud charges.
Thorn, Alvis, Welch, Inc., and Derryl Peden	Thorn, a Jackson, Miss., public finance firm, failed to disclose that $20 million in low-income housing bonds that were sold as tax-free might actually be taxable.	At this time, the case is before an administrative law judge.

Source: The New York Times, November 10, 1995, p. C1.

		TABLE 13.6	**Moody's and Standard & Poor's Bond Ratings**
Moody's	**S&P**	**Category**	**Explanation**
Aaa	AAA	Highest Grade	Extremely strong capacity to pay principal and interest
Aa	AA	High Grade	Very strong capacity to pay principal and interest
A	A	Medium-High	Strong financial capacity but susceptible to adverse events
Baa	BBB	Medium Grade	Adequate capacity but weakened under adverse events
Ba	BB	Low-Medium	Contains speculative elements
B	B	Speculative	Predominantly speculative
Caa	CCC	Very Speculative	Poor standing, may be in default
Ca	CC	Highly Speculative	Often in default
C	C	Income bonds	No interest is being paid
D	D	In default	Interest payment and/or principal repayment is in arrears

varying interpretations, it is likely that there will be a legal dispute over the management of the trust. Alternatively, a trustee may be instructed to invest in bonds with ratings of A or better. This instruction eliminates divergent interpretations of the goal of the trust. Any violation from the stated goal can be observed and settled with a minimum transaction cost.[10]

Who pays for the cost of rating? The issuing company does. If ratings are used by investors, why not charge them directly for the service? Imagine a situation in which investors purchase rating services directly from rating agencies. Since an individual investor generally does not have sufficient funds to purchase a large fraction of an issue, the investor may use the rating acquired and subsequently sell it to another investor for a fee. Since the rating agency is no longer able to collect all of the revenues from the investing public who use its ratings, the price of the service increases for those few who purchase it from the rating agency. Ultimately, when the number of investors who purchase the service from ratings agencies declines considerably, the market for credit ratings will collapse. This problem is caused by the "public-good" nature of information. If the value of information acquired by an investor does not diminish from its use by other investors, the information is deemed to have a public-good nature. To avoid this problem, the credit rating service is sold once to the issuing company.

Convertibles and Callables

A corporate bond may contain an option for the buyer or the seller of the bond. A *convertible bond* gives the right to the holder to convert the bond to a certain number of equity shares. Conversion will occur if the equity price increases to a level that makes the equity value of the investment greater than its straight bond value. For example, suppose that you purchase a seven-year convertible bond with a face value of $1,000 at par. The conversion feature provides you with the right to exchange the bond for 20 shares of stocks. The current price of the stock

---

[10] Wakeman (1981).

is assumed to be $40. You have no incentive for conversion today because the equity value is only $20 \times \$40 = \$800$, compared to the bond value of $1,000. Suppose that the bond price increases to $1,100 and the stock price increases to $60 in two years. The equity value of the investment increases to $20 \times \$60 = \$1,200$, which is greater than the bond value of $1,100. You now have the incentive to convert your bond to 20 shares of the stock.

A convertible bond investor acquires two instruments simultaneously: a straight bond with an option for common stock. Since options are valuable, the price of a convertible bond is expected to be greater than the price of a straight bond with similar features. Why do firms issue convertibles in lieu of straight bonds? The answer lies with the incentive problems between stockholders and bondholders that we discussed in Chapter 2. The conversion feature mitigates incentive problems for stockholders who otherwise might take actions that would increase the value of the stock while decreasing the value of the bond. Since convertible bondholders could convert their bonds into stocks, there would be less expropriation of wealth by stockholders with convertible bonds than those with straight bonds.[11] By mitigating the agency problems, convertibles carry less restrictive bond covenants than does straight debt. This conclusion is consistent with empirical observations.

Another example of hybrid bonds are **callable bonds**. When a company issues callable bonds, it is selling a straight debt to the bondholders and buying back an option from them. The option in a callable bond gives the right to the issuing company to buy back its debt at a prespecified price over a prespecified period of time. In contrast to convertible bonds that involve selling a bond and an option to the investor, a callable bond involves selling the bond but buying the option. The price of a callable bond should, therefore, be less than the price of the straight debt.

Why do firms issue callable bonds? With straight debt, there are more restrictive covenants to protect bondholders. This may prevent the firm from certain value-enhancing transactions such as acquiring another firm or spinning off a division of the company. If covenants in straight debt are sufficiently restrictive, shareholders may lose because of foregone positive net present value projects. With callable bonds, however, the company can buy back the bonds at the call price and proceed to take advantage of a profitable investment opportunity.[12]

Junk Bonds

Bonds that receive a Ba (BB) rating or lower are known as **junk bonds**. These bonds are also known as *high-yield* or *low-grade* bonds. Originally offered in the early 1900s to finance growth industries, these bonds virtually disappeared during the Great Depression. Junk bonds did not resurface until the 1970s. Prior to 1977, the junk bond market was composed almost exclusively of "fallen angels," investment-grade bonds that subsequently fell to the speculative-grade level because of increased default risk. The size of the fallen angel junk bond market was $8.5 billion in 1977. At the beginning of 1994, fallen angels comprised about 17% of the $240 billion publicly owned junk bond market.

Beginning in 1977, growth-oriented companies began issuing junk bonds for the purpose of financing high-risk projects. Early examples of junk bond issuers include energy-related firms, cable TV companies, airlines, and long-distance phone carriers. While most investment banking firms ignored this market until

---

[11] Barnea, Haugen, and Senbet (1985), Chapter VI.
[12] Bodie and Taggart (1978).

	TABLE 13.7 Junk Bond Activities: 1984–1994				
Year	Par Value Outstanding ($ Millions)	Par Value of Default ($ Millions)	Default Rate (%)	Weighted Price After Default	Default Loss (%)
1994	235,000	3,418	1.45%	39.9	.96%
1993	206,907	2,287	1.11	56.6	.52
1992	163,000	5,545	3.40	50.1	1.91
1991	183,600	18,862	10.27	36.0	7.16
1990	181,000	18,354	10.14	23.4	8.42
1989	189,258	8,110	4.29	38.3	2.93
1988	148,187	3,944	2.66	43.6	1.66
1987	129,557	7,486	5.78	75.9	1.74
1986	90,243	3,156	3.50	34.5	2.48
1985	58,088	999	1.71	45.9	1.04
Weighted Average 85–94	—	—	4.55	—	2.88

Source: Altman (1995).

1983–1984, Drexel Burnham Lambert and its junk bond chief, Michael Milken, expanded the market for junk bonds by organizing an extensive list of issuers and institutional investors. Milken argued that the interest-rate spread of junk bonds over investment-grade bonds was greater than what the extra default risk would justify, making junk bonds attractive to institutional investors.

Recent junk bond activities are summarized in Table 13.7.

The rise in original-issue junk bonds in the last two decades is attributed to two factors: first, expansion in deregulated and new industries; and second, accelerated corporate restructuring. With deregulation in industries such as telecommunications, airlines, trucking, among others, new firms entered into the respective markets. In order to compete with their well-established competitors, new firms had to raise large sums of capital, often in the form of junk bonds. Investments in new technologies, including computer hardware and software and cable television, also required substantial capital, making the issuing companies' debt speculative.

Corporate restructuring in the 1980s and 1990s often left the emerging firms with substantial debt. Increasingly, corporate acquisitions resulted in huge debt classified as junk bonds. Leveraged buyouts (LBOs), where a firm is taken private, and leveraged recapitalization, where debt is swapped for equity, are often financed by issuing large amounts of new junk bonds. A typical LBO financing will use 60% in senior debt, 30% in junk bonds, and 10% in equity. With the 1989 LBO of RJR Nabisco at a cost of $25 billion, the share of junk bond financing accounted for $7.5 billion of the funds needed.

In the second half of 1989, the economic environment became less friendly toward junk bonds. Regulators took action against S&Ls to restrict their holding of junk bonds. As economic growth slowed, the junk bond default rate increased. The default rate reached 4.29% in 1989 and climbed to 10.14% in 1990 and 10.27% in 1991. The government also exacted civil and criminal convictions and levied huge fines on Michael Milken and Drexel for various misdealing, resulting in the total collapse and bankruptcy of Drexel in February 1990.

As the economy recovered in 1992, the prospects for junk bonds also improved. The amount of new-issue junk bonds increased to $38 billion in 1992 and

$50 billion in 1993, bringing the total amount of junk bonds outstanding to $240 billion in 1994. The default rate also decreased from the high of 10.27% in 1991 to 1.45% in 1994 (see Table 13.7).

In the previous discussion, we concentrated on annual default rates in the junk bond market. The default risk in junk bonds can also be measured by evaluating the default rate over the entire life of junk bond issues. For example, of junk bonds issued in 1977 and 1978, 34% had defaulted by the end of 1988.[13] One would expect that the high default risk in junk bonds should be traded off against high returns. Do junk bonds provide sufficient returns for the default risk they contain? According to a junk bond performance study of 1977–1986, the answer is yes.[14] This study suggests that the average rate of return on low-grade bonds adjusted for the risk is higher than the average rate of return on high-grade bonds. This implies that junk bonds hold attractive investment features. At default rates of 1%–1.50% and returns of 15%–20% in the mid-1990s, junk bonds demonstrate favorable risk-return characteristics, proving that this form of financing is here to stay.

Eurobonds and Foreign Bonds

The *Eurobond market* is different from the domestic bond market in that Eurobonds are issued and sold in a jurisdiction outside the country of the underlying currency. The introduction and subsequent growth of the Eurobond market have had a great deal to do with the regulatory constraints imposed on domestic bond issues. Domestic regulations involving capital controls, issuance and trading restrictions, costly registration requirements, and taxes are among the factors that have influenced the market for Eurobonds.

Similar to most domestic bonds, Eurobonds are medium- to long-term coupon-paying instruments issued by creditworthy corporate and sovereign borrowers. Unlike Eurobonds, *foreign bonds* are issued within the domestic market of the underlying currency by nonresident borrowers. The issuance of foreign bonds follows the regulatory guidelines of the domestic country. In contrast, the Eurobond market is not tied to any particular location and does not follow the same regulations that the foreign bond market has to follow.

The origin of the Eurobond market can be traced back to the U.S. adoption of the Interest Equalization Tax in 1963. The tax was intended to slow the flow of long-term capital to other countries and to mitigate a balance-of-payments problem. This reduced after-tax returns for U.S. investors in foreign bonds and made it uneconomical for foreign borrowers to issue bonds in the U.S. market. An alternative was devised in the form of the Eurobond, which allows funds to be raised in a given national currency without being subjected to its restrictive regulations. The first series of Eurobonds were issued and marketed in 1964.

While the Interest Equalization Tax was dismantled in 1974, other restrictions kept the domestic and Eurobond markets segmented. For example, a "withholding tax" on foreign holders of domestic bonds was imposed on bond issuers, effectively reducing the coupon to investors with a 30% U.S. withholding tax from 8% to 5.6%. In 1984, the withholding tax was also removed in the United States, providing an opportunity for Eurobonds and domestic bonds of similar credit quality to converge in price.

While the development of the Eurobond market was in response to domestic regulations, one should not assume that the Eurobond market is totally free of

---

[13] Asquith, Mullins, and Wolff (1989).
[14] Blume and Keim (1987).

the rules of the country in whose currencies Eurobonds are denominated. For example, Japan and Switzerland actively opposed the issue of Eurobonds in their respective currencies for a long period of time. Since the clearing of a currency generally goes through the country of the underlying currency, it would be difficult to launch an issue without the tacit approval from the government of the underlying currency. Japan relaxed its objection to Euroyen bonds in the 1980s, but the Swiss government still does not sanction the issuance of Swiss franc–denominated Eurobonds. Other countries may attempt to restrict the Eurobond issues denominated in their currencies. For example, the government of Portugal currently exercises tight control over the volume and timing of the Euroescudo bond market. France permitted no Euro French franc bonds to be issued during the late 1970s and early 1980s. Other countries continue to impose restrictions on Eurobond issuance.

Countries with Eurobond market activities in their currencies, including the United States, the United Kingdom, Canada, Australia, and the Netherlands, have adopted varying rules when it comes to the investment of their citizens in these bonds. For example, due to the U.S. Securities Act of 1933, all domestic bonds must be registered with the SEC. Eurobonds, however, are not registered: Eurobond ownership belongs to the bearer of the physical certificate. The SEC actively prohibits the sale of Eurobonds to U.S. citizens on the grounds that it wants to protect investors. However, the enforceability of this restriction is in question. Investors may buy and sell Eurobonds freely among themselves, and it would be very difficult to track down who owns these instruments. In addition, the prohibition of dollar-denominated Eurobonds to U.S. nationals may be waived if the issue meets the requirements for private placement Eurobonds. (The private placement of securities involves the direct sale of an issue to a small number of sophisticated, large investors who are believed to be capable of sustaining the risk of losses.) Rule 144A, adopted by the SEC, allows the sale and subsequent trading of Eurobonds among investors who meet the private placement criterion.

What are the procedures to issue new Eurobonds? Suppose that Guinness wants to issue DM120 million in a DM-denominated Eurobond. Guinness has to first approach a bank to arrange the issue. Suppose that Guinness selects Swiss Bank Corp. as the "lead manager" of the Eurobond. With the instruction of Guinness, Swiss Bank may invite several other banks as the "comanagers." Swiss Bank and comanagers (the management group) negotiate the terms of the bond, including its coupon interest, in such a way as to make it acceptable to potential investors. If Guinness is also interested in a foreign exchange swap contract to swap DM to Pound Sterling, a swap counterparty must be lined up as well. Suppose that the coupon is set at 6.75%. The bond may be nominally "listed" in a location like Luxembourg where listing is inexpensive and there is no withholding tax. The listing is a formality and will take place only if the issue is to be sold to institutional investors who are required to invest in listed securities.

Subsequently, the management group invites a group of commercial banks, investment banks, and securities companies to form an "underwriting group." The underwriting group, which may include 25, 50, or more banks from different countries in addition to the management group, is selected on the basis of its ability to place the bonds with various investors. The underwriting group also commits itself to purchase bonds at a prespecified price if the price of the bond falls below the set value and/or if the bonds are not fully sold. This is analogous to underwriters selling a "put option" to the issuer.

A third group of participants consists of the "selling group" and includes managers, underwriters, and dealers who sell the bonds to the ultimate investors. The selling group does not have a commitment to purchase the bonds if the price falls. The three groups of participants in the issue and sale of the Eurobonds have overlapping responsibilities. If the issue amount is small, it is not uncommon for a group of banks to provide all three functions themselves.

In the next step, a preliminary version of the bond prospectus named a "red herring" is issued and used by salespeople in their efforts to line up prospective investors. Depending on the demand for the issue, the selling group provides feedback to the lead manager, who refines the original terms of the issue and signs the agreement with the issuer on the "offering day." Two weeks after signing the agreement, on the "closing day" the securities are delivered to the investors for cash and the borrower receives the proceeds. Total fees paid by the issuer are a management fee, an underwriting fee, and a selling concession. The fees range from ½% for each deal to 2½% for more complex issues.

Each Monday of the week, the *Financial Times* of London publishes a list of newly issued Eurobonds. Table 13.8 presents the list that appeared on March 6, 1995. Eurobonds were issued in 11 different currencies. The price of Eurobonds is calculated like that of domestic bonds. While most U.S., Canadian, and Japanese bonds pay semiannual coupons, other countries often have annual coupon payments with their bonds. The price of the bond is determined by the credit quality of the borrower and the coupon rate. In our example, Guinness issued DM120 million bonds to mature in April 1998 with a coupon rate of 6.75%. Based on the credit quality of Guinness, the market expected a yield of 6.29%, which corresponds to a price of $101.224. The Guinness bond is sold at a premium over its face value.

The current system of issuing Eurobonds through syndicates faces uncertainty due to increasing tensions between lead managers and their junior underwriting partners. With the fixed-price reoffer system, syndicate members agree to sell bonds at a prespecified price until the lead manager determines that the issue is largely placed, or until the market moves significantly. When the lead manager breaks the syndicate, the bonds are freed to trade at market prices. This system works without problems as long as interest rates are falling and bond prices are rising. Under these conditions, syndicate members can find investors who are interested in buying the bonds; if not, syndicate members are happy to hold on to their allotments. However, when rates are increasing and bond prices are decreasing, the syndicate members, instead of taking the bonds, hedging the exposure, and trying to place them with investors, simply wait until the syndicate breaks. They then sell their allotments anonymously through brokers back to the lead firm at the preoffer price, and pocket the usual 25 basis points underwriting fee. Subsequently, if their sales teams manage to place some bonds with investors, they can contact the lead manager and ask for more bonds to fill the new orders and pretend to have performed well by placing more than their original allotments. Given this scenario, why bother with comanagers and underwriting syndicates? Recent issues of Eurobonds indicate that there is indeed a trend toward a system in which three or four banks issue and place Eurobonds on their own, forgoing syndicates altogether.[15]

While Eurobond issues generally avoid the specific regulations of the countries of the underlying currencies, the central banks of some countries exert significant influence on new issues by specifying guidelines related to, among other things, issuing calendars and underwriting syndicates. In the United States, the Fed does not set such guidelines.

Both primary and secondary markets are self-regulated by trade associations.

---

[15] "Who Needs Syndicates?" *Euromoney*, March 1995, pp. 30–36.

TABLE 13.8 A Sample of Weekly Issues of Eurobond

NEW INTERNATIONAL BOND ISSUES

Borrower	Amount M.	Maturity	Coupon %	Price	Yield %	Launch Spread BP	Book Runner
U.S. DOLLARS							
Autobacs Seven Co.(a)Φ	100	Mar. 1999	4.125	100.00	—	—	Nomura International
Cariplo(c)‡	150	Nov. 1999	(c1)	99.80R	—	—	Swiss Bank Corp.
Korea Intl. Merchant Bank(d)*‡	50	Mar. 2000	(d1)	100.00	—	—	KEB International
LTCB of Japan, Tranche A(g)	25	Mar. 2005	(g1)	101.50	—	—	LTCB International
LTCB of Japan, Tranche B(h)	30	Mar. 2000	8.50	101.50	—	—	LTCB International
YEN							
Republic of Portugal*	70bn	Mar. 2002	4.50	100.00R	4.500	—	Daiwa Europe/IBJ Intl.
Fuji Finance (Cayman)(j)*‡	20bn	Jun. 2005	(j1,s)	100.00	—	—	Fuji Intl. Finance
Fuji Finance (Cayman)(k,s)*	10bn	Jun. 2005	4.90	100.00	—	—	Fuji Intl. Finance
Tokai Fin. (Curacao), A(m)*‡	10bn	Jun. 2005	(m1,s)	100.00	—	—	Nikko Europe
Tokai Fin. (Curacao), B(m)*‡	10bn	Jun. 2005	(m1,s)	100.00	—	—	Salomon Brothers Intl.
D-MARKS							
Guinness	120	Apr. 1998	6.75	101.224	6.290	—	Swiss Bank Corp. Ffrt.
Republic of Austria	1bn	Apr. 2000	6.875	99.9375R	6.890	+9(7%–99)	WestLB
First Austrian Bank	150	Mar. 2000	7.00	101.64	6.604	—	Commerzbank
Sudwestdeutsche LB Cp. Mkts.	500	Mar. 2000	7.00	99.875R	7.031	+20(7%–99)	Swiss Bank Corp. Ffrt.
Samsung Electronics Co.	300	Mar. 2000	7.50	101.75	7.072	—	Bayerische Landesbank
FRENCH FRANCS							
Usinor Sacilor	1.8bn	Mar. 2002	8.50	99.24R	8.649	+80(i)	Société Générale
GECC	1.5bn	Mar. 1997	7.25	100.00R	7.250	+10(8½%–97)	Banque Paribas
Catalonia	1.1bn	Mar. 2005	8.25	98.815R	8.430	+40(7½%–05)	Société Générale
DSL Bank(l)	1bn	Apr. 1997	7.25	99.91R	7.300	+14(8½%–97)	CCF
Depfa Bank(l)	1bn	Apr. 1997	7.25	99.74R	7.39	+20(8½%–97)	CCF

	Amount m.	Maturity	Coupon %	Price	Yield %	Spread	Book runner
SWISS FRANCS							
SXL Corp.(b,l)*Φ	200	Mar. 1999	2.00	100.00	—	—	Credit-Suisse
ESRA(e,s)*	100	Dec. 1999	5.75	101.75	—	—	Merrill Lynch Cap. Mkts.
Philip Morris Companies	200	Apr. 1999	5.50	102.50	4.798	—	Credit Suisse
STERLING							
GECC(s)	100	Dec. 1996	8.125	99.975R	8.175	+30(10%–96)	Deutsche/ HSBC Mkts.
ITALIAN LIRE							
Sudwestdeutsche LB(l)	150bn	Sep. 1997	11.50	100.895	—	—	Paribas Capital Markets
International Finance Corp.	150bn	Apr. 1997	11.25	101.125	10.60	—	Paribas/SBC
Electricité de France	150bn	Apr. 1998	11.40	101.205	10.91	—	Paribas/SBC
CANADIAN DOLLARS							
GE Capital Canada(s)	100	Dec. 2000	8.25	99.615R	8.35	+9.3(8½%–00)	ScotiaMcLeod
Bayerische Vereinsbank(s)	100	Dec. 2000	8.50	99.42R	8.65	+9(8½%–00)	Wood Gundy
LUXEMBOURG FRANCS							
Cregem International Bank(s)	2.5bn	Dec. 2000	7.75	102.55	7.20	—	Cregem Intl. Bank
Kredietbank Luxembourg	2bn	Apr. 2002	7.875	102.35	7.432	—	Kredietbank Lux.
Crédit Local de France(s)	2bn	Dec. 1999	7.625	102.375	7.017	—	BCEE
GECC	3bn	Apr. 2005	8.125	102.75	7.720	—	Crédit Européen
AUSTRALIAN DOLLARS							
Crédit Local de France	100	Apr. 2005	10.25	101.77	9.962	—	Hambros. Bank
DRACHMAS							
European Investment Bank‡	20bn	Mar. 2000	(f)	100.00	—	—	Bayer.Vereins, Athens

Final terms, non-callable unless stated. Yield spread (over relevant government bond) at launch supplied by lead manager. § Convertible. ‡ Floating-rate note. # Semi-annual coupon and yield. * Unlisted. * With equity warrants. Φ With equity warrants. a) Denom: $5,000 + 1 wrt. Ex price: Y8,723. FX: 98.10Y/$. b) Denom: SFr50,000 +50 wrts. Ex price: Y754. FX: 79.07Y/SFr. Refix:7/2/97. c) Fungible with $150m. c1) 3-mth Libor +1/8%. (1st coupon: 2-mth Libor + ⅛%). b) Denom: 3 yrs at par. d1) 6-mth Libor +40bp. e) European Sovereign Repackaged Assets. f) 3-mth Athibor −40bp, max 30%. g) Callable on 17/3/98 at par. g1) 6-mth Libor +75bp for 1st 3 yrs and 8½%pa thereafter. h) Callable on 17/3/97 at par. i) Over interpolated yield. j) Callable on 15/6/00 at par. j1) 3-mth Libor +15bp to 15/6/00 and +40bp thereafter. k) Callable on 23/6/00 at par. l) Long 1st coupon. m) Callable on coupon dates from 15/6/00 at par. m1) 6-mth Libor +15bp to +50bp thereafter. s) Short 1st coupon. Note: Yields are calculated on ISMA basis.

The primary market is regulated by the International Primary Markets Association (IPMA), while the secondary market is regulated by the International Securities Market Association (ISMA). The bond prospectus generally specifies the governing law (e.g., English law or that of the issuer country) to be applied in the event of legal dispute.

Floating-Rate Notes

Floating-rate notes (FRNs) issued outside of the country of the underlying currency are generally grouped in the Eurobond category, which is part of the global capital market. However, since FRNs are priced in part like money market instruments (repriced more than once a year), one may think of them as part of the global money market, with an emphasis on the pricing of the instruments.

FRNs were introduced in the 1970s in response to rapid changes in interest rates. These instruments are of interest to both borrowers and investors. Benefits for the borrowers include the following:

- FRNs have lower transaction costs than rolling over short-term debt.
- FRNs provide a guaranteed source of funding.
- FRNs allow the borrower to lock in a financial spread relative to a benchmark rate (e.g., LIBOR) regardless of changes in credit quality.
- FRNs provide for matching the cash flows from floating-rate assets.
- FRNs require lower liquidity premiums than comparable fixed-rate instruments.

Benefits for the investors are as follows:

- FRNs have lower transaction costs than a comparable series of short-term instruments.
- FRNs allow for locking in credit spreads over long periods.
- FRNs have lower interest-rate risk than comparable fixed-rate instruments.
- FRNs provide for matching cash flows from floating-rate liabilities.

Financial intermediaries, especially commercial banks, have been major customers of FRNs both as borrowers and as investors. Sovereign borrowers are also interested in FRNs as an alternative to the syndicated loan market.

Despite the popularity of FRNs, the valuation of these instruments is not always well understood. To understand the valuation process, we first need to specify a "reference" rate that the FRN is tied to, usually the LIBOR for Euromarket notes and the Treasury bill rate for domestic notes. The "term" of the reference rate must be defined (e.g., one month, three months, or six months). The "frequency of coupon payment" is often the same as the term of the reference rate, but not always. The "frequency of the coupon reset" (e.g., weekly, monthly, quarterly, or semiannually) is also typically similar to the term of the reference rate. Finally, there is a "margin" over the reference rate, which is a function of the issuer's credit rating. A "plain vanilla" FRN issued in the Euromarket has the attributes of fixed maturity; the LIBOR as reference rate and a margin of $\frac{1}{8}$ to $\frac{1}{4}$ above LIBOR; and term, frequency of coupon payment, and frequency of coupon reset are all the same length. A numerical example will illustrate the pricing system.

Suppose that UNOCAL (Union Oil Company of California) has issued $200 million FRNs at par in the Euromarket paying semiannual coupons with a spread of 50 basis points over the prevailing six-month LIBOR. The coupon payments are due on March 23 and September 23 of each year, and the face value is due on March 23, 2002. The coupon of September 23, 1997, is set on March 23, 1997, based on the LIBOR of the second business day prior to the beginning of the coupon period, or March 21, 1997. On this day, the agent bank collects the offered quotations prevailing at 11 A.M. for interbank deposits with the London branches of the leading banks listed in the prospectus. The arithmetic mean of these rates, rounded to the nearest 16th, is used as LIBOR. Similarly, the coupon for March 23, 1998, is set in September 1997.

The price is set at 100 on the issue date. Assume that the appropriate credit risk spread remains at 50 basis points at the time the next coupon payment is made on September 23, 1997. At the repricing date, this security would be priced at par. In other words, UNOCAL could issue a new March 2002 floater at 50 basis points over LIBOR at the next repricing date.

Now suppose the credit risk does not remain the same, but changes after issuance. The note will no longer be repriced at par on the next coupon reset date. Instead, the FRN will be priced at a discount if the borrower's credit risk has deteriorated, and at a premium if it has improved. Suppose the credit risk has deteriorated to the extent that if UNOCAL issues new debt, the new current rate would be 150 basis points above LIBOR. The holder of the original FRN continues to receive the original 50 basis points spread specified at the time of the issue. The FRN, therefore, will be priced below par on the coupon reset date.

Suppose that the six-month LIBOR is 8.5%. The new par floater will require a coupon of 10%. The existing FRNs pay only 9%. Suppose that the FRNs have five years to maturity. The new price will be par minus the present value of an annuity of $(10\% - 9\%) \times \$100 = \$1$ per year (or $0.50 per six months) for five years, discounted semiannually at a rate of 10%. This annuity has a value of $3.86, indicating the new price for the FRN of $100 - \$3.86 = \$96.14$.

For a perpetual floater, the reset price is calculated using the following formula:

$$P = 100 \times [(\text{LIBOR} + S) / (\text{LIBOR} + S')],$$

where

S = credit spread at issuance
S' = new credit spread after a change in credit quality

With LIBOR = 8.5%, S = .5%, and S' = 1.5%, the price of the perpetual floater will be

$$P = 100 \times [(0.085 + 0.005) / (0.085 + 0.015)] = \$90$$

As you can see, the price change due to credit quality deterioration is greater when we switch from an annuity to a perpetual floater. In general, the longer the maturing of the floater, the greater the price impact of any changes in credit quality.

FRNs may also have option features. Some have a minimum coupon level, called a **floor**. Others may have a maximum coupon level, called a **cap**. FRNs that have both a floor and a cap are called **collared**. Finally, many FRNs are issued with a call option for the issuer, indicating that at some point the issuer may elect to redeem all outstanding notes at a "redemption date" before the maturity of the notes. The redemption is generally at a price equal to 100% of face value. Interest on the notes due on or prior to the redemption date is paid at the time of redemption.

FRNs carry characteristics of both money market and capital market instruments. Similar to money market instruments, their prices are affected by the short-term interest rates. Like capital market instruments, their prices are also affected by the long-term credit risk premiums. As short-term interest rates change, the coupon payments are adjusted at each reset date in order to keep the prices at par. However, the prices will diverge from par if the market's view of the long-term credit risk of the borrower changes.

The Global Equity Market

In this section we examine the world's major stock markets, the development of the emerging equity markets, and the merit of global portfolio diversification. We further review the evidence comparing the risk and return payoffs from investing in a portfolio of domestic stocks vs. a portfolio of global stocks.

Global equity markets refer to two distinct markets: the primary market, which includes the market for new issues, dominated by investment banks; and secondary markets or exchange markets, where outstanding equity shares are traded.

The Global Equity Market: The Primary Market

When companies that have not previously issued common stock to the public initiate stock offerings for the first time, the process is referred to as an *initial public offering (IPO)*. Besides corporations, other entities that also issue common stock to the public include governments and supranational entities such as the World Bank and the Asian Development Bank. Because of the worldwide movement toward market economies and away from state ownership of corporations, government-initiated privatization plans currently account for a substantial segment of total IPO activities. In 1987, for instance, the U.S. government sold 58 million shares of its railroad company, Conrail, raising $1.65 billion. Other examples include the U.K. government sale of British Telecom for $4.7 billion, Chile's sale of Pacifica, and France's sale of Paribas. In 1995, French voters elected a market-oriented president, Jacques Chirac, who promised, along with the new prime minister, Alain Juppé, to accelerate the process of privatizing many state-owned enterprises including the banking, insurance, automobile, and airlines industries. Large-scale privatization is also currently under way in Eastern Europe and in the independent states of the former Soviet Union.

Traditionally, investment banking firms have been the main force behind IPOs. Their services include advising the issuer on the terms, timing, and pricing of the new shares; providing sales guarantees in the form of standby agreements; and distributing the issue to the public. Investment banking firms often serve two distinct parties with differing interests: the IPO issuer and the ultimate buyers of the stock. In their former capacity, they advise the issuer on, among other things, setting the price at which they believe the entire issue can be sold. In principle, they should set the price as high as they can without impeding the sale. On the other hand, they also serve their investment clients, who expect to purchase the issue at the lowest possible price. This creates incentive problems for the investment banker. Some have argued that investment banking firms intentionally set the initial price too low. In the banks' defense, others have argued that IPOs are inherently risky transactions and the investment banking firms should set the initial price low to provide a return for the investor commensurate with the underlying risk.

The incentive problems described exist primarily in the U.S. IPO market. In contrast, British and French IPOs involve fewer incentive problems. In the case of the United Kingdom, investment banking firms do not decide on the identity of the investors in the issue. The news of an impending IPO is publicly announced with a full description of the terms of the offering, including the volume of the offer and its set price. Prospective investors can file requests for their desired shares at that price. Depending on the number of shares requested, the issue is distributed on a pro rata basis. While this procedure partially eliminates the incentive problems of the investment banking firms by confining their allegiance to the issuer of the stock, it creates a problem for the investing public who may subscribe to either too many shares (if they perceive the issue to be underpriced) or

TABLE 13.9	Average IPO Returns for 25 Countries		
Country	Sample Size	Time Period	Average Initial Return
Australia	266	1976–89	11.9%
Belgium	28	1984–90	10.1%
Brazil	62	1979–90	78.5%
Canada	258	1971–92	5.4%
Chile	19	1982–90	16.3%
Finland	85	1984–92	9.6%
France	187	1983–92	4.2%
Germany	170	1978–92	10.9%
Hong Kong	80	1980–90	17.6%
Italy	75	1985–91	27.1%
Japan	472	1970–91	32.5%
Korea	347	1980–90	78.1%
Malaysia	132	1980–91	80.3%
Mexico	37	1987–90	33.0%
Netherlands	72	1982–91	7.2%
New Zealand	149	1979–91	28.8%
Portugal	62	1986–87	54.4%
Singapore	66	1973–87	27.0%
Spain	71	1985–90	35.0%
Sweden	213	1970–91	39.0%
Switzerland	42	1983–89	35.8%
Taiwan	168	1971–90	45.0%
Thailand	32	1988–89	58.1%
United Kingdom	2,133	1959–90	12.0%
United States	10,626	1960–92	15.3%

Source: Loughran et al. (1994).

too few shares (if they perceive the issue to be overpriced). French IPOs solve this problem by auctioning the new shares. The procedure is similar to that of standard auctions, where the issue is announced and a minimum price is set. The prospective investors file orders for shares at varying prices. The order of the highest bidder is filled first, followed by the order of the second highest bidder, and so on until all shares are sold.

If the underpricing of IPOs in the United States is due to the incentive problems described above, we should observe marked differences between IPO returns in the United States and those in the United Kingdom and France. Table 13.9 provides average initial returns for 25 countries. While the initial returns for U.S. IPOs averages 15.3%, it is 12.0% for the United Kingdom and only 4.2% for France. This discrepancy would seem to support the theory that incentive problems exist in the U.S. IPO market. Other possible explanations for the average initial return discrepancies among the 25 countries listed include differences in binding regulations, contractual mechanisms, and the characteristics of the firms going public.[16]

---

[16] For an interesting discussion on these issues, see Loughran et al. (1994).

The Global Equity Market: The Secondary Market

From an investor's perspective, the function of a secondary market is to provide liquidity at a fair price. Liquidity in the equity market depends on the allocational and operational efficiencies of the market structure.[17] The structure of equity markets varies by country, with the differences having a strong impact on the allocational and operational efficiencies of the different equity markets.

Allocational efficiency means the pricing of equities reflects "true" values of the underlying projects (an information issue). For the market to be allocationally efficient, it has to be informationally efficient, which means that the marginal benefit to society of gathering that information is equal to its marginal cost. In such a market, traders would react quickly to the announcement of any new information by trading in the shares of the relevant security and causing its price to fully reflect the new information. Equity prices in an informationally efficient market provide reliable signals for the allocation of resources.

Operational efficiency means the bid-ask spreads and commissions are minimal relative to the services provided (a competitive market structure issue). The bid-ask spread refers to the difference between the price an investor pays to buy the stock (the dealer's "ask" price) and the price at which the investor sells the stock (the dealer's "bid" price). The total revenues of the securities industry are calculated as:

Securities industry revenues =
$$\text{(ask price} - \text{bid price} + 2 \times \text{commissions)} \times \text{(number of shares traded)}$$

The size of the securities industry revenue is related to the size of the bid-ask spread, the level of commissions charged, and the number of shares traded. For a market to be operationally efficient there needs to be a large number of securities firms that compete for customers on the basis of the commissions they charge. In addition, an operationally efficient market requires a mechanism by which market makers compete with one another in setting bid-ask spreads. The trader will choose a market maker who provides the narrowest bid-ask spreads. Market efficiency benefits society directly by reducing the cost of capital for firms, allocating capital to its best use by means of market pricing, and providing liquidity for investors. The efficiency of the market is directly linked to the optimal design of the markets.

Table 13.10 presents information on stock exchanges, trading procedures, settlement issues, and regulatory agencies for major global equity markets including the United States, the United Kingdom, Japan, Germany, Canada, Australia, France, and Switzerland. The U.S. stock market, dominated by the New York Stock Exchange (NYSE), is the principal force in the global equity market by virtue of its size, depth, diversity, liquidity, and the extent of protection provided by its chief regulator, the SEC. By the mid-1990s, the total market capitalization (shares outstanding multiplied by their market prices) of the U.S. stock market reached $4.5 trillion. U.S. exchanges are privately owned, including the New York Stock Exchange, which has 85% of the market value listings, and the American Stock Exchange (AMEX), which has 3%. In addition, 12% are listed with the National Association of Securities Dealers Automated Quotations (NASDAQ). There are also regional exchanges including Philadelphia, Chicago Stock Exchange, Pacific Coast, Boston, Cincinnati, Inter-Mountain, and Spokane Exchanges. Most of the companies that are listed on the regional exchanges are also listed on the NYSE and AMEX; those listed solely on regional exchanges are few in number. The opening prices for equities in the U.S. exchanges are determined through a call auction among brokers. Subsequent transactions take place in a

---

[17] Copeland and Stoll (1995) and O'Hara (1995).

continuous market where market makers (specialists) set the bid-ask quotations at levels that reflect the supply and demand for securities and their own inventory. On U.S. exchanges, all stock trading occurs through a specialist. In the case of the NYSE, the specialist has a monopoly for a given stock, while on the other exchanges a group of market makers compete with each other in establishing bid-ask levels for a particular stock.

While U.S. exchanges use physical locations where transactions take place through an open outcry system on the floors of the exchanges, the over-the-counter (OTC) market uses a computer network of dispersed dealers, brokers, and traders, who make up the market. Established in 1971, NASDAQ included 4,902 companies with equity values in excess of $821 billion by the end of 1994.[18] Prior to the establishment of NASDAQ, dealers issued daily quotations in OTC stocks on "pink sheets" reflecting the previous day's closing prices. Currently, NASDAQ is a dealer market composed of approximately 425 dealers who stand ready to buy or sell the securities in the system. Each stock has at least two dealers, with the average stock having 10 dealers. There are 290 stocks that have more than 20 dealers. The average dealer makes a market in 300–400 stocks.

Access to NASDAQ takes place through three types of terminals. Level 1 terminals allow brokers to determine the inside quote, which amounts to the highest bid and lowest ask price for a given security. Level 2 terminals provide brokers with information on the bid-ask price of each dealer in a stock. Level 3 terminals, which are used by dealers in the system, permit dealers to post price quotations for the stocks in which they make a market. Trading information provided by NASDAQ includes bid-ask prices for all of the listed OTC stocks and volume information for more than 2,500 securities considered to be national market securities. On the OTC market, dealers post their bid-ask quotes and stand ready to buy and sell from their inventory of stocks. While a stock exchange resembles an auction market with trades taking place on the floor of the exchange, an OTC market is a negotiated interdealer market, which does not require a centralized trading floor. OTC dealers, therefore, can be located anywhere as long as they have computer-based communication links with other brokers and dealers.

In the United States, securities are registered and physical delivery is not necessary. A trade settlement takes place on the third business day after the trade. The purchaser delivers the cash and the seller delivers the stock to the broker, who in turn delivers it to the purchasers broker. Securities are kept in a "street name," which means that the broker keeps the stock in the brokerage firm's name on behalf of the client. The existence of a clearinghouse further simplifies the procedure. A brokerage firm, which is a member of the exchange, settles with the clearinghouse after all members' transactions are netted out.

Settlement procedures may change in the United States in the near future.[19] At the time of this writing, the SEC has issued a proposal for a "direct-registration system," which is an electronic book-entry alternative: Instead of leaving the purchased shares with a broker, they are transferred to the issuing company or its transfer agent. The investor's name is recorded on the company's books and the investor receives a statement from the company similar to that now issued by mutual funds. When the investor wants to sell the stock, the transfer agent is instructed to route the shares back to a broker, who sells them. This alternative has several advantages over the current system. First, the proposal allows the investor to buy additional stock directly from the company at a transaction cost

18 1995 NASDAQ Fact Book & Company Directory, p. 3.
19 "SEC Mulls 'Direct Registration' of Certificates," The Wall Street Journal, March 22, 1995, p. C1.

TABLE 13.10 Operating Features of Major Global Stock Markets

Country	Stock Exchanges	Method of Execution	Settlement Procedures	Regulator
U.S.	NYSE, American, NASDAQ, and regional exchanges	Private exchanges. Open outcry on exchanges, electronic trading for OTC. Shares are registered. Commissions are negotiable. Continuous quotation.	Third business day after the trade.	SEC
U.K.	International Stock Exchange (London, Birmingham, Manchester, Liverpool, Glasgow, Dublin); unlisted securities markets	Private exchanges. Electronic trading (SEAQ). Most shares are registered. Commissions are negotiable. Continuous quotation.	2–3-week account period.	Dept. of Trade
Japan	Tokyo, Osaka, Nagoya, five others	Private exchanges. Open outcry on exchange. Shares are registered. Commissions are fixed. Continuous quotation.	Fourth business day after the trade.	Finance Ministry
Germany	Frankfurt, Dusseldorf, Munich, Hamburg, Stuttgart, Hanover, Berlin, Bremen, and OTC market. Frankfurt's Deutsche Boerse plans to create a fully electronic trading system by 1998, which is expected to end the business of the regional exchanges.	Bankers' exchange. Shares are registered. Commissions are fixed. Continuous quotation in large stocks. Fixed quotation through call auction for small stocks. The planned fully electronic trading system is expected to end the open outcry system.	Two business days or five business days by arrangement.	Stock Exchange Board
Canada	Toronto, Montreal, Alberta, Vancouver, Winnipeg, and OTC market for unlisted shares.	Private exchanges. Between member firms on exchange. Shares are registered. Commissions are negotiable.	Five business days after the trade.	Provincial Securities Commission.

Australia	Australian Stock Exchange, which includes Sydney, Melbourne, Adelaide, Brisbane, Hobart, and Perth.	Private exchanges. Between brokers on exchange. Automated trading system in Sydney and Melbourne for actively traded shares. Shares are registered. Physical delivery. Commissions are negotiable.	Five business days normally. No official settlement period.	AASE
France	Paris, Lyons, Bordeaux, Lille, Marseille, Nancy, Nantes.	Public exchange. Forward market, some cash trade. Shares are registered. Commissions are negotiable. Fixed quotation through call auction.	Last working day of month for forward. Immediately after trading for cash.	COB
Switzerland	Zurich. In summer 1995 a fully electronic trading system was implemented, which ended the business of the regional exchanges.	Bankers' exchange. Cash market for 70% of trades and forward market up to 9 months for the rest. A fully electronic trading system put in place recently ended the practice of open outcry.	Last working day of month for forward and three days for cash.	Swiss National Bank

Source: The Wall Street Journal, May 31, 1995, p. C12; Giddy (1994) and Solnik (1996).

significantly less than a broker's commission. Second, the new system allows investors to keep the securities in their own names, thus enabling them to negotiate discounts with brokers. Since stocks are not held at any firm, the investors can sell them through any broker who offers the best deal. Third, investors who want to switch brokers can do so easily when securities are registered in investors' names. Currently, the transfer may take weeks or months. The heart of the plan is the creation of an electronic book-entry system. Obviously, the brokerage industry is not supportive of this proposal.

Finally, the U.S. security markets provide for a system of negotiable commissions. This system was adopted in 1975 and since then commissions have declined significantly. The negotiable commission system has brought a healthy dose of competition into the security markets in the United States.

Established in 1773, the United Kingdom's equity market is the second oldest, after the Netherlands. It is the world's third largest stock market (after the United States and Japan), where 12% of global equity trading by value takes place. The United Kingdom equity market today is one of the most modern systems in the world, incorporating state-of-the-art technology and trading in North American and Japanese shares, as well as those of continental Europe. By the mid-1980s, the United Kingdom abandoned the trading floor in favor of telephone and computer trading through a network called SEAQ. With its advanced and efficient equity and bond markets and its dominant role in the foreign exchange and derivatives markets, Britain has emerged as the financial center of Europe.

In July 1994, the United Kingdom exchange abandoned its traditional settlement at the end of two- or three-week account periods and moved to rolling settlement 10 days after each transaction. The move to shorten the settlement time is a step toward more efficiency if settlements occur on time. According to the U.S.-based Global Securities Consulting Service and U.K.-based Lee Schwartz Associates, there has been a marked decline in the efficiency of the London market since it switched to a shorter settlement period.[20] In 1994, before the exchange abandoned its previous settlement policy, 95.27% of trades settled on time. One year later, it has fallen to 84.97%. Considering the fact that after June 26, 1995, all shares in the London market have to be settled five days after their respective trades, the settlement efficiency may further deteriorate. The shorter settlement period, however, is essential to the efficiency and liquidity of the market. Since June 1995, the U.S. equity market has shifted to a three-day settlement period without significant problems.

The Japanese stock market has grown significantly in recent years, surpassing the U.S. market in market capitalization before its 1990–1992 stock market collapse. Despite its size, the Japanese stock market retains inefficient features that have long been abandoned in the United States and the United Kingdom. For example, entry to the securities business in Japan is strictly limited, and fixed commissions still prevail. The "big four" securities firms—Nomura, Daiwa[21], Nikko, and Yamaichi—have dominated the market by both trading in and setting equity prices. Cross holdings of industrial and financial firms are prevalent. These factors have contributed to the erosion of control mechanisms like those observed in the United States and United Kingdom, leading to financial scandals including the bribery of government officials (the 1989 Recruit Cosmos case), in-

---

[20] *Financial Times*, June 12, 1995, p. 8.

[21] In 1995, it was discovered that Daiwa Bank in New York had covered up, through unlawful accounting practices, more than $1 billion in losses in bond trading over a 10-year period. The Federal Reserve ordered the operation of Daiwa Bank to be closed down. Since the New York operation was essential for Daiwa's global operation, the long-run effect of this development may be far-reaching.

sider trading by top-level government officials in the early 1990s, and the revelation in 1991 that large securities firms were compensating certain customers for losses they had incurred in the market.

In Germany and Switzerland, banks are effectively the only force in securities trading. In Germany, the Banking Act gives banks a monopoly in brokerage activities. Bankers' exchanges, which may be privately or publicly owned, are convenient places for bankers to meet. Banks may even trade among themselves without going through an exchange. In Germany, shares are registered and commissions are fixed. Settlement takes place three days after the trade, but it may be five days by arrangement. In Switzerland, 70% of equity trading occurs in the cash market and the rest takes place in the forward market. Settlement takes place three days after the trade in the cash market and on the last working day of the month in the forward market.

In the summer of 1995, Switzerland launched a fully electronic trading system that replaced the open-outcry system and shut down its three remaining regional exchanges. Germany's Deutsche Boerse, which controls both the Frankfurt stock exchanges and Germany's DTB futures and options exchange, is set to create an electronic system for German shares and bonds by 1998.[22] The move will probably end the country's eight regional exchanges. The electronic system, according to Deutsche Boerse, will enhance market efficiency by improving price transparency and eliminating price discrepancies. The move toward electronic trading is part of a broader strategy to make Germany the leading financial market in Europe. Currently, the German equity market is relatively small because midsize firms are reluctant to go public, partially for tax reasons, and investors consider equity investing too risky. This has left Germany in the second position behind London, despite its economic superiority. Electronic trading will facilitate foreign links. Deutsche Boerse's DTB futures and options exchange has already established trading screens in the Netherlands, France, Switzerland, and the United Kingdom. In addition, Deutsche Boerse and the Paris-based Societé des Bourses Française have suggested plans to integrate their stock markets.

Equity markets in Canada and Australia follow many of the procedures that we observe in the U.S. market. Both have private exchanges where members trade with each other. Shares are registered and commissions are negotiable. Settlements take place five days after the trade in both markets.

France has a public exchange (bourse). Trades are mostly in the forward market even though there are some trades in the cash market as well. Shares are registered and commissions are negotiable. A call auction is used to set fixed quotations. Settlements on forward trades take place on the last working day of the month. For cash trades, settlement is immediate.

Markets are allocationally efficient when new information is rapidly disseminated in the market and transactions by competing traders cause security prices to fully reflect new information. Equity markets with continuous trading among a large number of traders provide allocational efficiency; examples include the markets of the United States, the United Kingdom, Canada, and Australia. Operational efficiency depends on the competitiveness of the commissions charged and the size of the bid-ask spreads. In this regard, the Japanese equity market stands out as the least efficient among industrialized countries, with fixed commissions and only a handful of securities firms dominating all trading and setting the bid-ask spreads. Due to the bank monopolies in equity markets, German and Swiss markets are operationally inefficient: Their limited competition has widened bid-ask spreads and fixed commissions reduce liquidity. Recent move-

---

[22] *The Wall Street Journal*, May 31, 1995, p. C12.

TABLE 13.11 Means and Standard Deviations of Returns[a] on Equities for Three Global Regions (1970–1991)

Region/Country	Geometric Mean	Standard Deviation
Pacific Basin		
Australia[b]	11.81%	29.41%
Hong Kong	20.46	52.78
Japan	19.34	32.17
New Zealand[c]	(6.62)	25.84
Singapore/Malaysia	15.56	53.99
Europe		
Austria	13.85	43.57
Belgium	15.75	25.53
Denmark	15.59	32.07
Finland[c]	(11.27)	24.17
France	12.70	32.52
Germany	11.95	33.06
Italy	6.09	43.77
Netherlands	15.53	20.18
Norway	13.33	54.08
Spain	8.87	34.62
Sweden	15.48	25.64
Switzerland	11.83	26.73
United Kingdom	13.60	33.82
North America		
Canada	10.15	17.48
Mexico	15.97	52.99
United States	10.93	16.76

[a] Returns are calculated after conversion to U.S. dollars.
[b] For 1974–1991.
[c] For 1988–1991.

Source: Ibbotson et al. (1995), p. 202.

ments in Switzerland and Germany toward an electronic trading system may challenge the British dominance in the European equity and bond markets. Overall, the entire European capital market seems to be moving toward an integrated electronic trading system.

Risk-Return Trade-Offs and Portfolio Diversification in the Global Equity Market

The relative performance of global equity markets can be measured in the paradigm of risk and return.[23] Table 13.11 provides means and standard deviations of returns for 21 countries for the period 1970–1991. Hong Kong and Japan had the highest and second highest returns for the period. The United States, with a 10.93% return, ranked 16th on the list. However, the U.S. market had the least volatility with a standard deviation of 16.76%.

---

[23] This section draws from Roll (1992) and Ibbotson et al. (1995).

TABLE 13.12	Emerging Stock Market Returns and Market Capitalizations[a]			
Region/Country	Compound Annual Return	Annualized Standard Deviation	Period	9/30/1992 Market Capitalization
Asia				
India	19.7%	27.1%	1/76–5/92	$ 83.6
Indonesia	(8.1)	33.4	1/90–5/92	12.1
South Korea	20.3	31.8	1/76–5/92	81.2
Malaysia	13.5	26.2	1/85–5/92	85.5
Pakistan	25.3	22.7	1/85–5/92	7.7
Philippines	53.4	38.5	1/85–5/92	15.6
Taiwan	30.6	55.2	1/85–5/92	102.4
Thailand	23.1	26.3	1/76–5/92	54.0
Americas				
Argentina	20.5%	92.3%	11/77–4/89	$ 18.5
Brazil	9.1	64.1	1/76–5/92	52.0
Chile	36.0	39.9	1/76–5/92	31.5
Colombia	53.9	33.2	1/85–5/92	5.9
Mexico	22.5	44.3	1/76–5/92	109.4
Venezuela	31.1	50.0	1/85–5/92	8.6
Europe, Middle East, and Africa				
Greece	3.4%	36.3%	1/76–5/92	$ 11.0
Jordan	10.6	19.0	1/79–5/92	3.0
Nigeria	(7.1)	36.0	1/85–5/92	1.3
Portugal	41.0	51.8	2/86–5/92	12.2
Turkey	73.3	102.6	1/87–5/92	11.0
Zimbabwe	5.2	34.2	1/76–5/92	0.8

[a] Returns expressed as percentage after conversion to U.S. dollars; capitalizations in billions of dollars.

Source: Ibbotson et al. (1995), p. 203.

While many individual markets had higher volatility than the U.S. market, an equally weighted or capitalization-weighted portfolio of non-U.S. stocks had a standard deviation close to that of the U.S. market. This points to the low correlations among the returns in these markets. Various studies have shown that a diversified portfolio of global stocks is superior to a portfolio of all U.S. stocks.[24]

The importance of global portfolio diversification becomes more evident in view of the rapid growth of equity markets outside the United States. For example, in 1970 worldwide stock market capitalization stood at $929 billion, 66% of which was in the United States. By 1993, the United States equity market represented only 36% of the $12,572 billion worldwide total. U.S. stock market capitalization may become even a smaller percentage of the global markets as other markets continue to grow rapidly.[25]

Global equity portfolios provide higher returns for a given level of risk than

---

[24] For a review of the evidence, see Solnik (1996), Chapter 4.
[25] Merrill Lynch, "A Case for Equities: Global Diversification," *Global Investing*, March 1994, p. 1.

do domestic portfolios because portfolio risk is reduced by global diversification. This strategy has been recognized by U.S. pension funds. In 1979, U.S. pension funds invested only $1.8 billion in foreign securities. This figure increased to $110 billion by 1991 and is expected to reach $270 billion by the end of 1995.[26] There is sufficient evidence to suggest that a portfolio of domestic and foreign stocks provides a risk-return outcome that is superior to that of a portfolio of purely domestic stocks.

Finally, it is instructive to examine briefly the development of emerging equity markets. These markets are called "emerging" because their respective countries have just begun to be integrated into the world economy. Table 13.12 provides information on returns and market capitalizations for emerging stock markets. Mexico and Taiwan have the two largest markets, followed by Malaysia, India, and South Korea. As it became evident in the case of Mexico in early 1995, these markets are highly sensitive to the various political and economic uncertainties that face emerging economies.

SUMMARY

Money markets, markets for short-term instruments, include Treasury bills, commercial paper, commercial letters of credit, banker's acceptances, Eurocurrencies, Eurocommercial paper, and Euronotes. Treasury bills are available in denominations of $10,000 or more with maturities of three months to one year. Commercial paper is unsecured corporate securities with maturities of less than 270 days. Commercial letters of credit are issued to facilitate imports and exports, and banker's acceptances are commercial letters that are stamped "accepted" by the issuing bank.

Eurocurrency markets developed out of the market for expatriated dollar deposits in Europe in the 1950s. From the beginning, the Eurocurrency market has been closely allied with foreign exchange markets and the development of offshore banking. Both Eurocurrency and offshore banking are wholesale forms of intermediation, and interbank transactions constitute about 70% of the volume of business in both.

Euronotes developed in the 1970s, and are generally issued through "note issuance facilities" or NIFs. NIFs are temporary facilities set up between underwriting banks and the borrower that permit the borrower to sell notes over a three- to five-year period. Eurocommercial paper is generally comparable to U.S. commercial paper, except that it typically has longer maturity, since Eurocommercial paper is not subject to SEC regulations. Both notes and paper are priced on a discount basis.

Capital market instruments include Treasury notes and bonds, agency securities, municipal bonds, corporate bonds, hybrid bonds, junk bonds, Eurobonds, foreign bonds, floating-rate notes (FRNs), and equity shares. Treasury notes are available in maturities of 1 to 10 years. Treasury bonds have maturities of seven years and longer. Treasury notes and bonds, along with Treasury bills, are auctioned in the primary market and traded in the secondary market by dealers. Agency securities are issued by entities that were established by Congress to facilitate flow of credit for farming, housing, and educational purposes. Municipal bonds are issued by states and local governments to finance necessary government projects such as building facilities or repairing roads and bridges. They are also used by states as low-cost debt incentives to attract corporations to their lo-

---

[26] Ibid.

cale. Corporations issue a variety of bonds ranging from straight debt to convertible and callable bonds, and high-yield junk bonds.

Foreign bonds are issued in the domestic market and currency of a given country by a foreign borrower. Eurobonds are issued and sold outside the country of the bond's currency. Eurobonds thus escape virtually all regulatory constraints imposed on both domestic and foreign bonds. Some countries restrict the issuance of Eurobonds in their currencies; others, such as the United States, prohibit the sale of Eurobonds to their citizens. The issuance of Eurobonds involves the borrower's selection of a "lead manager" and "comanagers" (typically banks), and "underwriting group" of banks, as well as a "selling group" of banks and dealers who place the bonds. Both primary and secondary Eurobond markets are self-regulated by trade associations.

Floating-rate notes (FRNs) represent a hybrid between the capital (bond) and money markets, in that they are issued for extended periods comparable to bonds, but are also repriced at frequent intervals—monthly, quarterly, or semiannually. FRNs issued outside of the country of the currency of the note are considered to be part of the Eurobond market.

The global equity market, like domestic markets, has primary and secondary segments. The international primary market has seen a recent upsurge of "IPOs" by governments pursuing privatization plans for state-owned industries. Investment banking firms dominate the IPO market; returns to purchasers of IPOs vary by country. The secondary equity markets vary even more by country, with differences in their structure having a strong impact on the allocational and operational efficiency of the different equity markets. Allocational efficiency means the pricing of equities reflects "true" values (an information issue); operational efficiency means that bid-ask spreads and commissions are minimal relative to the service provided (a competitive market structure issue). In the United States, the NYSE, AMEX, and NASDAQ (OTC) markets constitute the secondary market. Bid-ask spreads are set by specialist market makers in the exchanges, and commissions are negotiable (since 1975). In contrast, competition is limited in the Japanese equity market, and controls are minimal, with the result that operational efficiency is reduced. In Germany and Switzerland, bank monopolies in the equity markets have the same effect as they do in Japan.

REVIEW QUESTIONS

1. Classify financial markets in terms of maturity, the nature of the claim, scope of the market, delivery dates, and trading organization.

2. As of the second quarter of 1995, what were the total amounts of Treasury debt, Treasury bills, Treasury notes, and Treasury bonds?

3. Discuss the procedure for auctioning Treasury securities.

4. Discuss abuses in the market for Treasury securities. Define a "short squeeze." Discuss the anatomy of Salomon's short squeeze.

5. What are agency securities? For what purposes are they issued? Do they carry the full faith and credit of the U.S. government? What is the credit risk in these instruments?

6. Define munis. Discuss the purposes for which munis are issued. What were the abuses in issuing munis prior to 1986? What was the government's response in the 1986 tax law to mitigate the problem? What are the categories of munis specified in the 1986 law?

7. Identify the four classes of corporate bond issuers.

8. What are the bond rating classifications issued by Moody's and Standard & Poor's. Which ratings indicate investment grade bonds? Which ratings signal speculative bonds?

9. Define junk bonds. What kinds of investments are financed by junk bonds? What are the factors that contribute to the growth of junk

bonds? In the mid-1995s, what was the junk bond default rate and what was the average return?

10. What should be the price quote for a Eurocommercial paper maturing in 180 days at a rate of 8%?

11. Consider three FRNs issued in 1997 that are similar in all their characteristics except for their maturities. The first FRN is set to mature in 5 years, the second in 10 years and the third in perpetuity. The coupon payments are semiannual at a spread of 100 bp over the six-month LIBOR. The coupon payments are scheduled for June 1 and December 1 of each year. The coupon of December 1, 1997, is set on June 1, 1997, and the coupon of June 1, 1998, is set on December 1, 1997. Suppose that at the time of the issue, the six-month LIBOR is 8%. If the credit risk is to remain constant at 100 bp, the price of the floaters will be set at par ($100) at each of the future repricing dates. Suppose that after one year, the credit risk of the borrower deteriorates. Calculate the new price for each floater if the new rate is 150 bp, 200 bp, or 350 bp above the prevailing LIBOR. Show that the size of the discount depends on the size of the change in credit risk and the maturity of the bond.

REFERENCES

Altman, E. 1995. "Defaults and Returns on High Yield Bonds: Analysis Through 1994." New York University Salomon Center.

Asquith, P., D. Mullins Jr., and E. Wolff. 1989. "Original Issue High Yield Bonds: Aging Analysis of Defaults, Exchanges, and Calls." *Journal of Finance* (September): 923–952.

Barnea, A., R. Haugen, and L. Senbet. 1985. *Agency Problems and Financial Contracting*. New Jersey: Prentice Hall.

Bodie, Z., and R. Taggart. 1978. "Future Investment Opportunities and the Value of the Call Provisions on a Bond." *Journal of Finance*: 1187–1200.

Blume, M., and D. Keim. 1987. "Lower Grade Bonds: Their Risks and Returns." *Financial Analysts Journal* (July/August): 26–33.

Copeland, T., and H. Stoll. 1995. "Trading Markets." in *Financial Markets*, edited by Dennis Logue. Cincinnati, OH: Warren, Gorham & Lamont, 285–324.

Giddy, I., 1994. *Global Financial Markets*. Lexington, MA: D.C. Heath and Company.

Ibbotson, R., S. Lummer, and L. Siegel. 1995. "Historical Returns on Investment Instruments." in *Securities & Investment Management*, edited by Dennis Logue. Cincinnati, OH: Warren, Gorham & Lamont, 192–208.

Loughran, T., J. Ritter, and K. Rydqvist. 1994. "Initial Public Offerings: International Insights." *Pacific-Basin Finance Journal* (March).

O'Hara, M. 1995. *Market Microstructure Theory*. Cambridge, MA: Blackwell Publishers.

Roll, R., 1992. "Industrial Structure and the Comparative Behavior of International Stock Market Indexes." *Journal of Finance*, vol. 47, no. 1 (March): 3–41.

Solnik, B., 1996. *International Investments*, 3rd edition. Reading, MA: Addison-Wesley Publishing Company.

Wakeman, L. M., 1981. "The Real Function of Bond Rating Agencies." *Chase Financial Quarterly* (Fall): 18–26.

CHAPTER
14

Major Capital Market Transactions: Takeovers, Defensive Tactics, and Insider Trading

OBJECTIVES

In the previous chapter, we examined money and capital markets with an emphasis on financial instruments. In this chapter, we continue our discussion of capital markets with an emphasis on major market transactions, including corporate takeovers, defensive tactics, and insider trading. Corporate takeovers are transactions in which acquirers purchase majority shares of target firms and gain corporate control. Since change in corporate control generally involves replacement of the target firm managers, they often employ a variety of defensive tactics to block the effort. Defensive tactics take many forms, including issuing contingent claims (e.g., poison pills) that remain harmless as long as the firm stays independent but become claims on the acquiring party when control changes hands. Intertwined with takeovers and defensive tactics is insider trading based on material, nonpublic information. Despite being illegal, insider trading prior to public announcement of takeovers has continued over the years because of large profits.

Since takeovers, defensive tactics, and insider trading are often intertwined transactions, we examine them in the context of a unified framework. To do so, we begin with a discussion of incentive problems within corporate governance and demonstrate the role of corporate takeovers in mitigating managerial incentive problems. An obstacle to a successful takeover resolution may appear in the form of a defensive tactic used by the target management. We examine six categories of defensive tactics that are widely used by target firms. Takeover efforts are further complicated by the lingering problem of illegal insider trading. Various federal and state laws restrict takeover activities for a variety of reasons, such as the legal objection to insider trading, which is considered rampant around takeover events. We discuss legal and financial issues related to these transactions throughout the chapter.[1]

THE STRUCTURE OF THE PUBLIC CORPORATION

As defined in Chapter 2, a firm is composed of contractual relationships among stockholders, bondholders, and management. Each contracting party behaves out of self-interest, which may conflict with the interests of other parties. Our main focus here is on the stockholder-management conflict.

The modern corporation embodies an important set of incentive problems between professional managers and shareholders. This phenomenon, referred to as the problem of separation of ownership and control, has concerned students of corporate governance literature for more than half a century. Managers who run the typical modern corporation often own an insignificant fraction of the company's stock, while stockholders who own the corporation often have little control in the enterprise.[2] For example, a manager who works only half a day and enjoys the rest of the day socializing with friends behaves in a self-serving manner. A manager who hires relatives and friends for important positions while other, more talented candidates are turned away behaves in a self-serving fashion. A manager who draws high salaries compared to industry standards and imposes high personal expenses on the company is also demonstrating self-interest that is in conflict with the interest of shareholders. These problems are management perquisite problems.[3]

Managers may also prefer low-risk, low-return projects over high-risk, high-return alternatives because of concerns over the security of their own employment with the firm. Since stockholders of a leveraged company generally prefer riskier projects, they may be worse off if the manager systematically avoids risk.

Self-serving behavior by managers is also reflected in their investment and financing decisions. Managers may make specific investments to increase their own value to shareholders. Investments with entrenchment value reduce the probability of being replaced, provide greater latitude in setting corporate strategy, and produce higher wages and perquisites for managers. For example, in declining industries such as oil, managers may invest in nonvalue-maximizing projects that have entrenchment value.[4] The issuance of bonds on favorable terms, with a covenant that the debt is due if management is replaced or if the firm is acquired, is an example of a financing decision with entrenchment value. Other forms of managerial deviation from market-value maximization strategies include resistance to takeovers by managers with low ownership stakes[5] and the incidence of wealth-decreasing acquisitions by poorly performing managers who are willing to overpay for acquisitions with the hope of retaining their jobs.[6]

Left unmitigated, stockholder-management conflict will reduce the value of the firm and the price of the stock. Mechanisms that function to discipline managers exist in both internal and external forms. The internal mechanism for disciplining management is in the form of monitoring by the board of directors. The external mechanism for disciplining management is in the form of the market for corporate control or takeover market. We describe each of these mechanisms next.

---

[1]This chapter draws from Arshadi and Eyssell (1995).

[2] Berle and Means (1932), p. 8–9.

[3] Jensen and Meckling (1976).

[4] McConnell and Muscarella (1985), Jensen (1986), Shleifer and Vishny (1989), and Jensen (1993).

[5] Walkling and Long (1984).

[6] Lewellen, Loderer, and Rosenfeld (1985); Roll (1985); Lang, Stulz, and Walkling (1989); Morck, Shleifer, and Vishny (1990); and Servaes (1991).

The Internal Mechanism for Disciplining Management

323

Major Capital Market
Transactions: Takeovers,
Defensive Tactics, and
Insider Trading

One of the most important internal mechanisms for disciplining management is the board of directors. State chartering authorities require a board of directors composed of three or more individuals. The Model Business Corporation Act sets forth the following legal definition of the role of the board of directors:

> All corporate powers shall be exercised by or under authorities of, and the business and affairs of a corporation shall be managed under the direction of, a board of directors. . . . The fundamental responsibility of the individual corporate director is to represent the interests of the shareholders as a group, as the owners of the enterprise, in dealing with the business and affairs of the corporation within the law.[7]

Directors are fiduciaries who owe a *duty of care* to the corporation and a *duty of loyalty* to the shareholders.

The standard by which duty of care is measured is called the *business judgment rule*, which suggests that "[a]bsent bad faith or some other corrupt motive, directors are normally not liable to the corporation for mistakes of judgment, whether those mistakes are classified as mistakes of fact or mistakes of law." In practice, the rule serves more as a standard of judicial restraint to prevent courts from interfering in the activities of corporate directors and managers than as a restrictive duty imposed on directors and managers. The widespread application of the business judgment rule implies that management and board actions might not be reviewed at all.

In contrast to judicial restraint under the business judgment rule, courts have taken an active role in transactions that create conflicts of interest and threaten to breach the duty of loyalty. Directors' votes on matters related to their own business relationships with the firm are reviewed and scrutinized by the court to ensure the *fairness* of the decision. The fairness standard, however, has been shown to be inadequate in providing for the duty of loyalty in extreme circumstances, such as a change in control due to an outside takeover. In sum, when the self-interest of board members is at issue, the guidance of the business judgment rule and the fairness standard may not provide a value-maximizing decision by the directors for the shareholders.

There is some empirical support for the effectiveness of the board of directors in disciplining managers when the board includes a significant number of outside directors.[8] It has also been shown that the existence of large share blocks may provide an effective control mechanism[9] except when the blockholder is an institution such as a bank or an insurance company that has a significant business relationship with the current management.[10] Banks with multiple loans to a corporate customer may seek board membership in order to monitor managerial performance. When executives from lending institutions become board members of the borrowing firm or vice versa, they have an opportunity for mutual monitoring, leading to improved efficiency for both.[11] There is evidence that links management replacements to board monitoring, involvement by large block

---

[7] American Bar Association (1978), pp. 12 and 37.
[8] Weisbach (1988), Kaplan and Minton (1994), and Byrd and Hickman (1995).
[9] Shleifer and Vishny (1986) and Agrawal and Mandelker (1990).
[10] Brickley, Lease, and Smith (1988). Slovin and Sushka (1993) suggest that the presence of large blockholders may reduce the likelihood of a takeover bid.
[11] Kummer, Arshadi, and Lawrence (1989), and Chapter 3 in this book.

shareholders, and competition among top managers.[12] Proxy contests may also discipline managers. A study of 60 proxy contests for board representation during 1978–1985 found that proxy contests were often followed by managerial resignations, even when the dissidents were unable to obtain a majority on the board.[13] According to this study, three years after a proxy contest only one-fifth of firms in the sample had the same management. Bond covenants are also used to reduce incentive problems within firms. There are cases in which the creditors of firms with poor performances were involved in the removal of top managers.[14]

Morck, Shleifer, and Vishny (1988) examined the relationship between management and board ownership and firm performance. They found evidence of a significant nonlinear relationship, in which firm performance rises as the percent of management and board ownership of the firm increases from 0% to 5%, then declines as ownership increases from 5% to 25%, and then rises again as management and board ownership increases beyond the 25% level. They conjecture that the initial rise in firm performance is due to stock bonuses that are provided to management for high performance. The mid-range ownership, which is correlated with a decline in firm performance, may reflect management entrenchment, such as the case when a founding family is part of the board. Morck et al. suggest that the positive link between ownership stakes of greater than 25% and increased firm performance reflects the actual convergence of interests between managers and shareholders.

To the extent that internal control mechanisms resolve managerial incentive problems, no additional control system is needed. There is, however, evidence to show that internal systems do not fully mitigate managerial incentive problems.[15] Under such circumstances, an external control mechanism in the form of a corporate takeover may provide the necessary solutions.

The External Mechanism for Disciplining Management: Corporate Takeovers

Manne (1965) suggests that the firms most likely to be acquired will be those most requiring improvement. That is, the market for corporate control serves, in part, as an extension of the managerial labor market. Given this orientation, we will focus on one important method for effecting a change in control that does not require the consent of incumbent management—the tender offer.

In 1979, the SEC provided the following guidelines to legally identify a transaction as a tender offer:

1. The offer is made to more than 10 shareholders.
2. The offer is announced publicly.
3. It involves at least 5% of a class of securities.
4. The offer is nonnegotiable.
5. The tender price exceeds the market value by at least $2 or 5%.
6. The offer involves a limited time frame for consideration (approximately 45 days).[16]

In the next section we examine the laws concerning tender offers, the wealth consequences for parties associated with target and bidding firms, and the tax consequences of tender offers.

---

[12] Warner, Watts, and Wruck (1988) and Barclay and Holderness (1991).

[13] DeAngelo and DeAngelo (1989).

[14] Gilson (1988).

[15] Herman (1981) and Jensen (1993).

[16] Ratner (1988), p. 110.

Laws Concerning Tender Offers

The federal regulation of tender offers is manifested in various sections of the Williams Act (1968, 1970), and through numerous district and circuit court decisions. Several laws have been passed at the state level concerning tender offers, including some on which the Supreme Court has ruled.

In 1968, Congress amended the Securities Exchange Act of 1934 with the objective of protecting the interests of shareholders during a change in corporate control. Known as the Williams Act, the amendment requires acquirers to publicly disclose certain information, which is specified in Sections 13(d) and 14(d, e) of the act, in order to assure shareholders of an informed decision-making process during a tender offer.[17]

The main objective of Section 13 is to require that shareholders be informed when any significant block (5% or more) of outstanding shares is acquired by an outside individual or firm. Section 13(d) stipulates that within 10 days of such share acquisition, the following information must be disclosed: (1) the identity and background of the purchaser; (2) the source and amount of funds spent on the acquisition; (3) the number of shares owned; (4) the intentions of the acquirer (investment, takeover, etc.); and (5) planned changes in the target firm in the event of a successful takeover.

The rules of Section 13 pertain to virtually any initial acquisition of 5% or more of a firm's outstanding shares, and to subsequent acquisitions of 2% or more. Section 14(d) of the act, on the other hand, deals specifically with the acquisition of shares via tender offers. Under this section, share purchasers must file form 14d-1, which discloses information similar to that listed above, with the Securities and Exchange Commission. Additionally, it allows sellers the opportunity to change their minds within 60 days of the offer, or to withdraw their shares if they are misinformed. Further, all shareholders in the target class of securities must receive the same offer, and if the offer price is raised by the acquirer, the new price must also apply to shareholders who have already sold their shares. Section 14(e) requires the management of the target company to provide shareholders with a statement of the company's position on the tender offer and the reasons for that position within 10 days of the tender offer. This section also makes it unlawful for either the bidder or target management to attempt to deceive shareholders or manipulate share prices during the offer.

Enforcement of SEC tender offer regulations has been considered by some courts, primarily in cases of fraud or deception on the part of the bidder or the target. The Supreme Court has ruled, for example, that while bidders may not sue for damages when misleading statements are made by the management of target companies,[18] shareholders may initiate a civil suit if they are misled by those who make the tender offer.[19] In addition, target firm management cannot be sued by shareholders if a tender offer is abandoned as a result of misleading statements made by target management.[20] While these precedents are not necessarily clear-cut and may be subject to change in the future, they nevertheless present a judiciary sentiment that is generally sympathetic to target firms' management.

---

[17] The 1968 Williams Act (Pub. L. No. 90-439, 82 Stat. 454 July 29, 1968) and 1970 Amendments (Pub. L. No. 91-567, 84 Stat. 1497 December 22, 1970). It was specified in the Williams Act that the attempted acquisition must involve at least 10 percent of the securities. The 1970 amendment reduced the triggering proportion to 5 percent.

[18] *Piper* v. *Chris-Craft Industries*, 430 U.S. 1 (1977).

[19] *Plain* v. *McCabe*, 797 F. 2d 713 (9th Cir. 1986).

[20] *Lewis* v. *McGraw*, 619 F.2d 192 (2d Cir. 1980); *Panter* v. *Marshall Field*, 646 F.2d 271 (7th Cir. 1981).

In addition to federal regulation of tender offers through the Williams Act, tender offers are also subject to regulation at the state level, which often imposes greater restrictions. Required delays between public announcements and the commencement of tender offers (sometimes as long as 60 days) are not uncommon in state law. The criteria for disclosure are also typically more expansive than are SEC provisions. In addition, administrative review hearings for tender offers have been established in several states.

Changes in state and federal takeover regulations can be expected to have some impact on the price of premiums paid in takeovers. Evidence concerning these effects is somewhat mixed, however. One study has reported data suggesting that the first generation of state takeover laws may have had the effect of deterring some bidders.[21] Other studies have concluded that first-generation state laws and the Williams Act significantly increased the premiums paid to the shareholders of target firms.[22] On the other hand, recent work suggests that the average tender premiums in cash tender offers rose significantly in 1974, possibly due to "events such as the oil crisis and subsequent unexpected inflation [which] increased the heterogeneity of investors' beliefs about firm value."[23] Increases in takeover premiums for mergers in the United Kingdom after 1968 suggest that the passage of the Williams Act may have been a coincident, rather than causal, event.[24] Interestingly, a substantial amount of empirical evidence suggests that foreign investors pay higher premiums than do domestic investors.[25]

In 1982, a U.S. Supreme Court decision ruled the tender offer statute of Illinois unconstitutional.[26] This decision helped to create the environment necessary for the passage of a wave of second-generation state laws designed to pass the constitutional test set by the Supreme Court. Recent data shows that more than 35 states have passed laws intended to protect local companies from hostile takeovers. Many of these laws were upheld by the Court.[27] Subsequently, many states passed a "third generation" of laws designed to restrict takeovers.

Given sufficient antitakeover legislation, the shareholders of target firms may suffer. For example, stock prices of firms incorporated in the state of Ohio declined by an average of 3.24% following the passage of antitakeover laws in that state.[28] Another study examined the impact of one of the most severe of the second-generation antitakeover laws passed in Pennsylvania, which limits the ability of shareholders to challenge management through the proxy process and eliminates the traditional fiduciary obligation of the board of directors to promote shareholders' interests.[29] The results show significant decrease in share values of the Pennsylvania firms and estimate the loss to shareholders at $4 billion.

The Valuation Consequences of Tender Offers

From a social standpoint, it is crucial to consider the impact of tender offers on the wealth of the contracting parties (including but not limited to target firm stockholders, bondholders, top-level managers, employees, stockholders of the acquiring firm, and taxpayers) in any attempt to evaluate tender offers as a way

---

[21] Smiley (1981).

[22] Smiley (1975) and Jarrell and Bradley (1980).

[23] Nathan and O'Keefe (1989), p. 119.

[24] Franks and Harris (1989). However, see Malatesta and Thompson (1993) for contrasting results.

[25] Cebenoyan, Papaionnou, and Travlos (1992); Kang (1993); Swenson (1993); and Dewenter (1995).

[26] *Edgar* v. *Mite Corp.*, 457 U.S. (1982).

[27] Including Arizona, Florida, Indiana, Louisiana, Maryland, Massachusetts, Minnesota, Missouri, Nevada, North Carolina, Ohio, Oregon, Pennsylvania, Utah, Washington, and Wisconsin.

[28] Ryngaert and Netter (1987).

[29] Szewczyk and Tsetsekos (1992).

of effecting a change in control. In order to make a sound judgment about whether tender offers are "good" or "bad" we must examine the wealth consequences for the parties involved. The premiums paid in 663 successful tender offers averaged 19% in the 1960s, 35% in the 1970s, and 30% in the 1980s.[30] These figures are consistent with the findings of 13 other studies of pre-1980 data.[31] In addition, the Office of the Chief Economist of the SEC estimated that during 1981–1986, shareholders of target firms in successful tender offers received premiums in excess of $54 billion over the value of their pre-tender offer share prices. Thus, there is virtual unanimity in the conclusion that target firm shareholders profit from successful tender offers.[32]

The impact of merger bids on the value of target firm bonds led some classes of creditors (e.g., convertible bondholders) to enjoy significant wealth gains.[33] In addition, the holders of straight bonds suffered no significant losses. It should be noted, however, that the sample period for this study predates the advent of highly leveraged transactions; as a result, it is difficult to generalize their results to more recent events. The increasing popularity of Leveraged Buyouts (LBOs) and Management Buyouts (MBOs) in the latter part of the 1980s, along with high default rates on junk bonds used in these cases, have contributed to controversy about these transactions. An LBO is the purchase of a publicly held corporation, using a high level of debt financing, by a partnership of a small number of investors. MBOs are a subset of LBOs in which the acquiring group includes the incumbent managers of the acquired unit. The evidence suggests that LBOs create value by significantly improving the operating performance of the affected firms without widespread employee layoffs, wage reductions, or wealth transfers from bondholders.[34]

Target firm managers are often ousted as the result of takeover bids. According to one study, within three years of a successful takeover bid, 64% of target firms' top three managers departed.[35] Similarly, another study reported that 59% of the target firms experienced management changes within five years of a merger, compared to 33% for nonmerging firms.[36] Because the samples used in these studies included friendly as well as hostile acquisitions, it was highly probable that a sample composed only of hostile tender offers would provide a higher percentage of managerial turnover upon a successful bid.[37]

The finding that target firm managers are often displaced subsequent to a successful takeover bid is consistent with the argument that the market for corporate control acts as an external mechanism for transferring corporate resources to the hands of those best able to utilize them. Thus, the takeover market may serve as an effective monitoring system over managerial performance. From this, one may infer that corporate efficiency is an effective deterrent to tender offers, since it increases share prices and discourages takeover bids.

---

[30] Jarrell, Brickley, and Netter (1988).

[31] Summarized in Jensen and Ruback (1983).

[32] It should be noted, however, that this does not necessarily suggest that tender offers are sufficient to completely discipline target firm management. Smiley (1976) concludes that "the constraint posed by takeovers is far from binding." And Cotter and Zenner (1994) suggest that the probability of tender offer success is positively related to post-offer change in managerial wealth.

[33] Dennis and McConnell (1986).

[34] For evidence on post-buyout performance, see Palepu (1990) and Ofek (1994). Asquith and Wizman (1990) find bonds with strong covenant protection gain value in LBOs while those with no protection lose value. For other views see Asquith and Mullins (1989), Kaplan and Stein (1990), Lichtenberg and Siegel (1990), Smith (1990), Ippolito and James (1992), and Lee (1992).

[35] Martin (1986).

[36] Walsh (1988) and Martin and McConnell (1991).

[37] Weisbach (1995) documents that top management changes often lead to reversals of poor decisions.

A study on the impact of successful tender offers on the wages and employment of workers has reported that, as a result of mergers consummated in the state of Michigan in 1981–1982, the wages of the combined workforce in the state declined by about 4%, but total employment rose by about 2%.[38] While this study was based on only one state, it indicated that labor may be far less adversely affected than some antitakeover advocates have contended.

Tax benefits have long been considered an important source of takeover gains. The Tax Reform Act of 1986, however, reduced the incentives for takeovers by decreasing (1) the acquirer's ability to use the accumulated tax losses of the target firm to reduce its own tax liabilities, and (2) the acquirer's ability to step up the basis of depreciable assets without being subjected to capital gains tax. A study of the tax benefits of accumulated losses and credits in 318 successful takeovers, which occurred from 1968 to 1983, found that these tax benefits were not a significant factor in the majority of the transactions.[39] Thus, the role of tax benefits in even pre-1986 takeover gains may be relatively minor.

When it comes to the shareholders of acquiring firms, evidence concerning the wealth effects of takeover bids is mixed at best. The findings of 13 studies of pre-1980 data concluded that the acquiring firm in a tender offer earns significant positive returns, while those who acquire via merger earn neither positive nor negative excess returns.[40] Another study suggests a secular decline in the gains to successful bidders in tender offers.[41] The ambiguity of the empirical evidence may be attributable to methodological differences across studies because any answer to the question "are shareholders of acquiring firms better off after an acquisition than they were before?" is sensitive to both the choice of time intervals over which "before and after" performance is defined and the choice of a benchmark against which performance is measured.[42] More recent evidence on the performance of the 50 largest U.S. mergers between 1979 and mid-1984, however, suggests that merged firms have increased their postmerger operating cash flow returns due to improvements in asset productivity.[43]

Another study identified three types of acquisitions that show systematically lower and predominantly negative announcement period returns to acquiring firms.[44] These three categories of bad acquisitions are (1) those that cross industry lines (diversification acquisitions); (2) those involving rapidly growing targets; and (3) acquisitions made subsequent to a period of poor performance by bidding management. There is evidence that suggests that the acquirer in a value-reducing acquisition increases the likelihood that it will become a target.[45]

We conclude that takeover bids are, on balance, socially desirable transactions when they involve target firms that are crippled by inefficient management. There are, however, impediments that may effectively block a value-increasing tender offer. Besides federal and state antitakeover laws, the most significant impediments to tender offers are the defensive tactics employed by the managers and board members of target companies to thwart acquirers.

---

[38] Brown and Medoff (1988).
[39] Auerbach and Reishus (1988).
[40] Jensen and Ruback (1983).
[41] Jarrell, Brickley, and Netter (1988), p. 53.
[42] Magenheim and Mueller (1988), p. 41.
[43] Healy, Palepu, and Ruback (1992).
[44] Morck, Shleifer, and Vishny (1990).
[45] Mitchell and Lehn (1990).

ANTITAKEOVER DEFENSIVE TACTICS

329

Major Capital Market
Transactions: Takeovers,
Defensive Tactics, and
Insider Trading

The use of various techniques to thwart corporate acquirers has raised a good deal of controversy between those who believe that their principal purpose is to entrench incumbent management and those who believe that they serve to enhance the value of the target firm. Advocates of the "managerial entrenchment" hypothesis provide empirical evidence suggesting that antitakeover amendments may serve to sabotage the legitimate workings of the market for corporate control, with the result that precisely those managers least deserving of retention keep their positions.[46]

Others have argued, however, that the ability of target firm management to repel initial offers may serve to facilitate subsequent (larger) offers. Consider, for example, the Marathon Oil case, in which the bid rose from $85 to $125 following the use of a lock-up agreement.[47] "Discriminatory" defenses (i.e., those that may be used to increase the costs of bidding to one acquirer but not to another) may also be shareholder wealth-enhancing.[48] It has also been posited that the existence of takeover defenses may be a necessary condition for managerial investment in firm-specific human capital. According to this hypothesis, high-level managers will not expend large amounts of time and effort preparing themselves for positions they can be forced out of at any time.[49]

In this section we examine six frequently employed defensive tactics, including shark repellents, poison pills, lock-up options, litigation, targeted share repurchases or corporate greenmail, and discriminatory repurchases. The first three tactics are undertaken prior to the announcement of a takeover bid; the rest are employed subsequent to the bid. We briefly discuss institutional arrangements, review the results of empirical research on such tactics, and conclude by evaluating the legal status of each defense.

Shark Repellents

"Shark repellents" are designed to make it difficult for potential acquirers to (1) obtain majority representation on the target firm's board, (2) acquire minority shares cheaply, or (3) gain the approval of the target firm's shareholders for the planned acquisition. The popularity of shark repellents is widespread. It is reported that over 40% of the firms listed in the Fortune 500 and nearly half of all NYSE-listed firms had adopted one or more repellents by the end of 1986.[50]

"Classification" of the board of directors entails segregating directors into three groups (the maximum allowed by the NYSE), each of which is elected to a staggered three-year term. As a result, potential acquirers may find it impossible to obtain majority representation on the firm's board for several years. "Supermajority" provisions are often implemented in conjunction with the adoption of a classified board. The most common type of supermajority provision requires that an affirmative vote by a large proportion (often 75% to 90%) of the firm's stockholders is required to change the number of directors or to remove a director from the board. This ensures that a hostile acquirer, faced with a classified board, is unlikely to be able to simply change the number and/or identities of the directors to sidestep the classification provision. Other supermajority provisions

---

[46] Pound (1987).
[47] Michel and Shaked (1986).
[48] Berkovitch and Khanna (1990).
[49] Copeland and Weston (1988).
[50] Pound (1987).

require large voting majorities in the event of major asset sales, mergers, or consolidations.[51]

"Fair price" provisions require the acquiring firm to pay at least the announced tender price to those shareholders not tendering their shares at the time of the initial takeover bid. The effect of a fair price provision is to increase the cost of the completed acquisition and to reduce the uncertainty felt by the target shareholders with respect to the value of their shares. It also has the effect of negating the "gun-to-the-head" aspect of two-tier tender offers, in which those shareholders who do not tender immediately run the risk of receiving substantially less than those who do.

The use of shark repellents may be viewed either favorably or unfavorably. Market participants can interpret their adoption as good news, since it signals management's belief that a takeover bid is likely. Alternatively, shark repellents can be seen as "preemptive" defenses signaling management's intention to entrench itself.

The empirical evidence, unfortunately, is as conflicted as these interpretations. One study investigates the wealth effects associated with the announcement of several anticipatory defenses over the 1960–1980 period, and upon finding primarily nonnegative returns concludes:

> From a public policy perspective, the implication is that public concern over the use of antitakeover amendments by large U.S. corporations is misplaced. Such amendments do not have an adverse impact on the wealth of the shareholders of the firms that adopt them, nor do they lead to a misallocation of real corporate assets.[52]

Others, on the other hand, report small negative excess returns around the implementation of shark repellents.[53]

In a discussion of the legality of shark repellent amendments, it has been noted that while the lower Delaware courts have generally affirmed their validity, "the Delaware Supreme Court has remained curiously silent" on the issue of the validity of antitakeover amendments, taking care to express no opinion at all on the legality of the shark repellent amendments challenged in the *Martin Marietta Corp.* v. *Bendix Corp.* case.[54]

Poison Pills

Poison pill plans have evolved over the years with the development of the takeover market. Early poison pill plans entailed issuing a dividend in the form of convertible preferred stock to holders of the firm's common stock. The newly issued preferred stock in these plans was typically noncallable for several years and carried voting rights equal to that of the common stock. At the occurrence of a "triggering event" (e.g., the acquisition of a large block of shares by an outside party), the preferred stock became redeemable for cash, or, in a merger, convertible to the acquirer's common stock.

In subsequent "flipover" plans, the shareholders of the target firm received stock rights allowing the purchase of additional shares of the target firm. Since the exercise price was set above the current market price, the current value of the

---

[51] Gordon and Pound (1993) examine the effects of information and ownership structure on a broad range of shareholder-sponsored corporate governance proposals.

[52] Linn and McConnell (1983), p. 398.

[53] DeAngelo and Rice (1983) and Jarrell and Poulsen (1987).

[54] Gilson (1986), p. 741.

stock right was nil. Should a merger be consummated, however, the rights would "flip over" to allow target shareholders to acquire a substantial amount (often an amount equal to twice the exercise value) of the acquirer's outstanding shares.

Similarly, in "back-end rights" plans, stock rights were distributed to the shareholders of the potential target. The amendment then allowed all rights holders except the third-party acquirer to redeem their rights for cash and securities in the event that the third-party acquirer's holdings surpassed a prespecified limit. Voting plans also acted to exclude large, third-party acquirers. In this case, preferred stock with voting rights was issued to common stockholders of the potential target firm. For any given shareholder, however, once a prespecified ownership level was passed, the voting rights of that shareholder were voided.

"Poison puts" are a financial innovation analogous to the poison pill. "Poison put" bonds are debt securities that allow bondholders to put the bonds to the issuer at par, or that require the borrower to raise the coupon rate until the bond's market price reaches par, in the event of losses in value attributable to merger activity. As such, investors are protected against "event risk," i.e., the risk of loss due to takeover or recapitalization.

Evidence suggests that the adoption of poison pills is associated with significant decreases in the price of the adopting firm's stock. One study examined 113 firms that adopted poison pills in the 1982–1986 period and found that the adoption of the pill reduced shareholder wealth on average by –0.93% on the announcement date.[55] Conversely, the firms abandoning plans to adopt a pill experienced stock price increases. Another study found a statistically significant stock price decline when a firm's pill was upheld by the court, and a price increase of 3.4% when it was ruled invalid.[56] A closer examination of the composition of the board of directors shows that the negative relationship between the adoption of poison pills and stock price exists only when the board has a majority of inside directors. However, when the board has a majority of outside directors, the average stock market reaction to announcements of poison pills is positive.[57] To date, the wealth effects of the inclusion of poison puts in bond indentures remain unknown, but intuition suggests that these bonds will sell at slightly lower yields than similar nonprotected issues.

The legal status of poison pill amendments remains unclear due to a lack of agreement regarding the criteria by which such measures should be evaluated. As with most of the other takeover defenses described here, the courts have been loath to second-guess directors and top-level managers; rather, they have deferred to managerial discretion, citing the principle of the "business judgment rule."

Lock-Up Options

Target firms wishing to deter potential bidders may grant an option on a large block of (possibly unissued) stock or on other desirable firm assets to a friendly firm, or "white knight." As a result, the hostile bidder is forced to deal with two firms rather than one, and faces increased uncertainty with regard to the likelihood of success in a takeover bid. Lock-up agreements have also been constructed after the announcement of a hostile takeover bid in order to preclude further bidding by outsiders in situations where the target firm has reached agreement with an acquirer. This practice is increasingly tenuous, however: An asset lock-up agreement between Macmillan Inc. (the target) and Kohlberg,

---

[55] Malatesta and Walkling (1988).
[56] Ryngaert (1988).
[57] Brickley, Coles, and Terry (1994).

Kravis, Roberts, Inc. (the bidder) was invalidated by the Delaware Supreme Court on the grounds that "its only purpose was to end an active auction for Macmillan and drive away an unwanted suitor." [58]

Lock-up agreements are strongly criticized by those who contend that, by their very nature, the agreements stifle competition in the takeover market. By preemptively removing from the playing field large blocks of stock or prime corporate assets, target firm managers gain a substantial edge in their dealings with bidders. However, if a lock-up option is adopted in order to make the takeover more difficult for some bidders than for others, target management could get a higher price for target shares.[59]

The legal status of lock-up options is no clearer. The federal court system and the courts of appeals are divided with respect to the current state of the law. At issue is whether or not a lock-up agreement constitutes an attempt to manipulate the price of the target firm's stock. For example, in Mobil's attempt to acquire Marathon Oil, Marathon Oil entered into a lock-up arrangement with U.S. Steel. The arrangement was subsequently struck down by the Court of Appeals for the Sixth Circuit as a violation of the Williams Act. On the other hand, the lock-up agreement between Enstar Corp. and Unimar Corp. was upheld by the Delaware Chancery Court because "the plaintiffs [had] not sustained their burden of showing a reasonable probability that the approval of lock-up agreements is not fair to the shareholders or that the director acted unreasonably in adopting them." [60] It is unlikely that a definitive resolution to the question is forthcoming.

Litigation

Frequently, the first response of target firm managers is an attempt to slow the takeover process by means of litigation, which generally has two main effects. First, it imposes significant costs on the bidding firm, reducing the expected return from the acquisition and, as a result, making the target less desirable. Second, it delays the completion of the bid, allowing the managers of the target firm to present their case for continued independence to their shareholders, or, alternatively, to seek a "white knight."

There are numerous legal grounds for litigation. Since acquisitions via tender offer are regulated by the Williams Act (1968, 1970) amendment to the Securities Exchange Act of 1934, acquirers must disclose publicly such information as the purpose of the offer, the financing source(s), and any possible impact(s) on existing federal or state regulations. Failure to disclose fully or completely all relevant aspects of the offer may provide the target firm with significant delays while it seeks injunctive relief based on any violations of federal law.

Acquirers often obtain funds for takeover bids from large commercial banks, although doing so leaves the banks vulnerable to charges of conflict of interest if business relationships are maintained with both the bidder and the target. In addition, borrowing for stock purchases is regulated by the Federal Reserve System through margin purchase requirements.

Finally, target firms may contend that the acquisition, if completed, will be in violation of one or more antitrust statutes. Even though antitrust arguments are one of the most frequently used defenses, they are often ultimately unsuccessful.

An empirical study of the effects of litigation by target firms in response to unwanted bids found that (1) litigious targets are usually acquired in spite of le-

---

[58] *The Wall Street Journal*, May 8, 1989, p. B5, "Delaware High Court Rules a Company Can't Use 'Lock-Up' Just to Stop a Suitor."
[59] Berkovitch and Khanna (1990).
[60] Michel and Shaked (1986), p. 89.

gal maneuvering; (2) target litigation resulted in higher total takeover premiums; and (3) subsequent target management turnover was higher than normal for at least some of the sample firms that remained independent.[61] This study concluded that litigation might be in the interest of target shareholders.

Targeted Share Repurchases or Corporate Greenmail

The repurchase of shares from an acquiring firm is an obvious response to a takeover bid. When the repurchase offer is restricted to the bidder, the procedure is called a "targeted repurchase" or "corporate greenmail" because the bidder typically receives a substantial premium over the current market price for his block of shares. The fact that targeted repurchases are often undertaken as a means of "buying off" a hostile bidder is supported by the "standstill agreements," in which the bidder promises to refrain from further acquisition activities that often accompany targeted repurchases.

Studies of the effects of corporate greenmail associated with merger termination provide inconclusive results. While one study reported significant wealth losses to nonparticipating shareholders,[62] another study reported positive wealth effects for nonparticipating shareholders in the period preceding the targeted repurchase.[63]

Discriminatory Repurchases

Under this strategy, management of a target firm offers a repurchase plan to all shareholders at a price substantially higher than the current market price, with the exception of a potential bidder who has accumulated shares of the firm for a possible takeover. The legality of this plan was tested in the case of Unocal vs. Mesa, where the Delaware Supreme Court upheld Unocal's discriminatory repurchase offer designed to defeat Mesa's hostile takeover. A study of the share price reactions of target firms to the announcement of the Delaware Supreme Court ruling found that Delaware-chartered firms' shares declined in value while non-Delaware targets were not affected.[64] These results suggest that investors perceive discriminatory repurchases as harmful since the plan provides target managers with an effective tool for fending off unwanted takeovers.

In sum, the use of costly defensive tactics to defeat takeover bids may create a serious impediment to the effectiveness of the takeover market in resolving managerial incentive problems.

INSIDER TRADING

Corporate control transactions frequently involve both the creation of nonpublic information and the possibility of substantial share price increases. This combination of factors lends itself to preannouncement trading by some management in the firms involved, as well as by investment bank employees, risk-arbitrageurs, etc. While insider trading is neither caused by takeovers nor limited to them, the presence of a takeover bid creates substantial profit opportunities for insider trading despite the existence of laws prohibiting such transactions.

Insider trading refers to securities purchases or sales based on material, non-public information. Information is deemed "material" if its subsequent public release results in significant changes in market prices. Thus, persons with access to material nonpublic information ("insiders") have an opportunity to profit by

[61] Jarrell (1985).
[62] Bradley and Wakeman (1983).
[63] Klein and Rosenfeld (1988).
[64] Kamma, Weintrop, and Wier (1988).

transacting in the shares of their respective firms before the information is released publicly.

Insiders are defined in two categories. Registered insiders, or "inside-insiders," as defined by the Securities Exchange Act of 1934, include corporate officers, directors, and owners of 10% or more of a firm's outstanding shares. SEC Rule 3b-2 requires these individuals to report any transactions in their own firms' shares in a timely manner.[65] A second category of insiders, "outside-insiders," refers to those who are neither corporate officers nor large shareholders but who may have access to nonpublic information due to their relationship with the firm. Included in this group are the firm's legal counsel, investment advisers, and accountants. The outside-insider group also includes friends, relatives, and the acquaintances of inside-insiders who, by virtue of this relationship, obtain access to material nonpublic information. Finally, the outside-insider group may include market professionals who gather information about firms and industries, and arbitrageurs, who speculate on certain events through stock transactions. These market participants may be tipped by inside-insiders about impending events that may affect firm value.

Insider Trading Laws

Prior to 1933 there were virtually no U.S. regulations prohibiting insider trading, possibly due to the widespread belief that insider trading was an acceptable "perk" granted to corporate insiders. In the 1933 case of *Goodwin* v. *Agassiz*,[66] for instance, a plaintiff sold his shares after reading in a newspaper article that the company had discontinued its copper exploration in a certain area. Corporate directors knew, however, that the company was planning further exploration, and were buying additional shares based on their nonpublic information. When the value of the firm's shares rose upon the release of this information, the plaintiff sued for damages. The Massachusetts Supreme Court denied recovery, arguing that the directors did not have a face-to-face transaction with the plaintiff since the transaction was done through the stock exchange.

Following the crash of 1929, an attempt was made to address issues of fraud and manipulation in the securities markets. The Securities Act of 1934 tackled these problems largely through strict disclosure requirements and restrictions on the transactions of insiders. Section 12(b) of the act requires directors, officers, and large shareholders to report their ownership in the firm at the time of their appointments. Section 16(a) requires insiders to file statements with the SEC within 10 days of the close of each calendar month, disclosing any changes in their ownership in the firm; Section 16(b) makes any "short-swing" profits gained by insiders recoverable by the issuing firm. (A short-swing transaction consists of a matching purchase and sale, or sale and purchase within a six-month period.) Section 16(c) prohibits short selling by insiders of their own firms' shares.

---

[65] It should be noted that the titles "director" and "officer" refer to any individuals who perform functions usually associated with those positions, although one need not necessarily have that title to be considered an insider by the SEC. In *Colby* v. *Klune* the title "production manager" was treated as that of a corporate officer in that the employed performs "important executive duties of such character that he would be likely in discharging those duties, to obtain confidential information about the company's affairs that would aid him if he engaged in personal market transactions" (*Colby* v. *Klune*, 178 F.2d 872 [2d Cir. 1949]). Conversely, in *Merrill Lynch* v. *Livingston* the title "vice president" was found to be merely an honorary designation of a person whose real position was that of a "securities salesman who had none of the powers of an executive officer of Merrill Lynch" (*Merrill Lynch* v. *Livingston*, 566 F.2d 1119 [9th Cir. 1978]).

[66] *Goodwin* v. *Agassiz*, 283 Mass. 358, 186 N.E. 659 (1933).

The 1934 act contained some loopholes, weakening its effectiveness as a deterrent to insider trading. For example, while the SEC has control over the content of the disclosure requirements under Section 16(a), it has no power to force the disgorgement of short-swing profits. Rather, it is up to management or the directors to sue for disgorgement. This same group, however, constitutes the insiders whose actions the act sought to control.

While the SEC is thus limited in its use of Section 16(b) of the act, it does have broad latitude in the enforcement of Section 10(b), which makes it unlawful for any person to use the mails or facilities of interstate commerce

> to use or employ, in connection with the purchase or sale of any security . . . any manipulative or deceptive device or contrivance in contravention of such rules and regulations as the Commission may prescribe as necessary or appropriate in the public interest or for the protection of investors.[67]

The adoption of Rule 10b-5 was an important step in augmenting the enforcement powers of the SEC. In 1942, the president of a company was buying the shares of his firm from other shareholders at low prices by misrepresenting the company's financial condition. Existing antifraud rules dealt only with the sale of securities, and remained silent on transactions involving insider purchases. The SEC used the language of Section 17(a), adding "in connection with the purchase or sale of any security," and adopted it as Rule 10b-5. Thus, the Rule makes it

> unlawful for any person, directly or indirectly, by the use of any means or instrumentality of interstate commerce, or of the mails, or of any facility of any national securities exchange, 1) to employ any device, scheme, or artifice to defraud, 2) to make any untrue statement of a material fact or to omit to state a material fact necessary in order to make the statements made, in the light of circumstances under which they were made, not misleading, or 3) to engage in any act, practice, or course of business which operates or would operate as fraud or deceit upon any person, in connection with the purchase or sale of any security.[68]

The SEC has an important role in the enforcement of Rule 10b-5. It can take administrative actions against registered traders such as brokers and dealers; it can ask the federal courts to force the disgorgement of profits and to impose penalties; and it can refer violators of Rule 10b-5 to the Department of Justice for criminal prosecution.[69] Rule 10b-5 was applied for the first time in the case of Cady, Roberts & Co.,[70] in which the SEC brought administrative proceedings to determine whether a news leak by a board member to a stockbroker regarding a dividend cut and the subsequent sale of securities by the broker violated the rule. The broker was suspended for 20 days from the New York Stock Exchange. The case established what is now known as the "disclose or abstain" rule. This rule instructs those who have access to material nonpublic information either to disclose it or to abstain from any trading that is based on that information. The "disclose or abstain" rule was later applied successfully in the *SEC* v. *Texas Gulf Sul-*

---

[67] Ratner (1988), p. 129.
[68] Ibid, p. 130.
[69] Prentice (1987), pp. 628–29.
[70] Cady, Roberts & Co., 40 SEC 907 (1961).

phur Co.[71] case. An insider's duty to disclose information, or the duty to abstain from dealing in the company's securities, arises only in "those situations which are essentially extraordinary in nature and which are reasonably certain to have a substantial effect on the market price of the security if disclosed."

More recently, the Supreme Court has ruled on three occasions on the scope of Rule 10b-5. In 1980, it ruled in the *Chiarella* v. *United States*[72] case involving a printer, Vincent Chiarella, who as a "markup-man" in a printing firm had identified the concealed names of several tender offer targets on documents submitted for printing. He subsequently traded in the target firms' shares and netted a profit of $30,000. The SEC discovered the transactions and asked the Department of Justice to bring criminal charges against Chiarella for violation of Rule 10b-5. The trial court convicted him and the second circuit court affirmed the conviction. The conviction was overturned in an appeal to the U.S. Supreme Court. The Court argued that the duty to disclose or abstain per Rule 10b-5 is only applicable when there is a fiduciary duty involved.

The Supreme Court's "Chiarella rule" prompted the SEC to adopt Rule 14e-3 in September 1980, prohibiting trading based on nonpublic knowledge of impending tender offers by anyone inside or outside the firm. In 1983, the Supreme Court ruled in *Dirks* v. *SEC*[73] by referring to its decision in the Chiarella case. The Dirks case involved a financial analyst who discovered massive fraud involving the Equity Funding Corporation, a large insurance firm. After attempting to disclose the information he uncovered, he instructed his clients to sell their shares in the firm. Shortly thereafter, California insurance authorities discovered the fraud and their disclosure of it lowered the share price from $26 to $15. The SEC censured Dirks for violating Rule 10b-5, and the District of Columbia Court of Appeals ruled against him. In response to his appeal to the Supreme Court, the Court referred to its decision in the Chiarella case and ruled that the defendant did not have any fiduciary duty to the firms' stockholders and, therefore, had no obligation either to disclose the information or to abstain from trading.

In addition, the Supreme Court heard a case in 1986 involving a *Wall Street Journal* reporter and coauthor of the "Heard on the Street" column, who leaked advance information about companies to be mentioned in forthcoming articles to brokers employed by Kidder, Peabody, Inc.[74] The brokers netted $690,000 on subsequent trades, $31,000 of which was paid to the reporter. The government alleged that the reporter had misappropriated information that was the property of *The Wall Street Journal* for personal profit. However, the "misappropriation theory," first applied in 1982, had been neither legislated by Congress nor affirmed by the Supreme Court.[75] The Court ruled 8-0 in favor of mail and wire fraud convictions, but 4-4 on the securities fraud issue. Nonetheless, the tie was sufficient to affirm the earlier conviction. The Court indicated that "the object of the scheme was to take the *Journal*'s confidential business information—the publication schedule and contents of the 'Heard' column and its intangible nature does not make it any less 'property' protected by the mail and wire fraud status." It was further argued that "the *Journal* has been deprived of its right to exclusive use of the information, for exclusivity is an important aspect of confidential busi-

---

[71] *SEC* v. *Texas Gulf Sulphur Co.*, 401 F. 2d 833 (2d Cir. 1968).

[72] *Chiarella* v. *United States*, 445 U.S. 222 (1980).

[73] *Dirks* v. *SEC*, 463 U.S. 646 (1982).

[74] *United States* v. *Carpenter*, 108 S.Ct. 316 (1987).

[75] Prior examples of the application of the misappropriation theory include *United States* v. *Newman*, 664 F.2d 12 (2d Cir. 1981); *SEC* v. *Materia*, 745 F.2d 197 (2d Cir. 1984).

ness information and most private property, for that matter." The fact that the Court did not overturn the misappropriation theory, even when it included a reporter, provided government prosecutors with a powerful new weapon to indict stockbrokers, arbitrageurs, and other employees of the investment banking community on the basis that the misappropriation of information constitutes a fraud.

In 1984, Congress passed the Insider Trading Sanctions Act,[76] which increased the financial penalties for insider trading to $100,000. In 1986, the SEC and the Department of Justice started their most significant crackdown on insider trading, which continues to this day. In October 1988 Congress passed, and then President Reagan signed into law, the Insider Trading and Securities Fraud Enforcement Act, which increased maximum prison terms to 10 years, provided bounties for informers, and increased the maximum fine to $2.5 million.

Other Laws Applicable to Insider Trading: The Case of RICO

Prosecutors have sought to use laws other than existing anti-insider trading legislation in their attempts to reduce insider trading. The application of the Racketeer Influenced and Corrupt Organizations (RICO) law to insider trading is a prime example of this. Passed in 1970, RICO was intended for use against the criminal infiltration of legitimate businesses and labor unions by organized crime. In recent years, however, civil filings under RICO have increased substantially: More than 90% of the nearly 1,000 RICO cases filed during 1988 were against legitimate businesses and non-Mafia individuals.[77] Chief Justice William Rehnquist of the Supreme Court has summarized an emerging consensus:

> Virtually everyone who has addressed the question agrees that civil RICO is now being used in ways that Congress never intended when it enacted the statute in 1970. Most of the civil suits filed under the statute have nothing to do with organized crime. They are garden variety civil fraud cases of the type traditionally litigated in state courts. Why does the statute work this way? In part, because it creates a civil counterpart for criminal wire fraud and mail fraud prosecutions. It does this by stating that acts indictable under those provisions, as well as many other types of criminal acts, are capable of establishing the 'pattern of racketeering' that is the predicate for a civil RICO action.[78]

The criminal "predicate acts" that give rise to civil suits include robbery, murder, securities fraud, and using the telephone or the mail for illegal purposes. Since almost all securities transactions involve the mail or telephones, they can be alleged to be fraudulent acts under RICO.

The severity of the conditions imposed under RICO may have contributed to the notoriety of some cases. Those convicted under RICO must forfeit their profits from the scheme, including interest, salaries earned during the period, and any property used to facilitate the racketeering activities. Perhaps equally important is that, upon indictment, the government can ask for a significant portion of the defendant's assets as a security for assets that the government will be entitled to if it wins the conviction. The size of the bond may be substantial and the time

---

[76] Public Law 98-376 (98th Congress).
[77] "Second Thoughts on RICO," *The Wall Street Journal*, May 19, 1989, p. A10.
[78] William Rehnquist, "Get RICO Cases Out of My Courtroom," *The Wall Street Journal*, May 19, 1989, p. A10.

between the indictment and the posting of the bond can pose great uncertainty for a business.

The first RICO charges involving securities law violations were brought in August 1988 against five partners of Princeton/Newport L.P. and a former Drexel Burnham Lambert trader who were allegedly involved in a racketeering conspiracy to create tax losses using bogus stock deals. The combination of posting bond and business uncertainty ultimately forced Princeton/Newport into liquidation in December 1988, even though the defendants had yet to be convicted.

A similar threat of RICO forced Drexel Burnham Lambert to plead guilty to other nonracketeering charges, including six criminal counts of mail, wire, and securities fraud, and to agree to pay $650 million in fines.

The most significant securities-related RICO case to date is probably that brought against Michael Milken, formerly of Drexel Burnham Lambert. The 98-count indictment handed up by a federal grand jury provides the government with a claim on over $1.2 billion of Milken's assets. This forced Milken to plead guilty to six counts of technical offenses rather than enduring a RICO trial.

There have been a series of actions by the three branches of the government in response to criticism of the way in which RICO has been used. These actions have included court opinions, legislative proposals, and submissions to Congress seeking to reform civil RICO. For example, in July 1991 all RICO charges against Princeton/Newport partners, including tax and conspiracy charges, were dropped. More significantly, the Internal Revenue Service concluded that the firm had actually overpaid its taxes during the disputed period. The fact, however, remains that the firm itself was forced into liquidation because of the RICO indictment. This is the type of concern that is reflected in the Chief Justice's final remarks regarding RICO:

> I think that the time has arrived for Congress to enact amendments to civil RICO to limit its scope to the sort of wrongs that are connected to organized crime, or have some other reason for being in federal court.[79]

It is apparent that the laws against insider trading have become increasingly stringent in the last decade. Moreover, while direct and indirect laws concerning insider trading are numerous, it remains to be shown empirically whether such laws have been effective in deterring insider trading.

Empirical Evidence on the Effectiveness of Insider Trading Regulation

The advent of SEC prosecution of inside traders in the early 1960s generated interest among academic researchers seeking to determine (1) the degree to which the "strong form" of the efficient markets hypothesis (EMH) holds, and (2) the efficacy of insider trading regulation as a deterrent to those in possession of material nonpublic information. With respect to the former issue, the empirical results have been virtually unanimous in rejecting the strong-form EMH: Those with inside information have been able systematically to exploit that information to earn returns in excess of those without the informational advantage.[80]

Seeking to test the efficacy of insider trading regulation, one study examined

---

[79] Ibid.
[80] Research by Pratt and DeVere (1978), Seyhun (1986), and Rozeff and Zaman (1988) provides strong support for this contention.

the transactions of inside-insiders before and after three significant events in the history of insider trading regulation at the time: (1) the Cady, Roberts case; (2) the indictment of corporate officers and employees of the Texas Gulf Sulphur Co.; and (3) the Supreme Court's ruling in the Texas Gulf Sulphur case.[81] The study found little evidence that inside-insiders in general were deterred by the increased regulatory activity and concluded: "The results of this paper do not suggest that the recent regulation of insiders is effective, casting doubt on the value of this regulation to society."

Empirical studies of preannouncement run-ups in target firm stock prices suggest trading by those with nonpublic information about the impending takeover bid as the cause of the run-ups.[82] Two other studies examined the effects of the increasing number and severity of restrictions on insider trading by segregating the period from 1975 to 1990 into four regulatory "regimes" and considering changes in the nature of insider trading coincident with the announcement of tender offers occurring during each subperiod. The results indicated that in regimes 1 and 2 (in which insider trading regulation was relatively lax), inside-insiders were heavy purchasers of their firms' shares preceding the announcement of a tender offer. The transaction patterns of inside-insiders changed dramatically, however, after the imposition of sharply higher penalties associated with the passage of the ITSA in 1984. Inside-insiders were generally net sellers around tender offer announcements after 1984. This is more typical of insider transactions, and would suggest that the increasing stringency of the post-1984 federal laws against insider trading did deter trading by inside-insiders. Given the similarity of preannouncement stock price increases across all regulatory regimes, however, the authors concluded that insider trading had simply shifted to those not required to report their transactions to the SEC—the outside-insiders.[83]

Policy Implications in Insider Trading

The continuation of insider trading despite increasing penalties can be attributed to two factors. One, trading based on inside information is very profitable, and the probability of getting caught as an outside-insider is small, notwithstanding tips to authorities by individuals who are aware of the transaction. While it is relatively simple to scrutinize and control trading by inside-insiders (because of the SEC's disclosure requirements), it becomes substantially more complicated when the trading involves outside-insiders who do not face disclosure requirements or fiduciary responsibilities. Two, the Supreme Court has not provided a consistent opinion on this matter, leaving many loopholes that allow market professionals and their attorneys to sidestep anti-insider trading laws.

Actual prosecution of insider trading, despite tremendous publicity generated by the Department of Justice and the SEC about the deterring effects of their anti-insider trading activities, led to approximately 50 major indictments in the 1980s. Most of these cases have been settled out of court through guilty pleas involving lesser charges of securities laws violations; very few have gone to trial, and even fewer have produced convictions.

The high number of out-of-court settlements in insider trading cases can

---

[81] Jaffe (1974), p. 115.
[82] Keown and Pinkerton (1981) and Haw, Pastena, and Lillian (1990).
[83] Arshadi and Eyssell (1991) and Eyssell and Arshadi (1993).

be attributed to two interrelated factors. First, existing anti-insider trading laws are vague and there is no real consensus among various state and federal courts on the coverage of these laws. It is therefore unclear whether any of the indicted cases could be prosecuted successfully in court. Thus, prosecutors put pressure on defendants to settle on lesser charges, with the agreement that the defendants will cooperate with the authorities as witnesses in cases pending against others. Second, faced with the prospect of being indicted on RICO charges and having most of their assets frozen as a result, defendants see no other alternative than settlement with the authorities. This heavy-handed use of the RICO laws has created an uproar among legal scholars, judges, legislators, and even the justices of the Supreme Court. It is highly likely that Congress will revise RICO to limit its reach. If this happens, the Department of Justice will lose the powerful weapon it has used so often in recent years to obtain plea bargains.

If defendants are no longer threatened by RICO-type indictments, there will be less cooperation with the authorities, making it increasingly difficult to catch the outside-insiders involved in insider trading.[84] A major policy reevaluation may be required in order to examine other alternatives, including a serious study of the option of decriminalizing insider trading.[85]

SUMMARY

This chapter analyzes several important issues in corporate governance using a unified framework that synthesizes the legal and financial aspects of corporate governance, including corporate acquisitions, defensive tactics, and insider trading. Such an integration provides useful insights into the socioeconomic consequences of these transactions and into our understanding of the interrelationships among factors that affect corporate governance.

This chapter supports the following conclusions: First, takeovers play a positive role in encouraging corporate efficiency. As such, societal welfare is enhanced, although some sectors may be disrupted in the short run. Second, defensive tactics have a negative effect on corporate efficiency to the extent that they defeat takeover bids and neutralize the external control system. Third, the persistence of insider trading despite increasingly stringent anti-insider trading laws merits policy reevaluation.

The market solution to problems in corporate governance has been severely hampered by the passage of various federal and state antitakeover laws and by the implementation of legally accepted defensive tactics. Consequently, the costs of takeovers have become prohibitive in all but the most desperately perverse managerial incentive situations.

While antitakeover laws and corporate defenses have provided the management of inefficient firms with effective weapons for neutralizing the discipline of the market, the problem of market inefficiency has been exacerbated by abuses in the use of insider information. Recent anti-insider trading laws seem only to have had the effect of shifting insider trading from inside-insiders to outside-insiders, with management retaining sufficient latitude to continue to affect both the magnitude of information leaked and the identity of the "tipees."

---

[84] Kempf, Arshadi, and Eyssell (1992).
[85] Manne (1966) and Arshadi and Eyssell (1993).

REVIEW QUESTIONS

1. Explain the managers incentive problems in publicly held corporations due to separation of ownership and control.
2. Examine the role of each of the following factors in controlling management incentive problems:
   a. bond covenants
   b. labor market
   c. ownership structures such as franchising
   d. board of directors
3. Describe implications of duty of care and duty of loyalty and explain the standards by which these duties are measured.
4. When the self-interest of the board of directors is at issue, does the guidance of the business judgment rule provide for value maximizing decision by management? Explain.
5. Examine the wealth effects of tender offers on
   a. target firm stockholders
   b. acquiring firm stockholders
   c. target firm managers
   d. target firm bondholders
   e. target firm employees
6. Explain why each of the following descriptions of takeovers is or isn't true.
   a. an efficient method of resolving management incentive problems
   b. a sign of greed in Wall Street
   c. a sign of decay in business ethics
   d. bad for the economy
7. Which of the following answers constitutes the three pretakeover defensive tactics?
   a. lock-up options, shark repellents, and greenmail
   b. greenmail, discriminatory repurchases, and litigation
   c. shark repellents, lock-up options, and poison pills
   d. shark repellents, poison pills, and greenmail
8. Define poison pills and poison puts and examine their impact on target firm share prices.
9. Define insider trading.
10. Define the following categories of insiders and their respective legal obligation pertaining to insider trading.
    a. registered insiders
    b. outside-insiders
    c. temporary insiders
11. RICO was initially intended for use against the criminal infiltration of legitimate businesses and labor unions by organized crime. Describe the rationale for its application to the violations of the securities laws.
12. Which of the following statements is consistent with the empirical evidence?
    a. Insider trading laws have been effective in deterring insider trading activities.
    b. Insider trading laws have been effective in deterring insider trading by outside-insiders but not insider trading by inside-insiders.
    c. Insider trading laws have been effective in deterring insider trading by inside-insiders but not outside-insiders.
    d. Insider trading laws have been totally ineffective.

REFERENCES

American Bar Association. 1978. *Corporate Director's Guidebook.*

Agrawal, A., and G. Mandelker. 1990. "Large Shareholders and the Monitoring of Managers: The Case of Antitakeover Charter Amendments." *Journal of Financial and Quantitative Analysis,* vol. 25, no. 2:143–161.

Arshadi, N., and T. Eyssell. 1991. "Regulatory Deterrence and Registered Insider Trading: The Case of Tender Offers." *Financial Management,* vol. 20, no. 2:30–39.

Arshadi, N., and T. Eyssell. 1993. *The Law and Finance of Corporate Insider Trading: Theory and Evidence.* Boston: Kluwer Academic Publishers.

Arshadi, N., and T. Eyssell. 1995. "On Corporate Governance: Public Corporations, Corporate Takeovers, Defensive Tactics, and Insider Trading." *Financial Markets, Institutions, and Instruments,* vol. 4, no. 5:74–102.

Asquith, P., D. Mullins, and E. Wolff. 1989. "Original Issue High Yield Bonds: Aging Analyses of Defaults, Exchanges, and Calls." *Journal of Finance,* vol. 44, no. 4:923–952.

Asquith, P., and T. Wizman. 1990. "Event Risk, Covenants, and Bondholder Returns in Leveraged Buyouts." *Journal of Financial Economics,* vol. 27, no. 1:195–213.

Auerbach, A., and D. Reishus. 1988. "The Effects of Taxation on Merger Decisions." in *Corporate Takeovers: Causes and Consequences,* A. Auerbach, ed. Chicago, IL: University of Chicago Press, pp. 157–183.

Baker, G., M. Jensen, and K. Murphy. 1988. "Compensation and Incentives: Practice vs. Theory." *Journal of Finance,* vol. 43, no. 3:593–616.

Barclay, M., and Holderness, C. 1991. "Negotiated Block Trades and Corporate Control." *Journal of Finance,* vol. 46, no. 3:861–878.

Berkovitch, E., and N. Khanna. 1990. "How Target Shareholders Benefit from Value-Reducing Defensive Strategies in Takeovers." *Journal of Finance,* vol. 45, no. 1:137–156.

Berle, A., and G. Means. 1932. *The Modern Corporation and Private Property.* New York: Macmillan Publishing.

Bradley, M., and L. Wakeman. 1983. "The Wealth Effects of Targeted Share Repurchases." *The Journal of Financial Economics,* vol. 11, no. 1:301–328.

Brickley, J., and F. Dark. 1987. "The Choice of Organizational Form: The Case of Franchising." *Journal of Financial Economics,* vol. 18, no. 2:401–420.

Brickley, J., R. Lease, and C. Smith. 1988. "Ownership Structure and Voting on Antitakeover Amendments." *Journal of Financial Economics,* vol. 20, no. 1/2:267–291.

Brickley, J., J. Coles, and R. Terry. 1994. "Outside Directors and the Adoption of Poison Pills." *Journal of Financial Economics,* vol. 35, no. 3:371–390.

Brown, C., and J.L. Medoff. 1988. "The Impact of Firm Acquisitions on Labor." in *Corporate Takeovers: Causes and Consequences,* A. Auerbach, ed. Chicago, IL: University of Chicago Press, pp. 9–28.

Byrd, J., and K. Hickman. 1995. "Do Outside Directors Monitor Managers?" *Journal of Financial Economics,* vol. 32, no. 1:195–221.

Cannella, A., D.R. Fraser, and D.S. Lee. 1995. "Firm Failure and Managerial Labor Markets: Evidence from Texas Banking." *Journal of Financial Economics,* vol. 38, no. 2:185–210.

Cebenoyan, A.S., G.J. Papaioannou, and N.G. Travlos. 1992. "Foreign Takeover Activity in the U.S. and Wealth Effects on Target Firm Shareholders." *Financial Management,* vol. 21, no. 3:58–68.

Copeland, T., and J.F. Weston. 1988. *Financial Theory and Corporate Policy.* Reading, MA: Addison-Wesley Publishing Company.

Cotter, J., and M. Zenner. 1994. "How Managerial Wealth Affects the Tender Offer Process." *Journal of Financial Economics,* vol. 35, no. 1:63–97.

DeAngelo, H., and E. Rice. 1983. "Antitakeover Charter Amendments and Stockholder Wealth." *Journal of Financial Economics,* vol. 11, no. 1: 329–359.

DeAngelo, H., and L. DeAngelo. 1989. "Proxy Contests and the Governance of Publicly Held Corporations." *Journal of Financial Economics,* vol. 23, no. 1:29–59.

Dennis, D., and J. McConnell. 1986. "Corporate Mergers and Security Returns." *Journal of Financial Economics,* vol. 16, no. 2:143–187.

Dewenter, K.L. 1995. "Does the Market React Differently to Domestic and Foreign Takeover Announcements?

Evidence from the U.S. Chemical and Retail Industries." *Journal of Financial Economics,* vol. 37, no. 3:421–441.

Eyssell, T., and N. Arshadi. 1993. "Insiders, Outsiders, or Trend Chasers: An Investigation into the Causes of Pre-Takeover Price and Volume Run-Ups." *Journal of Financial Research,* vol. 15, no. 2:49–59.

Fama, E. 1980. "Agency Problems and the Theory of the Firm." *Journal of Political Economy,* vol. 88, no. 2:288–307.

Franks, J., and R. Harris. 1989. "Shareholder Wealth Effects of Corporate Takeovers: The U.K. Experience 1955–1985." *Journal of Financial Economics,* vol. 23, no. 2:225–249.

Gilson, R. 1986. *The Law and Finance of Corporate Acquisitions.* New York: Foundation Press.

Gilson, S. 1988. "Optimal Capital Structure and Management-Borne Cost of Financial Distress." Unpublished manuscript, University of Rochester.

Gordon, L., and J. Pound. 1993. "Information, Ownership Structure, and Shareholder Voting: Evidence from Shareholder-Sponsored Corporate Governance Proposals." *Journal of Finance,* vol. 48, no. 2:697–718.

Haw, I., V. Pastena, and S. Lillian. 1990. "Market Manifestation of Nonpublic Information Prior to Mergers: The Effect of Ownership Structure." *Accounting Review,* vol. 2, no. 1:432–451.

Healy, P., K. Palepu, and R. Ruback. 1992. "Does Corporate Performance Improve after Mergers?" *Journal of Financial Economics,* vol. 31, no. 2:135–175.

Herman, E. 1981. *Corporate Control, Corporate Power.* Cambridge: Cambridge University Press.

Ippolito, R., and W.M. James. 1992. "LBOs, Reversions, and Implicit Contracts." *Journal of Finance,* vol. 47, no. 1:139–167.

Jaffe, J. 1974. "The Effect of Regulation Changes on Insider Trading." *Bell Journal of Economics,* vol. 5, no. 1:93–121.

Jarrell, G., and M. Bradley. 1980. "The Economic Effects of Federal and State Regulation of Cash Tender Offers." *Journal of Law and Economics,* vol. 23, no. 2:371–388.

Jarrell, G., 1985. "The Wealth Effects of Litigation By Targets: Do Interests Diverge in a Merge?" *Journal of Law and Economics,* vol. 28, no. 1:151–177.

Jarrell, G., and A. Poulsen. 1987. "Shark Repellents and Stock Prices: The Effects of Antitakeover Amendments Since 1980." *Journal of Financial Economics,* vol. 19, no. 1:127–168.

Jarrell, G., J. Brickley, and G. Netter. 1988. "The Market for Corporate Control: The Empirical Evidence Since 1980." *Journal of Economic Perspectives,* vol. 7, no. 1/3:49–68.

Jensen, M. 1986. "Agency Costs of Free Cashflow, Corporate Finance and Takeovers." *American Economic Review Papers and Proceedings,* vol. 76, no. 2:323–329.

Jensen, M. 1993. "Presidential Address: The Modern Industrial Revolution, Exit, and the Failure of Internal

Control Systems." *The Journal of Finance,* vol. 48, no. 3:831–880.

Jensen, M., and W. Meckling. 1976. "Theory of the Firm: Managerial Behavior, Agency Costs and Ownership Structure." *Journal of Financial Economics,* vol. 3, no. 4:305–360.

Jensen, M., and R.S. Ruback. 1983. "The Market for Corporate Control: The Scientific Evidence." *Journal of Financial Economics,* vol. 11, no. 1:5–50.

Jensen, M., and J. Zimmerman. 1985. "Management Compensation and the Managerial Labor Market." *Journal of Accounting and Economics,* vol. 7, no. 1/3: 3–9.

Jensen, M., and K. Murphy. 1990. "Performance Pay and Top-Management Incentives." *Journal of Political Economy,* vol. 98, no. 2:225–264.

John, T., and K. John. 1993. "Top-Management Compensation and Capital Structure." *The Journal of Finance,* vol. 48, no. 3:949–974.

Kamma, S., J. Weintrop, and P. Wier. 1988. "Investors' Perceptions of the Delaware Supreme Court Decision in Unocal v. Mesa." *Journal of Financial Economics,* vol. 20, no. 1/2:419–430.

Kang, J.K. 1993. "The International Market for Corporate Control: Mergers and Acquisitions of U.S. Firms by Japanese Firms." *Journal of Financial Economics,* vol. 34, no. 3:345–372.

Kang, J., and A. Shivdasani. 1995. "Firm Performance, Corporate Governance, and Top Executive Turnover in Japan." *Journal of Financial Economics,* vol. 38, no. 1:29–58.

Kaplan, S., and J. Stein. 1990. "How Risky Is the Debt in Highly Leveraged Transactions?" *Journal of Financial Economics,* vol. 27, no. 1:215–245.

Kaplan, S., and B. Minton. 1994. "Appointments of Outsiders to Japanese Boards: Determinants and Implications for Managers." *Journal of Financial Economics,* vol. 36, no. 3:225–258.

Kempf, K., N. Arshadi, and T. Eyssell. 1992. "It Is Insider Trading, But the Offenders Are Really Outsiders." *Journal of Crime and Justice,* vol. 15, no. 2:111–138.

Keown, A., and J. Pinkerton. 1981. "Merger Announcements and Insider Trading Activity: An Empirical Investigation." *Journal of Finance,* vol. 36, no. 4:855–869.

Klein, B. 1980. "Transaction Cost Determinants of 'Unfair' Contractual Arrangements." *American Economic Review, Papers and Proceedings,* vol. 70, no. 2:356–362.

Klein, A., and J. Rosenfeld. 1988. "The Impact of Targeted Share Repurchases on the Wealth of Nonparticipating Shareholders." *Journal of Financial Research,* vol. 11, no. 2:89–97.

Kummer, D., N. Arshadi, and E. Lawrence. 1989. "Incentive Problems in Bank Insider Borrowing." *Journal of Financial Services Research,* vol. 3, no. 1:17–31.

Lang, L., R. Stulz, and R. Walkling. 1989. "Managerial Performance, Tobin's Q, and the Gains from Successful Tender Offers." *Journal of Financial Economics,* vol. 24, no. 1:137–154.

Lee, D. 1992. "Management Buyout Proposals and Inside Information." *Journal of Finance,* vol. 47, no. 3:1061–1079.

Lewellen, W., C. Loderer, and A. Rosenfeld. 1985. "Merger Decisions and Executive Stock Ownership in Acquiring Firms." *Journal of Accounting and Economics,* vol. 7, no. 1/3:209–231.

Lichtenberg, F., and D. Siegel. 1990. "The Effects of Leveraged Buyouts on Productivity and Related Aspects of Firm Behavior." *Journal of Financial Economics,* vol. 27, no. 1:165–194.

Linn, S., and J. McConnell. 1983. "An Empirical Investigation of the Impact of Antitakeover Amendments on Common Stock Prices." *Journal of Financial Economics,* vol. 11, no. 1:361–399.

Magenheim, E., and D. Mueller. 1988. "Are Acquiring Firm Shareholders Better Off After an Acquisition?" in *Corporate Takeovers: Causes and Consequences,* A. Auerbach, ed. Chicago, IL: University of Chicago Press, pp. 171–193.

Malatesta, P., and R. Walkling. 1988. "Poison Pill Securities: Stockholder Wealth, Profitability and Ownership Structure." *Journal of Financial Economics,* vol. 20, no. 1/2:347–376.

Malatesta, P., and R. Thompson. 1993. "Government Regulation and Structural Change in the Corporate Acquisitions Market: The Impact of the Williams Act." *Journal of Financial and Quantitative Analysis,* vol. 28, no. 3:363–379.

Manne, H. 1965. "Mergers and the Market for Corporate Control." *Journal of Political Economy,* vol. 73, no. 1:110–120.

Manne, H. 1966. *Insider Trading and the Stock Market.* New York: Free Press.

Manne, H. 1967. "Our Two Corporation Systems: Law and Economics." *Virginia Law Review,* vol. 53, no. 1:259–285.

Martin, K. 1986. "Firm Performance and Managerial Discipline in Contests for Corporate Control." Unpublished manuscript, Purdue University.

Martin, K., and J. McConnell. 1991. "Corporate Performance, Corporate Takeovers, and Management Turnover." *Journal of Finance,* vol. 46, no. 2:671–687.

McConnell, J., and C. Muscarella. 1985. "Corporate Capital Expenditure Decisions and the Market Value of the Firm." *Journal of Financial Economics,* vol. 14, no. 3:399–422.

Mayers, D., and C. Smith. 1981. "Contractual Provisions, Organizational Structure, and Conflict Control in Insurance Markets." *Journal of Business,* vol. 54, no. 3:407–434.

Mayers, D., and C. Smith. 1987. "Corporate Insurance and the Underinvestment Problem." *Journal of Risk and Insurance,* vol. 54, no. 1:45–54.

Michel, M., and I. Shaked. 1986. *Takeover Madness*. New York: John Wiley and Sons.

Mitchell, M., and K. Lehn. 1990. "Do Bad Bidders Become Good Targets? *Journal of Political Economy*, vol. 98, no. 1:75–90.

Morck, R., A. Shleifer, and R. Vishny. 1988. "Management Ownership and Market Valuation." *Journal of Financial Economics*, vol. 20, no. 1/2:293–315.

Morck, R., A. Shleifer, and R. Vishny. 1990. "Do Managerial Objectives Drive Bad Acquisitions?" *Journal of Finance*, vol. 45, no. 1:31–48.

Nathan, K., and T. O'Keefe. 1989. "The Rise in Takeover Premiums." *Journal of Financial Economics*, vol. 23, no. 1:101–119.

Ofek, E. 1994. "Efficiency Gains in Unsuccessful Management Buyouts." *Journal of Finance*, vol. 49, no. 2:637–654.

Palepu, K. 1990. "Consequences of Leveraged Buyouts." *Journal of Financial Economics*, vol. 27, no. 1:247–262.

Pound, J. 1987. "The Effects of Antitakeover Amendments on Takeover Activity: Some Direct Evidence." *Journal of Law and Economics*, vol. 30, no. 2:353–367.

Pratt, S., and C. DeVere. 1978. "Relationship Between Insider Trading and Rates of Return for NYSE Common Stocks, 1960–66." in *Modern Developments in Investment Management*, J. Lorie and R. Brealey, eds. Hinsdale, IL: Dryden Press, pp. 259–272.

Prentice, R. 1987. *Law of Business Organizations and Securities Regulation*. Englewood Cliffs, NJ: Prentice-Hall, Inc.

Ratner, D. 1988. *Securities Regulation*. St. Paul, Minnesota: West Publishing Company.

Roll, R. 1986. "The Hubris Hypothesis of Corporate Takeovers." *Journal of Business*, vol. 59, no. 2:197–216.

Rozeff, M., and M. Zaman. 1988. "Market Efficiency and Insider Trading: New Evidence." *Journal of Business*, vol. 61, no. 1:25–44.

Ryngaert, M. 1988. "The Effect of Poison Pill Securities on Shareholder Wealth." *Journal of Financial Economics*, vol. 20, no. 1/2:237–266.

Ryngaert, M., and J. Netter. 1987. "Shareholder Wealth Effects of the Ohio Anti-Takeover Law." Unpublished manuscript.

Securities and Exchange Commission, Office of the Chief Economist. 1985. "The Economics of Any-or-All, Partial, and Two-Tier Tender Offers." Washington, DC.

Servaes, H. 1991. "Tobin's Q and the Gains from Takeovers." *Journal of Finance*, vol. 46, no. 1:409–419.

Seyhun, H. 1986. "Insiders' Profits, Costs of Trading, and Market Efficiency." *Journal of Financial Economics*, vol. 16, no. 2:189–212.

Shleifer, A., and L.H. Summers. 1988. "Breach of Trust in Hostile Takeovers." in *Corporate Takeovers: Causes and Consequences*, A. Auerbach, ed. Chicago, IL: University of Chicago Press, pp. 33–68.

Shleifer, A., and R. Vishny. 1986. "Large Shareholders and Corporate Control." *Journal of Political Economy*, vol. 94, no. 3:461–488.

Shleifer, A., and R. Vishny. 1989. "Managerial Entrenchment: The Case of Manager-Specific Investments." *Journal of Financial Economics*, vol. 25, no. 1:123–139.

Slovin, M., and M. Sushka. 1993. "Ownership Concentration, Corporate Control Activity, and Firm Value: Evidence from the Death of Inside Blockholders." *Journal of Finance*, vol. 48, no. 4:1293–1321.

Smiley, R. 1975. "The Effect of the Williams Act Amendment and Other Factors on Transactions Costs in Tender Offers." *Industrial Organization Review*, vol. 3, no. 2:138–145.

Smiley, R. 1976. "Tender Offers, Transactions Costs and the Theory of the Firm." *Review of Economics and Statistics*, vol. 58, no. 1:22–32.

Smiley, R. 1981. "The Effect of State Securities Statutes on Tender Offer Activity," *Economic Inquiry*, vol. 19, no. 3:426–435.

Smith, A. 1990. "Corporate Ownership's Structure and Performance: The Case of Management Buyouts." *Journal of Financial Economics*, vol. 27, no. 1:143–164.

Swenson, D. 1993. "Foreign Mergers and Acquisitions in the United States." in *Foreign Direct Investment*, K.A. Froot, ed. Chicago IL: University of Chicago Press, pp. 255–286.

Szewczyk, S., and G. Tsetsekos. 1992. "State Intervention in the Market for Corporate Control: The Case of Pennsylvania Senate Bill 1310." *Journal of Financial Economics*, vol. 31, no. 1:3–23.

Walkling, R., and M. Long. 1984. "Agency Theory, Managerial Welfare, and Takeover Bid Resistance." *Rand Journal of Economics*, vol. 15, no. 1:54–68.

Walsh, J. 1988. "Top Management Turnover Following Mergers and Acquisitions." *Strategic Management Journal*, vol. 9, no. 3:173–183.

Warner, J., R. Watts, and K. Wruck. 1988. "Stock Prices and Top Management Changes." *Journal of Financial Economics*, vol. 20, no. 1:461–492.

Weisbach, M. 1988. "Outside Directors and CEO Turnover." *Journal of Financial Economics*, vol. 20, no. 1:431–460.

Weisbach, M. 1995. "CEO Turnover and the Firm's Investment Decisions." *Journal of Financial Economics*, vol. 37, no. 1:159–188.

C H A P T E R

15

Derivatives and the Management of Financial Risk

OBJECTIVES

This chapter examines the expansion of financial risk in the past two decades and presents financial derivatives as a means of hedging and redistributing risk. In the 1970s, three events significantly increased financial risk. First, the 1973 dismantling of the Bretton Woods Agreement, which had held foreign exchange rates stable for three decades, resulted in a significant increase in volatility of the exchange rate. Second, the 1974 oil embargo by the Organization of Petroleum Exporting Countries (OPEC) increased commodities prices and their volatility. And third, the 1979 shift in Fed policy from controlling interest rates to monitoring money supply increased the level and volatility of interest rates. In response to the increased volatility, derivatives products such as forwards, futures, swaps, and options were introduced to hedge against currency, interest-rate, and commodities price risks. Futures and options are primarily exchange-traded instruments, whereas forwards and swaps are generally customized, over-the-counter (OTC) products designed by financial intermediaries. This chapter examines the economic rationale for using derivatives and provides supporting data for the growth in their use. In addition, this chapter describes the characteristics of the major dealers in the derivatives market, including money-center banks, securities firms, and insurance companies. As the largely unregulated OTC derivatives market has expanded, major derivatives-related blowups have occurred, creating legal battles between dealers and end-users. A critical review of some of the best-known cases, including Barings, Orange County, and others, provides useful insights into the causes of the losses and ways to improve the derivatives market. The chapter concludes with an appendix, which reviews a set of recommendations for good industry practices. These recommendations were made by the Group of Thirty, a diverse cross-section of end-users, dealers, academics, accountants, and lawyers involved in derivatives.

THE EXPANSION OF FINANCIAL RISK SINCE THE 1970s

Foreign Exchange Risk

The first major change in the structure of financial risk in recent years occurred in 1973 when the Bretton Woods Agreement, which had provided a system of fixed exchange rates, was dismantled. The three-decade-old agreement had linked the values of all currencies to the dollar, and the value of the dollar to gold. This system of fixed exchange rates was established in July 1944 in Bretton Woods, New Hampshire, by 44 countries. The impetus for the agreement came from an interpretation of the reasons for the rise of the Nazi party in Germany and the factors that had led to the war. During the 1920s and early 1930s, the German economy experienced severe hyperinflation with an inflation rate exceeding 50% a month. The situation was further aggravated by successive changes in exchange rates in the 1931–1936 period when countries such as the U.K. and France devalued their currencies to increase their exports and employment at the expense of the exports and employment of their trading partners. During this period, Germany faced severe economic downturn, high unemployment, and general social decay. These conditions bolstered the rise of the Nazis, who promised economic prosperity, law and order, and the restoration of national pride.[1]

The United States emerged from WWII with its economy relatively unscathed. With the cooperation of its allies, the United States launched a series of economic plans for the postwar period. At the heart of these plans was the establishment of three multinational institutions: the International Monetary Fund (IMF), to deal with exchange rates and international payments; the International Bank for Reconstruction and Development (World Bank), to provide financing for the postwar reconstruction; and the International Trade Organization, now known as the World Trade Organization, to reduce tariffs and trade barriers, which led to the General Agreement on Tariffs and Trade (GATT).

In 1944, the Bretton Woods Agreement was initiated by the IMF following a U.S. proposal to establish a pool of national currencies from which member countries with payment deficits could borrow. A country with a balance-of-payment deficit could borrow from the pool instead of following the prewar practice of devaluing its currency. Each member country was obliged to set an exchange rate between its currency and the U.S. dollar and to prevent any deviation from this parity of more than one-quarter of 1% in its domestic spot exchange market. The foreign exchange value of each member's currency could only change through strict guidelines established by the IMF, which required evidence of fundamental economic disequilibrium. The Bretton Woods Agreement effectively established a system of stable exchange rates.

The fixed exchange rate system functioned well as long as inflation rates in the economies of the member countries remained relatively stable. As the United States entered into various conflicts, first in Korea at the end of 1950s and then in Vietnam in the 1960s, the financing of war brought inflation into the economy. Other countries had their conflicts, too. In the 1960s, France became deeply involved in the Algerian civil war and Israel engaged in war with several Arab countries. Since wars are generally inflationary, warring countries experienced declines in the purchasing power of their currencies. This in turn made retaining fixed exchange rates difficult. In November 1967, the U.K. devalued the pound.

---

[1] For an excellent description of the economic and social chaos in pre–WWII Germany see *Berlin Alexanderplatz* by Alfred Döblin (1961). Rainer Werner Fassbinder, the late German film director, adapted the book into an impressive 15-hour film of the same title.

TABLE 15.1	National Currency Indexes and Their Values Relative to the Dollar			
	Exchange Rate (1990 Index = 100)		Currency Units per $	
Country	April 1994	April 1995	April 1994	April 1995
Australia	87.0	77.3	1.39	1.37
Austria	103.3	108.5	11.80	9.60
Belgium	104.3	110.9	34.60	28.10
Britain	89.7	84.1	0.67	0.62
Canada	84.3	82.5	1.38	1.37
Denmark	104.1	110.8	6.60	5.38
France	104.3	109.9	5.77	4.82
Germany	105.1	114.1	1.68	1.37
Holland	103.8	110.9	1.89	1.53
Italy	79.2	64.4	1,611	1,686
Japan	147.8	174.7	103.0	81.6
Spain	81.1	79.6	137.0	122.0
Sweden	82.2	75.8	7.85	7.35
Switzerland	103.7	114.8	1.43	1.13
United States	99.3	86.8	—	—

Source: *The Economist*, April 29, 1995, p. 123.

In the United States, inflationary pressures increased the demand to convert dollars to gold. In April 1970, Canada allowed its dollar to float. A year later, Germany and the Netherlands also freed their currencies from the fixed exchange rate system. In August 1971, the U.S. Treasury stopped selling gold to official institutions at $35 per ounce. Later in the same year, the currencies of most industrial countries were revalued by 12%, that of the United States was devalued by 12%, and the price of gold was increased to $38 per ounce. The new exchange rates, however, did not last very long. Early in 1973, West Germany ceased pegging the deutschemark to the dollar and other industrial countries followed suit. This was the beginning of the move toward floating exchange rates.

Since the first quarter of 1973, when exchange rates were allowed to float, the values of all currencies in general and that of the dollar in particular have experienced large and abrupt movements. Table 15.1 presents national currency indexes and their values relative to the dollar. There are two major points apparent in this table. First, in the absence of a fixed exchange rate system, movements in exchange rates have been abrupt and large. Second, the volatility of movements in the foreign exchange value of the U.S. dollar has been large. Using an index value of 100 for 1990, all currencies listed in the table show significant movements in the foreign exchange values of their currencies. The Japanese yen had the largest appreciation in value, while Italy experienced the largest depreciation in value. Within a 12-month period, the dollar declined in value from 99.3 in 1994 to 86.8 in 1995. Considering the fact that during the same 12-month period the rate of inflation was about 3% in the United States and around 2% in Germany, it is clear that the changes in exchange rates are considerably larger than the differences in the changes in national price levels. The volatility of exchange rates can no longer be fully explained by differences in the inflation rates of national economies. Furthermore, there is little evidence that changes in exchange rates are due to intervention by the central banks of various countries.

Despite rapid changes in exchange rates, world trade has grown significantly in recent years, necessitating strategies to limit the foreign exchange risk exposure of those involved in international trade and investment. For example, in the first three months of 1995, the value of the dollar declined by 20% against the Japanese yen and 17.5% against the deutschemark. Salomon Brothers forecast that every 10% rise in the yen and in the deutschemark against the dollar would reduce the profits of car makers in Japan and Germany in the following year by 42% and 30%, respectively.[2]

Commodities Price Risk

Commodities price represents a second source of financial risk that was aggravated by the events of the 1970s. In 1974, following an embargo, OPEC successfully increased the price of oil from about $12 a barrel to about $28. Industrialized nations that relied heavily on oil for a wide range of products experienced a significant increase in the price of raw material. It is estimated that the 1974 oil price increase contributed to inflation in industrialized countries by 2% to 3%. The ability of OPEC to dictate new and significantly higher prices created uncertainty in the oil market. Individual members of OPEC also pursued different national policies and often did not hesitate to use oil as a political weapon in an effort to influence the policies of industrialized nations. The result was increased volatility in commodities prices.

The sharp increase in the price of oil resulted in a substantial payment surplus for oil-producing countries. The increased cash inflows were partially used to increase imports from industrialized countries. The remaining funds, which approached $200 billion from 1974 to 1982, were deposited in the major international banks. The non-oil-producing countries were faced with higher prices in imported goods and larger balance-of-payment deficits. International banks with large amounts of petrodollar deposits were ready to make loans to the developing countries that needed the funds to pay for the higher prices of their imports. Loans to developing countries increased from $120 billion in 1972 to $850 billion in 1982. Banks had severely underestimated the risk in lending to countries whose external debt was larger than their export earnings.[3] Since the debtor countries were unable to service their debt, banks had to write off significant portions of these loans by the end of the 1980s.

Interest Rate Risk

The third source of financial risk is interest rate risk. While persistent and volatile inflation in the U.S. economy was an important cause of the breakdown of the Bretton Woods Agreement, the post–Bretton Woods period in the mid-1970s is characterized by surprisingly stable interest rates. Toward the end of the 1970s, however, high levels of inflation caused interest rates to increase to record levels. During this period, the Federal Reserve Board attempted to control inflation by targeting short-term interest rates. The Fed policy involved purchasing large quantities of U.S. Treasury securities to increase their prices and to reduce interest rates.

The policy of targeting short-term interest rates in order to affect long-term interest rates proved to be futile. By late 1970s, the U.S. economy was faced with double-digit inflation. On October 6, 1979, shortly after being appointed as the Chairman of the Federal Reserve Board, Paul Volcker abandoned the Fed prac-

---

[2] *The Economist*, April 15, 1995, p. 67.
[3] The frenzy to lend to developing countries during the late '70s was due to the mistaken notion that sovereigns do not default!

tice of targeting interest rates and began to target money supply in the conduct of monetary policy. Upon the announcement of the new policy, interest rates increased substantially and became very volatile. One of the early victims of this increased interest-rate risk was the savings and loan industry. Accustomed to the practice of borrowing short term and lending long term, the industry suffered tremendously when the prices of its long-term assets declined more than the value of its short-term liabilities, forcing one-third of the institutions into insolvency.

The increased volatility of interest rates, foreign exchange rates, and commodities prices contributes to financial risk not only individually, but also as a group. In fact, these three factors are very much interrelated.

THE LINK BETWEEN INTEREST RATES, FOREIGN EXCHANGE RATES, AND COMMODITIES PRICES

As depicted in Figure 15.1, the three elements of financial risk are interrelated. The relationship between interest rates and commodities prices is referred to as the *Fisher Effect.* Prices of commodities are determined by supply and demand. Holding supply and demand for commodities constant, prices should remain constant unless there is inflation in the economy. Changes in price levels depend on the difference between the rate of growth in real output and the growth in the money supply. As economic output increases, there is a need for additional liquidity to keep prices constant. If the increase in the supply of money is greater than the increase in the level of output, prices will increase. Conversely, if the increase in money supply is less than the increase in the level of output, prices will decline. Inflation is caused by an excessive increase in money supply.

As inflation affects price levels, it also affects interest rates. Interest rates have two components. First, the real rate is paid to the holders of loanable funds to induce them to postpone their consumption for one period. The second component is an adjustment for price-level changes or the rate of inflation. If prices do not change (no inflation), interest rates will include only the real rates. But if prices are expected to increase (because of an excessive supply of money), lenders will expect to be compensated for inflation in order to protect their expected real returns. A change in interest rates is therefore equal to the percentage change in expected price levels, which in turn equals the increase in money supply that is in excess of the increase in the level of output.

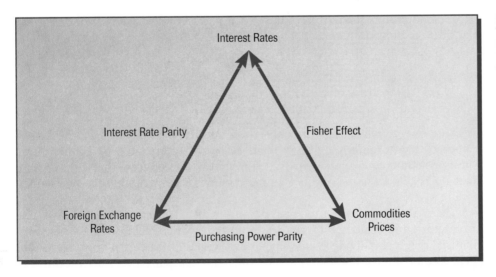

FIGURE 15.1
The Link Between Interest Rates, Foreign Exchange Rates, and Commodities Prices

The relationship between commodities prices and exchange rates is usually characterized by the **purchasing power parity (PPP) theorem.** The theory of PPP holds that changes in exchange rates parallel changes in relative price levels in the two countries. A simple example will illustrate the substance of the PPP argument. Suppose that the current price of an identical bundle of commodities is $P_\$$ in the United States and P_{FF} in France. In addition, suppose the spot exchange rate between the two currencies is S. According to PPP the following relationship should hold:

$$P_\$ \times S = P_{FF}$$

If the cost of the bundle of commodities is cheaper in the United States ($P_\$ \times S < P_{FF}$), French buyers will have an incentive to buy U.S. dollars and import U.S. commodities instead of buying them in France. This will bid up the price of commodities in the United States, bid up the spot exchange rate, and bid down the price of commodities in France, eventually restoring equality of the price in the two countries:

$$\uparrow P_\$ \times \uparrow S = \downarrow P_{FF}$$

The law of one price holds only if we can exclude the costs of transportation, tariffs, and other expenses that may cause prices to vary in the two countries.

The relationship between interest rates and exchange rates is referred to as **interest rate parity.** Suppose that the interest rate in the Eurocurrency market for a six-month dollar is 6%, while for a six-month deutschemark it is 4%. In addition, assume that the spot rate for the two currencies is $1 = DM1.50. According to the interest-rate-parity argument, the following relationship holds:

$$(1 + r_{DM})/(1 + r_\$) = F/S$$

where $r_\$$ and r_{DM} represent interest rates in U.S. dollars and German marks and F and S represent forward and spot exchange rates between the two currencies. In our example, the forward exchange rate should be

$$(1 + 0.04 \times 0.5)/(1 + 0.06 \times 0.5) = F/1.5 \text{ and } F = 1.4854$$

If the expected spot exchange rate in six months is higher than 1.4854, there will be an incentive for German investors to lend dollars rather than marks. As the investors sell marks and buy dollars, the spot exchange rate will be bid down (more marks required to buy one dollar).

The three sets of relationships described here suggest that change in the volatility of each source of financial risk is expected to affect the volatility of the other two sources of risk as well. Consequently, increased volatility in exchange rates, commodities prices, and interest rates affects total risk both individually and through their contagion effects on one another.

THE DEVELOPMENT AND EXPANSION OF DERIVATIVES IN RESPONSE TO INCREASED FINANCIAL RISK

Derivatives are financial instruments whose returns are derived from the performance of some underlying asset such as bonds, currencies, or commodities. These instruments are vehicles for redistributing already existing risk. Derivatives do not increase risk in the economy; rather, they reallocate the risk among willing parties.

There are three groups of participants in the derivatives market: hedgers, speculators, and arbitrageurs. **Hedgers** are parties who shield themselves against financial risk by taking derivatives positions with offsetting cash flows relative to their core positions. For example, an American company that sells products in

Britain expects to receive 5 million pounds every six months from its distributors. The company is concerned about the volatility of pound/dollar exchange rate. In order to hedge, the company enters into a currency futures position that requires it to pay 5 million pounds every six months in exchange for a prespecified dollar amount. If the pound depreciates against the dollar, the company will lose in its core position but will gain in its derivative position. Conversely, if the pound appreciates against the dollar, the company will gain in its core position but will lose in its derivative position. The hedging strategy can eliminate the risk exposure by locking the company into a fixed exchange rate at the present. In general, a party that has a long pound-based asset position will take a short pound-based derivatives position to hedge against unwanted exchange-rate risk.

Speculators are parties who take positions in derivatives without having offsetting core positions, betting that the underlying risk in derivatives will have positive payoffs. Speculators often get in and out of a position in a relatively short period of time, and, in the process, they increase the liquidity of the market. For example, in the CBOT's futures floor, speculators trade with one another and with hedgers.

Arbitrageurs are parties who buy and sell the same derivatives instruments in two different markets if there are sufficient price differentials to cover the transaction costs and to earn a small profit. Arbitrageurs help to bring together prices of the same instruments in different markets.

The basic building blocks of derivatives are forwards, futures, swaps, and options. These instruments will be examined in detail in the next three chapters. Here, we provide a brief review of these instruments in Table 15.2, which includes the markets in which they trade, their definitions, and examples of their usage. Futures and options are primarily exchange-traded instruments where market participants deal with the clearinghouses of the exchanges. Exchange-traded instruments are standardized contracts with relatively few available choices in order to create sufficiently large demand and thus the liquidity needed in this market. Forwards and swaps are over-the-counter (OTC) instruments that are designed by financial intermediaries to the exact specifications required by the clients.

All four instruments can be used to hedge against each of the three categories of risk. The decision about which instrument or combination of instruments should be used depends on the risk configuration in each case and the transaction costs involved. While exchange-traded instruments generally have lower transaction costs and greater liquidity, their standardized features may not provide a sufficient hedge against the underlying risk. OTC instruments, on the other hand, can be designed to the exact specifications of the underlying asset risk, but are generally more costly and less liquid.

In recent years, corporations, state and local governments, and retirement funds have increased their use of derivatives to manage their own increasing risk. Tables 15.3 and 15.4 present the notional[4] amounts of derivatives held in 1989–1992 by asset types and product groups. Between 1989 and 1992, the notional amount of derivatives increased by 145%, reaching $17.6 trillion in 1992. Interest-rate instruments constituted the largest percentage of derivatives held in 1992 at 62%, and foreign exchange instruments ranked second with 37%. Commodities and equity instruments accounted for only 1% of the total volume of derivatives. In terms of product types, forwards had the largest share with 42%, swaps ranked second with 27%, and futures and options held third and fourth place with 18% and 13%.

---

[4] The word notional is used instead of principal because this amount usually does not change hands.

TABLE 15.2   The Four Major Types of Derivatives

Derivatives	Market	Definition	Example
Forwards	OTC markets for custom-ized contracts	Forwards and futures obligate the holder to buy or sell a specific amount or value of an under-lying asset, reference rate, or index at a specified price on a specified future date.	A U.S. importer promises to buy ma-chinery at a future date for a price quoted in German currency. The importer can use a forward con-tract—or a futures contract, if one is available that meets the firm's needs—to fix the dollar cost of con-verting to German currency at that future date. Thus, the importer avoids a loss if the dollar cost of German currency increases between the purchase and delivery dates.
Futures	Organized exchanges, standardized contracts.	The same	The same
Options	OTC and exchanges	Options contracts grant their pur-chasers the right but not the obligation to buy or sell a spe-cific amount of the underlying asset at a particular price within a specified period.	A mutual fund buys an option on a given amount of Treasury bills. The fund will benefit if the price of the Treasury bills moves in a favorable direction. If the price moves in an unfavorable direction, the fund will not recover the option's price.

| Swaps | OTC | Swaps are agreements between counterparties to make periodic payments to each other for a specified period. In a simple interest rate swap, one party makes payments based on a fixed interest rate, while the counterparty makes payments based on a variable rate. The contractual payments are based on a notional amount that for interest-rate swaps is never actually exchanged. | A bank has a portfolio of loans whose floating rates must be adjusted frequently because they are tied to changes in market interest rates. The bank also has deposits that pay customers at rates that are adjusted infrequently. This bank has interest-rate risk, because a decline in interest rates reduces the interest receipts on its loans but not the interest payments the bank must pay depositors. The bank may enter into an interest-rate swap with another financial institution to hedge the risk. |

Source: United States General Accounting Office, *Financial Derivatives: Actions Needed to Protect the Financial System,* May 1994, p. 5.

TABLE 15.3	Notional Amounts of Derivatives Held by Type of Underlying Assets, 1989–1992 ($ Billions)					
Type of Underlying	1989	1990	1991	1992	% of 1992	% Increase, 1989–1992
Interest Rate	$4,311	$6,087	$8,404	$10,923	62%	153%
Foreign Exchange Rate	2,779	3,927	5,415	6,475	37	133
Equity/Commodity Price	108	158	209	245	1	127
Total	$7,198	$10,172	$14,028	$17,643	100%	145%

Source: BIS, ISDA, Federal Reserve Bank of New York, Swaps Monitor Publications, Inc., Derivatives Strategy & Tactics, Inc., and GAO.

In the following three sections, we provide examples of derivative instruments available to hedge against exchange rate, interest-rate, and commodities price risks. The basic instruments—forwards, futures, swaps, and options—were defined in Chapter 5. More complex versions of these instruments will be briefly introduced here and their detailed descriptions will be provided in Chapters 16–18.

Derivatives Products for Exchange Rate Risk

Derivatives based on foreign currencies first appeared in May 1972 with the introduction of futures contracts on the British pound, Canadian dollar, deutschemark, Japanese yen, and Swiss franc by the International Monetary Market of the Chicago Mercantile Exchange (CME). In December 1982, options contracts on foreign currencies were offered for the first time by the Philadelphia Stock Exchange on the British pound. This was followed by options on the Canadian dollar, deutschemark, Japanese yen, and Swiss franc in January and February 1983. The CME also offered options on foreign currencies, including the deutschemark (January 1984), British pound and Swiss franc (February 1985), Japanese yen (March 1986), and Canadian dollar (June 1986).

OTC derivatives on foreign currencies were initiated with the introduction of World Bank-IBM swaps in August 1981. Next came bank OTC products includ-

TABLE 15.4	Notional Amounts of Derivatives Held by Product Type, 1989–1992 ($ Billions)					
Type of Product	1989	1990	1991	% of 1992	1992	% Increase, 1989–1992
Forwards	$3,034	$4,437	$6,061	$7,515	42%	148%
Futures	1,259	1,540	2,254	3,154	18	151
Options	953	1,305	1,841	2,263	13	137
Swaps	1,952	2,890	3,872	4,711	27	141
Total	$7,198	$10,172	$14,028	$17,643	100%	145%

Source: BIS, ISDA, Federal Reserve Bank of New York, Swaps Monitor Publications, Inc., Derivatives Strategy & Tactics, Inc., and GAO.

TABLE 15.5	Chronology of the Exchange-Traded Interest-Rate Derivatives		
	Date of the Offer	**Underlying Asset**	**Exchange**
Futures:	October 1975	GNMA	CBOT
	January 1976	T-Bills	CME
	August 1977	T-Bonds	CBOT
	December 1981	Eurodollars	CME
	May 1982	T-Notes	CBOT
Options:	October 1982	T-Bond Futures	CBOT
	October 1982	T-Bonds	CBOE
	March 1985	Eurodollar Futures	CME
	May 1985	T-Note Futures	CBOT
	July 1985	T-Notes	CBOE
	April 1986	T-Bill Futures	CME

ing foreign exchange options, forwards, and forwards with optionlike characteristics.

Derivatives Products for Interest Rate Risk

The 1979 shift in monetary policy by the Fed increased the volatility of interest
rates. In response to increased interest rate risk, the Chicago Board of Trade
(CBOT) and the Chicago Mercantile Exchange (CME) offered the interest rate futures and options depicted in Table 15.5.

In the early 1980s, banks followed the lead of the organized exchanges and
offered OTC interest rate derivatives, customized according to client specifications. Banks offered fixed-to-floating interest rate swaps in 1982, forward contracts on interest rates or forward-rate agreements (FRAs) in 1983, and OTC options including caps, floors, and collars, also in 1983. A cap is an upper limit and
a floor is a lower limit on interest rates. A collar is a combination of a cap and a
floor whereby a borrower receives protection against interest-rate increases by
giving up the benefits of interest rate decreases. Other complex derivatives were
offered in the form of swaptions (options on swaps), captions (options on interest-rate caps), futures on interest rate swaps, and diff swaps (swaps on the differences between two interest rates). Hybrid securities were also offered in the form
of debt securities combined with derivatives such as putable bonds in 1976,
extendable bonds in 1982, convertible floating-rate notes in 1985, and inverse
floating-rate notes in 1986.

Derivatives Products for Commodities Price Risk

The increase in the price and volatility of oil prices in the mid-1970s was
followed by the introduction of heating oil futures by the New York Mercantile
Exchange (NYMEX) in November 1978, and West Texas Intermediate (WTI)
crude oil futures in March 1983. Options on WTI crude oil futures were offered in
November 1986, and options on heating oil futures were introduced in June 1987.

Commodities OTC derivatives products began with the introduction of bank
oil swaps in 1986. In 1987, the Commodity Futures Trading Commission (CFTC)
effectively blocked bank swap trades in the United States, causing the market to
move abroad. In 1993, the CFTC issued new rules allowing bank activities in the
development of new products.

DETERMINANTS OF DEMAND FOR DERIVATIVES BY PUBLICLY HELD CORPORATIONS

Corporate finance literature suggests that stockholders in publicly traded corporations receive returns proportionate to the market risk of their holdings. Accordingly, rational stockholders are advised to diversify their portfolios in order to eliminate the unique or firm-specific risks of their stocks. A fully diversified portfolio, the argument goes, is indifferent to the unique risk of individual stocks and is only susceptible to market risk.

Financial risk-hedging generally involves efforts to reduce or eliminate the unique risk of individual companies. Since hedging is costly, why should stockholders go along with the management of corporations in reducing the unique risk that they can so easily eliminate in their portfolios by means of diversification? Stated differently, is risk-hedging an optimal strategy for a publicly held corporation? The answer lies with the assumptions we make about the capital market. In a perfect capital market where firms pay no taxes and face no incentive problems among stockholders, bondholders, and management, there is indeed no need for financial risk-hedging. However, the real world is plagued with these frictions. In the following sections, we will demonstrate how the implementation of risk-hedging strategies can increase the value of the firm by reducing its tax liabilities and alleviating its agency problems.

Financial Risk-Hedging Reduces Corporate Taxes

Although U.S. corporations are currently subject to a virtual flat tax schedule, when tax loss carries forwards, investment tax credits, and the alternate minimum tax provisions are considered, most firms face an effective tax function that is convex. With a convex tax function, the effective tax rate is an increasing function of pretax income.

A firm without a risk-hedging strategy faces volatility in its pretax income. If the firm's tax function is convex, the expected tax liability of the firm is reduced by implementing a risk-hedging strategy that reduces the volatility of its pretax income. The reason for this proposition is simple. Without the hedge, in some periods the firm's income may be too low to take advantage of all its tax deductions. Consequently, the firm will lose some tax benefits. With a hedge, the firm reduces the volatility of its pretax income, diminishing the probability that deductions may not be used. A numerical example will demonstrate the tax advantage of hedging.

Suppose that a corporation without a risk-hedging strategy faces two possible outcomes with equal probabilities: It will earn a pretax income of either $200,000 or $1,000,000. In addition, assume that the firm faces a convex tax function where tax rates are 24% and 34% on income levels of $200,000 and $1,000,000, respectively. Accordingly, the firm's expected tax liability will be

Expected tax liability without a risk-hedging strategy = $1/2 \times 0.24 \times (\$200,000) +$
$$1/2 \times 0.34 \times (\$1,000,000) = \$194,000$$

Alternatively, the firm may implement a risk-hedging strategy that promises a certain pretax income of $600,000 ($1/2 \times \$200,000 + 1/2 \times \$1,000,000$). Assume that the convex tax function produces a 29% tax rate for $600,000 of pretax income. Under this scenario, the expected tax liability amounts to

Tax liability with a risk-hedging strategy = $\$600,000 \times .29 = \$174,000$

In this example, the value of the firm is increased by $20,000 ($194,000 − $174,000) a year due to a lower tax liability.

In Chapter 2 we discussed incentive conflicts between stockholders and bond-holders, including risk incentives, investment incentives, and bankruptcy dis-putes. To the extent that these conflicts are left unmitigated, the resulting agency costs will reduce the value of the firm. Any strategy that reduces or eliminates these conflicts will increase the value of the firm. In this section, we will demon-strate how implementing a risk-hedging strategy can reduce conflicts of interest between stockholders and bondholders and increase the value of the firm.

The risk incentive problem exists when stockholders and their agents, the managers, can replace existing assets with riskier projects. As assets become riskier, bond prices decline due to the increased default risk, while stock prices increase. This potential transfer of wealth from bondholders to stockholders causes investors to discount the price they are willing to pay for the bond. This price discount is the agency cost of the risk incentive problem. If the firm em-ploys a risk-hedging strategy to reduce the volatility of its cash flows, the risk in-centive problem will be greatly diminished, causing the value of the firm to in-crease. A numerical example will demonstrate the substance of this argument.

Suppose that today a firm issues $500 of debt securities to mature in three years and $500 of equity securities. The firm invests $1,000 in assets for two years. At the end of one year, assume that the firm faces some losses and is left with assets with a total expected value of $600 ($0.60 \times \$400 + 0.40 \times \$900$). At time two, the firm will collect one of the two possible asset returns, either $400 or $900. In either case, it has to invest in another set of assets to mature at the end of year three. If the time two value is $900, there is no incentive problem. However, if the asset value at time two is only $400, stockholders and their managers will have a risk incentive problem. With $400 to invest, suppose there are two proj-ects available: one project with $100 NPV with certainty, and another project with −$60 NPV ($0.20 \times \$500 + 0.80 \times -\$200$). Obviously, if there were no incentive problem, the first project would be chosen because it has a positive NPV of $100 instead of a negative NPV of −$60 with the second project. But if the first project is undertaken, at the end of the third year the asset value will be

$$\$400 + \$100 = \$500,$$

all of which will go to the bondholders. With the second project, however, there is a 20% chance that the NPV will be $500, bringing the assets to a total value of

$$\$400 + \$500 = \$900,$$

out of which $500 goes to bondholders and $400 is left for stockholders. There is, however, an 80% probability that the firm will have a negative NPV of −$200, which will bring total asset value to

$$\$400 - \$200 = \$200,$$

all going to the bondholders, who will lose

$$\$500 - \$200 = \$300$$

on their investment. With risk incentive problems, the stockholders have an in-centive to take on a negative NPV project if it has a sufficiently large risk, and forgo the smaller but certain returns of the project with positive NPV and no risk. The difference between $100 profit in the first project and a $60 loss in the second project is $160, which is the agency cost of the stockholder-bondholder risk in-centive problem. Of course, bondholders are aware of this opportunistic behav-ior and will accordingly discount the bond prices at the time of purchase. Enter a risk-hedging strategy: With a hedged portfolio, the firm will have at time two with certainty. Since the asset value is greater than the debt value, the equity holders will choose the positive NPV project with its certain $100 profit. At time three, the total asset value will be

$$\$600 + \$100 = \$700,$$

$500 of which will go to bondholders, with the remaining $200 going to stockholders.

The second agency problem between stockholders and bondholders involves an investment incentive problem. This problem generally arises in financially distressed firms where positive NPV projects are rejected because the expected profits will go to bondholders. To illustrate the problem, we will use the example presented for the risk incentive problem. We pick up the problem at time one when the firm is left with two assets with an expected value of

$$0.60 \times \$400 + 0.40 \times \$900 = \$600$$

to mature in time two. If the time two value is $400, and an investment with a positive NPV of $100 comes along, there will be no incentive for stockholders to invest because the $100 in profits plus the $400 will be paid to the bondholders, who have a $500 claim on the firm. However, if the firm implements a risk-hedging strategy in time one, which will guarantee a value of

$$0.60 \times \$400 + 0.40 \times \$900 = \$600$$

in time two, the asset value will be greater than the debt value, and stockholders will take advantage of the positive NPV project. In this case the value of the firm will increase by $100, the otherwise forgone profit.

The third agency problem between stockholders and bondholders involves bankruptcy disputes. When a firm is in financial distress, bondholders are concerned that stockholders may take self-serving actions including those described in the previous paragraphs as well as paying themselves liquidating dividends, further increasing losses to bondholders. As risk-hedging strategies align the interests of stockholders and bondholders, fewer disputes will end up in bankruptcy courts, avoiding that costly process.

A Look at the Derivative Activities of Corporations

In the previous section, we discussed the economic rationale for the use of derivatives by corporations. In this section, we provide information on the derivative activities of some of the largest corporations in the United States. In addition, we examine the credit standing of the users of derivatives. Finally, we provide the results of a survey of corporate derivative practices.

Table 15.6 presents derivative positions of the 10 largest U.S. industrial companies in 1993. Ford Motor Company, with $45 billion in notional amounts, is the largest user of derivatives, followed by GE and GM with $27 billion and $25 billion, respectively. The three oil companies on the list, Mobil, Exxon, and Texaco, show a relatively low use of derivatives, with less than $10 billion. The extent of derivative use depends on the kind of financial risk facing these companies. In the case of large automobile manufacturers, those with extensive foreign market activities such as GM and Ford are heavy users of derivatives. Chrysler, with a much smaller presence overseas, makes less use of derivatives at only $2 billion. The oil companies, while faced with some foreign exchange risk, are predominantly concerned with commodities price risk, which is a relatively small percentage of total derivatives products (see Table 15.3).

Opponents of the use of derivatives have implied that derivatives are highly risky instruments used by high-risk corporations. The next table rejects this

TABLE 15.6 Derivative Positions of the 10 Largest Industrial Companies in 1993	
Company	Notional Value ($ Billions)
General Motors	25.5
Ford Motor	45.1
Exxon	1.6
IBM	18.1
General Electric	27.0
Mobil	9.9
Philip Morris	1.4
Chrysler	2.3
Texaco	1.8
Du Pont	11.7

Source: The Swaps Monitor Handbook.

proposition. Table 15.7 presents the credit ratings of 200 companies with more than $1 billion in swaps outstanding. Investment-grade companies comprised 97.5% of this group, while speculative, unrated, and noninvestment-grade companies constituted only 2.5% of this group of corporate derivatives users.

A 1994 survey of corporate end-users in the derivatives market by the Group of Thirty provides interesting insights into industry practices. The results are summarized in Table 15.8. A questionnaire was mailed to 149 companies in 17 different countries. Out of 149 firms, 146 responded to the questionnaire. Hedging seems to be the most important reason for the use of derivatives followed by reducing funding costs and speculative purposes.

The global nature of derivative activities is evident from the multiple currencies used in derivatives. The survey also shows that participating firms use derivatives primarily to manage interest-rate and foreign-exchange-rate risks, followed with less frequency by commodities and equity price risks. Among the instruments used, swaps are the most popular, followed by options. Among

TABLE 15.7 Credit Ratings of 200 Companies with More Than $1 Billion in Swaps Outstanding, 1993 ($ Billions)			
Credit Rating	Number of Companies	Outstanding Notional Amounts of Swaps	Percent
AAA or Aaa	21	$535	9.7%
AA or Aa	34	1,747	31.7
A	78	2,023	36.7
BBB or Baa	38	1,066	19.4
Total Investment Grade	**171**	**$5,371**	**97.5%**
Speculative	15	30	0.6
Unrated	14	106	1.9
Total Non-Investment Grade	**29**	**$136**	**2.5%**

Source: Swaps Monitor Publications Inc., Derivatives Strategy & Tactics, Inc., and various annual reports.

TABLE 15.8   Corporate End-Users in the Derivatives Market: Survey Results

Country	No.	Objectives in Derivative Activities	
United States	82	Hedge normal operation	86%
Australia	11	Hedge financial operations	90%
Britain	11	Reduce funding costs	77%
Germany	8	Speculative	33%
Canada	7		
Switzerland	7	**No. of Currencies in Derivative Activities**	
Japan	5		
Sweden	4	1–2 currencies	60%
Norway	3	3–5 currencies	32%
France	2	More than 5 currencies	8%
Ireland	2		
Italy	2	**Underlying Risk Managed by Derivatives**	
Austria	1		
Hong Kong	1	Interest rates	97%
Netherlands	1	Foreign exchange rates	92%
Philippines	1	Commodity prices	40%
South Africa	1	Equity	29%
Total	149		

Total Assets of Participants		Derivative Products Used	
Less than $1 billion	20	Swaps	93%
$1 billion–$5 billion	33	Options purchased	89%
$5 billion–$10 billion	23	Options sold	66%
$10 billion–$20 billion	27	Others	66%
Greater than $20 billion	46		
Total	149		

Source: The Group of Thirty (December 1994), pp. 161–250.

derivatives used, OTC products were used by 98% of the participants, while exchange-traded instruments were used by 53% of the firms.

DETERMINANTS OF DEMAND FOR DERIVATIVES BY LOCAL GOVERNMENTS AND PENSION PLANS

Beside corporations, state and local governments, public retirement funds, and pension plans also use derivatives. These entities have a different set of incentives in using derivatives. Unlike corporations, they pay no taxes and face no incentive conflicts between different claimants.

The General Accounting Office (GAO) conducted a survey of 4,600 state and local government entities as well as public and private pension plans, including 156 of the largest private pension funds in the United States, to determine their incentives for using derivatives. The results are summarized in Table 15.9. There were 3,727 respondents, of which 288 reported using derivatives. The percentage of these entities that use derivatives varies significantly, from a low of 4% of

3,400 localities (municipalities, special districts, and counties) to a high of 72% among the 114 largest private pension plans.

Local governments mostly use interest-rate instruments, while state governments use all products in relatively even proportions. The public retirement funds and private pension funds primarily use futures, foreign exchange instruments and options. As one might expect, asset size is an important factor in the extent of derivative use between state and local governments as well as public and private retirement funds. Derivatives users generally have greater asset size than nonusers in each of the categories.

The reasons government entities and public and private retirement plans engage in derivative activities vary among entities. Since retirement funds do not generally raise money in capital markets, they did not state that reducing the cost of capital was a reason for using derivatives. However, hedging was an important factor for retirement funds as well as for state and local governments. Increasing the returns on investments was also stated as an important reason for using derivatives by all entities. Other reasons, including a desire to take a position in the options and market index futures, were also mentioned.

Since volatility in financial markets is generally more severe in the short run than in the long run, why are retirement funds so concerned with hedging given their long-run investment horizons? A possible reason why managers in retirement funds may be concerned with the short-run volatility is that their performance is often judged on a short-term basis.

DETERMINANTS OF THE SUPPLY OF DERIVATIVES
BY FINANCIAL INTERMEDIARIES AS DEALERS

As discussed in Chapter 5, the new era of banking has witnessed a decline in traditional bank products such as loans and an increase in new and highly technical off-balance-sheet activities. One of the most important elements of bank off-balance-sheet activities involves derivatives. Derivatives include the information production and risk-bearing functions of bank loans and exclude the funding and servicing functions.

The main role of financial intermediaries in the derivatives market is that of a dealer. While small and medium-sized banks may function as end-users in order to manage interest-rate and foreign-exchange-rate risks in their loan portfolios, the magnitude of these activities is relatively small. As we showed in Chapter 5, a substantial portion of the derivatives activity in the banking industry occurs in a small number of money-center banks that function as dealers in the derivatives market. In this capacity, they provide hedging instruments to their clients and create liquidity. As we will demonstrate later in this section, dealers may also use exchange-traded derivatives to hedge the residual exposure of their derivatives portfolios.

Dealing in derivatives requires not only extensive technological expertise, including highly skilled employees with access to sophisticated computers, but also ample capital and credit evaluation experience. Large, money-center banks are uniquely qualified as dealers in the derivatives market. They are skilled in producing the relevant information, including an assessment of the credit risk of the end-user; the market risk of the unhedged portion of the derivatives portfolio; the legal risk that contracts may not be enforceable; and the administrative risk of inadequate internal control systems. They are also in the position of risk-bearing, which requires significant capital to withstand the risk inherent in derivatives activities.

Table 15.10 presents 15 major U.S. OTC derivatives dealers. The seven banks

TABLE 15.9 State and Local Governments and Pension Funds as End-Users in the Derivatives Market: Survey Results

Percentage of State and Local Governments and Pension Plans Using Derivatives

Local government	4%
State government	18%
Public Retirement Systems	45%
Private Pension Plans	72%

Derivative Usage by Asset Size

Asset Size	% Using Any Derivatives
$5 billion or more	76%
$1 billion–$5 billion	50%
$100 million–$1 billion	13%
$10 million–$100 million	4%
Less than $10 million	1%

Asset Size of Users and Nonusers of Derivatives

Type of Entity	Users (Dollars in Millions)	Nonusers (Dollars in Millions)
State government	$14,259	$2,803
Local government	491	80
Public retirement	9,442	3,333
Private pension plans	5,297	2,600

Objectives in Derivative Activities

Derivative Products	As a Hedge	To Reduce Cost of Capital	Speculative
Interest rate swaps	73%	44%	71%
FX instruments	94%	8%	55%
Forwards	69%	50%	50%
Futures	82%	11%	81%
Options	72%	14%	81%

Derivative Products Used

Type of Derivative	Local Gov.	State Gov.	Public Retirement	Private Pensions
Futures	10%	33%	48%	80%
FX instruments	10%	40%	70%	60%
Options	17%	32%	50%	50%
Interest rate swaps	50%	25%	10%	8%
Forwards	12%	25%	20%	5%

Source: United States General Accounting Office (May 1994), pp. 130–139.

**TABLE 15.10   15 Major U.S. OTC Derivatives Dealers
and Their Notional/Contract Derivatives Amounts
December 1992 ($ Millions)**

Banks	
Chemical Banking Corporation	$1,620,819
Citicorp	1,521,400
J.P. Morgan & Co., Inc.	1,251,700
Bankers Trust New York Corporation	1,165,872
The Chase Manhattan Corporation	886,300
Bank America Corporation	787,891
First Chicago Corporation	391,400
Banks as a Percentage of Total	**69.35%**
Securities Firms	
The Goldman Sachs Group, L.P.	752,041
Salomon, Inc.	729,000
Merrill Lynch & Co., Inc.	724,000
Morgan Stanley Group, Inc.	424,937
Shearson Lehman Brothers, Inc.[a]	337,007
Securities Firms as a Percentage of Total	**27.00%**
Insurance Companies	
American International Group, Inc.	198,200
The Prudential Insurance Company of America	121,515
General Re Corporation	82,729
Insurance Companies as a Percentage of Total	**3.65%**
Total	**$10,994,811**

[a] Shearson Lehman no longer exists under this name.

Source: Annual reports for 1992

on the list—Chemical Banking Corporation, Citicorp, J.P. Morgan, Bankers Trust, Chase Manhattan, Bank of America, and First Chicago—constitute 70% of the total volume of derivative activities. Securities firms—Goldman Sachs, Salomon, Merrill Lynch, Morgan Stanley, and Lehman—hold the next largest market share, with 27%. Insurance companies—American International, Prudential, and General Re Corporation—have 3% of the market. This should not be surprising, considering the expertise of large banks and the size of their equity capital. At the end of 1994, Bank of America, Citibank, and Chemical had shareholders' equity worth $18.9 billion, $17.8 billion, and $10.8 billion, respectively. In contrast, the best capitalized securities firm on Wall Street, Merrill Lynch, had only $5.5 billion, and the smallest securities firm on the list, Lehman, had $2.1 billion in equity.[5]

The magnitude of notional amounts in derivatives positions has alarmed many. However, it is important to note that notional amounts are not subject to risk. Instead, they are reference amounts, which form the basis for the calculation of payments. The exposure of an intermediary to risk due to derivatives can be

[5] *Euromoney,* May 1995, p. 27.

TABLE 15.11   Gross Replacement Costs[a] of Derivatives Exposure by Lead Banks of 50 Largest U.S. Bank Holding Companies, 1990–1992

Year	Interest Rate Contracts		Currency Contracts		Combined $ Billion
	$ Billion	% of Notional Amount	$ Billion	% of Notional Amount	
1990	26.2	1.15	76.3	2.82	102.5
1991	47.8	1.61	99.4	3.70	147.2
1992	49.7	1.61	94.3	2.98	144.0

[a] The gross replacement cost is the mark-to-market value for OTC derivatives contracts with positive replacement cost, including swaps, forwards, purchased options, when-issued securities, and forward deposits accepted. Exchange-traded contracts and foreign exchange contracts with less than 14 days maturity are excluded.

Source: Call Reports.

better observed by examining the replacement costs of derivatives. Replacement costs are marked-to-market values of contracts that have become assets because of changes in interest rates or foreign exchange rates. Table 15.11 presents replacement costs for the 50 largest banks in the United States. These costs range from 1% to 4% of the total notional amounts. In 1992, the combined replacement cost of derivatives for the 50 largest banks in the United States was $144 billion.

The Evolution of Derivatives Intermediation: Brokerage, Warehousing, and Portfolio Management

Financial intermediaries began their derivative activities by offering a simple brokerage service to their customers. For example, a U.S. exporter, due to receive British pounds in the future, wants to hedge its foreign exchange exposure. A U.S. importer, which is due to pay British pounds in the future, also wants to hedge its foreign exchange exposure. An intermediary simply brokers the deal by bringing the two parties together. In the brokerage function, the intermediary produces the necessary information regarding the counterparties but takes neither credit risk nor market risk.

Since finding counterparties with exactly offsetting positions is difficult, the size of brokerage activities in the derivatives market remained small. Intermediaries figured out that they could expand their derivatives business by acting as counterparties to their clients. Subsequent to entering into a contract with the first customer, the intermediary would look for another customer whose hedging needs required a position opposite that of the first customer. The contract with the second customer enabled the intermediary to unwind its derivative position with the first customer. Thus, the intermediary kept a book of paired contracts. Although cash flows from these contracts offset one another, the intermediary bore the credit risk and to a lesser extent the market risk in dealing with two sets of customers. Because of the inherent risk exposure, the intermediary assumed a dealership position.

The next step in the evolution of derivatives intermediation occurred when the intermediaries began to "warehouse" their derivative positions. In warehousing, the dealer temporarily hedges a derivative position (e.g., a swap) with a cash security or an exchange-traded position (e.g., a futures) until a matching position is found to replace the temporary hedge.

Finally, major intermediaries moved from a simple warehousing of derivatives to creating a portfolio of derivative positions. A portfolio approach to derivatives intermediation involves the dealer taking counterparty positions with various clients without trying to match each transaction with an offsetting position. The dealer simply creates a portfolio of diverse derivatives positions. By the simple rule of portfolio diversification, the residual risk is less than the sum of individual risks. The residual risk of the portfolio can subsequently be hedged, using exchange-traded instruments. We will elaborate on this issue in later chapters.

THE REGULATION OF OTC DERIVATIVES

While the parameters of exchange-traded derivatives are clearly defined and regulated by the Commodities Futures and Trading Commission (CFTC), those of OTC derivatives are far from clear. As it stands today, the CFTC does not have jurisdiction over OTC derivatives. Depending on the trade group affiliation of the dealer, a varying degree of regulatory oversight is applied to these transactions.

Table 15.12 presents the regulatory status of OTC derivatives as of April 1994. Bank derivative activities are regulated along with other bank activities in terms of examination, capital, and reporting requirements by the Fed, the FDIC, OCC, and by state banking commissions. Quarterly reporting requirements include the notional amount of each derivative category and its replacement cost. Since March 1994, a 3% capital requirement has been levied against the replacement cost of certain contracts.

Securities firms and insurance companies do not face examination and capital requirements. Since October 1992, securities firms' affiliates have been required to report the notional amount and replacement cost of each derivative category. Information on the derivatives activities of the affiliates of insurance companies is consolidated with parent company reports. Table 15.13 presents the regulatory requirements for OTC derivatives dealers in industrialized countries. These requirements are not significantly different from those in the United States.

Legislative and regulatory entities have been concerned about the potential risks of OTC derivatives for some time. The main concern revolves around two interrelated issues: first, the concentration of derivatives activities in a small number of firms; and second, the fear of systemic risk. On the issue of concentration, the OTC derivatives of eight money-center banks account for 90% of all OTC derivatives in the United States and 60% of the activities worldwide. With the "too big to fail" policy in effect, major derivatives losses in a money-center bank may force a regulatory rescue, which may in turn threaten the viability of the FDIC insurance fund. The systemic risk involves the external effects that the failure of several large banks may have on the viability of the financial system. If dealer banks take similar positions in derivatives and collectively face large losses, the payment system may break down and the credit market could collapse.

EXAMPLES OF DERIVATIVES BLOWUPS

The Collapse of Barings PLC[6]

The 1995 failure of Barings Bank in Britain provides important lessons to dealers, end-users, and regulators about risks in derivatives activities. In early 1992, Nick

---

[6] The factual information about Barings is drawn from news reports published in various issues of *Financial Times*, *The Economist*, and *Euromoney*.

TABLE 15.12 Regulatory Oversight of OTC Derivatives Activities

Type of Intermediary	Examination Requirements	Capital Requirements	Reporting Requirements
Banks	Banks are subject to annual examinations. Major OTC derivatives dealers regulated by the OCC are subject to continuous on-site examinations.	For credit risk, banks are to hold capital against their derivatives' positions equal to 8 percent of the adjusted value of their positions. The adjustments serve to reduce required capital, depending on the type of counterparty and the maturity of the contract. Since March 1994, these firms also must hold at least 3 percent of the unadjusted replacement cost of certain contracts.	Banks are to report quarterly their total derivatives' notional amounts by product type. They are also required to report the total gross replacement cost of these positions. Reporting on individual counterparty credit exposures is not required, but exposures may be reviewed by regulatory staff during periodic examinations.
Securities Firms	None	None	Since October 1992, securities firm affiliates have been required to report quarterly their total derivatives notional amounts by product type. They also were to report the total gross replacement cost of those positions. Information on individual counterparty credit exposures is to be reported only when exposures are above a certain threshold.
Insurance Firms	None	None	Insurance firm affiliates' financial information is consolidated with parent company reports.

Source: GAO, Financial Derivatives: Actions Needed to Protect the Financial System, May 1994, p. 11.

TABLE 15.13   **Regulatory Requirements for Major OTC Derivatives Dealers in Selected Countries**

Country	Requirements for Reporting Notional/Contract Amounts	Requirements for Reporting Amounts for Credit or Market Risk
Australia	Banks report quarterly on forwards, futures, options, and swaps for foreign currencies, interest rates, gold, equities, and other contracts. Banks also make weekly reports on foreign currency derivatives. Securities firms do not report any derivatives positions.	Banks report quarterly on the credit equivalent amount of outstanding transactions.
France[a]	Banks report quarterly on derivatives, grouped as interest rate or currency, exchange-traded or OTC, and hedging or proprietary positions.	Banks report quarterly on unhedged positions.
Germany[a]	Banks report monthly on forwards, futures, options, and swaps related to foreign currencies, interest rates, equities, and other contracts. The information is subdivided by major types of exchange-traded and OTC contracts, by maturity, and by type of counterparty.	Banks report monthly on the delta value of options,[b] the credit equivalent amount of other reported contracts, and three ratios that reflect the extent of foreign exchange risk, interest-rate risk, and other market risks.
Japan	Banks and securities firms report monthly on exchange-traded derivatives.[c]	Banks and securities firms report monthly on the market value of exchange-traded derivatives.
Singapore	Banks and securities firms report monthly a combined total for exchange-traded and OTC derivatives.	Banks report monthly on the market value of their unhedged foreign exchange positions for capital purposes.
Switzerland[a]	Banks report monthly on foreign currency derivatives and annually on foreign currencies, forwards, and OTC interest rate contracts.	An annual audit report to regulators comments about risks undertaken and how they are managed.

[a] No separate reporting requirements apply to securities firms because only firms licensed as banks can conduct securities activities.
[b] The delta value of an option measures the sensitivity of the option's price to changes in the price of the underlying contract.
[c] This reporting is by numbers of contracts.

Country	Requirements for Reporting Notional/Contract Amounts	Requirements for Reporting Amounts for Credit or Market Risk
U.K.	Banks report monthly on activities related to foreign currencies and quarterly on forwards, OTC options, and swaps related to interest rates, foreign currencies, precious metals, equities, and other contracts. Depending on the overall nature of their business, some banks provide more detailed information, biweekly or monthly, about derivatives. Securities firms report monthly on the market value of futures, options, and swaps, and submit quarterly reports that provide more detail about specific types of derivatives.	Banks report quarterly on the credit equivalent amount of their contracts. Depending on the overall nature of their business, some banks provide more detailed analyses of their market and credit risks. Securities firms report monthly and quarterly on the amount of capital held to cover market and credit risks with quarterly reports providing more detail on specific types of derivatives.

TABLE 15.13 Regulatory Requirements for Major OTC Derivatives Dealers in Selected Countries (Continued)

Source: Regulatory agencies of various countries.

Leeson, a back-office employee of Barings in London, was sent to Baring Futures, a Barings subsidiary in Singapore, to manage accounting and settlement operations. By the end of 1992, Leeson received a Simex (Singapore International Monetary Exchange) trading licence and began trading in options and futures. In a clear violation of one of the most important rules of the derivatives business, he continued his work as the manager of accounting and settlement operations while expanding his trading activities. According to an internal audit report in the summer of 1994, the Singapore team was to engage in arbitrage activities and "[was] not authorized to carry overnight positions in any instrument traded." The arbitrage activities were based on exploiting slight differences in pricing between Nikkei 225 futures on Simex and those on the Osaka securities exchange in Japan, where similar contracts were traded. For example, buying 7,000 futures contracts in Simex could be matched by selling 3,500 futures contracts in Osaka (where contracts are twice the size); the long and short positions exactly offset each other and the trader is not exposed to market risk.

By January 1994, Leeson began a trading strategy that involved selling call and put options on the Nikkei 225 index, receiving premiums into an unauthorized and unreported trading account known as error account number 88888. Both the call and the put options were usually written at the same exercise price and expiration date, a combination known as a "straddle." This straddle strategy represents a bet on volatility that the market will not experience sharp upward and downward movements. Leeson also heavily purchased Nikkei futures during the autumn and winter of 1994, betting that Nikkei would rise in value. During 1994, Nikkei moved in a narrow range of 19,000 and 21,000 and, consequently, Leeson performed reasonably well in his straddle strategy.

In the early hours of January 17, 1995, a powerful earthquake hit Kobe and Osaka, two industrial cities in Japan, killing more than 5,000 people. On Monday, January 23, Nikkei 225 dropped by 1,000 points to 17,950. At this point, Leeson began heavy purchasing of the Nikkei March and June 1995 futures contract for account number 88888. By February 23, 1995, the error account contained 55,399 Nikkei contracts expiring in March and 5,640 contracts expiring in June. As time went by, Nikkei declined in value and its volatility increased. The decline in the value of Nikkei caused large losses in the futures position and the increase in volatility created enormous losses in the straddle position. What is not clear is why Leeson held a long position in futures and a short position in straddles, two contradictory strategies where the former is betting on an increase in Nikkei while the latter is betting on no significant change in Nikkei. Usually, a trader with a losing straddle in a falling market will sell futures in order to protect the position from further downward movement. The only explanation may be that Leeson was following a time-honored tradition among losing gamblers: Double up the bet in an effort to salvage an otherwise hopeless position.

By February 24, 1995, losses amounted to £850 million ($1.3 billion). Over the weekend of February 25–26, the Bank of England made a last-minute effort to find an investor who was willing to inject the necessary capital in the bank in order to prevent its collapse. The effort did not succeed. On Monday, February 27, the Bank of England announced the failure of the bank. The bank was finally acquired by Internationale Nederlanden Group.

With hindsight, the derivatives losses in Baring Futures could have been prevented through an adequate system of managerial control. The appendix to this chapter discusses the Group of Thirty's recommendations for good business practices in derivatives. A review of these recommendations shows that had Baring Futures followed these recommendations, it could have prevented the losses and avoided the ultimate collapse of the bank.[7]

While losses exceeding $1.3 billion in the Japanese stock index futures forced the bank into insolvency, there were no spillover effects on the payment system, the liquidity of the market, and the viability of other banks involved in derivatives. The cooperative efforts of the Bank of England, the FDIC, and the authorities in Singapore and Japan mitigated the potential systemic risk resulting from the Barings failure. The lesson learned in the Barings case was that one bank's failure can be contained and the systemic risk can be avoided.

Hammersmith and Fulham's Losses in Derivatives and Legal Risk

The lack of clear regulatory guidelines on derivatives has created uncertainties for dealers and end-users. One of the byproducts of regulatory ambiguity is legal risk, where a counterparty is legally incapable of entering into the underlying contract. The case of Hammersmith and Fulham provides an example of this legal risk. The London borough of Hammersmith and Fulham entered into interest-rate swap contracts during the 1980s and suffered large losses. Since the Local Government Act of 1972 did not provide any express power for local authorities to enter into derivatives contracts, the United Kingdom House of Lords nullified the contracts in January 1991 on the grounds that the municipality did not have the legal capacity to enter such contracts.[8]

The ruling of the House of Lords had the effect of voiding agreements be-

---

[7] Baring Futures' conduct seems to have breached the Group of Thirty's recommendations # 1, 8, 12, 16, 17, 18, and 20. For more details, see the appendix to this chapter.
[8] The Group of Thirty (July 1993b), pp. 46–47.

tween more than 130 councils and 75 of the world's largest banks. It covered more than 600 business transactions going back as far as 1981. The decision not only caused large losses for financial intermediaries, but also cost valuable hedging positions and unrealized gains for local authorities. The Hammersmith and Fulham decision has made dealers leery of entering into derivatives contracts with government entities in jurisdictions where the capacity to enter into derivatives contracts is not clear.

Orange County's Losses in Derivatives and the Legal Battle with Merrill Lynch

A test of legal risk in derivatives activities in U.S. municipalities came about in the case of Orange County. On December 6, 1994, Orange County, a wealthy municipality south of Los Angeles with a population of 2.3 million, filed for bankruptcy under Chapter 9 (the public sector's equivalent to Chapter 11) of the Bankruptcy Code. The filing came only days after Robert Citron, the county's treasurer, admitted that Orange County's $7.7 billion investment pool had lost $1.5 billion since the beginning of the year due to rises in interest rates.

At the time of filing for bankruptcy, the Orange County investment pool had 187 participants. For the past 15 years, Citron had delivered a 10.1% average annual return for the county while California's own treasury department played it safe and averaged 5% to 6% on its portfolio. Citron, an elected official, was popular among his predominantly conservative electorate, which had demanded and received tax cuts in previous years.

Orange County had $7.7 billion in its investment pool. By using a type of financial arrangement known as a "reverse-repurchase agreement," the county bought securities on credit, increasing the fund's holdings. This involved buying instruments such as five-year Treasury bonds and simultaneously pledging them to an investment bank as a collateral for a loan. A total of $12.9 billion of the agreements was accumulated, increasing the fund's holdings to about $20 billion.

The Orange County portfolio was a highly leveraged fund that had taken a chance on declining interest rates. Its interest-rate sensitivity was further enhanced by purchasing some $8 billion of a type of bond known as an inverse floater from investment bankers headed by Merrill Lynch. An inverse floater is a hybrid security composed of a floating-rate note and an interest-rate swap. The notional amount of the swap is twice as large as that of the floating note. The payoff of the inverse floater at any settlement date was equal to twice the fixed payment minus the floating-rate payment. The holder of an inverse floater will benefit when interest rates decrease and will lose when interest rates increase. In the case of Orange County, inverse floaters further increased the funds bet on decreasing rates. A highly leveraged portfolio, coupled with inverse floaters, worsened the fund's problems as interest rates increased.

Initially, Citron blamed the investment bankers for the large losses. He claimed that the investment bankers had sold him complex instruments including derivatives without his full understanding of the underlying risk. Merrill Lynch, as the main investment banker, had a multifaceted relationship with Orange County, including providing loans and underwriting and distributing its securities. It also sold many of the hybrid securities to the fund, such as inverse floaters, that ended up losing money. In May 1995, Citron pleaded guilty to six felony charges of misappropriating funds and misleading investors, but most of those crimes were committed in a desperate effort to prop up his collapsing fund. Citron's former deputy, Matthew Raabe, was also indicted on six counts of similar charges.

Metallgesellschaft Hedges Long-Term Commitments
with Short-Term Derivatives

371

Derivatives and
the Management
of Financial Risk

On November 23, 1994, Metallgesellschaft AG (MGAG), one of Germany's largest industrial conglomerates, announced losses of DM2.8 billion ($1.8 billion) by its U.S. subsidiary MG Corporation for the year ended September 1994. These losses were attributed primarily to derivatives positions that MG Corp. had entered into. Ironically, this amounted to a $10 loss on each barrel of the oil or oil products that MG Corp. had been trying to hedge in December 1993, when margin calls on its futures positions and the resulting liquidity crisis forced the parent company to close out its derivatives positions at a huge loss.

MG Refining & Marketing (MGRM) of Maryland, a subsidiary of MG Corp., had used short-term energy futures to hedge long-term commitments to deliver fuel. Hedging a long-term commitment with a short-term contract creates what is known as basis risk—the risk that the magnitude of price changes in the derivatives instruments may differ from those of the asset being hedged, as short-term futures contracts nearing maturity have to be rolled over and short-term gains or losses have to be realized. If the futures market is in normal backwardation (spot prices are higher than contracted futures prices), there will be gains in rolling over the futures contracts. Conversely, if the market is in contango (spot prices are lower than contracted futures prices), there will be losses in rolling over futures contracts.

By December 1993, MGRM had sold customers 180 million barrels of oil and oil products, to be delivered in 5–10 years. It had hedged its position by taking long positions in energy derivatives equivalent to 185 million barrels of oil. Since the derivatives positions had shorter maturities, they had to be rolled over in order to maintain the hedged position. As the price of oil in the spot market fell, rolling over the futures contracts cost the firm a total of $88 million in October and November alone.

The merit of hedging long-term commitments with short-term derivatives has sparked debates in academic circles. Merton Miller and Christopher Culp of the University of Chicago have argued that the management of the parent company made a mistake in closing out the derivatives positions, thus forcing the realization of the losses. They contended that gains in the long-term commitments could have canceled out any losses in the derivatives contracts. Their argument relies on the notion that short-term derivatives instruments could indeed be used to hedge long-term commitments. John Parsons, a visiting professor at Columbia University, has argued that the maturity mismatch in MGRM's hedge does indeed matter. According to Parsons, the often slow movements in long-term oil prices, compared with short-term futures prices, could create enormous rollover losses due to basis risk. He estimated that a drop in the oil price by $.75 in one month would have created $49 million in rollover losses on MGRM's contracts while raising profits on that month's oil deliveries by only $300,000. Parsons concluded that MGRM was not just hedging but also gambling on cash profits from backwardation in the oil market.[9]

These conflicts have inescapably ended up in the courts. On January 20, 1994, Heinz Schimmelbusch, the firm's former boss, filed a lawsuit in New York alleging that the parent company and its major shareholder, Deutsche Bank, were in part responsible for the financial troubles of the firm. A week later, an auditor's report, commissioned by shareholders including Deutsche Bank, faulted Schimmelbusch and other former MG Corp. executives on the matter.

---

[9] Cited in *Euromoney*, January 1995, pp. 36–38. See also *The Economist,* February 4, 1995, p. 71.

Bankers Trust's Court Battles with Equity Group Holdings, Gibson Greetings, and Procter & Gamble

In the early 1990s, Bankers Trust was more closely associated with the business of derivatives than any other financial intermediary. For over a decade, Bankers Trust carefully built a set of high-profit, wholesale banking ventures, including derivatives, proprietary trading, leveraged finance, Latin American debt, and asset management. At the same time, Bankers Trust completely withdrew from retail banking and credit card businesses that were characterized by repeat business and small profit margins. The importance of each profit function to Bankers Trust can be ascertained by examining the net income for each category as presented in Table 15.14.

While 1993 was an impressive year for Bankers Trust with profits exceeding $1 billion, 1994 was a year that threatened its very survival. A series of legal battles with clients and subsequent negative publicity and a dramatic ($523 million) decline in proprietary trading profits reduced its net income from $1.07 billion in 1993 to $615 million in 1994, a drop of 40%. By the end of 1994, most of the high-profit leveraged derivatives that Bankers Trust was known for had dried up and what was left were plain vanilla derivatives that produced low profit margins. Yet, at the end of 1994, Bankers Trust's derivative account totaled $1.98 trillion in notional amounts, an amount equal to that of J.P. Morgan, which has twice as much in capital. The replacement cost of Bankers Trust's derivatives amounted to $10.9 billion. It is obvious that, despite its troubles, Bankers Trust remains an important player in the derivatives business.

Bankers Trust's problems started in March 1994, when Equity Group Holdings, an investment firm, sued Bankers Trust after it had lost $11.2 million on derivatives products purchased from the bank. In September, Gibson Greetings, a greeting card maker, sued the bank for derivatives-related losses of $20 million and damages. And, in October, Procter & Gamble, a consumer-goods firm, sued the bank for the $195 million that it had lost in derivatives transactions. These lawsuits depicted Bankers Trust as the symbol of what was wrong with derivatives, and propelled regulators and legislators into trying to restrict the activities of derivatives dealers.

For Bankers Trust, the problems began when the bank marketed highly complex derivatives products with large profit margins to clients who wanted to take their chances with an element of financial risk such as interest rates. In the case of Gibson Greetings, the bank had sold leveraged interest-rate swaps that would have increased in value if interest rates had remained lower than the market ex-

TABLE 15.14 Bankers Trust's Net Income by Business Functions ($ Millions)		
Category	Year-End 1993	Year-End 1994
Client finance	76	140
Client advisory	63	87
Client risk management	336	259
Client transaction processing	60	99
Trading and positioning	594	71
Other	−59	−41
Income before cumulative effects	1,070	615

Source: 1994 annual reports.

pectation and would have produced huge losses if interest rates had increased above market expectations. The increase in interest rates in 1994, partially due to Fed actions, created significant losses for Gibson Greetings as well as other Bankers Trust clients.

Gibson Greetings argued that the officers at the bank had willfully misled them in their risk exposure. Initially, Bankers Trust fought the accusation, but when an internal tape was discovered that pointed to officers' wrongdoing, it settled the case with Gibson Greetings.

In December, Bankers Trust was fined $10 million by the SEC and the CFTC and forced to sign an "agreement" with the Federal Reserve Bank of New York to follow strict rules of transparency in selling leveraged derivatives and to be certain that the clients understand the products. Consequently, Moody's, a credit-rating agency, reduced the long-term rating of Bankers Trust from Aa2 to Aa3, citing its heavy dependance upon derivatives-generated earnings.

Britain Fines Morgan Stanley on Derivatives Misconduct

On May 29, 1995, Britain's Securities and Futures Authority (SFA), the regulator of London's investment markets, announced a settlement with Morgan Stanley, the U.S. investment bank, which included a fine of £240,000 ($376,000).[10] The firm also made "a substantial payment" to cover the cost of the investigation by SFA and offered compensation of about $30 million to private clients who had incurred losses on their investments. The settlement took place after an investigation by the regulatory authority concluded that the investment bank had failed to supervise the conduct of one of its foreign exchange derivatives traders, resulting in a $28 million loss for its clients.

While the size of the fine paid by Morgan Stanley is small relative to similar cases in the United States, the fact that it involved one of the most powerful investment banking houses operating in Europe makes it a significant affair. The implicit reputational cost of the settlement may be much greater for Morgan Stanley, especially in light of the details of the case.

While previous cases discussed in this section were associated mainly with government or corporate entities, the Morgan Stanley case involved private clients. The case involved five clients and resulted from trading in highly leveraged currency derivatives. In one case, the Universal Consult's account, the leverage reached 22.6 times, which was more than double Morgan Stanley's in-house limit. All five cases involved a broker, Burkhard Brauch, who magnified discretionary client accounts through leverage and who apparently traded in derivatives without the authorization of the investors. For example, in one case, Peter Ackerman, a German lawyer and a director of Universal Consult (UK), a London-based consulting firm, initially invested $818,000 in an account that was supposed to be used for straightforward, unleveraged investment with no speculative currency transactions. In less than six months, the gross value of transactions in the account reached $600 million, a huge volume for an initial investment of less than $1 million. What makes the case even more troublesome is the fact that most of the derivatives transactions involved currency forward and option contracts where the counterparty was Morgan Stanley itself. The incentive problem for the broker is obvious. If commissions are based on the volume of trading, a highly leveraged account with active trading can produce substantial commissions for the trader.

The investigation showed that Morgan Stanley had monitored the aggregate

---

[10] *Financial Times*, May 30, 1995, pp. 1 and 13, and *Financial Times*, May 31, pp. 1 and 14.

private client account, without supervising individual accounts. Since most of the settlement details were kept secret, several important questions remain unanswered. Were the losses incurred because of exceptional market circumstances? How did the broker violate house rules on leverage trading without his superiors' knowledge? How could Morgan Stanley not know about these trades while it was the counterparty to client transactions?

SUMMARY

This chapter examined three sources of financial risk: interest-rate, foreign exchange, and commodities-price risks. As was shown, the three types of financial risk are not independent. Commodity price levels are influenced by monetary policy. The resulting level of inflation impacts interest rates, which in turn affect currency exchange rates.

Derivatives were presented as a means of redistributing risk. The basic building blocks of derivatives are forwards, futures, swaps, and options. Futures and options are largely exchange-traded instruments, while forwards and swaps are typically designed by financial intermediaries to the exact specifications of client demand. The use of derivative instruments has increased greatly in just the last few years.

The economic rationale for derivatives use was explored for end-users including corporations and state and local governments. In a world of less than perfect financial markets, derivatives can be used to reduce the tax liability of corporations, to reduce conflicts between stock and bondholders, and to improve the potential performance of financial portfolios.

Unfortunately, performance is not always improved when derivatives are utilized by portfolio managers. Major derivatives blowups of the early 1990s were examined. The most famous case to date in the United States is the bankruptcy of Orange County, California. The collapse of Barings Bank of Britain from derivatives trades by an unsupervised trader is almost as well known as the Orange County debacle and indicates derivative problems are not confined to the United States. The chapter concludes with an appendix discussing recommendations made by the Group of Thirty to improve derivative industry practices.

REVIEW QUESTIONS

1. What are the benefits of corporate risk-hedging for stockholders?
2. Define the brokerage, warehousing, and portfolio management functions in derivatives intermediation.
3. Briefly describe the causes of derivatives-related problems in Barings and Orange County.
4. Explain the benefits of using one master agreement for dealers and end-users of derivatives.
5. Describe briefly the events of the 1970s that led to increased financial risk.

REFERENCES

Döblin, A. 1983. *Berlin Alexanderplatz.* New York: Frederick Ungar Publishing Co.

Group of Thirty, Global Derivatives Study Group. 1993a. *Derivatives: Practices and Principles* (July).

Group of Thirty, Global Derivatives Study Group. 1993b. *Derivatives: Practices and Principles, Appendix I: Working Papers* (July).

Group of Thirty, Global Derivatives Study Group. 1993c. *Derivatives: Practices and Principles, Appendix II: Legal Enforceability: Survey of Nine Jurisdictions* (July).

Group of Thirty, Global Derivatives Study Group. 1994a. *Derivatives: Practices and Principles, Appendix III: Survey of Industry Practice* (March).

Group of Thirty, Global Derivatives Study Group. 1994b. *Derivatives: Practices and Principles, Follow-up Surveys of Industry Practice* (December).

United States General Accounting Office. 1994. *Financial Derivatives: Actions Needed to Protect the Financial System.* GAO/GGD-94-133 (March).

APPENDIX

THE GROUP OF THIRTY'S RECOMMENDATIONS FOR GOOD INDUSTRY PRACTICE

In 1993, based on a survey of industry practices and a careful analysis of the derivatives business, the Group of Thirty, a diverse cross-section of end-users, dealers, academics, accountants, and lawyers involved in derivatives, provided 24 recommendations to help dealers and end-users to manage their derivatives activities. In light of the cases discussed in this chapter, it will be apparent that if all parties had followed these recommendations, they could have avoided many of their ensuing problems. Below, we provide a summary of these recommendations with a brief explanation of each.[11]

Recommendation 1: The Role of Senior Management

Dealers and end-users should use derivatives in a manner consistent with the overall risk management and capital policies approved by their boards of directors. These policies should be reviewed as business and market circumstances change. Policies governing derivatives use should be clearly defined, including the purposes for which these transactions are to be undertaken. Senior management should approve procedures and controls to implement these policies, and management at all levels should enforce them.

Surprisingly, this important recommendation is often overlooked. In the cases involving Barings, Metallgesellschaft, Bankers Trust, and Morgan Stanley, senior management was not fully informed about transactions that led to problems.

Recommendation 2: Marking to Market

Dealers should mark their derivatives positions to market, on at least a daily basis, for risk management purposes.

Marking to market, the practice of valuing positions based on current market prices, is essential in determining market risk and appropriate hedging actions. The Group of Thirty's Survey of Industry Practice (the survey) shows that dealers often use daily, intraday, or even real time valuation of their derivative positions.

Recommendation 3: Market Valuation Methods

[The] derivatives portfolios of dealers should be valued based on mid-market levels less specific adjustments, or on appropriate bid or offer levels. Mid-market valuation adjust-

---

[11] The Group of Thirty (July 1993a,b,c, March 1994, and December 1994).

ments should allow for expected future costs such as unearned credit spread, closeout costs, investing and funding costs, and administrative costs.

The Survey reveals diverse practices between dealers and end-users. The most common adjustments made are credit and administrative costs.

Recommendation 4: Identifying Revenue Sources

Dealers should measure the components of revenue regularly and in sufficient detail to understand the sources of risk.

This involves identifying and isolating the individual sources of revenue including revenue from origination, risk-bearing, and trading. This will help the dealer to identify various sources of risks. The survey results show that dealers rarely isolate the various sources of their revenue.

Recommendation 5: Measuring Market Risk

Dealers should use a constant measure to calculate daily the market risk of their derivatives positions and compare it to market risk limits. Market risk is best measured as "value at risk" using probability analysis based upon a common confidence interval (e.g., two standard deviations) and time horizons (e.g., a one-day exposure). Components of market risk that should be considered across the term structure include: absolute price or rate change (delta); convexity (gamma); volatility (vega); time decay (theta); basis or correlation; and discount rates (rho).

Determining different components of market risk, setting a confidence level, and deciding on the tolerance for losses based on capital resources and liquidity are among the most important decisions that dealers make. The survey indicates that most dealers consider some components of market risk. However, a consistent use of a measure of market risk such as "value at risk" occurs only in the domain of large dealers. Various components of market risk will be examined in detail in later chapters.

Recommendation 6: Stress Simulations

Dealers should regularly perform simulations to determine how their portfolios would perform under stress conditions.

Simulations of improbable market conditions are important in order to examine the consequences of changes in normal market assumptions and also in periods of abnormally large market swings or prolonged market inactivity. The survey indicates that large dealers simulate stress conditions, and the application of this practice by a wider group of dealers seems to be on the horizon.

Recommendation 7: Investing and Funding Forecasts

Dealers should periodically forecast the cash investing and funding requirements arising from their derivatives portfolios.

The survey indicates that currently only half of the dealers conduct cash flow forecasts.

Recommendation 8: Independent Market Risk Management

Dealers should have a market risk management function, with clear independence and authority, to ensure that the following responsibilities are carried out:

- *The development of risk limit policies and the monitoring of transactions and positions for adherence to these policies (see Recommendation 5).*
- *The design of stress scenarios to measure the impact of market conditions, however improbable, that might cause market gaps, volatility swings, or disruptions of major relationships, or might reduce liquidity in the face of unfavorable market linkages, concentrated market making, or credit exhaustion (see Recommendation 6).*

- *The design of revenue reports quantifying the contribution of various risk components, and of market risk measures such as value at risk (see Recommendations 4 and 5).*
- *The monitoring of the variance between actual volatility of portfolio value and that predicted by the measure of market risk.*
- *The review and approval of pricing models and valuation systems used by front- and back-office personnel, and the development of reconciliation procedures if different systems are used.*

The survey shows that a majority of dealers already have such functions in place and many more plan to implement them. Barings and Orange County, however, did not.

Recommendation 9: Practices by End-Users

As appropriate to the nature, size, and complexity of their derivatives activities, end-users should adopt the same valuation and market risk management practices that are recommended for dealers. Specifically, they should consider: regularly marking to market their derivatives transactions for risk management purposes; periodically forecasting the cash investing and funding requirements arising from their derivatives transactions; and establishing a clear independent and authoritative function to design and [ensure] adherence to prudent risk limits.

The survey indicates that currently only half of the end-users mark their derivatives to market. Cases involving Gibson Greetings and Procter & Gamble indicate that end-users pay less than adequate attention to these issues.

Recommendation 10: Measuring Credit Exposure

Dealers and end-users should measure credit exposure on derivatives in two ways:

- Current exposure, *which is the replacement cost of derivatives transactions, that is, their market value.*
- Potential exposure, *which is an estimate of the future replacement cost of derivatives transactions. It should be calculated using probability analysis based upon broad confidence intervals (e.g., two standard deviations) over the remaining terms of the transactions.*

The survey shows that dealers use various methods including worst-case scenarios. End-users rely on simpler methods based primarily on notional amounts.

Recommendation 11: Aggregating Credit Exposures

Credit exposures on derivatives, and all other credit exposures to a counterparty, should be aggregated taking into consideration enforceable netting arrangements. Credit exposures should be calculated regularly and compared to credit limits.

According to the survey, aggregating current and potential exposures by a counterparty on a net basis is not common among dealers. End-users monitor credit exposures at least once a month.

Recommendation 12: Independent Credit Risk Management

Dealers and end-users should have a credit risk management function with clear independence and authority, and with analytical capabilities in derivatives, responsible for:

- *Approving credit exposure measurement standards.*
- *Setting credit limits and monitoring their use.*
- *Reviewing credits and concentrations of credit risk.*
- *Reviewing and monitoring risk reduction arrangements.*

The intent of this recommendation is the reduction of conflict of interest among salespeople in dealer banks. For example, in the case of Morgan Stanley described earlier, one broker was the culprit for losses in five individual client accounts. With an independent credit risk management group, such trades would have been monitored and discovered much sooner. In the Barings case, effective independent credit risk management did not exist at all. Otherwise, the bank would have known sooner that the trader's positions were not arbitrage but speculative.

Recommendation 13: Master Agreements

Dealers and end-users are encouraged to use one master agreement as widely as possible with each counterparty to document existing and future derivatives transactions, including foreign exchange forwards and options. Master agreements should provide for payments netting and closeout netting, using a full two-way payments approach.

A single master agreement that documents all transactions between two parties reduces credit risk and provides legal certainty that credit exposure will be netted. Separate agreements for each transaction is not a good practice. According to the survey, two-fifths of all dealers use a single master agreement, and more plan to do so in the future.

Recommendation 14: Credit Enhancement

Dealers and end-users should assess both the benefits and costs of credit enhancement and related risk-reduction arrangements. Where it is proposed that credit downgrades would trigger early termination or collateral requirements, participants should carefully consider their own capacity and that of their counterparties to meet the potentially substantial funding needs that might result.

The methods that can be used to reduce the credit risk of a counterparty include collateral and margin arrangements, third-party credit enhancements such as letters of credit, and structural credit enhancement by establishing special-purpose vehicles to conduct derivatives activities. The survey indicates that about two-thirds of the dealers accept credit enhancements with cash or securities as collateral or third-party letters of credit.

Recommendation 15: Promoting Enforceability

Dealers and end-users should work together on a continuing basis to identify and recommend solutions for issues of legal enforceability, both within and across jurisdictions, as activities evolve and new types of transactions are developed.

Because the market for OTC derivatives is an evolving phenomenon where new products are produced, legal risk is a source of concern. Highly leveraged derivatives of the kind produced and marketed by Bankers Trust became controversial in the cases involving Equity Group Holdings, Gibson Greetings, and Procter & Gamble. The legal battle over these products revolved around the issue of transparency and whether the dealer had disclosed sufficiently the nature of the risk the end-users were getting into. Uncertainty about new products may also create incentive problems for end-users, who when faced with large losses are tempted to blame the dealer and try to get out of their contractual agreements by means of legal action. Legal risk is also present in the case of government entities as end-users, as in the Hammersmith and Fulham case, if the courts rule that these entities have no legal capacity to enter certain contracts.

In the Survey, the enforceability of netting provisions was named by 43% of dealers as a serious legal concern, while another 45% of dealers expressed some concern with this issue. End-users also named netting as a source of legal concern.

Recommendation 16: Professional Expertise

Dealers and end-users must ensure that their derivatives activities are undertaken by professionals in sufficient number and with the appropriate experience, skill levels, and degree of specialization. These professionals include specialists who transact and manage the risks involved, their supervisors, and those responsible for processing, reporting, controlling, and auditing activities.

The survey indicates that professionals in charge of derivatives activities in dealer banks are sufficiently trained in the field. What is not always clear is whether their supervisors or senior management are knowledgeable enough about derivatives. Senior management in Barings claimed that they were not aware of risks undertaken by the trader. They either knew more than they claim, or were genuinely ignorant of the risks involved. End-users may suffer from similar deficiencies as dealers. In addition, they have an incentive to plead ignorance when faced with large losses. In the Orange County case, Robert Citron, the treasurer, originally claimed that he had not understood the risk he was taking and blamed Merrill Lynch for the losses. He later changed his story and accepted responsibility. It turned out that he was a sophisticated investor who got involved in highly speculative transactions and lost. Similar claims were also made by Gibson Greetings and Procter & Gamble. As the OTC derivatives market matures, it is expected that contracts will be more carefully designed in order to mitigate these types of problems.

Recommendation 17: Systems

Dealers and end-users must ensure that adequate systems for data capture, processing, settlement, and management reporting are in place so that derivatives transactions are conducted in an orderly and efficient manner in compliance with management policies. Dealers should have risk management systems that measure the risks incurred in their derivatives activities including market and credit risks. End-users should have risk management systems that measure the risks incurred in their derivatives activities based upon their nature, size, and complexity.

The survey shows that 40% of dealers currently use an automated system to confirm transactions, while 10% indicated future plans for automation. Another 45% of dealers use a manual system. End-users have less sophisticated systems for handling their derivatives positions.

Recommendation 18: Authority

Management of dealers and end-users should designate who is authorized to commit their institutions to derivatives transactions.

According to the survey, two-thirds of the dealers require a person from senior management to authorize the traders to commit the firm to a derivatives position.

Recommendation 19: Accounting Practices

International harmonization of accounting standards for derivatives is desirable. Pending the adoption of harmonized standards, the following accounting practices are recommended:

- *Dealers should account for derivatives transactions by marking them to market, taking changes in value to income each period.*
- *End-users should account for derivatives used to manage risks so as to achieve a consistency of income recognition treatment between those instruments and the risks being managed. Thus, if the risk being managed is accounted for at cost (or, in the case of an anticipatory hedge, not yet recognized), changes in the value of a qualifying risk management instrument should be deferred until a gain or loss is recognized on the risk being managed. Or, if the risk being managed is marked to market with changes in value being taken to income, a qualifying risk management instrument should be treated in a comparable fashion.*

- *End-users should account for derivatives not qualifying for risk management treatment on a mark-to-market basis.*
- *Amounts due to and from counterparties should only be offset when there is a legal right to set off or when enforceable netting arrangements are in place.*

Where local regulations prevent adoption of these practices, disclosure along these lines is nevertheless recommended.

The survey results show that inconsistency because of accounting standards and the economics of the derivatives business are considered sources of concern by senior management.

Recommendation 20: Disclosures

Financial statements of dealers and end-users should contain sufficient information about their use of derivatives to provide an understanding of the purposes for which transactions are undertaken, the extent of the transactions, the degree of risk involved, and how the transactions have been accounted for. Pending the adoption of harmonized accounting standards, the following disclosures are recommended:

- *Information about management's attitude to financial risks, how instruments are used, and how risks are monitored and controlled.*
- *Accounting policies.*
- *[An] analysis of positions at the balance sheet date.*
- *[An] analysis of the credit risks inherent in those positions.*
- *For dealers only, additional information about the extent of their activities in financial instruments.*

According to the survey, about three-fifths of dealers' senior management have some concern, or serious concern, about inadequate public disclosure of counterparty exposures.

Recommendation 21: Recognizing Netting

Regulators and supervisors should recognize the benefits of netting arrangements where and to the full extent that they are enforceable, and encourage their use by reflecting these arrangements in capital adequacy standards. Specifically, they should promptly implement the recognition of the effectiveness of bilateral closeout netting in bank capital regulations.

This recommendation was implemented by regulators. On December 28, 1994, the OCC issued an amendment to the risk-based capital standards for national banks, which recognizes the risk-reducing benefits of qualifying bilateral netting contracts.[12] Effective immediately, for off-balance-sheet transactions that are subject to a qualifying bilateral netting contract, banks are permitted to net positive and negative market values when calculating their capital ratios. This net market value is used in determining the credit equivalent amount for off-balance-sheet transactions, which is then included in a bank's total risk-weighted assets. The amendment was similarly implemented in the Basle Accord.

Recommendation 22: Legal and Regulatory Uncertainties

Legislators, regulators, and supervisors, including central banks, should work in concert with dealers and end-users to identify and remove any remaining legal and regulatory uncertainties with respect to:

---

[12] *Federal Register*, 12 CFR Part 3, December 28, 1994.

- *The form of documentation required to create legally enforceable agreements (statute of frauds).*
- *The capacity of parties, such as governmental entities, insurance companies, pension funds, and building societies, to enter into transactions (ultra vires).*
- *The enforceability of bilateral closeout netting and collateral arrangements in bankruptcy.*
- *The enforceability of multi-branch netting arrangements in bankruptcy.*
- *The legality/enforceability of derivatives transactions.*

The concern about the "legal capacity" of government entities to enter into derivatives transactions was heightened with the Hammersmith and Fulham ruling. Implementing this recommendation is a crucial step toward an efficient derivatives market.

Recommendation 23: Tax Treatment

Legislators and tax authorities are encouraged to review and, where appropriate, amend tax laws and regulations that disadvantage the use of derivatives in risk management strategies. Tax impediments include the inconsistent or uncertain tax treatment of gains and losses in derivatives, in comparison with the gains and losses that arise from the risks being managed.

In October 1993, the IRS issued both Temporary Regulations and Proposed Regulations on Hedging Transactions.[13] The Temporary Regulations state that "most business hedges give rise to ordinary gain or loss." And the Proposed Regulations define a "hedging transaction" as one entered in the normal course of business that would reduce interest-rate, foreign exchange rate, and commodities price risk. Hedging transactions would give rise to ordinary gains and losses regardless of whether the hedging instrument would otherwise be regarded as a capital asset.

Recommendation 24: Accounting Standards

Accounting standards–setting bodies in each country should, as a matter of priority, provide comprehensive guidance on [the] accounting and reporting of transactions in financial instruments, including derivatives, and should work toward [the] international harmonization of standards on this subject. Also, the international Accounting Standards Committee should finalize its accounting standards on financial instruments.

In July 1993, the FASB issued tentative conclusions that would change hedge accounting in the following manner:

- Include all hedges in which the hedging instruments are financial derivatives.
- Permit hedge accounting for cross-currency hedges.
- Limit deferral of gains and losses based on the effectiveness of the hedge.
- Eliminate the requirement to assess correlation on an ongoing basis and discontinue hedge accounting if the correlation is less than "high."
- Clarify that hedging means reducing the risk of adverse events that are assessed at the business unit on an ongoing basis.

---

[13] *Federal Register,* 26 CFR Part 1, October 18, 1993.

16

Forwards and Futures

OBJECTIVES

This chapter is the first of three on pricing and hedging strategies based on derivatives. The focus of this chapter is on forwards and futures, which have many similar features. We begin with a description of the contractual features of forward contracts and continue with forward-based pricing and hedging strategies involving foreign currencies, interest rates (forward-rate agreements), and commodities. Forwards are generally over-the-counter instruments designed to meet the specific needs of the customer. The uniqueness of these individual contracts reduces their liquidity. They are also credit instruments that carry default risk. The liquidity, credit risk, and transaction cost problems associated with forward contracts have provided the impetus for the design and development of futures contracts that carry features similar to those of forwards without the underlying problems. Futures, however, also have their shortcomings. In order to create liquidity, futures contracts have to be standardized instruments with few underlying assets and a limited number of maturities. Futures pricing and hedging strategies are provided for foreign currencies, Treasury bills, Treasury notes, Treasury bonds, and commodities.

FORWARD CONTRACTS

A forward contract is an agreement between two parties to exchange a designated amount of a financial asset or a commodity at a prespecified price on a predetermined future date. The party agreeing to buy is said to take a *long position* and the party agreeing to sell is said to take a *short position* in the underlying asset. Some contracts require an actual exchange of assets, while others require only a cash settlement.

A forward contract is an obligation for each of the contracting parties. The settlement price is established by setting the NPV of the transaction equal to zero. As time passes, the market value of the underlying asset changes, creating a positive value for one party and a negative value for the other party in the contract. For example, if the value of the underlying asset increases, the party with a long position will gain an amount equal to the loss incurred by the party with a short position. No money changes hands until maturity. The relevant information, therefore, is the price at the settlement date; any fluctuation in price from the date the contract is entered into until shortly before the settlement date is of no consequence.

Foreign Exchange Forwards

Foreign exchange forward contracts are available for most major currencies. As Table 16.1 shows, there is a reasonably liquid market for currency forwards with maturities ranging from one month to one year. Other maturities, including two, four, six, and nine months, also exist for major currencies such as the dollar, pound sterling, yen, and deutschemark.

In a foreign currency forward contract, the buyer agrees to buy and the seller agrees to sell a certain quantity of a currency at a prespecified price on a predetermined future date. The forward exchange rate is a function of the spot exchange rate, the spot domestic interest rate, and the spot foreign interest rate. At the outset, the transaction is a zero-NPV proposition, requiring no exchange of funds between the parties. The forward pricing equation is based on the *interest-rate parity theorem*.

The interest-rate parity formula, described in Chapter 15, provides the following relationship between spot and forward exchange rates and domestic and foreign interest rates:

$$F = S \frac{(1+r_f)}{(1+r_d)}$$

where

F = forward currency rate = foreign currency / domestic currency
S = spot currency rate = foreign currency / domestic currency
r_f and r_d = foreign and domestic interest rates

The logic behind this relationship is as follows: A forward contract allows a party to take a long (short) position with an obligation to purchase (sell) a certain quantity of the underlying currency at a prespecified price on a predetermined future date. For example, a party who is interested in purchasing deutschemarks one year from today can borrow one dollar today at the rate of r_d, convert it to $S_{DM/\$}$ deutschemarks, and invest the $S_{DM/\$}$ deutschemarks at the rate of r_f for one year. At the end of the year, the deutschemark investment will be worth $S_{DM/\$}(1 + r_f)$ and the loan obligation will be equal to $\$1(1 + r_d)$. In order to pay off the loan, the investor will exchange the deutschemarks for dollars at the exchange rate of $F_{DM/\$}$, which will produce

$$\frac{S_{DM/\$}(1+r_f)}{F_{DM/\$}}$$

dollars. The interest-rate parity relationship requires that this amount be equal to the principal and interest of the dollar loan:

$$1(1+r_d) = \frac{S_{DM/\$}(1+r_f)}{F_{DM/\$}}$$

and

$$F_{DM/\$} = S_{DM/\$} \frac{(1+r_f)}{(1+r_d)}$$

Suppose we are interested in a long forward contract to purchase deutschemarks in one year. From Tables 16.1 and 16.2 the following information is extracted:

$$S_{DM/\$} = 1.4007$$
$$r_f = 4\tfrac{1}{2} = 0.0450$$
$$r_d = 5\tfrac{7}{8} = 0.0588$$

TABLE 16.1 Spot and Forward Prices of Foreign Currencies Against the Dollar
June 16, 1995

DOLLAR SPOT FORWARD AGAINST THE DOLLAR

June 16		Closing Mid-point	Change on Day	Bid/Offer Spread	Day's Mid High	Day's Mid Low	One Month Rate	One Month %PA	Three Months Rate	Three Months %PA	One Year Rate	One Year %PA	J.P. Morgan Index
Europe													
Austria	(Sch)	9.8494	−0.0696	462–525	9.9105	9.8420	9.8374	1.5	9.8174	1.3	9.7229	1.3	106.9
Belgium	(BFr)	28.7430	−0.233	340–520	28.9150	28.7300	28.708	1.5	28.653	1.3	28.533	0.7	109.4
Denmark	(DKr)	5.4696	−0.0315	678–713	5.4940	5.4663	5.4733	−0.8	5.4816	−0.9	5.5171	−0.9	109.1
Finland	(FM)	4.3020	−0.021	015–025	4.3282	4.2720	4.3002	0.5	4.297	0.5	4.2965	0.1	85.9
France	(FFr)	4.9183	−0.0302	178–188	4.9415	4.9110	4.9248	−1.6	4.9373	−1.5	4.9673	−1.0	108.1
Germany	(DM)	1.4007	−0.0099	003–010	1.4100	1.3995	1.3989	1.5	1.3952	1.6	1.3819	1.3	111.2
Greece	(Dr)	226.050	−1.6	800–300	228.060	225.790	228.05	−10.6	231.8	−10.2	247.55	−9.5	67.7
Ireland	(I£)	1.6358	+0.0112	345–370	1.6405	1.6315	1.6363	−0.4	1.6381	−0.6	1.643	−0.4	—
Italy	(L)	1648.25	−1.75	750–900	1652.75	1644.00	1654.75	−4.7	1667.5	−4.7	1727.75	−4.8	66.7
Luxembourg	(LFr)	28.7430	−0.233	340–520	28.9150	28.7300	28.708	1.5	28.653	1.3	28.533	0.7	109.4
Netherlands	(Fl)	1.5675	−0.012	672–677	1.5777	1.5665	1.5654	1.6	1.5614	1.5	1.5493	1.2	108.8
Norway	(NKr)	6.2390	−0.031	365–415	6.2658	6.1936	6.2402	−0.2	6.233	0.4	6.2255	0.2	97.9
Portugal	(Es)	147.430	−0.995	380–480	148.520	147.320	147.88	−3.7	148.88	−3.9	154.68	−4.9	95.6
Spain	(Pta)	121.650	−0.4	600–700	122.260	121.490	121.99	−3.4	122.79	−3.7	127.125	−4.5	80.6
Sweden	(SKr)	7.2531	−0.0238	485–577	7.2925	7.2461	7.2688	−2.6	7.3046	−2.8	7.4906	−3.3	77.4
Switzerland	(SFr)	1.1599	−0.0066	594–604	1.1679	1.1590	1.1571	2.8	1.152	2.7	1.1326	2.3	112.1
U.K.	(£)	1.6080	+0.0125	076–083	1.6106	1.5975	1.6076	0.3	1.6058	0.5	1.589	1.2	84.1
Ecu	(—)	1.3206	+0.0096	203–208	1.3210	1.3130	1.3204	0.1	1.3203	0.1	1.3163	0.3	—
SDR†	(—)	0.64067	—	—	—								—

Americas

Country		Closing mid-point	Change on day	Bid/offer spread	Day's high	Day's low	One month rate	%PA	Three month rate	%PA	One year rate	%PA	Index
Argentina	(Peso)	0.9999	-0.0001	998–999	0.9999	0.9997	—	—	—	—	—	—	—
Brazil	(R$)	0.9085	+0.003	080–090	0.9090	0.9080	—	—	—	—	—	—	—
Canada	(C$)	1.3819	+0.0046	816–821	1.3825	1.3798	1.3834	-1.3	1.3865	-1.3	1.3984	-1.2	80.8
Mexico	(New Peso)	6.1850	-0.02	700–000	6.2000	6.1700	6.1872	-0.4	6.1904	-0.4	6.1953	-0.2	—
U.S.A.	($)	—	—	—	—	—	—	—	—	—	—	—	90.1

Pacific/Middle East/Africa

Country		Closing mid-point	Change on day	Bid/offer spread	Day's high	Day's low	One month rate	%PA	Three month rate	%PA	One year rate	%PA	Index
Australia	(A$)	1.3736	-0.0013	732–742	1.3822	1.3732	1.3752	-1.4	1.3791	-1.6	1.4003	-1.9	80.0
Hong Kong	(HK$)	7.7353	-0.0008	348–358	7.7370	7.7345	7.7335	0.3	7.733	0.1	7.7488	-0.2	—
India	(Rs)	31.3950	-0.001	900–000	31.4170	31.3740	31.475	-3.1	31.72	-4.1	—	—	—
Israel	(Shk)	2.9671	-0.0123	651–690	2.9830	2.9651	—	—	—	—	—	—	—
Japan	(Y)	84.5350	-0.27	000–700	84.7700	84.3700	84.18	5.0	83.47	5.0	80.565	4.7	170.5
Malaysia	(M$)	2.4420	-0.0015	415–425	2.4445	2.4410	2.44	1.0	2.4376	0.7	2.432	0.4	—
New Zealand	(NZ$)	1.4928	-0.0011	923–934	1.5015	1.4909	1.4962	-2.7	1.503	-2.7	1.5222	-2.0	—
Philippines	(Peso)	25.6750	—	000–500	25.7500	25.6000	—	—	—	—	—	—	—
Saudi Arabia	(SR)	3.7505	—	503–507	3.7508	3.7502	3.7515	-0.3	3.7536	-0.3	3.7655	-0.4	—
Singapore	(S$)	1.3958	-0.001	953–963	1.3980	1.3950	1.3905	4.5	1.3823	3.9	1.3558	2.9	—
South Africa	(R)	3.6678	-0.004	670–685	3.6710	3.6670	3.6888	-6.9	3.7398	-7.9	3.9958	-8.9	—
South Korea	(Won)	761.050	-0.85	000–100	762.100	761.000	764.05	-4.7	767.55	-3.4	786.05	-3.3	—
Taiwan	(T$)	25.7860	+0.0085	830–890	25.8000	25.7800	25.806	-0.9	25.846	—	—	—	—
Thailand	(Bt)	24.6600	—	500–700	24.6800	24.6540	24.681	-1.0	24.7075	-0.8	24.795	-0.5	—

+ SDR rate per $ for Jun 15. Bid/offer spreads in the Dollar Spot table show only the last three decimal places. Forward rates are not directly quoted to the market but are implied by current interest rates. U.K., Ireland & ECU are quoted in U.S. currency. J.P. Morgan nominal indices June 15. Base average 1990 = 100.

Source: Financial Times, June 19, 1995, p. 27.

TABLE 16.2 Bid–Ask Spread in Euro Currency Interest Rates June 16, 1995

EURO CURRENCY INTEREST RATES

June 16	Short Term	7 Days Notice	One Month	Three Months	Six Months	One Year
Belgian Franc	$4\frac{5}{8}$–$4\frac{1}{2}$	$4\frac{5}{8}$–$4\frac{1}{2}$	$4\frac{5}{8}$–$4\frac{1}{2}$	$4\frac{11}{16}$–$4\frac{9}{16}$	$4\frac{3}{4}$–$4\frac{5}{8}$	5–$4\frac{7}{8}$
Danish Krone	7–$6\frac{1}{2}$	$6\frac{3}{4}$–$6\frac{1}{2}$	$6\frac{11}{16}$–$6\frac{7}{16}$	$6\frac{3}{4}$–$6\frac{1}{2}$	$6\frac{3}{4}$–$6\frac{1}{2}$	$6\frac{3}{4}$–$6\frac{1}{2}$
D-Mark	$4\frac{5}{8}$–$4\frac{1}{2}$	$4\frac{9}{16}$–$4\frac{7}{16}$	$4\frac{1}{2}$–$4\frac{3}{8}$	$4\frac{1}{2}$–$4\frac{3}{8}$	$4\frac{1}{2}$–$4\frac{3}{8}$	$4\frac{9}{16}$–$4\frac{7}{16}$
Dutch Guilder	$4\frac{3}{16}$–$4\frac{1}{16}$	$4\frac{3}{16}$–$4\frac{1}{16}$	$4\frac{3}{16}$–$4\frac{1}{8}$	$4\frac{1}{4}$–$4\frac{3}{16}$	$4\frac{1}{4}$–$4\frac{3}{16}$	$4\frac{7}{16}$–$4\frac{3}{8}$
French Franc	$7\frac{7}{16}$–$7\frac{5}{16}$	$7\frac{1}{2}$–$7\frac{3}{8}$	$7\frac{7}{16}$–$7\frac{5}{16}$	$7\frac{5}{16}$–$7\frac{3}{16}$	7–$6\frac{7}{8}$	$6\frac{11}{16}$–$6\frac{9}{16}$
Portuguese Esc.	$9\frac{1}{16}$–$8\frac{7}{8}$	$9\frac{1}{4}$–9	$9\frac{1}{2}$–$9\frac{5}{16}$	10–$9\frac{7}{8}$	$10\frac{1}{2}$–$10\frac{5}{16}$	$10\frac{15}{16}$–$10\frac{3}{4}$
Spanish Peseta	$9\frac{9}{16}$–$9\frac{7}{16}$	$9\frac{9}{16}$–$9\frac{7}{16}$	$9\frac{9}{16}$–$9\frac{7}{16}$	$9\frac{3}{4}$–$9\frac{5}{8}$	10–$9\frac{7}{8}$	$10\frac{7}{16}$–$10\frac{5}{16}$
Sterling	$6\frac{7}{8}$–$6\frac{5}{8}$	$6\frac{5}{8}$–$6\frac{1}{2}$	$6\frac{1}{2}$–$6\frac{7}{16}$	$6\frac{11}{16}$–$6\frac{5}{8}$	$6\frac{15}{16}$–$6\frac{13}{16}$	$7\frac{1}{4}$–$7\frac{1}{8}$
Swiss Franc	$2\frac{1}{2}$–$2\frac{1}{4}$	$2\frac{3}{4}$–$2\frac{5}{8}$	$3\frac{1}{16}$–$2\frac{15}{16}$	$3\frac{1}{8}$–3	$3\frac{3}{16}$–$3\frac{1}{16}$	$3\frac{5}{16}$–$3\frac{3}{16}$
Can. Dollar	7–$6\frac{13}{16}$	$7\frac{1}{8}$–$6\frac{15}{16}$	$7\frac{1}{16}$–$6\frac{15}{16}$	$6\frac{15}{16}$–$6\frac{13}{16}$	$6\frac{13}{16}$–$6\frac{11}{16}$	$6\frac{7}{8}$–$6\frac{3}{4}$
U.S. Dollar	$6\frac{1}{16}$–$5\frac{15}{16}$	$6\frac{1}{16}$–$5\frac{15}{16}$	$6\frac{1}{16}$–$5\frac{15}{16}$	$6\frac{1}{16}$–$5\frac{15}{16}$	$5\frac{15}{16}$–$5\frac{13}{16}$	$5\frac{15}{16}$–$5\frac{13}{16}$
Italian Lira	$10\frac{1}{2}$–$10\frac{3}{8}$	$10\frac{1}{2}$–$10\frac{3}{8}$	$10\frac{3}{4}$–$10\frac{5}{8}$	11–$10\frac{7}{8}$	$11\frac{1}{4}$–$11\frac{1}{8}$	$11\frac{1}{2}$–$11\frac{3}{8}$
Yen	$1\frac{9}{16}$–$1\frac{7}{16}$	$1\frac{9}{16}$–$1\frac{7}{16}$	$1\frac{1}{4}$–$1\frac{3}{16}$	$1\frac{3}{16}$–$1\frac{1}{8}$	$1\frac{1}{8}$–$1\frac{1}{16}$	$1\frac{3}{32}$–$1\frac{1}{32}$
Asian $Sing	$1\frac{1}{2}$–$1\frac{3}{8}$	$1\frac{1}{4}$–$1\frac{1}{8}$	$1\frac{1}{4}$–$1\frac{1}{8}$	$1\frac{3}{8}$–$1\frac{1}{4}$	$1\frac{5}{8}$–$1\frac{1}{2}$	$2\frac{1}{8}$–2

Short term rates are call for the U.S. Dollar and Yen, others: two days' notice.

Source: Financial Times, June 19, 1995, p. 27.

The forward exchange rate will be:

$$F = S\frac{(1+r_f)}{(1+r_d)} = 1.4007\frac{(1+0.0450)}{(1+0.0588)} = 1.3824$$

In the example described previously, we assumed that two parties conducted a face-to-face transaction. In reality, each party deals with its own financial intermediary. The intermediary takes a short position against the party who is taking the long position and a long position against the party who is taking the short position. The intermediary's positions cancel out, leaving it a profit equal to the bid-ask spread.

Let us introduce the intermediary in the previous example. For each variable we used previously, we will have two values, a lower bid value, when the intermediary is buying, and a higher ask value, when the intermediary is selling:

$$S_{DM/\$} = 1.4003 - 1.4010$$
$$r_f = 4\tfrac{7}{16} - 4\tfrac{9}{16} = 0.0444 - 0.0456$$
$$r_d = 5\tfrac{13}{16} - 5\tfrac{15}{16} = 0.0581 - 0.0594.$$

The spot exchange rates are drawn from Table 16.1 and the Eurocurrency rates are extracted from Table 16.2. The bid-ask spread for major currencies in the spot market is usually very small. In our example, the spread is only seven pips, a pip being 1/10,000 of a deutschemark. The bid-ask forward prices are calculated as follows:

$$F_{\text{bid}} = S_{\text{bid}}\frac{(1+r_{f(\text{bid})})}{(1+r_{d(\text{ask})})} = 1.4003\frac{(1+0.0444)}{(1+0.0594)} = 1.3805$$

$$F_{\text{ask}} = S_{\text{ask}}\frac{(1+r_{f(\text{ask})})}{(1+r_{d(\text{bid})})} = 1.4010\frac{(1+0.0456)}{(1+0.0581)} = 1.3844$$

The wider bid-ask spread in the forward market compared to the narrower spread in the spot market reflects the fact that forward contracts carry credit risk for the intermediary, thus requiring a risk premium. The forward price of 1.3819 reported in Table 16.1 is the midpoint value of the bid-ask prices we just calculated.

Interest Rate Forwards: Forward-Rate Agreements

A forward-rate agreement (FRA) is a contract between two parties intent on locking in future borrowing costs. The terms of the contract will typically specify the notional amount, interest rate, and maturity. An FRA does not involve making loans or taking deposits. There is a cash settlement at a specified future date, the amount of which is determined by the size of the notional amount, the spread between the contract rate and the settlement rate, and the length of the contract period. Since only the net interest flows are exchanged, FRAs contain very little credit risk.

FRAs exist in most major currencies, including U.S. dollars, British pounds, German marks, Swiss francs, and Japanese yen. Most FRA activities are concentrated in London. Consequently, the "terms and conditions" recommended by the British Bankers' Association (BBA) are widely accepted by market participants.[1] An example will illustrate pricing and settlement procedures.

Suppose that party A wants to lock in its dollar-denominated LIBOR borrowing costs for three months, six months into the future. Party A signs a forward-rate agreement with Citibank. The contract stipulates a settlement in six months based on the three-month dollar LIBOR, a contract rate set today, and the notional amount. The rate set today is the three-month forward rate six months from today, which is calculated from spot LIBOR rates. At the settlement date, if the outstanding rate is higher than the contract rate, party A will receive cash from Citibank. Conversely, if the outstanding rate is lower than the contract rate, party A will pay cash to Citibank.

Suppose that six-month and nine-month spot U.S. dollar LIBOR rates are 6% and 6.5%, respectively. The forward rate on a three-month LIBOR six months from today is calculated using the formula presented in Chapter 12:

$$_6R_9 = \left[\frac{(1+{_0}R_9)^{9/12}}{(1+{_0}R_6)^{6/12}}\right]^{12/3} - 1 = \left[\frac{(1+0.065)^{9/12}}{(1+0.060)^{6/12}}\right]^{12/3} - 1 = 0.075 = 7.5\%$$

Suppose that six months from today (settlement) the three-month rate turns out to be 8.5%. Party A gains by

$$3/12 \times (8.5\% - 7.5\%) = 0.25\%$$

On the notional amount of $1,000,000, the interest settlement is equal to

$$\$1,000,000 \times 0.0025 = \$2,500$$

in three months, with a present value of

$$PV = \frac{\$2,500}{\left(1+0.085 \times \dfrac{3}{12}\right)} = \$2,448$$

This solution could have been reached using a simple formula that the BBA has recommended:

[1] British Bankers' Association, *London Interbank Forward Rate Agreements: Recommended Terms and Conditions*, August, 1985.

$$\frac{(L-R)\times D\times A}{(B\times 100)+(L\times D)}$$

where

L = interest settlement rate
R = contract rate
D = days in contract period
A = notional amount
B = 360 or 365 days, according to market custom

Using the data from our example, we can calculate the amount party A will receive at the settlement date:

$$\frac{(8.5-7.5)\times 90\times \$1,000,000}{(360\times 100)+(8.5\times 90)} = \$2,448$$

As discussed earlier, FRAs involve the exchange of the net interest flows, which contain little credit risk since the notional amount of the contract is not at risk. This provides for narrower bid-ask spreads in FRAs. A typical broker screen in Reuters presents quotes for three- and six-month U.S. dollar FRAs commencing in three months, four months, five months, and six months. For example, a quote of

6 v 9 7.50/7.45

indicates an FRA from month six to month nine (a three-month rate in six months) at a spread of five basis points.

Contracting Issues in the Forward Market

Forward contracts are customized for a variety of underlying assets, contract sizes, and settlement dates. The customized nature of forward contracts contributes to contracting problems associated with size, settlement date, default risk, and liquidity.

A party seeking a long forward position of a particular size and settlement date may have difficulty finding a counterparty who is looking for the exact opposite position. In addition, forward contracts encompass default risk. Hedgers are protected against risk only if the parties to the contract honor their respective obligations. To the extent that the losing party in a forward contract has an incentive to default, the contract is a credit instrument with default risk.

There are also liquidity problems in the forward market. A party who has entered into a forward contract may decide to exit the contract prior to its settlement date. Since the contract is customized, there is no active secondary market. This limits his alternatives to the following:[2]

1. **Canceling the contract**. The party who is interested in exiting the contract may solicit an early settlement with the counterparty. However, a counterparty who has entered into the contract in order to hedge against an exposure is not likely to agree on an early settlement. With an intermediary as a counterparty, there is a better chance for an early settlement if the party is willing to incur the transaction cost.
2. **Finding another party to take over the position**. If a third party needs that particular position, the first party may be able to exit the contract by transferring its position to the third party. The complicating factor is the credit risk. The third party has to have a credit risk acceptable to the second party. Again, finding a third party who needs the same exact position and has the same credit risk as the first party may be difficult.

---

[2] Campbell and Kracaw (1993), pp. 111–113.

3. **Taking an offsetting position**. A party with a long position may close out the position by entering into a short contract of the same size, settlement date, and underlying asset. The transaction cost involved includes the bid-ask spread and other fees.

If the parties to a forward contract are both hedgers, any disturbance to the contract may expose at least one of them to risk. Consequently, an early exit based on any of the above scenarios will only be remotely feasible.

Financial intermediaries, by virtue of their expertise in information production, risk assessment, size, maturity, and liquidity intermediation, are in a unique position to mitigate the aforementioned contracting problems. The uniqueness in size and settlement date makes finding matching counterparties to a forward contract difficult. Consequently, a customized forward contract is usually obtained from a financial intermediary. Since unwinding each position individually is difficult, the intermediary is likely to create a portfolio of forwards and other OTC derivatives and hedge the residual risk of the entire portfolio through exchange-traded derivatives. Financial intermediaries with expertise in credit assessment are also well suited to handle the default risk inherent in forward contracts.

The liquidity problem is also significantly reduced when the counterparty to a forward contract is a financial intermediary. Having a financial intermediary as the counterparty makes an early exit easier. This increased liquidity, however, comes at a substantial transaction cost. Consequently, forward contracts are generally available in sizable denominations for large entities such as corporations, institutional investors, and other wealthy clients. The customized nature of forward contracts along with credit and liquidity risks make financial intermediaries natural suppliers of forward contracts. To provide the service, financial intermediaries charge a fee in the form of a bid-ask spread that reflects both their credit risk and a liquidity premium.

FUTURES

Futures contracts were designed partially in response to the contracting problems of the forward market. While the history of modern commodities futures goes back to the establishment of the Chicago Board of Trade in the mid-19th century,[3] financial futures have a much shorter history, having been developed in the 1970s.

During the 1840s, Chicago was the center of trade for agricultural goods produced in the Midwest. The Board of Trade of the City of Chicago was established by 1850 to facilitate trade in farm products. During the 1850s, farm products were traded by means of "to arrive" contracts, which later became known as forward contracts. These contracts were agreements to exchange farm products at a future date at a pre-specified price. Initially, these contracts were private, non-transferable agreements between the buyer and the seller. By the 1870s, the Chicago Board of Trade (CBOT) had developed rules and printed documents that specified the grade, quantity, and time of delivery in its forward contracts.

As described in the previous section, default risk is one of the contracting problems in the forward market. In order to reduce default risk, performance bonds were set up in the form of money deposits with a third party. In 1891, the Minneapolis Grain Exchange organized the first complete clearinghouse system as the third party to all transactions in the exchange.

---

[3] Actually, futures contracts were traded in Japan in the 1700s and in Holland during the tulip bulb bubble.

The clearinghouse system was principally organized to ensure the integrity of contracts through a series of centralized, efficient procedures, which continue in practice today. Buyers and sellers are required to post margins with the clearinghouse. An *initial margin*, the amount of which is determined by the historical daily fluctuations of the price, is deposited in the account of each contracting party at the exchange. A limit is imposed on the maximum one-day loss in each contract in order to shield the clearinghouse from default risk. The clearinghouse also specifies a *maintenance margin*—a minimum balance in the margin account. In addition, the clearinghouse requires a daily settlement of all open positions, a practice now known as marking-to-market. At the end of each trading day, the clearinghouse settles each contract at the closing price by transferring funds from the account of the party who loses to the account of the party who gains. If an account's balance falls below the maintenance margin, the clearinghouse issues a *margin call*, requiring the account holder to post additional deposits, called *variation margin*, to bring the account back to its initial margin level. If a party fails to meet the margin call, the account is closed out by executing an offsetting transaction, and the remaining balance is returned to the account holder.

The development of the clearinghouse system combined with the public price auction system on the exchange floor constitute the final steps in the evolution of the forward market into the futures market. The default risk inherent in the forward market is absent in the futures market because of the clearinghouse system, margin requirements, and the daily marking-to-market of all positions. An active market in a relatively small number of standardized contracts creates liquidity in the futures market. A party with a long position in a futures contract who wants to exit the contract prior to the settlement date can enter into a short position in a similar contract and the clearinghouse would simply close out the two matching positions at the end of the day.

In contrast to commodities futures, financial futures were not developed until the 1970s. As discussed in Chapter 15, increased volatility in the foreign exchange and interest-rate markets increased the demand for hedging instruments, including futures contracts. Today, there is a wide variety of short- and long-term futures contracts available, among them foreign exchange futures; interest-rate futures, including 90-day Treasury bill futures, Treasury bond and note futures, municipal bond index futures, and Eurodollar futures; commodities futures; and stock index futures.

Foreign Exchange Futures

The International Monetary Market (IMM) of the CME opened the first foreign currency futures in 1972. As the volatility of currency exchange rates increased following the breakdown of the Bretton Woods Agreement, so did the demand for currency futures to mitigate the risk. The IMM quotes currency futures prices in terms of the U.S. dollar. In order to explain the institutional features of currency futures, actual quotations for Japanese yen from the July 12, 1995, issue of *The Wall Street Journal* for trades on July 11 are presented in Table 16.3.

Each contract amounts to 12.5 million yen. The price quotes are in cents per yen. For example, the September settlement quote of 1.1546 means a price per contract of ¥0.011546 × 12,500,000 = $144,325. In the columns preceding the open interest column, lifetime high and low prices are provided. The volume of open interest in the contract with the nearest maturity is largest, with 42,994 September contracts. This volume declines significantly to 3,604 contracts for December and to less than 10% of that for the later maturities.

Other currency futures traded on the IMM include the German mark, Canadian dollar, British pound, Swiss franc, and Australian dollar. There are also cur-

TABLE 16.3	Japan Yen (CM)—12.5 Million Yen; $ Per Yen (.00)							
	Open	High	Low	Settle	Change	High	Low	Open Interest
Sept	1.1614	1.1625	1.1536	1.1546	−0.0059	1.2670	1.0175	42,994
Dec	1.1688	1.1753	1.1680	1.1685	−0.0059	1.2813	1.0300	3,604
Mr96	1.1825	1.1825	1.1825	1.1825	−0.0059	1.2990	1.0465	302
June	1.1955	1.1960	1.1954	1.1965	−0.0059	1.3130	1.0780	333

Est. vol. 9,975; vol. 25,164; open int. 47,233, +1,842.

rency index futures contracts available. For example, the U.S. Dollar Index (USDX), which began trading on the Financial Instrument Exchange (FINEX) in late 1985, is a weighted geometric average of the foreign exchange rates of 10 currencies. Delivery procedures follow those of other financial futures traded on the IMM.

Interest Rate Futures

Treasury Bill Futures Three-month T-bill futures were first offered by the International Monetary Market (IMM) of the Chicago Mercantile Exchange (CME) on January 2, 1976. Contract expiration months are March, June, September, and December; contracts are available for up to two years in the future. Actual quotations for T-bill futures, based on July 11, 1995, trades, are presented in Table 16.4.

On July 11, 1995, T-bill futures contracts were available for delivery in September and December 1995 and in March 1996. Each contract requires the delivery of $1 million in face value of three-month T-bills. The prices quoted are points of 100%. For example, the September contracts opened at 94.81% of their face values, fluctuated in price between a high of 94.82% and a low of 94.78%, and closed at 94.79%. The settlement price was 0.04% lower than the previous day's price.

T-bill futures prices are quoted as discounts over face values. For example, the settlement price of a September contract was 94.79, which means it was sold at a 5.21% discount from 100% face value: 100 - 5.21 = 94.79. The 5.21% is the annualized discount rate that needs to be adjusted for the actual maturity of the underlying T-bill, which is three months. On the delivery date in September, the price paid for a $1 million face value of a three-month to maturity T-bill will be:

$$\text{Three-month discount rate} = 5.21 (90/360) = 1.3025$$
$$\text{Price in points of } 100\% = 100 - 1.3025 = 98.6975$$
$$\text{Price per contract} = 98.6975(\$1,000,000/100) = \$986,975$$

TABLE 16.4	Treasury Bills (CME)–$1 mil.; pts of 100%							
						Discount		Open Interest
	Open	High	Low	Settle	Chg	Settle	Chg	
Sept	94.81	94.82	94.78	94.79	−.04	5.21	+0.04	9,753
Dec	94.96	94.97	94.93	94.93	−.06	5.07	+0.06	9,993
Mr96	95.01	95.01	94.97	94.99	−.04	5.01	+0.04	681

Est. vol. 885; vol. 403; open int. 20,429, −87.

On July 11, 1995, the September contracts declined in value by 0.04% over the previous day's price. This amounts to four basis points. The change in the price of a three-month T-bill futures contract due to a one basis point or one tick move in the quoted price is:

$$0.0001 \times (90/360) \times \$1,000,000 = \$25$$

In our example, the −0.04 change amounts to a decline in the price of futures contract by $4 \times \$25 = \$100$. The party who has a long position pays $100 to the party with a short position when the contracts are marked-to-market.

The last column of the price table shows the number of bilateral contracts that exist between buyers and sellers for each settlement date. For example, on July 11, 1995, there were 9,753 separate $1 million contracts in three-month T-bills for the September 1995 settlement date. The figures reported at the bottom of the table show the number of contracts executed on the trading day. At the time of the publication of the report, settlements for the day were not fully accounted for. Therefore, an estimated number (885) is provided along with the previous day's actual volume of 403. The previous day's total open interest was 20,429, which was 87 contracts below the open interest of the day before.

Treasury Bond and Note Futures   Treasury bond futures contracts were offered by the Chicago Board of Trade (CBOT) for the first time in 1977. T-bond futures are based on Treasury bonds with maturities of at least 15 years, if not callable, or bonds that are not callable for at least 15 years. T-note futures are based on intermediate-term Treasury notes with maturities of 2, 5, or 10 years. T-bond and T-note futures are identical in their design with the exception of their maturities and margin requirements. On July 12, 1995, *The Wall Street Journal* reported the July 11 T-bond futures trades presented in Table 16.5.

Several obvious differences exist between T-bond and T-bill futures. Each contract in T-bond futures has a denomination of $100,000, versus $1,000,000 for T-bill futures. Each decimal point in T-bond futures is worth $\frac{1}{32}$ of 100. For example, the September contract's settlement price is calculated as

$$\$100,000\ [(114 + 20/32)/100] = \$114,625$$

which means that the buyer of the September contract will receive $100,000 (face value) in U.S. T-bonds (standard 8% coupon) in September at a price of $114,625.[4] A price move of 00-01, or 1/32% of face value, results in a

$$\$100,000/100 \times 1/32 = \$31.25$$

change in the price of each contract.

The number of open interest contracts for September futures was 394,927. The volume of open interest dropped sharply for later dates, indicating lower demand. The last settlement date reported is September 1996, a year and a half in the future with only 31 open positions. Positions with later dates were not available due to lack of demand.

Another important difference between T-bond and T-bill futures lies with the deliverable securities. While T-bill futures require delivery of three-month T-bills, T-bond futures provide the short party a choice of delivery from a wide range of coupons and maturities. The maturity of the deliverable T-bond has to be 15 years or longer, if the bond is not callable, and if callable, it has to have at least 15 years from the first day of the delivery month before it becomes callable. For delivery at the settlement date, the short would choose from the list of eligi-

---

[4] The long will not actually receive an 8% coupon but will receive the equivalent. We will return to this later.

						Lifetime		Open
	Open	**High**	**Low**	**Settle**	**Chg**	**High**	**Low**	**Interest**
Sept	115–14	115–14	114–19	114–20	–27	116–06	94–10	394,927
Dec	114–29	114–29	114–05	114–06	–27	115–22	93–27	21,107
Mr96	—	—	—	113–23	–27	115–06	93–13	1,834
June	—	—	—	113–06	–27	114–05	93–06	306
Sept	—	—	—	112–22	–27	113–26	102–06	31

TABLE 16.5   Treasury Bonds (CBT)–$100,000; pts, 32nd of 100%

Est. vol. 215,000; vol. Mn 145,750; open int. 418,261, –2,841.

ble T-bonds the cheapest-to-deliver (CTD) bond. Since the contract provisions are specified in terms of an 8% coupon bond, a system of conversion factors is designed to determine the number of deliverable T-bonds needed to be the equivalent of the standard 8% coupon bonds. More detail about conversion factors will be provided later.

While less than 1% of T-bond and T-note futures result in delivery, everyone with an outstanding position as of the delivery date must buy or sell the underlying instrument to meet the requirements of the legally binding futures contract. A party who uses futures for hedging purposes may liquidate the futures position before the delivery date by means of an "offsetting trade." An offsetting trade requires the long (short) to sell (buy) an equal number of contracts in the same delivery month. Despite the fact that only a small fraction of total futures contracts are delivered, the possibility of delivery converges futures prices and cash market prices to the extent that, in the delivery month, prices in both markets are approximately equal.

The actual delivery process is a fixed sequence of events established by the futures exchange. Delivery of T-bond and T-note futures is a three-day process that provides time for the short, the long, and the Clearing Corporation to make the necessary arrangements for the delivery. The short has the right to initiate the three-day delivery process any time during a period that begins two business days prior to the first business day of the delivery month and ends two business days before the last business day of the month. While the last day of the delivery is the last business day of the delivery month, trading in the deliverable contract ends on the seventh business day before the last business day of the delivery month. The sequence of the three-day delivery process is as follows:[5]

Day 1: Position Day
> The short notifies the Clearing Corporation about the intention to make delivery.

Day 2: Notice of Intention Day
> The Clearing Corporation matches the oldest long to the delivering short and then notifies both parties. The short invoices the long.

Day 3: Delivery Day
> The short delivers the financial instrument that was previously acquired by the long. The long pays the invoice price and title is passed to the long, who now assumes ownership.

To facilitate the delivery from a range of eligible securities, the CBOT has developed a *conversion factor* system. The conversion factor is the present value of a $1 face value bond discounted at 8%. The conversion factor with an 8% coupon

---

[5] Chicago Board of Trade, *The Delivery Process in Brief: Treasury Bond and Treasury Note Futures*, 1990.

rate is approximately equal to 1.0000. If the instrument used in the delivery has a coupon greater than 8%, the conversion factor will be greater than 1.0000 to reflect the premium. Conversely, if the coupon is lower than 8%, the conversion factor will be less than 1.0000 to reflect the discount.

The CBOT provides conversion factor tables for various coupons and maturities. A sample of conversion factors is provided in Table 16.6.[6] The computation of conversion factors is a relatively simple task. Strictly speaking, a conversion factor is the present value of coupon payments and the face value on a $1 bond. For example, suppose that the short decides to deliver the 8⅞% August 2017 cash bond against the September 1995 futures contract. On September 1, 1995, 8⅞% bonds of August 2017 have a term-to-maturity of 21 years, 11 months, and 14 days. The procedure in computing the conversion factor requires rounding down the maturity to the nearest quarter, which translates into 21 years, 9 months. The bond in our example has coupon payment dates of February 15 and August 15. The conversion factor is calculated (CF_9)

$$CF_9 = \frac{0.08875}{2}\left[\frac{1}{0.04} - \frac{1}{0.04(1+0.04)^{21.75 \times 2}}\right] + \frac{1}{(1+.04)^{21.75 \times 2}} = 1.0893$$

The invoice price— the amount the long pays to the short for the bond—is calculated by multiplying the settlement price by the conversion factor, plus the accrued interest from the last coupon payment date until the delivery date:

Invoice price = settlement price × conversion factor + accrued interest

Suppose that the bond has coupon payments on February 15 and August 15. The short has the choice of the delivery day during the month of delivery. Suppose that on Tuesday, September 5, 1995 (day 1: position day), the short notifies the Clearing Corporation of the intention to make delivery. Assume that on position day, the settlement price is 113-20 or $113,625. On Wednesday, September 6, 1995 (day 2: notice of intention day), the short invoices the long. On Thursday, September 7, 1995 (day 3: delivery day), the short delivers the 8⅞% coupon bonds of August 2017 (the cheapest-to-deliver bond, see below) at a settlement price of $113,625. Since delivery takes place on September 7 and the last coupon payment was on August 15, 1995, there are 22 days of accrued interest—counting from, but not including, August 15 to, and including, September 7. The coupon payments are on August 15 and February 15 and there are 184 days between two coupon payments. The accrued interest is calculated as:

Accrued interest = $100,000(0.08875/2)22/184 = $531

The invoice price is

Invoice price = $113,625 × 1.0893 + $531 = $124,303

At any settlement time, there are some 30 bonds that are eligible for delivery. Since the short has the right to choose the bond to be delivered, the choice will be the cheapest-to-deliver bond. In the previous example, the short received the invoice price (cash inflow) and paid for the price of the bond delivered (cash outflow):

The short's cash inflow = invoice price = settlement price
× CF + accrued interest

The short's cash outflow = quoted price of the bond delivered
+ accrued interest

The short's net cash outflow = settlement price × CF
− quoted price of the bond delivered

---

[6] Chicago Board of Trade, *Conversion Factors*, 1994.

TABLE 16.6   Conversion Factor to Yield 8%

Coupon Rate

Yrs–Mos	8%	8⅛%	8¼%	8⅜%	8½%	8⅝%	8¾%	8⅞%
15–0	1.0000	1.0108	1.0216	1.0324	1.0432	1.0540	1.0648	1.0757
15–3	0.9998	1.0107	1.0216	1.0325	1.0434	1.0543	1.0652	1.0761
15–6	1.0000	1.0110	1.0220	1.0330	1.0440	1.0550	1.0660	1.0769
15–9	0.9998	1.0109	1.0220	1.0330	1.0441	1.0552	1.0663	1.0774
16–0	1.0000	1.0112	1.0223	1.0335	1.0447	1.0559	1.0670	1.0782
16–3	0.9998	1.0111	1.0223	1.0336	1.0448	1.0561	1.0673	1.0786
16–6	1.0000	1.0113	1.0227	1.0340	1.0454	1.0567	1.0681	1.0794
16–9	0.9998	1.0112	1.0226	1.0341	1.0455	1.0569	1.0683	1.0798
17–0	1.0000	1.0115	1.0230	1.0345	1.0460	1.0575	1.0690	1.0805
17–3	0.9998	1.0114	1.0230	1.0346	1.0461	1.0577	1.0693	1.0809
17–6	1.0000	1.0117	1.0233	1.0350	1.0467	1.0583	1.0700	1.0817
17–9	0.9998	1.0115	1.0233	1.0350	1.0468	1.0585	1.0702	1.0820
18–0	1.0000	1.0118	1.0236	1.0355	1.0473	1.0591	1.0709	1.0827
18–3	0.9998	1.0117	1.0236	1.0355	1.0474	1.0592	1.0711	1.0830
18–6	1.0000	1.0120	1.0239	1.0359	1.0479	1.0598	1.0718	1.0837
18–9	0.9998	1.0118	1.0239	1.0359	1.0479	1.0600	1.0720	1.0840
19–0	1.0000	1.0121	1.0242	1.0363	1.0484	1.0605	1.0726	1.0847
19–3	0.9998	1.0120	1.0241	1.0363	1.0485	1.0607	1.0728	1.0850
19–6	1.0000	1.0122	1.0245	1.0367	1.0490	1.0612	1.0734	1.0857
19–9	0.9998	1.0121	1.0244	1.0367	1.0490	1.0613	1.0736	1.0859
20–0	1.0000	1.0124	1.0247	1.0371	1.0495	1.0619	1.0742	1.0866
20–3	0.9998	1.0122	1.0247	1.0371	1.0495	1.0620	1.0744	1.0868
20–6	1.0000	1.0125	1.0250	1.0375	1.0500	1.0625	1.0750	1.0875
20–9	0.9998	1.0124	1.0249	1.0375	1.0500	1.0626	1.0751	1.0877
21–0	1.0000	1.0126	1.0252	1.0378	1.0505	1.0631	1.0757	1.0833
21–3	0.9998	1.0125	1.0251	1.0378	1.0505	1.0632	1.0758	1.0885
21–6	1.0000	1.0127	1.0255	1.0382	1.0509	1.0637	1.0764	1.0891
21–9	0.9998	1.0126	1.0254	1.0382	1.0509	1.0637	1.0765	1.0893

Coupon

Yrs–Mos	10½	10⅝	10¾	10⅞	11%	11⅛	11¼	11⅜
20–0	1.2474	1.2598	1.2722	1.2845	1.2969	1.3093	1.3216	1.3340
20–3	1.2484	1.2608	1.2733	1.2857	1.2981	1.3106	1.3230	1.3354
20–6	1.2499	1.2624	1.2749	1.2874	1.2999	1.3124	1.3249	1.3374
20–9	1.2509	1.2634	1.2760	1.2885	1.3011	1.3136	1.3262	1.3387
21–0	1.2523	1.2649	1.2776	1.2902	1.3028	1.3154	1.3280	1.3406
21–3	1.2532	1.2659	1.2786	1.2912	1.3039	1.3166	1.3293	1.3419
21–6	1.2546	1.2674	1.2801	1.2928	1.3056	1.3183	1.3310	1.3438
21–9	1.2555	1.2683	1.2811	1.2939	1.3066	1.3194	1.3322	1.3450

In choosing which bond to deliver, the short will attempt to minimize the net cash outflow. Suppose that in the preceding example, the short has the following bonds presented in Table 16.7 to choose from

TABLE 16.7 A List of Available Bonds to Deliver					
Bond	Quoted Price	Settlement Price	CF	Settlement Price × CF	Net Cash Outflow
1	90.78	113.625	0.8173	92.87	−2.09
2	99.66	113.625	0.8727	99.16	+0.50
3	102.69	113.625	0.9175	103.68	−0.99
4	120.97	113.625	1.0893	123.77	−2.80

The cheapest-to-deliver bond is bond 4, which is the one the short chose to deliver.

Municipal Bond Index Futures The CBOT introduced Municipal Bond Index futures in June 1985. Prior to the introduction of the muni-bond contracts, those who wanted to hedge their portfolios of muni-bonds had to use other instruments, such as T-bonds. Because of the inherent differences between muni-bonds and T-bonds in risk, liquidity, and tax treatment, the price movements in T-bond contracts and muni-bonds did not adequately match, diminishing T-bond futures' usefulness for hedging muni-bond portfolios. The introduction of muni-bond index contracts addressed this problem. The Municipal Bond Index futures is based on *The Bond Buyer* Index of 40 actively traded, general obligation, and revenue, tax-exempt bonds. For a bond to be included in the index composition, it must satisfy the following criteria:[7]

- be A− or better rated by Standard & Poor's or A or better rated by Moody's
- have a term amount that equals, or exceeds, $50 million in size ($75 million for housing issues)
- have a remaining maturity of at least 19 years
- be callable prior to maturity, with the first call between 7 and 16 years, upon inclusion in the index
- have a fixed coupon with semiannual interest payments
- be re-offered, out of syndicate, with prices ranging from 95 to 105

Private bonds and bonds with unusual features are not eligible to be included in the index. An example of the muni-bond index futures price quotation from July 11, 1995, trading is presented in Table 16.8.

Each contract is worth $1,000 times the Bond Buyer's muni-bond index. Since the muni-bond contract is based on an index, the settlement always takes place in cash.

Eurodollar Futures Eurodollar deposit futures began trading on the IMM in December 1981. A partial listing of price quotations for July 11, 1995, is presented in Table 16.9.

Eurodollar contracts call for delivery in March, June, September, and December

---

[7] *CBOT Financial Instrument Guide*, Chicago Board of Trade, 1994, p. 74.

TABLE 16.8	Muni-Bond Index (CBT)–$1,000; Times Bond Buyer MBI							
	Open	High	Low	Settle	Chg	High	Low	Open Interest
Sept	116–07	116–24	116–05	116–15	–2	117–06	109-05	20,486
	Est. vol. 5,000; vol. Mn 2,729; open int. 20,488, +566.							
	The Index: Close 116–16; Yield 6.13.							

of each year for 10 years into the future. Similar to T-bill futures, prices for Eurodollar contracts are quoted as 100 minus the annualized Eurodollar futures rate. Each contract has $1 million in denomination. For example, the September 1995 contract with the settlement of 94.42 and annual yield of 5.58% has a three-month yield of

$$5.58(90/360) = 1.3950\%,$$

which is the actual discount on the 90-day Eurodollar futures contract. The actual settlement price in dollars is

$$\$1,000,000 \ (1 - .01395) = \$986,050$$

The final settlement is made in cash, based on the average three-month LIBOR quoted on a random selection of 12 banks from the top 20 banks in the London Eurodollar market. The settlement goes through the IMM Clearinghouse.

Commodities Futures

A variety of commodities futures are traded, including grains and oilseeds, livestock and meat, food and fiber, metals and petroleum. Commodities futures have been traded for a much longer period of time than financial futures. An example of a commodities futures listing for July 11, 1995, is presented in Table 16.10.

Heating oil futures are traded on the New York Mercantile Exchange. Each contract amounts to 42,000 gallons of heating oil no. 2. The prices are quoted in dollars per gallon. Contracts are available for each month, and actively traded for the next 12 months.

Stock Index Futures

The first stock index futures was offered by the Kansas City Futures Exchange on the Value Line Index in February 1982. The Nikkei Stock Average futures was the first foreign stock index futures; it opened on the CME in June 1987. Today, the CME, the NYSE, and the CBOT trade stock index futures contracts based on the S&P 500, NYSE indexes, and the Major Market Index (MMI), respectively. The July 11, 1995, quotes for S&P 500 index futures are presented in Table 16.11.

TABLE 16.9	Eurodollar (CME)–$1 Million; Pts of 100%							
	Open	High	Low	Settle	Chg	Yield Settle	Chg	Open Interest
Sept	94.47	94.47	94.41	94.42	–0.05	5.58	+0.05	389,199
Dec	94.56	94.56	94.49	94.50	–0.07	5.50	+0.07	346,054
Mr96	94.60	94.60	94.55	94.56	–0.07	5.44	+0.07	286,723
June	94.52	94.52	94.46	94.47	–0.06	5.53	+0.06	203,201
	Est. vol. 200,087; vol. 251,220; open int. 2,265,124, –12,488.							

TABLE 16.10	Heating Oil No. 2 (NYM) 42,000 Gallons; $ Per Gallon							
						Lifetime		Open Interest
	Open	High	Low	Settle	Change	High	Low	
Aug	0.4715	0.4760	0.4690	0.4696	−0.0014	0.5400	0.4600	41,776
Sept	0.4780	0.4810	0.4750	0.4752	−0.0014	0.5310	0.4670	19,753
Est. vol. 31,196; vol. Mn 29,890; open int. 131,049, − 120.								

The S&P 500 index futures' contract price is calculated by multiplying the price quoted by 500. For example, the September contract with a settlement price of 557.75 indicates a contract price of 557.75 × 500 = $278,875. A one-point change in the quoted price amounts to a $500 change in the price of one contract. The two columns immediately preceding the open interest column present the lifetime high and low prices for the contract.

Unlike most futures contracts, stock index futures contracts do not require the delivery of the underlying assets. The reason for not delivering the stock index is that such an exchange would create substantial transaction costs in buying baskets of shares and might even create liquidity problems in the market. Thus, all stock index positions are closed out at maturity and a cash settlement is made, based on the value of the index at that time. For MMI, NYSE, and Value Line stock index futures, the termination time is 4 P.M. Eastern time of the last trading day. To mitigate the impact of the cash settlement of stock index futures on the securities markets, S&P 500 index futures are settled on the basis of the opening price on that Friday, while trading in the expiring futures ends on the prior day.

The Pricing of Futures Contracts

The Cost of Carry   Futures prices are linked to spot prices throughout the life of the contract. At any point during the contract period, there is a difference between the cash price and the futures price on the underlying asset that is known as the *basis*. Theoretically, the basis is equal to the cost of carrying the asset, or the *cost of carry*. The reasoning behind this relationship can be explained by a simple example. Suppose you are interested in owning a certain asset in six months. You have two choices: Either borrow the money today and purchase the asset, or take a long futures position on the asset for six months. Both alternatives will produce ownership of the asset in six months. Since the two outcomes are identical, their cost should be the same. The cost of the first alternative is the price of the asset today, or the spot price, plus the interest cost of the loan. Since the asset serves as

TABLE 16.11	S&P 500 Index (CME) $500 Times Index							
	Open	High	Low	Settle	Chg	High	Low	Open Interest
Sept	560.05	560.80	556.80	557.75	−3.45	562.50	556.30	198,489
Dec	564.10	564.35	561.20	561.85	−3.45	566.10	474.50	8,500
Mar	—	—	—	565.50	−3.45	568.80	511.00	2,816
June	—	—	—	569.40	−3.75	572.00	544.25	181
Est. vol. 65,807; vol. 51,189; open int. 209,986, +2,680.								
Indx prelim High 557.17; Low 553.80; Close 554.78, −2.41.								

collateral for the loan, it is reasonable to assume that the interest cost will be equal to the risk-free rate. Thus, the futures price should be equal to the spot price, adjusted for the financing charges:

$$F_0 = S_0(1 + r)^T$$

In this equation, F_0 is the futures price today, S_0 is the current spot price and r is the annual risk-free rate. Since the futures price is equal to the cash price of the underlying asset, net of carry, the investor will be indifferent between futures and cash markets.

In the preceding example, we assumed that there were no intermediate cash flows. Examples of contracts without intermediate cash flows include T-bill and Eurodollar futures. For assets that generate intermediate cash flows—T-bonds, stock indexes, and currencies (if invested), for example—the equation should be adjusted to reflect the present value of the intermediate cash flows. While finance charges increase the cost of buying the asset today and, hence, the price of the futures contract, intermediate cash flows reduce the cost of buying the asset in the spot market and, therefore, reduce the futures price. The futures price for an asset with intermediate cash flows, therefore, is the spot price plus financing charges, minus cash flows to be received while holding the asset. For commodities, the cost of storage is added to the financing cost to arrive at the total cost of carry.

A Simple Proof of the Relationship Between Prices in the Spot and Futures Markets For financial futures, the cost of carry is the net financing cost. The most basic form of financial futures involves an asset that provides no income during the contract period. The futures price for such a contract is calculated by the following equation:

$$F_0 = S_0(1 + {}_0r_T)^T$$

which indicates that the investor is indifferent between borrowing money and purchasing the asset today and purchasing a futures contract on the same asset. To prove that this equation holds, suppose that $F_0 > S_0(1 + {}_0r_T)^T$. An investor can borrow S_0 at the risk-free rate of ${}_0r_T$, purchase the asset, and take a short position in the futures contract. At time T, the investor delivers the asset, receives F_0, pays off the loan in the amount of $S_0(1 + {}_0r_T)^T$, and makes an arbitrage profit of $F_0 - S_0(1 + {}_0r_T)^T$. The exploitation of the arbitrage profit forces the futures price and the spot price, adjusted for the cost of carry, to be equal.

Now suppose that $F_0 < S_0(1 + {}_0r_T)^T$. An investor can sell the asset short at the price of S_0, invest the proceeds for T years at the rate of ${}_0r_T$, and take a long position in the futures contract. At time T, the investor takes delivery of the asset at F_0, returns the asset to cover the short position, receives $S_0(1 + {}_0r_T)^T$, and earns an arbitrage profit of $S_0(1 + {}_0r_T)^T - F_0$. Again, arbitrage trading forces prices in the cash market adjusted for the cost of carry and the futures market to be equal.

Futures Prices on Assets with Intermediate Cash Flows For contracts on assets with intermediate cash flows such as stock index futures, the basic futures price equation described above is adjusted by subtracting the present value of the intermediate cash flows

$$F_0 = S_0(1 + {}_0r_T)^T - PV(D)$$

If intermediate cash flows constitute a constant percentage of the asset price, as is the case with dividend yield, the futures price will be calculated as

$$F_0 = S_0 \frac{(1 + {}_0r_T)^T}{(1 + \delta)^T}$$

where δ is the annual dividend yield.

Futures Prices for Commodities with Storage Costs   For commodities, the equation is adjusted by adding the present value of the storage costs

$$F_0 = S_0(1 + {_0r_{T)}}^T + PV(C)$$

Futures Prices for Currencies   For currencies, the basic futures price equation is adjusted by the interest income that is earned by investing the currency

$$F_0 = S_0 \frac{(1 + {_0r_T})^T}{(1 + {_0r_f})^T}$$

where $_0r_f$ is the risk-free interest rate on the foreign currency.

HEDGING STRATEGIES

The purpose of risk management is to redistribute risk arising from holding fixed-income securities (interest-rate risk), currencies (foreign exchange risk), and real assets and equity (commodities price risk). This involves altering the risk/return profile of a core cash position to suit the investor's risk preference. Forward and futures contracts are used to protect the value of the underlying position, limit opportunity losses, and/or enhance returns. Figure 16.1 demonstrates the sensitivity of the underlying position (ΔV) to changes in interest rates, foreign exchange rates, or commodities prices (ΔP). To set up a hedge, a forward or futures position opposite to that of the underlying exposure should be taken. For example, if the hedge is to protect the value of a long portfolio, a short hedge is needed.

Faced with financial risk, management must focus on the following factors:

- The nature of the risk exposure (micro or macro);
- The desired risk/return profile;
- The market expectations;
- The magnitude of basis risk with the optimal futures contract; and
- The number of futures contracts required.

After evaluating the risk exposure, management needs to determine the preferred risk/return profile. Depending on the amount of risk management is willing to take, the decision is made as to whether to use over-the-counter instruments such as forward contracts that eliminate basis risk or to use exchange-traded instruments such as futures contracts. While forward contracts are written

FIGURE 16.1
Change in Value as Function of Change in Interest Rates, Foreign Exchange Rates, or Commodities Prices

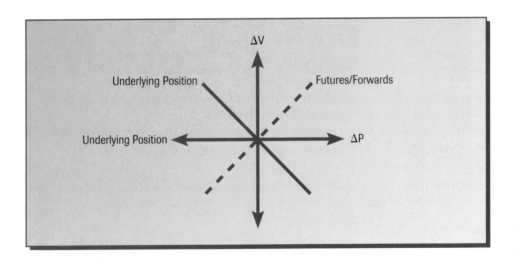

to meet the specific needs of the investor, futures contracts are standardized instruments that can be bought and sold in a liquid market. The standardized features of futures contracts reduce their transaction costs, relative to forward contracts. The standardized features that make futures contracts more liquid and less costly than forward contracts are also responsible for the differences between cash and futures price movements, or basis risk. Management has to evaluate the trade-off between the liquidity available in the futures market and the basis risk inherent in futures hedging.

The presence of basis risk necessitates the use of a *hedge ratio,* which indicates the number of futures contracts required to hedge against changes in the underlying cash position. Basis risk is managed by carefully choosing a minimum variance hedge ratio.

Methods of Calculating Hedge Ratios

In order to hedge an underlying position, an investor has to employ a sufficient number of futures contracts to ensure the following:

$$\Delta\text{cash price} = -\Delta\text{futures price}$$

The purpose of a hedge is to ensure that any change in the price of the underlying position is matched with an equal change in the opposite direction in the price of the futures position. Since futures prices do not behave exactly like cash prices, a hedge ratio (HR) is calculated that indicates how many futures contracts are required to obtain the desired hedge. The relationship is depicted as follows:

$$\Delta\text{cash price} = -\Delta\text{futures price} \times \text{HR}$$

For example, if the cash position is twice as volatile as the futures contract, the HR will be 2. Accordingly, a 20% change in the price of the cash instrument would correspond to a 10% change in the futures price. The HR adjusts for this disparity:

$$20\% \; \Delta\text{cash price} = -10\% \; \Delta\text{futures price} \times 2$$

or

$$20\% \; \Delta\text{cash price} = -20\% \; \Delta\text{futures price}$$

Hedge ratios are sensitive to time and price. As time passes and price changes, the hedge ratio needed to mitigate the basis risk has to be adjusted. We now describe various methods of calculating the hedge ratio.

Conversion Factor as Hedge Ratio   A conversion factor (CF) determines the relative price sensitivity of the cash instrument as compared to that of the futures contract. As such, a conversion factor can be used to determine the hedge ratio:

$$\Delta\text{cash price} = -\Delta\text{futures price} \times \text{HR}$$
$$\Delta\text{cash price} = -\Delta\text{futures price} \times \text{CF}$$

For example, a conversion factor of 1.45 indicates that the price sensitivity of the cash instrument is 145% of the price sensitivity of the futures contract. Accordingly, 1.45 futures contracts would be required for every $100,000 face value of the cash position.

While conversion factor weighting is a simple way of determining the hedge ratio, the hedger has to be aware of its shortcomings. The problem lies with the fact that a futures contract tracks the price movements of the cheapest-to-deliver bond, while the conversion factor adjusts for the volatility of the cash instrument that may or may not be the same as the cheapest-to-deliver bond. If the cash instrument being hedged is not the cheapest-to-deliver instrument, the futures position will not accurately hedge the cash position, subjecting the hedger to basis risk. In order to avoid this problem, we can use other methods to determine the hedge ratio, including *basis point value* and *duration*.

Basis Point Value as the Basis for Determining a Hedge Ratio Basis point value (BPV) refers to the price change of a debt instrument, given a one basis point (0.01%) change in the yield of the same instrument. When yields change, the price change can be calculated by multiplying the BPV by the yield change measured in basis points. A BPV remains accurate only within a narrow range of yields. As time passes and yield changes, the BPV has to be adjusted.

The HR using basis point value is calculated as:

$$HR = \frac{BPV_{cash\ security}}{BPV_{futures\ contract}}$$

$$where \quad BPV_{futures\ contract} = \frac{BPV_{CTD}}{CF}$$

For example, suppose that your portfolio of cash instruments with a face value of $500,000 has a BPV of $80 per $100,000, or a total BPV of $400. Further assume that the BPV of the cheapest-to-deliver BPV_{CTD} instrument is $60 per $100,000 face value and the conversion factor is 1.5. The HR is calculated as

$$BPV_{futures\ contract} = \frac{60}{1.5} = 40$$

$$HR = \frac{400}{40} = 10$$

Accordingly, 10 contracts are required to hedge the portfolio.

Duration Weighting as the Basis for Determining a Hedge Ratio *Duration* is the weighted average maturity of an instrument's cash flows. The present values of the cash flows serve as the weights. The original duration, developed by Macaulay in 1938, is calculated as:

$$D = \frac{\sum_{t=1}^{n} \frac{t \times c_t}{(1+r)^t}}{\sum_{t=1}^{n} \frac{c_t}{(1+r)^t}} = \frac{\sum_{t=1}^{n} \frac{t \times c_t}{(1+r)^t}}{PV}$$

where

$$D = duration$$
$$t = time$$
$$c = periodic\ cash\ flow$$
$$r = discount\ rate$$
$$PV = current\ price\ of\ the\ bond$$

In this equation, the numerator is the sum of the discounted cash flows in each period multiplied by the time of the cash flows divided by the market price of the bond. For example, suppose that a debt instrument has a coupon rate of 10% (paid semiannually), face value of $1,000, yield-to-maturity of 8%, and term-to-maturity of four years. The market price of the bond today is the present value of all of the future cash flows, which amounts to $1,067.33. The duration of this instrument is calculated as

$$D = \frac{\dfrac{1\times50}{(1+.04)^1} + \dfrac{2\times50}{(1+.04)^2} + \dfrac{3\times50}{(1+.04)^3} + \dfrac{4\times50}{(1+.04)^4} + \dfrac{5\times50}{(1+.04)^5} + \dfrac{6\times50}{(1+.04)^6} + \dfrac{7\times50}{(1+.04)^7} + \dfrac{8\times50}{(1+.04)^8}}{1,067.33}$$

$$= \frac{7,291.19}{1,067.33} = 6.83$$

The duration of the debt instrument equals 6.83 six-month periods, or 3.4 years.

Duration provides a measure of price sensitivity to changes in the yield of the underlying security. As such, the change in price is

$$\Delta price = \left[-\frac{D}{(1+r/m)}\right][\Delta yield \times price]$$

Suppose that the yield in the above example increases by one basis point. For a portfolio composed of $1,000,000 in face value of such bonds, the resulting change in price is

$$\Delta price = \left[\frac{-6.83}{(1+0.08/2)}\right][0.0001]\left[\$1,067.33 \times \frac{1,000,000}{1,000}\right] = -\$700.95$$

What we just calculated is the equivalent of a BPV. In an example in the previous section we used a futures contract with BPV of 40. If we use the same contract in this example, the HR can be calculated as

$$HR = \frac{BPV_{duration}}{BPV_{futures}} = \frac{700.95}{40} = 17.52$$

In order to hedge this portfolio, we need to short 18 contracts, which is the rounded value of 17.52. The combined portfolio, composed of the securities and futures contracts, is hedged. A hedged portfolio has a duration of zero because a long position in securities and a short position in futures with equal durations (with opposing signs) results in a net duration of zero. Duration is a measure of interest-rate risk, where the longer the duration, the greater the exposure to interest-rate risk.

Cross-Hedging and the Hedge Ratio   The methods we have described thus far, including conversion factor, BPV, and duration, are useful when hedging a portfolio composed of Treasury instruments. The arrangement works well because the cash position and the futures position are homogenous in their credit risks, callability, and other features. However, if Treasury bond futures are used to hedge non-Treasury instruments such as Eurobonds, corporate bonds, and mortgage-backed securities, further adjustments are needed in the HR.

For purposes of cross-hedging, the yield changes of the hedged instrument are regressed against the yield changes of the cheapest-to-deliver bonds or notes, using historical data. The estimated slope of the regression is subsequently multiplied by the HR that was calculated using one of the previous methods. As is often observed, Eurobonds have slope coefficients of less than one. Suppose that the slope coefficient for a portfolio of Eurodollar bonds is estimated to be 0.8. The HR, the value of which was previously calculated as 17.52, needs to be adjusted:

Adjusted HR = HR × slope coefficient of the regression model
Adjusted HR = 17.52 × 0.8 = 14.02

This means that, to hedge the portfolio of Eurodollar bonds, we need only 14 contracts as opposed to the 18 contracts needed when the underlying portfolio consisted of Treasury instruments.

A note of caution must be made in using regression analysis. Since the slope coefficient is calculated using historical data, the assumption is that future movements in market variables will be similar to the historical pattern. While this assumption may be realistic in some cases, the assumption may not hold in other cases, especially when the hedging is for a short term. In such cases, HRs may be adjusted based on management's expectations of the future.

Examples of Hedging Strategies

The Long Hedge Using a Conversion Factor to Determine the Hedge Ratio
Suppose that in February 1995 an insurance company plans to invest $1 million in the 11¼% February 2015 Treasury bonds. The fund, however, will not be available for six months. Using Treasury futures, the investor can lock in the yield today. The details of the cash and futures positions are as follows:

Input	T	T + 180
The 11¼% Feb. 2015 T-bond to be purchased:		
Price	137–01	145–28
Conversion factor	1.3216	
T-bond futures price	102–20	110–15
Investment amount	$1,000,000	

Steps:

1. Calculate the price of T-bonds today:
$$\$1 \text{ million @ } 137\text{--}01 = \$1,370,312.50$$
2. Calculate the number of futures contracts to be purchased:
No. of contracts to be purchased = CF × (par value of cash bonds/par value of futures contracts) = 1.3216 × ($1,000,000/$100,000) = 13.216 ≈ 13 contracts

Results:

1. Cash position: The investor purchases T-bonds in six months at the price of:
$$\$1 \text{ million at time T} + 180 \text{ @ } 145\text{--}28 = \$1,458,750$$
$$\$1 \text{ million at time T @ } 137\text{--}01 = \$1,370,312$$
Extra cost of purchasing T-bonds = $1,458,750 – $1,370,312 = $88,438
2. Futures position: The investor settles the futures contract:
Futures price @ 110–15 = 13 × 100,000 [(110 + 15/32)/100] =$1,436,093
Contractual price @ 102–20 = 13 × 100,000 [(102 + 20/32)/100] = $1,334,125
The gain in futures contract = $1,436,093 – $1,334,125 = $101,968
3. The net gain:
Gains from futures – extra cost of purchasing T-bonds = $101,968 – $88,438
$$= \$13,530$$

The purchase of the futures contract enabled the insurance company not only to lock in the current price but also to make an additional profit of $13,530.

The Short Hedge Using BPV to Determine the Hedge Ratio In June 1996, a money manager at a bank is planning to sell $10 million of 10⅝ August 2017 Treasury bonds in 30 days, but is worried about a decrease in the price prior to the sale. To lock in the current price, she shorts September 1996 T-bond futures. The input data is as follows:

Input	T	T + 30
Treasury bond to be sold:		
Price	132–27	131–00
BPV (per $100,000)	$132.65	
T-bond futures:		
Price	103–27	102–14
Conversion factor	1.2649	
BPV (CTD per $100,000)	130.66	
Portfolio amount	$10 million	

Steps:

1. Find the BPV of the T-bond futures:

$$BPV_{futures} = \frac{BPV_{CTD}}{CF} = \frac{130.66}{1.2649} = 103.30$$

2. Find the number of T-bond futures to sell:

$$\frac{BPV_{cash\ instrument}}{BPV_{futures}} = \frac{13,265\ (for\ \$10\ million)}{103.30} = 128.41 \approx 128$$

Results:	T	T + 30
Without futures:		
Price of the bonds to be sold		
$(132^{27}\!/_{32} \times 10,000,000/100) =$	$13,284,375	
	$(131.00 \times 10,000,000/100) = \$13,100,000$	
Decrease in price $=(\$13,284,375 - \$13,100,000) =$ $184,375		
With futures:		
Price of bond to be sold	$13,284,375	$13,100,000
Futures gain $= (103^{27}\!/_{32} - 102^{14}\!/_{32}) \times 128 \times 100,000/100 =$		$180,000
Total amount received		$13,280,000
Net loss $= (\$180,000 - \$184,375) =$		$4,375
The short hedge reduced the loss to $4,375.		

Cross-Hedging Corporate Bonds with T-Notes Futures The CFO of a publicly held company is planning to issue $50 million of 10-year debt in three months. He is concerned that the interest rate may increase over this period. He would like to effectively fix the cost of debt at the current level. The detail of the case is as follows:

Input	T	T + 90
8¾% corporate bond		
Yield	9%	10%
BPV (of $50 million)	$32,149.66	
12% 10-year note futures		
(CTD)		
Yield	7.31%	
BPV (per $100,000)	79.35	
Conversion factor	1.0510	
Price	103–07	99–11

Steps:

1. Determine the BPV of the 10-year note futures:

$$BPV_{futures} = \frac{BPV_{CTD}}{CF} = \frac{79.35}{1.0510} = 75.50$$

2. Determine the number of futures contracts to short:

$$HR = \frac{BPV_{cash}}{BPV_{futures}} = \frac{32,149.66}{75.50} = 425.82 \approx 426 \ contracts$$

3. Based on regression analysis of historical data, the beta coefficient of T-note futures regressed on the corporate bond is 1.2. Adjust the number of contracts accordingly:

$$426 \times 1.2 = 511 \ contracts$$

Results:

1. In T + 90, calculate the gain in futures contracts:

$$(103\text{–}07) - (99\text{–}11) \times 511 \times 100,000 \ / \ 100 = \$1,980,125$$

2. Determine the new cost of borrowing:
   While the actual cost of borrowing has increased to 10%, the gain from the futures contracts reduced the cost of borrowing by approximately

$$\frac{\$1,980,125}{\$32,149.66} = 62 \ basis \ points$$

which brings the cost of borrowing to $10 - 0.62 = 9.38\%$.

Using a Short Hedge to Protect the Value of a Portfolio with Duration Determining the Hedge Ratio   Suppose that a pension fund manager plans to liquidate a T-bond portfolio with a face value of $100 million in six months. The manager is concerned that interest rates may increase during the next six months, resulting in a decline in the value of the portfolio. The manager would like to hedge the portfolio using duration as the basis for calculating the hedge ratio. The details of the manager's position are as follows:

Input	T	T + 180
Portfolio duration (Macaulay)	14.20	
Portfolio face value	$100,000,000	
T-bond cash price	145–28	137–01
T-bond futures price	110–15	102–00
Portfolio yield	7.50%	
BPV of futures	130.66	

Steps:

1. Convert portfolio duration to BPV:

$$BPV_{duration} = \frac{14.20}{\left(1 + \frac{0.075}{2}\right)}(\$100,000,000)(.0001) = \$136,867.47$$

2. Calculate the number of short contracts:

$$HR = \frac{BPV_{duration}}{BPV_{futures}} = \frac{136,867.47}{130.66} = 1,047.50 \approx 1,048 \ contracts$$

Results:	T	T + 180
Without futures:		
Price	$145,875,000	$137,031,250
Loss		$8,843,750
With futures:		
Price	$145,875,000	$137,031,250
Futures gain = [(110–15) – (102–00)] × 1,048 × 100,000/100 =		$8,875,250
Net gain = ($8,875,250 – $8,843,750) =		$31,500

The pension fund manager has eliminated the potential loss and has increased the value of the portfolio by $31,500.

Hedging Strategy Using Duration to Immunize a Portfolio In the last example, we used duration to determine the hedge ratio in order to hedge the portfolio by setting its aggregate duration equal to zero. Duration can also be used to lock in a certain yield in a portfolio of securities regardless of what happens to interest rates. The process of using duration to guarantee a certain yield for a portfolio is called *immunization*. Consider a coupon bond. As interest rates rise, the price of the security declines, while the reinvestment rate for coupon payments increases. If the investor's anticipated holding period of the security is set equal to the duration of the security, for a given increase in interest rate, the loss from the decline in security price is exactly offset by the gain in the reinvestment income. The strategy of equating holding period and duration is called immunization.

For example, suppose that we have a pension fund manager who has a portfolio of securities with a par value of $10,000,000. Further assume that the portfolio has a duration of 15 six-month periods. If the anticipated holding period for the portfolio is 15, changes in interest rates will not affect the yield the manager is currently expecting to earn, which means that the portfolio is immunized. However, if the desired holding period is 20, the manager has to extend the portfolio duration from 15 to 20 periods in order to guarantee the current yield. To extend the duration of the portfolio, we have two choices: Either replace some or all of the existing securities in the portfolio with those with higher duration, or use futures contracts to extend the duration.

Replacing current securities with those that would provide the desired duration may impose high transaction costs. A simpler way of achieving the same objective is to keep the existing portfolio intact and to use futures positions to extend the duration of the portfolio. An example will illustrate the point. Assume the following information:

Input	T
Portfolio duration	15 six-month periods
Target duration	20 six-month periods
Portfolio value	$10,000,000
Portfolio yield-to-maturity	7.50%
BPV of futures	130.66

Steps:

1. Convert portfolio duration to a BPV:

$$\frac{Duration}{\left(1+\frac{yield}{2}\right)}(Portfolio\ Value)(0.0001) = \frac{15}{\left(1+\frac{.075}{2}\right)}(\$10,000,000)(0.0001) = \$14,457.83$$

2. Convert target portfolio duration to a BPV:

$$\frac{20}{\left(1+\frac{0.075}{2}\right)}(\$10,000,000)(0.0001) = \$19,277.11$$

3. Find the number of contracts required to extend the duration of the portfolio:

$$\frac{\$19,277.11-\$14,457.83}{\$130.66} = 36.88$$

If the pension fund manager takes a long position in 37 contracts, the duration of the portfolio will be extended to 20 periods and the portfolio will be immunized.

The problem above could have been solved directly using duration without converting it to BPV. Suppose the following information is available:

Input	T
Portfolio duration	15
Target duration	20
Portfolio value	$10,000,000
Portfolio yield-to-maturity	7.50%
Futures duration	13.56
Futures price	99–31

The number of long futures contracts needed to extend the duration of the portfolio from 15 to 20 is:

$$\frac{S}{F} \times \frac{D_{2(spot)} - D_{1(spot)}}{D_{futures}} = \frac{\$10,000,000}{99,968.75} \times \frac{(20-15)}{13.56} = 36.88 \approx 37$$

where S is the spot price or market value of the portfolio, F is the futures price per contract (99–31 or 99.9687 × \$100,000 / 100), and D is the duration for respective positions.

SUMMARY

This is the first of three chapters on pricing and hedging strategies using derivatives. Forward and futures contracts are agreements between two parties to exchange certain assets at a prespecified price on a predetermined date. The party who agrees to buy is said to take a long position and the party who agrees to sell is said to take a short position in the contract.

Forward contracts are over-the-counter instruments designed to meet the specific needs of their customers. As such, forward contracts provide an opportunity to eliminate risk entirely. The customized nature of forward contracts, however, makes them relatively illiquid. Forward contracts are also credit instruments that encompass default risk. These contracting issues have provided a unique opportunity for financial intermediaries to become the main suppliers of forward contracts because of their expertise in credit assessment and their long-standing role in maturity and size intermediation. The profits made by financial intermediaries in offering forward contracts are drawn from their bid-ask spreads.

Forward contracts are available on a variety of underlying positions, including currency forwards and interest-rate forwards (forward rate agreements). Due to their customized nature, hedging through forwards incurs higher transaction costs than hedging through futures contracts.

Futures contracts in general, and financial futures in particular, were developed and marketed partially in response to the contracting problems encountered in the forward market. Futures markets are characterized by liquidity, a lack of default risk, and low transaction costs. The clearinghouse system, along with margin requirements and the daily marking-to-market of positions, virtually eliminates default risk and contributes to the liquidity of the futures market. In order to create liquidity, however, contracts are standardized, meaning that the use of futures contracts may not fully hedge an underlying risk exposure. A less than fully hedged position exposes the hedging party to basis risk because the underlying cash position may change in value differently from the futures contract. A hedger must consider the trade-off between liquidity and basis risk in using futures contracts.

Futures contracts are available on a variety of financial and real assets. Currency futures, interest-rate futures (T-bill, T-bond, Eurodollar, and muni-bond futures), commodity, and equity futures are readily available. The presence of basis risk in futures contracts necessitates the computation of a hedge ratio, which determines the number of futures contracts needed to hedge against changes in the underlying cash position. Determining a minimum variance hedge ratio is one of the most crucial aspects of futures hedging. Various weighting systems are used to calculate hedge ratios, including conversion factor (CF), basis point value (BPV) and duration. Risk-hedging using futures is a dynamic process that requires monitoring of the performance of the hedged portfolio.

1. Compare and contrast forward and futures contracts.

2. Discuss the contracting problems in forward contracts.

3. Explain the trade-off between liquidity and basis risk in transactions involving futures contracts.

4. Examine the role of financial intermediaries in reducing the contracting problems in forward contracts. Explain the rationale for the dominant role financial intermediaries play in the over-the-counter derivatives market in general and the forward market in particular.

5. Analyze the basic pricing equation for foreign exchange forwards. How does the interest-rate parity theorem apply to foreign exchange forward pricing?

6. Explain the notion of *cost of carry* and its role in the pricing of futures contracts.

7. Define *hedge ratio, basis point value, conversion factor,* and *duration*. Explain the significance of the hedge ratio in hedging strategies.

8. We are interested in a forward contract to purchase Ffr1,000,000 in one year. Use the following information, extracted from Tables 16.1 and 16.2, to calculate the forward price.

$$S_{Ffr/\$} = 4.9183$$
$$r_f = .0663$$
$$r_d = .0588$$

Suppose that in one year, the exchange rate is 5Ffr per dollar. Calculate the gain from the forward contract.

9. Suppose that a financial intermediary has posted the following bid-ask prices and one-year interest rates:

$$S_{Ffr/\$} = 4.9178 - 4.9188$$
$$r_f = 6\%_{16} - 6^{11}\%_{16}$$
$$r_d = 5^{13}\%_{16} - 5^{15}\%_{16}$$

Calculate the bid-ask prices for a one-year forward contract.

10. You are given the following spot rates on six-month and three-month U.S. dollar LIBOR:

$$_0R_6 = 5\%\%; \text{ and}$$
$$_0R_3 = 6\%$$

Suppose that you would like to lock in $2,000,000 LIBOR borrowing cost for three months, three months from today. Calculate the forward rate on a three-month borrowing period, three months from today. You enter into a forward rate agreement based on the data given above. Assuming that in three months, the cost of borrowing for three months is 5%, calculate the gain or loss that you will incur from your FRA.

11. Using today's *Wall Street Journal*, calculate the price per December futures contract for the Japanese yen, British pound, German mark, French franc, and Australian dollar on the delivery date.

12. The March T-bill futures contract is quoted as 94.99. On the delivery date, what will the dollar price be per contract?

13. The settlement price for June T-bond futures is quoted as 113-06. What is the dollar value of this contract? At the settlement date, suppose the short decides to deliver 11% T-bonds with a remaining maturity of 21 years and six months. Using the conversion factor table in this chapter, calculate the invoice price for a 100 T-bond futures contract. Assume that the most recent coupon payment took place 15 days ago, and there are 184 days in the relevant six-month period.

14. The closing yield on December Eurodollar futures is quoted as 5.50. What is the dollar amount of the settlement price for one contract?

15. The settlement price for March S&P 500 index futures is quoted as 565.50. What is the dollar amount of the settlement price for one contract?

16. Suppose that the futures price for an S&P 500 index deliverable in six months is 567.50. If the risk-free interest rate is 8% per year and the dividend yield on the stock index is 5% per year, what is the equilibrium price of the index today?

17. Three-month interest rates in the United States and Switzerland are 6% and 3% per year, respectively. If the spot exchange rate is $S_{Sfr/\$} = 1.1599$ and the futures price for a contract deliverable in three months is 1.1559, is there an arbitrage opportunity?

18. The futures price of gold deliverable in four months is $389 per ounce. The storage cost is $24 per ounce per year, paid at the end of the period. If the interest rate is 6% per year, what is the equilibrium spot price for gold?

19. Suppose you have a portfolio of securities with a face value of $10,000,000. You plan to sell these securities in three months but you are concerned about a possible decline in the value of the portfolio. You would like to protect the value of your portfolio by taking a futures position. The following information is available about your portfolio and the T-bond futures you are interested in:

Input	T
The cash price of your securities	130–11
Conversion factor	1.3183
T-bond futures price	101–00
Face value of the portfolio	$10,000,000

a. Should you take a long or a short position in T-bond futures in order to hedge? Use the conversion factor as the basis for determining the hedge ratio and calculate the number of contracts you need for hedging.
b. Assume the following information is available in three months:

Input	T + 90
The price of your securities	122–16
T-bond futures price	94–22

Evaluate the performance of your hedging strategy.

20. You plan to invest $5,000,000 in bonds in six months but you are concerned about a possible increase in the price of the bonds. You would like to hedge the risk by taking a position in T-bond futures. Currently, the following information is available to you:

Input	T
Bonds to be purchased	
Price	134–00
Conversion factor	1.3450
BPV (per $100,000)	132.50
T-bond futures	
Price	101–16
BPV (CTD per $100,000)	110.00
Investment amount	$5,000,000

a. In order to hedge your position, should you take a long or a short position?

b. How many contracts would you need?
c. In six months, the following information is available to you:

Input	T + 180
The price of bonds to be purchased	135–20
T-bond futures price	102–16

Calculate the result of your hedged position.

21. Suppose you are holding $1,000,000 of Treasury bonds (cheapest-to-deliver) and plan to sell them in 60 days. To ensure that the price of the bonds will not decline, you take a short position in T-bond futures. The following information is available:

Input	T
Treasury bonds to be sold (CTD)	
Price	132–27
BPV (per $100,000)	130.00
Conversion factor	1.2776
T-bond futures price	102–27
Portfolio amount	$1,000,000

In 60 days, suppose you have the following information:

Input	T + 60
Treasury bonds price	131–16
T-bond futures price	101–27

a. Calculate the result of your hedged position. (Note that your portfolio consists of cheapest-to-deliver T-bonds; therefore, the BPVs of the cash and futures positions are identical.)

22. A fund manager would like to hedge the value of a $100,000,000 portfolio for the next three months. The following information is available:

Input	T
Portfolio duration	10
Portfolio face value	$100,000,000
Portfolio cash price	130–16
T-bond futures price	112–11
Portfolio yield (semiannual coupon)	8%
BPV of futures	120.19

411

a. Calculate the number of short futures contracts the manager needs to hedge the portfolio. Use duration as the basis for determining the hedge ratio.

b. In three months, assume the following information:

Input	T+90
Portfolio cash price	122–16
T-bond futures price	102–22

Calculate the net gain or loss in the portfolio.

23. Suppose that you have a portfolio consisting of $10,000,000 in five-year, 8% semiannual coupon bonds that are priced at par. You would like to hedge the portfolio with T-note futures with a duration of seven years and a market price of 95-00. Your desired holding period is 10 years.

a. Calculate the duration of the portfolio.

b. Calculate the number T-note futures you need to immunize the portfolio.

REFERENCES

British Bankers' Association. 1985. *London Interbank Forward Rate Agreements: Recommended Terms and Conditions* (August).

Campbell, T., and W. Kracaw. 1993. *Financial Risk Management: Fixed Income and Foreign Exchange*, New York: Harper Collins College Publishers.

Chicago Board of Trade. 1990. *The Delivery Process in Brief: Treasury Bond and Treasury Notes Futures.*

Chicago Board of Trade. 1994. *CBOT Financial Instrument Guide.*

Chicago Board of Trade. 1994. *CBOT Conversion Factor.*

Macaulay, F. 1938. *The Movement of Interest Rates, Bonds, Yields, and Stock Prices in the United States Since 1865.* New York: Columbia University Press.

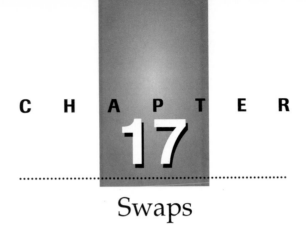

Swaps

OBJECTIVES

This chapter presents swaps as the newest of the derivative products. Similar to other derivatives, swaps are designed to redistribute risk arising from fluctuations in interest rates, exchange rates, and commodities prices. We include an analysis of the origin and subsequent growth of swaps, the economic rationale for their existence, and the dominant role played by banks in the market. Market structure, pricing conventions, and swap-based hedging strategies are also presented. The chapter concludes with a discussion of the regulatory issues surrounding swap transactions.

THE ORIGIN AND SUBSEQUENT DEVELOPMENT OF THE SWAP MARKET

A swap is an agreement between two parties to exchange a series of cash flows over a period of time. The frequency of the exchange and the size of the cash flows are contract-specific. The first widely publicized swap agreement was between IBM and the World Bank in 1981. Earlier, IBM had issued debt securities denominated in deutsche marks and Swiss francs. Subsequently, when the dollar appreciated against the two currencies, IBM decided to lock in its currency gains. At the same time, the World Bank, having saturated German and Swiss markets with its debt issues, proceeded to issue dollar-denominated securities with the intention of converting them to deutsche marks and Swiss francs. Salomon Brothers brokered a transaction in which IBM agreed to make a series of payments to the World Bank in deutsche marks and Swiss francs in exchange for a series of payments by the World Bank to IBM in dollars. This simple transaction, which hedged both parties against their future exposure to currency fluctuations, became known as the first currency swap. Interest-rate swaps were developed a year later. Other swaps, including commodities, followed shortly thereafter.

Table 17.1 demonstrates the 1990–1994 data reported for interest-rate and currency swaps. These figures were compiled by the International Swaps and

TABLE 17.1 Year-End Data Reported for Interest-Rate and Currency Swaps, 1990–1994 $Trillions			
Year	Interest-Rate Swap	Currency Swap	Total
1990: Activity	$1.23	$0.21	$1.44
Outstanding	2.31	0.58	2.89
1991: Activity	1.62	0.33	1.95
Outstanding	3.06	0.81	3.87
1992: Activity	2.82	0.30	3.12
Outstanding	3.85	0.86	4.71
1993: Activity	4.10	0.30	4.40
Outstanding	6.18	0.90	7.08
1994: Activity	6.24	0.38	6.62
Outstanding	8.82	0.91	9.73

Derivatives Association, based on data from 88 dealers in more than 17 currencies, worldwide.[1]

Interest-rate swaps constitute the largest segment of total swap transactions. In every year since 1990, interest-rate swap activities and outstanding balances have increased. At year-end 1994, interest-rate swaps had a total outstanding balance of $8.82 trillion. The growth of currency swaps has been slower than that of interest-rate swaps, with an outstanding amount of $0.91 trillion at the end of 1994. The combined value of interest-rate and currency swaps has increased every year since 1990 to a total value of $9.73 trillion outstanding at the end of 1994.

MAJOR SWAP PRODUCTS

Some of the most popular swap products are

- Interest-rate swaps
    -fixed-to-floating-rate swaps
    -floating-to-floating-rate swaps (basis swaps)
- Currency swaps
    -fixed-to-floating-rate swaps
    -fixed-to-fixed-rate swaps
    -floating-to-floating-rate swaps
- Commodity swaps
- Equity swaps

In a single-currency, fixed-to-floating swap, counterparties agree to exchange a fixed percentage of a notional amount with a floating percentage of the same notional amount in the same currency. The floating-rate index used is often LIBOR, but other indices are also available, including rates on Treasury instruments and commercial paper. In a single-currency, floating-to-floating-rate swap, one party makes a series of payments based on one floating rate (e.g., six-month dollar-based LIBOR) in exchange for payments by the counterparty based on another

---

[1] Source: International Swaps and Derivatives Association, *ISDA Survey of Global Swap Transactions: 1994*, News Release, June 12, 1995.

floating rate (e.g., the three-month dollar-based commercial paper rate). This type of swap is known as a *basis swap*.

A generic currency swap involves a fixed-to-floating swap in two different currencies. For example, two parties agree to exchange fixed-rate payments in pounds sterling with floating-rate payments in U.S. dollars. This swap redistributes exchange rate and interest-rate risks. A fixed-to-fixed-currency swap involves the exchange of fixed-rate cash flows in one currency for fixed-rate cash flows in another. This swap only redistributes exchange-rate risk. In a floating-to-floating currency swap, cash flows exchanged are calculated based on floating rates in two different currencies. For example, one party agrees to make a series of payments based on a six-month pound sterling LIBOR in exchange for a series of payments based on a six-month dollar LIBOR.

Commodity swaps are designed to alter risk exposure in commodities prices. Among commodities swaps, energy-related swaps have been in high demand. Crude oil, heating oil, gasoline, natural gas, jet fuel, and coal are among the commodities that have been hedged using swaps. Commodities swaps are commonly written as fixed-to-floating swaps. For example, an oil producer, who sells oil in the spot market, enters into a swap agreement with an intermediary to receive a series of cash flows based on a fixed price per barrel of oil in exchange for payments based on the future floating price in the market. As the oil price fluctuates, the net cash flows for the oil producer stays constant because the floating cash flows from sale of oil in the spot market are used to make payments to the intermediary in exchange for a series of fixed payments. The oil producer, therefore, is hedged against oil price changes. Commodities swaps are also available in copper, aluminum, nickel, and zinc. Commodities swap maturities range from one month to five years.

Equity swaps involve agreements in which one party pays on the basis of the return on an equity index (e.g, S&P 500) and the other party pays on the basis of a fixed or a floating rate (e.g., dollar LIBOR). Equity swaps can also be arranged to swap cash flows based on one equity index (e.g, S&P 500) in exchange for cash flows in a different equity index (e.g, Nikkei 225). Another variation of equity swaps has recently been designed that involves a single equity rather than an equity index.

THE ECONOMIC RATIONALE FOR THE EXISTENCE OF SWAPS

Why Do Currency Swaps Exist?

Long before generic fixed-to-floating-currency swaps were introduced, parallel loans were used to hedge against currency risk. Consider a fixed-to-floating-currency swap where one party makes fixed-rate payments in pounds sterling and the other party makes payments in dollars based on a six-month dollar LIBOR. Alternatively, the first party can obtain a pound-denominated loan from the second party at a fixed rate that requires payments in pounds, while the second party receives a dollar-denominated loan from the first party at a floating LIBOR that requires payments in dollars. Suppose that both loans are for two years with semiannual payments. At the end of the two-year period, each party will pay off the principal of the respective loan: The first party pays off the pound-denominated loan, while the second party pays off the dollar-denominated loan. For each party, the combined cash flows will be similar to the cash flows arising from a swap contract.

If two parallel loans provide the same function as a currency swap, what is the rationale for the development of swaps? Despite similarities in cash flows, parallel loans contain the following shortcomings that can be avoided by using swaps:

1. The *default risk in parallel loans*. Since the two loans are independent, default by one party does not absolve the other party of its responsibility for making payments.
2. The *balance-sheet limitations of parallel loans*. Parallel loans are included in the balance sheet of the contracting parties and may cause problems with financial covenants, even though the two loans effectively cancel each other out.

The default risk in parallel loans is significantly higher than the default risk in swaps. With parallel loans, a counterparty's default in payments does not absolve the other party of its payment obligations. Swaps require counterparties to exchange cash flows at each settlement date. A counterparty's failure to make payments will automatically relieve the other party of its payment obligations. Swaps also carry less default risk than do parallel loans because even if a counterparty faces financial distress, default may occur only if the distressed party is the loser at the settlement date.

Accounting and regulatory disclosure rules treat swaps as off-the-balance-sheet items. Swaps, therefore, do not inflate the balance sheet. Reduced default risk, along with the off-the-balance-sheet nature of swaps, make them superior alternatives to parallel loans.

For a product to be viable as a financial innovation, it must either expand the set of available investment choices (i.e., complete the markets) or improve the operational efficiency of those markets that already exist.[2] Currency swaps meet the conditions set for an innovative product by improving the operational efficiency of parallel loans.

Why Do Interest-Rate Swaps Exist?

In 1982, one year after the introduction of the first currency swap, interest-rate swaps were developed. Various explanations have been presented for the existence of interest-rate swaps, including comparative advantage, agency cost, and product innovation.

The comparative advantage argument,[3] borrowed from trade theory, states that each transacting party has a comparative advantage in one market. For example, the rate differential in the long-term, fixed-rate loan market for a AAA-rated borrower and a BBB-rated borrower may be higher than the rate differential in the long-term, floating-rate loan market. This being the case, it is advantageous for an AAA-rated party to borrow in the long-term fixed-rate loan market and for a BBB-rated party to borrow in the long-term, floating-rate market. If the AAA-rated borrower wishes to hold a floating-rate loan and the BBB-rated borrower wishes to hold a fixed-rate loan, they could enter into a swap agreement wherein the AAA-rated borrower pays based on a floating rate in exchange for receipts based on a fixed rate, while the BBB-rated borrower pays based on a fixed rate in exchange for receipts based on a floating rate. Combined with the original loan, the AAA-rated borrower ends up with a series of cash flows similar to holding a floating-rate loan while the BBB-rated borrower ends up with a series of cash flows similar to holding a fixed-rate loan. In the meantime, the savings in the cost of the loans due to the swap transaction can be split between the two parties.

The comparative advantage theory of swaps is challenged on the grounds that it neglects arbitrage.[4] With no barriers to capital flows, arbitrage would elim-

---

[2] Van Horne (1985).
[3] Bicksler and Chen (1986).
[4] Smith, Smithson, and Wakeman (1986).

TABLE 17.2 Combined Risk-Free Rates and Credit-Risk Premiums		
	Floating Risk-Free Rate	**Fixed Risk-Free Rate**
Fixed credit-risk premium	L-T term floating rate	L-T fixed-rate loan
Floating credit-risk premium	Short-term loan	Swap + S-T

inate any comparative advantage. Furthermore, a synthetic, swap-induced, long-term, fixed-rate loan precludes a valuable prepayment option that exists in the loan if it is directly acquired in the long-term, fixed-rate loan market. The apparent savings in obtaining a long-term, fixed-rate loan through a swap transaction is therefore explained by the fact that the borrower is giving up a valuable option.

Another explanation for swaps lies with the differences in the agency costs between a long-term and a short-term debt.[5] When a lower-rated borrower applies for a long-term loan, the rate charged includes a credit risk premium to account for the risk-incentive problem (see Chapter 2). To avoid the extra cost in the long-term, fixed-rate loan, the lower-rated borrower can borrow in the short-term debt market and enter into a swap contract to pay based on a fixed rate and to receive based on a floating rate. With a short-term debt, the borrower will be under closer scrutiny by the lender, who will be deciding whether to renew the loan, thus mitigating the risk-incentive problem. To mitigate the interest-rate risk of a short-term loan, the borrower enters into a swap agreement to create a combined position that resembles a long-term, fixed-rate loan. The short-term loan provides a binding promise to the lender that the borrower will not alter its asset-risk configuration after the loan is obtained.

There is yet another explanation for swaps.[6] Simply stated, the expected return on a risky loan can be divided into a risk-free rate and a credit-risk premium. A borrower has three alternatives in the credit market: (1) to borrow in the long-term, fixed-rate loan market; (2) to borrow in the long-term, floating-rate loan market; or (3) to borrow in the short-term loan market. Table 17.2 provides all the combinations of risk-free rate and credit-risk premium.

In order to fix only the credit-risk premium, the borrower may take a long-term, floating-rate loan. In a floating-rate loan, a fixed spread is added to a floating-rate index to determine the appropriate rate. While the risk-free portion of the rate will vary based on changes in market interest rates, the spread over the index will not. This loan is suitable for a borrower who predicts a decrease in the risk-free rate but is concerned that the credit-risk premium may increase. Therefore, the borrower chooses to fix the credit-risk premium segment of the rate and allows for the risk-free portion to float. If the borrower is concerned that both the risk-free part of the rate and the credit-risk premium part of the rate may increase, the optimal choice will be a long-term, fixed-rate loan that keeps both parts constant.

If the borrower believes that both the risk-free rate and credit-risk premium will decline in the future, the choice will be a short-term debt that keeps both parts of the rate floating. Finally, if the borrower believes that the risk-free rate may increase but the credit-risk premium may decline, the choice will be a short-term debt coupled with an interest-rate swap where the borrower pays fixed and

---

[5] Wall (1989).
[6] Arak, Estrella, Goodman, and Silver (1988).

receives floating. The combination of a short-term debt and an interest-rate swap creates a series of payments that are fixed in the risk-free segment and floating in the credit-risk premium. In this way, swaps provide borrowers with previously unattainable alternatives. This makes swaps a new and enduring financial innovation.

REASONS FOR THE DOMINANT ROLE OF COMMERCIAL BANKS IN THE SWAP MARKET

In the IBM–World Bank swap agreement, Salomon Brothers acted as the broker that provided technical expertise and facilitated the transaction without bearing risk. This was the norm in the early days of swap transactions, when brokers brought together parties whose opposite risk exposures could be hedged by entering into a swap agreement. It is no surprise that investment banks, which are experts in the brokerage function, played a major role in the early stages of swap market development. As the market expanded, finding matching counterparties became a difficult task. Financial intermediaries, therefore, began to act as temporary counterparties to client swaps until a suitable party could be found to take on the position. In effect, intermediaries were temporarily *warehousing* swap positions. While warehousing swaps provided an element of flexibility, finding ultimate parties who were willing to take the warehoused swaps remained a formidable task and an obstacle to the growth of the swap market.

Once the intermediary adopted the counterparty position on a permanent basis, the final necessary step was taken for the creation of a fully flexible swap market. As the intermediary became the counterparty for various contracts, a portfolio of swaps (along with other OTC derivatives) was created. Portfolio diversification reduced the risk exposure to some degree. Ultimately, the residual risk of the portfolio was managed by using exchange-traded derivatives such as futures and options.

As derivative intermediation moved from the relatively straightforward task of brokerage to a more complex job of asset transformation and portfolio management (information production and risk-bearing), investment banks were no longer the best-suited intermediaries for the job. Investment banks were effective in the early stages of swap market development when they were required to serve only as brokers. However, their capital base was too small to support their taking positions as counterparties; another group of intermediaries was needed to perform the asset transformation function.

This intermediary was the commercial bank. With its long-standing experience in information production and credit-risk assessment, and its stronger capital base, the commercial bank gradually became the dominant force in the market for OTC derivatives in general and swaps in particular. Because new swaps required the intermediary to act as the counterparty, higher capital levels were needed to absorb the risk. Commercial banks have historically held a stronger capital position than investment banks. As was reported in Chapter 15, at the end of 1994, Bank of America, Citibank, and Chemical had shareholders' equity worth $18.9 billion, $17.8 billion, and $10.8 billion, respectively. In contrast, the best-capitalized investment banking firm on Wall Street, Merrill Lynch, had only $5.5 billion in capital.[7] By the early 1990s, commercial banks dominated the OTC derivatives market with 70%. Investment banks and insurance companies held distant second and third places, with 27% and 3% of the market, respectively.

---

[7] *Euromoney*, May 1995, p. 27.

Interest-Rate Swaps

A basic, plain vanilla interest-rate swap involves a series of payments based on a fixed rate in exchange for a series of payments based on a floating rate (e.g., six-month LIBOR). By convention, the floating side of the payments is generally quoted flat (i.e., LIBOR flat). The fixed side of the swap is quoted in terms of two components: a base rate and a swap spread. The base rate is the yield of a recently issued Treasury instrument with a maturity or tenor similar to that of the swap contract. The swap spread, reported in basis points, is added to the base rate to arrive at the swap market rate. A typical schedule of swap market quotations is presented in Table 17.3.

As the maturity of the swap lengthens, the effective fixed swap rates also rise. This is due to both the term structure of Treasury yields and the term structure of swap spreads at any point in time. The spread serves as the intermediary's profit margin. In the vocabulary of swaps, the party that pays fixed swap rates and receives floating swap rates is said to have bought or to have taken a *long position,* and the party that pays floating swap rates and receives fixed swap rates is said to have sold or to have taken a *short position* in the swap agreement. The bid and ask quotes are the intermediary's bid and ask prices. For example, in a five-year swap, if the intermediary pays fixed and receives floating, the effective fixed rate will be 6.45%. Conversely, if the intermediary pays floating and receives fixed, the effective fixed rate will be 6.52%.

The day count for fixed and floating rates is often different. The fixed-rate day count is based on the convention used for Treasury notes and bonds that assumes a 365-day year, while the floating rate is based on a 360-day year, similar to money market instruments. While day counts stated here are the most commonly observed arrangements, others may also exist through bilateral agreements between the contracting parties.

Currency Swaps

There are distinct differences between currency swaps and interest-rate swaps. Apart from the obvious difference that currency swaps are in two currencies while interest-rate swaps are in one currency, there are two other major differences. First, in contrast to the absence of any exchange of notional amounts in interest-rate swaps, currency swaps almost always require the exchange of the principal amounts, both at the initiation date and at the termination date. Second, because two sets of currencies are involved, there are two sets of interest rates and therefore more possible combinations in basic currency swaps. For example,

TABLE 17.3 A Sample of Interest-Rate Swap Market Quotations

Maturity	Treasury Yield %	Bid-Ask Spread (Basis Points)	Effective Fixed Swap Rate
1 year	5.22%	55–62	5.77–5.84%
2 year	5.35	59–64	5.94–5.99
3 year	5.48	66–70	6.14–6.18
4 year	5.57	69–77	6.26–6.34
5 year	5.71	74–81	6.45–6.52

TABLE 17.4 Day Count in Currency Swaps			
Currency	**Floating Day Count[9]**	**Fixed Day Count**	**Payment Frequency**
Australian dollar	Actual/365	Actual/365	Semiannual
British pound	Actual/365	Actual/365	Semiannual
Canadian dollar	Actual/365	Actual/365	Semiannual
Deutsche mark	Actual/360	30/360	Annual
Dutch guilder	Actual/360	30/360	Annual
ECU	Actual/360	30/360	Annual
French franc	Actual/360	30/360	Annual
Italian lira	Actual/360	30/360	Annual
Japanese yen	Actual/365	Actual/365	Semiannual
New Zealand dollar	Actual/365	Actual/365	Semiannual
Swiss franc	Actual/360	30/360	Annual
U.S. dollar	Actual/360	30/360	Semiannual

a dollar/yen currency swap may take one of the following patterns: fixed-rate dollar-to-fixed-rate yen, floating-rate dollar-to-fixed-rate yen, fixed-rate dollar-to-floating-rate yen, and floating-rate dollar-to-floating-rate yen.

The market convention for day count in currency swaps is presented in Table 17.4.[8]

The most popular form of currency swaps involves floating U.S. dollar-to-fixed-non-U.S. dollar, where a series of payments are made based on a non-U.S. fixed rate in exchange for a series of payments based on the floating dollar LIBOR. By convention, the floating side of the payments is generally quoted flat (i.e., LIBOR flat), while the intermediary's markup is built into the bid-ask spreads. A typical schedule of currency swap market quotations for various maturities and currencies is presented in Table 17.5.

There is a unique swap yield curve for each currency. In our sample of swap quotations, the level of fixed rates for each currency increases as the maturity of the swap lengthens. This implies that at the time the swap quotations were posted, the swap yield curve in each market was upward sloping. The bid and ask quotes are the intermediary's bid and ask prices. For example, in a five-year pound sterling swap, the intermediary is willing to pay a pound-based bid rate of 7.25% in exchange for receiving U.S. dollar LIBOR. Conversely, the intermediary is willing to accept a pound-based rate of 7.37% in exchange for paying U.S. dollar LIBOR.

SWAP PRICING

Pricing a Fixed-to-Floating Interest-Rate Swap

Fixed-to-floating interest-rate swaps are used to redistribute the interest-rate risk of the underlying position. We will use an example to demonstrate how a generic interest-rate swap is designed between counterparties.

---

[8] Johnson and Showers (1992), pp. 361–362.

[9] Floating indexes are all LIBOR-based for the respective currencies except for the Canadian dollar (banker's acceptances), Dutch guilder (Dutch guilder Amsterdam Interbank Offered Rate), French franc (Paris Interbank Offer Rate), and New Zealand dollar (New Zealand dollar bills).

TABLE 17.5 A Sample of Currency Swap Market Quotations

Currency		Swap Maturity				
		1 year	2 years	3 years	4 years	5 years
D mark	Bid	4.25%	4.33%	4.63%	4.85%	5.20%
	Ask	4.35	4.43	4.69	4.90	5.32
Pound	Bid	6.84	7.02	7.08	7.15	7.25
	Ask	6.94	7.12	7.19	7.27	7.37
Swiss franc	Bid	3.06	3.37	3.69	3.95	4.22
	Ask	3.10	3.43	3.76	4.03	4.29
Yen	Bid	2.50	2.57	2.74	2.92	3.12
	Ask	2.56	2.64	2.82	3.04	3.20
U.S. dollar	Bid	5.77	5.94	6.14	6.26	6.45
	Ask	5.84	5.99	6.18	6.34	6.52

Consider the following information:

Notional amount	$100 million
Maturity	2 years
Floating index	Six-month dollar LIBOR
Fixed coupon	?
Payment frequency	Semiannual
Day count	30/360 for fixed, actual/360 for floating
LIBOR determination	Determined in advance, paid in arrears

The spot LIBOR yield curve at the origination of the swap provides the following (annualized) rates:

$$_0R_6 = 6.00\%$$
$$_0R_{12} = 6.50\%$$
$$_0R_{18} = 6.80\%$$
$$_0R_{24} = 7.20\%$$

We are interested in designing a two-year fixed-to-floating swap with a notional amount of $100 million. The frequency of settlements is semiannual; thus, there will be four settlements. The floating rate is a six-month dollar LIBOR, determined in advance, and paid in arrears. The unknown variable here is the fixed rate that will be used to determine the fixed payments in the swap. Suppose that the origination date is June 15, 1996, which requires the following four settlement dates:

First settlement	December 15, 1996	No. of days = 183
Second settlement	June 15, 1997	No. of days = 182
Third settlement	December 15, 1997	No. of days = 183
Fourth settlement	June 15, 1998	No. of days = 182

At the origination date, the swap contract is set in terms that make the net present value of the swap cash flows equal to zero for both parties. As indicated earlier, the floating payments are calculated in advance and paid in arrears. Accordingly, the first floating payment, to accrue on December 15, 1996, is based on a six-month LIBOR today, or 6%. The second floating payment, to accrue on June 15, 1997, will be based on the six-month LIBOR on December 15, 1996, and so on. The LIBOR used for the first settlement date is known with certainty but the others will not be known until later. However, at the present time, we can use the

LIBOR spot rates to calculate a series of forward rates that will serve as the best proxy for future floating rates. Accordingly, the following rates will be used to calculate the floating payments:

First floating rate $= 6.00\%$

$$\text{Second floating rate} = \left[\frac{(1+ {_0R_{12}}/2)^2}{(1+ {_0R_6}/2)} - 1\right] \times 2 = \left[\frac{(1+0.065/2)^2}{(1+0.06/2)} - 1\right] \times 2 = 7.00\%$$

$$\text{Third floating rate} = \left[\frac{(1+ {_0R_{18}}/2)^3}{(1+ {_0R_{12}}/2)^2} - 1\right] \times 2 = \left[\frac{(1+0.068/2)^3}{(1+0.065/2)^2} - 1\right] \times 2 = 7.40\%$$

$$\text{Fourth floating rate} = \left[\frac{(1+ {_0R_{24}}/2)^4}{(1+ {_0R_{18}}/2)^3} - 1\right] \times 2 = \left[\frac{(1+0.072/2)^4}{(1+0.068/2)^3} - 1\right] \times 2 = 8.40\%$$

The present value of the floating payments can be calculated as follows:

PV(floating) =

$$100\left[\frac{(0.06 \times 183/360)}{(1+0.06/2)} + \frac{(0.070 \times 182/360)}{(1+0.065/2)^2} + \frac{(0.074 \times 183/360)}{(1+0.068/2)^3} + \frac{(0.084 \times 182/360)}{(1+0.072/2)^4}\right]$$

PV(floating) = $13.37

For a zero net present value swap, the present value of the floating payments should equal the present value of the fixed payments:

$$\text{PV(fixed)} = C\left[\frac{1}{(1+0.06/2)} + \frac{1}{(1+0.065/2)^2} + \frac{1}{(1+0.068/2)^3} + \frac{1}{(1+0.072/2)^4}\right] = 13.37$$

$$C = 3.6316, \text{ fixed rate} = \frac{3.6316}{100} \times 2 = 7.2632\% \approx 7.26\%$$

The results are summarized in Table 17.6.

The procedure that we just completed is called *at-market* swap pricing, which indicates that the net present value of the swap is zero for both parties. As time passes and the floating rate fluctuates, the swap will no longer be a zero net present value contract for the two parties. The process of calculating the value of the swap when the floating rate has changed from its initial level is referred to as *out-of-market* swap pricing.

Suppose that after the exchange of the second payment, the parties want to close out the swap. In order to determine the value of the swap, we have to calculate the present values of both the floating and the fixed payments. Assume that the zero coupon LIBOR yield curve provides the following rates:

$$_0R_6 = 5.00\%$$
$$_0R_{12} = 5.50\%$$

TABLE 17.6

Date	Zero Coupon	Floating Rate	Floating Payments	$PV_{floating}$	Fixed Payments	PV_{fixed}
12/15/96	6.00%	6.00%	$3.0500	$2.9612	$3.6316	$3.5258
06/15/97	6.50%	7.00%	$3.5389	$3.3196	$3.6316	$3.4066
12/15/97	6.80%	7.40%	$3.7617	$3.4027	$3.6316	$3.2850
06/15/98	7.20%	8.40%	$4.2467	$3.6865	$3.6316	$3.1525
				$13.37		$13.37

The next floating payment will be based on 5% LIBOR, and the last floating payment will be based on the following forward rate:

$$\text{Last floating rate} = \left[\frac{(1+{}_0R_{12}/2)^2}{(1+{}_0R_6/2)} - 1\right] \times 2 = \left[\frac{(1+0.055/2)^2}{(1+0.05/2)} - 1\right] \times 2 = 6.0\%$$

The present value of the floating payments is calculated as

$$\text{PV(floating)} = 100\left[\frac{(0.05 \times 183/360)}{(1+0.05/2)} + \frac{(.060 \times 182/360)}{(1+0.055/2)^2}\right] = \$5.3528$$

The present value of the fixed payments is calculated as

$$\text{PV(fixed)} = 3.6316\left[\frac{1}{(1+0.05/2)} + \frac{1}{(1+0.055/2)^2}\right] = \$6.9828$$

The party that pays fixed has to pay $6.9828 − $5.3528 = $1.63 in order to close out the position.

Pricing a Currency Swap

A generic currency swap is a fixed-to-floating swap in which one party makes payments in one currency based on a fixed rate in exchange for the second party's payments in another currency based on a floating rate. Other popular forms of currency swaps are fixed-to-fixed and floating-to-floating currency swaps.

In order to demonstrate the pricing schemes for currency swaps, we will work through a numerical example. Assume the following information about a currency swap that involves the U.S. dollar and the Japanese yen:

	Dollar	Yen
Notional amount	$100 million	¥8,500 million
Maturity	2 years	2 years
Floating index	6-month $LIBOR	6-month ¥LIBOR
Fixed coupon	?	?
Payment frequency	Semiannual	Semiannual
Day count (fixed)	30/360	Actual/365
Day count (floating)	Actual/360	Actual/365
LIBOR determination	Determined in advance paid in arrears	The same as $

The spot LIBOR yield curve at the origination of the swap provides the following (annualized) rates for the two currencies:

	Dollar	Yen
${}_0R_6 =$	6.00%	4.00%
${}_0R_{12} =$	7.00%	5.00%
${}_0R_{18} =$	7.50%	5.25%
${}_0R_{24} =$	8.00%	6.00%

Suppose initially we are interested in a fixed-to-fixed currency swap of $100 million in exchange for ¥8,500 in notional amounts over the next two years. (We are assuming that the spot exchange rate is 85 yen per dollar.) The frequency of settlements is semiannual; thus there will be four settlements. The floating rate is a six-month LIBOR, determined in advance, paid in arrears. The day count for dollar payments is 30/360 for fixed and actual/360 for floating; yen payment day counts are actual/365 for both fixed and floating.

We calculate forward rates based on the zero coupon spot LIBOR rates provided for each currency. As mentioned earlier, in the absence of actual future rates, forward rates reflect the market's best estimate of LIBOR rates.

Dollar:

$$\text{First floating rate} \quad = 6.00\%$$

$$\text{Second floating rate} = \left[\frac{(1+{_0}R_{12}/2)^2}{(1+{_0}R_6/2)} - 1\right] \times 2 = \left[\frac{(1+0.07/2)^2}{(1+0.06/2)} - 1\right] \times 2 = 8.00\%$$

$$\text{Third floating rate} \quad = \left[\frac{(1+{_0}R_{18}/2)^3}{(1+{_0}R_{12}/2)^2} - 1\right] \times 2 = \left[\frac{(1+0.075/2)^3}{(1+0.07/2)^2} - 1\right] \times 2 = 8.50\%$$

$$\text{Fourth floating rate} = \left[\frac{(1+{_0}R_{24}/2)^4}{(1+{_0}R_{18}/2)^3} - 1\right] \times 2 = \left[\frac{(1+0.08/2)^4}{(1+0.075/2)^3} - 1\right] \times 2 = 9.51\%$$

Yen:

$$\text{First floating rate} \quad = 4.00\%$$

$$\text{Second floating rate} = \left[\frac{(1+{_0}R_{12}/2)^2}{(1+{_0}R_6/2)} - 1\right] \times 2 = \left[\frac{(1+0.05/2)^2}{(1+0.04/2)} - 1\right] \times 2 = 6.00\%$$

$$\text{Third floating rate} \quad = \left[\frac{(1+{_0}R_{18}/2)^3}{(1+{_0}R_{12}/2)^2} - 1\right] \times 2 = \left[\frac{(1+0.0525/2)^3}{(1+0.05/2)^2} - 1\right] \times 2 = 5.75\%$$

$$\text{Fourth floating rate} = \left[\frac{(1+{_0}R_{24}/2)^4}{(1+{_0}R_{18}/2)^3} - 1\right] \times 2 = \left[\frac{(1+0.06/2)^4}{(1+0.0525/2)^3} - 1\right] \times 2 = 8.27\%$$

We must next calculate the present values of the floating payments, and set them equal to the present values of the fixed payments in order to arrive at the fixed rates used for the dollar and yen payments:

Dollar:

$$\text{PV(floating)} =$$
$$100\left[\frac{(0.06 \times 183/360)}{(1+0.06/2)} + \frac{(0.080 \times 182/360)}{(1+0.07/2)^2} + \frac{(0.085 \times 183/360)}{(1+0.075/2)^3} + \frac{(0.0951 \times 182/360)}{(1+0.080/2)^4}\right] = \$14.7155$$

$$\text{PV(fixed)} = C\left[\frac{1}{(1+0.06/2)} + \frac{1}{(1+0.07/2)^2} + \frac{1}{(1+0.075/2)^3} + \frac{1}{(1+0.08/2)^4}\right] = \$14.7155$$

$$C = 4.0265, \textit{ fixed rate} = 4.0265/100 \times 2 = 0.080531 \approx 8.05\%$$

$$\text{PV(floating)} =$$

$$8,500\left[\frac{(0.04\times183/365)}{(1+0.04/2)} + \frac{(0.06\times182/365)}{(1+0.05/2)^2} + \frac{(0.0575\times183/365)}{(1+0.0525/2)^3} + \frac{(0.0827\times182/365)}{(1+0.06/2)^4}\right] = ¥947.33$$

$$\text{PV(fixed)} = C\left[\frac{1}{(1+0.04/2)} + \frac{1}{(1+0.05/2)^2} + \frac{1}{(1+0.0525/2)^3} + \frac{1}{(1+0.06/2)^4}\right] = ¥947.33$$

$$C = 252.90, \; \textit{fixed rate} = 252.90/8500\times2 = 0.059505 \approx 5.95\%$$

Now that the fixed rates for dollar- and yen-denominated cash flows are known, we can construct cash flows for fixed-dollar-to-fixed-yen swaps. Table 17.7 presents the results.

On June, 15, 1996 (the origination date of the swap), there is an exchange of currencies. Two years later, on June 15, 1998, there will be another exchange of currencies, which is the reverse of the first exchange. At the origination date, the dollar-paying party pays the principal amount of the swap, ¥8,500 million, and receives $100 million. On June 15, 1998, the same party will pay $100 million and receive ¥8,500 million.

Other varieties of currency swaps can also be devised, including floating dollar-to-fixed yen and floating dollar-to-floating yen. Using the same example, we will next devise a floating-dollar-to-fixed-yen swap. The fixed-yen payments are already calculated. As discussed, the day count for floating-dollar payments is actual/360. Floating-dollar payments depend on the future levels of LIBOR. Since floating payments are determined in advance and paid in arrears, the first floating-dollar payment is based on the six-month dollar LIBOR for today, or 6%. Using a series of hypothetical future LIBOR rates, we construct cash flows for the dollar-paying party in Table 17.8.

Finally, we devise a floating-dollar to floating-yen swap using the same information. The floating rates for yen payments are also hypothetical, except for the first payment, which is based on the six-month yen LIBOR for today. Table 17.9 represents the results.

HEDGING STRATEGIES USING SWAPS

Interest-Rate Risk-Hedging with Swaps

The following example illustrates how swaps can be used for hedging interest-rate risk. Suppose the Bell company has issued short-term securities that need to

TABLE 17.7		**Fixed-Dollar-to-Fixed-Yen Swap Cash Flows**				
		(from the Dollar Payer's Perspective) (in Millions)				
Date	**$ Day Count**	**$ Fixed Rate**	**$ Fixed Payments**	**¥ Day Count**	**¥ Fixed Rate**	**¥ Fixed Receipt**
06/15/96	—	—	−¥8,500	—	—	$100
12/15/96	180/360	8.05%	−$4.0265	183/365	5.95%	¥253.57
06/15/97	180/360	8.05%	−$4.0265	182/365	5.95%	¥252.18
12/15/97	180/360	8.05%	−$4.0265	183/365	5.95%	¥253.57
06/15/98	180/360	8.05%	−$4.0265	182/365	5.95%	¥252.18
06/15/98	—	—	−$100	—	—	¥8,500

TABLE 17.8	**Floating-Dollar-to-Fixed-Yen Swap Cash Flows (from the Dollar Payer's Perspective) (in Millions)**					
Date	**$ Day Count**	**Hypoth. $ LIBOR**	**$ Floating Payments**	**¥ Day Count**	**¥ Fixed Rate**	**¥ Fixed Receipt**
06/15/96	—	6.00%	−¥8,500	—	—	$100
12/15/96	183/360	6.50%	−$3.05	183/365	5.95%	¥253.57
06/15/97	182/360	7.00%	−$3.29	182/365	5.95%	¥252.18
12/15/97	183/360	7.25%	−$3.56	183/365	5.95%	¥253.57
06/15/98	182/360	—	−$3.67	182/365	5.95%	¥252.18
06/15/98	—	—	−$100	—	—	¥8,500

be rolled over frequently. Bell is concerned that the cost of its debt will increase in the future, and plans to hedge against this interest-rate risk. Bell approaches Citibank for a hedging strategy. Citibank suggests the following swap:

Initiation date	June 15, 1996
Maturity	Two years
Notional amount	$10 million
Fixed-rate payer	Bell
Fixed rate	5.97%
Fixed-payment day count	Actual/365
Fixed-rate receiver	Citibank
Floating-rate index	Six-month LIBOR
Floating-payment day count	Actual/360
Payment frequency	Semiannual
Settlement dates	12/15/1996, 06/15/1997, 12/15/1997, 06/12/1998
LIBOR determination	Determined in advance, paid in arrears

The fixed and floating settlement payments are calculated as follows:

$$\text{Fixed-rate payment} = (.0597)(\text{actual days}/365)(\$10 \text{ million})$$
$$\text{Floating-rate payment} = (\text{LIBOR})(\text{actual days}/360)(\$10 \text{ million})$$

The fixed and floating rates are stated in annual terms and need to be converted to semiannual rates using the actual number of days. The following actual days apply to the four settlement dates:

TABLE 17.9	**Floating Dollar-to-Floating-Yen Swap Cash Flows (from the Dollar Payer's Perspective) (in Millions)**					
Date	**$ Day Count**	**Hypoth. $ LIBOR**	**$ Floating Payments**	**¥ Day Count**	**Hypoth. ¥ Floating Rate**	**¥ Floating Receipt**
06/15/96	—	6.00%	−¥8,500	—	4.00%	$100
12/15/96	183/360	6.50%	−$3.05	183/365	5.00%	¥170.47
06/15/97	182/360	7.00%	−$3.29	182/365	5.50%	¥211.92
12/15/97	183/360	7.25%	−$3.56	183/365	6.00%	¥234.39
06/15/98	182/360	—	−$3.67	182/365	—	¥254.30
06/15/98	—	—	−$100	—	—	¥8,500

TABLE 17.10		Swap Cash Flows for Bell			
Settlement Date	No. of Days	Hypothetical LIBOR	Fixed-Rate Payment	Floating-Rate Receipt	Net Cash Flows
06/15/96	—	5.5%	—	—	—
12/15/96	183	5.75	−$299,318	$279,583	−$19,735
06/15/97	182	6.00	−$297,682	$290,694	−$6,988
12/15/97	183	6.25	−$299,318	$305,000	$5,682
06/15/97	182	—	−$297,682	$315,972	$18,290

Initiation date	June 15, 1996	
First settlement	December 15, 1996	No. of days = 183
Second settlement	June 15, 1997	No. of days = 182
Third settlement	December 15, 1997	No. of days = 183
Fourth settlement	June 15, 1998	No. of days = 182

We now have sufficient information to calculate the fixed payments. Floating payments, however, depend on the future levels of LIBOR. The convention used in calculating the floating payments calls for the floating rate to be determined one period before the actual settlement. In our example, the first floating settlement, on December 15, 1996, is based on the LIBOR rate for June 15, 1996, and so on. Table 17.10 presents the fixed payments and floating receipts (with a hypothetical LIBOR series) for Bell.

Note that no exchange of the notional amount is necessary in interest-rate swaps. Also, on each settlement date a *difference check* will be written and paid by one party to the other. For example, on the first and second settlement dates, Bell has to pay $19,735 and $6,988, respectively, to Citibank, while on the third and fourth settlement dates, Citibank will pay Bell $5,682 and $18,290, respectively.

Currency Risk-Hedging with Swaps

The following example demonstrates how a fixed-to-floating currency swap can be used to hedge interest-rate and currency risks. Suppose that Spirit, an American manufacturing company, has signed a contract with a British company to deliver a product at a fixed pound sterling price. Spirit has raised the necessary financing for manufacturing this product through a floating-rate loan. Spirit faces two sets of risks: First, it is concerned that the dollar may appreciate against the pound, reducing its dollar equivalent of sale revenues in Britain. Second, it is concerned that interest rates may increase in the dollar market, increasing its financing costs. To hedge against these risks, Spirit enters into a currency swap agreement with Bankers Trust in which it will make payments based on a fixed pound rate and will receive cash flows based on a floating dollar LIBOR. As Spirit receives the proceeds of its sale in Britain, it will pass them along to Bankers Trust as the contractual fixed pound payments require, and receive floating-dollar payments based on a dollar LIBOR in return. The currency risk is mitigated because Spirit will receive cash flows based on a notional amount in dollars that is fixed in advance. The interest-rate risk is also mitigated because the rate used in computing the cash flow receipts for Spirit is a dollar LIBOR. If dollar-based interest rates increase, Spirit will be worse off in its cost of debt and better off in its swap receipts. Conversely, if interest rates decline, the cost of its debt will decline for Spirit, making it better off, while swap cash flows will also decline, making Spirit worse off. The combined effect is that Spirit can fix its future cash flows from the sale of its product to Britain today, and avoid the underlying currency and interest-rate risks. The details of the swap agreement between Spirit and Bankers Trust are as follows:

Currency Swap: Fixed British Pound vs. Floating U.S. Dollar LIBOR

Initiation date	June 15, 1996
Maturity	Four years (termination date: June 15, 2000)
Principal amounts	£50 million and $77.5 million
Fixed-rate payer	Spirit
Fixed rate	7.27% in pounds
Fixed-payment day count	Actual/365
Fixed-rate receiver	Bankers Trust
Floating-rate index	Six-month $LIBOR
Floating-payment day count	Actual/360
Payment frequency	Semiannual
Settlement dates	June 15 and December 15
LIBOR determination	Determined in advance, paid in arrears

The fixed and floating payments are calculated as follows:

$$\text{Fixed-rate payments} = 0.0727(\text{actual days}/365)(£50 \text{ million})$$
$$\text{Floating-rate payments} = \text{LIBOR}(\text{actual days}/360)(\$77.5 \text{ million})$$

We have sufficient information to calculate the pound-based fixed payments. The floating payments depend on the future levels of LIBOR. The dollar-based floating payments are determined by dollar LIBOR, one period before the actual settlement. In our example, the first floating settlement on December 15, 1996, is based on the dollar LIBOR of June 15, 1995, and so on. Table 17.11 presents the fixed payments and floating receipts (with a hypothetical LIBOR series) for Spirit.

Note that the principal amounts were exchanged at the swap initiation date, with a reverse exchange occurring at the swap termination date.

While most commonly traded currency swaps are floating-dollar to fixed-nondollar currency swaps, there are other combinations of cash flows that may be suitable for a party's risk exposure. For instance, in the above example, suppose we revise the scenario a bit by assuming that Spirit's debt is a fixed-rate

TABLE 17.11   Currency Swap Cash Flows for Spirit (Fixed-Rate Pound Payments in Exchange for Floating Dollar LIBOR)

Settlement Date	No. of Days	$ LIBOR (Hyp.)	Spirit Pays	Spirit Receives
06/15/96	—	5.5%	−$77.50	£50.00
12/15/96	183	5.75	−£1.8225	$2.1668
06/15/97	182	6.00	−£1.8125	$2.2529
12/15/97	183	6.25	−£1.8225	$2.3638
06/15/98	182	6.50	−£1.8125	$2.4488
12/15/98	183	6.75	−£1.8225	$2.5607
06/15/99	182	6.50	−£1.8125	$2.6447
12/15/99	183	6.25	−£1.8225	$2.5607
06/15/2000	183	6.00	−£1.8225	$2.4622
06/15/2000	—	—	−£50.00	$77.50

TABLE 17.12 Currency Swap Cash Flows for Spirit (Fixed-Rate Pound Payments in Exchange for Fixed-Rate Dollar Receipts) (in Millions)

Settlement Date	No. of Days for £	No. of Days for $	Spirit Pays	Spirit Receives
06/15/96	—	—	-$77.50	£50.00
12/15/96	183	180	-£1.8225	$2.4258
06/15/97	182	180	-£1.8125	$2.4258
12/15/97	183	180	-£1.8225	$2.4258
06/15/98	182	180	-£1.8125	$2.4258
12/15/98	183	180	-£1.8225	$2.4258
06/15/99	182	180	-£1.8125	$2.4258
12/15/99	183	180	-£1.8225	$2.4258
06/15/2000	183	180	-£1.8225	$2.4258
06/15/2000	—	—	-£50.00	$77.50

loan, thus limiting the company's exposure to currency risk. This risk can be mitigated by a fixed-dollar-to-fixed-pound currency swap. Note the following details for the swap:

Currency Swap: Fixed-Rate British Pound vs. Fixed-Rate U.S. Dollar

Initiation date	June 15, 1996
Maturity	Four years (termination date: June 15, 2000)
Principal amounts	£50 million, and $77.5 million
Pound payer	Spirit
Pound fixed-rate	7.27%
Pound day count	Actual/365
Dollar payer	Bankers Trust
Dollar fixed rate	6.26%
Dollar day count	30/360
Payment frequency	Semiannual
Settlement dates	June 15 and December 15

The payments are calculated as follows:

Pound fixed-rate payments = 0.0727(actual days / 365)(£50 million)
Dollar fixed-rate payments = 0.0626(180/ 360)($77.5 million)

The results are presented in Table 17.12.

Again, note that the principal amounts were exchanged at the swap initiation date, with a reverse exchange occurring at the swap termination date.

THE REGULATION OF SWAPS

According to the Commodity Exchange Act (CEA), all futures and options contracts are supposed to be traded on organized exchanges. This point is relevant to our discussion of swaps because there is some risk that U.S. courts may yet construe swaps and other OTC derivatives to be futures contracts, thus making swaps in their present form off-market, illegal contracts. This ambiguity may also cause the losing parties in swap contracts to walk away from their obligations on the grounds that the contracts were not legal. These fears were realized in 1987 when the Commodities Futures Trading Commission (CFTC) issued an Advance

Note of Proposed Rulemaking in which it questioned the legality of commodity swaps. The immediate result was that commodity swaps moved offshore. A similar problem surfaced in the forward market in 1990.

In July 1989, the CFTC reversed its original stand on swaps by declaring that although swaps contained some elements of futures contracts, they could not be appropriately regulated under the CEA. In 1992, Congress passed the Futures Trading Practice Act that authorized the CFTC to exempt swaps from regulations under the CEA. Subsequently, in January 1993, the CFTC declared that swaps had a separate identity from futures and were therefore exempt from the exchange trading requirements of the CEA. This finally relieved the market of its uncertainty with regard to the CFTC.

Concerns about possible regulation in swaps, however, have not been fully dispelled. In May 1994, the U.S. General Accounting Office (GAO) published recommendations on how to limit the largely unregulated OTC derivative market.[10] Currently, various bills are under consideration in the banking committees of both chambers of the U.S. Congress to legislate OTC derivative activities. This legislation may determine what types of firms can deal in which products, and some products may be flagged as too risky for some entities.

Most OTC derivatives (70%) are issued by large depository intermediaries that are closely supervised by the Fed, the OCC, and the FDIC. A revised version of the Risk-Based Capital Standards has established an elaborate system for calculating the underlying risk exposures of OTC derivatives, which is then used to establish minimum capital requirements.[11]

The GAO has recommended that the other suppliers of OTC derivatives, including securities firms and insurance companies, be brought under the purview of one or more of the existing federal financial regulators. With regard to end-users of OTC derivatives, the GAO compels the SEC to require major corporate end-users of derivatives to establish audit committees and provide public reporting on their derivative activities. While private trade organizations, such as the International Swaps and Derivatives Association, and private research groups, such as the Group of Thirty, have taken significant steps in recommending sound industry practices, the likelihood of legislation and regulation remains high.

SUMMARY

Swaps constitute the newest and fastest growing segment of the derivatives market. By the end of 1994, the combined volume of interest-rate and currency swaps exceeded $9 trillion, more than four times the 1990 volume of $2 trillion. This rapid market growth points to the significance of swaps in risk-hedging strategies and confirms that swaps are innovative, enduring products.

In 1981, the first well-publicized currency swap was brokered by Salomon Brothers between IBM and the World Bank. A year later, the first interest-rate swap was introduced. At the early stages of market development, swaps involved two end-users who were brought together by a broker. It soon became apparent that matching counterparties imposed major limitations on the development of the swap market. Consequently, intermediaries began to act as tempo-

---

[10] U.S. General Accounting Office, *Financial Derivatives: Actions Needed to Protect the Financial System*, May 1994.
[11] Federal Reserve System, *Final Amendments to the Risk-Based Capital Standards in Regulations H and Y*, 12 CFR Parts 208 and 225 (Regulations H and Y; Docket No. R-0845), September 11, 1995.

rary counterparties by warehousing the contracts until a matching party could be found at a later date. Greater flexibility was brought into the market when intermediaries created a diversified portfolio of swaps and other OTC derivatives and used exchange-traded derivatives to hedge their residual risks.

As intermediaries began to assume the role of counterparties and bore the inherent risk, they needed to have a stronger capital base and an increased ability to evaluate risk. These developments brought large depository intermediaries into the market. Due to their stronger capital position, large commercial banks replaced investment banks as the major suppliers of swap products. Today, the market for interest-rate and currency swaps is dominated by large commercial banks, which control 70% of the market.

Both the narrow bid-ask spreads and the significant rise in volume of swap activities suggest that the swap market is an efficient and competitive market. A growing number of corporations and public entities find swaps to be an effective hedging tool.

Swap transactions by depository intermediaries are monitored along with other off-the-balance-sheet activities by banking supervisory agencies. New Risk-Based Capital Standards require banks to maintain a minimum level of capital against their derivative positions, including swaps. The OTC activities of securities firms and affiliates of insurance companies are currently unregulated. Recommendations by the U.S. GAO have stressed the importance of subjecting these entities to regulation by federal financial agencies.

REVIEW QUESTIONS

1. Briefly describe the incentives for IBM and the World Bank to enter into a transaction that became known as the first currency swap.
2. Explain the criteria for an innovative financial instrument.
3. Using the criteria discussed in question 2, explain whether swaps meet the requirements of a new product.
4. Explain the reasons behind commercial banks' dominant position in the swap market.
5. Describe the reasons for the phenomenal growth of the swap market.
6. Explain the basic steps in calculating the fixed rate in an interest-rate swap.
7. Briefly define the following varieties of swaps:
   a. single-currency fixed-to-floating interest-rate swaps
   b. single-currency floating-to-floating interest-rate swaps (basis swaps)
   c. double-currency fixed-to-floating swaps
   d. double-currency fixed-to-fixed swaps
8. Describe the types of risk that can be hedged using the following varieties of swaps:
   a. single-currency fixed-to-floating interest-rate swaps
   b. single-currency floating-to-floating interest-rate swaps (basis swaps)

   c. double-currency fixed-to-floating swaps
   d. double-currency fixed-to-fixed swaps
9. Examine the current regulatory environment for swaps. Does the fact that commercial banks play a dominant role in the swap market increase or decrease the likelihood of further regulation?
10. Consider the following information:

Initiation date	June 15, 1998
Termination date	June 15, 2000
Notional amount	$10 million
Maturity	Two years
Floating index	Six-month dollar LIBOR
Fixed coupon	?
Payment frequency	Semiannual
Day count	30/360 for fixed, actual/360 for floating
LIBOR determination	Determined in advance, paid in arrears

The spot LIBOR yield curve at the origination of the swap provides the following (annualized) rates:

$$_0R_6 = 4\%$$
$$_0R_{12} = 4.5\%$$
$$_0R_{18} = 5\%$$
$$_0R_{24} = 5.5\%$$

The day count for each settlement date is as follows:

First settlement	December 15, 1998	No. of days = 183
Second settlement	June 15, 1999	No. of days = 182
Third settlement	December 15, 1999	No. of days = 183
Fourth settlement	June 15, 2000	No. of days = 183

Calculate the fixed rate to be used in the swap contract and set up the fixed and floating cash flows.

11. Suppose that a mortgage company, First Mortgage, has issued a total of $50 million in variable-rate mortgages. First Mortgage is concerned that interest rates may decline in the future, resulting in a decline in its cash inflows. To avoid interest-rate risk, First Mortgage approaches J.P. Morgan for a swap contract. J.P. Morgan suggests the following swap:

Initiation date	June 15, 1998
Maturity	Two years
Notional amount	$50 million
Floating-rate payer	First mortgage
Fixed-rate	6.5%
Fixed-payment day count	Actual/365
Fixed-rate payer	J.P. Morgan
Floating-rate index	Six-month LIBOR
Floating payment day count	Actual/360
Payment frequency	Semiannual
Settlement dates	12/15/1998, 06/15/1999, 12/15/1999, 06/12/2000
LIBOR determination	Determined in advance, paid in arrears

The fixed and floating settlement payments are calculated as follows:

Fixed-rate payment =
   (0.065)(actual days/365)($50 million)
Floating-rate payment=
   (LIBOR)(actual days/360)($50 million)

The fixed and floating rates are stated in annual terms and need to be converted to semiannual rates using the actual number of days. The following actual days apply to the four settlement dates:

Initiation date	June 15, 1998	
First settlement	December 15, 1998	No. of days = 183
Second settlement	June 15, 1999	No. of days = 182
Third settlement	December 15, 1999	No. of days = 183
Fourth settlement	June 15, 2000	No. of days = 183

Suppose that LIBOR rates observed in the future are as follows:

First settlement	December 15, 1998	5.50%
Second settlement	June 15, 1999	6.00%
Third settlement	December 15, 1999	6.75%
Fourth settlement	June 15, 2000	7.00%

Calculate payments and receipts for First Mortgage at each of the settlement dates. Determine the amounts of each check.

12. Consider the following information:

Currency Swap: Fixed Deutschemark vs. Floating U.S. Dollar LIBOR

Initiation date	June 15, 1996
Maturity	Four years (termination date: June 15, 2000)
Principal amounts	DM145 million, and $100 million
Fixed-rate payer	ZZZ
Fixed-rate	4.85% in Deutschemarks
Fixed-payment day count	30/360
Fixed-rate receiver	Bank of America
Floating-rate index	Six-month $LIBOR
Floating-payment day count	Actual/360
Payment frequency	semiannual
Settlement dates	June 15 and December 15
LIBOR determination	Determined in advance, paid in arrears

The fixed and floating payments are calculated as follows:

Fixed-rate payments=
$$.0485(180 / 360)(DM145 \text{ million})$$
Floating-rate payments =
$$LIBOR(\text{actual days} / 360)(\$100 \text{ million})$$

Assume the following hypothetical U.S. dollar LIBOR rates:

06/15/96	5.00%
12/15/96	5.25%
06/15/97	5.75%
12/15/97	6.00%
06/15/98	6.50%
12/15/98	6.75%
06/15/99	7.00%
12/15/99	7.25%
06/15/2000	7.50%

Prepare the schedule of cash flows for ZZZ, from 06/15/96 to 06/15/2000.

REFERENCES

Arak, M., A. Estrella, L. Goodman, and A. Silver. 1988. "Interest Rate Swaps: An Alternative Explanation," *Financial Management* (Summer): 12–18.

Bicksler, J., and A.H. Chen. 1986. "An Economic Analysis of Interest Rate Swaps." *Journal of Finance* (July): 645–655.

Federal Reserve System. *Final Amendments to the Risk-Based Capital Standards in Regulations H and Y*, 12 CFR Parts 208 and 225 (Regulations H and Y; Docket No. R-0845). September 11, 1995.

International Swaps and Derivatives Association. *ISDA Survey of Global Swap Transactions: 1994*, News Release, June 12, 1995.

Johnson, C., and J. Showers. 1992. "Currency Swap Pricing and Valuation." In *Cross Currency Swaps*, edited by C. Beidleman. Homewood, IL: Business One Irwin, pp. 331–363.

Smith, Jr., C.W., C.W. Smithson, and L.M. Wakeman. 1986. "The Evolving Market for Swaps." *Midland Corporate Finance Journal*, vol. 3: 20–32.

U.S. General Accounting Office. 1994. *Financial Derivatives: Actions Needed to Protect the Financial System.* (May).

Van Horne, J. 1985. "Of Financial Innovations and Excesses." *Journal of Finance* (July): 621–631.

Wall, L. 1989. "Interest Rate Swaps in an Agency Theoretic Model with Uncertain Interest Rates." *Journal of Banking and Finance*, vol. 13: 261–270.

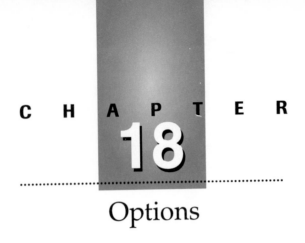

Options

OBJECTIVES

Unlike forwards, futures, and swaps, which convey obligations to both contracting parties, options provide rights for the buyer and obligations to the seller only. Options present unique opportunities for the financial manager to hedge against the unwanted downside risk while holding the rights to the profitable upside risk. Similar to other derivative products, options can be written on a wide variety of assets including interest-rate instruments, currencies, commodities, and equities. This chapter provides the institutional details of options, pricing methods for various contracts, and hedging strategies to mitigate interest-rate, foreign-exchange-rate, commodity, and equity risks.

UNIQUE FEATURES OF OPTIONS

Unlike forwards, futures, and swaps, which initially have zero net present values for both contracting parties, the buyer of an option pays a price (*premium*) to the seller at the time the parties enter into the contract. During the contract period, the option is exercised only if it is profitable for the buyer. Otherwise, it will be left to expire without exercise. Exercise may take place on any day during the life of the contract if it is an *American-style option*. But exercise can only take place at expiration if it is a *European-style option*.

Options are available on a wide variety of instruments, including contracts written on interest-rate products, currencies, commodities, and equities. Since the most widely written area of options literature involves equity options, we first describe the institutional details and pricing models for equity options and then generalize the discussion to include other underlying positions.

Buy-a-Call Option

The buyer of an equity call option contract has the right to purchase 100 shares of the underlying stock at a prespecified price (exercise price) over a preset period of time (term to expiration of the option). The call holder will exercise the option only if the share price exceeds the exercise price. At maturity, the value of the call option is:

$$C = \max(0, S_t - X)$$

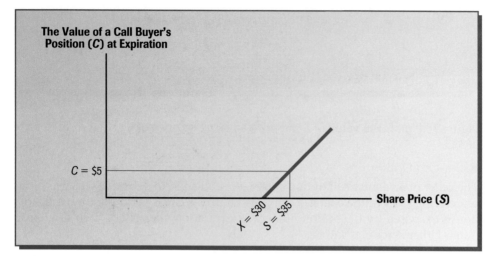

FIGURE 18.1
The Payoff for a Call
Option Holder on
Expiration

where

$$C = \text{call value}$$
$$S_t = \text{stock price}$$
$$X = \text{exercise price}$$

If $S_t < X$, the call will expire without exercise because the option holder has no incentive to purchase a share of the stock at X when its market price is only S_t. If $S_t > X$, the option holder has the incentive to exercise the option to purchase a share of the stock at X when its market value is S_t, thereby receiving $S_t - X$. The payoff of a call option at expiration is summarized as follows:

Payoff for a Buy-a-Call Position at Expiration		
	If $S_t \leq X$	**If $S_t > X$**
Buyer's Call Option Value	0	$S_t - X$

Figure 18.1 plots the value of a call with an exercise price of $30 and a share price of $35.

Buy-a-Put Option

The buyer of a put option has the right to sell a share of the underlying stock at a prespecified price over a prespecified period of time. The buyer will exercise the option only if the share price is below the exercise price. At expiration, the value of the put option will be

$$P = \max(0, X - S_t)$$

where P = put value. If $S_t > X$, the put will expire without exercise because the option holder has no incentive to sell a share of the stock at X when its market price is S. If $S_t < X$, the option holder has the incentive to exercise the option to sell a share of the stock at X when its market value is S_t, thereby receiving $X - S_t$. The payoff for a put option is summarized as follows:

Payoff for a Buy-a-Put Position at Expiration		
	If $S_t < X$	**If $S_t \geq X$**
Buyer's Put Option Value	$X - S_t$	0

Figure 18.2 plots the value of a put with an exercise price of $30 and a share price of $25.

Sell-a-Call Option

The seller of an equity call option contract is obligated to deliver 100 shares of the underlying stock at the exercise price over a prespecified period of time if the option is exercised by the option holder. At expiration, the seller's cash flow position is either zero or negative:

$$\text{Cash flows for the seller of a call} = \min(0, X - S_t)$$

On the option expiration date, if $S_t \leq X$, the call will expire without exercise. However, if $S_t > X$, the call will be exercised at the exercise price of X. The payoff of a sell-a-call is summarized as follows:

Payoff for a Sell-a-Call Position at Expiration		
	If $S_t \leq X$	**If $S_t > X$**
Seller's Call Option Value	0	$X - S_t$

Figure 18.3 plots cash flows for a sell-a-call position.

Sell-a-Put Option

The seller of a put option contract on common stock is obligated to purchase 100 shares of stock at the exercise price over a preset period of time if the option is exercised by the option holder. On the expiration date, the seller's cash flow position will be either zero or negative:

FIGURE 18.2
The Payoff for a Put Option Holder at Expiration

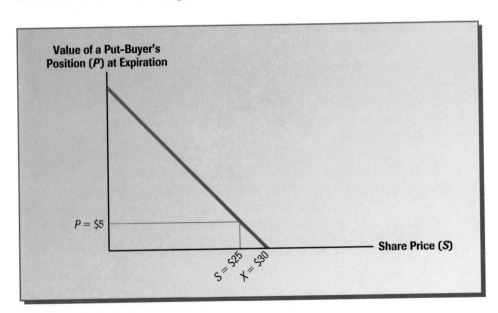

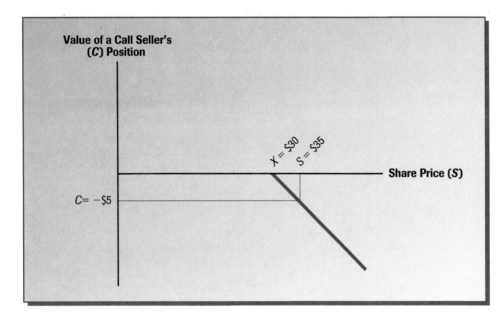

FIGURE 18.3
The Payoff to the Seller of a Call (C)

Cash flows for the seller of a put = min $(S_t - X, 0)$

On the expiration date, if $S_t < X$, the option will be exercised at the price of X. However, if $S_t \geq X$, the option will expire without exercise and the liability of the seller is zero. The payoff for a short put position is as follows:

Payoff for a Sell-a-Put Position at Expiration		
	If $S_t < X$	If $S_t \geq X$
Seller's Cash Flows	$S_t - X$	0

Figure 18.4 plots the cash flows for a sell-a-put position.

Combined Options: Buy a Share and a Put, Buy a Call and Sell a Put, Sell a Call and Buy a Put

Calls, puts, and shares can be combined as building blocks to create other products. Consider a portfolio made up of a share of stock and a put option with an exercise price of $50 expiring in one year. Suppose that the share price at option expiration will be either $45 or $55, resulting in a portfolio value of:

Payoff for a Portfolio of a Put and a Share		
	$S_t = \$45$	$S_t = \$55$
Share	$45	$55
Put	$5	0
Total Value of Portfolio	$50	$55

Combining a put and a share creates a portfolio with a floor value of $50 regardless of what happens to the share price at expiration. If the share price is $45, the

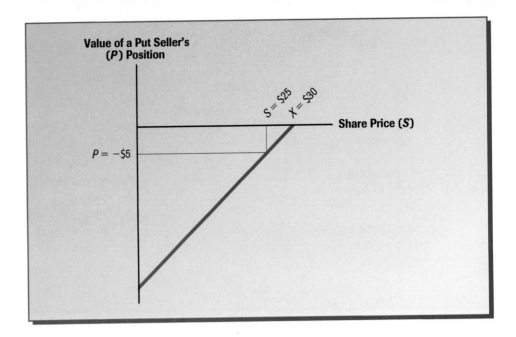

FIGURE 18.4
The Payoff to the Seller
of a Put Position (P)

put option will be exercised to sell the share for $50. If the share price is $55, the put option will be worthless and the share can be sold for $55. The strategy of combining a share of stock with a put on the stock guarantees that the value of the portfolio will not decline below the exercise price of the put. This strategy is known as *portfolio insurance*. This combination is plotted in Figure 18.5.

Consider another strategy in which you purchase a one-year call option on the stock at the exercise price of $50. You also invest the present value of the exercise price in a safe bank account that pays a continuously compounded risk-free rate of 6% per year:

$$PV\ (X) = \$50/e^{.06} = \$47.09$$

At expiration of the option, the price of the stock will be either $45 or $55, resulting in a portfolio value of:

FIGURE 18.5
The Payoff for a Buyer
of a Share and a Put

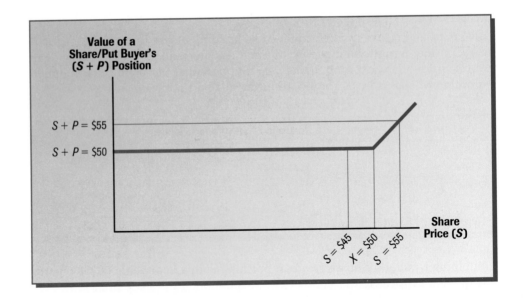

Payoff for a Portfolio of a Call and PV (X)		
	$S_t = \$45$	$S_t = \$55$
Call	0	$5
PV (X)	$50	$50
Total Value of Portfolio	$50	$55

Since the outcome of the second strategy is identical to that of the first strategy, the current values of the two portfolios should be identical:

$$Call + PV(X) = put + share$$

which is known as the **call-put parity formula**. This equation is very important because if you have one of the two options, you can create the other one. If puts are traded but calls are not, you can create a synthetic call:

$$Call = put + share - PV(X)$$

which indicates that you can create a call by buying a put, buying a share of the stock, and borrowing the present value of the exercise price. Conversely, if calls are traded but puts are not, you can create a synthetic put:

$$Put = call + PV(X) - share$$

which indicates that you can create a put by purchasing a call, investing the present value of the exercise price in a safe account, and selling a share short. This equation is also useful when pricing options. Instead of calculating the call and put prices separately, we can calculate one and then use the call-put parity formula to calculate the other.

Another useful option combination strategy involves purchasing a call option and selling a put option at the same exercise price. As shown in Figure 18.6, this combination resembles a long forward position:

$$Buy\ a\ call + sell\ a\ put = a\ long\ position\ in\ forwards$$

Conversely, if you buy a put and sell a call, your portfolio will resemble a short forward position as shown in Figure 18.7:

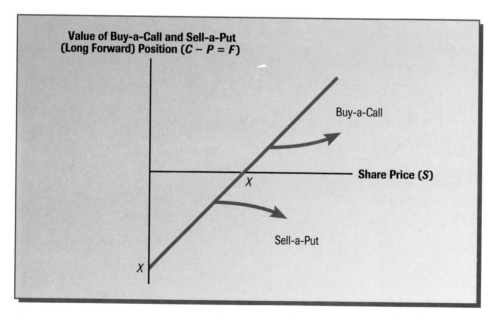

Value of Buy-a-Call and Sell-a-Put
(Long Forward) Position ($C - P = F$)

Buy-a-Call

Share Price (S)

X

Sell-a-Put

X

FIGURE 18.6
The Payoff for a
Buy-a-Call and
Sell-a-Put (Long
Forward) Position

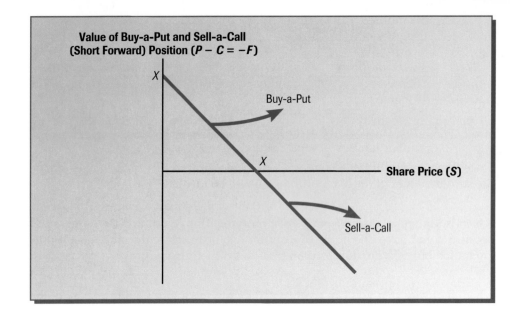

FIGURE 18.7
The Payoff for a
Buy-a-Put and
Sell-a-Call (Short
Forward) Position

Sell a call + buy a put = a short position in forwards

Since options are rights and forwards are obligations, it can be reasoned that forwards consist of a long option (right) and a short option (obligation). At expiration, if the forward contract is in the money, the net position constitutes a right. Conversely, if the forward contract is out of the money, the net position constitutes a commitment.

PRICE QUOTATIONS FOR EQUITY OPTIONS

Closing option prices for Citicorp from the Friday, September 29, 1995, issue of *The Wall Street Journal* for trades on the previous day are presented in Table 18.1.

The first column presents the stock's name and its closing price. Citicorp shares closed at $71⅞ on September 28, 1995. Next, the strike (exercise) prices are presented. On the day of trading, Citicorp options ranged in exercise prices from $45 to $75. The next column represents expiration dates. There are three separate expiration cycles—January, February, and March. The January cycle comprises quarterly expirations in January, April, July, and October. The February cycle comprises quarterly expirations in February, May, August, and November. The

TABLE 18.1	Listed Options Quotations					
Option	Strike	Exp.	Call Vol.	Call Price	Put Vol.	Put Price
Citicorp	45	Jan	509	26⅞	—	—
71⅞	65	Jan	63	8	23	1
71⅞	70	Oct	230	2⅝	290	¹⁵⁄₁₆
71⅞	70	Jan	42	5	27	2½
71⅞	75	Nov	301	1¼	42	4⅜
71⅞	75	Jan	45	2⅝	10	5¾
71⅞	75	Apr	71	4¼	5	6⅜

March cycle comprises quarterly expirations in March, June, September, and December. Each equity option belongs to one of the three cycles. Citicorp belongs to the January cycle. Short-term equity options are available for two near-term months plus two additional months of the January, February, or March cycle. For example, on September 29, 1995, option expiration months for Citicorp consisted of October, November, January, and April.

The next two columns show the trading volume and the closing price for each call option. The unit of trade is a contract, made up of 100 shares of the underlying stock. For January 45s, the total volume was 509 contracts of 100 shares each. The next column is the price of the call. For January 45s, the call price was $26⅞, which means that each contract of 100 shares was worth $2,687.50. There were no puts traded on January 45s. The last row reports prices for the April 1996 options at an exercise price of $75. There were 71 call contracts traded at a price of $4¼ per call and 5 put contracts traded at a price of $6⅜ per put.

Market Risk in Options: Delta, Vega, and Gamma

The value of an option is sensitive to changes in the market price, volatility, and price convexity of the underlying asset. Since an equity option is a right to purchase (sell) a share of stock at a prespecified price, the higher the market price of the stock, the higher (lower) the price of the call (put). The sensitivity of the option price to changes in the price of the underlying asset is called *delta risk*.

Since ownership of an option is a right and not an obligation, the option holder will benefit from greater volatility in the share price because as volatility increases, so does the likelihood that the option will be in the money at expiration. The relationship between volatility of the underlying asset and the price of an option is referred to as *volatility risk* or *Vega risk*.

Convexity or *gamma risk* refers to a property that, as the market price of the underlying asset gets closer to the exercise price, the price of the option becomes very sensitive to small changes in the price of the underlying asset. When the option is way out of the money, the value of the option does not change very much for small changes in the price of the underlying asset.

Determinants of Option Prices

The price of a call is a function of five variables: price of the underlying asset (S), exercise price (X), volatility of the underlying asset (σ), term to expiration (T), and risk-free rate (r). The relationship for a European call can be summarized as follows:

$$C = F(\overset{+}{S}, \overset{-}{X}, \overset{+}{\sigma}, \overset{+}{T}, \overset{+}{r})$$

The value of a call option when exercised is the amount by which the stock price exceeds the exercise price. A call option, therefore, becomes more valuable as the stock price increases and less valuable when the exercise price increases. For example, given an exercise price of $30, a call value is greater when the underlying stock price is $25 than when the stock price is $20. In the first case, the share price has to appreciate by $5 to be at the money, while in the second case the share price has to appreciate by $10 to be at the money. In general, the higher the stock price, the higher the value of the call, with other factors held constant.

The value of a call is a negative function of the exercise price. Suppose that the stock price is $25. At an exercise price of $30, the share price has to appreciate by $5 to be at the money. With an exercise price of $35, the share price has to increase by $10 to be at the money. Therefore, the call with a $30 exercise price is more valuable than the call with an exercise price of $35. In general, the higher the exercise price, the lower the price of the call, with other variables held constant.

The relationship between the value of a call and the risk of the underlying asset is positive. Since the ownership of a call is a right and not an obligation, a call holder will benefit from greater volatility in the share price, because as volatility increases, there is a greater likelihood that the call will be in the money at expiration.

The relationship between the value of a call and the term to expiration of the option is also positive. Consider two call options that are identical in every aspect except term to expiration. At the expiration of the shorter-term option, the value of the longer-term option is either equal to or greater than the value of the shorter-term option. For example, assume that at the expiration of the shorter-term call the stock price is $35. If the exercise price is $30, the value of the shorter-term call at expiration will be $5. The value of the longer-term call is at least $5 and, depending on the other four factors, it may be greater than $5. Overall, the longer the time to expiration of a call, the greater will be its value.

Finally, the relationship between the price of a call and the risk-free interest rate is positive. Suppose you plan to own shares of a certain stock in six months. Consider two alternatives: First, borrow money at the risk-free rate today and purchase the stock. The cost of this alternative (the cost of the loan) is the interest rate. Second, buy a six-month call option on the stock. The cost of the second alternative is the premium paid to purchase the call. Since both alternatives provide the same result—ownership of the stock in six-months—their costs should be identical. The higher the cost of borrowing, or interest rate, the higher the cost of buying the call, or the call premium.

The relationship between the value of a put and the five factors we described above is as follows:

$$P = F(\overset{-}{S}, \overset{+}{X}, \overset{+}{\sigma}, \overset{+/-}{T}, \overset{+/-}{r_f})$$

The value of a put option at expiration depends on the amount the exercise price exceeds the stock price. The put value, therefore, becomes less valuable as the stock price increases and more valuable as the exercise price increases.

Similar to call options, put options benefit from increased volatility in the underlying asset. Since the ownership of a put is a right and not an obligation, the put holder will benefit from greater volatility in the share price, because as volatility increases there is a greater likelihood that the put will be in the money at expiration.

The effect of the term to expiration and the risk-free interest rate on the price of a put is indeterminate. Consider the price of a put derived from the call-put parity formula:

$$P = C + PV(X) - S$$

Since the effect of both T and r on the value of a call are positive, their impact on the value of a put should also be positive. However, T and r affect $PV(X)$ negatively, reducing the value of the put. Thus, the net impact of T and r on the value of a put may be either positive or negative.

THE BOUNDARIES OF OPTION VALUES

A call option at any time prior to expiration has a lower-bound and an upper-bound value. The lower-bound value of a call is determined by

$$C = \max(0, S - X)$$

The upper-bound value of a call option is the price of the underlying asset. The price of a call option will never exceed the price of its underlying asset. At the extreme, when the exercise price is equal to zero, the value of the call is equal to the

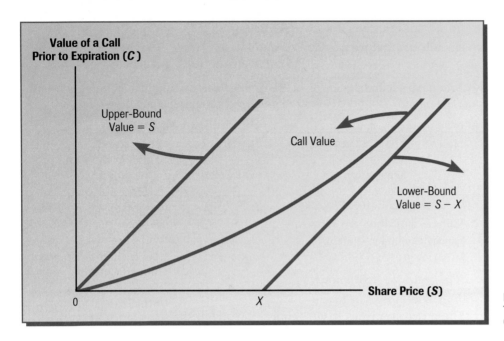

Value of a Call Prior to Expiration (C)

Upper-Bound Value = S

Call Value

Lower-Bound Value = S − X

Share Price (S)

0

X

FIGURE 18.8
The Boundaries of Call Option Values

value of the underlying asset. The upper- and lower-bound values for a call option are presented in Figure 18.8.

The lower-bound value of a put is determined by

$$P = \max(0, X - S)$$

The upper-bound value of a put is the value of its exercise price when the share price nears zero.

OPTION PRICING

The option pricing model presented in this section is the famous Black-Scholes option pricing model. Before we begin discussing the Black-Scholes model, we present a simple two-state model of option pricing that serves as the foundation for the more complex Black-Scholes model.

A Two-State Option Pricing Model

Suppose that the current price of a given stock is $30 per share. Further assume that the price within a year can only take one of two values: It will be either $35 or $25. We examine two investment strategies:

1. Buy a call option contract to purchase 100 shares at the exercise price of $30 and an expiration date of one year;
2. Buy 50 shares of the stock at the price of $30 and borrow a *duplicating* amount, the repayment of which in a year will make the payoffs from the two strategies identical.

In order to determine the duplicating amount, we need to find the payoff from the first strategy. If the stock price is $35 in one year, the value of the call will be

$$100(\$35 - \$30) = \$500$$

From the second strategy, the value of 50 shares of the stock will be

$$50 \times \$35 = \$1{,}750$$

In order to make the payoffs from two strategies equal, we need to have a loan repayment of

$$\$1{,}750 - \$500 = \$1{,}250$$

which indicates that we need to borrow

$$\$1{,}250/(1 + .05) = \$1{,}190$$

today to have a loan balance of $1,250 in one year, assuming a 5% annual interest rate. The payoffs from the two strategies are summarized as follows:

Strategy	S = $35		S = $25
1. Value of the calls: 100($35 – $30) =	$500	$100 \times 0 =$	$0
2. Value of the shares: 50 × $35 =	$1,750	$50 \times \$25$	$1,250
Principal and interest of the loan:			
$1,190 (1 + 0.05) =	–$1,250		–$1,250
Total cash flows from Strategy 2	$500		$0

These two strategies have identical payoffs. If the stock price in one year is $35, in the first strategy, the call value will be the difference between the stock price and the exercise price, $5, multiplied by 100, or $500. In the second strategy, the value of the stocks owned will be $1,750, the loan obligation will be $1,250, resulting in a net portfolio value of $500.

If the price of the stock in one year is $25, the investment value in the first strategy will be zero because the price at the option expiration date is below the exercise price of $30. The value of the portfolio in the second strategy is also zero because the stock value is $1,250 and the loan has a balance of $1,250, resulting in a net portfolio value of zero. Since the two strategies produce identical results in one year, their costs today also should be equal:

$$\text{Cost of strategy } 1 = 100 \times C$$
$$\text{Cost of strategy } 2 = (50 \times \$30) - \$1{,}190 = \$560$$
$$100 \times C = \$560, \text{ or } C = \$560/100 = \$5.60$$

which indicates that the price of one call today should be $5.60.

This simple method of calculating the price of a call option has a fundamental appeal but little practical use because the stock price in one year will not be limited to only two levels; instead, it may take many other values. However, if we shorten the length of time between time zero and one, we can significantly reduce the number of stock price possibilities. To allow for a plausible two-state pricing, we may reduce the length of the time between now and the first period to an infinitesimal instant.

The appeal of the Black-Scholes model is that it duplicates a call by a combination of stock and borrowing over an infinitesimal time horizon. By adjusting the combination from moment to moment, the Black-Scholes model enables us to value a call in the real world as we have shown how to value the call in our simple two-state model.

The Black-Scholes Option Pricing Model

The Black-Scholes model provides a valuation formula for European-style equity options.[1] The model is based on the following assumptions:

1. The stock pays no dividends
2. There are no transaction costs

[1] Black and Scholes (1973).

3. There are no taxes
4. Interest rates are constant
5. There are no penalties or restrictions against short selling
6. The market operates continuously and the share price follows a continuous pattern
7. The stock price is "lognormally" distributed

The restrictive nature of these assumptions does not diminish the significance of the model considering the fact that these assumptions were later relaxed in extensions made to the original model.

The Black-Scholes model provides the following equations to calculate the value of European-style equity call and put options:

$$C = SN(d_1) - \frac{X}{e^{rT}} N(d_2), \; P = \frac{X}{e^{rT}} N(-d_2) - SN(-d_1)$$

$$d_1 = \frac{\ln\left(\dfrac{S}{X}\right) + \left(r + \dfrac{\sigma^2}{2}\right)T}{\sqrt{\sigma^2 T}}$$

$$d_2 = \frac{\ln\left(\dfrac{S}{X}\right) + \left(r - \dfrac{\sigma^2}{2}\right)T}{\sqrt{\sigma^2 T}} = d_1 - \sqrt{\sigma^2 T}$$

The variables in the equations are defined as

S = current stock price
X = exercise price
r = risk-free rate (annualized, continuously compounded)
σ^2 = variance of the continuous return on the stock (per year)
T = time to expiration (in years)
$N(d)$ = probability that a standardized, normally distributed, random variable will be less than or equal to d

Example 1: The Pricing of an Out-of-the-Money Call and an In-the-Money Put

On June 12, 1995, we are interested in calculating the prices for January 1996 calls and puts for Citicorp (CCI). The expiration date is the third Thursday of the expiring month, or January 18, 1996. The following information is also provided:

$$S = \$55$$
$$X = \$60$$
$$\sigma^2 = 10\%$$
$$r = 6\%$$
$$T = 220 \text{ days}$$

We take the following steps:

1. Calculate d_1 and d_2.
2. Find $N(d_1)$ and $N(d_2)$.
3. Use the formula to calculate the value of the call.
4. Use the call-put parity formula to calculate the value of the put.

Step 1: Calculate d_1 and d_2.

$$d_1 = \frac{\ln\left(\dfrac{55}{60}\right) + \left(0.06 + \dfrac{0.10}{2}\right)220/365}{\sqrt{0.10(220/365)}} = -0.0844$$

$$d_2 = -0.0844 - \sqrt{0.10(220/365)} = -0.3299$$

Step 2: Find $N(d_1)$ and $N(d_2)$. The values of $N(d_1)$ and $N(d_2)$ are cumulative probabilities of the standard normal distribution with an expected value of 0 and a standard deviation of 1. The probability that a drawing from a standard normal distribution will be between −1 and +1 (within one standard deviation of the mean) is 68.25%. Since the normal distribution is symmetric, the probability that a drawing will be below 0 is 50%, which means that $N(0) = 0.50$. Since d_1 and d_2 are slightly negative, we expect $N(d_1)$ and $N(d_2)$ to be below 0.50. Table 18.2 presents the cumulative probabilities of the standard normal distribution function. Using d_1 and d_2, we find the appropriate values from the table. Since d_1 and d_2 are negative, the values found in the table will be subtracted from 0.50:

$N(d_1)$:

$$N(-0.08) = 0.50 - 0.0319 = 0.4681$$
$$N(-0.09) = 0.50 - 0.0359 = 0.4641$$

By interpolation:

$$N(-0.0844) = 0.4681 - 0.44 \times (0.4681 - 0.4641) = 0.4663$$

$N(d_2)$:

$$N(-0.3299) = N(-0.33) = 0.50 - 0.1293 = 0.3707$$

Step 3: Calculate the value of the call.

$$C = 55(0.4663) - \frac{60}{e^{0.06 \times 220/365}}(0.3707) = \$4.19$$

Step 4: Calculate the value of the put based on the call-put parity formula.

$$Put = call + PV(x) - share\ price$$

$$P = 4.19 + \frac{60}{e^{0.06 \times 220/365}} - 55 = \$7.06$$

Example 2: The Pricing of an In-the-Money Call and an Out-of-the-Money Put

We use the information provided in the previous example with one exception: We change the exercise price from $60 to $50. Now the call is in the money and the put is out of the money. Again, on June 12, 1995, we are interested in calculating the prices for January 1996 calls and puts for Citicorp. The expiration date is the third Thursday of the expiring month or January 18, 1996. The rest of the information is provided as follows:

$$S = \$55$$
$$X = \$50$$
$$\sigma^2 = 10\%$$
$$r = 6\%$$
$$T = 220\ days$$

We follow the four-step procedure to calculate the values of a call and a put.

Step 1: Calculate d_1 and d_2.

$$d_1 = \frac{\ln\left(\frac{55}{50}\right) + \left(0.06 + \frac{0.10}{2}\right)220/365}{\sqrt{0.10(220/365)}} = .6583$$

$$d_2 = 0.6583 - \sqrt{0.10(220/365)} = 0.4128$$

Step 2: Find $N(d_1)$ and $N(d_2)$. Since d_1 and d_2 are positive, $N(d_1)$ and $N(d_2)$ will be greater than 0.50. Therefore, we add the figures found from Table 18.2 to 0.50.

$N(d_1)$:

$$N(0.65) = 0.50 + 0.2422 = 0.7422$$
$$N(0.66) = 0.50 + 0.2454 = 0.7454$$

By interpolation:

$$N(0.6583) = 0.7422 + 0.83 \times (0.7454 - 0.7422) = 0.7449$$

$N(d_2)$:

$$N(0.41) = 0.50 + 0.1591 = 0.6591$$
$$N(0.42) = 0.50 + 0.1628 = 0.6628$$

By interpolation:

$$N(0.4128) = 0.6591 + 0.28 \times (0.6628 - 0.6591) = 0.6601$$

Step 3: Calculate the value of the call.

$$C = 55(0.7449) - \frac{50}{e^{0.06 \times 220/365}}(0.6601) = \$9.14$$

Step 4: Calculate the value of the put based on the call-put parity formula.

$$P = 9.14 + \frac{50}{e^{0.06 \times 220/365}} - 55 = \$2.36$$

MODELS RELAXING THE ASSUMPTIONS OF THE BLACK-SCHOLES MODEL

The development of the basic equity-based option pricing model led to other extensions that relaxed the original assumptions of the Black-Scholes model. Below, we discuss the option pricing model for stocks that pay dividends.[2]

Pricing of Equity Options with Dividends

The original Black-Scholes model was designed to price a European-style option that paid no dividends. Allowing for dividends the model is revised as follows:[3]

$$C = \frac{S}{e^{\delta T}} N(d_1) - \frac{X}{e^{rT}} N(d_2)$$

$$d_1 = \frac{\ln\left(\dfrac{S}{X}\right) + \left(r - \delta + \dfrac{\sigma^2}{2}\right)T}{\sqrt{\sigma^2 T}}$$

$$d_2 = d_1 - \sqrt{\sigma^2 T}$$

where δ is the constant dividend yield. The reasoning behind the changes made in the original model is simple. Dividend payments reduce the stock value to the holder of the option by the PV of the foregone dividends while reducing the cost of holding the stock by the same amount.

---

[2] Other extensions that relaxed the Black-Scholes assumptions include constant interest rates (Merton, 1973), no taxes or transaction costs (Ingersoll 1976), continuous trading and price distribution (Merton, 1976, Cox and Ross, 1976), and lognormally distributed stock prices (Jarrow and Rudd, 1982).

[3] Merton (1973).

	TABLE 18.2	Cumulative Probabilities of the Standard Normal Distribution Function			
d	**0.00**	**0.01**	**0.02**	**0.03**	**0.04**
0.0	0.0000	0.0040	0.0080	0.0120	0.0160
0.1	0.0398	0.0438	0.0478	0.0517	0.0557
0.2	0.0793	0.0832	0.0871	0.0910	0.0948
0.3	0.1179	0.1217	0.1255	0.1293	0.1331
0.4	0.1554	0.1591	0.1628	0.1664	0.1700
0.5	0.1915	0.1950	0.1985	0.2019	0.2054
0.6	0.2257	0.2291	0.2324	0.2357	0.2389
0.7	0.2580	0.2611	0.2642	0.2673	0.2704
0.8	0.2881	0.2910	0.2939	0.2967	0.2995
0.9	0.3159	0.3186	0.3212	0.3238	0.3264
1.0	0.3413	0.3438	0.3461	0.3485	0.3508
1.1	0.3643	0.3665	0.3686	0.3708	0.3729
1.2	0.3849	0.3869	0.3888	0.3907	0.3925
1.3	0.4032	0.4049	0.4066	0.4082	0.4099
1.4	0.4192	0.4207	0.4222	0.4236	0.4251
1.5	0.4332	0.4345	0.4357	0.4370	0.4382
1.6	0.4452	0.4463	0.4474	0.4484	0.4495
1.7	0.4554	0.4564	0.4573	0.4582	0.4591
1.8	0.4641	0.4649	0.4656	0.4664	0.4671
1.9	0.4713	0.4719	0.4726	0.4732	0.4738
2.0	0.4773	0.4778	0.4783	0.4788	0.4793
2.1	0.4821	0.4826	0.4830	0.4834	0.4838
2.2	0.4861	0.4866	0.4830	0.4871	0.4875
2.3	0.4893	0.4896	0.4898	0.4901	0.4904
2.4	0.4918	0.4920	0.4922	0.4925	0.4927
2.5	0.4938	0.4940	0.4941	0.4943	0.4945
2.6	0.4953	0.4955	0.4956	0.4957	0.4959
2.7	0.4965	0.4966	0.4967	0.4968	0.4969
2.8	0.4974	0.4975	0.4976	0.4977	0.4977
2.9	0.4981	0.4982	0.4982	0.4982	0.4984
3.0	0.4987	0.4987	0.4987	0.4988	0.4988

$N(d)$ represents areas under the standard normal distribution function. For example, if $d_1 = 1.53$, $N(d_1) = 0.5000 + 0.4370 = 0.9370$. If d_1 is equal to 1.5344, the probability is estimated by interpolating between $N(1.53)$ and $N(1.54)$.

0.05	0.06	0.07	0.08	0.09
0.0199	0.0239	0.0279	0.0319	0.0359
0.0596	0.0636	0.0675	0.0714	0.0753
0.0987	0.1026	0.1064	0.1103	0.1141
0.1368	0.1406	0.1443	0.1480	0.1517
0.1736	0.1772	0.1808	0.1844	0.1879
0.2088	0.2123	0.2157	0.2190	0.2224
0.2422	0.2454	0.2486	0.2517	0.2549
0.2734	0.2764	0.2794	0.2823	0.2852
0.3023	0.3051	0.3078	0.3106	0.3133
0.3289	0.3315	0.3340	0.3365	0.3389
0.3531	0.3554	0.3577	0.3599	0.3621
0.3749	0.3770	0.3790	0.3810	0.3830
0.3944	0.3962	0.3980	0.3997	0.4015
0.4115	0.4131	0.4147	0.4162	0.4177
0.4265	0.4279	0.4292	0.4306	0.4319
0.4394	0.4406	0.4418	0.4429	0.4441
0.4505	0.4515	0.4525	0.4535	0.4545
0.4599	0.4608	0.4616	0.4625	0.4633
0.4678	0.4686	0.4693	0.4699	0.4706
0.4744	0.4750	0.4756	0.4761	0.4767
0.4798	0.4803	0.4808	0.4812	0.4817
0.4842	0.4846	0.4850	0.4854	0.4857
0.4878	0.4881	0.4884	0.4887	0.4890
0.4906	0.4909	0.4911	0.4913	0.4916
0.4929	0.4931	0.4932	0.4934	0.4936
0.4946	0.4948	0.4949	0.4951	0.4952
0.4960	0.4961	0.4962	0.4963	0.4964
0.4970	0.4971	0.4972	0.4973	0.4974
0.4978	0.4979	0.4979	0.4980	0.4981
0.4984	0.4985	0.4985	0.4986	0.4986
0.4989	0.4989	0.4989	0.4990	0.4990

The call-put parity formula for a stock with dividend payments is as follows:

$$C + \frac{X}{e^{rT}} = P + \frac{S}{e^{\delta T}}$$

Example 3: The Pricing of European Options with Dividends

In Example 2, we assumed there were no dividends. Now use the information from Example 2 with the assumption of a 3% continuously compounded annual dividend yield. On June 12, 1995, we are interested in calculating the prices for January 1996 calls and puts for Citicorp (CCI). The expiration date is the third Thursday of the expiring month, or January 18, 1996. The following information is also provided:

$$S = \$55$$
$$X = \$50$$
$$\sigma^2 = 10\%$$
$$r = 6\%$$
$$T = 220 \text{ days}$$
$$\delta = 3\%$$

We follow the four necessary steps to calculate the values of the call and the put.

Step 1: Calculate d_1 and d_2.

$$d_1 = \frac{\ln\left(\frac{55}{50}\right) + \left(0.06 - 0.03 + \frac{0.10}{2}\right)220/365}{\sqrt{0.10(220/365)}} = 0.5845$$

$$d_2 = 0.5845 - \sqrt{0.10(220/365)} = 0.3390$$

Step 2: Using Table 18.2, find $N(d_1)$ and $N(d_2)$:

$N(d_1)$:

$$N(0.58) = 0.50 + 0.2190 = 0.7190$$
$$N(0.59) = 0.50 + 0.2224 = 0.7224$$

By interpolation:

$$N(0.5845) = .7190 + .45 \times (.7224 - .7190) = .7205$$

$N(d_2)$:

$$N(0.33) = 0.50 + 0.1293 = 0.6293$$
$$N(0.34) = 0.50 + 0.1331 = 0.6331$$

By interpolation:

$$N(0.3390) = 0.6293 + 0.90 \times (0.6331 - 0.6293) = 0.6327$$

Step 3: We now can calculate the value of the call.

$$C = \frac{55}{e^{0.03 \times 220/365}}(0.7205) - \frac{50}{e^{0.06 \times 220/365}}(0.6327) = \$8.41$$

Remember from Example 2 that the value of the call was $9.06. The decline in the call value is due to the expected dividend payments to stockholders that will reduce the price of the stock. Since call holders do not receive dividends, the value of a call option on a dividend-paying stock is less than the value of a call on a similar but nondividend-paying stock.

Step 4: Calculate the value of the put on a dividend-paying stock.

$$P = 8.41 + \frac{50}{e^{0.06 \times 220/365}} - \frac{55}{e^{0.03 \times 220/365}} = \$2.62$$

The value of the put in this example is greater than the value of the put in Example 2 because the price of the dividend-paying stock is lower than a non-dividend-paying stock, causing the price of the put to increase.

EQUITY INDEX OPTIONS

The market for equity index options includes the S&P 500 Index (CBOE), the S&P 100 Index (CBOE), and the Major Market Index (AMEX), among others. While some index options follow movements in the market, others are based on the performance of a particular sector (e.g., biotechnology, computer, pharmaceutical, semiconductor, and utility).

The S&P 500 contracts are European-style; the S&P 100 and the Major Market Index are American-style options. Each contract is a right to buy or to sell 100 times the index at a preset exercise price. Stock index options are settled in cash. When exercised, the value of a call for the owner is determined by max(0, S − X) while the value of the put for the owner is determined by max(0, X − S). For example, suppose that one call on S&P 100 at an exercise price of $550 is exercised when the index is at $557. The call payoff will be ($557 − $550) × 100 = $700.

The length of time before expiration of the exchange-traded equity options generally does not exceed four months. For example, in October 1995, stock index options are traded with expiration dates of October, November, and December 1995, and January 1996. There are also long-term exchange-traded equity index options known as LEAPs (Long-Term Equity Anticipation Securities) with maturities of up to three years. Stock index LEAPs expire once a year in December.

Another category of the stock index options introduced by the CBOE is *caps*. These are European options on the S&P 500 and the S&P 100 where the payout is capped at $30. A call cap is automatically exercised on the day that the index closes $30 more than the exercise price. A put cap is automatically exercised on the day that the index closes $30 below the exercise price. CBOE has also introduced a new stock index option known as a *flex option*, where the exercise price and the maturity of the option are determined by the traders and not by the exchanges.

The Pricing of Stock Index Options

The pricing model for stock index options is similar to the pricing model for dividend-paying equity options. The original Black-Scholes model is adjusted for dividends, as presented previously:

$$C = \frac{S}{e^{\delta T}} N(d_1) - \frac{X}{e^{rT}} N(d_2)$$

$$d_1 = \frac{\ln\left(\frac{S}{X}\right) + \left(r - \delta + \frac{\sigma^2}{2}\right)T}{\sqrt{\sigma^2 T}}$$

$$d_2 = d_1 - \sqrt{\sigma^2 T}$$

The call-put parity formula is as follows:

$$C + \frac{X}{e^{rT}} = P + \frac{S}{e^{\delta T}}$$

where

S = current price of the index
X = exercise price of the option

σ^2 = volatility of the index
r = annual continuously compounded risk-free rate
T = term to expiration of the option
δ = average annualized dividend yield on the index

Example 4: Pricing Equity Index Options

Based on the following information, calculate the values of a call and a put for a S&P 500 index option:

$$S = \$582$$
$$X = \$600$$
$$\sigma^2 = 4\%$$
$$r = 6\%$$
$$T = 90 \text{ days}$$
$$\delta = 5\%$$

We follow the four necessary steps to calculate the values of the call and the put.

Step 1: Calculate d_1 and d_2.

$$d_1 = \frac{\ln\left(\frac{582}{600}\right) + \left(0.06 - 0.05 + \frac{0.04}{2}\right)90/365}{\sqrt{0.04(90/365)}} = -0.2322$$

$$d_2 = -0.2322 - \sqrt{0.04(90/365)} = -0.3315$$

Step 2: Using Table 18.2, find $N(d_1)$ and $N(d_2)$.

$N(d_1)$:

$$N(-0.23) = 0.50 - 0.0910 = 0.4090$$
$$N(-0.24) = 0.50 - 0.0948 = 0.4052$$

By interpolation:

$$N(-0.2322) = 0.4090 - 0.22 \times (0.4090 - 0.4052) = 0.4082$$

$N(d_2)$:

$$N(-0.33) = 0.50 - 0.1293 = 0.3707$$
$$N(-0.34) = 0.50 - 0.1331 = 0.3669$$

By interpolation

$$N(-0.3315) = 0.3707 - 0.15 \times (0.3707 - 0.3669) = 0.3701.$$

Step 3: Calculate the value of the call.

$$C = \frac{582}{e^{0.05 \times 90/365}}(0.4082) - \frac{600}{e^{0.06 \times 90/365}}(0.3701) = \$15.86$$

One call contract will cost $15.86 \times 100 = \$1,586$.

Step 4: Calculate the value of the put based on the call-put parity formula.

$$P = 15.86 + \frac{600}{e^{0.06 \times 90/365}} - \frac{582}{e^{0.05 \times 90/365}} = \$32.18$$

One put contract will cost $32.18 \times 100 = \$3,218$.

CURRENCY OPTIONS

The Philadelphia Stock Exchange began trading in currency options in 1982. By 1995, options were traded in the following currencies: Australian dollar, British pound, Canadian dollar, French franc, German mark, Japanese yen, and Swiss

TABLE 18.3 Philadelphia Currency Options **Friday, October 6, 1995**	Call		Put	
	Vol.	**Last**	**Vol.**	**Last**
Australian dollar (76.18)				
50,000 Australian dollar–European style				
77 Nov.	16	0.43	—	—
50,000 Australian dollar–cents per unit				
77 Nov.	30	0.44	—	—
British pound (158.46)				
31,250 British pounds–European style				
157 Oct.	—	—	32	0.33
158 Oct.	5	1.10	—	—
159 Oct.	32	0.49	—	—
31,250 British pounds–cents per unit				
157 Oct.	—	—	42	0.30
158 Oct.	500	1.16	—	—
159 Oct.	64	0.49	—	—
Japanese yen (99.44)				
6,250,000 Japanese yen–100th of a cent per unit				
93 Dec.	—	—	22	15.78
99 Oct.	8	1.66	8	0.70
100 Oct.	8	1.10	8	1.12
105 Dec.	1	1.48	40	5.55
6,250,000 Japanese yen–European style				
98 Oct.	—	—	100	0.52
102 Nov.	5	1.55	—	—
Call Vol. = 15,704 Open Interest = 256,118				
Put Vol. = 20,982 Open Interest = 278,968.				

franc. A sample of traded currency options reported in the October 9, 1995, issue of *The Wall Street Journal* based on trades conducted on October 6, 1995, is presented in Table 18.3.

Currency options are traded with expiration months of March, June, September, and December for up to nine months in the future. In addition, during any month, there are options with maturities in each of the next two months. For example, in October 1995, the available currency option expiration months are December, March, June, October, and November. In the price table above, currency names are followed by spot exchange rates in American cents in parentheses. Currency options are available in both European and American styles. For example, on October 6, 1995, the spot exchange rate for the British pound was 158.46 cents per pound. Each option contract has a denomination of 31,250 pounds. There were 32 European-style October put contracts with an exercise price of 157 cents traded at the closing price of 0.33. The put holder has the right to sell £31,250 at a price of £31,250 × 157/100 = US$49,062.50. Each put contract costs £31,250 × 0.0033 = $103.125. The total volume of calls and puts for the trading day in the exchange were 15,704 and 20,982 contracts with open interest of 256,118, and 278,968, respectively.

In addition to the exchange-traded currency options, over-the-counter currency options are available through financial intermediaries. The OTC currency options are designed to maturity and exercise price specifications of the clients.

Pricing of Currency Options

The pricing model for European-style currency options is similar to the model for dividend paying equity options with the following specifications:[4]

$$C = \frac{S}{e^{r_f T}} N(d_1) - \frac{X}{e^{rT}} N(d_2)$$

$$d_1 = \frac{\ln\left(\dfrac{S}{X}\right) + \left(r - r_f + \dfrac{\sigma^2}{2}\right)T}{\sqrt{\sigma^2 T}}$$

$$d_2 = d_1 - \sqrt{\sigma^2 T}$$

where

S = spot exchange rate (one unit of foreign currency in U.S. dollars)
X = exercise price
r = domestic risk-free interest rate (annual continuously compounded)
r_f = foreign risk-free interest rate (annual continuously compounded)
σ^2 = volatility of the exchange rate (annual variance)
T = term to expiration of the option (annual)

The valuation formula for foreign currency options is similar to the model for a dividend-paying stock in that the owner of a foreign currency receives a "dividend yield" equal to the foreign risk-free rate (r_f). We therefore substitute r_f for δ in the pricing model for dividend-paying stock options to obtain the pricing model for currency options. The call-put parity formula for currency options is as follows:

$$C + \frac{X}{e^{rT}} = P + \frac{S}{e^{r_f T}}$$

Example 5: The Pricing of European Currency Options

Based on the following information, calculate the European call and put option values for British pounds:

$$S = 1.58$$
$$X = 1.60$$
$$r = 5.60\% \ (USA)$$
$$r_f = 6.87\% \ (UK)$$
$$\sigma^2 = 20\%$$
$$T = 70/365$$

We follow the four necessary steps to calculate the values of the call and the put.

Step 1: Calculate d_1 and d_2.

$$d_1 = \frac{\ln\left(\dfrac{1.58}{1.60}\right) + \left(0.0560 - 0.0687 + \dfrac{0.20}{2}\right)70/365}{\sqrt{0.20(70/365)}} = 0.0213$$

$$d_2 = 0.0213 - \sqrt{0.20(70/365)} = -0.1745$$

---

[4] Garman and Kohlhagen (1983).

Step 2: Using Table 18.2 we find $N(d_1)$ and $N(d_2)$.

$N(d_1)$:

$$N(0.02) = 0.50 + 0.0080 = 0.5080$$
$$N(0.03) = 0.50 + 0.0120 = 0.5120$$

By interpolation:

$$N(0.0213) = 0.5080 + 0.13 \times (0.5120 - 0.5080) = 0.5085$$

$N(d_2)$:

$$N(-0.17) = 0.50 - 0.0675 = 0.4325$$
$$N(-0.18) = 0.50 - 0.0714 = 0.4286$$

By interpolation:

$$N(-0.1749) = 0.4325 - 0.45 \times (0.4325 - 0.4286) = 0.4307$$

Step 3: Calculate the value of the call.

$$C = \frac{1.58}{e^{0.0687 \times 70/365}}(0.5085) - \frac{1.60}{e^{0.0560 \times 70/365}}(0.4307) = \$0.11$$

The price for one call contract will be: $31{,}250 \times 0.11 = \$3{,}437.50$.

Step 4: Calculate the value of the put based on the call-put parity formula.

$$P = 0.11 + \frac{1.60}{e^{0.0560 \times 70/365}} - \frac{1.58}{e^{0.0687 \times 70/365}} = \$0.13$$

The price for one put contract will be $31{,}250 \times 0.13 = \$4{,}062.50$.

INTEREST-RATE OPTIONS

Exchange-Traded Interest-Rate Options: T-Bond Futures Options, Eurodollar Futures Options, and Others

The payoff in interest-rate options depends on the level of interest rates. Two general categories of interest-rate options are: exchange-traded interest-rate options; and over-the-counter interest-rate options. The exchange-traded interest-rate options are presented in Table 18.4.

Among the exchange-traded interest-rate options, the most active are those written on interest-rate futures contracts. The CBOT's T-Bond futures and CME's Eurodollar futures have the largest volume and open interest. Options on

TABLE 18.4   The Chronological Development of Exchange-Traded Interest-Rate Options

Options On	Exchange	Year	Level of Activity
T-Bond Futures	CBOT	Oct. 1982	High
Eurodollar Futures	CME	Oct. 1982	High
Treasury Bonds	CBOE	Oct. 1982	Low
T-Notes and T-Bills	AMEX	Oct. 1982	Low
10-Yr T-Note Futures	CBOT	May 1985	High
Muni Index Futures	CBOT	June 1987	High
5-Yr T-Note Futures	CBOT	May 1990	High
2-Yr T-Note Futures	CBOT	May 1992	High

TABLE 18.5 Futures Options Prices Interest Rates

T-Bonds (CBOT)

$100,000; points and 64ths of 100%

Strike Price	Calls-Settle			Puts-Settle		
	Nov.	Dec.	Mar.	Nov.	Dec.	Mar.
114	2–11	2–45	3–37	0–06	0–38	1–57
118	0–06	0–41	1–45	—	2–35	3–61

Est. vol. 60,000; Wed vol. 25,184 calls; 33,861 puts; Open Interest Wed 358,938 calls; 332,348 puts.

Eurodollar (CME)

$million; points of 100%

	Calls-Settle			Puts-Settle		
	Dec.	Mar.	June	Dec.	Mar.	June
9,375	0.50	0.69	0.75	0.02	0.06	0.14
9,500	0.01	0.06	0.14	0.77	0.66	0.75

Est. Vol. 72,971; Wed vol. 35,439 calls; 20,421 puts; Open Interest Wed 775,269 calls; 885,201 puts.

interest-rate futures are American-style options. Upon exercise, the option holder on T-bond futures takes a long or a short position in the nearby futures contract. Exercise of the options on Eurodollar futures results in taking a position in the Eurodollar futures contract of the same maturity.

A sample of trading in options written on interest-rate futures reported in the October 13, 1995, edition of *The Wall Street Journal* based on trading on October 12, 1995, is presented in Table 18.5.

The trading unit for options on T-bond futures is one T-bond futures contract of a specified delivery month with a face value at maturity of $100,000 or a multiple thereof. The tick size is one sixty-fourth (¹⁄₆₄) of a point ($15.625 per contract) rounded up to the nearest cent per contract. Strike prices (exercise prices) are set in one point per T-bond futures contract to bracket the current T-bond futures price. For example, if T-bond futures are at 116-00, strike prices may be set at 114, 115, 116, 117, 118.

The daily price fluctuation limit is three points ($3,000 per contract) above or below the previous day's settlement premium (expandable to 4½ points). Limits are lifted on the last trading day. Contract months are the front month of the current quarter plus the next three contracts of the regular quarterly cycle (March, June, September, and December). For example, in October 1995, contract months available are the front month of the current quarter, November, and the next three contracts of the regular quarterly cycle, December, March '96, and June '96.

In the price quotations above, trades were available in three out of four contract months—November, December, and March. The monthly options contract exercises into the current quarterly futures contract. For example, a November T-bond option will exercise into a December futures position.

The reported T-bond futures call option price for December contract at an exercise price of 114 is 2-45. This means that the cost of the option is $2^{45}\!/_{64} \times \$1,000$ or $2,703.13. (On October 12, 1995, the settlement price for a December T-bond futures contract was $116^{3}\!/_{32}$.)

Eurodollar futures options are also American-style contracts. The trading unit is one Eurodollar futures contract of the same maturity at a face value of $1 million. Similar to the underlying Eurodollar futures contract, the expiration day of the Eurodollar futures option is the second London business day before the third Wednesday of the contract month. Upon exercise, the option holder takes a position in the Eurodollar futures contract of the same maturity. The Eurodollar futures fix the price or the yield on a three-month Eurodollar deposit.

The Eurodollar futures option price quotations from above report a price of 0.50 for a December contract at the exercise price of 9,375. The price is in basis points. As explained in Chapter 15, since the face value per unit of Eurodollar contract is $1 million and the maturity of the contract is 90 days, each basis point of the price is worth: $0.0001 \times \$1,000,000 \times 90/360 = \$25$. Therefore, the price of the December 9,375 call is $50 \times \$25$, or $1,250. The call-holder has the right to purchase a Eurodollar futures contract at 9,375, which implies an index level of 93.75. (On the October 12, 1995, trading session, the December futures contract was settled at 94.23.)

Over-the-Counter Interest Rate Options: Caps, Floors, Collars, and Swaptions

A cap is an upper limit, while a floor is a lower limit on interest rates. Consider a bank customer who receives a $25,000,000 loan for three years. The interest paid on the loan is based on the quarterly floating-rate index of LIBOR. There will be 12 settlement dates. To avoid the risk of increasing interest rates, the borrower purchases a cap from the bank that limits the cost of the loan to 6%. Under the cap agreement, the bank has to pay the customer at the end of each quarter the following amount:

$$\text{Bank pays} = \tfrac{1}{4} \times \$25,000,000 \times \max(\text{LIBOR} - 0.06, 0)$$

where LIBOR is the three-month rate at the beginning of the quarter. For example, if the three-month LIBOR at the beginning of the quarter is 7%, the bank must pay

$$\tfrac{1}{4} \times \$25,000,000 \times (0.07 - 0.06) = \$62,500$$

at the end of the quarter. If the rate is 5%, the bank does not have to pay anything. A *cap* consists of a portfolio of call options on interest rates with payoffs occurring in arrears.

An interest-rate floor consists of a portfolio of put options on interest rates. From the perspective of a lender, a put option on interest rates will protect against declining interest rates in the future. Suppose that in the previous example the payoff on an interest-rate floor is tied to the three-month LIBOR with an exercise rate of 4%. At the end of each quarter, the payoff on a floor will be

$$\tfrac{1}{4} \times \$25,000,000 \times \max(0.04 - \text{LIBOR}, 0)$$

where LIBOR is determined at the beginning of the quarter and paid in arrears. For example, if the three- month LIBOR at the beginning of the quarter is 3.5%, the holder of a floor will receive

$$\tfrac{1}{4} \times \$25,000,000 \times (0.04 - 0.035) = \$31,250$$

at the end of the quarter. If the rate is 4.5%, the floor is left unexercised. A *floor* consists of a portfolio of put options on interest rates with payoffs occurring in arrears.

An interest-rate collar is a combination of a cap and a floor. Suppose that in our example the bank customer purchases a cap limiting the upper-bound cost of the interest rate to 6% at a fee equal to the price of a call option. The bank customer may simultaneously sell a put on interest rates, or a floor, limiting the lower-bound cost of the interest rate to 4% at a fee equal to the price of a put option. Buying a cap and selling a floor creates a *collar*, limiting the fluctuations in interest cost to 200 basis points. The premium received from selling a floor helps offset the cost of the cap. It is possible to structure the exercise rates in the collar in such a way that the premium paid on the purchase of the cap equals the premium received from the sale of the floor, creating a zero cost collar.

Swaptions are another category of interest-rate options, which give the right to the holder to enter into an interest-rate swap contract at a preset future date. Swap dealers usually offer to buy or to sell swaptions along with underlying swaps. For example, suppose that a company is planning to enter a swap agreement in six months to make payments based on a fixed rate and receive payments based on a floating-rate index. This is an effort by the company to hedge its interest-rate risk arising from a loan whose interest cost is adjusted periodically. Waiting for six months to enter into a swap agreement, however, carries the risk that the fixed rate may increase in the interval. To avoid the risk, the company may enter into a swaption agreement today with a right to enter into a fixed-to-floating interest-rate swap where it will pay based on a 6% fixed rate in exchange for payments based on a floating-rate index. In six months, if the fixed rate is higher than 6%, the company will exercise its swaption to enter into a swap that requires payments based on 6%. If the fixed rate is lower than 6%, the company will leave the swaption unexercised and enter the swap at the lower fixed rate.

Swaptions provide a function similar to forward swaps, alternatively called deferred swaps. While a deferred swap does not cost anything at the outset, it obliges the party to enter into the contracted swap at a later date regardless of whether it is beneficial to the party. In contrast, the buyer of a swaption pays a premium to acquire a right that will be exercised only if it is profitable for the option holder.

Table 18.6 presents the 1990–1994 data reported for caps, floors, collars, and swaptions. The data were compiled by the International Swaps and Derivatives Association, based on information from 88 dealers in more than 17 countries.[5] Both the activity levels and the outstanding amounts have increased significantly over the five-year period, with the outstanding amount reaching $1.57 trillion in 1994.

The Pricing of Interest-Rate Futures Options

The original Black-Scholes model was later extended to price European-style options on futures.[6] The option price is calculated as

$$C = \frac{F}{e^{rT}} N(d_1) - \frac{X}{e^{rT}} N(d_2)$$

$$d_1 = \frac{\ln \frac{F}{X} + \frac{\sigma^2}{2} T}{\sqrt{\sigma^2 T}}$$

$$d_2 = d_1 - \sqrt{\sigma^2 T}$$

where F is the forward (futures) price. A comparison of the formula for options on futures with the basic Black-Scholes model reveals two changes. First, in the

[5] *ISDA Survey of Global Swap Transactions: 1994*, News Release, June 12, 1995.
[6] Black (1976).

**TABLE 18.6 Year-End Data Reported for Caps, Floors, Collars, and Swaptions
$ Trillions**

Year	Activity	Outstanding
1990	$0.30	$0.56
1991	$0.38	$0.58
1992	$0.60	$0.63
1993	$1.12	$1.40
1994	$1.51	$1.57

call equation, S, the spot price of the underlying asset, is replaced with F/e^{rt}. With no dividends, we presented in Chapter 16:

$$F = Se^{rT}$$

$$S = \frac{F}{e^{rT}}$$

which implies that we can substitute F/e^{rt} for S in the original Black-Scholes model. Second, in the revised model, d_1 does not include the continuously compounded risk-free rate, r, as it does in the original Black-Scholes model. In the original model, r reflects the opportunity cost of funds invested in the stock. In the option on futures model, no funds are invested in the futures and there is no opportunity cost.

Example 6: The Pricing of Options on Futures

We are interested in calculating the March 118 call and put option values on T-bond futures. The underlying futures price is 115, and the risk-free rate of return is 5%. As of October 12, 1995, the option has 156 days remaining to expiration. The variance of T-bond futures is estimated to be 0.01.

$$d_1 = \frac{\ln\dfrac{115}{118} + \dfrac{0.01}{2}\left(\dfrac{156}{365}\right)}{\sqrt{0.01 \times \dfrac{156}{365}}} = -0.3612$$

$$d_2 = -0.3612 - \sqrt{0.01 \times \frac{156}{365}} = -0.4266$$

$$N(d_1) = 0.3590, \ N(d_2) = 0.3348$$

$$C = \left[\frac{115}{e^{0.05 \times 156/365}}\right][0.3590] - \left[\frac{118}{e^{0.05 \times 156/365}}\right][0.3348] = 1.74$$

$$P = 1.74 + \frac{118}{e^{0.05 \times 156/365}} - \frac{115}{e^{0.05 \times 156/365}} = 4.68$$

The Pricing of Caps and Floors

As discussed earlier, an interest-rate cap places an upper limit on the interest rate and an interest-rate floor places a lower limit on the interest rate. An interest-rate collar provides both upper and lower limits on interest rates. A cap is a portfolio of call options, and a floor is a portfolio of put options on interest rates. The cap and the floor are usually constructed so that their premiums are equal, which results in a zero net cost for the collar.

Suppose a bank customer, who has a LIBOR-based adjustable-rate loan, enters into an agreement with the bank to cap the interest rate at an annual rate of 6%. At each settlement date, the bank has to pay the customer the following:

$$\text{Bank pays} = \frac{1}{4} \times \$25{,}000{,}000 \times \max(\text{LIBOR} - 6\%, 0)$$

where $\frac{1}{4}$ signifies a quarter of one year and the expression $\max(\text{LIBOR} - 6\%, 0)$ indicates the payoff from a call option on LIBOR. The cap is basically a portfolio of call options with payoffs calculated at the beginning of each quarter and paid in arrears. Since the payoff takes place three months later and not at the maturity of the call, the value of the option's payoff is calculated by discounting the amount for three months. To generalize the model, we define the following variables:

$$L = \text{the principal of the loan}$$
$$m = \text{the number of settlements per year}$$
$$r = \text{the risk-free rate}$$
$$R_F = \text{the reference floating rate}$$
$$R_x = \text{cap rate}$$

The principal amount for each option is therefore:

$$\frac{\dfrac{L}{m}}{1 + \dfrac{R_F}{m}}$$

and the option payoff should be

$$\frac{\dfrac{L}{m}}{1 + \dfrac{R_F}{m}} \max(R_F - R_X, 0)$$

where the expression $\max(R_F - R_X)$ is the value of the call per unit of the principal.[7]

The pricing of a cap involves the pricing model for futures options multiplied by the principal of the options:

$$\text{Price of caps} = \frac{\dfrac{L}{m}}{1 + \dfrac{R_F}{m}} \left[\frac{R_F}{e^{rT}} N(d_1) - \frac{R_X}{e^{rT}} N(d_2) \right]$$

$$d_1 = \frac{\ln \dfrac{R_F}{R_X} + \dfrac{\sigma^2}{2} T}{\sqrt{\sigma^2 T}}$$

$$d_2 = d_1 - \sqrt{\sigma^2 T}$$

where r is the risk-free rate, and σ^2 is the variance of the forward rate.

Example 7: The Pricing of an Interest-Rate Cap

Suppose that we want to cap the interest rate on a $25,000,000 loan at 6% per year with quarterly compounding for three months beginning in one year. The forward interest rate for a three-month period one year from today is 5% per year

---

[7] If the bank that makes the loan also provides the cap, the cost of the option is incorporated into the interest charged. If the cap is obtained from another party, the cost of the cap has to be paid up front.

with quarterly compounding; the current one-year risk-free interest rate is 4.5% per year with continuous compounding; and the variance of the three-month forward rate is 0.04 per year. The information is summarized as:

$$L = \$25,000,000$$
$$m = 4$$
$$r = .045$$
$$R_F = .05$$
$$R_x = .06$$
$$\sigma^2 = .04$$
$$T = 1.0$$

$$d_1 = \frac{\ln\frac{0.05}{0.06} + \frac{0.04}{2} \times 1}{\sqrt{0.04 \times 1}} = -0.8116$$

$$d_2 = -0.8116 - \sqrt{0.04 \times 1} = -1.0116$$

$$N(d_1) = 0.2085, \ N(d_2) = 0.1558$$

$$C = \frac{0.05}{e^{0.045 \times 1}}(0.1558) - \frac{0.06}{e^{0.045 \times 1}}(0.1128) = 0.000977$$

$$Principal\ amount = \frac{\dfrac{\$25,000,000}{4}}{1 + \dfrac{.05}{4}} = \$6,172,840$$

$$Price\ of\ the\ cap = \$6,172,840 \times .000977 = \$6,031$$

which is the value of the interest rate cap.

Example 8: The Pricing of an Interest Rate Floor

An interest rate floor is a portfolio of put options on interest rates. Consider an interest rate floor at 4%. Using the information in Example 7, we can calculate the price of a floor:

$$d_1 = \frac{\ln\frac{0.05}{0.04} + \frac{0.04}{2} \times 1}{\sqrt{0.04 \times 1}} = 1.2157$$

$$d_2 = 1.2157 - \sqrt{0.04 \times 1} = 1.0157$$

$$N(d_1) = 0.8880, \ N(d_2) = 0.8451$$

$$C = \frac{.05}{e^{0.045 \times 1}}(0.8880) - \frac{0.04}{e^{0.045 \times 1}}(0.8451) = 0.01013$$

$$Using\ call\text{-}put\ parity\ formula\ P = 0.00057$$

$$Principal\ amount = \frac{\dfrac{\$25,000,000}{4}}{1 + \dfrac{0.05}{4}} = \$6,172,840$$

$$Price\ of\ the\ floor = \$6,172,839 \times 0.00057 = \$3,519$$

Example 9: The Pricing of an Interest Rate Collar

In order to create a collar, one has to buy a cap and sell a put. It is possible to create a zero cost collar by choosing an exercise rate that will make two premiums equal. Suppose that in Examples 7 and 8 above we would like to keep the cap at 6%. We have already shown that a floor of 4% generates $3,518.67 in option premium, significantly less than the $6,031 that we have to pay to purchase the cap. To increase the value of the floor, we have to increase the floor rate. Through an iterative search we find that a floor rate of 4.25% generates a premium of approximately $6,391. Therefore, buying an interest-rate cap at 6% and simultaneously selling an interest-rate floor at 4.25% creates a near zero cost collar.

The Pricing of Bond Options

Consider the following variables for a bond option:

$$B = \text{current bond price}$$
$$X = \text{exercise price of the option}$$
$$r = \text{risk-free interest rate}$$
$$\sigma^2 = \text{variance of the bond price}$$
$$T = \text{time to expiration of the option (in years)}$$

If the underlying asset is a zero-coupon bond, the Black-Scholes model will provide the following pricing equations for European-style calls and puts:

$$C = BN(d_1) - \frac{X}{e^{rT}} N(d_2)$$

$$d_1 = \frac{\ln\left(\dfrac{B}{X}\right) + \left(r + \dfrac{\sigma^2}{2} T\right)}{\sqrt{\sigma^2 T}}$$

$$d_2 = d_1 - \sqrt{\sigma^2 T}$$

If the underlying asset is a coupon-paying bond, the present value of coupon payments during the life of the option must be subtracted from the current price of the bond, B, before using the above formula.[8]

Example 10: The Pricing of Bond Options

Consider a one-year European option on a coupon-paying bond with a face value of $100,000 with a remaining term to maturity of 10 years. Assume that the current price of the bond is $115,863, and the exercise price is $100,000. The one-year risk-free rate today is 5.9% per year, and the variance of the bond price is 0.01 per year. The bond pays a semiannual coupon of 8% a year and coupon payments of $4,000 are expected in three months and in nine months. The three-month and nine-month risk-free rates are 5% and 6% per year, respectively. We would like to calculate the price of a call and a put option on the bond.

Since the underlying asset for the option is a coupon-paying bond, we need to calculate the present value of the two coupon payments that will be made during the life of the options:

$$\text{PV (coupon payments)} = 4000e^{-0.25 \times 0.05} + 4000e^{-0.75 \times 0.06} = \$7,774$$
$$B = \$115,863 - \$7,774 = \$108,089$$

The variables for option pricing are as follows:

$$B = \$108,089$$
$$X = \$100,000$$
$$r = 5.9\% \text{ per year}$$
$$\sigma^2 = 0.01$$
$$T = 1 \text{ year}$$

---

[8] In the model presented above, B is the actual price to be paid if the bond is purchased today and X is the *actual* exercise price that needs to be paid to acquire the bond when the option is exercised. If X is the *quoted* price, as it is in the exchange-traded bond options, X should be calculated as the exercise price plus the accrued interest at the expiration date of the option.

The prices of the call and the put are calculated as follows:

$$d_1 = \frac{\ln\left(\dfrac{108,089}{100,000}\right) + \left(0.059 + \dfrac{0.01}{2}\right)1}{\sqrt{0.01 \times 1}} = 1.4179$$

$$d_2 = 1.4179 - \sqrt{0.01 \times 1} = 1.3179$$

$$N(d_1) = 0.9219, \ N(d_2) = 0.9062$$

$$C = (108,089)(.9219) - \frac{100,000}{e^{0.059 \times 1}}(0.9062) = \$14,219$$

$$P = 14,219 + \frac{100,000}{e^{0.059 \times 1}} - 108,089 = \$401$$

HEDGING STRATEGIES USING OPTIONS

In hedging strategies using forwards, futures, and swaps, the hedger forgoes a potential profit in exchange for protection against a probable loss. Using options as hedging tools, the hedger mitigates the downside risk while retaining a position to profit from an upside turn. While the purchase of an option requires the payment of a premium, the hedger has the flexibility to modify the cost by selling the coverage it does not need. The availability of options in standardized form through exchanges and in customized form in the over-the-counter market further increases their appeal as hedging tools.

Hedging Foreign Exchange Risk Using Options

Consider an American computer software company that is planning to market its new software product in Germany next year. An agreement with local distributors has resulted in a 10 million deutsche mark sale of the product to be delivered in March of the next year. If the exchange rate remains at the current level of $0.70 per DM, the company will receive $7 million in March and earn a reasonable profit. However, if the dollar appreciates vs. the deutsche mark, the estimated profit may easily turn into a loss. At the exchange rate of 0.65, the company will break even in the transaction. To hedge against the exchange-rate risk, the company considers options. The Philadelphia Options Exchange trades March currency options at a denomination of DM62,500 per contract. In order to hedge DM10 million, the company needs 10,000,000/62,500 = 160 contracts. The company considers the following four strategies:

Strategy 1:	Buy 160 at-the-money March 70 puts @ 1.85 cents.
Strategy 2:	Buy 160 out-of-the-money March 66 puts @ 0.88 cents.
Strategy 3:	Buy 160 at-the-money March 70 puts @ 1.85 cents, and sell 160 out-of-the money March 76 calls @ 0.68 cents.
Strategy 4:	Buy 160 out-of-the-money March 66 puts @ 0.88 cents, and sell 160 out-of-the-money March 76 calls @ 0.68 cents.

The cost of each strategy is as follows:

Cost of Strategy 1:	$160 \times 0.0185 \times 62,500$ =	$185,000
Cost of Strategy 2:	$160 \times 0.0088 \times 62,500$ =	$88,000
Cost of Strategy 3:	$160 \times 0.0185 \times 62,500$ =	$185,000
less: call premium	$160 \times 0.0068 \times 62,500$ =	$68,000
net cost:		$117,000

				TABLE 18.7			
DM/$	Price	Do Nothing	Strategy 1	Strategy 2	Strategy 3	Strategy 4
70	Asset	7,000,000	7,000,000	7,000,000	7,000,000	7,000,000
	Put	—	0	0	0	0
	Call	—	—	—	0	0
	Total	7,000,000	7,000,000	7,000,000	7,000,000	7,000,000
78	Asset	7,800,000	7,800,000	7,800,000	7,800,000	7,800,000
	Put	—	0	0	0	0
	Call	—	—	—	−200,000	−200,000
	Total	7,800,000	7,800,000	7,800,000	7,600,000	7,600,000
62	Asset	6,200,000	6,200,000	6,200,000	6,200,000	6,200,000
	Put	—	800,000	400,000	800,000	400,000
	Total	6,200,000	7,000,000	6,600,000	7,000,000	6,600,000
	Cost	0	185,000	88,000	117,000	20,000

Cost of Strategy 4: $160 \times 0.0088 \times 62,500 = \$88,000$
less: call premium $160 \times 0.0068 \times 62,500 = \$68,000$
net cost: $\$20,000$

Strategy 1 locks in the exchange rate at 70 cents per deutsche mark, completely hedging the risk, but it is the most expensive hedging strategy. Strategy 2 allows for some loss due to the exchange-rate fluctuations while creating a floor at 66 cents per deutsche mark, guaranteeing the company a small profit. Strategy 3 creates a floor of 70 cents per deutsche mark by purchasing at-the-money puts while reducing the cost by selling out-of- the-money March 76 calls. This strategy is cheaper than Strategy 1, but it gives up part of the profit potential if the dollar depreciates compared with the deutsche mark. Strategy 4 creates a minimum and a maximum for the exchange-rate fluctuations by buying an out-of-the-money put and selling an out-of-the-money call. This is the least expensive strategy.

Suppose that in March the exchange rate will be 70, 78, or 62. The outcome under each scenario is presented in Table 18.7.

Under a "do nothing" scenario, cash flows range from $6,200,000 to $7,800,000 with a potential for a maximum loss of $300,000.[9] With Strategy 1, cash flows range from $7,000,000 to $7,800,000, suggesting a complete hedge against the downside risk and an opportunity for additional profits on the up-side. The cost of Strategy 1 is the highest among the alternatives with $185,000. In Strategy 2, with a cost of $88,000, cash flows range from $6,600,000 to $7,800,000, guaranteeing that the transaction will generate profits in the range of $100,000–$1,300,000. With Strategy 3, cash flows range from $7,000,000 to $7,600,000. The purchase of the in-the-money put guarantees minimum cash flows of $700,000 and the sale of the call at the exercise price of 76 requires the company to pay $200,000 to the callholder when the price is 78, limiting the up-side potential to $7,600,000. Strategy 3 has the second highest cost of $117,000. With Strategy 4, cash flows range from $6,600,000 to $7,600,000. When the ex-change rate is 62, the put is in the money, generating a profit of $300,000. When

---

[9] As we mentioned earlier, the break even exchange rate is 65 cents per deutschemark. When the ex-change rate declines to 62 cents, there will be a loss of 3 cents per deutschemark, or $300,0000.

the exchange rate is 78, the call is in the money, requiring the company to pay $200,000. Strategy 4 is the least costly alternative with $20,000 net cash outflow due to buying a put and selling a call. Which strategy is most suitable for the company? It depends on its risk preferences.

Hedging Interest Rate Risk Using Options

Consider a company that has a $50,000,000 floating-rate loan. The rate applied to the loan will be reset in one year. The company is concerned that the interest rate may increase by the time of the rate reset. The company is interested in an interest rate cap to mitigate the risk of an increasing interest rate. However, it is concerned about the cost of purchasing a cap. Since interest rate caps are over-the-counter instruments, the company calculates its potential cost of purchasing a cap with the following information:

$$L = \$50,000,000$$
$$m = 1$$
$$r = 0.055$$
$$R_F = 0.06$$
$$R_x = 0.07$$
$$\sigma^2 = 0.09$$
$$T = 1.0$$

$$d_1 = \frac{\ln\frac{0.06}{0.07} + \frac{0.09}{2} \times 1}{\sqrt{0.09 \times 1}} = -0.3640$$

$$d_2 = -0.3640 - \sqrt{0.09 \times 1} = -0.6640$$

$$N(d_1) = 0.3579, \quad N(d_2) = 0.2533$$

$$C = \frac{0.06}{e^{0.055 \times 1}}(0.3579) - \frac{0.07}{e^{0.055 \times 1}}(0.2533) = 0.003543$$

$$Principal\ amount = \frac{\$50,000,000}{1 + 0.06} = \$47,169,811$$

$$Price\ of\ the\ cap = \$47,169,811 \times 0.003543 = \$167,123$$

The company considers the cost of the cap too high. In order to reduce the cost, the company decides to sell a floor at 4%.

$$d_1 = \frac{\ln\frac{0.06}{0.04} + \frac{0.09}{2} \times 1}{\sqrt{0.09 \times 1}} = 1.5016$$

$$d_2 = 1.5016 - \sqrt{0.09 \times 1} = 1.2016$$

$$N(d_1) = 0.9334, \quad N(d_2) = 0.8852$$

$$C = \frac{0.06}{e^{0.055 \times 1}}(0.9334) - \frac{0.04}{e^{0.055}}(0.8852) = 0.019494$$

$$P = 0.000564$$

$$Principal\ amount = \frac{\$50,000,000}{1 + 0.06} = \$47,169,811$$

$$Price\ of\ the\ floor = \$47,169,811 \times 0.000564 = \$26,604$$

The net cost of buying a cap and selling a floor is $167,123 − 26,604 = $129,519. While this is less than the cost of only purchasing a cap, the company may further reduce its net cost by increasing the exercise rate of the floor. A zero cost solution is also available in the form of a collar.

SUMMARY

Options constitute the last set of products in derivatives. Options are unique in that they are rights for the buyer and obligations to the seller. This feature has provided a degree of flexibility to options untenable to other hedging products. In addition, options are traded on both organized exchanges and over the counter. Exchange-traded options are available on a variety of underlying positions including interest-rate instruments, currencies, commodities, and equities. Over-the-counter options are available on interest-rate instruments and currencies. OTC options are customized to the specifications of each client in terms of maturity, exercise price, and denomination. Interest-rate caps, floors, collars, and swaptions are available only in the over-the-counter market. The volume of caps, floors, collars, and swaptions exceeded $1.5 trillion by mid-1995.

Options on futures are among the most popular hedging instruments. Actively traded futures options include agricultural products, livestock, metals, oil, currencies, and stock indices. The main reason for the popularity of futures options is their superior liquidity over spot options. Options on futures are easier to price because futures prices are readily known from trading on the futures exchanges, whereas spot prices of the underlying assets may not be immediately available.

Exchange-traded and over-the-counter options are priced using various versions of the classic Black-Scholes model. This model, despite its simplicity, has been surprisingly effective in providing pricing models for a large number of underlying positions. Later extensions of the Black-Scholes model have relaxed the restrictive assumptions in the original model. Options play a powerful role in hedging strategies and serve an important purpose in the price discovery system.

REVIEW QUESTIONS

1. What is the difference between an American call option and a European call option?
2. Define a cap, a floor, and a collar.
3. What is a swaption?
4. The market price of a share of stock is $40 and its standard deviation is 10%. The risk-free rate is 6%. Calculate the premium values for a call and a put at the exercise price of $45.
5. Recalculate the call and put premiums in problem 4 assuming a continuously compounded annual dividend yield of 5%.
6. Based on the following information, calculate the values of a call and a put for a S&P 500 index option:

$$S = \$580$$
$$X = \$560$$
$$\sigma^2 = 4\%$$
$$r = 6\%$$
$$T = 180 \text{ days}$$
$$\delta = 5\%$$

7. Based on the following information, calculate the European call and put option values for German marks:

$$S = .70$$
$$X = .75$$
$$r = 5.00\% \text{ (U.S.A.)}$$
$$r_f = 3.00\% \text{ (Germany)}$$
$$\sigma^2 = 20\%$$
$$T = 90 \text{ days}$$

8. Calculate call and put option values on T-bond futures with following information: The underlying futures price is 110, the exercise price is 115, the risk-free rate is 6%, the variance of T-bond futures is 0.03, and 120 days remain to expiration of the option.
9. Suppose that we want to cap the interest rate on a $10,000,000 loan at 7% per year with semiannual compounding for six months beginning in one year. The forward interest rate for a six-month period one year from today is 6% per year with semiannual compounding, the current one-year risk-free rate is 5% per year with continuous compounding, and the variance of the six-month forward rate is 3% per year. Calculate the cost of an interest-rate cap.

10. Use the information provided in problem 9 to calculate the price of a floor at 4%.
11. Suppose you want to create a costless collar using information provided in problem 8. If the interest-rate cap is kept at 7%, what should be the floor rate?

REFERENCES

Black, F., and M. Scholes. 1973. "The Pricing of Options and Corporate Liabilities." *Journal of Political Economy*, vol. 81: 637–659.

Black, F. 1976. "The Pricing of Commodity Contracts." *Journal of Financial Economics*, vol. 3: 167–179.

Cox, J., and S.A. Ross. 1976. "The Valuation of Options for Alternative Stochastic Processes." *Journal of Financial Economics*, vol. 3 (January–March): 145–166.

Garman, M.B., and S.W. Kohlhagen. 1983. "Foreign Currency Option Values." *Journal of International Money and Finance*, vol. 2 (December): 231–253.

Ingersoll, J. 1976. "A Theoretical and Empirical Investigation of the Dual Purpose Funds: An Application of Contingent Claims Analysis." *Journal of Financial Economics*, vol. 3 (January/March): 83–123.

Jarrow, R., and A. Rudd. 1982. "Approximate Option Valuation for Arbitrary Stochastic Processes." *Journal of Financial Economics*, vol. 10 (November): 347–369.

Merton, R.C. 1973. "Theory of Rational Option Pricing." *Bell Journal of Economics and Management Science*, vol. 4 (Spring): 141–183.

Merton, R.C. 1976. "Option Pricing When Underlying Stock Returns are Discontinuous." *Journal of Financial Economics*, vol. 3 (January/March): 125–144.

19

Future Trends in Financial Intermediaries and Markets

OBJECTIVES

In the first 18 chapters, we described modern functions of financial intermediaries and markets. In this chapter, we focus on the future and provide our predictions of how financial intermediaries and markets may evolve. In projecting trends, we consider the individual and combined effects of globalization of the economy, advances in technology, and deregulation of the economic activity on the intermediation process. Consistent with the structure of the text, we organize our discussion of future trends into three parts: financial intermediaries, financial markets, and financial derivatives.

TRENDS IN FINANCIAL INTERMEDIARIES

Globalization of the economy and resulting competition in financial intermediation significantly affect the structure of financial intermediaries in the United States. For many years, financial intermediaries of European countries have enjoyed a wide range of powers unavailable to U.S. intermediaries. The competitive pressure will further accelerate as the European Community (EC) moves toward implementing the framework for a single banking, insurance, and investment market.[1] As a single market with a population of 368 million, the EC is a major competitive force, controlling 20% of world trade.[2] Individual EC member states have permitted their banks to offer insurance and investment banking products in addition to the traditional banking services. From 1979 through 1994, foreign banks doubled their share of lending to U.S. corporations. Foreign banks are now almost on par with U.S. banks with 48% share of total nonfarm, nonfinancial cor-

---

[1] As of early 1996, the European Community (EC) included the following 15 countries: Austria, Belgium, Denmark, Finland, France, Germany, Greece, Ireland, Italy, Luxembourg, The Netherlands, Portugal, Spain, Sweden, and the United Kingdom. The framework for a single EC-wide market in banking, insurance, and investment services was established over the 1993–1995 period.

[2] Zimmerman (1995), p. 35.

porate loans.[3] Globalization of the economy has forced U.S. intermediaries to find ways to compete effectively with their foreign counterparts.

Technological advances also affect the intermediation process. Computer banking is now available through select banks and will be more prevalent in the near future. Most bank transactions such as moving funds between accounts, checking balances, reviewing previous transactions, paying bills, and applying for loans can be conducted by a computer and a free 800 modem line. Some brokerage houses currently offer their customers free computer software to conduct securities transactions without the assistance of a broker. Computerized delivery of banking and brokerage services reduces transaction costs and provides the convenience of 24-hour-a-day banking. This is in addition to the well-developed ATM systems that enable the customer to receive many bank services virtually anywhere in the world without having to personally deal with a bank employee.[4]

How will financial information technology develop in the near future? On the computer hardware front, the power of the processor will continue to increase, perhaps doubling every 18 months. In early 1996, the chip of choice was Intel Pentium. A much faster version, Pentium Pro, has already been launched, which operates at 320 million instructions per second, more than three times faster than the current popular Pentium chip.

As the computer industry is looking at ways to further increase the power of the chip in the future, it is clear that there are few, if any, banking applications for which sufficient processing speed is not already available. Increasingly, banking application of technology tends to be network oriented. Since bank products are primarily information driven, knowledge-based systems, new types of interfaces, and data warehousing within the framework of networks will be used increasingly to connect banks with one another and bank staff within one bank with one another. While the Internet is not yet secure enough for widespread bank transactions, it will be in the future.

As banks increasingly rely on computer networks to offer both wholesale and retail banking services, their computer network providers such as Microsoft may become competitors with banks whose transactions they are facilitating. As banking becomes more and more electronic, those organizations that currently enable banks to become virtual entities may decide to go into the banking business themselves. The sign of banks becoming more and more virtual entities is already apparent. In the aftermath of its acquisition of First Interstate Bancorp, Wells Fargo & Co. announced its plans to close more than four-fifths of First Interstate's branches and lay off 85% of its staff. The banking expansion of the future seems to be driven more by technology than by people.

Globalization of the economy and advancements in technology have brought up once again the question of the proper role for government in the conduct of private enterprise. Most banking and securities laws in the United States were put in place in the aftermath of the Great Depression of the 1930s. Despite later amendments and liberalizations in certain areas, depository intermediaries are still heavily regulated and nondepository intermediaries are perhaps more strictly regulated today than in the 1930s.[5]

One of the most influential legislative banking reforms in recent times is the Interstate Branching Act of 1994. This act allows domestic and foreign banks to

---

[3] Berger, Kashyap, and Scalise (1995), pp. 76–77.

[4] The number of ATMs in the United States increased from 13,800 in 1979 to 109,080 in 1994. See Berger, Kashyap, and Scalise (1995), p. 69.

[5] Securities laws related to takeovers and insider trading have become more restrictive in recent years.

TABLE 19.1	Number of Depository Institutions for Selected Years		
Year	Banks	Savings Banks	Savings & Loans
1960	13,126	502	4,098
1970	13,511	493	4,365
1975	14,385	475	4,078
1980	14,435	460	4,002
1985	14,417	394	2,944
1986	14,209	472	2,817
1987	13,722	484	2,648
1988	13,137	492	2,328
1989	12,709	489	2,291
1990	12,345	474	2,257
1991	11,921	436	2,096
1992	11,462	414	1,855
1993	10,958	404	1,860
1994	10,450	387	1,765

Source: FDIC, *Historical Statistics on Banking, 1934–1994;* U.S. League of Savings Institutions, *Savings Institutions Source Book,* 1990, p. 28; RTC, *Annual Reports,* various issues.

launch cross-border takeovers and to merge their operations into national networks. While in the past two decades all states except Hawaii had allowed out-of-state banks to do business within their borders, they often required separate subsidiaries within each state. The act makes interstate branching less costly by brushing aside subsidiary requirements. The passage of the Interstate Branching Act led to a feverish and continuing consolidation in the banking industry.

Consolidation in the Banking Industry

Table 19.1 presents the number of depository intermediaries for the 1960–1994 period. From 1980 through 1994, the total number of savings and loan associations shrunk from 4,002 to 1,765, a decline of 56%. During the same period, savings banks shrunk from 460 to 387, a decline of 16%. The primary reason for the decline in the number of savings and loans and savings banks was financial insolvency.

The number of banks shrunk from 14,435 in 1980 to 10,450 in 1994, a decline of 28%. The decline in the number of banks is attributed to a number of factors, including an increase in the number of bank failures, bank mergers, and a decrease in the number of newly chartered banks. Table 19.2 details the change in bank charters. During the 1989–1994 period, a total of 671 banks were closed due to financial difficulties, while 662 new banks were opened. During the same period, bank mergers reduced the total number of banks by 2,666, resulting in a net decline of 2,675 banks. Therefore, at the end of 1994, the total number of banks had declined to 10,450.

After the Interstate Banking Act went into effect in 1995, bank merger activities increased substantially. Six decades of restrictions on interstate banking ended and many banks rushed to enter into markets that were previously closed to them.

Traditionally, consolidation in the banking industry has been examined in the context of economies of scale. Economies of scale exist if the average cost per unit of output declines as the level of output of a firm increases. If economies of

TABLE 19.2	The Decline of Bank Charters			
Year	Closed Banks	New Charters[a]	Mergers[b]	Net Change
1989	−206	+192	−410	−424
1990	−168	+183	−383	−368
1991	−124	+106	−406	−424
1992	−120	+72	−412	−460
1993	−42	+59	−509	−492
1994	−11	+50	−546	−507
Total	−671	+662	−2,666	−2,675

[a]New charters also include conversions from bridge banks.
[b]Mergers exclude failed banks merged with healthy institutions.

Source: FDIC, *Historical Statistics on Banking, 1934–1994;* and FDIC, *Annual Reports, 1989–94.*

scale exist, then combining two banks should lead to a lower average cost per unit of bank output. Previous studies of economies of scale in banking suggest that scale economies are exhausted at around $100 million in deposits. Bank profitability studies find results similar to cost studies. While smaller banks typically have higher risk-adjusted returns on assets than larger banks, there are no discernable differences in returns on equity across size groups because of larger banks' greater use of financial leverage. Cost and profitability studies therefore do not explain consolidation among multibillion dollar banks.

The modern view of consolidation in the banking industry is that banks may expand at a constant cost rather than at a diminishing cost with the objective of diversifying their operations and reducing the variability of their cash flows.[6] Under this scenario, large and small banks may coexist. Deregulation of geographic restrictions and advances in technology enable large banks to expand for the purpose of diversification, while small banks survive by developing a niche in information production about local customers.

The Future of Financial Intermediaries

The size of an intermediary and its product mix are affected fundamentally by the state of technology. As computer technology advances, firms that produce information-based products, such as financial intermediaries, rapidly embrace the new technology in their product lines. As bank products change to reflect the new technology, the delivery system of products also changes. For example, the delivery of computer-based bank products does not require a particular geographic location and can be accessed from anywhere via a modem. Generating computer-based products requires appropriate technology. The cost of such technology may prohibit banks below a critical size from offering certain technology-based services.

Bank products and the way they are delivered and their organizational structure reflect the technology. A conducive regulatory environment would speed the process of change. A restrictive regulatory environment, on the other hand, may only slow the process of change in the short run but will not be able to block

---

[6] See, for example, Robertson (1995).

it in the long run. Network banking will redefine the geographic issues. As NASDAQ circumvented the need for a geographic location for stock trading, advances in technology will make banking through a computer network a viable alternative to traditional banking through a branch. In this context, a large bank with national and global networks will provide a wide array of bank services through the convenience of computer banking.

Since the ban on interstate banking was lifted, the pace of consolidation in the banking industry has picked up significantly. In the first 10 months of 1995, 283 acquisitions occurred at a value of $60 billion. The largest bank merger of 1995 was between Chemical Banking Corporation and Chase Manhattan Bank. Another large bank merger between First Interstate Bancorp of Los Angeles and Wells Fargo was initiated late in 1995 and was consummated in 1996.

Merger activity in the U.S. banking market will be hastened if the Glass–Steagall Act, which prohibits commercial banks from investment banking activities, and the section of the Bank Holding Company Act, which limits bank insurance activities, are repealed. While there seems to be wide support for repealing the Glass–Steagall Act, there is less agreement on allowing banks to enter insurance business without restrictions. Interestingly, banks are already in the insurance business to varying degrees. For example, state bank insurance laws allow state banks to sell credit, accident, and health insurance. In addition, 16 of the largest national banks have "grandfathered" some insurance powers under the Bank Holding Company Act. Since the high court ruling in *Nationsbank* v. *Valic*, annuities are considered as investment products as opposed to insurance products and thus can be sold by banks.

European banks, which are not constrained in their investment banking and insurance activities, are increasingly moving into these businesses due to the erosion of margins and the lack of loan growth in their commercial banking business. With the current restrictions on their investment banking and insurance activities, the large U.S. banks have aggressively sought fee-based activities primarily in the area of over-the-counter derivatives. It is only a matter of time before restrictions on bank activities will be lifted, and the U.S. banks will emulate the universal banking model of the Swiss and German banks.

With these changes on the horizon, the process of restructuring in the U.S. banking industry will continue. Reaction to further deregulation in banking activities may resemble that of London's Big Bang when deregulation in the mid-1980s set off a wave of mergers and acquisitions among commercial and investment banks and insurance companies.

Table 19.3 presents the results of a survey of industry officials on bank consolidation conducted by Andersen Consulting for the Bank Administration Institute. It is projected that by the year 2000, the number of depository intermediaries will decline significantly. The number of commercial banks is expected to decline by 24% to 7,312 banks. The number of thrift institutions is expected to decline by 66%. Credit unions are expected to have 31% fewer entities by the year 2000.

What is even more interesting about the survey result is that few of the respondents saw a continuing role for thrifts in the financial services industry. Only about one-third of officials in banks, federal and state banking agencies, and nonbank institutions thought there would be a thrift industry in the year 2000. Even fewer thought there should be a thrift industry. Thrift institutions no longer provide a function uniquely different from commercial banks to justify a separate entity.

Successful banks of the future must either be very large or fill a niche. The very large banks will function as universal banks, providing an array of services

TABLE 19.3   Expected Number of Depository Institutions—Survey Results

Type of Institution	Number Expected by the Year 2000	Percentage Change 10 Years
Commercial Banks—total	7312	−24%
> $250 billion	2	—
$100–$250 billion	5	+67%
$25–$100 billion	40	+60%
$1–$25 billion	265	+10%
< $1 billion	7000	−25%
Saving and Loans	1000	−66%
Credit Unions	10,000	−31%

Source: *Vision 2000: The Transformation of Banking,* Andersen Consulting.

including commercial, investment, and insurance products. Fee-based products will play an important part in the business of these large banks. Large banks will be heavy users of technology, providing banking products over computer networks. The smaller, niche banks will provide services uniquely designed and packaged for a smaller community of customers. Their product lines may not be as extensive as larger banks, but their services will appeal to customers who prefer more traditional face-to-face banking transactions. Mid-sized banks will probably disappear.

TRENDS IN FINANCIAL MARKETS

Financial markets are also affected by the globalization of the economy, advances in technology, and deregulation. An aspect of the financial markets that is most affected by the underlying changes involves secondary markets where seasoned securities are bought and sold. Secondary markets, including organized exchanges, over-the-counter markets, and proprietary electronic systems, offer varying levels of market liquidity. Issuing corporations seek more liquid markets because greater liquidity results in narrower bid-ask spreads, lower trading costs, and lower required rates of return.[7] In general, market liquidity is believed to result in the efficient allocation of resources.

    While organized exchanges have been the only outlet for trading seasoned securities at some point, their share of trading volume has declined steadily over time. The new players include not only NASDAQ, which has been around for a quarter of a century, but also other sources of electronic trading such as Posit and Instinet. In order to evaluate trends in the secondary market activities we examine trading activities in the following four markets: *the first market*, which refers to securities exchanges where listed stocks and bonds are traded; *the second market*, which alludes to the over-the-counter trading of unlisted securities; *the third market*, which entails the over-the-counter trading of listed securities; and *the fourth market*, which involves trading of securities without using a broker.

The First Market

The first market refers to the trading of exchange-listed securities on the organized exchanges. The New York Stock Exchange (NYSE), now more than 200

---

[7] See Demsetz (1968), Amihud and Mendelson (1986), and Reinganum (1990).

years old, is the largest and the oldest exchange in the United States. More than 2,600 companies, including 200 non-U.S. companies, have listed their shares on the NYSE. The NYSE-listed companies constitute more than 85% of the $5 trillion capitalization value of all U.S. companies. The American Stock Exchange (AMEX) has 3% of the market value listings. There are also seven regional exchanges, including Philadelphia, Chicago, Pacific Coast, Boston, Cincinnati, Inter-Mountain, and Spokane, which primarily trade securities that are listed on the NYSE and AMEX.

The NYSE is a customer-driven, auction system where a group of traders, also known as specialists, maintain an orderly market in the securities assigned to them. The interaction of buyers' and sellers' orders determines the price of the listed stocks. Specialists are also expected occasionally to buy and to sell from their own inventory in order to improve the liquidity in the market and to reduce the bid and ask spreads. The NYSE requires its member firms to execute their trades of the listed securities on the exchange. Trading costs on the NYSE including bid-ask spreads and commissions are generally higher than those of regional exchanges and proprietary electronic systems. Furthermore, trading on the NYSE reveals traders' identities. Some traders who prefer anonymity choose alternative trading locations, including foreign exchanges. We will return to this issue in a later section.

The Second Market

Trading of unlisted securities on the over-the-counter market is referred to as the second market. More than 4,900 over-the-counter securities with a capitalization value exceeding $900 billion or 12% of all U.S. companies are traded on the National Association of Securities Dealers Automated Quotation (NASDAQ) system. Established in 1971, NASDAQ is made up of a network of dispersed dealers, brokers, and traders who conduct their transactions over computer terminals without the need for a centralized geographic location.

The main reason for the development and subsequent growth of NASDAQ was to create a stock market that would serve small- and medium-sized companies that could not meet the listing requirements of the NYSE.[8] Today, some small companies of the early days have become giants in their fields. Technology firms such as Intel, Microsoft, and MCI are a few examples of firms that are listed currently on the NASDAQ stock market.

The over-the-counter market is a dealer-driven market in which dealers quote their bid and ask prices and stand ready to buy for and sell from their own accounts. In a dealer market all trades are subject to a bid-ask spread.

NASDAQ is owned by the National Association of Securities Dealers (NASD).[9] Registered under the Securities and Exchange Act of 1934 (Exchange Act), NASD is the nation's only registered securities association. The Exchange Act requires every broker or dealer engaged in a securities business with the public to be a member of the NASD. The NASD is a self-regulatory organization

---

[8] As of 1995, the NYSE required the following as a minimum for initial listing: (1) pretax income of $2.5 million, (2) net tangible assets of $18 million, (3) market value of publicly held shares of $9 million, (4) a total of 1,100,000 publicly held common shares, and (5) 2,000 holders of 100 shares or more (*New York Stock Exchange Fact Book,* April 1995, p. 33). In contrast, NASDAQ national market required the following as a minimum for initial listing: (1) pretax income of $750,000, (2) net tangible assets of $4 million, (3) market value of publicly held shares of $3 million, (4) a total of 500,000 common shares publicly held, and (5) 400 public shareholders (*NASDAQ Fact Book and Directory,* 1995, p. 44).
[9] For further details on the NASD and its governance rules, see Rudman, et al. (1995).

(SRO) overseeing 5,400 securities firms and 500,000 registered securities professionals. NASD members include securities firms involved in corporate debt and equities, municipal and federal government securities, derivative instruments, insurance products (e.g., annuities), and limited partnership interests.

In its capacity as the largest SRO, the NASD establishes Rules of Fair Practice governing securities trades among broker-dealers and between broker-dealers and private investors, and trading rules for the over-the-counter market. It sets up operational rules for its member firms and examines the firms for possible violations of federal securities law and SEC regulations. The NASD is the main arbitration forum for securities disputes. It also administers qualification testing for all securities principals and registered representatives.

The SEC has to review and approve every NASD rule before it goes into effect and oversees the overall operation of the NASD. The SEC has the authority to take disciplinary action against the NASD or even to revoke the NASD's registration if it fails to meet the requirements of the Exchange Act.

The NASD has been subjected to criticism in the academic and popular press on the grounds that its regulation of the NASDAQ stock market, which it also owns, has been flawed and its monitoring of its member firms has been ineffective. In addition, criticism has been levied against traders in the NASDAQ stock market, accusing them of collusion in setting wider than usual bid-ask spreads. In a study of the 100 most active NASDAQ stocks in 1991, research results showed that spreads of one-eighth were virtually nonexistent for 70 of the 100 most actively traded stocks, including Intel, Apple Computers, and Lotus Development.[10] The lack of one-eighth spreads resulted in the absence of bid and ask quotes ending in odd-eighths ($\frac{1}{8}$, $\frac{3}{8}$, $\frac{5}{8}$, $\frac{7}{8}$). In contrast, a sample of 100 NYSE and AMEX firms of similar price and market value were shown to consistently use the full spectrum of the eighths. The research concluded that the observed lack of odd-eighth quotes was the result of an implicit agreement among market makers to avoid using odd-eighths in quoting bid and ask prices. The findings of apparent price collusion among NASDAQ dealers were published in several national newspapers including *The Wall Street Journal* and *The Los Angeles Times* on May 25 and 26, 1994. On May 27, dealers in several stocks in the original study, including Amgen, Cisco Systems, and Microsoft, sharply increased their use of odd-eighth quotes, resulting in a 50% decline in the bid-ask spreads. The following day, the same pattern was repeated for Apple Computer and a month later Intel stock was quoted in odd-eighth spreads. The evidence suggests that the negative publicity of collusion in the NASDAQ stock market caused the dealers to abandon their implicit agreement to avoid odd-eighth spreads.[11]

Further evidence of higher trading costs in the NASDAQ is observed in a study of firms that choose to move from the NASDAQ to the NYSE (AMEX). It is shown that, on average, trading costs declined by 4.7 cents per share for firms that made the switch.[12] These trading practices resulted in a rash of lawsuits alleging price-fixing among dealers. The SEC conducted an investigation of the NASD and the NASD itself commissioned a study of the NASDAQ's operating procedures that was culminated in a report by the Rudman Committee. The overall conclusions of this committee are summarized as follows:

> The Select Committee does find, however, that the NASD's governance structure has failed to keep pace with the significant

---

[10] Christie and Schultz (1994).
[11] Christie, Harris, and Schultz (1994).
[12] Christie and Huang (1994).

growth and continuing evolution of the NASDAQ market, and the concomitant expansion of the NASD's regulatory responsibilities. In some cases, the existing governance structure has led to ineffective rulemaking for the NASDAQ market. In others, it has required the NASD to mediate economic clashes among its members arising from their divergent interests in the NASDAQ market—a daunting role which the NASD, as a membership association and regulator of the entire broker-dealer profession, did not seek and was never designed to play. The current structure has also placed the NASD, as the owner of NASDAQ's trading systems, in the unenviable position of regulating the competing systems owned by NASD members.[13]

The major recommendations of the Rudman Committee are as follows:

- The NASD and the NASDAQ market should not be divorced, but regulation of the broker-dealer profession should otherwise be separated from and performed independently of regulation of the NASDAQ and other OTC markets.
- To this end, the governing Board charged with regulating the NASD's member firms should be separate and independent from the governing Board responsible for overseeing the NASDAQ market. So, too, should their respective professional staffs. Those two governing Boards and staffs, however, should remain associated within a single SRO structure. This will maintain the strength of the existing NASD organization in linking commercial and technical expertise to regulation so that each informs and enhances the other.
- In all events, enforcement should be independent of responsibility for the NASDAQ and other OTC markets and should be the paramount task of the Board charged with regulating the broker-dealer profession.
- The separate governing Boards responsible for regulating the broker-dealer profession and for regulating the NASDAQ market should each have 50% public membership. The parent (or equivalent) Board should have a majority of public members. Other governing bodies with substantial policymaking or oversight authority also should have strong public representation, as appropriate to their specific tasks.[14]

The core of the recommendations made by the Rudman Committee was later adopted by the NASD.

The Third Market

Trading of the exchange-listed securities on the over-the-counter market is referred to as the third market. The third market grew in an environment where exchange members were required to execute their trades on the exchanges and to charge commissions according to a fixed schedule. Brokerage firms who were not members of the exchanges realized that they could trade NYSE-listed securities over-the-counter at significantly lower transaction costs. The growth of the third market slowed after May 1, 1975, when commissions on all NYSE orders became negotiable.

Recently, some third market players have begun to pay brokers to funnel their customers' orders through their systems. For example, Bernard L. Madoff

---

[13] Rudman, et al. (1995), p. 21.
[14] Rudman, et al. (1995), p. 22.

Investment Securities, a New York firm, pays brokers a rebate of one cent a share on orders of 3,000 shares or less.

The practice of matching customers' buy and sell orders away from the primary exchanges and in the process pocketing the difference between the buy and sell prices along with commissions is referred to as *order preferencing*. Order preferencing may take place in a regional exchange (e.g., the Cincinnati Stock Exchange) or through a proprietary system (e.g., Madoff Investment Securities). Proponents of the third market argue that by paying for the order flow they create the right incentives for the brokers to seek alternative trading channels with superior prices for their customers. The SEC seems to agree because it continues to issue permits for pilot programs in regional exchanges and other electronic systems that favor "preference" trades. The NYSE opposes the practice, arguing that it benefits securities professionals while hurting customers. The NYSE is not simply concerned about customers. Instead, the NYSE is defending its turf. In 1995, the NYSE's share of the transaction volume declined to 70%. Only a few years earlier, it had enjoyed a market share of greater than 80%.

The Fourth Market

Trading securities between investors without the benefit of a broker is referred to as the fourth market. Institutional investors avoid paying the brokers' fees by going through electronic trading systems that match single stocks and stock portfolios of traders without participation of a broker. The best-known examples of the fourth market include Instinet and Posit. Instinet is owned by Reuters, whose Crossing Network began its operation in 1987. Posit, which is owned by West Coast-based broker Jefferies & Co., started its operation in 1988. In a typical trading day, Instinet and Posit handle more than 10% of the volume in the NYSE-listed issues. Their share of program trading, which includes many types of investing based on indexes, reaches 50%.

The direct impact of the alternative trading systems, such as the fourth market electronic enterprises, is seen on the power and profitability of the NYSE. In 1987, before the stock market crash, a NYSE seat was sold at $1.5 million. In 1991, the price of a seat had declined to $350,000. While the price of a seat rebounded to $760,000 by 1994, in the long run the fourth market imposes a serious challenge to the monopoly the NYSE enjoyed for nearly 200 years.

Instinet and Posit do not entirely avoid the NYSE. Institutional investors may enter their large buy and sell orders into these systems without revealing their identities to the market. Then once a day the orders are matched and priced based on the NYSE prices. For example, Posit crosses its trades at a randomly selected time between 1 P.M. and 2 P.M. at whatever the market prices are at that exact moment. The Instinet Crossing Network crosses its trades at 5:45 P.M. based on the market's closing prices. Posit's trades are reported on the national market system's consolidated tape the same day while Instinet's trades are reported the following day.

A more recent electronic system, the Arizona Stock Exchange (ASE), formerly known as the Spaworks (Single Price Auction Network), goes a step further than Instinet and Posit in bypassing the NYSE by establishing its own prices. Established in 1991, the ASE accepts buy and sell orders throughout the day from traders at the price range they want to trade. At 5:15 P.M. on Mondays and Wednesdays and at 9:00 A.M. on Fridays, buy and sell orders are matched at a price that gets most of the orders executed. In contrast to the NYSE, where only the specialist knows the relative strength of buy and sell orders, the ASE provides its participants an opportunity to monitor the supply and demand curves for the underlying stocks. The ASE also provides anonymity to their traders.

In addition to offering traders a degree of anonymity, the main advantage of the fourth market system lies in its lower transaction costs. With the NYSE's specialist system, a buyer would pay the asked price while a seller would receive the bid, leaving the spread to the specialist. With Posit, for example, the price for the buyer and the seller of the same stock is set midway between the bid-ask price. At a typical spread of ¼ point, the buyer pays ⅛ less and the seller receives ⅛ more as the buyer and the seller split the specialist's fee. The buyer and the seller of 50,000 shares each save $6,250. In addition, the commission on Posit—2 cents a share—is at least 2 cents less than what a trader pays to go through the NYSE, or a savings for each trader of $1,000. Each trader would save a total of $6,250 + $1,000 = $7,250. A one cent-a-share savings in transaction costs on each side of the trade on the NYSE would have resulted in a savings to investors of $1.5 billion in 1994, based on the trading volume exceeding 73 billion shares.

The Future of Financial Markets

Is the fourth market the wave of the future? No. It is more realistic to think of the fourth market as the starting point for a more efficient, technologically oriented market of the future. The future system will likely be a continuous electronic market without exchange floors. The future system will also be available to retail traders in addition to the institutional traders that the fourth market serves today.

Since the fourth market avoids brokers, it is instructive to unbundle brokerage services to understand whether the brokerage function will be obsolete in the future. A typical broker provides some or all of the following functions:

- Matching of orders, which involves bringing buyers and sellers together.
- Margin lending, which refers to lending to investors on the basis of securities purchased.
- Trusteeship, which points to holding and verifying the ownership of the securities on behalf of investors.
- Short selling, which alludes to lending shares from the margin accounts of investors to others.
- Investment advice, which deals with making buy and sell recommendations to investors.

Consider an investor who wants to purchase stocks on margin. The investor contacts a broker and asks for advice. The broker inquires about the investor's risk preferences and makes investment recommendations accordingly. After the investor makes the portfolio choice, the broker matches the investor's buy order with someone else's sell order on the floor of an exchange, over-the-counter, or through other electronic systems. The broker also provides the margin lending and retains the securities purchased as collateral in its own name, known as the "street name." It holds the shares and provides periodic reporting of the ownership to the investor. As a custodian of street-name shares, the broker may loan these shares to someone else (e.g., a short seller) without the knowledge of the investor. Dividends are still paid to the original investor by the short seller, but voting rights are generally lost when the shares are loaned. The short seller deposits the funds received from the sale of the shares in an escrow account. The interest earned in this account is split between the short seller and the broker who lent the shares. Currently, the original investor has no claim over the interest that was split between the broker and the short seller. At some point in the future, the short seller will have to purchase the shares in the market and return them to the broker.

While the five functions described here are currently provided by the same broker, there is no reason to believe that is going to be the case in the future. It is conceivable for an investor to use (1) one broker to purchase the shares, (2) a second firm to borrow on margin, (3) a third firm to act as a custodian for the shares, (4) a fourth firm to short sell the shares, and (5) a fifth firm to sell the shares. Why then are these functions joined together? The answer lies with the current practice of using street name registration as the only alternative to holding paper certificates to prove ownership. An investor borrowing on margin has to allow the shares to be held in the name of the lending broker. This practice makes it difficult and costly to unbundle various functions provided by a broker. Currently, the transfer of securities from one brokerage firm to customer accounts at another firm can take months. While adequate technology exists to speed up the process significantly, it is to the advantage of the brokerage firm to discourage the switch. This may be changing, however. A recent proposal by the SEC,[15] if adopted, will alter the nature of ownership registration from the current practice of street name to direct registration. Instead of keeping securities in the broker's name, it will leave them in the name of the issuer at a depository. Changes in the ownership of securities will be reported by a transfer agent on behalf of the issuing company and the securityholder. The investor will receive a confirmation statement similar to the one currently sent by brokerage firms. Of course, one may choose to hold security certificates or have the shares held in street name.

Direct registration is a significant step toward a market without brokers.[16] If the ownership is held in the issuer's name, an investor no longer has to use the same firm for all the five functions described above. Matching trades between buyers and sellers can be separated from the responsibility of trusteeship. Margin lending can also be handled separately. An investor will have an opportunity to shop around and find the best available borrowing rate. While a firm that provides a margin loan will hold title to the shares (street name), transferring the shares to another broker for the purpose of selling them will take much less time than it currently takes. Upon selling the shares, the margin lender will receive its fund. Short selling, which currently benefits only the brokers and short sellers to the total exclusion of the retail investors, will be possible for retail investors where separate entities may coordinate the task of pooling shares from small investors and offering them to short sellers. In such a system, the interest earned on the funds raised from short selling will be split among the investor, the intermediary that coordinates the pooling, and the short seller.

Technological advances have enabled retail investors to submit their trades directly to a brokerage firm via a computer and a modem 24-hours-a-day without the benefit of professional advice from a broker. Proliferation of discount brokerage houses in the past two decades is a clear indication that a significant number of investors make their own portfolio choices independent of professional investment advisors.

By unbundling the five functions of brokerage firms, an investor may shop around and purchase services on an as-needed basis at competitive prices from various venders. Transaction costs will decline, leading to increased liquidity in the market. At some point in the future, institutional and retail investors will be able to trade at a continuous electronic market without the benefit of a trading floor or a broker.

---

[15] "Transfer Agents Operating Direct Registration System," SEC release No. 34-35038, File No. S7-34-94.

[16] For an interesting discussion of the benefits of Direct Registration, see Brown (1996).

TRENDS IN DERIVATIVES AND THE MANAGEMENT
OF FINANCIAL RISK

Two decades ago, there was very little activity in the financial derivatives market. As the volatility of interest rates, foreign exchange rates, and commodity prices increased in the 1970s, many financial and nonfinancial firms began to take positions in derivatives in order to hedge against their risk exposure. For example, a U.S. company with significant foreign sales is exposed to the foreign exchange risk. Even though the firm may forecast successfully the volume of its foreign sales, fluctuations in the exchange rates will significantly affect the dollar value of its revenues. If the dollar appreciates versus the foreign currency, sales revenues will be less than projected. If the dollar depreciates versus the foreign currency, sales revenues will be more than the estimated amount. Strategic decisions such as the amount of investment in R&D often depend on cashflows generated from sales. Consequently, those plans will be affected by the unforeseen changes in the exchange rates. For such a firm, hedging foreign exchange risk is a sound idea.

The value of a firm increases because of good investment decisions. Investments require financing, which needs to be raised either internally or externally. If the source of financing is internal, the use of derivatives will reduce the uncertainty of future cashflows and enable the firm to implement its strategic investment plans.[17] If the source of financing is external, the use of derivatives will reduce the uncertainty faced by creditors (bondholders and lenders) and facilitate external financing.[18]

Derivatives are used for a variety of reasons, including the following: (1) to hedge an underlying cash position; (2) to speculate on the direction of interest rates, exchange rates, and commodity prices; and (3) to arbitrage price differences across markets. The most common use of derivatives is for hedging the firm's exposure to risk arising from changes in interest rates, foreign exchange rates, and commodity prices.[19]

Using derivatives for the purpose of hedging the underlying risk is similar to drawing an insurance policy against losses due to adverse events. Hedging involves taking on a new risk that offsets the existing risk in the underlying business. As such, derivatives used for hedging purposes are a means of reducing risk. The total risk in the economy, however, does not change. Hedging provides for the redistribution of risk among willing parties. This scenario of risk, however, seems to be at odds with a barrage of negative publicity on derivatives-related losses in recent years. Table 19.4 presents a list of firms that have revealed their derivatives losses. Among the most publicized cases are the $1.3 billion loss at the German industrial firm Metallgesellschaft, the $100 million loss at Procter and Gamble, and the $1.4 billion loss at the British bank Barings.

The negative publicity about a few large losses has induced regulators to try to restrict derivatives activities. In a study of derivatives, the United States General Accounting Office (GAO) recommended sweeping regulation of the market.[20] The GAO's recommendation to Congress was to bring the currently

---

[17] See Froot, Scharfstein, and Stein (1993).

[18] Derivatives may be used to reduce agency problems associated with external financing and to reduce taxes. For more detail, see Chapter 15.

[19] See "Derivatives: Practices and Principles, Appendix III: Survey of Industry Practice," Group of Thirty, Washington, DC (March 1994); and "A Survey of Derivatives Usage by U.S. Non-Financial Firms," The Wharton School (March 1995).

[20] United States General Accounting Office Report to Congressional Requesters, *Financial Derivatives: Actions Needed to Protect the Financial System*, May 1994.

TABLE 19.4   A List of Organizations with Large Derivatives-Related Losses

Date	Organization	Event
1986–88	Hammersmith & Fulham Local Authority, Britain	Losses of $900 million on interest rate swaps. In 1991 the House of Lords ruled that local authorities did not have the power to enter into swaps contracts
March 1991	Allied Lyons	Losses of $265 million in foreign exchange options
February 1993	Showa Shell Sekiyu	$1.4 billion write-off for foreign exchange forward contracts
December 1993	Metallgesellschaft	Oil futures trading resulted in losses of up to $1.3 billion
January 1994	Codelco	Losses of $207 million in a copper futures deal
April 1994	Kashima Oil	$1.5 billion losses on dollar derivatives
April 1994	Procter & Gamble	Losses of over $100 million in highly leveraged interest rate swaps designed by Bankers Trust
May 1994	Air Products & Chemicals	Losses of $60 million on interest rate derivatives
May 1994	Sandoz	Losses of $78.5 million in derivatives arranged by Bankers Trust
1st half of 1994	Gibson Greetings	Losses of $19.7 million on interest rate derivatives; sued Bankers Trust for damages of $23 million, settled out of court
July 1994	Glaxo	Losses of $180 million and $25 million on derivatives and asset-backed bonds
December 1994	Orange County	Losses of $1.7 billion in leveraged interest rate derivatives
February 1995	Barings	Losses of $1.4 billion in Nikkei-index contracts, leading to the bank's insolvency

Source: Adapted from *The Economist,* February 10, 1996, p. 4 of survey.

unregulated over-the-counter (OTC) derivatives activities of securities firms and insurance company affiliates under the purview of the SEC or some other federal agency. To financial regulators, the GAO recommended the application of minimum capital standards to derivatives dealers. The GAO also recommended that the Financial Accounting Standards Board (FASB) come up with a financial disclosure scheme for derivatives based on market value accounting.

Politicians and regulators often believe that an unregulated market is doomed to face disaster. In response to the GAO report, several bills were initiated in Congress, including legislation introduced by Rep. Edward Markey (D., Mass.), that would require unregulated derivatives dealers such as affiliates of securities firms and insurance companies to register with the SEC. Rep. Jim Leach (R., Iowa) and Rep. Henry Gonzales (D., Texas), the chairman and ranking Democrat, respectively, of the House Banking Committee, also introduced legislation aimed at expanding regulation of financial institutions engaged in derivatives activities.

Regulatory efforts have been channeled into two areas. First, there is a proposed disclosure requirement for end users of derivatives issued by FASB. This proposal, which is likely to be adopted by 1997, requires end users to report their derivatives at current market prices. Since current GAAP accounting requires the underlying assets and liabilities to be carried at historical cost, a market value reporting of derivatives will lead to increased volatility in earnings, even when hedging reduces variability in the firm value. The problem was partially mitigated in a modified version of the FASB proposal where it permitted using gains or losses in the value of underlying assets or liabilities to offset changes in the values of derivatives.

Second, there is an even greater regulatory burden in the proposal to impose risk-based capital requirement on derivatives dealers. Currently, derivatives activities of commercial banks are subjected to a minimum risk-based capital requirement. The proposal extends the risk-based capital requirement to derivatives activities of securities firms, insurance companies, and nonbank affiliates of bank holding companies. Without debating over the effectiveness of the risk-based capital requirement in banking, which is already in place, we examine the shortcomings of its application to derivatives activities of nonbank derivatives dealers.

The rule applies risk weights to the total volume of derivatives without considering the credit standing of the counterparties. In addition, the rule does not differentiate between a derivatives contract issued to a customer who uses it to hedge and one who uses it for the purpose of speculating. For example, the risk-based capital rule would treat a derivatives contract issued to a client with an AAA rating who uses it to hedge its underlying risk exposure the same as a contract issued to a client with a BBB rating who uses it for the purpose of speculating in the direction of interest rates, foreign exchange rates, or commodity prices. This type of regulation, which applies a rigid rule across the board regardless of the specific nature of each contract, may also create incentive problems for some dealers. For example, capital guidelines, which require dealers to hold capital against the notional amount of their derivatives, may encourage them to issue leveraged derivatives of the kind sold by Bankers Trust to Procter & Gamble since leveraged derivatives enable the dealer to support a larger exposure with the same amount of capital.

The derivatives market is a competitive market. U.S. regulators should be concerned that any excessive regulation of the market may impose a significant burden on dealers to the extent that they may lose business to their global competitors. For example, in 1987, the Commodities Futures Trading Commission (CFTC) ruled swaps as OTC futures and effectively shut down the market. This did not end the market, however; it simply moved the market overseas. When the CFTC reversed itself in 1993, making swaps legal contracts, U.S. dealers experienced a costly process to get the market reestablished in the United States again.

All the evidence available today suggests that derivatives are here to stay. In fact the market has enjoyed double digit growth for many years. The publicity about a few large losses may convince end users and dealers to concentrate on simpler derivatives designed primarily for hedging purposes.

TRENDS IN REGULATORY REFORM

Advances in technology and globalization of the economy follow a rational and to some degree a predictable course in contributing to the evolution of financial intermediaries and markets. Regulatory reform, however, is more difficult to predict. The overlapping regulatory oversight contributes to piecemeal changes initiated by one agency that may or may not be consistent with changes initiated by another agency. Regulatory reform is also affected by the political incentives of each agency and the turf battle among agencies.

Depository financial intermediaries are currently regulated by the OCC, the Fed, the FDIC, and the state banking commissions. The OCC issues national bank charters and supervises their operations. The Fed oversees the operation of bank holding companies and state banks that are members of the Fed. The FDIC regulates state nonmember banks. This division, however, does not work as neatly as it is described here. The FDIC insures more than 98% of all banks and has the power to issue, maintain, or cancel deposit insurance, which is essential for the survival of banking firms. It also influences what is disclosed in Call Reports. The Fed acts as the lender of last resort for practically every depository institution and therefore exerts tremendous influence over them. State banking commissions, which issue state bank charters, often follow the lead from the OCC in chartering requirements and follow-up regulation of institutions under their jurisdictions.

Each agency has its own regulatory agenda based on philosophical orientation, political persuasion, and self-interest. For example, the OCC, as part of the Department of Treasury, is influenced by the policies of the executive branch of the government. Since banks choose to be either nationally chartered, falling under the jurisdiction of the OCC, or state chartered, the OCC has the incentive to be accommodating toward national banks in order to attract a larger constituency. As a government agency, the OCC also has an incentive to increase its regulatory influence in order to justify a larger budget. If recent history is any indication, the OCC will continue to follow a permissive and accommodating policy toward bank activities.

The FDIC carries its mandate from Congress and operates within certain guidelines as to the size of the insurance fund relative to total insured deposits held in banks. In its daily operations, however, it has tremendous leeway in setting up policies and implementing them. Recently, the FDIC has reduced the insurance premium to a statutory minimum of $2,000 per year for the majority of banks while aggressively seeking a permanent solution to the savings and loan insurance fund. The FDIC seeks to receive the necessary funding from Congress to restore the savings associations' insurance fund and ultimately convert them all to banks. Their agenda seems to be gaining ground in Congress and even among other regulatory agencies. Overall, the current policy pursued by the FDIC seems to be accommodating toward banks.

The Fed has greater power over depository intermediaries than other agencies. As the nation's central bank, it sets the monetary policy and short-term interest rates, which affect not only banks but every sector of the economy. It is the only agency that operates independently of the executive branch of the government. It offers services to banks at monopoly or near monopoly terms and earns over $20 billion a year in revenues. After paying its own expenses of over $300 million a year, the remainder of its revenues are turned over to the Treasury. Financial independence gives the Fed an unprecedent autonomy in its operation. While it is best known for its monetary policy efforts, most of the Fed's resources (90%) are spent on bank regulation and supervision.

With its political and financial independence, its role in conducting monetary policy, and its purview over bank holding companies including the largest banking organizations, the Fed is in a unique position to play a crucial role in the future of financial intermediaries and markets. It can either play a reactive role or a proactive role. A reactive role would amount to an act of catch-up with changes brought by advances in technology and globalization of the economy. Such efforts are generally initiated by the legal department, which concerns itself with the consistency of various laws and regulations. For example, when the 1994 interstate banking act went into effect, it influenced other regulations involving state member banks (Regulation H) that needed editing and streamlining to be consistent with the new law. While these efforts are needed and useful, they play a very minor role in the long run in the evolution of financial intermediaries and markets. A regulator in reactive mode is inherently suspicious of the activities of its constituents and only grudgingly accepts minor changes when it becomes obvious that what is left in the books is obsolete.

An alternative role for the Fed would be a proactive one in which reform proposals are initiated by financial economists who have the necessary technical skills to understand the dynamics of the current activities and future trends in the intermediation process. A proactive role will enable the regulator to understand and support positive change while ensuring the safety and soundness of the financial system. Cooperation with the legal division is necessary to ensure internal consistency of various regulations and to meet the statutory requirements. As it stands today, the Fed plays more of a reactive role in its bank regulatory function. This is curious, given that the Fed employs some of the best economists in the world.

Financial markets are primarily regulated by the SEC and the CFTC. The SEC regulates the activities of public corporations, securities brokers and dealers, and securities markets. In recent years, the SEC has pursued a proactive role by issuing to public comment some of the best forward-looking reform proposals in decades. As discussed earlier, the adoption of the Direct Registration is an example of how a regulatory agency can alter the regulation to accommodate and facilitate the conversion of the existing exchange-based secondary markets into a continuous electronic market of the future. Recently, the SEC issued to public comment a staff proposal containing 140 major changes that will simplify and reduce regulatory burden on public corporations, securities professionals, and financial markets. Among other things, the recommendations would:[21]

- Eliminate 81 Rules and 22 Forms, and modify many others
- Make it easier for smaller, less-seasoned companies to move quickly in accessing the public markets by expanding some shelf registration concepts to such companies
- Facilitate capital-raising by small businesses by, for example, liberalizing the exemption from registration available to offerings that cross state lines but remain within a prescribed area

---

[21] The SEC, "Publications of the Report of the Task Force on Disclosure Simplification and Implementation of Certain of its Recommendations," March 5, 1996.

- Increase the flexibility of larger, seasoned issuers in accessing the public markets
- Adopt a plain-English format for the opening pages of disclosure documents, such as prospectuses, which are often written in a manner that has been described as "turgid" and "opaque"
- Replace the trading practices rules that restrict trading during a securities distribution, which have been criticized for being difficult to understand and unnecessarily restrictive, with a new regulation that would be narrower in scope and easier to follow.

The current practice of the SEC is a good example of how a progressive and proactive regulatory policy can succeed in promoting positive change while maintaining the safety and the soundness of the financial market.

The record of the CFTC is less impressive. Its well-publicized flip-flop on swaps is a good example of a reactive regulatory philosophy that is suspicious of innovations initiated by economic agents. The CFTC has also spent a significant amount of its energy in fighting the SEC over their respective jurisdictions related to various financial instruments. The endless debate over which financial claim is an instrument, which implies a CFTC jurisdiction, and which one is a security indicating an SEC jurisdiction is an example of fighting over turfs that only serves the self-interest of the parties involved. It is no surprise, therefore, that the best innovations in financial derivatives have come from a segment of the industry that is outside the jurisdiction of the CFTC, namely the OTC derivatives, and not from the exchange-traded futures and options markets supervised by the CFTC.

SUMMARY

Advances in technology, globalization of the economy, and regulatory reforms are three interrelated forces behind changes in financial intermediation and markets. Within the next decade, the banking industry will go through a rapid pace of consolidation, leading to a reduction of at least one-third of independently owned banks. The intermediaries of the future will be either large universal banks offering traditional bank services, along with new securities and insurance products, or small, niche banks operating in small communities offering a limited number of services with greater direct interactions with their customers.

Financial markets of the future will be more electronic and less exchange-floor based. Advances in technology have made electronic markets a reality. The rapid acceptance of the Internet along with changes in the regulatory structure will contribute to a system of trading without brokers or exchanges. European securities markets have been moving toward a complete electronic system for a number of years. In some countries they have abandoned exchange floors altogether in favor of an electronic system. In the United States this process will be slower. The NYSE with its more than 200 year history is by far the largest and best-known organized exchange. It will lose its market share slowly but will remain a major force for some time to come. Investors in U.S. markets will likely have alternative trading choices in the future, ranging from the traditional broker-facilitated exchange floor trades to fully electronic brokerless systems. Efficiency and competition will be healthy for the evolution of the U.S. financial markets.

Financial derivatives are here to stay, despite the negative publicity surrounding a few large losses. They will remain because financial risk arising from interest rates, foreign exchange rates, and commodity prices will continue to expose financial and nonfinancial firms to risk. With a greater knowledge of risk involved in derivatives, the share of hedgers versus speculators and arbitragers will increase. The share of simpler contracts will be greater and complex leveraged instruments will have a smaller share of the total derivatives market.

REVIEW QUESTIONS

1. Describe the three factors that contribute to rapid changes in financial intermediation and markets.
2. What are the theories explaining recent consolidations in the banking industry?
3. Explain the role of technology in the future of banking business.
4. Define a universal bank.
5. Describe the economics of small, niche banks.
6. Describe four categories of the secondary market.
7. It is argued that trading on the floor of the NYSE is more expensive than trading through alternative systems such as the fourth market. Discuss.

8. What are the accomplishments and shortcomings of the NASDAQ stock market?
9. What was the basis for the specific accusations made against the NASDAQ?
10. What has the NASDAQ done to address its critics?
11. How does a brokerless stock market function? What are the regulatory changes that will make a brokerless system feasible?
12. Describe the role derivatives play in hedging, speculating, and arbitrage.
13. In the aftermath of a few large losses in the derivatives market and the resulting negative publicity, how do you foresee the future of this market?

REFERENCES

Amihud, Y., and H. Mendelson. 1986. "Asset Pricing and the Bid-Ask Spread." *Journal of Financial Economics*, vol. 17: 223–249.

Berger, A.N., A.K. Kashyap, and J.M. Scalise. 1995. "The Transformation of the U.S. Banking Industry: What a Long, Strange Trip It's Been." *Brookings Papers on Economic Activity*, vol. 2:55–218.

Brown, D.P. (1996, forthcoming). "Why Do We Need Stock Brokers?" *Financial Analysts Journal*.

Christie, W.G., and P.H. Schultz. 1994. "Why Do NASDAQ Market Makers Avoid Odd-Eighth Quotes?" *The Journal of Finance*, vol. 49, no. 5 (December): 1813–1840.

Christie, W.G., J.H. Harris, and P.H. Schultz. 1994. "Why Did NASDAQ Market Makers Stop Avoiding Odd-Eighth Quotes?" *The Journal of Finance*, vol. 49, no. 5 (December): 1841–1860.

Christie, W.G., and R.D. Huang. 1994. "Market Structures and Liquidity: A Transactions Data Study of Exchange Listings." *Journal of Financial Intermediation*, vol. 3, no. 3 (June): 300–326.

Demsetz, H. 1986. "The Cost of Transacting." *Quarterly Journal of Economics*, vol. 2: 33–53.

Froot, K.A., D.S. Scharfstein, and J. C. Stein. 1993. "Risk Management: Coordinating Corporate Investment and Financing Policies." *The Journal of Finance*, vol. 48, no. 1 (March): 16–29.

Reinganum, M.R. 1990. "Market Microstructure and Asset Pricing: An Empirical Investigation of NYSE and NASDAQ Securities." *Journal of Financial Economics*, vol. 28:127–147.

Robertson, D. 1995. "Are Banks Converging to One Size?" *Federal Reserve Bank of Philadelphia Working Paper No. 95-29* (December).

Rudman, W.B., J.W. Gleason, S.L. Hammerman, P.S. Lynch, R.H. Mundheim, I.M. Pollack, and A.A. Sommer Jr. 1995. "The NASD Select Committee on Structure and Governance." Paul, Weiss, Rifkind, Wharton & Garrisson Report.

Zimmerman, G.C. 1995. "Implementing the Single Banking Market in Europe." *Federal Reserve Bank of San Francisco Economic Review*, no. 3:35–49.

INDEX